Ed Cape's

Defending suspects at police stations

the practitioner's guide to advice and representation

Ed Cape is a solicitor and Emeritus Professor of Criminal Law and Practice at the University of the West of England, Bristol. Formerly a partner in a legal aid practice in Bristol, and a duty solicitor for 10 years, Ed taught and researched in the area of criminal procedure and criminal justice for most of his academic career. Ed was a contributing author to *Blackstone's Criminal Practice*, and wrote case commentaries for the *Criminal Law Review* for many years, and is also co-author of the bi-annual Police Station Update in *Legal Action* (Legal Action Group). Ed has carried out, and published, research in the field of criminal justice in the UK and internationally, including in Europe, Latin America, China and Japan, and has also worked for the United Nations and international NGOs on early access to legal aid and the right to a lawyer.

Matthew Hardcastle is a partner at Kingsley Napley. He is on the editorial board of the *Criminal Law Review*; the Chair of *Criminal Law Week: Live*; and a case commentator for *Lloyd's Law Reports: Financial Crime*. Matt acted as a Specialist Adviser for the House of Commons Justice Committee's inquiry into the disclosure of evidence in criminal cases. Matt is co-author, with Tony Edwards, of *Police Station Adviser's Handbook* (Legal Action Group, 2020) and writes, with Ed Cape and Sandra Paul, the Police Station Update in *Legal Action* (Legal Action Group). Before joining Kingsley Napley, Matt was a duty solicitor at a large legal aid practice in East London.

Sandra Paul is a partner at Kingsley Napley. Her serious and general crime practice concentrates on pre-charge work. She has been an accredited police station representative since 2001. Sandra has a particular interest in representing children and young adults. Prior to joining Kingsley Napley, she was a duty solicitor and solicitor advocate at a busy legal aid practice in central London. In 2021, she chaired the JUSTICE working party that reported on the over-representation of minoritised children in the Youth Justice System. She is an Advisory Board member for the Youth Justice Legal Centre. Between 2024 and 2025, she was a member of the Times' Crime and Justice Commission. Sandra is a lay member of the House of Lords Conduct Committee. Sandra co-authors the bi-annual Police Station Update in *Legal Action* (Legal Action Group).

Jawaid Luqmani is a partner at Luqmani Thompson LLP in London specialising in immigration law. He was an executive member of the Immigration Law Practitioners' Association (ILPA) and an assessor for the Law Society Immigration Panel (1999–2003) and on the advisory panel of the Office of the Immigration Services Commission (now IAA) from 2001–2005. He was appointed as an assessor to the Law Society Immigration and Asylum Accreditation Scheme (and is an Advanced Level Practitioner) and served as Chief Assessor on the scheme from 2011–2014. He is a member of the Legal Aid Practitioners Group (LAPG) advisory committee and a member of the Law Society Access to Justice committee. Jawaid has contributed to *Legal Action* (Legal Action Group) for more than 25 years and lectures on immigration and related topics.

The Legal Action Group is a national, independent charity which campaigns for equal access to justice for all members of society. Legal Action Group:

- Strengthens the voice of people and communities denied access to justice
- Supports frontline charities, lawyers and advisers to deliver access to justice
- Influences law and policy to improve access to justice and create a fair legal system for all.

APPENDICES

Table of cases

McDaniel & Co v Clarke [2014] EWHC 3826 (QB), [2014] 10 WLUK 416, [2014] 6 Costs LR 963 — 1.14
McDonnell v Commissioner of Police of the Metropolis [2015] EWCA Civ 573, [2015] 5 WLUK 327 — 2.42
McGowan v B [2011] UKSC 54, [2011] 1 WLR 3121, 2012 SC (UKSC) 182, 2012 SLT 37, 2012 SCL 85, 2012 SCCR 109, [2011] 11 WLUK 666, [2012] HRLR 7, (2011) 155(45) SJLB 31, (2011) *Times*, November 25 — 2.133
McLeod v United Kingdom (App No 24755/94) [1998] 9 WLUK 211, [1998] 2 FLR 1048, [1999] 1 FCR 193, (1999) 27 EHRR 493, 5 BHRC 364, [1999] Crim LR 155, [1998] HRCD 878, [1998] Fam Law 734, (1998) *Times*, October 1, ECtHR — 13.52
McMillan v Crown Prosecution Service [2008] EWHC 1457 (Admin), [2008] 5 WLUK 229, (2008) 172 JP 485, [2008] LLR 513, (2008) 172 JPN 646, (2008) 172 JPN 694 — 2.39
McNamee and McDonnell's Application for Judicial Review, Re [2014] NICA 13, [2014] 2 WLUK 273 — 2.155
Mader v Croatia (App No 56185/07) (2011) 21 September, ECtHR — 2.141
Magee v United Kingdom (App No 28135/95) [2000] 6 WLUK 66, (2001) 31 EHRR 35, 8 BHRC 646, [2000] Po LR 188, [2000] Crim LR 681, (2000) *Times*, June 20, ECtHR — 13.55
Mandalia v Secretary of State for the Home Department [2015] UKSC 59, [2015] 1 WLR 4546, [2016] 4 All ER 189, [2015] 10 WLUK 352, [2016] Imm AR 180, [2016] INLR 184, (2015) *Times*, October 26 — 12.4
Mansfield v DPP [2021] EWHC 2938 (Admin), [2022] QB 335, [2022] 2 WLR 229, [2022] 2 All ER 1164, [2021] 11 WLUK 20, [2022] 1 Cr App R 8, [2022] LLR 767, [2022] Crim LR 163, [2022] ACD 6, CLW/21/42/1 — 10.133
Marsh v DPP [2006] EWHC 1525 (Admin), [2006] 5 WLUK 174, [2007] Crim LR 162 — 13.42
Martin v Chief Constable of Avon and Somerset (1997) 29 October (unreported), CA — 2.64
Mepstead v DPP [1995] 6 WLUK 301, (1996) 160 JP 475, [1996] COD 13, (1996) 160 JPN 448, QBD — 2.39
Michalko v Slovakia (App No 35377/05) [2010] ECHR 2078, ECtHR — 13.54
Miller v DPP [2018] EWHC 262 (Admin), [2018] 2 WLUK 331, [2018] RTR 19, [2018] MHLR 96, [2018] Crim LR 472 — 11.24, 13.30
Minio-Paluello v Commissioner of Police of the Metropolis [2011] EWHC 3411 (QB), [2011] 12 WLUK 541 — 2.42
Morris v DPP [2014] EWHC 105 (Admin), [2014] 1 WLUK 278, [2014] 2 Cr App R 21 — 5.62
Mouncher v Chief Constable of South Wales [2016] EWHC 1367 (QB), [2016] 6 WLUK 318 — 2.20
Murray v United Kingdom (App No 18731/91) [1996] 2 WLUK 139, (1996) 22 EHRR 29, (1996) *Times*, February 9, (1996) *Independent*, March 1, ECtHR — 5.66, 13.55
Myles v DPP [2004] EWHC 594 (Admin), [2004] 2 All ER 902, [2004] 3 WLUK 645, [2005] RTR 1, (2004) *Independent*, May 3 — 2.142
Neale v DPP [2021] EWHC 658 (Admin), [2021] 2 WLUK 586, [2021] 2 Cr App R 9, [2021] Crim LR 878, [2021] ACD 52, CLW/21/14/5 — 2.22
Nikonovs v Governor of Brixton Prison [2005] EWHC 2405 (Admin), [2006] 1 WLR 1518, [2006] 1 All ER 927, [2005] 11 WLUK 40, [2005] Extradition LR 125 — 10.136

Roberts v Chief Constable of Kent [2008] EWCA Civ 1588, [2008] 12 WLUK 501, [2009] Po LR 8	2.42
Roques v Commissioner of Police of the Metropolis September 1997 *Legal Action* 23	1.7, 2.147
RSPCA v Eager [1995] Crim LR 59, [1994] 1 WLUK 506, (1994) *Times*, January 27, DC	1.69
Rudall v Crown Prosecution Service [2018] EWHC 3287 (QB), [2018] 11 WLUK 553, [2019] Lloyd's Rep FC 115, CLW/19/11/5	13.16
S v Switzerland (App No A/220) [1991] 11 WLUK 390, (1992) 14 EHRR 670, ECtHR	13.57
ST v Chief Constable of Nottinghamshire [2022] EWHC 1280 (QB), [2022] 5 WLUK 310	2.18, 2.19, 2.22, 2.61, 2.70, 6.128, 11.4
Salduz v Turkey (App No 36391/02) [2008] 11 WLUK 716, (2009) 49 EHRR 19, 26 BHRC 223, [2010] Crim LR 419, CLW/09/33/28, ECtHR	1.1, 2.129, 13.55
Samuels v Commissioner of Police of the Metropolis June 1999 *Legal Action* 14, CA	2.15
Searson v Chief Constable of Nottingham [2025] EWHC 1982 (KB), [2025] 7 WLUK 595, CLW/25/29/4	2.18, 2.80
Sebalj v Croatia (App No 4429/09) [2011] ECHR 1048, ECtHR	2.141, 13.55
Secretary of State for Trade and Industry v Crane (No 2) [2001] 4 WLUK 338, [2004] BCC 825, [2001] 2 BCLC 222, (2001) 98(23) LSG 40, (2001) *Times*, June 4, (2001) *Daily Telegraph*, April 24, ChD	5.73
Selmouni v France (App No 25803/94) [1999] 7 WLUK 617, (2000) 29 EHRR 403, 7 BHRC 1, ECtHR	13.59
Sheldrake v DPP [2004] UKHL 43, [2005] 1 AC 264, [2004] 3 WLR 976, [2005] 1 All ER 237, [2004] 10 WLUK 328, [2005] 1 Cr App R 28, (2004) 168 JP 669, [2005] RTR 2, [2004] HRLR 44, [2005] UKHRR 1, 17 BHRC 339, [2005] LLR 198, [2005] Crim LR 215, (2005) 169 JPN 19, (2004) 101(43) LSG 33, (2004) 148 SJLB 1216, (2004) *Times*, October 15	5.61
Shields v Chief Constable of Merseyside Police [2010] EWCA Civ 1281, [2010] 11 WLUK 410, (2011) *Times*, March 3	2.14, 2.39
Simpson v Chief Constable of South Yorkshire [1991] 2 WLUK 339, (1991) 135 SJ 383, (1991) *Times*, March 7, (1991) *Independent*, March 14, CA	2.42
Sneyd v DPP [2006] EWHC 560 (Admin), [2006] 2 WLUK 635, (2006) 170 JP 545, [2007] RTR 6, (2006) 170 JPN 998	4.40
Sobczak v DPP [2012] EWHC 1319 (Admin), [2012] 5 WLUK 34, (2012) 176 JP 575, [2013] Crim LR 515, [2012] ACD 73	2.7
Soe Thet v DPP [2006] EWHC 2701 (Admin), [2007] 1 WLR 2022, [2007] 2 All ER 425, [2006] 10 WLUK 504, [2007] INLR 71, (2006) *Times*, November 1	12.36
Sowande v Crown Prosecution Service [2017] EWHC 1234 (Admin), [2017] 2 WLUK 603	2.23
Spicer v Holt [1977] AC 987, [1976] 3 WLR 398, [1976] 3 All ER 71, [1976] 7 WLUK 166, (1976) 63 Cr App R 270, [1976] RTR 389, [1976] Crim LR 139, (1976) 120 SJ 572, HL	2.39
Stanford International Bank Ltd v Director of the Serious Fraud Office [2010] EWCA Civ 137, [2011] Ch 33, [2010] 3 WLR 941, [2010] Bus LR 1270, [2010] 2 WLUK 712, [2011] BCC 211, [2010] Lloyd's Rep FC 357, [2010] BPIR 679	4.23
Steel v United Kingdom (App No 24838/94) [1998] 9 WLUK 214, (1999) 28 EHRR 603, 5 BHRC 339, [1998] Crim LR 893, [1998] HRCD 872, (1998) *Times*, October 1, ECtHR	2.26, 2.27, 13.52

Table of statutes

Table of statutory instruments

Children (Secure Accommodation) (Amendment) (England) Regulations 2015 SI No 1883—	
reg 2	11.65
Children (Secure Accommodation) Regulations 1991 SI No 1505—	
reg 6	11.65
Children (Secure Accommodation) (Wales) (Amendment) Regulations 2016 SI No 312 (W 102)—	
reg 2(8)	11.65
Children (Secure Accommodation) (Wales) Regulations 2015 SI No 1988 (W 298)—	
reg 15(1)	11.65
Civil Legal Aid (Remuneration) Regulations 2013 SI No 422—	
reg 5A	12.120
Civil Procedure Rules 1998 SI No 3132—	
Pre-Action Protocol for Judicial Review	10.2
Counter-Terrorism Act 2008 (Code of Practice for the Video Recording with Sound of Post-Charge Questioning) Order 2012 SI No 1793	10.38
Crime and Courts Act 2013 (Application and Modification of Certain Enactments) Order 2014 SI No 1704—	
art 3	1.67
Sch 1	1.67
Crime and Disorder Act 1998 (Youth Conditional Cautions: Code of Practice) Order 2013 SI No 613	11.56
Crime and Disorder Act 1998 (Youth Conditional Cautions: Financial Penalties) Order 2013 SI No 608	11.56
Criminal Justice Act 2003 (Conditional Cautions: Code of Practice) Order 2013 SI No 801	10.77
Criminal Justice Act 2003 (Conditional Cautions: Financial Penalties) Order 2013 SI No 615	10.79
Criminal Justice and Courts Act 2015 (Simple Cautions) (Specification of Either-Way Offences) Order 2015 SI No 790—	
Sch 1	10.60
Criminal Justice and Public Order Act 1994 (Application to the Armed Forces) Order 2009 SI No 990	5.63
Criminal Legal Aid (Remuneration) Regulations 2013 SI No 435	9.2
Criminal Procedure Rules 2020 (CrimPR) SI No 759—	
r5.7	4.23
r14.6	10.148
Drug Driving (Specified Limits) (England and Wales) (Amendment) Regulations 2015 SI No 911	6.74
Drug Driving (Specified Limits) (England and Wales) Regulations 2014 SI No 2868	6.74
Extradition Act 2003 (Codes of Practice and Transit Code of Practice) Order 2021 SI No 530	1.74
Family Procedure Rules 2010 SI No 2955—	
PD 12D	11.11

Table of European and international legislation

EU Regulations ***continued***

Regulation) as it forms part of the law of England and Wales, Scotland and Northern Ireland by virtue of section 3 of the European Union (Withdrawal) Act 2018) (UK GDPR)	4.19, 4.20

EU Directives

Directive 2012/13/EU of the European Parliament and of the Council of 22 May 2012 on the right to information in criminal proceedings	2.60, 4.58

Table of Police and Criminal Evidence Act 1984 Codes of Practice

Table of Legal Aid Agency Standard Crime Contract 2022

Table of Legal Aid Agency Draft Standard Crime Contract 2025

Table of Legal Aid Agency Standard Civil Contract 2024

Table of Immigration Rules

Abbreviations

ACPO	Association of Chief Police Officers (replaced in 2015 by the National Police Chiefs' Council)
ARC	asylum application registration card
BA 1976	Bail Act 1976
BRP	biometric residence permit
CA 1989	Children Act 1989
CA 2004	Children Act 2004
CCA 2013	Crime and Courts Act 2013
CCMS	Client and Cost Management System
CCP	Code for Crown Prosecutors
CCU	Command and Control Unit
CDA 1998	Crime and Disorder Act 1998
CDD	Criminal Defence Direct
CIO	chief immigration officer
CJA 1988	Criminal Justice Act 1988
CJA 2003	Criminal Justice Act 2003
CJCA 2015	Criminal Justice and Courts Act 2015
CJPA 2001	Criminal Justice and Police Act 2001
CJPOA 1994	Criminal Justice and Public Order Act 1994
CLAS	Criminal Litigation Accreditation Scheme (Law Society)
CLR	controlled legal representation
CPIA 1996	Criminal Procedure and Investigations Act 1996
CPP	Code for Crown Prosecutors
CPS	Crown Prosecution Service
CR Guidance	*Community Resolutions (CR) Guidance 2022* (National Police Chiefs' Council)
CrimPR	Criminal Procedure Rules 2020
CSA 2010	Crime and Security Act 2010
CSO	community support officer
CSV	community support volunteer
CTA 2008	Counter-Terrorism Act 2008
C-TBSA 2019	Counter-Terrorism and Border Security Act 2019
DA 2005	Drugs Act 2005
DAA 2021	Domestic Abuse Act 2021
DAC	detained asylum casework
DAPN	domestic abuse protection notice
DAPO	domestic abuse protection order
DBS	Disclosure and Barring Service
DPA	deferred prosecution agreement
DPP	Director of Public Prosecutions
DSCC	Defence Solicitor Call Centre
DVPN	domestic violence protection notice

DVPO	domestic violence protection order
DWP	Department for Work and Pensions
EA 2003	Extradition Act 2003
ECHR	European Convention on Human Rights
ECO	entry clearance officer
ECtHR	European Court of Human Rights
FACT	Federation Against Copyright Theft
FCA	Financial Conduct Authority
FTT	First-tier Tribunal
FTT Rules 2014	Tribunal Procedure (First-tier Tribunal) (Immigration and Asylum Chamber) Rules 2014
HEO	higher executive officer
HMCPSI	His Majesty's Crown Prosecution Service Inspectorate
HMIC	His Majesty's Inspectorate of Constabulary
HMICFRS	His Majesty's Inspectorate of Constabulary and Fire & Rescue Services
HMRC	His Majesty's Revenue and Customs
HRA 1998	Human Rights Act 1998
IA 1971	Immigration Act 1971
IA 2016	Immigration Act 2016
IAA	Immigration Advice Authority
IAA 1999	Immigration and Asylum Act 1999
IAAS	Immigration and Asylum Accreditation Schem
IAC	Immigration and Asylum Chamber
IO	immigration officer
IOPC	Independent Office for Police Conduct
LAA	Legal Aid Agency
LASPO	Legal Aid, Sentencing and Punishment of Offenders Act 2012
MCA 1980	Magistrates' Courts Act 1980
MCQ	Magistrates' Court Qualification
MDA 1971	Misuse of Drugs Act 1971
MHA 1983	Mental Health Act 1983
MoJ	Ministry of Justice
MoJ guidance	*Simple cautions for adult offenders* (Ministry of Justice)
MoJ PND Guidance	*Penalty notices for disorder (PNDs)* (Ministry of Justice)
MOPAC	Mayor's Office for Policing and Crime
NAAN	National Appropriate Adult Network
NCA	National Crime Agency
NFA	no further action
NfG	note for guidance
NIAA 2002	Nationality, Immigration and Asylum Act 2002
NPCC	National Police Chiefs' Council
NSA 2023	National Security Act 2023
OISC	Office of the Immigration Services Commissioner
OOCD	out-of-court disposal
PACE	Police and Criminal Evidence Act 1984
PCA 2017	Policing and Crime Act 2017
PCE	pre-charge engagement
PCSCA 2022	Police, Crime, Sentencing and Courts Act 2022
PDS	Public Defender Service
PND	penalty notice for disorder
POA 1985	Prosecution of Offences Act 1985

POCA 2002	Proceeds of Crime Act 2002
PRA 2002	Police Reform Act 2002
PSQ	Police Station Qualification
PSRAS	Police Station Representative Accreditation Scheme
Refugee Convention	United Nations Convention Relating to the Status of Refugees 1951
REL	registered European lawyer
RFL	registered foreign lawyer
RIPA 2000	Regulation of Investigatory Powers Act 2000
ROA 1974	Rehabilitation of Offenders Act 1974
RTA 1988	Road Traffic Act 1988
RUI	release under investigation
SA 2020	Sentencing Act 2020
SCC	Standard Crime Contract (Legal Aid Agency)
SFO	Serious Fraud Office
SIAC	Special Immigration Appeals Commission
SOA 2003	Sexual Offences Act 2003
SPA 2019	Stalking Protection Act 2019
SPO	stalking protection order
SRA	Solicitors Regulation Authority
SVRO	serious violence reduction order
TA 2000	Terrorism Act 2000
TIC	(offence to be) taken into consideration
TIE	trace, interview and elimination
TPIMA 2011	Terrorism Prevention and Investigation Measures Act 2011
UK GDPR	UK General Data Protection Regulation
UKBA 2007	UK Borders Act 2007
UKVI	UK Visas and Immigration
VIPER procedure	Video Identification Parade Electronic Recording procedure
YJB	Youth Justice Board for England and Wales
YJCEA 1999	Youth Justice and Criminal Evidence Act 1999
YOT	youth offending team

CHAPTER 1

Defending the client

continued

Role of the defence lawyer

1.1 The trial, especially jury trial, has traditionally been regarded as the crowning glory of our adversarial criminal justice system. For many years, the emphasis placed on the trial justified the view that advising at police stations was relatively unimportant, not requiring the skills or deserving the knowledge and experience expected of courtroom lawyers. As a result, until the late 1980s, few suspects asked for a lawyer at the police station, and law firms were not organised to deliver advice at the police station. In reality, however, what happens at the police station is often more important than what occurs in the courtroom in terms of determining the outcome of the case. Most cases are won or lost at the police station rather than at court. Confessions, sometimes false, are obtained from suspects, evidence is gathered, deals are done, and decisions are made which will inevitably influence the course of subsequent events. The Court of Appeal has described police interrogation and the trial as being 'part of a continuous process in which the suspect is engaged from the beginning'.[1] In a leading case in 2008, the European Court of Human Rights explained the importance of the investigative stage in the following terms:

> ... the evidence obtained during this stage determines the framework in which the offence charged will be considered at the trial [and at] the same time, an accused often finds himself in a particularly vulnerable position at that stage of the proceedings, the effect of which is amplified by the fact that legislation on criminal procedure tends to become increasingly complex, notably with respect to the rules governing the gathering and use of evidence.[2]

1.2 Defending at police stations is not easy. Clients may be vulnerable, nervous, apprehensive, resentful, angry, rude or all of these things. Police officers may be unco-operative, secretive, difficult, dismissive or aggressive. The lawyer is on police territory, subject to a police agenda, and may be regarded as someone who will interfere with both the investigation and the course of justice. On top of this, it may be late at night or in the early hours of the morning, and the lawyer is alone, unsupported by professional colleagues.

1.3 It is essential that lawyers working in this environment are clear about their role, are confident in their knowledge of relevant law and procedure, and possess the skills necessary to be effective. The importance of the lawyer's role is classically underlined by two Court of Appeal decisions. In the first, *R v Paris, Abdullahi and Miller*,[3] Stephen Miller and his two co-defendants were found guilty of murder largely because of Miller's false confession, made as a result of considerable and illegitimate pressure from the police. As the then Lord Chief Justice Taylor said at the successful appeal: 'Short of physical violence, it was hard to conceive of a

1 *R v Howell* [2003] EWCA Crim 1.

2 *Salduz v Turkey* (App No 36391/02) (2008) 49 EHRR 421 at para 54, ECtHR. This principle has, in effect, also been accepted by the United Nations. See *Basic principles on the role of lawyers*, adopted by the Eighth United Nations Congress on the Prevention of Crime and the Treatment of Offenders on 7 September 1990 and welcomed by the General Assembly in Resolution 45/121 of 14 December 1990. For the domestic implications of *Salduz*, see *Cadder v HM Advocate* [2010] UKSC 43.

3 (1993) 97 Cr App R 99, CA.

more hostile approach by officers to a suspect.' The defendant, during most of the interviews, was accompanied by his solicitor and the Court of Appeal was unimpressed:

> [T]he solicitor who sat in on the interviews, seems to have done that and little else . . . Otherwise, his presence may actually render disservice. We can only assume that in the present case the officers took the view that unless and until the solicitor intervened, they could not be criticised for going too far.[4]

The fact that an inactive lawyer can do the client a disservice is also shown by a second case, that of *R v Dunn*,[5] in which it was held that the presence of a lawyer may nullify the otherwise adverse effects for the prosecution of a breach of the Police and Criminal Evidence Act 1984 (PACE) or the PACE Codes of Practice since, in the view of the court, the presence of the lawyer was sufficient to protect the suspect's interests.[6] The more recent judgment in Oliver Campbell's case[7] demonstrates how long it can take to overturn a miscarriage of justice.

1.4 It is for these reasons that this book is called *Defending suspects at police stations*. The proper role of the defence lawyer is not, as some would have it, merely that of an observer.[8] If that were the case, the lawyer could be replaced by a video camera. Neither is it to maintain some kind of balance between police and suspect – it is unlikely that the defence will ever have the powers and resources to match those of the police. Nor is the defence lawyer's function merely, as the Court of Appeal has sometimes implied,[9] that of a provider of legal information. Rather, the role of the lawyer is to act in the best interests of their client, to protect and advance the client's legal rights and, in so doing, to seek to ensure a fair and just criminal process. In our adversarial system, in which the police actively pursue the interests of the prosecution, the defence lawyer must actively pursue the interests of the suspect. To the extent that the lawyer does not do so, the lawyer will, as the Lord Chief Justice indicated in the case of *Paris*, be doing a disservice to the client – but will also be doing a disservice to the cause of justice.

Objectives of the defence lawyer

Introduction

1.5 The defence lawyer, as with any other lawyer, is under a duty to act in the best interests of each client.[10] This means that the lawyer must treat the

4 (1993) 97 Cr App R 99 at p110, CA.
5 (1990) 91 Cr App R 237, CA.
6 It is not suggested that the lawyer in this case acted anything other than properly, since she denied that the disputed confession, which the police said was made in her presence, took place at all. For a further discussion of this case, see para 13.23 below.
7 *R v Campbell* [2024] EWCA Crim 1036.
8 See, for example, D Newman, *Legal Aid Lawyers and the Quest for Justice* (Hart, Oxford, 2013).
9 See, for example, *R v Alladice* (1988) 87 Cr App R 380, CA; and *R v Dunford* (1990) 91 Cr App R 150, CA.
10 Solicitors Regulation Authority (SRA) Principles Principle 7.

interests of the client as paramount, provided that this does not conflict with the lawyer's professional conduct obligations or the public interest in the administration of justice. While, for example, a client may be advised in strong terms of the advantages of admitting an offence to the police, whether the client does so is a matter for the client, and the lawyer should not apply any undue pressure to accept their advice. After all, it is the client who has to live with the consequences. If the lawyer feels strongly that the client's decision is contrary to the advice given, one safeguard is for the lawyer to put the advice in writing and ask the client to read it and sign it. Acting in the client's best interests also involves trying to secure the best possible outcome for the client. This may include advising the client in such a way as to avoid disclosing information or evidence to the police that would be detrimental to the client's interests; trying to persuade the police or prosecutor not to charge; seeking to minimise the length of detention; trying to secure the client's release; and ensuring that relevant mitigating factors are put forward. The specific objectives of the defence lawyer may be summarised as:

- securing information;
- advising in private;
- advising on matters arising during the period of detention;
- presence at police interviews;
- safeguarding the client's rights; and
- acting ethically.

Securing information

1.6 The lawyer should seek to obtain as much relevant information from the police as possible. The police well understand the power of information and, more particularly, the utility of withholding information. It will usually be impossible to advise a client adequately in the absence of information, particularly about the evidence in the hands of the police, but also in relation to the circumstances of the arrest and detention. This takes on added significance in the context of the 'inference from silence' provisions of the Criminal Justice and Public Order Act (CJPOA) 1994, particularly since the Court of Appeal has held that failure of the police to supply information will not necessarily render a decision not to answer police questions reasonable. See further chapters 4 and 5 below.

Advising in private

1.7 Giving advice to the client in private is of paramount importance, and is a basic right under PACE s58, Terrorism Act (TA) 2000 Sch 8 para 7 and National Security Act (NSA) 2023 Sch 6 para 7. Police tactics that have the effect of undermining this right should be firmly resisted.[11] See further paras 2.146–2.148 below.

11 It has been held that this right is capable of enforcement by way of an action for breach of statutory duty (*Roques v Commissioner of Police of the Metropolis* September 1997 *Legal Action* 23).

Advising on matters arising during the period of detention

1.8 In most cases the need for advice is unlikely to be confined to the initial consultation with the client, whether on the telephone or in person. Matters may arise throughout the period that the client is in police custody on which they may want or need advice. In particular, advice should not stop when the client enters the police interview or after the lawyer has left the police station. As PACE s58 makes clear, the suspect is entitled to legal advice 'at any time'. Furthermore, the lawyer should not wait until the client asks for advice. There are many occasions when the lawyer should take the initiative.

Presence at police interviews

1.9 Police interviews are crucial, both to the police and to the client. There are relatively few occasions when a lawyer would be justified in not attending them. The fact that they are electronically recorded is certainly no justification for absence. The fact that the client is intending not to answer questions is an important indication that the lawyer's presence is required. See further chapter 7 below.

Safeguarding the client's rights

1.10 Securing police observance of the rights of a suspect under PACE, the TA 2000, the NSA 2023 and the Codes of Practice is not necessarily an easy task since, in particular, they provide no mechanisms for enforcement that can be put into effect at the police station. However, the duty to safeguard a client's rights follows directly from the general duty to act in the client's best interests. If the defence lawyer does not take appropriate action, no one else will.

Acting ethically

1.11 High ethical standards are important for the defence lawyer, particularly in view of the nature of the work. One aspect of this principle is that the lawyer should do nothing that will compromise the interests of their client. The lawyer is under a professional duty to keep the client's affairs confidential,[12] and under a duty to pass on to the client all material information regardless of the source of that information.[13] This means that the lawyer must not pass on information about the client to the police unless authorised to do so by the client, and must pass on relevant information to the client even if the police have given the lawyer the information 'in confidence'. See further paras 1.16 and 4.30 below. The principle of acting ethically also means that the lawyer must not compromise themself in relation to the client. The lawyer must be clear, for example, about the difference between pointing out the weaknesses of a client's version of events and

12 SRA Code of Conduct for Solicitors, RELs and RFLs para 6.3.

13 SRA Code of Conduct for Solicitors, RELs and RFLs para 6.4. Note that this paragraph contains important qualifications to this requirement.

helping the client to concoct a story. The former is perfectly proper; the latter probably illegal. The lawyer must always remember that an act performed with intent to impede the apprehension or prosecution of a person who has committed a 'relevant offence' is itself a serious criminal offence.[14] Finally, the lawyer must take care to avoid acting for more than one client where there is a conflict of interests. See further para 5.42 below.

Dealing with the client

General approach

1.12 Specific information about dealing with a client at the police station is given throughout this book, but some general points about the lawyer/client relationship are considered here. As noted earlier, the client may be in a variety of emotional states, which will require an approach that is both empathetic and inspires confidence. Empathy may be demonstrated by being willing to listen to what the client has to say even if it does not appear directly relevant to the issues. This is not to say that the lawyer should allow the client to ramble on indefinitely, but it will usually be appropriate to allow the client the time and the opportunity to express how and what they are feeling. In any case, this will then allow the consultation to proceed in a calmer and more constructive fashion. At the same time, the lawyer must also take appropriate action to ensure their own safety. See further para 5.8 below.

1.13 If the lawyer is to be effective, they will need to be able to inspire confidence in their skills and abilities. An adequate knowledge of the law governing police detention is a prerequisite, but is not, in itself, sufficient. While some might argue that a casual approach, both in dress and manner, means that the lawyer will be 'closer' to the client, in the context of the police station this is often likely to be counterproductive. A lawyer who looks professional and acts professionally, whose demeanour is calm, and who is willing to stand up to the police where necessary, is likely to inspire much greater confidence than one who is casual, uses 'street' talk or who is easily knocked off course by confrontation with the police. This is especially important since the police will often be competing with the lawyer in terms of status. If the police are successful in this regard, it will be easier for them to influence the suspect in the direction they want, which may entail encouraging the suspect to ignore the lawyer's advice.

SRA Standards and Regulations

1.14 The lawyer should be aware of the relevant provisions of the Solicitors Regulation Authority's (SRA) Standards and Regulations, in particular the Code of Conduct for Solicitors, RFLs and RELs, and the Transparency

14 Criminal Law Act 1967 s4; and see further para 5.37 below. For an example of the difficulties that a lawyer can get into by asserting facts to the police that may not be true, see *R v Williams* [2002] EWCA Crim 2208.

Rules.[15] Although certain aspects of the code and rules are not applicable at the police station, generally the rules may be suitably adapted to police station advice. The lawyer should:

- tell the client their name and status;
- clearly identify the client's objectives in relation to the work to be done for them;
- give the client a clear explanation of the issues involved and the options available to them;
- if the case is not covered by legal aid, tell the client the likely cost – and that advice is available for free under the police station advice and assistance scheme;[16]
- keep the client informed of progress; and
- when the client is to be released from police custody, agree with them the next steps to be taken, inform them of any continuing consequences and write to them confirming the position.

1.15 The lawyer should, where appropriate, confirm relevant information in writing once the client has been released from police custody. If the lawyer, or their firm, continues to act for the client in respect of criminal proceedings resulting from the period in the police station, the relevant requirements of the SRA Standards and Regulations should be followed in full.

Client confidentiality and privilege

1.16 There is a number of important issues regarding the confidentiality of communications between a defence lawyer and their client:

(1) The first concerns the professional duty of a solicitor not to disclose communications between them and their client, and the related question of whether the lawyer can ever be required to divulge such information.
(2) The second concerns the power of the police to obtain material that may be privileged.
(3) The third issue, which concerns whether the police can listen to communications between a lawyer and client, is dealt with at paras 2.146–2.148 below.

1.17 In relation to the first issue, it is important to distinguish between the duty of confidentiality, which is an obligation governed by the SRA Code of Conduct for Solicitors, RFLs and RELs, and legal professional privilege, which is an evidential rule governing the question whether a lawyer can be required to divulge information that is otherwise confidential. Solicitors and their staff are under a professional duty to keep their clients', and former clients', affairs in connection with the retainer in which they are

15 SRA Standards and Regulations, available at: www.sra.org.uk/solicitors/standards-regulations.

16 In *McDaniel & Co v Clarke* [2014] EWHC 3826 (QB), the High Court upheld the decision of a Master who had assessed a solicitor's bill of costs at nil in circumstances where the solicitor had failed to advise their client of the availability of union funding (which would have meant that her legal representation was free).

instructed confidential.[17] Confidentiality does not extend to information unrelated to the retainer; for example, if whilst acting for the client the lawyer observes them committing an offence. No information that has been communicated to the lawyer by or on behalf of a client, including the client's address, may be disclosed to anyone outside the firm without the client's agreement. The duty continues to apply even after the solicitor/client relationship comes to an end. For problems that may arise where the solicitor/client relationship may be terminated while the lawyer is at the police station, see para 5.38 below.

1.18 The duty of confidentiality is overridden where disclosure is permitted or required by law, which may include the following:

(1) where disclosure is necessary to prevent the client or a third party committing a criminal act which the solicitor reasonably believes is likely to result in serious bodily harm;
(2) in exceptional circumstances involving children, where the client is a child and discloses continuing sexual or other physical abuse but refuses to allow disclosure of such information, or where the client is an adult and discloses abuse of a child by them or another adult and refuses to allow disclosure of such information;
(3) where disclosure is required by statute, for example, under the Proceeds of Crime Act (POCA) 2002, or the Money Laundering Regulations;[18]
(4) where the lawyer believes that their client is genuine in their intention to commit suicide or serious self-harm and there is no other way of dealing with the issue;[19] or
(5) where a court orders confidential information to be disclosed, or issues a warrant that authorises the seizure of confidential information.

1.19 Quite separately from the professional duty of confidentiality, the law recognises that certain communications between a lawyer and their client, or with a third party, should be protected from enforced disclosure, and this is contained within rules concerning legal professional privilege. In some respects these rules cover a narrower range of communications than the duty of confidentiality. Whereas the confidentiality rule covers all confidential information about a client's affairs, legal professional privilege is confined to communications between a lawyer and the client that are made for the purpose of enabling the client to obtain, or the lawyer to give, legal advice.[20] If a communication is privileged, neither the police

17 SRA Guidance, *Confidentiality of Client Information* (first published 25 November 2019), available at: www.sra.org.uk/solicitors/guidance/confidentiality-client-information.

18 Money Laundering, Terrorist Financing and Transfer of Funds (Information on the Payer) Regulations 2017 SI No 692, as amended by the Money Laundering and Terrorist Financing (Amendment) Regulations 2019 SI No 1511. See the Financial Conduct Authority's *Money Laundering Regulation*, available at: www.fca.org.uk/firms/financial-crime/money-laundering-regulations; and the Law Society's *Quick Guide to the Money Laundering Regulations 2017*, available at: www.lawsociety.org.uk/topics/anti-money-laundering/quick-guide-to-the-mlrs.

19 SRA Guidance, *Confidentiality of Client Information* (first published November 2019).

20 Which could include a document prepared by a lawyer for the purposes of providing advice, even if at the time the document was prepared, the lawyer's ultimate intention was to show the document to the police (*Director of the Serious Fraud Office v Eurasian Natural Resources Corp Ltd* [2018] EWCA Civ 2006).

nor a court can force either the lawyer or client to divulge the communication.[21] The client, but not the lawyer, can expressly waive privilege and thus allow its disclosure, but it is important to note that privilege can be waived by implication – that is, disclosure of some privileged material may result in other material losing its privileged status. If privilege is lost in this way, a court could order disclosure of such material. For a discussion of this in relation to disclosure of legal advice given to a client, see para 5.103 below.

1.20 It follows from the above that the police can never directly force a lawyer to disclose to them information that is covered by legal professional privilege and, in view of the duty of confidentiality, a lawyer must never (subject to the exceptions noted above) volunteer confidential information without their client's consent. However, the police will sometimes seek to persuade a lawyer, possibly in forceful terms, to supply information and/or hand over documents that the lawyer has prepared or obtained while acting for a client. If the client consents then, of course, the information can be given or the documents handed over. If the client does not consent, the lawyer should consider the following questions:

(1) Is the information or are the documents covered by the duty of confidentiality? If the information or documents have been received from the client, or prepared in the course of giving advice, they almost certainly will be unless an exception applies (see above). The lawyer should insist on the police obtaining a witness summons or subpoena unless the lawyer has strong prima facie evidence that they have been used by the client to perpetrate a fraud or other crime.
(2) Will the lawyer commit an offence if they do not give the information or documents to the police? Generally, a lawyer will not be committing an offence merely by refusing to hand over information or documents that they believe to be covered by the duty of confidentiality. It is highly unlikely that a court would conclude that a lawyer is guilty of wilfully obstructing a police officer in such circumstances. There are provisions in the TA 2000 that make it an offence not to disclose to the police a belief or suspicion that a person has committed an offence under TA 2000 ss15–18 (offences relating to terrorist property), where that belief or suspicion is based on information obtained in the course of a trade, profession, business or employment (TA 2000 s19(1) and (2)). Other non-disclosure offences are to be found in TA 2000 ss21A and 38B. Generally, however, disclosure is not required where the information is obtained in circumstances that are covered by legal professional privilege.[22] There is a number of provisions in the POCA 2002 which impose extensive disclosure obligations in relation to the proceeds of crime. In particular, POCA 2002 s328(1) makes it an offence for a person to enter into or become concerned in an arrange-

21 See *R v Derby Magistrates' Court ex p B and Another* [1995] 4 All ER 526, HL; and *R v Crown Court at Manchester ex p Rogers* [1999] 4 All ER 35, QBD. Legal professional privilege also covers communications between a lawyer or client and a third party (for example, a potential witness or expert) where the dominant purpose is preparation for pending or contemplated litigation.

22 TA 2000 s19(5) and (6). See also the Law Society's *Anti-terrorism* practice note, available at: www.lawsociety.org.uk/topics/criminal-justice/anti-terrorism.

ment which the person knows or suspects facilitates the acquisition, retention, use or control of criminal property by or on behalf of another person. 'Criminal property' is widely defined to include property that itself constitutes a person's benefit from criminal conduct or which represents such a benefit, wholly or partly and whether directly or indirectly. However, it was held in *Bowman v Fels*[23] that section 328 was not intended to cover or affect the ordinary conduct of litigation by legal professionals, and that even if this conclusion was incorrect, that it did not override the duty of confidentiality or legal professional privilege. Therefore, provided the information is obtained in, or documents are created for the purposes of, the proper conduct of the case, the lawyer will not commit an offence under the POCA 2002 by failing to disclose them.

(3) Do the police have the power to seize documents in the lawyer's possession? This may arise in respect of documents in the lawyer's possession while still at the police station, or in respect of documents retained elsewhere, such as in their office. Unless the lawyer is arrested, the police have no power to seize documents or other material from them whilst they are at the police station.[24] With regard to documents or other material held elsewhere, if such documents or material have been created in the course of a lawyer/client relationship, or have been passed to the lawyer by a client in connection with the matter on which legal advice is sought, they are likely to amount to legally privileged material (unless held with the intention of furthering a criminal purpose) or special procedure material. In this case, the power of the police to search for or require production of such material is circumscribed by PACE Part II, and generally the police would have to obtain a production order or a search warrant.

Dealing with the police

1.21 The attitude of police officers to lawyers varies, but some officers have a negative attitude towards lawyers. This largely results from their 'crime control' values. Their job, as they see it, is to control crime. The best way to control crime is to catch criminals. Anyone, or anything, that interferes with that mission is on the side of the criminal against the police. An important aspect of the police perspective is the need to demand deference from, and to be in control of, those people who they see as 'police property'. By acting for, and speaking on behalf of, such people, defence lawyers challenge this perspective. The objectives of investigative interviewing have been described by the police as obtaining 'accurate and reliable accounts from . . . suspects about matters under police investigation'.[25] However, the evidence demonstrates that the police are often more inter-

23 [2005] EWCA Civ 226.

24 For the application of these principles to a statement prepared for the purposes of a police interview, see para 5.160 below.

25 College of Policing, *Authorised professional practice: Investigative interviewing* Principle 1, available at: www.college.police.uk/app/investigation/investigative-interviewing/investigative-interviewing.

ested in securing proof than in discovering truth, and the involvement of Crown prosecutors in crime investigation and charge decisions reinforces the view that the police are acting on behalf of the prosecution. Seen from this standpoint, unless defence lawyers can be harnessed to the values of the police, they are bound to interfere with these crime control objectives.[26] Furthermore, the police have developed strategies such as phased (or managed) disclosure and intelligence-led investigation that have the effect, if not the purpose, of making the work of defence lawyers more difficult.

1.22 The defence lawyer, having recognised why the police act as they do towards them, needs to develop strategies for dealing with such conduct. This may, on occasion, require personal qualities of courage and perseverance. The words of the then Lord Chief Justice, Lord Taylor, in *R v Paris, Abdullahi and Miller*[27] should be borne in mind by all defence lawyers acting at the police station. Having commented on the fact that the lawyer in that case appeared to have done little in the police interview, he went on to say:

> Guidelines for solicitors published by the Law Society provided that a solicitor might need to intervene if the questions were oppressive, threatening or insulting: that a solicitor should intervene if the officer was not asking questions but only making comments or if the questions were improperly put: and that the solicitor should advise the suspect of his right to remain silent if improprieties remained uncorrected or continued. A solicitor fulfilling the exacting duty of assisting a suspect during interviews should follow the guidelines and discharge his function responsibly and courageously. Otherwise his presence might actually render a disservice.[28]

The defence lawyer should need no further endorsement of the legitimacy of and necessity for a proactive and interventionist role.

1.23 One matter of general importance is the extent to which defence lawyers can expect the police to respect the confidentiality of consultations with their clients. There is evidence that the police have, sometimes, placed listening devices in cells and consultation rooms and have recorded telephone conversations. For this reason, lawyers should always be aware of the possibility that conversations with their clients may be listened to by the police and, in particular, should never assume that a telephone or web-based conversation with a client in a police station is private. Lawyers should also warn clients of the possibility that any conversation that they have in their cell may be 'bugged'.[29] For the use of covert surveillance in respect of lawyer/client consultations see para 2.148 below.

26 See L Skinns, *Police custody: governance, legitimacy and reform of the criminal justice process* (Willan, Abingdon, 2011); and J Blackstock, E Cape, J Hodgson, A Ogorodova and T Spronken, *Inside police custody: an empirical account of suspects' rights in four jurisdictions* (Intersentia, Cambridge, 2014).

27 (1993) 97 Cr App R 99, CA.

28 (1993) 97 Cr App R 99 at p110, CA.

29 See *R v Ali* (1991) Times, February 19, CA; *R v Bailey* [1993] 3 All ER 513, CA; *R v Roberts* [1997] Crim LR 222, CA; and *R v Mason* [2002] EWCA Crim 385.

Preparing for the defence lawyer's role

Organisation by the firm

1.24 Effective and efficient organisation is essential for firms providing a service to those detained at a police station because:

- police station work is both individually and organisationally demanding;
- it is unpredictable – clients are often arrested at inconvenient times and frequently in the middle of the night;
- it is required by the Legal Aid Agency's (LAA) Standard Crime Contract (SCC) Specification 2022 (draft Standard Crime Contract Specification 2025), which governs the provision of criminal legal aid services; and
- it may well make the difference between the work being profitable and unprofitable.

In order to satisfy these various requirements, any firm that provides legal advice at the police station must develop structures and procedures to cater for the following (explained below):

- availability 24 hours per day;
- full record-keeping;
- prompt allocation of cases to appropriately qualified staff;
- appropriate supervision;
- appropriate training;
- file and case management; and
- arrangements with doctors, interpreters, etc.

Availability 24 hours per day

1.25 Systems are necessary to ensure that a lawyer is available and can be contacted at any time of the day or night in order to deal with police station calls, including back-up arrangements to cater for busy periods.

Full record-keeping

1.26 Systems are necessary to ensure that all relevant information, from first contact onwards, is recorded in an accessible and retrievable form. This will necessitate appropriate training of all staff, including relevant administrative staff, and the use of pro formas and checklists (see appendix 2).

Prompt allocation of cases to appropriately qualified staff

1.27 This will involve having systems to ensure that:

- cases are allocated without delay;
- cases are allocated to appropriate staff having regard to the actual or potential seriousness of the case, and the status and experience of the staff member; and
- duty solicitor cases are allocated to staff who are appropriately qualified.

Appropriate supervision

1.28 Police station lawyers, especially those with less experience, should have prompt access to a more experienced lawyer who can be consulted in respect of difficult or complex issues that arise while advising a client at the police station. In addition, a system should be in place to ensure that police station lawyers routinely discuss their cases, or a selection of them, with a supervising lawyer. This should involve face-to-face discussion, providing the lawyer with an opportunity to reflect on the way in which they dealt with specific cases, and to provide an opportunity to take any necessary remedial action.

Appropriate training

1.29 The need for relevant training is self-evident, and mechanisms should be in place for all staff engaged in police station work to access such training. Training should cover not only substantive law, procedure and evidence, but also appropriate skills.

File and case management

1.30 Good file and case management systems are necessary for what is, in many firms, high volume work. Particular attention should be paid to systems that:

- enable files, in particular the most recent, to be retrieved quickly where an existing client has been arrested;
- enable conflict of interests checks to be made without undue delay;
- ensure that information obtained at the police station is available to the court advocate as soon as the client appears in court; and
- ensure that information resulting from police station attendance is placed in any subsequent file.

Arrangements with doctors, interpreters, etc

1.31 Firms should ensure that police station lawyers have up-to-date information on the availability of doctors, interpreters, etc. Firms should consider making suitable arrangements with such professionals in order to ensure their availability at short notice.

Personal organisation

1.32 In addition to the firm being organised appropriately for police station work, the individual lawyer needs to be organised as well. A number of matters are relevant here, discussed below:

- expertise and skills; and
- comprehensive and legible notes.

Expertise and skills

1.33 As noted above, firms are responsible for ensuring that all staff are appropriately trained so that they have the necessary knowledge, expertise and skills to do their job well. It is also the responsibility of individual police station lawyers to ensure that they are adequately prepared for defending clients at police stations.

Comprehensive and legible notes

1.34 The importance of comprehensive and legible note-taking cannot be overstated. The defence lawyer, and all staff involved in any way with a police station case – such as the person who takes the initial telephone message – must take a contemporaneous note of what is said and done, the date and time, and the initials or signature of the note-maker. This will be made easier by the use of a standard police station form. There is a number of reasons why comprehensive record-keeping is important.

- It helps to ensure that all work done in respect of a particular case can be included in a claim for work done (where an itemised claim can be made).
- It facilitates the passing of a case from one lawyer to another. The second lawyer will be able to see, at a glance, what has been done and said before the handover. If it is in the form of a standard case form, it will also ensure that the second lawyer is aware of such important details as the review times and when the detention time limit expires.
- Events that occur at the police station may be relevant at trial, and the police station lawyer may have to give evidence. For example, in *R v Samuel*[30] the defendant's lawyer was able to give evidence of the times that he had contacted the police station in order to try to gain access to his client and of the conversations that took place, and this was crucial in persuading the court that evidence of the police interviews should have been excluded at trial.

1.35 All events must be noted and all conversations with the police and other people recorded, even if they appear insignificant at the time. Indeed, it may be appropriate on occasions to record that nothing was said or done. In *R v Dunn*[31] the lawyer gave evidence that there had been no confession by her client at the end of the police interview, as was alleged by the police (although apparently she was disbelieved by the jury). Thus, in police interviews, the time that the interview ended and the time that the parties left the interview room should be recorded, and the content of any conversation – or the fact that there was no conversation – also noted.

1.36 Guidance concerning what information should be sought is given in subsequent chapters, and in the checklists in appendix 2, but the following lists the type of information that should be carefully recorded:

- the time and place of all relevant conversations and events;
- the physical and mental state of the client;
- the general conduct of the police and the 'atmosphere' in which the investigation is being conducted;

30 [1988] QB 615, CA.

31 (1990) 91 Cr App R 237, CA, discussed at para 13.23 below.

- anything the police allege has been said by the client before attendance by the lawyer;
- anything the police assert has been said to the client by them, for example, a request to account for an object, substance or mark, etc, and what reply, if any, was made;
- information given by the police to the lawyer;
- requests for information made to the police by the lawyer;
- any request for information to be recorded in the custody record, and any representations made to the custody officer;
- information given to the lawyer by the client;
- the client's apparent understanding of the significance of the allegation, the caution, and the significance of their reply or failure to reply;
- advice given by the lawyer to the client, and the reasons for that advice;
- the wording of any caution or special warning, or explanation of any caution or special warning given, and any response by the client;
- what was said during the course of a police interview; and
- anything said at the time of charge/informed that may be prosecuted.

Police station toolkit

1.37 Lawyers who do police station work should have a 'toolkit' – hard copy or electronic – which is easily available and ready to hand for whenever they are called out to a police station. This toolkit should contain the following, discussed below:

- sources of reference;
- headed notepaper;
- identification;
- standard case forms;
- mobile telephone, laptop and other electronic devices; and
- useful addresses and telephone numbers.

Sources of reference

1.38 An up-to-date version of PACE and the Codes of Practice is essential. An up-to-date version of PACE and the current versions of the Codes of Practice are available online.[32] A reference resource containing at least common crimes and defences should also be included. See, for example, *Police Station Adviser's Handbook*.[33] The following should be readily available (or the current version of these codes and circulars where they have been revised since the date of publication of this book):[34]

- Director's guidance on charging;
- Code for Crown prosecutors;

32 Available at: www.legislation.gov.uk/ukpga/1984/60/contents, and www.gov.uk/guidance/police-and-criminal-evidence-act-1984-pace-codes-of-practice respectively.

33 A Edwards and M Hardcastle, Legal Action Group, London, 2021.

34 Current versions of the *Code for crown prosecutors* and the *Director's guidance* are available via: www.cps.gov.uk. The Ministry of Justice guidance *Simple cautions for adult offenders* is available at: https://assets.publishing.service.gov.uk/media/5afeacfc40f0b6561ce44093/cautions-guidance-2015.pdf. *Code of practice for adult conditional cautions* is available at: www.gov.uk/government/publications/code-of-practice-for-adult-conditional-cautions.

- Ministry of Justice guidance: Simple cautions for adult offenders;
- Code of Practice for adult conditional cautions; and
- Director's guidance on adult conditional cautions.

Headed notepaper

1.39 Even if a lawyer uses a laptop or tablet to record relevant information, notepaper may be needed to write a letter to a client to whom access is being denied, to make written representations or a written record of oral representations, or to make a formal complaint. It is important always to keep a copy of any letter or written representation made, since it may be needed for future reference or for evidential purposes. This may be done by taking a photograph or using a scanning application.

Identification

1.40 A form of identification is useful, particularly if the lawyer is attending at a police station where they are not known. Non-solicitors doing police station work should carry a letter of authorisation from the firm or solicitor on whose behalf they attend the police station. The contents of such a letter must be taken into account if the police are considering excluding a representative from the police station (Code C para 6.13; Code H para 6.15; Code I para 6.14; and see para 4.6 below). In duty solicitor cases, staff undertaking police station advice must carry an identification card as specified by the LAA.[35]

Standard case forms

1.41 A standard police station form has a number of functions. A standard police station form:

- acts as a checklist, both helping to ensure that relevant information has been obtained and prompting the lawyer in relation to events that are coming up, such as review times or expiry of custody time limits;
- enables efficient transfer to another lawyer;
- provides a readily available source of information for use at any subsequent trial;
- makes the process of billing quicker since all the relevant information is contained in one document; and
- helps satisfy the requirements of the SCC.

1.42 When completed, the standard case form should be placed in the case file as soon as it is opened. Other standard forms, and checklists (such as an identification procedure checklist (see appendix 2)), should also be included.

Mobile telephone, laptop and other electronic devices

1.43 The Law Society and the Association of Chief Police Officers (ACPO) issued joint guidance on lawyers taking mobile telephones, laptops and

35 SCC Specification 2022 para 6.63 (draft SCC Specification 2025 para 6.62).

other electronic devices into police stations.[36] The main provisions of the guidance are as follows:

- lawyers must disclose to the custody officer what electronic communication or recording devices they have in their possession if required to do so by the custody officer;
- the presumption is that lawyers should be allowed to retain and use such devices, unless there is a good reason why they should not be allowed to do so;
- surrender of such devices will only be required where there are reasonable grounds to believe that surrender is necessary to prevent unauthorised communications being made by or on behalf of a detainee, and the lawyer must be informed of the reasons for any such decision; and
- where the lawyer is permitted to retain such a device, they must agree that they will not allow any detainee to have access to the device, nor use the device to communicate with anyone on behalf of the detainee, and to report any breach of this condition to the custody officer as soon as practicable after the breach took place.

Useful addresses and telephone numbers

1.44 The toolkit should include a list of addresses and telephone numbers, such as those for police stations in the area, the social services duty team and other lawyers in the firm. The list should also include details of appropriate doctors, experts and interpreters.

Qualification for police station advice

Police station qualification for solicitors

1.45 The Law Society operates a Criminal Litigation Accreditation Scheme (CLAS),[37] consisting of a Police Station Qualification (PSQ) and a Magistrates' Court Qualification (MCQ). The LAA does not require solicitors who conduct publicly funded own-solicitor cases to have gained the PSQ.[38] However, in duty solicitor cases a solicitor who is not a duty solicitor and who does not have the PSQ cannot accept the initial call from the Defence Solicitor Call Centre (DSCC), provide initial telephone advice or attend the police station to give advice in person.[39]

36 *Mobile telephones and laptops being taken into custody suites by solicitors* (August 2011), available at: www.policestationreps.com/Docs/LegalUpdates/ACPO%20Mobile%20Phones.pdf. ACPO has since been replaced by the National Police Chiefs' Council, but it would seem that the guidance is still in force.

37 Details of the CLAS can be obtained at: www.lawsociety.org.uk/career-advice/individual-accreditations/criminal-litigation-accreditation.

38 SCC Specification 2022 para 9.28 (draft SCC Specification 2025 para 9.25).

39 SCC Specification 2022 para 9.28 (draft SCC Specification 2025 para 9.25).

Accreditation for representatives

1.46 Non-solicitors who provide police station advice must be registered with the LAA in order for their work to be paid for out of public funds. This is the case in respect of both own-solicitor and duty solicitor work.[40] Following registration, and before obtaining accreditation, they are known as probationary representatives. Once they have obtained accreditation, they are known as accredited representatives.[41] The accreditation scheme for police station representatives (known as PSRAS) is operated by the SRA, and consists of three assessments: (i) a portfolio of police station cases; (ii) a written test; and (iii) a critical incidents test.[42]

1.47 There is a number of limitations and restrictions that apply to representatives. Accredited and probationary representatives are treated as solicitors for the purposes of the PACE Codes, but they can be excluded from a police station in certain circumstances that do not apply to solicitors (Codes C and H paras 6.12–6.14; Code I paras 6.13–6.15; Code D para 2.6; and see para 4.4 below). Codes C and I para 6.12 and Code H para 6.13 do not include in the definition of 'solicitor' a representative who is neither a probationary nor an accredited representative, and it is unclear whether the police are required to permit access to a suspect by such a person who has been sent to the police station on behalf of a solicitor in a privately funded case.

1.48 In publicly funded cases, the SCC imposes a number of restrictions and obligations. A probationary representative may only provide advice and assistance on behalf of a provider (that is, the firm that has a contract with the LAA) at which their supervising solicitor is based, cannot accept the initial call or provide advice or assistance in duty solicitor cases, and cannot provide advice and assistance in respect of an indictable-only case.[43] The provider is responsible for the standard of work of representatives employed by them, and also for those representatives who are not directly employed under a contract of employment, and in the case of the latter there are certain restrictions on claiming for travel time.[44] Before attending a police station, the representative must have the telephone number of their supervising solicitor and must be able to contact them, or another solicitor in the firm with sufficient experience of police station work, in case the representative needs guidance.[45] Once a case has been concluded, the representative must provide a written report to the conducting solicitor

40 SCC Specification 2022 paras 9.26 and 9.27 (draft SCC Specification 2025 paras 9.23 and 9.24).

41 SCC Specification 2022 para 1.2 (draft SCC Specification 2025 para 1.2).

42 Details of the accreditation scheme can be obtained at: www.sra.org.uk/solicitors/resources/specific-areas-of-practice/police-station-representative-accreditation-scheme. The SRA issued a consultation on amendments to the accreditation scheme: see www.sra.org.uk/sra/consultations/consultation-listing/psras-consultation. The outcome of the consultation was not known at the date of publication.

43 SCC Specification 2022 paras 9.28, 9.34 and 9.35 (draft SCC Specification 2025 paras 9.25, 9.28 and 9.30).

44 SCC Specification 2022 paras 9.29 and 9.30 (draft SCC Specification 2025 para 9.26) (SCC Specification 2022 para 9.29 not included in draft SCC Specification 2025).

45 SCC Specification 2022 para 9.31 (draft SCC Specification 2025 para 9.27).

no later than the next working day.[46] A representative must not be employed as a special constable, nor in any other capacity that may cause a conflict of interest with their work as a representative.[47]

The Duty Solicitor Scheme

1.49 The police station Duty Solicitor Scheme is regulated by the SCC. A 'duty solicitor' is defined as a person who has previously been a member of a scheme under a previous contract or is a current member of the Law Society's CLAS and has passed the PSQ (see para 1.45 above).[48] As with accredited representatives, duty solicitors must not be special constables.[49] Detailed rules regarding the operation of the scheme are set out in the SCC 2022 section 6. The obligation to participate in the scheme is imposed on providers that have a contract with the LAA rather than on individual duty solicitors,[50] and duty slots on rota schemes and places on duty solicitor panels are allocated to providers rather than to individual duty solicitors.[51] It is for the LAA to determine whether and where rota and panel schemes should operate, and also to allocate slots on rota schemes.[52]

1.50 Obligations under the SCC concerning taking duty calls, accepting cases and attendance at the police station are set out in the relevant sections of chapter 3 below. Once a request for the duty solicitor has been accepted, the provider must normally continue to act for the suspect until the end of the investigation.[53] A duty solicitor case can only be handed back to the DSCC before the end of the investigation if:

- the duty solicitor is unable to continue to act personally and there is no other suitable person in the organisation who is able to act and it is not possible to instruct an agent;
- the client removes or rescinds their instructions;
- there is legitimate concern about breach of the professional code of conduct; or
- the provider confirms that the provider will not claim remuneration in respect of the case.[54]

Where a case is handed back to the DSCC, the reasons must be clearly recorded on the case file.[55]

46 SCC Specification 2022 para 9.32 (draft SCC Specification 2025 para 9.22).
47 SCC Specification 2022 para 9.36 (draft SCC Specification 2025 para 9.31).
48 SCC Standard Terms 2022 para 1.1 (draft SCC Specification 2025 para 1.1).
49 SCC Specification 2022 para 6.20 (draft SCC Specification 2025 para 9.26).
50 SCC Specification 2022 para 6.1 (draft SCC Specification 2025 para 6.1).
51 SCC Specification 2022 paras 6.2–6.7 (draft SCC Specification 2025 paras 6.2–6.8).
52 SCC Specification 2022 paras 6.51–6.59 (draft SCC Specification 2025 paras 6.49–6.59).
53 SCC Specification 2022 para 9.51 (draft SCC Specification 2025 para 9.43).
54 SCC Specification 2022 para 9.52 (draft SCC Specification 2025 para 9.44).
55 SCC Specification 2022 para 9.53 (draft SCC Specification 2025 para 9.45).

Legal aid

Introduction

1.51 Those people who are entitled to legal advice and assistance in connection with criminal investigations – which includes those who are arrested and held in custody by the police (see para 2.131 below); HM Revenue and Customs (HMRC) officers (see para 1.65 below); volunteers (see para 2.164 below); persons being interviewed in connection with a service offence (see para 1.72 below); those detained under TA 2000 s47 and Sch 7 (see para 2.131 below); and those detained under NSA 2023 s27 – are entitled to legal aid to pay for that advice and assistance without reference to their financial resources.

1.52 The provision of legally aided advice and assistance is governed by the terms of the LAA's SCC. The contract (together with certain provisions of Codes C, H and I) imposes significant limitations and conditions both on the right to legal advice at police stations and on the ability of lawyers to provide it. Reference is made to relevant parts of the contract throughout the book, but three important features are dealt with here: (i) the provisions regarding who initial instructions can be received from in legal aid cases; (ii) the Criminal Defence Direct (CDD) scheme; and (iii) the 'sufficient benefit' test.

Who instructions can be received from

1.53 Where a suspect who is held in police custody requests legal advice to be paid for by public funds, the police are required to contact the DSCC (Codes C and H note for guidance (NfG) 6B; Code I NfG 6C).[56] The DSCC determines whether the case is covered by the CDD scheme (see para 1.54 below), and if it is not the DSCC then refers the request to the solicitor requested or to the duty solicitor. Generally, payment under the SCC can only be claimed if the instructions are initially received from the DSCC.[57] However, this rule does not apply where:

- a suspect attends a police station by prior agreement with the police and requests the solicitor to represent them, although the solicitor must inform the DSCC within 48 hours of the first attendance at the police station, and must actually represent them at the police station; or
- instructions are received from a member of the suspect's immediate family or a third party of similar status (including an appropriate adult under the PACE Codes of Practice), although the solicitor must report the matter to the DSCC prior to telephoning or attending the client; or
- the solicitor is already at the police station when a suspect requests advice from them, as own-solicitor or duty solicitor, although the solicitor must

56 Although the LAA appears to accept that the police may pass a request directly to the nominated solicitor, or a duty solicitor, if they are already at the police station since SCC Specification 2022 para 9.20(c) (draft SCC Specification 2025 para 9.14(c)) provides that the solicitor may claim payment for work done in such circumstances provided that they inform the DSCC within 48 hours of receiving the instructions.

57 SCC Specification 2022 paras 9.18–9.19 (draft SCC Specification 2025 paras 9.12–9.13).

report the matter to the DSCC within 48 hours of receiving instructions.[58]

The Criminal Defence Direct scheme

1.54 Cases that fall within the scope of the CDD scheme are excluded from the scope of the SCC 2022, so that a claim for work carried out in respect of such cases cannot be made unless one of the exceptions set out in the contract applies. As noted above, when contacted by the police the DSCC determines whether the case is within the scope of the CDD scheme. If it is, the DSCC will refer the request to CDD to provide advice.

1.55 Cases that fall within the scope of CDD are those where the suspect:

- is detained in respect of a non-imprisonable offence;
- was arrested on a bench warrant for failing to appear and is being held for production before a court, except where the solicitor has clear documentary evidence that would result in the suspect being released from custody (in which case, payment for attendance may be allowed provided that the reason is recorded on file);
- was arrested on suspicion of:
  - driving with excess alcohol and was taken to the police station to provide a specimen (Road Traffic Act (RTA) 1988 s5);
  - failure to provide a specimen (RTA 1988 ss6, 7 and 7A); or
  - driving while unfit/drunk in charge of a motor vehicle (RTA 1988 s4);
- is detained in relation to breach of police or court bail conditions.[59]

However, a claim for payment may be made in respect of such cases if the sufficient benefit test is satisfied (see para 1.57 below) and one of the following exceptions applies:

- an interview or an identification procedure is to be held;
- the suspect is eligible for assistance from an appropriate adult (see paras 11.17 and 11.88 below);
- the suspect is unable to communicate over the telephone;
- the suspect complains of serious maltreatment by the police;
- the investigation includes another alleged offence which is not within the scope of the CDD scheme;
- the solicitor or representative is already at the same police station (in which case the claim cannot exceed the police station telephone advice fixed fee);
- the advice relates to an indictable offence; or
- the request is a 'special request'.[60]

A 'special request' is a request identified to the lawyer as such by the DSCC. Special requests may include, for example, requests where CDD considers that, because of a conflict of interest, the request should be dealt with by a duty or own-solicitor, or considers that advocacy assistance is

58 SCC Specification 2022 para 9.20 (draft SCC Specification 2025 para 9.14).

59 SCC Specification 2022 para 9.9 (draft SCC Specification 2025 para 9.3).

60 SCC Specification 2022 para 9.10 (draft SCC Specification 2025 para 9.4).

required, or considers that one of the other exceptions specified above applies.[61]

1.56 If any of the specified exceptions apply, the solicitor must endorse the file with the reasons for attendance.[62] In addition, a case is not treated as a CDD scheme case if CDD is unable to provide telephone advice, but this does not apply if the reason for this is that the suspect refused to accept advice from them.[63] Where CDD refers a case to the suspect's own-solicitor (for example, because they are informed that the police do intend to interview the suspect or discover that the suspect is eligible for assistance from an appropriate adult) it ceases to be a CDD case, and the normal rules apply.[64] Although it is not specifically provided for in the SCC 2022 (draft SCC 2025), the definition of 'special request' implies that this is also the case where CDD refer the case to a duty solicitor.

The sufficient benefit test

1.57 Advice and assistance may only be claimed for under the SCC 2022 (draft SCC 2025) if there is 'sufficient benefit' to the client, having regard to the circumstances of the matter, including the personal circumstances of the client, to justify work or further work being carried out.[65] The sufficient benefit test is automatically satisfied for the purposes of initial advice in respect of a person who has a right to legal advice or who is a volunteer under PACE or the equivalent legislation applying to the armed forces in the case of military investigations. After initial advice has been given, the solicitor must consider whether, and what, further work is justified by reference to there being 'sufficient benefit' for the client.[66] The contract states that the test is satisfied where further legal advice is given to a client immediately following charge. However, it goes on to state that attendance upon the client thereafter while fingerprints, photographs and swabs are taken will not meet the sufficient benefit test except where the client requires further assistance owing to their particular circumstances, in which case the relevant factors must be noted on file. It also, in effect, provides that the test would be satisfied where the lawyer remains at the police station in order to make representations about bail, again provided that this justification is noted on file.[67]

61 SCC Specification 2022 para 1.2 (draft SCC Specification 2025 para 1.2).
62 SCC Specification 2022 para 9.11 (draft SCC Specification 2025 para 9.5).
63 SCC Specification 2022 para 9.12 (draft SCC Specification 2025 para 9.6).
64 SCC Specification 2022 para 9.13 (draft SCC Specification 2025 para 9.7).
65 SCC Specification 2022 para 3.10 (draft SCC Specification 2025 para 3.10).
66 SCC Specification 2022 para 3.15 (draft SCC Specification 2025 para 3.10).
67 SCC Specification 2022 para 9.15 (draft SCC Specification 2025 para 9.10). In most cases these limitations are irrelevant because remuneration is by way of a fixed fee, but may be relevant if a case qualifies for an 'escape fee'. See SCC Specification 2022 paras 9.95–9.98 (draft SCC Specification 2025 paras 9.92–9.95).

Who does this book apply to?

Introduction

1.58 This book is primarily concerned with advising a person who has been arrested on suspicion of a criminal offence and is being held in custody in a police station or other authorised place of detention. The detention and treatment of a suspect in these circumstances is governed by PACE and Codes of Practice C–F. One of the key definitions in PACE is that concerning 'police detention'. A person is in police detention for the purposes of PACE if the person:

- has been taken to a police station after being arrested for an offence or under TA 2000 s41 or 43B, or NSA 2023 s27; or
- is arrested at a police station after attending voluntarily or accompanying a constable to it and they are detained there or detained elsewhere in the charge of a constable (PACE s118(2)).

However, where a person is arrested and detained under TA 2000 s41 or s43B, or under NSA 2023 s27, the arrest and detention is governed by those legislative regimes respectively and associated Codes of Practice, although since such a person is treated as being in police detention, those powers and duties under PACE that apply to a person in police detention also apply to persons arrested under those Acts (see paras 1.61–1.64 below).

1.59 A person is treated as being in police detention if they are in the custody of a designated civilian officer by virtue of the Police Reform Act (PRA) 2002.[68] A person who is at court after being charged is not in police detention (PACE s118(2)).

1.60 Many of the procedures and police powers in PACE relate only to persons in police detention. However, the right of intimation under PACE s56 (see para 2.126 below) and the right to consult a solicitor under PACE s58 (see para 2.129 below) apply to any person arrested and held in custody at a police station or other premises whether or not the arrest was for an offence. Furthermore, a volunteer (see para 2.164 below) is always entitled to legal advice and ought to be treated with no less consideration than a detainee.[69] Code C applies to people in custody at a police station in England and Wales whether or not they have been arrested,[70] and it also applies to persons removed to a police station as a place of safety under Mental Health Act (MHA) 1983 ss135 and 136. However, Code C section 15 (reviews and extensions of detention) applies only to persons in police detention. Code C does not directly govern the treatment of volunteers, but the code should be regarded as establishing minimum standards

68 PRA 2002 Sch 4 para 34(1) or 35(3) (PACE s118(2A)).

69 Code C NfG 1A.

70 Code C para 1.10, subject to certain exceptions set out in Code C para 1.12. It was held in *Williamson v Chief Constable of the West Midlands* [2003] EWCA Civ 337 that Code C did not apply to a person detained at a police station following arrest for breach of the peace because such a person was not arrested for an offence, and was therefore not in police detention. However, Code C para 1.10 states that the code applies to people in custody at police stations 'whether or not they have been arrested'.

governing their treatment (see Code C NfG 1A). Persons who are designated civilian officers under the PRA 2002 (see para 2.54 below), and those who are accredited under PRA 2002 s41, must have regard to any relevant provision of the PACE Codes in the exercise or performance of their powers (PACE s67(9A)). For the application of Code C where a person is being investigated by others charged with the duty of investigating offences or charging offenders, see para 1.68 below.

Persons examined, detained or arrested under terrorism legislation

1.61 A person who is at a port or border area may be examined, and detained for examination, by an examining officer (which includes a police constable, immigration officer and designated customs officer) who believes that their presence at that place is connected with entering or leaving the country, to enable the officer to determine whether the person is or has been concerned in the commission, preparation or instigation of acts of terrorism. A person may also be detained for examination if they are detained under the Immigration Acts or are in custody having been arrested under Immigration Act (IA) 1971 Sch 2 para 17(1) (TA 2000 s53 and Sch 7 para 2). The person may initially be questioned for up to an hour, but if they are detained under TA 2000 Sch 7 para 6, they may be detained for questioning for up to six hours beginning with the time when the examination began (TA 2000 Sch 7 para 6A). The treatment of a person so detained is governed by TA 2000 Sch 8 Part 1. The person is not treated as being in police detention for the purposes of PACE, and the PACE Codes of Practice do not apply to them. There is a separate code of practice for examining officers issued under TA 2000 Sch 14 para 6.[71] The detainee is entitled to have a person informed of their detention (TA 2000 Sch 8 para 6). They are also entitled to consult a solicitor, normally in person, and where they have requested a solicitor they should not normally be questioned until they have consulted the solicitor (TA 2000 Sch 8 paras 7 and 7A). A person detained for examination under Schedule 7 is entitled to legal aid.

1.62 Similar powers of examination and detention for examination are available under Counter-Terrorism and Border Security Act (C-TBSA) 2019 s22 and Sch 3. An examining officer may question a person for the purpose of determining whether they appear to be a person who is, or has been, engaged in hostile activity provided one or both of the conditions set out in Schedule 3 para 1(2) and (3) is satisfied (C-TBSA 2019 Sch 3 para 1). The powers may be carried out irrespective of whether there are grounds to suspect that the person is or has been engaged in hostile activity (Sch 3 para 1(4)). 'Hostile activity' is defined in Schedule 3 para 1(5) and (6). Where a person is detained for examination, they are not treated as being

71 *Examining officers and review officers under Schedule 7 to the Terrorism Act 2000* (updated July 2025), available at: www.gov.uk/government/publications/codes-of-practice-for-officers-using-examination-powers-at-ports/examining-officers-and-review-officers-under-schedule-7-to-the-terrorism-act-2000-accessible-version#:~:text=An%20examining%20officer%20may%20only,is%20necessary%20for%20that%20purpose.

in police detention for the purposes of PACE and the PACE Codes of Practice. Instead, the applicable powers and rights are governed by C-TBSA 2019 Sch 3 and the Code of Practice issued under that Act.[72] A detained person (but not a person examined without being detained) does have the right to consult with a solicitor in private, but this is subject to certain limitations (Sch 3 paras 30–33).[73] A person detained for examination under Schedule 3 is entitled to legal aid.

1.63 A person may be arrested under TA 2000 s41(1) on suspicion of being a terrorist, or under section 43B on suspicion that they are a terrorist offender who is in breach of their licence (see paras 2.29 and 2.30 below). A person arrested under section 41 or 43B must be taken to a police station designated by the secretary of state for these purposes (see para 2.58 below). The person is not treated as having been arrested for an offence, but is treated as being in police detention for the purposes of PACE (s118(2)(a)). Detention is regulated by TA 2000 Sch 8 and Code H. Code H applies up until the time when a person so detained is charged, released without charge or transferred to prison (Code H para 1.2). Code C applies if and when the person is charged. PACE Code D does apply to persons arrested under TA 2000 s41, except for those provisions relating to photographs, fingerprints, skin impressions, body samples and impressions of people (Code D para 2.17). PACE Codes E and F do not apply, but there is a separate code of practice governing the video recording of interviews issued under TA 2000 Sch 8 para 3(4)(a).[74] There are special provisions concerning the length of detention without charge and review of detention (see paras 2.83 and 2.97 below). A person detained under these provisions has the right to have someone informed of their detention (TA 2000 Sch 8 para 6) and the right to consult a solicitor (TA 2000 Sch 8 para 7), but these rights may be delayed on the authority of a superintendent or above (TA 2000 Sch 8 para 8; and see para 2.156 below). A person arrested and detained under TA 2000 s41(1) or 43B and Sch 8 is entitled to legal aid.

Persons arrested or detained under the National Security Act 2023

1.64 A person may be arrested under NSA 2023 s27(1) where a constable reasonably suspects that they are, or have been, involved in a foreign power threat activity (see para 2.32 below). A constable who arrests a person under section 27 must take them as soon as is reasonably practicable to a police station that the constable considers the most appropriate (NSA 2023 Sch 6 para 1(4)), but the secretary of state may designate places at

72 *Revised Schedule 3 Code of Practice 2023* (Updated July 2025), available at: www.gov.uk/government/publications/codes-of-practice-for-officers-using-examination-powers-at-ports/revised-schedule-3-code-of-practice-2023-accessible-version.

73 And see the Code of Practice paras 132–143.

74 *Terrorism Act 2000 video recording code of practice (July 2012)*, available at: www.gov.uk/government/publications/terrorism-act-2000-video-recording-code-of-practice; and *Examining officers and review officers under Schedule 7 to the Terrorism Act 2000* (updated July 2025), available at: www.gov.uk/government/publications/codes-of-practice-for-officers-using-examination-powers-at-ports/examining-officers-and-review-officers-under-schedule-7-to-the-terrorism-act-2000-accessible-version.

which persons arrested under section 27 may be detained (Sch 6 para 1(1)). The person is not treated as having been arrested for an offence, but is treated as being in police detention for the purposes of PACE (s118(2)). Detention is regulated by NSA 2023 Sch 6, and there are special provisions concerning the length of detention and review of detention (see paras 2.84 and 2.101 below). The applicable code of practice is Code I,[75] which is closely modelled on Code H. PACE Code D does apply to persons arrested under NSA 2023 s27, except for those provisions relating to photographs, fingerprints, skin impressions, body samples and impressions of people (Code D para 2.17). PACE Codes E and F do not apply, but video recording, with sound, of interviews is mandatory (Sch 6 para 3), and is regulated by a dedicated code of practice.[76] A person detained under these provisions has the right to have someone informed of their detention (NSA 2023 Sch 6 para 6), and the right to consult a solicitor (NSA 2023 Sch 6 para 7). However, either or both rights may be delayed on the authority of a superintendent or above (NSA 2023 Sch 6 para 9), and a superintendent may also deny access to a particular solicitor (NSA 2023 Sch 6 para 8). A person arrested and detained under NSA 2023 s27(1) and Sch 6 is entitled to legal aid.

Persons arrested and detained by HM Revenue and Customs

1.65 PACE s114(2) provides that any provision of PACE relating to the investigation of offences or detention may, by order and with appropriate modifications, be applied to investigations conducted by HMRC officers or to a person detained by HMRC officers. Most of the relevant provisions of PACE are applied to such investigations by the Police and Criminal Evidence Act 1984 (Application to Revenue and Customs) Order 2015 ('the 2015 Order').[77] HMRC officers have a variety of powers of arrest under the Customs and Excise Acts[78] and have powers of detention under PACE s37. A person is in HMRC detention for the purposes of PACE if they have been taken to an HMRC office after having been arrested for an offence or they are arrested at an HMRC office after attending voluntarily or accompanying an officer to it and are detained there, or elsewhere, in the charge of an officer. A person in HMRC detention is entitled to consult a solicitor under PACE s58 (and to legal aid), and is entitled to have a friend or relative informed of their arrest and detention under PACE s56.

1.66 The PACE Codes of Practice are specifically applied to HMRC officers by the 2015 Order art 3 and Sch 1.[79] However, it has been held that they do

75 This is published as a PACE Code even though the governing legislation is the NSA 2023. It is available at: www.gov.uk/government/publications/pace-code-i-2023/pace-code-i-2023-accessible.

76 *National Security Act 2023: video recording code* (December 2023), available at: www.gov.uk/government/publications/national-security-act-2023-video-recording-code-of-practice/national-security-act-2023-video-recording-code-accessible-version.

77 SI No 1783.

78 As defined in Customs and Excise Management Act 1979 s1(1).

79 And see *R v Sanusi* [1992] Crim LR 43, CA; *R v Weerdesteyn* [1995] Crim LR 239, CA; and *R v Okafor* [1994] 3 All ER 741, CA.

not apply where a person is interviewed under Value Added Tax Act 1994 s60.[80] They also do not apply to the civil investigation of tax fraud procedure.[81] By virtue of Borders, Citizenship and Immigration Act 2009 s22, the PACE Codes also apply to criminal investigations conducted by designated customs officials relating to a general customs matter or customs revenue matter as they apply to relevant investigations conducted by HMRC officers.

Persons arrested by the National Crime Agency

1.67 The Director General of the National Crime Agency (NCA) has the power to designate a member of the NCA staff as a person having the powers of a constable, HMRC officer and/or an immigration officer (Crime and Courts Act (CCA) 2013 s10 and Sch 5). Where a person is designated as having the powers of a constable, they have all the common law and statutory powers of a constable (CCA 2013 Sch 5 para 11), and PACE applies to them and to the exercise of their powers.[82] For this purpose PACE is subject to the modifications set out in Schedule 1 to the Crime and Courts Act 2013 (Application and Modification of Certain Enactments) Order 2014. The most important modifications are as follows.

- References to 'police officer' and 'officer' are normally to be treated as references to a 'designated person' under the CCA 2013. One consequence of this is that CCA 2013 designated persons are governed by the PACE Codes of Practice when exercising their powers as police constables.
- Where authorisation is required for a search under PACE s18, reference to an inspector is replaced by reference to a grade 3 officer.
- References to 'police station', for example, in relation to voluntary attendance (PACE s29), and fingerprints and samples (PACE s63) are to be treated as references to an 'NCA office'.
- 'NCA office' means a place for the time being occupied by the NCA.

Persons investigated by others having a duty to investigate crime

1.68 The provisions of PACE relating to investigation and detention apply only to police officers (and, subject to amendments and exceptions, Revenue and Customs officers, designated NCA staff, labour abuse prevention officers,[83] and to investigations under the Armed Forces Act 2006). However, any person who is 'charged with the duty of investigating offences or charging offenders' must, in the discharge of that duty, have regard to any relevant provisions of the Codes of Practice (PACE s67(9)).

80 *Khan v Revenue and Customs Commissioners* [2006] EWCA Civ 89.

81 See HMRC, *Code of Practice 9: where HMRC suspects fraud (COP9)* (June 2023), available at: www.gov.uk/government/publications/code-of-practice-9-where-hmrc-suspects-fraud-cop9.

82 Crime and Courts Act 2013 (Application and Modification of Certain Enactments) Order 2014 SI No 1704 art 3, applied by virtue of CCA 2013 Sch 8 Part 4.

83 See Police and Criminal Evidence Act 1984 (Application to Labour Abuse Prevention Officers) Regulations 2017 SI No 520.

This could include officers of the Department for Work and Pensions (DWP), the Serious Fraud Office[84] or certain local government officers such as trading standards officers[85] and environmental health officers, provided in each case that they do in fact have a duty of investigating offences. Thus, it has been held that inspectors appointed under Companies Act 1985 ss432 and 442 were not investigating officers within PACE s67(9).[86] A similar conclusion was drawn in respect of local tax inspectors.[87] Prison officers have been treated as persons charged with a duty of investigating offences, but not always.[88]

1.69 It has been held that the Codes apply to commercial investigators interviewing an employee,[89] store detectives[90] and investigators employed by the Federation Against Copyright Theft (FACT),[91] although in each case it is a question of fact whether the relevant personnel are charged with the duty of investigating offences. A senior line manager who interviewed an employee concerning suspicions that he was defrauding the company was treated, on the facts, as not having a duty to investigate offences.[92]

1.70 Where a person is interviewed by an official to whom PACE s67(9) applies, they are not covered by the police station advice and assistance scheme unless they are being held in custody at a police station or the interview is conducted in the presence of a police constable, although they will, subject to financial eligibility, qualify for assistance under the means-tested legal advice and assistance scheme.[93]

1.71 In recent years there has been an increase in the number of private prosecutions instigated by individuals (or corporations) instructing specialist firms. As part of the investigative process, a private prosecutor may invite a suspect to attend an interview 'under caution'. Any invitation should be critically assessed to identify whether PACE s67(9) will apply. If the section is found to apply, then an inference may be drawn from the accused's failure to mention, when questioned, any fact relied on in their defence in those proceedings.[94] However, an inference under CJPOA 1994 s34(1)(a) can only be drawn from a failure to mention a fact *when*

84 *R v Director of the Serious Fraud Office ex p Saunders* [1988] Crim LR 837, DC; and *R v Gill* [2003] EWCA Crim 2256.

85 *Dudley MBC v Debenhams* (1995) 159 JP 18, DC; and *R v Tiplady* (1995) 159 JP 548, CA.

86 *R v Seelig and Spens* [1991] 4 All ER 429, CA.

87 *R v Doncaster* [2008] EWCA Crim 5.

88 A prison officer was so treated in *R v Devani* [2007] EWCA Crim 1926, but not in *R v Taylor* [2001] EWCA Crim 2922. It has been held that a prison officer who merely hears an unsolicited comment by a prisoner is not investigating an offence, and is therefore not bound by the Codes (*R v Harper* [2019] EWCA Crim 343).

89 *R v Twaites and Brown* (1991) 92 Cr App R 106, CA.

90 *R v Bayliss* (1994) 98 Cr App R 235, CA.

91 *Joy v Federation Against Copyright Theft Ltd* [1993] Crim LR 588, DC. See also *Halawa v Federation Against Copyright Theft* [1995] 1 Cr App R 21, QBD. The RSPCA has accepted that its officers should comply with the Codes. See *RSPCA v Eager* [1995] Crim LR 59, DC, also reported as *Stilgoe v Eager* (1994) Times, January 27, DC.

92 *R v Welcher* [2007] EWCA Crim 480.

93 SCC Specification 2022 paras 9.54 and 9.113–9.140 (draft SCC Specification 2025 paras 9.51 and 9.109–9.136).

94 CJPOA 1994 s34(4).

interviewed and a refusal to attend questioning is insufficient for a section 34(1)(a) inference to be drawn.[95]

Service personnel

1.72 There is an important distinction between investigations conducted by Ministry of Defence police officers and those conducted by service police officers. Ministry of Defence police officers are deemed to be 'constables',[96] and PACE and the Codes apply to them in the normal way. In respect of investigations by service police officers, PACE s113(1) provides that the secretary of state may, by order, make provisions in relation to the investigation of 'service offences'[97] that are equivalent to the provisions of PACE Part V (the questioning and treatment of suspects). The Police and Criminal Evidence Act 1984 (Armed Forces) Order 2009[98] applies, with modifications, most of the PACE Part V provisions. A person arrested and held in custody is entitled to consult a legal adviser,[99] although this may be delayed for up to 36 hours in similar circumstances as those that apply under PACE (see para 2.151 below) where the person is in custody in respect of a serious service offence.[100] The ordinary PACE Codes of Practice do not apply, but dedicated codes have been issued under PACE s113(2) and (3).[101] A services person at a services establishment or elsewhere in the UK assisting with an investigation by the service police of an offence that cannot be dealt with summarily or suspected of a serious service offence is entitled to legal advice under the police station scheme.[102]

Immigration detainees

1.73 Where a person has been arrested for an immigration offence, PACE and the Codes of Practice will apply as normal, as will entitlement to advice and assistance under the police station scheme and the duty solicitor scheme. However, the SCC imposes restrictions. Advice and assistance may only be given under the police station scheme up to the point that the immigration authorities take over conduct of the investigation and it has been confirmed that no criminal offence or charge is being pursued. However, it may continue to be provided if the person remains in deten-

95 *R v Johnson* [2005] EWCA Crim 971. Note that this would not preclude an inference being drawn under section 34(1)(b) in appropriate circumstances.

96 Ministry of Defence Police Act 1987 s2(1).

97 Defined by Armed Forces Act 2006 s50(2).

98 SI No 1922.

99 The definition of 'legal adviser' in art 2(1) of the 2009 Order excludes non-solicitors or barristers.

100 2009 Order art 9. A 'serious service offence' is defined by art 2(1) to include offences that are equivalent to indictable offences, other service offences that may not be dealt with at a summary hearing by a commanding officer, and certain other specified service offences.

101 *Service police codes of practice* (November 2020), available at: www.gov.uk/government/publications/service-police-codes-of-practice.

102 SCC Specification 2022 paras 9.57–9.60 (draft SCC Specification 2025 paras 9.54–9.57)

tion and requires advice in respect of a criminal offence (including an immigration offence).[103] See further chapter 12.

Extradition Act 2003 Part 1 Warrant

1.74 Where a person has been arrested under an Extradition Act (EA) 2003 Part 1 warrant (formerly a European Arrest Warrant) under powers granted by EA 2003 Part 4, they must be taken before an appropriate judge as soon as is practicable (EA 2003 s4(3)), and may be held in custody at a police station until they are so produced. While at a police station, the person is not in police detention (see para 1.61 above), but is covered by dedicated EA 2003 Codes of Practice B, C and D.[104] A person who is arrested under a Part 1 warrant and held in custody at a police station is entitled to legal advice under the police station scheme.[105]

PACE and the Codes of Practice

1.75 PACE has been amended by numerous subsequent statutes, and the structure is therefore quite complex and, in places, confusing. An up-to-date version can be found at: www.legislation.gov.uk/ukpga/1984/60/contents. The PACE Codes of Practice are issued by the secretary of state under the authority of PACE ss66 and 67. Current versions of the Codes of Practice are available at: www.gov.uk/guidance/police-and-criminal-evidence-act-1984-pace-codes-of-practice. For applicability of the PACE Codes to persons examined, detained or arrested under terrorism legislation (see paras 1.61–1.64). Note that whilst PACE Code A does not apply to stop and search under the TA 2000, which is governed by a separate code of practice,[106] it does apply to powers under Terrorism Prevention and Investigation Measures Act (TPIMA) 2011 Sch 5 to search persons without them being arrested. PACE Code B includes powers to enter and search premises for the purposes of serving, monitoring and enforcing terrorism prevention and investigation measures. For the applicability of PACE Codes C and H in respect of a person arrested under TA 2000 s41(1) on suspicion of being a terrorist, see para 1.63 above. For applicability of the PACE Codes to persons arrested or detained under the NSA 2023, see para 1.64 above. For applicability of PACE and the PACE Codes

103 SCC Specification 2022 paras 9.61–9.66 (draft SCC Specification 2025 paras 9.58–9.63)

104 Extradition Act 2003 (Codes of Practice and Transit Code of Practice) Order 2021 SI No 530. The codes are available at: https://assets.publishing.service.gov.uk/media/6033e3f6d3bf7f264f23eb38/CCS001_CCS0221079802-001_Extradition_Act_2003_CoP_Web_Accessible.pdf.

105 This is not expressly referred to in SCC Specification 2022 para 9.1, but follows from para 9.99 (draft SCC Specification 2025 para 9.96 onwards).

106 Issued under the Terrorism Act 2000 (Alterations to the Search Powers Code for England and Wales and Scotland) Order 2022 SI No 1087. The code is available at: www.gov.uk/government/publications/police-stop-and-search-powers-code-of-practice/revised-code-of-practice-england-wales-and-scotland-for-the-exercise-of-stop-and-search-powers-accessible--6.

to persons arrested or detained by HMRC officers, see paras 1.65–1.66 above.

1.76 A failure by a police officer or other person required to have regard to provisions of the PACE Codes does not, of itself, render them liable to criminal or civil proceedings (PACE s67(10)). However, to the extent that they are relevant, the codes are admissible in evidence in criminal or civil proceedings (PACE s67(11)). See further chapter 13 below.

CHAPTER 2

Key provisions of PACE, the terrorism legislation and the Codes

continued

Introduction

2.1 This chapter sets out some of the key powers, and important terms and phrases, in the Police and Criminal Evidence Act 1984 (PACE), the Terrorism Act (TA) 2000, the Counter-Terrorism and Border Security Act (C-TBSA) 2019, the National Security Act (NSA) 2023, and the relevant codes of practice and explains their practical significance. The purpose is to provide a ready reference that is of immediate practical use. For a more extended consideration of them, see one of the guides to PACE or police powers.[1]

Stop and search

Introduction

2.2 The police have a range of powers to stop and search people without arresting them. The main general power of stop and search is governed by PACE Part I, but there are powers under other legislation, including the Criminal Justice and Public Order Act (CJPOA) 1994, the Misuse of Drugs Act (MDA) 1971 and the TA 2000. PACE Code of Practice A[2] applies to most police powers of stop and search other than those under Aviation Security Act 1982 s27(2), PACE s6(1) (relating to powers of constables employed by statutory undertakers on the premises of those statutory undertakers), and the TA 2000 (for which there is a separate code of practice) (see para 1.75 above). Examination under TA 2000 Sch 7 is also covered by a separate code of practice (see para 1.61 above), as is examination under the C-TBSA 2019 (see para 1.62 above). However, Code A does apply to search powers granted by Terrorism Prevention and Investigation Measures Act (TPIMA) 2011 Sch 5. Code A also applies, subject to modifications, to persons subject to a serious violence reduction order (SVRO).[3] For a list of powers to which Code A applies, see Code A Annex A. Community support officers do not have powers of stop and search under PACE, but do have powers under other legislation, which are summarised in Code A Annex C.

2.3 Different police forces make markedly different use of stop and search powers, but nationally around one in seven stop and searches under PACE results in an arrest. Although police station lawyers are not often called upon to advise on stop and search powers, it is important to understand the powers since the legality of an arrest may be affected by the legality of a stop and search that preceded it, and advice concerning a substantive

1 For example, M Zander, *Zander on PACE: The Police and Criminal Evidence Act 1984* (Sweet & Maxwell, London, 9th edn, 2023).

2 See para 1.71 above. See also the College of Policing, *Authorised professional practice: Stop and search* (updated 2017), available at: www.college.police.uk/app/stop-and-search/stop-and-search. Note that the version available on 30 June 2025 is not fully up to date.

3 See Code A Annex G. SVROs are governed by the Sentencing Code s342E, and on 30 June 2025 were being piloted only in the Thames Valley, Sussex, West Midlands and Merseyside police force areas. The pilot ends on 19 October 2025 after which a decision will be made on whether to apply SVROs nationally.

offence allegedly committed in the context of the exercise of stop and search powers (for example, assault on a police officer in the execution of their duty) may be affected by the conduct or legality of the stop and search.[4]

Powers to stop and search

2.4 PACE Code A para 1.5 provides that a police officer must not search a person where no power to search is applicable, even if the person consents to being searched.[5] Stop and search powers are of two types: (i) those that require reasonable suspicion; and (ii) those that do not.

Powers requiring reasonable suspicion

2.5 Reasonable suspicion is required for the exercise of stop and search powers under PACE Part I, MDA 1971 s23 and TA 2000 s43:

- Under PACE s1(2) a constable may search any person or vehicle, or anything that is in or on a vehicle, for stolen or prohibited articles, any article to which section 1(8A) applies, any substance to which section 1(8AA) applies, or any firework to which section 1(8B) applies. 'Prohibited articles' are specified in section 1(7) and (8)–(8C). By PACE s1(3) the constable must have reasonable grounds for suspecting that a relevant article will be found. For guidance on how the reasonable suspicion test must be applied, see Code A paras 2.4–2.6B.[6] A person may not be stopped or detained in order to find grounds for a search, but if during an 'ordinary' encounter with a member of the public suspicion emerges, a search may be conducted even though no grounds existed when the person was initially stopped (Code A para 2.11).
- Under MDA 1971 s23 a constable may stop and search a person whom they have reasonable grounds to suspect is in possession of a controlled drug in contravention of that Act or of any regulations made thereunder, and to search any vehicle or vessel in which the constable suspects that the drug may be found.
- Under TA 2000 s43 a constable may stop and search a person whom they reasonably suspect to be a terrorist to discover whether the person has in their possession anything that may constitute evidence that the

4 His Majesty's Inspectorate of Constabulary and Fire & Rescue Services (HMICFRS) has conducted a number of inspections of police use of stop and search powers. The most recent is HMICFRS, *Disproportionate use of police powers: A spotlight on stop and search and the use of force* (February 2021), available at: https://assets-hmicfrs.justiceinspectorates.gov.uk/uploads/disproportionate-use-of-police-powers-spotlight-on-stop-search-and-use-of-force.pdf. See also Metropolitan Police, *Stop and Search Charter* (February 2025), available at: www.met.police.uk/advice/advice-and-information/st-s/stop-and-search/met/the-stop-and-search-charter.

5 The only exception is where entry to a sports ground or other premises is conditional on consent to being searched.

6 And see *Howarth v Commissioner of Police of the Metropolis* [2011] EWHC 2818 (Admin), regarding stop and search of a person suspected to be part of a 'protest group'.

person is a terrorist.[7] For guidance on how the test must be applied, see the Terrorism Act Code of Practice[8] paras 3.4.1–3.4.11 (see para 1.75 above).

Powers not requiring reasonable suspicion

2.6 Reasonable suspicion is not required to stop and search a person under a number of statutory powers, including the following:

- CJPOA 1994 s60, which enables a constable in uniform to stop and search persons or vehicles for offensive weapons or dangerous instruments[9] where an inspector or above has given an authorisation under section 60, reasonably believing that incidents involving serious violence may take place or that persons are carrying dangerous instruments or offensive weapons, and that it is expedient to give such authorisation. Under Code A para 2.14A,[10] the selection of persons and vehicles to be stopped and, if appropriate, searched should reflect an objective assessment of the nature of the incident or weapon in question and the individuals and vehicles thought likely to be associated with that incident or those weapons. See further Code A paras 2.12–2.14C.
- CJPOA 1994 s60AA, which permits a constable in uniform to demand the removal of, and to seize (but not to search for), any item that the constable reasonably believes is being worn wholly or mainly for the purposes of concealing identity. This power is only available if authorisation has been given by an inspector or above under CJPOA 1994 s60 or 60AA(3). See Code A paras 2.15–2.18.
- Criminal Justice Act (CJA) 1988 s139B, which permits a constable to enter school or further education premises and search the premises or any person on those premises for any bladed or pointed article, or offensive weapon. The officer must have reasonable grounds for suspecting that an offence under CJA 1988 s139A or 139AA has been or is being committed, but does not have to have such a belief in relation to any person searched. See Code A paras 2.27–2.29.
- MDA 1971 s23(3), where a warrant specifically authorises the search of persons found on premises specified in the warrant.

7 'Terrorist' is defined by TA 2000 s40 as a person who has committed an offence under TA 2000 ss11, 12, 15–18, 54 and 56–63, or is or has been concerned in the commission, preparation or instigation of acts of terrorism.

8 Issued under the Terrorism Act 2000 (Alterations to Search Powers Code for England and Wales and Scotland) Order 2022 SI No 1087. The code is available at: www.gov.uk/government/publications/police-stop-and-search-powers-code-of-practice/revised-code-of-practice-england-wales-and-scotland-for-the-exercise-of-stop-and-search-powers-accessible--6.

9 Defined in CJPOA 1994 s60(11).

10 This paragraph was added following the decision in *Gillan and Quinton v UK* (App No 4158/05) (2010) 50 EHRR 45, ECtHR concerning similar powers under the TA 2000. In *R (Roberts) v Commissioner of Police of the Metropolis* [2015] UKSC 79 the Supreme Court confirmed the power under section 60 to be compatible with European Convention on Human Rights (ECHR) Article 8 (right to private and family life).

- TPIMA 2011 Sch 5 para 3, which permits a constable to detain a person to be searched under powers granted by paras 6(2)(a), 8(2)(a) and 10. See Code A paras 2.18–2.26.
- NSA 2023 Sch 11 paras 3 and 6, which permit a constable to detain and search a person when serving a Part 2 notice under section 39, or after having served such a notice, for anything that may contravene measures in the notice.
- TA 2000 s47A, which permits a constable in uniform to stop and search any person or vehicle where authorisation has been given by an assistant chief constable (or equivalent) or above on the grounds that they reasonably suspect that an act of terrorism will take place and consider that such authorisation is necessary to prevent it.[11]
- Public Order Act 2023 s11, which permits a constable in uniform to stop and search persons or vehicles for prohibited objects, that is, an object that is made or adapted for use in the course of, or in connection with, an offence specified in section 11(1)(a), or which is intended by the person having it with them for such use by them or by some other person. Authorisation, for a specific period and location, must have been issued by an inspector or above, who must have a reasonable belief that authorisation is necessary to prevent the commission of offences specified in section 11(1)(a) or the carrying of prohibited objects (section 11(4)). The selection of persons or vehicles to be stopped should reflect an objective assessment of the nature of activity in the locality or items in question and the individuals and vehicles thought likely to be associated with that local activity or those items (Code A para 2.42A). See Code A paras 2.40–2.44.

The conduct of stop and search

2.7 The various statutory powers contain different provisions regarding the conduct of searches (for example, some require the officer to be in uniform and others do not), but Code A sets out minimum requirements that apply to all searches covered by the Code (see para 2.2 above). Reasonable force may be used to carry out a search, but only after it has been established that the person is unwilling to co-operate or resists (PACE s117 and Code A para 3.2). A person may be detained for the purpose of carrying out the search, but the period for which the person is detained must be reasonable and must be kept to a minimum (PACE s1(2)(b) and Code A para 3.3).[12] The search must be conducted at or near the place where the person or vehicle was first detained (Code A para 3.4).[13] However, a place is 'near' if

11 For an analysis of the power to stop and search under TA 2000 s47A, see E Cape, 'The counter-terrorism provisions of the Protection of Freedoms Act 2012: preventing misuse or a case of smoke and mirrors?' [2013] Crim LR 385. For detention for the purposes of examination under TA 2000 Sch 7, see para 1.61 above.

12 It was held in *R (Gillan) v Commissioner of Police of the Metropolis and Secretary of State for the Home Department* [2006] UKHL 12 that a 'short detainment' of 20 minutes was acceptable.

13 Note that the power of stop and search under PACE Part I may only be exercised in places to which, at the time, the public or a section of it have access (PACE s1(1)); and see *Sobczak v DPP* [2012] EWHC 1319 (Admin).

it is within a reasonable travelling distance 'using whatever mode of travel (on foot or by car) is appropriate' (Code A note for guidance (NfG) 6). Therefore, a person could be taken to a police station for the search to be conducted if it is near the place where they were first detained. NfG 6 states that this is the case whether or not the search requires the removal of more than outer clothing. If a search does require the removal of more than outer clothing, this cannot be done in public.[14] Therefore, if a search does require the removal of more than outer clothing and there is no suitable place out of public view nearby, a search cannot be conducted under these powers (see Code A NfG 6).

2.8 Before a search of a person or an attended vehicle is conducted, the officer must take reasonable steps to give the person certain information (PACE s2; Code A para 3.8):

- that the person is being detained for the purposes of a search;
- the officer's name (except in cases linked to the investigation of terrorism, or where the officer reasonably believes that giving their name might put them in danger, in which case a warrant or other identification number must be given) and the name of the officer's police station;
- the legal power of search that is being exercised;
- a clear explanation of the object of the search, the ground for suspicion (where suspicion is required) or the nature of the power and any necessary authorisation (where suspicion is not required); and
- the person's right to a record of the search.

If the officer is not in uniform, the officer must produce documentary evidence that they are a constable (for example, a warrant card) (PACE s2(2); Code A para 3.8). The obligations under PACE s2 are mandatory and failure to comply with them may render the stop and search unlawful.[15] If the person to be searched, or the person in charge of the vehicle to be searched, does not appear to understand what is being said, or there is any doubt about their ability to understand English, the officer must take reasonable steps to bring information regarding their rights to their attention (Code A para 3.11).

Recording and monitoring

2.9 The officer must make a written record of the stop and search unless it is not practicable to do so (PACE s3). Code A para 4.1 puts this in stronger terms, stating that a record must be made unless there are exceptional circumstances that would make this wholly impracticable. If the search results in an arrest and the person is taken to a police station, the record should be made as part of their custody record. Otherwise, the record

14 PACE s2(9)(a). See Code A para 3.5 for the permissible extent of a search in public.

15 *R v Bristol* [2007] EWCA Crim 3214. The obligation to inform the person of the officer's name and station is mandatory even if they are known to each other (*R (Michaels) v Highbury Corner Magistrates' Court and Crown Prosecution Service* [2009] EWHC 2928 (Admin)). See also *B v DPP* [2008] EWHC 1655 (Admin), in which a stop and search was found to be unlawful where an officer in plain clothes failed to produce his warrant card. If the stop and search is unlawful, the officer will not be acting in the execution of their duty.

must normally be made 'on the spot' or, if this is not practicable, as soon as practicable afterwards (PACE s3(2); Code A para 4.1). If a record is made at the time, the person must be asked if they want a copy, and if they do, they must either be given a copy of the record or a receipt that explains how they can obtain a copy (PACE s3(7)–(9); Code A para 4.2). The information to be included in the record consists of:[16]

- the identity of the officer making the search (subject to the exceptions in Code A para 3.8(b));
- the object of the search and the grounds for making it (subject to additional requirements set out in Code A para 4.3(d));
- the date, time and place when it was made; and
- except in the case of a search of an unattended vehicle, the self-defined ethnicity of the person searched or the person in charge of the vehicle searched (and, if different, their ethnic origin as perceived by the officer).

There is, unfortunately, no obligation to record what, if anything, was found in a search. Subject to local police force requirements, there is no obligation on an officer to record a 'stop and account' (ie where an officer requests a person in a public place to account for themself without exercising statutory stop and search powers) (Code A para 4.12).

2.10 Supervising officers are required to monitor the use of stop and search powers, and must 'consider in particular where there is any evidence that they are being exercised on the basis of stereotyped images or inappropriate generalisations' (Code A para 5.1). Any apparent disproportionate use of the powers by particular officers or groups of officers or in relation to specific sections of the community must be identified and investigated (Code A para 5.3).[17] Arrangements must be made for the records to be scrutinised by representatives of the community, and for explanations to be given of the use of the powers at a local level (Code A para 5.4).

Powers of arrest

Introduction

2.11 Police powers of arrest without warrant are largely governed by PACE s24, although they also have powers of arrest under a number of other statutes, and also at common law in respect of breach of the peace. In addition, the police have powers of arrest in accordance with warrants issued under Magistrates' Courts Act (MCA) 1980 s1 or under other legislation. The legislative provisions are supplemented by PACE Code G (see para 2.18 below). In addition to specific obligations, the code sets out some general requirements directed at the need to comply with the Equality Act 2010 and with the ECHR. It stresses the importance of the right to liberty

16 PACE s3(6) and (6A); Code A para 4.3.

17 Official statistics show that stop and search powers are consistently used disproportionately against black and Asian people. See the *Ethnicity and the criminal justice system* series published by the Ministry of Justice, available at: www.gov.uk/government/collections/race-and-the-criminal-justice-system.

under ECHR Article 5, and provides that exercising the power of arrest 'represents an obvious and significant interference with' that right (Code G para 1.2). It also states that an arrest must be both necessary and proportionate: police officers must 'consider if the necessary objectives can be met by other, less intrusive means' (Code G para 1.3). Arrest must never be used simply because it can be used: 'it is essential that it is exercised in a non-discriminatory and proportionate manner' (Code G para 1.3). Thus the less serious the suspected offence, the less likely that arrest rather than, for example, the written charge and requisition procedure, will be justified. This is particularly important because PACE s24 provides the police with powers of arrest in respect of *all* offences.[18]

2.12 The following sections set out the major statutory powers of summary arrest:

- police powers of arrest under PACE;
- civilian powers of arrest under PACE;
- arrest for breach of the peace; and
- pre-PACE powers of arrest.

This is followed by:

- arrest on suspicion of being a terrorist;
- arrest under the NSA 2023;
- arrest under warrant;
- arrest under PACE s31; and
- arrest other than for a criminal offence.

Thereafter, there is a discussion of some general issues: what constitutes an arrest; use of force; the information to be given on arrest; caution on arrest; the consequences of an unlawful arrest; and action following arrest, including 'street bail'.

Police powers of arrest under PACE s24

Introduction

2.13 Police officers have powers of arrest without warrant in respect of any offence in three sets of circumstances (PACE s24(1)–(3)).

(1) A police officer can arrest anyone who is about to commit an offence, or whom they have reasonable grounds for suspecting to be about to commit an offence (PACE s24(1)(a) and (c)).
(2) A police officer can arrest anyone who is in the act of committing, or whom they have reasonable grounds for suspecting to be committing, an offence (PACE s24(1)(b) and (d)).
(3) If a police officer has reasonable grounds for suspecting that an offence has been committed, they may arrest any person whom the officer has reasonable grounds to suspect of being guilty of it (PACE s24(2)). Alternatively, if an offence has been committed, a police officer may

18 For a report critical of the over-use of arrest powers in one police force, see Dame Vera Baird KC, *The Baird Inquiry* (July 2024), available at: www.greatermanchester-ca.gov.uk/media/9861/the-baird-inquiry.pdf.

arrest anyone who is guilty of the offence or anyone whom the officer has reasonable grounds for suspecting to be guilty of it (PACE s24(3)).

2.14 The provisions in PACE s24(1)(a), (b) and (3) give police officers powers to arrest a person who is about to commit, is in the act of committing, or has committed, an offence. Provided that this can be proved, for example, by a subsequent conviction of the person for the offence for which they were arrested, the arrest will have been lawful even if the officer had no, or no reasonable, grounds for suspecting the person at the time of the arrest (subject to the necessity requirement in section 24(4)).[19] However, even if it cannot be proved that an offence was, as a matter of fact, about to be, was being, or had been, committed, an arrest would still be lawful under section 24(1)(c) or (d), (2) or (3) (subject to the necessity requirement) provided that it can be established that the officer had reasonable grounds for suspecting that the person was about to commit or was committing an offence, or had reasonable grounds for suspecting that an offence had been committed and for suspecting that the person the officer arrested had committed the offence. While the reasonable suspicion provisions sound like a due process safeguard preventing arbitrary arrest, in fact they largely operate as a safeguard for the police.

Reasonable grounds for suspicion

2.15 Where reasonable grounds for suspicion are required, it has been held that whether the officer carrying out the arrest had reasonable grounds for suspicion must be assessed by reference to a mixed subjective/objective test: did the officer actually suspect that the person was guilty of the offence for which they were arrested; and if so, would a reasonable person in possession of the same facts as the officer have suspected that person.[20] Unlike Code A in respect of stop and search, Code G does not attempt to define reasonable grounds for suspicion in respect of powers of arrest. However, it does state that the facts and information relied upon should include those that tend to dispel suspicion as well as those that tend to indicate guilt (NfG 2A). In practice, the reasonable suspicion requirement has often been given such a liberal interpretation by the courts as to provide very little protection against arbitrary arrest.[21] The arresting officer must be in possession of some facts or information that would satisfy an objective observer that the person concerned may have committed an

19 The police rarely rely on the powers that do not require reasonable suspicion when defending actions for wrongful arrest, although largely for tactical reasons. See *Shields (by his Litigation Friend, Rebecca Shields) v Chief Constable of Merseyside Police* [2010] EWCA Civ 1281, in which they were encouraged to do so. However, arguably arrest without reasonable suspicion amounts to a breach of ECHR Article 5(1)(c) which, in effect, requires reasonable suspicion to justify the interference with liberty represented by an arrest (see para 13.52 below).

20 *Castorina v Chief Constable of Surrey* (1988) 138 NLJ Rep 180, CA. See also *Plange v Chief Constable of South Humberside* (1992) Times, March 23, CA; and *R v Redman* [1994] Crim LR 914, CA.

21 But see *Samuels v Commissioner of Police of the Metropolis* June 1999 *Legal Action* 14, CA, where it was held that the mere fact that a person was walking through an area well-known for burglaries did not provide reasonable grounds for suspicion; and *Fittschen v Chief Constable of Dorset Police* [2022] EWHC 399 (QB), in which the court found that the objective test was not satisfied.

offence,[22] but the threshold is low;[23] it is lower than a prima facie case and far less than the evidence required to convict. Suspicion may also take into account information that could not be used as evidence.[24] The officer does not have to have identified the precise legal power under which they act.[25] They can take a 'broad brush' approach so that it is not necessary for them to have identified the specific offence of which they are suspicious,[26] although the officer must suspect the existence of facts amounting to an offence of a kind that they have in mind.[27] Account can be taken of 'information of particular opportunity for a suspect to have committed an offence',[28] and it has been held that the fact that a small number of people could be identified as the only ones capable of having committed an offence can, in principle, afford reasonable grounds to arrest all of them.[29]

2.16 A major issue concerns arrests that are based on information supplied by someone else – such as a witness, an informant, a store detective, another police officer or via a computer. A description given by a witness can be sufficient for suspicion to be reasonable, and even a description given in an anonymous telephone call can be sufficient provided that the person arrested corresponds with the description given in the message.[30] Information received from a police informant can be sufficient, although it should be treated with considerable reserve.[31] Suspicion based on information contained on the police national computer can support reasonable suspicion even if the information turns out to be incorrect.[32] Reliance may be placed on a briefing by another police officer,[33] or by another investigator such as an officer from the Serious Fraud Office.[34] In such circumstances, the arresting officer is not under a duty to check the information supplied, and an arrest will be lawful even if the information

22 *O'Hara v Chief Constable of the Royal Ulster Constabulary* [1997] 1 All ER 129, HL (NI); and *Chief Constable of Northern Ireland v Smith* [2019] NIQB 39.

23 See, for example, *Armstrong v Chief Constable of West Yorkshire* [2008] EWCA Civ 1582; *Alford v Chief Constable of Cambridgeshire* [2009] EWCA Civ 100; and *Andrews v Chief Constable of Suffolk* [2022] EWHC 3162 (KB).

24 *Parker v Chief Constable of Essex* [2018] EWCA Civ 2788.

25 *R (Rutherford) v Independent Police Complaints Commission* [2010] EWHC 2881 (Admin).

26 Thus, in *Coudrat v Revenue and Customs Commissioners* [2005] EWCA Civ 616 it was held to be sufficient to arrest for 'VAT fraud' without being more specific. Note, however, that if the police wish to exercise a power that is dependent upon the person being under arrest for an indictable offence, a decision as to the precise grounds for the arrest must be made before the power is exercised.

27 *Chapman v DPP* (1989) 89 Cr App R 190, QBD.

28 *Al Fayed and Others v Commissioner of Police of the Metropolis and Others* [2004] EWCA Civ 1579.

29 *Cumming and Others v Chief Constable of Northumbria* [2003] EWCA Civ 1844; *Parker v Chief Constable of Essex* [2018] EWCA Civ 2788.

30 *Jones v Chief Constable of Bedfordshire* (1999) 30 July (unreported), CA; *King v Gardner* (1980) 71 Cr App R 13, DC; and *DPP v Wilson* [1991] RTR 284, DC.

31 *James v Chief Constable of South Wales* (1991) 6 CL 80, CA.

32 *Hough v Chief Constable of Staffordshire* [2001] EWCA Civ 39.

33 *Alford v Chief Constable of Cambridgeshire* [2009] EWCA Civ 100.

34 *R (Rawlinson and Hunter Trustees) v Central Criminal Court* [2012] EWHC 2254 (Admin).

was incorrect.[35] However, an instruction or request to arrest made by another police officer, without supporting information, would not be sufficient,[36] although the existence of such an instruction or request does not necessarily undermine the arresting officer's subjective belief that grounds for arrest exist.[37] How much information has to be given in order to satisfy the reasonable suspicion test would appear to depend on the status and identity of the person providing the information. Even a small amount of information received from a senior police officer is likely to be regarded as sufficient,[38] but it is not enough for the arresting officer to believe that the superior officer is in possession of information that the officer has not disclosed.[39]

2.17 An arrest carried out for an ulterior purpose, for example, to enable the police to install a bugging device in the suspect's house for the purpose of investigating another offence, is lawful provided there are reasonable grounds for suspicion in relation to the offence for which the person was arrested.[40] However, the police must not mislead the suspect as to the true nature of the investigation, for example, by failing to inform a person arrested for burglary that the victim had died.[41]

Belief that an arrest is necessary

2.18 The powers of arrest under PACE s24(1), (2) and (3) can only be exercised if the arresting officer has reasonable grounds for believing that arrest is necessary for one or more of the reasons set out in PACE s24(5) (PACE s24(4)). The necessity for arrest creates a higher threshold than merely 'desirable' or 'convenient', and must be assessed by reference to a mixed subjective/objective test: did the officer honestly believe that arrest was necessary; if so, would a reasonable person in possession of the same information as the officer have concluded that arrest was necessary; and if so, was the arrest *Wednesbury* reasonable[42] (ie was the discretion exercised properly having regard only to relevant factors?).[43] The requirement of *reasonable belief* that arrest is necessary clearly implies a higher threshold than that for *reasonable suspicion*; it constitutes a 'high bar'.[44] The objective element requires the officer to have 'solid grounds' for believing that that arrest is necessary, for example, that the suspect would hide or destroy

35 *R (Tchenguiz) v Director of Serious Fraud Office* [2012] EWHC 2254 (Admin); and *R (Chatwani) v National Crime Agency* [2015] EWHC 1283 (Admin). An arrest would not be lawful if the officer supplying the information lied or was not acting in good faith (*Copeland v Commissioner of the Police of the Metropolis* [2014] EWCA Civ 1014); but see *Karalis v Chief Constable of Derbyshire* [2023] EWHC 1496 (KB).

36 *R v Olden* [2007] EWCA Crim 726.

37 *R (Hicks) v Commissioner of Police of the Metropolis* [2012] EWHC 1947 (Admin).

38 *O'Hara v Chief Constable of the Royal Ulster Constabulary* [1997] 1 All ER 129, HL (NI).

39 *Commissioner of Police of the Metropolis v Raissi* [2008] EWCA Civ 1237.

40 *R v Chalkley and Jeffries* [1998] QB 848, CA.

41 *R v Kirk* [2000] 1 WLR 567, CA.

42 See *Associated Provincial Picture Houses Ltd v Wednesbury Corp* [1948] 1 KB 223, HL.

43 *Graham v Chief Constable of West Mercia and Others* [2011] EWHC 4 (QB); and *Richardson v Chief Constable of the West Midlands* [2011] EWHC 773 (QB).

44 *Commissioner of Police of the Metropolis v MR* [2019] EWHC 888 (QB).

evidence; a theoretical possibility that they might do so is not sufficient.[45] The officer should have in mind the specific necessity conditions set out in PACE s24(5) and be able to explain why arrest is necessary by reference to one or more of those conditions, having regard to the particular facts of the case. It is not lawful for an officer retrospectively to seek to justify an arrest by reference to a necessity condition that was not in their mind when they carried out the arrest.[46] Necessity is an 'exacting test' and the pre-conditions for arrest are a key constitutional safeguard in the 'exceptionally important' area of the liberty of a suspect. An officer who fails properly to turn their mind to the pre-conditions for arrest is exposed to the 'plain risk' of liability.[47] In relation to the arrest of a child, it has been held that in determining the necessity for an arrest, special regard must be paid to the need to safeguard and promote the welfare of the child, and that the time of the arrest is a relevant consideration.[48]

2.19 Voluntary attendance at a police station may be, but is not necessarily, a viable alternative to arrest.[49] In deciding whether arrest is necessary, an officer does not have to consider that there is no viable alternative to arrest, but they must make some evaluation of the feasibility of achieving the object of arrest by some alternative means, such as by inviting the person to attend the police station as a volunteer.[50] Code G para 2.6 provides that the officer must 'examine and justify' the reason or reasons why a person needs to be arrested, and this means that the officer must consider that arrest is the 'practical, sensible and proportionate option in all the circumstances' (Code G NfG 2C). While the officer is not required to interrogate the suspect to determine whether they will attend a police station voluntarily in order to be interviewed, the officer must consider whether voluntary attendance is a practical alternative for carrying out the interview (Code G NfG 2F).

2.20 Where a person attends voluntarily at a police station for interview by arrangement, their arrest is only justified if new information which came to light after the arrangements were made indicates that voluntary attendance is no longer a practical alternative to arrest, and it was not reasonably practicable for the person to be arrested before attending the police station (Code G NfG 2G). The routine arrest of persons attending voluntarily at the police station is not lawful, since the officer considering arrest must always consider whether arrest is necessary and be able to justify it.[51]

45 *Hanningfield v Chief Constable of Essex* [2013] EWHC 243 (QB), cited with approval in *B and Others (Former Soldiers) v Chief Constable of Northern Ireland* [2015] EWHC 3691 (Admin).

46 See, in particular, *R (TL) v Chief Constable of Surrey* [2017] EWHC 129 (Admin); and *Alger v Commissioner of Police of the Metropolis* [2023] EWHC 1582 (KB).

47 See *ALK and Another v Chief Constable of Surrey* [2025] EWHC 1964 (KB) and *Searson v Chief Constable of Nottingham* [2025] EWHC 1982 (KB).

48 *ST v Chief Constable of Nottinghamshire* [2022] EWHC 1280 (QB).

49 *Hayes v Chief Constable of Merseyside* [2011] EWCA Civ 911.

50 *Re Alexander and Others' Applications* [2009] NIQB 20; *Richardson v Chief Constable of the West Midlands* [2011] EWHC 773 (QB); *ST v Chief Constable of Nottinghamshire* [2022] EWHC 1280 (QB); and *Alger v Commissioner of Police of the Metropolis* [2023] EWHC 1582 (KB).

51 See *Richardson v Chief Constable of the West Midlands* [2011] EWHC 773 (QB); and *R (TL) v Chief Constable of Surrey* [2017] EWHC 129 (Admin).

The possibility that a person might decide to leave during the interview is not a valid reason for arresting them before the interview is commenced (Code G NfG 2G).[52]

2.21 Note that where a suspect is dealt with as a volunteer, some of the protective provisions of PACE and Code C do not apply to them (see para 2.164 below). However, a suspect may prefer to be dealt with as a volunteer since arrest may have adverse consequences in respect of their employment or travel abroad, and because it may amount to bad character for the purposes of Criminal Justice Act (CJA) 2003 ss98–113 (see para 5.173 below). Furthermore, being dealt with as a volunteer will avoid them being locked in a cell.

2.22 The necessity conditions set out in PACE s24(5), as supplemented by Code G, are as follows (together with commentary on those conditions):

- *To enable the name or address of the person in question to be ascertained* (where the constable does not know, and cannot readily ascertain, the person's name or address, or has reasonable grounds for doubting whether a name or address given by the person as their name or address is their real name or address (PACE s24(5)(a) and (b)).[53] Code G para 2.9(b) states that an address is satisfactory for the purposes of serving a summons if the person will be at it for a sufficiently long period to facilitate service, or that some other person at the address given will accept service of the summons on their behalf. This condition should not justify an arrest simply because a person does not have proof of their name and address on them. It refers to reasonable grounds for doubting the name or address given, which implies that the officer must have some objective reason for doubting the information given. The mere fact that other persons suspected of a similar offence have, in the past, given incorrect particulars would not be sufficient.[54]
- *To prevent the person causing physical injury to themself or any other person, suffering physical injury, causing loss or damage to property, committing an offence against public decency (which only applies where members of the public going about their normal business cannot reasonably be expected to avoid the person in question), or causing an unlawful obstruction of the*

52 Note that this was inserted into Code G after the judgment in *Hayes v Chief Constable of Merseyside* [2011] EWCA Civ 911, which held that a fear that a volunteer would leave during an interview did justify an arrest. In *Mouncher and 14 Others v Chief Constable of South Wales* [2016] EWHC 1367 (QB), it was held that 'the statutory provisions relating to the "necessity test" would be nullified if it was open to a police officer to say that arrest in advance of an interview under caution was always necessary to prevent the person being interviewed attempting to leave' (para 877). However, in *Parker v Chief Constable of Essex* [2018] EWCA Civ 2788 it was held that the fact that a person who had previously co-operated with the police when interviewed as a witness was now to be interviewed as a suspect was 'sufficient to raise a serious question about whether [he] would continue to co-operate' (para 130). See also *B and Others (Former Soldiers) v Chief Constable of Northern Ireland* [2015] EWHC 3691 (Admin) at paras 19 and 62; and *Rashid v Chief Constable of West Yorkshire* [2020] EWHC 2522 (QB) at para 25.

53 It was reaffirmed in *Neale v DPP* [2021] EWHC 658 (Admin) that whilst there is no general obligation on a person to provide their name and address, if suspected of an offence they may be arrested to enable their name or address to be ascertained.

54 *G v DPP (1988)* [1989] Crim LR 150, DC.

highway (PACE s24(5)(c)). Since the officer must have reasonable grounds for believing that a necessity condition renders arrest necessary, and Code G para 1.3 requires officers to consider whether the necessary objective can be achieved by measure short of arrest, the officer should consider whether any of the consequences could be avoided by actions other than arrest.

- *To protect a child or other vulnerable person from the person in question* (PACE s24(5)(d)). Again, the officer should consider whether the circumstances necessitate arrest or whether protection can be achieved by other means that do not interfere with the liberty of the person.
- *To allow the prompt and effective investigation of the offence or of the conduct of the person in question* (PACE s24(5)(e)).[55] '[P]rompt and effective' are to be read conjunctively, so that arrest should be necessary for both a prompt and an effective investigation.[56] Code G para 2.9(e) states that the condition may be satisfied if further action considered necessary properly to investigate the person's involvement in the (suspected) offence would be frustrated, unreasonably delayed or otherwise hindered and therefore rendered impracticable, if a suspect is not arrested.[57] Code G para 2.9(e) gives examples of investigative actions that may render an arrest necessary. However, some of the actions cited – such as entering and searching premises occupied or controlled by the person, and taking fingerprints, photographs, footwear impressions or non-intimate samples – can be carried out with the consent of the person concerned without arresting them. Therefore, an officer should, at least, consider whether their desired objective could be achieved by consent.[58] It has been held that the fact that an officer *may* wish to place a person on conditional bail following interview does not, of itself, render an arrest necessary.[59] However, an arrest to enable pre-charge bail to be imposed could be regarded as necessary if the officer has grounds for believing that conditions are necessary, for example, to protect a witness from intimidation.[60] The necessity condition may not be satisfied if the police arrest a person to enable them to conduct a search of premises under PACE s18, in circumstances where they believe that a search warrant would not be granted.[61] However, it has

55 It is not clear what the second clause, to investigate the conduct of a person, adds since the conduct of a person could only justify an arrest if it amounts to, or provides evidence of, an offence.

56 *B and Others (Former Soldiers) v Chief Constable of Northern Ireland* [2015] EWHC 3691 (Admin) especially at paras 53–54; although see *DE v Chief Constable of the West Midlands* [2023] EWHC 146 (KB).

57 For example, arrest to prevent collusion between co-suspects who were members of the same family: *R (Norman and Others) v Crown Court at Chelmsford and Chief Constable of Essex* [2020] EWHC 3456 (Admin).

58 See, for example, *Rashid v Chief Constable of West Yorkshire* [2020] EWHC 2522 (QB) (seizing the suspect's mobile phone); and *ST v Chief Constable of Nottinghamshire* [2022] EWHC 1280 (QB) (search of premises).

59 *B and Others (Former Soldiers) v Chief Constable of Northern Ireland* [2015] EWHC 3691 (Admin).

60 *R (TL) v Chief Constable of Surrey* [2017] EWHC 129 (Admin); and *DE v Chief Constable of the West Midlands* [2023] EWHC 146 (KB).

61 *R (TL) v Chief Constable of Surrey* [2017] EWHC 129 (Admin).

been held that where the conditions for both an arrest followed by a search and a search warrant are satisfied, the police have a choice as to which procedure to use.[62] PACE s24(5)(e) should not be used to justify arrest where there is no investigative need. In the case of many minor, regulatory or motoring offences the taking of fingerprints, photographs or non-intimate samples is not necessary for investigation of the suspected offence. Furthermore, it may be difficult for the police to justify an arrest under this condition where the person is then to be granted 'street bail' (see para 2.48 below), although in these circumstances arrest may be justified under the next condition.

- *To prevent any prosecution for the offence from being hindered by the disappearance of the person in question* (PACE s24(5)(f)). Code G para 2.9(f) states that this may apply if it is thought that the person will fail to attend court if not arrested, or if the address given is not a satisfactory address for service of a summons or a written charge and requisition. Since PACE s24(4) requires an officer to have reasonable grounds for believing that arrest is necessary, the officer must have some concrete basis for fearing that the person would not appear in court.

Civilian powers of arrest under PACE s24A

2.23 Civilian powers of arrest are more limited than those of police officers. A civilian, which for these purposes includes community support officers and other designated civilians (see para 2.54 below), can arrest in two sets of circumstances:

(1) A civilian can arrest a person who is in the act of committing an indictable offence, or whom the civilian has reasonable grounds for suspecting to be committing an indictable offence (PACE s24A(1)).
(2) Where an indictable offence has been committed, a civilian can arrest a person who is guilty of the offence or whom the civilian has reasonable grounds for suspecting to be guilty of it (PACE s24A(2)).

Unlike a police officer, a civilian cannot arrest a person for an anticipated offence. If a civilian arrests a person for an offence they believe has been committed (as opposed to one that is being committed), the arrest will be unlawful if it cannot be established that the offence was, in fact, committed. It can be difficult in practice to determine when an offence is complete for this purpose. For example, if a store detective arrests a suspected shoplifter as soon as they leave the shop, it is likely that the person would be regarded as still in the act of committing the offence of theft. However, if the suspect was arrested 20 minutes later by a security guard from another shop who had been given a description by the store detective, it is unlikely that it could be validly maintained that the suspect was still in the act of committing the offence.[63] The arrest by the security guard is potentially lawful under PACE s24A(2), but would not be lawful if it could not

62 *R (Singh) v National Crime Agency* [2018] EWHC 1119 (Admin).

63 For a case in which the distinction between an offence that was being committed and an offence that had been committed was critical to the question of whether the arrest was lawful, see *Sowande v Crown Prosecution Service* [2017] EWHC 1234 (Admin).

be established that an indictable offence had been committed.[64] An arrest by a police officer in these circumstances is likely to be lawful since PACE s24(2) permits an officer to arrest a person if the officer has reasonable grounds for suspecting that an offence has been committed. Unlike police powers of arrest, civilians may only arrest for indictable offences, ie offences that are triable only on indictment or offences triable either-way.[65] Therefore, civilians cannot arrest in respect of summary-only offences.

2.24 The power of arrest under PACE s24A(1) or (2) can only be exercised if the person making the arrest has reasonable grounds for believing that arrest is necessary for one or more of the reasons set out in PACE s24A(4), and it appears to the person that it is not reasonably practicable for a constable to make it instead (PACE s24A(3)). The necessity conditions, which are more limited than those relating to arrest by a police officer, are as follows:

- to prevent the person causing physical injury to themself or any other person, or from suffering physical injury (PACE s24A(4)(a) and (b));
- to prevent the person causing loss of or damage to property (PACE s24A(4)(c)); and
- to prevent the person making off before a constable can assume responsibility for them (PACE s24A(4)(d)).

Arrest for breach of the peace

2.25 An arrest for breach of the peace under common law powers can be made where:

- a breach of the peace is committed in the presence of the person making the arrest; or
- the person effecting the arrest reasonably believes that such a breach will be committed in the immediate future by the person to be arrested;[66] or
- where a breach of the peace has been committed or the person effecting the arrest reasonably believes that a breach has occurred, and it is reasonably believed that a further breach is threatened.

Compliance with ECHR Article 5(1)(c) requires that an arrest must be for the purpose of bringing the person before a competent legal authority, but the fact that a person arrested for breach of the peace is released before they can be taken before a court does not amount to a breach of that requirement.[67] A breach of the peace occurs whenever harm is actually done or is likely to be done to a person or, in their presence, to their

64 See *R v Self* [1992] 3 All ER 476, CA, which was decided under a previous version of PACE s24, but the same principles apply to PACE s24A.

65 Low-value shoplifting (ie where the value of the goods does not exceed £200 (MCA 1980 s22A)), although a summary-only offence, is treated as an indictable offence for the purposes of PACE (Anti-social Behaviour, Crime and Policing Act 2014 s176(6)).

66 *R (Laporte) v Chief Constable of Gloucestershire* [2006] UKHL 55; *Rawlins v Crown Prosecution Service* [2018] EWHC 2533 (Admin). For action short of arrest, such as 'kettling', see *Austin v Commissioner of Police of the Metropolis* [2009] UKHL 5; and *R (Moos) v Commissioner of Police of the Metropolis* [2011] EWHC 957 (Admin).

67 *R (Hicks) v Commissioner of Police of the Metropolis* [2017] UKSC 9.

property, or a person is in fear of being harmed through an assault, an affray, a riot, an unlawful assembly or other disturbance.[68]

2.26 The power to arrest for an apprehended breach of the peace caused by apparently lawful conduct is exceptional,[69] in the sense that the lawful conduct must be wholly unreasonable and interfere in some way with another person's rights.[70] It was held in *Steel v UK*[71] that an arrest to prevent a breach of the peace did not contravene the ECHR, although it must be proportionate to the aims of preventing disorder and protecting the rights of others. The principles to be followed in 'exercising the now exceptional common law power of arrest' where the conduct is not itself unlawful were set out by the Court of Appeal in *Bibby v Chief Constable of Essex*[72] as follows:

- there must be the clearest of circumstances and a sufficiently real and present threat to the peace to justify the extreme step of depriving of their liberty a citizen who was not at the time acting unlawfully;
- the threat must be coming from the person who is to be arrested;
- the conduct must clearly interfere with the rights of others;
- the natural consequence of the conduct must be violence from a third party;
- that violence must not be wholly unreasonable; and
- the conduct of the person arrested must be unreasonable.

2.27 A person arrested for breach of the peace may be held in custody at a police station, under common law powers, in order to prevent a breach of the peace. However, for detention to be lawful, fear of a further breach of the peace must be real, and the officer making the decision must have an honest belief, based upon objective and reasonable grounds, that further detention is necessary in order to prevent a breach of the peace. If these conditions are not satisfied, and no other grounds for detention exist, the person must be released.[73] Although breach of the peace is criminal for the purposes of ECHR Article 5 (right to liberty and security) and Article 6 (right to a fair trial),[74] it is not a criminal offence under domestic law. One consequence of this is that detention at a police station of a person arrested for breach of the peace is not governed by PACE s37 unless the person is also, or subsequently, arrested for an offence. However, their treatment while held in custody is covered by Code C, although the review

68 *R v Howell* [1982] QB 416, CA. For guidance on immediacy in relation to conduct in a domestic setting, see *Wragg v DPP* [2005] EWHC 1389 (Admin); and *Demetriou v DPP* [2012] EWHC 2443 (Admin).

69 *Foulkes v Chief Constable of Merseyside* [1998] 3 All ER 705, CA.

70 *Redmond-Bate v DPP* [1999] Crim LR 998, QBD.

71 App No 24838/94 (1999) 28 EHRR 603, ECtHR.

72 (2000) 164 JP 297, CA.

73 *Chief Constable of Cleveland v McGrogan* [2002] EWCA Civ 86.

74 *Steel v UK* (App No 24838/94) (1999) 28 EHRR 603, ECtHR.

of detention provisions does not strictly apply but should be followed as a matter of good practice (see Code C para 1.10 and NfG 15B).[75]

Pre-PACE powers of arrest

2.28 PACE abolished most existing powers of arrest, but Schedule 2 specifically preserves certain powers of arrest governed by pre-PACE legislation. Preserved powers include the power to arrest under Bail Act (BA) 1976 s7 for absconding or breaching bail conditions, and the power under the Mental Health Act (MHA) 1983 to arrest a person who is absent without leave or who has absconded.

Arrest on suspicion of being a terrorist

2.29 A constable may arrest without warrant a person whom they reasonably suspect to be a terrorist (TA 2000 s41(1)). There is no equivalent of the necessity requirement under PACE s24(4). A 'terrorist' is defined as a person who has committed an offence under TA 2000 s11 or 12 (activities in relation to proscribed organisations), ss15–18 (financial activities relating to terrorism), s54 (involvement in weapons training), ss56–63 (various activities relating to terrorism) or s40(1)(b) (where the person is or has been concerned in the commission, preparation or instigation of acts of terrorism (s40(1)). 'Terrorism' means the use or threat of action where the action falls within TA 2000 s1(2), the use or threat is designed to influence the government or an international governmental organisation or to intimidate the public or a section of the public, and the use or threat is made for the purpose of advancing a political, religious, racial or ideological cause (TA 2000 s1(1)). Action falls within TA 2000 s1(2) if it involves serious violence against a person or serious damage to property, endangers another person's life, creates a serious risk to the health or safety of the public or a section of the public, or is designed seriously to interfere with or seriously to disrupt an electronic system. The power of arrest gives a broad discretion to the police since the arresting officer does not have to have a specific offence in mind.

2.30 A constable may arrest without warrant a terrorist offender who has been released on licence, if they have reasonable grounds for suspecting that the person has breached a condition of their licence and reasonably considers it necessary, for purposes connected with protecting members of the public from a risk of terrorism, to detain them until a recall decision is made (TA 2000 s43B(1)). 'Terrorist offender' is defined by section 43B(4). If the person is not recalled, or detained under any other power,

75 It was held in *Williamson v Chief Constable of the West Midlands* [2003] EWCA Civ 337 that Code C does not apply to a person detained at a police station following arrest for breach of the peace because such a person was not arrested for an offence, and was therefore not in police detention. However, Code C para 1.10 states that the code applies to people in custody at police stations 'whether or not they have been arrested', and it would be a strange result if a person arrested and detained for breach of the peace had less protection than a person who is in custody without having been arrested. See further para 2.144 below regarding the right to consult a solicitor.

they must be released no later than six hours from the time of arrest under this section (section 43B(2) and (6)).

2.31 Where a person is arrested under TA 2000 s41 or 43B, their detention and treatment is governed by TA 2000 Sch 8 rather than by PACE. The person is not treated as having been arrested for an offence, but is treated as being in police detention by virtue of PACE s118(2)(a). For application of the PACE Codes see para 1.61 above. Where a person is arrested under TA 2000 s41, they should be taken to a place designated by the secretary of state for the purpose of detention under this section (TA 2000 Sch 8 para 1).

Arrest under the National Security Act 2023

2.32 A constable may arrest without warrant a person whom they reasonably suspect is, or has been, involved in a foreign power threat activity (NSA 2023 s27(1)). There is no equivalent of the necessity requirement under PACE s24(4). '[F]oreign power threat activity' is defined in NSA 2023 s33, and includes the commission, preparation or instigation of acts or threats within section 33(3), conduct which facilitates or is intended to facilitate such conduct, or conduct which gives support or assistance to a person that the offender knows or believes to be involved in such conduct. A constable who arrests a person under section 27 must take them as soon as is reasonably practicable to a police station which the constable considers the most appropriate (NSA 2023 Sch 6 para 1(4)), but the secretary of state may designate places at which persons arrested under section 27 may be detained (NSA 2023 Sch 6 para 1(1)). The person is not treated as having been arrested for an offence, but is treated as being in police detention for the purposes of PACE (s118(2)). Detention is regulated by NSA 2023 Sch 6, and there are special provisions concerning the length of detention and review of detention (see paras 2.84 and 2.101 below). For the relevant codes of practice, see para 1.64 above.

Arrest under warrant

2.33 There is a number of statutes that provide for the issue of a warrant for arrest. The most important of the statutes that authorise arrest under warrant for a criminal offence is the MCA 1980. Section 1 empowers a justice to issue a warrant on the basis of written information substantiated on oath that a person has, or is suspected of having, committed an offence. Such a warrant may or may not be endorsed for bail. If endorsed for bail, the warrant will (if relevant) specify the amounts in which any sureties are to be bound. If bail is to be granted with sureties, the police must release the offender if the sureties approved by the officer enter into recognisances in accordance with the endorsement. The person bailed is then obliged to appear before a magistrates' court at the time and place named in the recognisance (MCA 1980 s117).

2.34 The power of a magistrates' court to issue a warrant for the arrest of any person who has attained the age of 18 years is limited by MCA 1980 s1(4). The offence concerned must be indictable (ie indictable-only or either-way), or punishable with imprisonment, or the person's address must be not sufficiently established for a summons to be served on them. A warrant to arrest any person for non-appearance before a magistrates' court must not be issued unless the offence to which the warrant relates is also punishable with imprisonment or where the court, having convicted the defendant, proposes to impose a disqualification upon them. Power is given under MCA 1980 s13 to issue a warrant for the arrest of a person who has failed to appear to answer a summons. Power to issue a warrant for arrest in respect of a person who has been granted bail and who fails to surrender to custody or who, having surrendered to custody, then leaves the court before the case is dealt with, is governed by BA 1976 s7.

Arrest under PACE s31

2.35 Where a person has been arrested for an offence and is at the police station in consequence of that arrest, and it appears to the police that, if released, they would be liable to arrest for some other offence, they must be arrested for that other offence (PACE s31). One effect of this requirement is that the detention time limit runs from the time applicable to the original offence and is not extended by the subsequent arrest (see para 2.76 below). Although powers of arrest are generally discretionary, PACE s31 has the effect of requiring arrest in circumstances where the section applies. However, generally, a person is liable to arrest only if the police have reasonable grounds for suspecting that the person is guilty (for example, under PACE s24(1)–(3)) and arrest is necessary under PACE s24(4) (see para 2.13 above). This gives the police some leeway. They could question a suspect about matters for which the suspect has not been arrested up to the point when (as a result of answers to the questions or otherwise) they form a reasonable suspicion that the suspect is guilty of the other matter(s), at which point the suspect must be arrested for the further offence(s) by virtue of PACE s31. For the obligation to caution the suspect, see paras 2.46 and 7.6 below.

Arrest other than for a criminal offence

2.36 In addition to the powers of arrest considered above, police constables and others have a range of powers to arrest people other than in respect of a criminal offence. For example, they may arrest a person for the purpose of taking fingerprints or samples (PACE s63A(4) and Sch 2A para 17) or for failure to surrender to police bail (PACE s30D or 46A). The police also have powers to arrest a person under MHA 1983 s136(1) (see para 11.97 below), and to arrest a child for breaking conditions of remand (Legal Aid, Sentencing and Punishment of Offenders Act 2012 (LASPO) s97).

2.37 Generally, the provisions in PACE Parts IV and V, governing detention, questioning and treatment, relate only to those who are in police detention (see para 1.58 above). The major exceptions to this are the right of intimation under section 56 and the right to consult a solicitor under section 58, which apply whatever the reason for the arrest. However (subject to the exceptions noted in the next paragraph), Code C (except section 15, governing reviews and extension of detention) is expressly applied to people who are in police custody, whether or not they have been arrested for an offence, and to those who have been removed to a police station as a place of safety under the MHA 1983 (Code C para 1.10). Therefore, subject to the exceptions noted in para 2.38 below, people arrested for any reason and held in custody in a police station must be treated in accordance with Code C.

2.38 Code C paras 1.11 and 1.12 provide that the code does not apply to the following groups of people in custody:

- persons detained to whom Code H applies (see para 1.63 above);
- persons detained to whom Code I applies (see para 1.64 above);
- persons detained for examination under C-TBSA 2019 Sch 3, to whom the code of practice issued under Schedule 3 para 56 applies (see para 1.62 above);
- persons detained for examination under TA 2000 Sch 7 (see para 1.61 above);
- persons who have been arrested on a warrant issued in Scotland by officers under CJPOA 1994 s136(2), or arrested or detained without warrant by officers from a Scottish police force under CJPOA 1994 s137(2) (when police powers and suspects' rights are the same as those in Scotland);
- persons arrested under Immigration and Asylum Act 1999 s142(3) for the purpose of having their fingerprints taken;
- persons whose detention is authorised by an immigration officer under Immigration Act 1971 Sch 2 or 3; or Nationality, Immigration and Asylum Act 2002 s62;
- convicted or remanded prisoners held in police cells on behalf of the Prison Service under the Imprisonment (Temporary Provisions) Act 1980; and
- persons detained for search under stop and search powers, except as required by Code A.

General issues

What is an arrest?

2.39 Although the police have long had extensive powers of arrest, the term 'arrest' is not defined by PACE, nor by any other legislation, and there is some inconsistency in the case-law. One approach is that a person is arrested if, as a result of what is said or done, they are under compulsion and are not free to go where they please.[76] Arrest, it is said, is an ordinary English word, and whether or not a person has been arrested depends not on the legality of the arrest but on whether they have been deprived of their liberty to go where they please.[77] A second approach is that context and purpose are relevant. In *Austin v Commissioner of Police of the Metropolis*,[78]

76 *Alderson v Booth* [1969] 2 QB 216, DC; *R v Inwood* (1973) 57 Cr App R 529, CA; *Spicer v Holt* [1977] AC 987, HL.

77 *Lewis v Chief Constable of South Wales* [1991] 1 All ER 206, CA.

78 [2009] UKHL 5.

the House of Lords distinguished between a deprivation of liberty and a restriction of movement. Whether a situation amounts to a deprivation of liberty as opposed to a restriction of movement is a matter of degree and intensity and is highly fact-sensitive. A whole range of factors has to be considered, including the individual's specific situation, the context in which the restriction occurs and the purpose of the confinement or restriction.[79] Taking hold of a person's arm for the purpose of simply drawing their attention to what is being said to them, without an intention to detain or arrest, is not an arrest unless it goes beyond what is acceptable by the ordinary standards of everyday life;[80] and the same is true where an officer takes a drunk person by the arm to steady them for their own safety.[81] However, if an officer takes hold of a person's arm to detain them while deciding whether to arrest them, that does amount to trespass.[82] Similarly, detaining a person by confining them to a restricted space, without intending to arrest them, amounts to unlawful imprisonment.[83] In *R v Iqbal* it was held that a person who was handcuffed by a police officer and told that he would be arrested later by other officers was not under arrest (although he was unlawfully detained).[84] Under the approach in *Lewis v Chief Constable of South Wales*,[85] the circumstances in *Iqbal* would clearly have amounted to an arrest, albeit an unlawful arrest because the appellant was not told that he was under arrest as required by PACE s28(1).

2.40 Despite the uncertainty as to the precise meaning of arrest, temporary deprivation of or interference with liberty – such as that under powers of stop and search (see para 2.2 above), or the power of a community support officer to require a person to wait for up to 30 minutes pending the arrival of a constable (see para 2.54 below) – is unlikely to be treated as an arrest either under domestic or ECHR law.

Use of force

2.41 The power of the police to use force in carrying out an arrest derives from PACE s117, which provides that where any provision of PACE confers a power on a constable and does not provide that the power may be exercised only with the consent of a person other than a police officer, the officer may use reasonable force, if necessary, in the exercise of the power.[86] A civilian designated under Police Reform Act (PRA) 2002 s38 may, in exercising powers in respect of which they have been designated, use reasonable force in the same circumstances as a constable (PRA 2002 s38(8) and Code C para 1.14). In addition, Criminal Law Act 1967 s3 empowers any person to use such force as is reasonable in the circumstances in the

79 See also *Austin v UK* (App No 39692/09) (2012) 55 EHRR 14, ECtHR; and *Shields v Chief Constable of Merseyside Police* [2010] EWCA Civ 1281.

80 *Mepstead v DPP* (1996) 160 JP 475, QBD.

81 *McMillan v Crown Prosecution Service* [2008] EWHC 1457 (Admin).

82 *Elkington v DPP* [2012] EWHC 3398 (Admin).

83 *Walker v Commissioner of Police of the Metropolis* [2014] EWCA Civ 897.

84 [2011] EWCA Crim 273.

85 [1991] 1 All ER 206, CA.

86 The use of force may be lawful even if used in relation to an unlawful arrest if, for example, the person being arrested uses unreasonable force in resisting that arrest (*Dixon v Crown Prosecution Service* [2018] EWHC 3154 (Admin)).

prevention of crime, or in effecting or assisting in the lawful arrest of an offender or suspected offender or of persons unlawfully at large. The use of force under either statutory provision must be both necessary and proportionate, and if the use of force is challenged, it is for the police to establish that the officer honestly believed that use of force was necessary, that their belief was objectively reasonable, and that the force used was no greater than was objectively reasonable in the circumstances.[87]

2.42 In determining what force is reasonable, a court may take into account all the circumstances, including:

- the nature and degree of the force used;
- the gravity of the offence for which arrest is to be made;
- the harm that would flow from the use of force against the suspect; and
- the possibility of effecting the arrest or preventing the harm by other means.[88]

The fact that the force used results in serious injury does not necessarily make it unreasonable,[89] although it will do so if the degree of force used was neither reasonable nor proportionate.[90] The use of excessive force does not render an otherwise lawful arrest unlawful.[91]

2.43 Handcuffs should be used only where they are reasonably necessary to prevent an escape or to prevent a violent breach of the peace by a prisoner.[92] For a stop and search, handcuffs must only be used when lawful, necessary and proportionate, and use as a matter of routine is likely to be unlawful.[93]

Information to be given on arrest

2.44 A person who is arrested (whether or not for an offence) must, unless the arrest is by way of informing them that they are under arrest, be informed that they are under arrest as soon as is practicable after the arrest (PACE s28(1)).[94] If the arrest is by a constable, this requirement applies even if the fact of the arrest is obvious (PACE s28(2)). Failure to inform the person renders the arrest unlawful. If an arrest is unlawful, any subsequent detention may be unlawful (see para 2.47 below).

2.45 In addition, a person who is arrested must be told of the ground for the arrest, either at the time of the arrest or as soon as is practicable afterwards (PACE s28(3)), and of the reason why arrest was believed to be necessary

87 *Afriyie v Commissioner of Police for the City of London* [2023] EWHC 1632 (KB).

88 For example, in *Roberts v Chief Constable of Kent* [2008] EWCA Civ 1588 it was held that reasonable force had been used despite the fact that a police dog had caused serious bite injuries.

89 *Roberts v Chief Constable of Kent* [2008] EWCA Civ 1588; *McDonnell v Commissioner of Police of the Metropolis* [2015] EWCA Civ 573.

90 *Minio-Paluello v Commissioner of Police of the Metropolis* [2011] EWHC 3411 (QB).

91 *Simpson v Chief Constable of South Yorkshire* (1991) Times, March 7, CA.

92 *R v Lockley* (1864) 4 F & F 155; and *Afriyie v Commissioner of Police for the City of London* [2023] EWHC 1632 (KB). The National Police Chiefs Council guidance on the use of handcuffs does not appear to be publicly available.

93 See: www.college.police.uk/app/stop-and-search/legal/legal-application#using-handcuffs-during-stop-and-search.

94 What is practicable depends upon the circumstances of the arrest. See, for example, *Wheeldon v Crown Prosecution Service* [2018] EWHC 249 (Admin).

(Code C NfG 10B; Code G paras 2.2, 3.3 and NfG 3). This information must also be recorded in the officer's pocketbook or by other methods used for recording information (Code G para 4.1) and, if the suspect is detained in a police station, in the custody record (Code C para 3.4). According to Code C NfG 10B and Code G NfG 3, where a person is arrested for an offence, they must be given sufficient information to enable them to understand the reason why they have been arrested, such as the nature of the suspected offence and when and where it was allegedly committed. It has been held that the words used will suffice even though they are apt to describe more than one offence,[95] and that informing a person that they were arrested for 'public order' was sufficient.[96] PACE s28(3) expressly provides that failure to inform the person of the grounds for arrest renders the arrest unlawful, unless it was not reasonably practical for them to be so informed because they escaped from arrest (PACE s28(5)).[97] An unlawful arrest may render subsequent detention unlawful, but an arrest that was unlawful for this reason becomes lawful when grounds for the arrest are given.[98]

Caution on arrest

2.46 A person who is arrested, or who is further arrested (for example, under PACE s31), must be cautioned at the time of the arrest or as soon as practicable afterwards unless it is impracticable to do so because of the person's condition or behaviour at the time, or the person has already been cautioned immediately before arrest (for example, where they were initially questioned regarding a suspected offence without being arrested) (Code C para 10.4; Code G para 3.4). The terms of the caution are set out in Code C para 10.4. The alternative caution set out in Code C Annex C para 2 (see para 5.69 below) does not apply unless the person is already in police detention (see para 1.58 above) at the time of the arrest. Failure to administer a caution does not render the arrest unlawful, but it may provide grounds for exclusion of evidence under PACE s76 or 78.[99]

Consequences of an unlawful arrest

2.47 An arrest may be unlawful for a number of reasons:

- the officer carrying out the arrest did not have reasonable grounds for suspicion;
- the necessity condition was not satisfied; or

95 *Abbassy v Commissioner of Police of the Metropolis* [1990] 1 All ER 193, CA; *Clarke v Chief Constable of North Wales* [2000] All ER (D) 477, CA.

96 *Walker v Commissioner of Police of the Metropolis* [2014] EWCA Civ 897. For an analysis, see E Cape, 'Transposing the EU Directive on the Right to Information: a firecracker or a damp squib?' [2015] Crim LR 48 at p54.

97 If the person is not notified of the grounds for arrest for this reason, the arrest does not become retrospectively unlawful because of a later failure to provide this information (*DPP v Hawkins* [1988] 3 All ER 673, QBD; *Lewis v Chief Constable of South Wales* [1991] 1 All ER 206, CA).

98 *Lewis v Chief Constable of South Wales* [1991] 1 All ER 206, CA. In this case, grounds for arrest were given 10 and 23 minutes after arrest. See also *DPP v L* [1999] Crim LR 752, DC.

99 *R v Miller* [2007] EWCA Crim 1891.

- the arrested person was not informed of the fact of or grounds for arrest.

If an arrest is unlawful, subsequent detention at the police station is arguably unlawful since the power to detain a person under PACE s37 (see para 2.56 below) depends on the person having been lawfully arrested. While some forms of unlawful arrest can be 'cured', in particular failure to inform the person of the grounds for arrest, this is not the case where, for example, the arrest was not necessary. If the defence lawyer believes an arrest to have been unlawful, they should consider making representations to the custody officer regarding detention, or bail, at the police station. It was held in *Hutt v Commissioner of Police of the Metropolis*[100] that where a person who has been unlawfully arrested is charged with an offence, bail under PACE s38(1) cannot be denied. Note that the custody officer must disclose documents and materials that are essential for challenging the legality of an arrest (Codes C and H para 3.4(b); and see para 2.62 below). The fact that an arrest was unlawful may amount to a defence against a charge of obstruction or assault arising from the arrest,[101] and this can include an assault on an officer who came to the aid of the officer carrying out the unlawful arrest.[102] An unlawful arrest may also provide grounds for the exclusion of evidence or for a civil action against the police (see chapter 13).

Action following arrest and 'street bail'

2.48 Where a person has been arrested by a police officer in a place other than a police station, or is taken into custody by a police officer after being arrested for an offence by a civilian, the officer must normally take them to a designated police station as soon as practicable after the arrest (PACE s30(1), (1A), (1B) and (2)).[103] In exceptional circumstances, they may be taken to a non-designated station (PACE s30(3)–(6)). The officer may delay taking the person to a police station or releasing them on street bail (see below) if their presence is necessary in order to carry out such investigations as it is reasonable to carry out immediately (PACE s30(10)–(11)). This could include a search of premises under PACE s32 (see para 6.117 below) or under PACE s18 (see para 6.123 below). A section 18 search normally requires prior authorisation by an inspector or above, but this may be dispensed with in these circumstances (PACE s18(5)(b) and (5A)),

100 [2003] EWCA Civ 1911.

101 Although assault on a police officer under Assaults on Emergency Workers (Offences) Act 2018 s1 does not depend on the officer acting in the execution of their duty. See *DPP v Ahmed* [2021] EWHC 2122 (Admin); *DPP v Price and Darby* [2024] EWHC 2864 (Admin).

102 *Cumberbatch v Crown Prosecution Service; Ali v DPP* [2009] EWHC 3353 (Admin); *Oraki v Crown Prosecution Service* [2018] EWHC 115 (Admin). Self-defence may be available even if an arrest is lawful, since the defence 'applies in accordance with the state of mind of the defendant, albeit mistaken and perhaps unreasonable' (*Wheeldon v Crown Prosecution Service* [2018] EWHC 249 (Admin) at para 40).

103 Failure to comply with PACE s30 may, but will not necessarily, result in the exclusion of evidence obtained during any period of delay (*R v King and Provan* [2012] EWCA Crim 805).

although the officer must then inform an inspector or above as soon as practicable after the search has been conducted (PACE s18(6)).

2.49 As an alternative to taking the arrested person to a police station, the officer may release them without bail, or on bail (known as 'street bail') to attend at a police station on a future date (PACE s30A). The release may only be on bail if the officer is satisfied that releasing the person on bail is necessary and proportionate in all the circumstances, and it is authorised by a custody officer (PACE s30A(1A)). In determining whether a release on bail is necessary and proportionate, the officer must have regard in particular to:

- the need to secure that the arrested person surrenders to custody;
- the need to prevent offending by the arrested person;
- the need to safeguard victims and witnesses;
- the need to safeguard the arrested person; and
- the need to manage risks to the public (PACE s30A(1B)).

2.50 Street bail may be unconditional or conditional. Such conditions may be imposed as appear to the police officer to be necessary for the purpose of securing surrender, preventing further offences, preventing interference with witnesses or obstruction of the administration of justice, or for the person's own protection (or if the person is aged under 18 years, for their own welfare or in their own interests) (PACE s30A(3B)). A surety or security cannot be required, nor a requirement that the person reside in a bail hostel (PACE s30A(3A)). An application to vary or remove conditions may be made to the police (normally the custody officer at the station at which the person is required to surrender) and, thereafter, to a magistrates' court (PACE ss30CA and 30CB).

2.51 Before releasing a person on street bail, the officer must give them a notice stating:[104]

- the offence for which they were arrested;
- the ground on which they were arrested;
- if conditions are imposed, the requirements imposed by those conditions and the right to apply for variation of those conditions;
- the fact that the person is required to attend a police station; and
- the time and police station where the person is to surrender.

The police station that the person is required to attend can be any police station (PACE s30A(5)). The period for which bail may be granted is limited to three months, beginning the day after the day on which they were arrested for the offence for which bail is granted, and there is no provision for this to be extended (PACE s30B(8)). The time and place for surrender may subsequently be varied (PACE s30B(6) and (7)), and the requirement to attend may be withdrawn (PACE s30C(1)). When a person answers to street bail, the custody officer must link any documentation held in relation to the arrest with the custody record (Code C para 3.25).

2.52 If the person fails to attend at the specified time, they may be arrested (PACE s30D(1)) and, in any event, may be re-arrested if new evidence has come to light or an examination or analysis of existing evidence has been

104 PACE s30B.

made which could not reasonably have been made before their release (PACE s30C(4)). The person may also be arrested if, in the case of conditional street bail, a constable has reasonable grounds for suspecting that they have broken any of those conditions (PACE s30D(2A)). If arrested under these provisions, the person must be taken to a police station (which may be the specified police station or any other police station) (PACE s30D(2B)). Although breach of conditions, and failure to attend a police station, are not criminal offences, an arrest under these provisions counts as an arrest for an offence for the purpose of PACE ss30 and 31 (PACE s30D(4)). There is no power of arrest for an anticipated breach of conditions or anticipated failure to surrender.

2.53 Where a client has been granted street bail, the lawyer should carefully scrutinise the reasons given by the police for why an arrest was necessary since, given the willingness of the officer to release the person on bail, it may be difficult for them to justify the necessity for the arrest by reference to PACE s24(4) and (5) (see para 2.18 above).

Powers of designated police civilians

2.54 Certain police powers can be exercised by civilians employed by the police authority, or by police volunteers, and designated by chief police officers as community support officers (CSOs) or community support volunteers (CSVs) or policing support officers (PRA 2002 Part 4).[105] Chief police officers have the authority to decide which police powers such officers or volunteers will have, and may confer any police power other than a 'core' power or duty listed in PRA 2002 Sch 3B Part 1. Excluded powers include the power of arrest, the power to stop and search, and the power to act as a custody officer. CSOs and CSVs may detain a person for up to 30 minutes to await the arrival of a police constable for certain purposes specified in PRA 2002 Sch 3C para 7.

2.55 A designated person may only use their powers if they are wearing an approved uniform (PRA 2002 s42(2)).[106] Where a designated person exercises a power which, if exercised by a constable, could be accompanied by the use of reasonable force, they are empowered to use reasonable force (PRA 2002 s38(8); Code C para 1.14). There are similar offences of assaulting, obstructing or impersonating designated police civilians as apply to police officers (PRA 2002 s46). Designated persons (and other civilian support staff) must have regard to any relevant provisions of the codes (PACE s67; Code C para 1.16).

105 There are also powers to designate civilians employed by organisations contracted by the authority to supply services as detention officers or escort officers (PRA 2002 s39); and powers to accredit civilians under community safety and other specified accreditation schemes, and who may be granted certain, more limited, powers. See PRA 2002 ss40–43.

106 Although by PRA 2002 s42(2A) an inspector or above may authorise a designated person not to wear a uniform for the purposes of a particular operation.

Power to detain without charge

Grounds for authorisation of detention

2.56 Following an arrest for an offence at a place other than a police station, the person arrested must normally be taken to a police station as soon as practicable (PACE s30(1), and see para 2.48 above). Where the person arrested is taken to a police station, the custody officer[107] must determine whether there is sufficient evidence to charge them, and may detain the person for such time as is necessary to enable them to do so (PACE s37(1)).[108] If the custody officer decides that there is sufficient evidence to charge the arrested person with the offence for which they were arrested, the person must either be charged or released without charge, either on bail or without bail (PACE s37(7)). If, however, the custody officer decides that they do not have before them sufficient evidence to charge, the arrested person must be released[109] unless the officer has reasonable grounds for believing that detention without charge is necessary:

- to secure or preserve evidence relating to an offence for which the person is under arrest; or
- to obtain such evidence by questioning the person (PACE s37(3)).

2.57 These grounds for detention apply to all persons, including children,[110] who have been arrested for an offence, and thus a person arrested for an offence cannot be detained without charge at a police station unless either or both of the grounds are satisfied. A person is deemed to have been arrested for an offence for the purposes of PACE s37 where they:

- were arrested under Road Traffic Act (RTA) 1988 s6D (arrest under the breath-test procedure) or Transport and Works Act 1992 s30(2) (arrest under the breath-test procedure of a person working on a transport system (PACE s34(6));
- have returned to the police station to answer to bail granted under PACE Part IV or are arrested under PACE s46A for failure to return to the police station to answer to bail; or
- have attended the police station having been granted bail under PACE s30A (street bail) or are arrested under section 30D having failed to attend (PACE s34(7)).

107 An officer designated as a custody officer must be of at least the rank of sergeant, although an officer of any rank can perform the functions if a custody officer is not readily available (PACE s36(3) and (4)). Normally, an officer acting as custody officer must not be involved in the investigation of an offence for which the person in respect of whom the officer is performing such duties is in detention, although there are exceptions (PACE s36(6)). If the person is taken to a non-designated police station (see PACE s35), any officer not involved in the investigation can perform the functions of custody officer (PACE s36(7)–(7B)).

108 Note that HMICFRS makes regular inspections of police custody facilities, and its reports may be accessed at: https://hmicfrs.justiceinspectorates.gov.uk/our-work/article/criminal-justice-joint-inspection/joint-inspection-of-police-custody-facilities/.

109 For the terms of such a release, see para 10.113 below.

110 'Juvenile' is defined as a person who appears to be under the age of 18 (PACE s37(15)).

PACE s37 does not apply to a person arrested other than for an offence in respect of whom the authority for detention will be governed by the common law, statute or, where a person has been arrested under the authority of a warrant, the warrant itself. Thus PACE s37 does not apply to:

- persons arrested for common law breach of the peace (see para 2.25 above);
- persons arrested under BA 1976 s7;
- persons arrested for breach of an injunction to which a power of arrest is attached; and
- convicted or remanded prisoners who are held in police cells on behalf of the Prison Service (Code C para 1.12(iv)),

although it does apply to prisoners brought to the police station having been arrested for an offence.

2.58 Where a person has been arrested under TA 2000 s41 or 43B, they must be taken as soon as is reasonably practicable to a police station designated by the secretary of state for these purposes (TA 2000 Sch 8 para 1).[111] The decision to detain a person arrested under TA 2000 s41 is governed by TA 2000 Sch 8 Part II, which provides that detention must initially be reviewed as soon as is reasonably practicable after arrest (TA 2000 Sch 8 para 21). The review officer can only authorise continued detention if satisfied that it is necessary (TA 2000 Sch 8 para 23):

(1) to obtain relevant evidence whether by questioning or otherwise;
(2) to preserve relevant evidence;
(3) pending the result of an examination or analysis of any relevant evidence or of anything the examination or analysis of which is to be or is being carried out with a view to obtaining relevant evidence;
(4) pending a decision whether to apply to the secretary of state for a deportation notice to be served on the detained person;
(5) pending the making of an application to the secretary of state for a deportation notice to be served on the detained person;
(6) pending consideration by the secretary of state whether to serve a deportation notice on the detained person; or
(7) pending a decision whether the detained person should be charged with an offence.

The review officer is an officer not directly connected with the investigation who, in the case of a review conducted within 24 hours of arrest, is of at least the rank of inspector, and in the case of any other review, is of at least the rank of superintendent (TA 2000 Sch 8 para 24). There is no equivalent to the obligation of a custody officer under PACE s37(7) to make a decision about charge if satisfied that there is sufficient evidence to charge. In the case of a person arrested under TA 2000 s41, subject to the overall detention time limits, detention can continue for so long as a review officer is satisfied that one or more of the above conditions applies, provided generally that the officer is satisfied that matters are proceeding diligently and expeditiously (TA 2000 Sch 8 para 23(2) and (3)). The review provisions do not apply to a person arrested under TA 2000 s43B, who must, in

111 See generally PACE Code H.

any event, be released no later than six hours[112] after the time at which they were arrested unless recalled or detained under another power (TA 2000 s43B(2) and (6)).

2.59 Where a person has been arrested under NSA 2023 s27, they must be taken as soon as is reasonably practicable to a police station designated by the secretary of state for these purposes (NSA 2023 Sch 6 para 1).[113] The decision to detain is governed by NSA 2023 Sch 6 Part 5, which provides that detention must initially be reviewed as soon as is reasonably practicable after arrest (NSA 2023 Sch 6 para 29). The conditions for authorisation of continued detention are similar to those for detention under TA 2000 s41 (see NSA 2023 Sch 6 para 31), as are the provisions regarding officers who can conduct reviews (NSA 2023 Sch 6 para 32).

2.60 Where a person is brought to a police station under arrest, or is arrested at a police station having attended voluntarily,[114] the custody officer must:

- open a custody record, and enter certain information such as the offence(s) for which the person has been arrested, and the grounds for the arrest and the detention (PACE s37(4)–(6); Code C paras 2.1 and 3.4; Code H paras 2.2 and 3.4; Code I paras 2 and 3.4; and see para 2.106 below);[115]
- inform the person of their right to consult a solicitor and to have someone informed of their arrest (and must ask them whether they wish to exercise those rights), of their right to interpretation and translation (if applicable) and right to consult the Codes of Practice; and must give the person a written notice setting out these and other rights (Codes C, H and I section 3);[116]
- determine whether the person is in need of medical attention or treatment, is a child and/or vulnerable, or wishes to speak in private with a member of the custody staff about any matter concerning their personal needs relating to health, hygiene and welfare (Code C para 3.5; Code H para 3.5; Code I para 3.6);
- conduct a risk assessment and take any necessary action (Codes C and H paras 3.6–3.9; Code I paras 3.7–3.12; and see para 4.24 below);
- if the person is a child, ascertain the person responsible for their welfare and inform that person of the arrest and detention (Code C para 3.13; Code H para 3.15; Code I para 3.18); and if the child is known

112 Twelve hours in Northern Ireland and Scotland (TA 2000 s43B(6)).

113 See generally PACE Code I.

114 In practice, the police normally only open a custody record for a person in respect of whom detention without charge is authorised. This is contrary to the provisions of the relevant codes, and in any event that approach would not be relevant in the case of a person arrested under TA 2000 s43B.

115 With regard to the grounds for detention, the standard practice for custody officers is simply to record either or both limbs of PACE s37(3), rather than the factual and legal basis for the decision. For an analysis of whether this satisfied Directive 2012/13/EU on the right to information in criminal proceedings, see E Cape, 'Transposing the EU Directive on the Right to Information: a firecracker or a damp squib?' [2015] Crim LR 48 at p53.

116 Note that the written notice of rights and entitlements is available in over 50 languages, and also in an easy-read English version, available at: www.gov.uk/guidance/notice-of-rights-and-entitlements-a-persons-rights-in-police-detention.

to be the subject of a court order under which a person or organisation is responsible for supervising or monitoring them, inform that person or organisation (Code C para 3.14; Code H para 3.16; Code I para 3.19);

- if the person is a child or a vulnerable person, inform them of the decision that an appropriate adult is required (Code C para 3.15; Code H para 3.17; Code I para 3.20);
- if the person appears to be someone who does not speak or understand English or who has a hearing or speech impediment, call an interpreter (Code C para 3.12; Code H para 3.14; Code I para 3.16); and
- if the person is a national of a foreign country, inform them of their rights of communication with their High Commission, embassy or consulate (Code C para 3.12A; Code H para 3.14A; Code I para 3.17).

PACE grounds in practice

Overview

2.61 A person arrested for an offence can only be detained without charge if:

- there is not sufficient evidence to charge the person with the offence for which they were arrested; and
- detention is necessary for one or both of the two purposes set out in PACE s37(3) (see para 2.56 above).

Despite the clear obligation on the custody officer under PACE s37(1) initially to determine whether there is sufficient evidence to charge, in practice the custody officer normally proceeds to consider the decision whether to detain without enquiring about or considering the lawfulness of the arrest or the strength of the evidence at that stage. It has been held that the custody officer is not under a proactive duty to seek information and is not required to enquire into the lawfulness of the arrest.[117] However, in the case of a child, it has been held that the custody officer is under a duty to seek information regarding the arrest before making a detention decision, and should not simply rely on the information provided by the arresting officer.[118] Furthermore, Code C NfG 3ZA imposes a duty on the investigating officer to bring to the attention of the officer making a relevant decision (which includes the custody officer) 'any documents and materials in their possession or control which appear to undermine the need to keep the suspect in custody'. In addition, Code G para 2.2 requires that the custody officer be informed of both the grounds for arrest and the grounds for believing that arrest was necessary. An unlawful arrest may, depending on the nature of the illegality, render detention unlawful (see para 2.47 above). Taken together, this suggests that the custody officer should consider the legality of the arrest, not just in the case of child

117 *DPP v L* [1999] Crim LR 752, DC; *Al Fayed and Others v Commissioner of Police of the Metropolis and Others* [2004] EWCA Civ 1579.

118 *ST v Chief Constable of Nottinghamshire* [2022] EWHC 1280 (QB). The court was critical of the custody officer.

suspects but also in the case of adults.[119] If the custody officer is reluctant to do so, the lawyer should consider submitting a written argument as to the legality of the arrest to the investigating officer who, by virtue of NfG 3ZA, must bring it to the attention of the custody officer.

2.62 The custody officer must determine, in consultation with the investigating officer, whether there are any documents and materials that are essential to challenging the legality of the arrest or detention, and must disclose them to the suspect or their lawyer. Documents are essential for this purpose 'if they are capable of undermining the reasons and grounds which make the detainee's arrest and detention *necessary*' (Codes C and H para 3.4(b), original emphasis). See further para 4.22 below.

2.63 If the conditions for detention cease to apply, and there are no other grounds on which the person can be detained, the custody officer must immediately release the suspect (PACE s34(2)). In effect, the conditions must continue to be satisfied at each review before charge and where it is proposed to authorise continued detention at the 24-hour stage. In practice, custody officers rarely, if ever, refuse to authorise detention on the grounds that they are not satisfied that PACE s37 grounds are made out.[120] However, there is some evidence that if the custody officer has doubts about whether the conditions are satisfied, they may put pressure on the arresting or investigating officers to expedite their inquiries. Furthermore, if the custody officer can be persuaded to proceed straight to charge, inferences under CJPOA 1994 ss34(1)(a), 36 and 37 may be avoided, although inferences under section 34(1)(b) would still be possible. For these reasons, although the custody officer is not under a duty to receive representations in respect of the decision to detain, the lawyer may wish to make representations about the grounds for detention, even if the initial decision to detain has already been taken.

Is there 'sufficient evidence to charge'?

2.64 The lawyer should consider whether there is sufficient evidence to charge their client with the offence for which they were arrested. The phrase 'sufficient evidence to charge' is not defined in PACE or in Code C. In fact, Code C does not provide any guidance on the initial detention decision. The Director of Public Prosecutions (DPP) has issued statutory guidance in respect of PACE s37(7) (see para 10.2 below), but this is not binding in respect of a decision under PACE s37(1) and (2).[121] The meaning of 'sufficient evidence to charge' for the purpose of the initial detention decision has received scant judicial attention. In *R v Mehmet*,[122] where the defendant was arrested for, and admitted, possession of an unlawful drug, the Court of Appeal decided that the custody officer was entitled to conclude that there was not sufficient evidence to charge until a forensic analysis

119 For more detailed consideration of this argument, see E Cape, 'Transposing the EU Directive on the Right to Information: a firecracker or a damp squib?' [2015] Crim LR 48 at p63.

120 See, for example, L Skinns, *Police custody: governance, legitimacy and reform in the criminal justice process* (Willan, Abingdon, 2011) p49.

121 *R (G) v Chief Constable of West Yorkshire* [2008] EWCA Civ 28.

122 (1989) 13 June (unreported), *Butterworth's PACE Act Cases*, IV 53, CA.

had been obtained. However, in *Martin v Chief Constable of Avon and Somerset Constabulary*,[123] it was held that the need for analysis did not mean that there was not sufficient evidence to charge. The similar phrase, 'sufficient evidence to prosecute', found in earlier versions of Code C para 16.1,[124] has been interpreted as involving some consideration of any explanation, or lack of explanation, coming from the suspect.[125] If this reasoning is applied to the custody officer's decision under PACE s37, it would seem to enable detention to be authorised for interviewing, at least to give the suspect an opportunity to provide an explanation, even where the evidence of guilt at the time the initial detention decision is being made is overwhelming. However, if this is correct, there would be few if any circumstances where detention for questioning under PACE s37(3) could not be justified.

2.65 It seems that the authorities want the expression 'sufficient evidence to charge' to represent a high threshold when it is relevant to the decision whether a person can be detained in order to conduct investigations (ie under PACE s37(3)), but to represent a low threshold when it is relevant to a decision to charge (ie under PACE s37(7)). Unless and until the matter is authoritatively decided, if the defence lawyer wishes to avoid their client being detained for questioning, they should argue that 'sufficient evidence to charge' means sufficient evidence to establish a prima facie case or, at most, sufficient evidence to provide a realistic prospect of conviction (irrespective of any explanation given by the client). See further the discussion at paras 10.9–10.10 below.

2.66 If a person has been arrested for an offence that has little or no 'mental element' (such as minor public order and strict liability offences), and where the only evidence is that of police officers who witnessed the incident and implicate the suspect, it can be strongly argued that there is sufficient evidence to charge when the person first arrives at the police station. The proper course of action for the custody officer is to make a decision about charge or otherwise under PACE s37(1) and (7) without detaining the person for the purpose of securing evidence.

2.67 Where a person has been arrested for a more serious offence, or in respect of an offence that involves a significant mental element, it will be easier for the custody officer to justify detention even though the apparent evidence is strong. In principle, the only question is whether the custody officer has before them sufficient evidence to charge the person with the offence for which they were arrested, and thus a response from the custody officer that they want to give the suspect the opportunity to comment on the allegation is not relevant. If, in these circumstances, the custody officer does authorise detention, the lawyer may seek to confine any interview to

123 (1997) 29 October (unreported), CA. For further discussion, see E Cape, 'Detention without charge: what does "sufficient evidence to charge" mean?' [1999] Crim LR 874.

124 Replaced by the phrase 'sufficient evidence to provide a realistic prospect of conviction' in para 16.1 of the current Code C.

125 See *R v Elliott* [2002] EWCA Crim 931 for a review of the relevant cases, and see para 5.77 below for their application to the question whether inferences may be drawn. Note that none of the cases dealt with PACE s37, dealing only with the relevant provisions of Code C.

offering the client an opportunity to give an explanation.[126] The custody officer may also be asked what their intentions are following any interview. If the officer states that they will charge the suspect, it is hard to resist the conclusion that the officer must have had sufficient evidence to charge them when they arrived at the police station, and that therefore detention should not be authorised. Even if this argument fails, it may be relevant to the advice to be given to the client concerning the strategy to adopt in the police interview (see para 5.148 below).[127]

2.68 It should also be noted that PACE s37(7) refers to there being sufficient evidence to charge the person with the offence for which they were arrested. Since PACE s37 is in mandatory terms, it should not be legitimate for a custody officer to authorise detention because the officer believes that, although there is sufficient evidence to charge in respect of the offence for which the person was arrested, evidence may subsequently arise which would justify the officer charging them with a different, perhaps more serious, offence. Code C para 16.1 provides that where a person is detained for more than one offence it is permissible to delay bringing them before the custody officer until the police are ready to charge in respect of all offences. However, this potentially conflicts with PACE s37(7), which requires the custody officer to make a charging decision once they are satisfied that there is sufficient evidence to charge a person with the offence for which they were arrested. In any event, this aspect of Code C para 16.1 only applies where a person has been detained for more than one offence, and the argument here is that the officer should not authorise detention in the first place. The proper course of action would be for the police to consider whether to arrest the suspect for the second offence. In fact, provided there were reasonable grounds for suspicion, the police would be obliged to do so under PACE s31.

2.69 Pursuing this with the custody officer is unlikely to persuade them to make a charge decision, but it may reveal the true purpose of the investigation. This, in turn, may prevent the client from being taken by surprise by unforeseen questions, or lines of enquiry, during the police interview.

Is detention 'necessary'?

2.70 If the lawyer is satisfied that there is insufficient evidence to charge, they should go on to consider whether detention is necessary for either or both of the reasons set out in PACE s37. In principle, the test is quite strong, since not only must the police be seeking to secure or preserve evidence or to obtain it by questioning, but detention must be necessary in order for them to do so. If these objectives can be achieved without the arrested

126 In *R v Coleman, Knight and Hochenberg* (1995) 20 October (unreported), CA (referred to in *R v Elliott* [2002] EWCA Crim 931), the Court of Appeal accepted there had been a breach of Code C where the police, having concluded that there was sufficient evidence successfully to prosecute the suspect, nevertheless Interviewed him rather than asking him simply whether he had anything to say. See also *R v Dellaway and Moriarty* (2000) 7 April (unreported), CA.

127 In *R v Dervish* [2001] EWCA Crim 2789, a case on inferences rather than PACE s37, the Court of Appeal accepted that there was a breach of Code C where the suspect was interviewed in circumstances where the police had decided that they would charge him irrespective of what he said in interview.

person's detention, then arguably that detention is not necessary. This was emphasised by Douglas Hurd, the Home Office minister at the time of the passage of the Police and Criminal Evidence Bill, who told the House of Commons that the provision required that 'detention is necessary – not desirable, convenient or a good idea but necessary'.[128] In practice it has rarely, if ever, been interpreted by custody officers in this way. In *Al Fayed and Others v Commissioner of Police of the Metropolis and Others*[129] it was held that while the question whether the custody officer has reasonable grounds for their belief that detention is necessary is an objective question, the question of necessity is to be determined by reference to whether the custody officer acted reasonably in determining that detention was necessary. In *Al Fayed* the appellant had attended at the police station voluntarily and indicated that he was willing to be interviewed. Nevertheless, the court found that the decision to arrest, and then to detain, him was reasonable. However, in the later case of *ST v Chief Constable of Nottinghamshire* the court stated that the custody officer's decision should be considered on the basis of 'the material facts which, on a reasonable analysis, he should have known; not as he mistakenly believed them to be (there being no explanation for the mistakes)'.[130] Given that both the arrest decision and the detention decision involve a necessity test, and that the decisions are closely linked, the test for the necessity for detention should mirror the test for the necessity of arrest (see para 2.18 above).

2.71 Thus in making the detention decision, the custody officer should have regard to the particular facts of the case, and consider whether the objectives (for example, securing or preserving evidence, conducting an interview, taking fingerprints and samples, etc) can be achieved by means that are less intrusive and restrictive than detention. Where the defence lawyer is present at the time the detention decision is taken, and the client is willing, and would prefer, to be treated as a volunteer, the lawyer should consider making representations to this effect. The custody officer might be asked what the particular features of the case are that make detention necessary. If the client has attended the police station as a volunteer, this should strengthen the argument that they should continue to be treated as a volunteer, and not detained. However, even if the client has been taken to the police station under arrest, this does not, in principle, prevent them from being treated as a volunteer once they arrive at the police station. Alternatively, if it is clear that the client is not willing to answer police questions, it might be argued that the custody officer cannot be satisfied that detention, or continued detention, is necessary for the purpose of obtaining evidence by questioning, although in view of cases such as *R v*

128 Hansard, HC, Standing Committee E, col 1229, 16 February 1984. See *R (TL) v Chief Constable of Surrey* [2017] EWHC 129 (Admin), in which it was held that the term 'necessary' in relation to arrest 'cannot be envisaged as a synonym for "desirable" or "convenient"' (at para 40).

129 [2004] EWCA Civ 1579.

130 '[o]therwise there would be a perverse incentive not to provide the custody officer with correct information and/or information beyond the most basic detail of the offence': [2022] EWHC 1280 (QB) at para 143.

McGuinness[131] and *R v Elliott*,[132] this argument is unlikely to be successful. However, if having been detained the client continues to refuse to answer questions, it is arguable that at some stage continued detention for the purpose of obtaining evidence by questioning must become oppressive.

2.72 A detention that is unlawful because there are no grounds to justify it may give rise to a civil action for false imprisonment and trespass to the person, and in appropriate cases it may be advisable to remind the custody officer of this. Furthermore, it may result in evidence obtained during the period of unlawful detention being excluded. See further chapter 13 below.

Power to detain after charge

2.73 Where a person (having been arrested for an offence) is charged, the custody officer must order their release from custody, either on bail or without bail, unless certain conditions are satisfied (PACE s38(1)). The relevant law and practical considerations relating to the decision whether to grant bail after charge are dealt with in detail in chapter 10 below. Note that while a lawyer may wish to make representations, there is no duty on the custody officer to seek them from the suspect or their lawyer. Note also the special rules that apply where a child is denied bail (see para 11.60 below).

Detention time limits

Detention under PACE

Overview

2.74 The normal maximum period for which a person can be detained without charge is 24 hours commencing with the relevant time. This period may be extended for up to a total of 36 hours from the relevant time on the authorisation of an officer of the rank of superintendent or above if the officer *has reasonable grounds for believing* that:

- detention without charge is necessary to secure or preserve evidence relating to an offence for which the suspect is under arrest, or to obtain such evidence by questioning the suspect;
- the person is under arrest for an indictable offence;[133] and
- investigation is being conducted diligently and expeditiously (PACE s42(1)).

If the suspect is under arrest for an indictable offence a magistrates' court may, on the application of the police, issue a warrant for further detention authorising detention without charge for up to a further 72 hours (PACE ss43 and 44; and see chapter 9 below).[134]

131 [1999] Crim LR 318.

132 [2002] EWCA Crim 931.

133 See para 2.23 above for definition of 'indictable'.

134 For the significance of the use of the term 'believing', as compared with 'suspecting', see para 2.18 above.

2.75 Time, for the purpose of calculating the period of detention, runs from the 'relevant time', which is generally the time the person arrived at the police station (but see para 2.76 below). Note that, for the purpose of reviews of detention, time does not run from the relevant time but from the time detention was authorised (see para 2.86 below). At the expiry of the maximum period of detention, the person must be charged or released, either on or without bail (PACE ss41(7), 42(10), 43(18)). The maximum period of detention without charge is always subject to the requirement that a person in police detention must be released by the custody officer if they are aware that the grounds for detention of that person no longer apply and that there are no other grounds justifying continued detention (PACE s34(2); Code C para 1.1). Note that PACE s45(2) provides that reference to a period of time is to be treated as approximate. Any delay must be justifiable and reasonable steps must be taken to prevent unnecessary delay (Code C para 1.1A). Code C NfG 1H states that Code C para 1.1A is intended to cover delays that may occur in processing detainees, such as those caused by a large number of detainees being brought to the police station at the same time, interview rooms being full, or by difficulties in contacting a lawyer, appropriate adult or interpreter.

'Relevant time'

2.76 Generally, the relevant time is the time an arrested person arrives at the first police station they are taken to, or 24 hours after arrest, whichever is the earlier (PACE s41(2)(a)). However, the following modifications to this rule apply.

(1) If the person initially goes to the police station as a volunteer (see para 2.164 below), and is arrested at the police station, the relevant time is the time of their arrest (PACE s41(2)(c)).
(2) Where a person attends a police station to answer to bail granted under PACE s30A (see para 2.49 above), the relevant time is the time they arrive at the police station (PACE s41(2)(ca)).
(3) If the person, having been detained in respect of one offence, is subsequently arrested at the police station in respect of another offence under PACE s31, the relevant time is that relating to the original arrest, so that the further arrest does not have the effect of prolonging the maximum period of detention (PACE s41(4)).
(4) If the person is arrested outside England and Wales, the relevant time is the time they arrive at the first police station that they are taken to in the police area in England and Wales in which the offence for which they were arrested is being investigated, or 24 hours after they entered England or Wales, whichever is the earlier (PACE s41(2)(b)).
(5) If the person is arrested in police area 1 in connection with an offence for which their arrest is sought in police area 2, provided that they are not questioned in police area 1 in order to obtain evidence concerning the offence, the relevant time is the time they arrive at the first police station to which they are taken in police area 2, or the time 24 hours after they were arrested, whichever is the earlier (PACE s41(3)). This has the effect of increasing the maximum period of detention by up to 24 hours. During transit, the person must not be questioned about the

offence except to clarify any voluntary statement made by them (Code C para 14.1). If the person is questioned about the offence in police area 1, the relevant time is calculated in the usual way even if they are subsequently taken to a police station in police area 2 to be questioned about the same offence.

(6) If the person is in police detention in police area 1, and their arrest in connection with another offence is sought by police area 2, and they are taken to police area 2 for the purpose of investigating that other offence without being questioned in police area 1 in order to obtain evidence in connection with that other offence, the relevant time is the time at which they arrive at the first police station to which they are taken in police area 2 or the time 24 hours after they leave the police station in which they have been detained in police area 1, whichever is the earlier (PACE s41(5)). This has the effect, where a person is sought by a number of different police forces, of allowing a series of detentions, the relevant time starting afresh in each police area to which they are taken. During transit, the person must not be questioned about the offence except to clarify any voluntary statement made by them (Code C para 14.1). Again, if the person is questioned about the offence in police area 1, the relevant time is calculated in the usual way.

(7) Where the person is released on bail subject to a duty to attend the police station on a future date under PACE s47(3)(b), if they are detained when they return to the police station, the relevant time is that relating to the initial detention. This is the case whether the person returns to the police station under the terms of their bail or is arrested under PACE s46A for failure to surrender to police bail (PACE s47(6)). However, if the person is re-arrested other than under PACE s46A, the relevant time will be that relating to the subsequent arrest (PACE s47(7); and see para 10.127 below). For example, PACE s47(2) provides that a person granted bail may be re-arrested if 'new evidence justifying a further arrest has come to light' since their release.

2.77 Generally, time runs continuously from the relevant time during periods that the person is in police detention, but does not run during any period when they are on police bail (PACE s47(6)). However if, having been detained, the person is in need of medical treatment and as a result is removed to hospital, time spent at the hospital or travelling to or from hospital will not count in calculating the period of detention except for any time spent questioning them for the purpose of obtaining evidence in respect of an offence (PACE s41(6)).[135] A person in police detention at a hospital must not be questioned without the agreement of a responsible doctor (Code C para 14.2), and is entitled to legal advice under PACE s58.

Detention beyond 24 hours

Grounds and procedure

2.78 The period of detention without charge may be extended for any period up to 36 hours from the relevant time by an officer of the rank of superintend-

135 'Medical treatment' includes psychiatric treatment (*Re XX's Application for Habeas Corpus* [2019] NIQB 31).

ent or above who is in charge of the police station in which the person is detained (PACE s42(1)). If the initial extension is for less than the maximum period, a further extension can be authorised up to the maximum period (PACE s42(2)). Extension of the period of detention can only be authorised if the conditions set out in para 2.74 above are satisfied.

2.79 Authorisation may be granted at any time after the second review of detention (PACE s40; and see below) and before the expiry of 24 hours from the relevant time (PACE s42(4)). If authorisation is granted, the officer must inform the person of the grounds for continued detention (PACE s42(5)); of the right of intimation under PACE s56; and of the right to advice under PACE s58 (if not already exercised) (PACE s42(9)); and record this in the custody record (PACE ss42(5)(b) and 42(9)).

Representations

2.80 Before deciding whether to grant authorisation, the officer must:

(1) make available to the detained person or their lawyer documents that are 'essential to challenging the lawfulness of the detainee's arrest and detention' (Code C para 15.0);[136] and
(2) give an opportunity to the detained person (unless they are unfit by reason of their condition or behaviour), or to their lawyer (if available at the time), to make representations (PACE s42(6), (7) and (8)).

The decision regarding an extension of detention must normally be dealt with by the officer in person (Code C NfG 15F). However, PACE s45ZA permits the decision to be made by live link,[137] but only if the custody officer considers it appropriate, the detained person has advice from a solicitor concerning its use and the detained person consents. If the detained person is likely to be asleep at the time the decision is made, the time should, if the legal obligations and time constraints permit, be brought forward, but the person should not be woken if they are asleep (Code C NfG 15C). The meaning of 'available at the time' is not defined in PACE. A former version of Code C defined 'available' in connection with the right to have a solicitor present at a police interview as 'present at the station or on his way to the station or easily contactable by telephone', although this does not appear in the current version. If a solicitor and a suspect are mid-interview, the correct course is for an inspector either to cause there to be a break in the interview for the review to take place or to delay the review under PACE s40(4)(b)(i).[138] The meaning of 'available at the time' is important since it has been held that PACE s42(6) is mandatory, rendering a purported authorisation following a failure to seek representations invalid.[139] If, after the second review, the lawyer has any concern that the

136 Documents and materials are 'essential' for this purpose if they are capable of undermining the reasons and grounds that make the detainee's arrest and detention necessary (Code C para 3.4(b)). See para 4.22 below.

137 See PACE s45ZA(8) for the definition of 'live link'.

138 *Searson v Chief Constable of Nottingham* [2025] EWHC 1982 (KB).

139 *Police v Mudd and McDonough* November 1987 *Legal Action* 19, also reported as *In the matter of an application for a warrant of further detention* [1988] Crim LR 296, although only a magistrates' court decision. See also *Searson v Chief Constable of Nottingham* [2025] EWHC 1982 (KB).

police may seek to extend the period of detention under PACE s42 and wishes to make representations, they should either leave written representations with the custody officer or, preferably, ask that the custody record be endorsed with a request for the solicitor to be contacted before authorisation is considered.

2.81 Representations at this stage should deal with (as appropriate):

(1) Whether there are any documents that are essential to challenging the lawfulness of the arrest or detention and whether the authorising officer has consulted with the investigating officer as required by Code C para 15.0, and with any issues arising from any documents disclosed.
(2) Whether there is sufficient evidence to charge. If the custody officer determines that there is sufficient evidence to charge, the suspect must be charged or released (PACE s37(7); and see para 2.64 above and para 10.9 below). In such a case, continued detention without charge could not be justified. Investigating officers sometimes say during interview that they have sufficient evidence to charge but want to give the suspect the opportunity to give their version of events, so the record of any police interview should be checked.
(3) Whether detention is necessary to secure, preserve or obtain evidence (see para 2.70 above). This raises questions such as:
   - What is the nature of the evidence that the police hope to secure during the further period of detention?
   - Is it necessary that the person be detained during this period, or could they be released on police bail?
   - If the person has demonstrated that they are unwilling to answer questions, how can further detention to obtain evidence by questioning be justified?
(4) Whether the offence for which the person is under arrest is an indictable offence (see para 2.23 above).
(5) Whether the investigation is being conducted diligently and expeditiously.[140] If there are periods during which the police appear to be doing nothing, how can this be justified? Although Code C para 12.2 provides that in any period of 24 hours a detained person must usually be allowed a period of at least eight hours for rest, this does not necessarily justify the police in not continuing with other aspects of the investigation during this period.
(6) The length of the proposed extension of detention, since this should be sufficient for the purpose for which the extension is being granted and no longer.

Detention beyond 36 hours

2.82 Detention without charge beyond 36 hours from the relevant time can only be authorised by a magistrates' court and only in respect of a person who is under arrest for an indictable offence (see para 2.23 above). See further chapter 9 below.

140 See *R (Wiles) v Chief Constable of Hertfordshire* [2002] EWHC 387 (Admin).

Detention under the Terrorism Act 2000

2.83 The normal maximum period for which a person arrested under TA 2000 s41 (see paras 2.29 and 2.58 above) can be detained without charge is 48 hours. This may initially be extended by a warrant for further detention for up to a total of seven days, and may be further extended up to a total of 14 days (see para 9.8 below). Where an application is intended to be made for a warrant of further detention, or is made, the person can be detained pending the making of the application or the conclusion of the proceedings (TA 2000 s41(5) and (6)). If the application is refused, the person may still be detained until the expiry of the 48-hour period (TA 2000 s41(8)). Time runs from the time of the arrest under TA 2000 s41 or, where the person was initially detained under a provision listed in section 41(3A) when arrested, the time when detention under that provision commenced (TA 2000 s41(3)). A person arrested under TA 2000 s43B must be released no later than six hours[141] after the time at which they were arrested unless recalled or detained under another power (TA 2000 s43B(2) and (6); and see paras 2.30 and 2.58 above).

Detention under the National Security Act 2023

2.84 A person arrested under NSA 2023 s27 (see paras 2.32 and 2.59 above) must normally be released no later than 48 hours beginning with the time of their arrest under section 27 or, where the person was initially detained under a provision listed in section 27(4) when arrested, the time when detention under that provision commenced (NSA 2023 s27(3)). This may initially be extended by a warrant of further detention for up to a total seven days, and may be further extended up to a total of 14 days (see para 9.12 below). Where an application is intended to be made for a warrant of further detention, or is made, the person can be detained pending the making of the application or the conclusion of the proceedings (NSA 2023 s27(6) and (7)).

Breach of the detention time limit provisions

2.85 If a person is kept in police detention beyond the time allowed by these provisions, the detention will be unlawful unless it is made lawful by any other power to detain. An unlawful detention may provide grounds for civil action for false imprisonment, or for complaint against the police, and may, if evidence is obtained during such period, provide grounds for exclusion of that evidence at trial under PACE s76, 78 or 82(3). Furthermore, there is authority to suggest that failure to abide by the correct procedures, such as seeking representations, renders the detention unlawful.[142] See further chapter 13 below.

141 Twelve hours in Northern Ireland and Scotland (TA 2000 s43B(6)).

142 See note 136 above. However, it was held in *DPP v Park* [2002] EWHC 1248 (Admin) that an unlawful detention resulting from failure to charge the accused within the time limit did not render the charges a nullity.

Review of detention

Review under PACE

Overview

2.86 A person who is in police detention (see para 1.58 above) must have their detention reviewed periodically in order to determine whether continued detention is justified. This is so whether or not the person has been charged, but it does not apply to volunteers, to people removed to a police station as a place of safety under the MHA 1983, or to those who have been arrested for something other than an offence, for instance, an arrest under a fine default warrant or an arrest for fingerprints or samples (PACE Sch 2A), since they are not in police detention (Code C NfG 15B; and see para 1.60 above). However, the detention of such people should still be reviewed periodically as a matter of good practice (Code C NfG 15B). The review provisions do apply to a person detained following an arrest for failure to answer police bail under PACE s46A, or following surrender to bail granted under PACE s30A (street bail) or under PACE Part IV, or following an arrest for failure to surrender under PACE s30D, since such a person is deemed to be arrested for an offence (PACE s34(7)). A review must initially be conducted six hours after detention is first authorised, and thereafter at nine-hour intervals, although there is provision for late review. References to periods of time are approximate only (see para 2.75 above). Note that time runs for review purposes from a different time than for the purpose of determining the maximum period of detention. Although the difference may often be only a matter of minutes, if a large number of arrested people arrive at the police station at the same time, the difference may be significant. The time that detention is authorised must be noted on the custody record (PACE s37(4)).

Review before charge

2.87 The first review must be carried out no later than six hours after detention was first authorised under PACE s37 (PACE s40(3)(a)). The second and subsequent reviews must be carried out no later than nine hours after the previous review (PACE s40(3)(b), (c)). Reviews must continue to be carried out during any period of extended detention, whether on the authority of a superintendent or a magistrates' court (see para 2.78 above and chapter 9 below).

2.88 A review may be postponed if it is not practicable to carry it out at the due time (PACE s40(4)(a)). PACE specifically provides that there may be a postponement if at the due time:

- the person is being interviewed and the review officer is satisfied that interruption would prejudice the investigation; or
- no review officer is readily available (PACE s40(4)(b)).

2.89 However, there may be other situations where it is not practicable to hold a review at the due time – for example, where there has been a large number of arrests following a public disturbance. A detainee who is asleep need not be woken for a review, but if they are likely to be asleep at the time a review is due to be conducted the reviewing officer should, if legal obligations and time constraints permit, bring the review forward so that the detainee can make representations (Code C NfG 15C). If a review is postponed, it must be carried out as soon as practicable (PACE s40(5)). The timing of subsequent reviews is not affected, and they must be carried out at the time they would have been conducted if there had been no postponement (PACE s40(6)).

2.90 Review before charge is carried out by an officer of at least the rank of inspector, except that continued detention at the 24-hour stage must be authorised by an officer of at least the rank of superintendent (see para 2.78 above). The primary purpose of the review is to ensure that the grounds for detention continue to apply. This involves consideration of the same factors as those to be taken into account by the custody officer at the time of initial detention. In particular, the review officer must decide whether there is sufficient evidence to charge and, if there is not, whether detention is necessary to secure or preserve evidence or to obtain evidence by questioning (PACE s40(8)). If the person has not been charged or released because they were unfit under PACE s37(9), the review officer must decide whether the person is yet in a fit state (PACE s40(9)). If there is a disagreement between the review officer and a more senior officer about the continued detention of a person in police detention, the review officer must immediately refer the matter to an officer of at least the rank of superintendent who is responsible for the police station concerned (PACE s40(11)). Before conducting a review, the review officer must, unless the detainee is asleep, remind the detained person of their right to legal advice (Code C para 15.4; and see para 2.80 below).

2.91 A review (other than a review by a superintendent at the 24-hour stage) may be conducted by video-conferencing facilities where the review officer has access to the use of such facilities, enabling the officer to communicate with persons at the police station (PACE s45A(1)).[143] Where such facilities are not available reviews, other than those conducted by a superintendent at the 24-hour stage or by the custody officer following charge, may be conducted by telephone (PACE s40A(1)). The decision whether to conduct a review in person, by telephone or by video-conferencing is a matter for the officer conducting the review. The officer should take into account the needs of the person in custody, and factors such as whether they are a child, are mentally vulnerable, have received medical attention (other than for a routine minor ailment), or whether there are 'presentational or community issues around' the person's detention (Code C para 15.3C). The precise meaning of the latter is not explained, but presumably means that a review should be conducted in person where the detention of the person is a sensitive matter because, for example, of concerns in the community. If a review is conducted by video-conferencing or telephone, there is provision for representations to be made either by means of telephone or video-conferencing or by fax (PACE ss40A(3), (4) and 45A(6), (7)). There is also provision for the record to be made in the custody record by another officer (PACE ss40A(3) and 45A(5)).

143 And see Police and Criminal Evidence Act 1984 (Remote Reviews of Detention) Regulations 2014 SI No 3279.

Review after charge

2.92 If the person has been charged, the review requirements set out above continue to apply with the following modifications:

- review is carried out by the custody officer (PACE s40(1)(a)); and
- the primary purpose of the review is to decide whether the decision to detain in custody rather than to release on bail continues to be justified (PACE s40(10)).

A review after charge must be conducted in person (PACE ss40A(1) and 45A(2)(b)).

Representations at review

2.93 Before making a decision at review, the review officer must make available to the detained person or their lawyer documents that are 'essential to effectively challenging the lawfulness of the detainee's arrest and detention' (Code C para 15.0(a)); and see para 2.62 above and para 4.22 below). The review officer must give the detained person (unless asleep or unfit because of their condition or behaviour) and their solicitor and appropriate adult (if relevant, and if available at the time of the review) the opportunity to make oral or written representations about the detention (PACE s40(12), (13), (14); Code C para 15.3).[144] If the detained person is likely to be asleep at the latest time for review, the review should if practicable be brought forward (see para 2.89 above). If the lawyer is not likely to be at the police station when the review is conducted, they should make it clear to the custody officer whether they wish to make representations at a future review, and ask that a note be made of this in the custody record. Alternatively, the lawyer could leave written representations (having taken a copy) with the custody officer, with instructions to bring them to the attention of the review officer.

2.94 Representations at reviews conducted before charge should deal with:

(1) Whether there are any documents that are essential to challenging the lawfulness of the arrest or detention and whether the review officer has consulted with the investigating officer as required by Code C para 15.0, and with any issues arising from any documents disclosed.

(2) Whether there is sufficient evidence to charge. If the custody officer determines that there is sufficient evidence to charge, the officer must do so or release the person (PACE s37(7); and see para 2.56 above). In such a case, continued detention without charge could not be justified.

(3) Whether detention is necessary to secure, preserve or obtain evidence (see para 2.70 above):
   - What is the nature of the evidence that the police hope to secure during the further period of detention?
   - Is it necessary for the person to be detained during this period, or could they be released on police bail?

144 While PACE s40(12) refers to the detainee or their solicitor, Code C para 15.3 refers to the detainee and their solicitor. For the meaning of 'available' see para 2.80 above.

- If the person has demonstrated that they are unwilling to answer questions, how can detention to obtain evidence by questioning be justified?

(4) Whether the investigation is being conducted expeditiously (Code C para 1.1). If there are periods during which the police appear to be doing nothing, how can this be justified? Although Code C para 12.2 provides that in any period of 24 hours a detained person must be allowed a period of at least eight hours for rest, this does not necessarily justify the police in not continuing other aspects of the investigation during this period.

(5) Whether a detention limit has expired or is about to expire.

2.95 Representations can be made orally or in writing (PACE s40(13); and see para 2.93 above), although oral representations are preferable where possible. If it is not possible to be at the police station at the appropriate time, representations could be made over the telephone. A written note must be made in the custody record of the grounds for and extent of any postponement of review (PACE s40(7); Code C para 15.13), of the fact that the detained person was reminded of their right to advice (Code C para 15.12) and of the outcome of the review (Code C para 15.16). If continued detention is authorised, the review officer must make a note of any comment made by the suspect or their lawyer (Code C para 15.5). The officer must also retain any written representation made (Code C para 15.15). In any event, the lawyer should keep a written record of the representations made and the review officer's comments. The review officer must not put specific questions to the suspect regarding the suspect's involvement in any offence, nor in respect of any comment the suspect may make in response to the decision to keep them in detention (Code C para 15.6).

2.96 Note that the right to make representations is conferred by PACE s40(12) on the detained person's 'solicitor', which is defined for the purposes of Code C as including an accredited or probationary representative included on the register of representatives maintained by the Legal Aid Agency (LAA) (Code C para 6.12). Once admitted to the police station (see Code C para 6.12A; and para 4.4 below), an accredited or probationary representative should be treated in the same way as a solicitor, and this includes the making of representations on review. If a review officer refuses to hear representations from an accredited or probationary representative, the officer should be asked to give reasons for this. If the review officer is still not willing to receive the representations, the instructing solicitor should be contacted and the review officer asked to consider postponing the review to allow time for this. See para 2.88 above regarding postponement of reviews.

Review under the Terrorism Act 2000

2.97 Where a person has been arrested and detained under TA 2000 s41 (see paras 2.29 and 2.83 above), review of detention is governed by TA 2000 Sch 8 Part II. Similar provisions to those in Code C regarding disclosure of documents and materials relevant to the necessity of arrest and detention apply (Code H para 3.4(b); and see para 2.61 above). The first review must be carried out as soon as is reasonably practicable following the arrest (TA 2000 Sch 8 para 21(2)). Subsequent reviews must be conducted at intervals of not more than 12 hours, but reviews are not required after a warrant of further detention has been issued under TA 2000 Sch 8 Part III (TA 2000 Sch 8 para 21(3) and (4); and see chapter 9 below). A review may be postponed if:

- the detained person is being questioned by police and interruption of the questioning would prejudice the investigation;
- no review officer is readily available; or
- it is not practicable for some other reason to carry out the review (TA 2000 Sch 8 para 22(1)).

If a review is postponed it must be carried out as soon as is reasonably practicable (TA 2000 Sch 8 para 22(2)), but this does not affect the timing of the next review, which must be held not later than 12 hours after the latest time that the postponed review should have been conducted (TA 2000 Sch 8 para 22(3)).

2.98 A review conducted within 24 hours beginning with the time of the arrest is conducted by an officer of at least the rank of inspector. Reviews conducted thereafter must be conducted by an officer of at least the rank of superintendent (TA 2000 Sch 8 para 24). A review officer must not be directly involved in the investigation in connection with which the person is detained (TA 2000 Sch 8 para 24(1)). Where a review is conducted by an officer of lower rank than superintendent and an officer of higher rank gives directions relating to the detained person that are at variance with those of the review officer, the latter must refer the matter immediately to an officer of at least the rank of superintendent (TA 2000 Sch 8 para 25).

2.99 The grounds for continued detention are set out at para 2.58 above. Before deciding whether to authorise continued detention the review officer must give the detained person (unless they are unfit because of their condition or behaviour) or their solicitor an opportunity to make representations, which may be oral or in writing (TA 2000 Sch 8 para 26). If authorising continued detention the review officer must inform the detained person of their right to have someone informed of their detention under TA 2000 Sch 8 para 6 and their right to legal advice under Schedule 8 para 7 if they have not yet been exercised or, where relevant, of the fact that they are being delayed (TA 2000 Sch 8 para 27(1)). Where exercise of one or more of these rights has been delayed, the review officer must consider whether the reason(s) for the delay continue to apply and, if the officer decides that they do not, must inform the officer who authorised the delay (unless delay was authorised by the review officer) (TA 2000 Sch 8 para 27(2)).

2.100 The review officer must make a written record of the outcome of the review, together with other relevant information, such as the grounds upon which continued detention is authorised, the reason for postponement of the review and the fact that the detainee has been informed of their rights as required by TA 2000 Sch 8 para 27(1) (TA 2000 Sch 8 para 28(1)). The review officer must inform the detained person whether the officer is authorising continued detention and, if so, the grounds for doing so, and must make the written record in the presence of the detained person, unless the detained person is incapable of understanding what is said to them, is violent or likely to become violent, or is in urgent need of medical attention (TA 2000 Sch 8 para 28(2) and (3)). Unlike a PACE review conducted before charge, there is no provision for the review to be conducted by telephone or video-link facilities.[145]

Review under the National Security Act 2023

2.101 Where a person has been arrested and detained under NSA 2023 s27 (see paras 2.32 and 2.59 above), review of detention is governed by NSA 2023 Sch 6 Part 5. Similar provisions to those in Code C regarding disclosure of documents and materials relevant to the lawfulness of arrest and detention apply (Code I paras 3.5 and 13; and see para 2.61 above). The first review must be carried out as soon as is reasonably practicable following the arrest (NSA 2023 Sch 6 para 29(2)). Subsequent reviews must be conducted at intervals of not more than 12 hours, but no reviews are to be conducted after a warrant of further detention has been issued under NSA 2023 Sch 6 Part 6 (NSA 2023 Sch 6 para 29(3) and (4); and see chapter 9 below). A review may be postponed if:

- the detained person is being questioned by police and interruption of the questioning would prejudice the investigation;
- no review officer is readily available; or
- it is not practicable for some other reason to carry out the review (NSA 2023 Sch 6 para 30(1)).

2.102 If a review is postponed, it must be carried out as soon as is reasonably practicable (NSA 2023 Sch 6 para 30(2)), but this does not affect the timing of the next review, which must be held not later than 12 hours after the latest time that the postponed review should have been conducted (NSA 2023 Sch 6 para 30(3)).

2.103 The conditions for authorisation of continued detention are similar to those for detention under TA 2000 s41 (NSA 2023 Sch 6 para 31), as are the provisions regarding officers who can conduct reviews (NSA 2023 Sch 6 para 32) (see para 2.58 above).

2.104 The provisions regarding information to be given to the suspect regarding their rights, delay of certain rights, recording of decisions and information regarding decisions made regarding detention, are also similar to those applicable where a person is detained under TA 2000 s41 (see paras 2.99 and 2.100 above). See, as relevant:

- the right of the suspect or their solicitor to make representations regarding detention (NSA 2023 Sch 6 para 34);
- the obligation to provide information to the suspect regarding their rights (NSA 2023 Sch 6 para 35);
- the right of the suspect to consult a solicitor (NSA 2023 Sch 6 para 7; Code I para 6), subject to delay under NSA 2023 Sch 6 para 9;

145 Although there is provision for the use of video-link in proceedings for a warrant of further detention (Code H NfG 14I).

- the right of the suspect to have someone informed of their detention (NSA 2023 Sch 6 para 6; Code I para 5), subject to delay under para 9; and
- the obligation to make a written record of the decision (NSA 2023 Sch 6 para 36).

Unlike a PACE review conducted before charge, there is no provision for the review to be conducted by telephone or video-link facilities.[146]

Breach of review provisions

2.105 Although the review provisions are expressed in mandatory terms, neither PACE, the TA 2000 nor the NSA 2023 provide any direct mechanism for enforcement. Breach of the review provisions, particularly failure to remind the suspect of their right to consult a solicitor, may provide grounds for exclusion of evidence under PACE s76, 78 or 82(3) at a subsequent trial. Breach may also provide grounds for a complaint, and may render the detention unlawful, thus giving rise to a civil action for damages or a criminal action for false imprisonment.[147] It has been held that a late review rendered continued detention unlawful, but that it was arguable that the detention was rendered lawful once the review was conducted.[148]

Custody records

Formalities

2.106 A separate custody record must be opened as soon as is practicable for each person who is brought to a police station under arrest, or who is arrested at the police station having attended voluntarily, or who attends at the police station in answer to street bail (Code C para 2.1).[149] This also applies to a person arrested under TA 2000 s41 (Code H para 2.2), or under NSA 2023 s27(1) (Code I para 2.1). A custody record does not have to be opened in respect of a person who attends voluntarily and who is not arrested. Information that is required to be recorded in the custody record (see para 2.111 below) must be recorded as soon as practicable unless otherwise specified, and entries must be timed and signed by the person making the entry or, where on computer, contain the operator's identification

146 Although there is provision for the use of video-link in proceedings for a warrant of further detention (NSA 2023 Sch 6 para 41; Code I NfG 13H).

147 See *R (Craik, Chief Constable of Northumbria) v Newcastle upon Tyne Magistrates' Court and Others* [2010] EWHC 935 (Admin), although there is no doctrine of vicarious liability in respect of a criminal offence.

148 *Roberts v Chief Constable of Cheshire* [1999] 1 WLR 662, CA. But see *DPP v Park* [2002] EWHC 1248 (Admin).

149 This applies to all persons brought to the police station under arrest, and to those arrested having attended as a volunteer, and not only those whose detention is then authorised. See also College of Policing, *Authorised professional practice: Detention and custody: Response, arrests and detention* para 3.3, available at: www.app.college.police.uk/app-content/detention-and-custody-2/response-arrest-and-detention/#detention-not-authorised.

(subject to limited exceptions) (Code C paras 2.1, 2.6 and 2.6A; Code H paras 2.2 and 2.3; Code I paras 2.2 and 2.3). The custody officer is responsible for the accuracy and completeness of the record (PACE s39; Codes C and I para 2.3; Code H para 2.4). If the detained person is transferred to another police station, the custody record or a copy of it must accompany them, and must show the time and reason for the transfer (Codes C and I para 2.3; Code H para 2.4). It is unclear whether a new custody record should be opened where a person is further detained on surrendering to custody following a release on police bail under PACE s47(3) or whether the original custody record should be continued. In any event, time in detention before the release on bail will normally count towards the maximum period of detention (see para 10.129 below).

Access to the custody record and other information

2.107 A solicitor (and an appropriate adult) must be permitted to inspect the custody record of their client as soon as practicable after their arrival at the police station, and at any other time while the client is detained. The right of inspection applies to the whole of the custody record, including information about the circumstances and reasons for arrest and the grounds for detention (Codes C and I para 2.4; Code H para 2.5). The lawyer has no right under the code to insist on an entry being made in the custody record (see further para 2.124 below). By PACE s54(2A), the requirement to record in the custody record everything that a person has with them when they are detained is at the discretion of the custody officer. If a record is made, it does not have to be made in the custody record (PACE s54(2A)), but a record made in a separate document is treated as being part of the custody record for all purposes, including that of inspection (Codes C, H and I para 4.4). The lawyer should ask the custody officer what property was taken from their client on arrival at the police station and ask to see the record.

2.108 Where a medical examination by a doctor or other healthcare professional has been requested or conducted, Code C para 9.15, Code H para 9.17 and Code I para 9.18 set out what must be recorded in the custody record:

- the arrangements made for an examination, and any complaint about treatment by police made by the suspect, and any relevant remarks by the custody officer;
- any arrangements made regarding clinical attention under Code C para 9.5, Code H para 9.6 or Code I para 9.7;
- any request for a clinical examination made by the suspect, and arrangements made in response;
- the injury, ailment, condition or other reason that made it necessary to make any of the above arrangements;
- any clinical directions and advice given to the police by the healthcare professional; and
- if applicable, the responses received when attempting to rouse a person who is suspected of being intoxicated through drink or drugs, or whose level of consciousness causes concern.

Where a healthcare professional is called in to see a suspect, the custody officer must ask them to advise, among other things, about when to carry out an interview (Code C para 9.13; Code H para 9.15; Code I para 9.16). Fitness for interview must be considered by reference to Codes C, H and I Annex G para 7, which states that the healthcare professional's determination and any advice or recommendations should be 'made in writing and form part of the custody record'. Subject to the above, the healthcare professional's own notes do not form part of the custody record, but if their clinical findings are not recorded in the custody record, the record must show where they are recorded (Code C para 9.16; Code H para 9.18; Code I para 9.19). While Codes C, H and I do not provide that the suspect or their lawyer has a right to see these if they are not in the custody record, it is difficult to see, subject to practicability, what justification there could be for refusing access to them. This is particularly so if the healthcare professional was called in for therapeutic, as opposed to evidential, reasons. In any event, the respective paragraphs of the three codes do state that information which is necessary to ensure the effective ongoing care and wellbeing of the suspect 'must be recorded openly in the custody record'.

2.109 The detained person or their legal representative or appropriate adult has a right to a copy of the custody record if a request is made when the person is taken before a court or within 12 months of release from detention. Such request must be satisfied as soon as practicable (Code C para 2.4A; Code H para 2.6; Code I para 2.5). If the police are seeking a warrant of further detention, the lawyer should request an up-to-date copy of the custody record. The detained person and their lawyer or appropriate adult also have a right to see the original custody record after the person has left police detention, provided reasonable notice is given (Code C para 2.5; Code H para 2.7; Code I para 2.6).

2.110 Note that any audio or video recording made in the custody area does not form part of the custody record (Codes C and I para 2.1; Code H para 2.2). Most police stations have audio-visual recording facilities covering custody areas, and some also have such facilities in some or all of the cells. Where they exist, clients should be advised of the potential implications, and the lawyer should consider the evidential potential they may represent which, depending on the circumstances, may be favourable or contrary to the interests of the client.

Information that must be recorded

2.111 The matters which must be recorded are extensive, and those required by PACE and/or the Codes include the following.[150]

Authorisation of detention

2.112 • The reason and grounds for detention of an arrested person (PACE s37(4); Codes C and I para 2.4(b); Code H para 2.5(b)).

150 Note that some recording requirements are set out more than once where they come under more than one heading.

- The reason for detention of a person charged and not released (PACE s38(3)).
- The reason for imposing or varying bail conditions (BA 1976 s5A(3)).
- The offence for which the person has been arrested and the reasons for the arrest (Codes C, H and I para 3.4(a)). In the case of arrest under PACE, this should include the reason why arrest was believed to be necessary (see Code C NfG 10B; Code G para 4.3). If the person is answering to street bail, the custody officer should link any documentation held in relation to the arrest with the custody record (Code C para 3.25).
- The fact that documents or materials that are essential to challenging the lawfulness of arrest or detention have been disclosed (Codes C and H para 3.4(b); Code I para 3.5).
- Grounds for authorising detention and extension of detention (PACE s42(5)(b); Code C para 15.16; Code H para 14.15; Code I para 13.4).
- The signature of the detained person confirming receipt of the notice setting out their rights (Codes C and H para 3.2A; Code I para 3.2).
- Any comment made by the detained person in relation to the arresting officer's account of the arrest, or in relation to the decision to detain the detained person (Codes C and H para 3.4(a); Code I para 3.4(b) and (c)).
- The signature of the detained person signifying whether or not they wish to receive legal advice at the time of initial detention (Codes C and H para 3.5(b); Code I para 3.6(b)).
- The decision taken as to whether the detained person is or might be in need of medical attention, or requires an appropriate adult or help to check documentation, or requires an interpreter (Codes C and H para 3.5(b); Code I para 3.6(b)).
- Details of special action taken in respect of detainees who are vulnerable (PACE refers to detainees who are deaf, children, mentally disordered or vulnerable, with a visual handicap, or unable to read (Code C para 3.20; Code H para 3.23; Code I para 3.27).

Conditions of detention and review

2.113
- The grounds and reasons for any delay in conducting a review (Code C para 15.13; Code H para 14.15; Code I para 13.4).
- The time of and reason for transfer to another police station and time the person is released from detention (Codes C and I para 2.3; Code H para 2.4).
- Details of replacement clothing and meals offered (Code C para 8.9; Code H para 8.11; Code I para 8.10).
- Arrangements made for examination of a detained person by a healthcare professional, requests made for medical examination by a detained person and arrangements made in response, clinical directions and advice given (including clinical findings or details of where these are recorded), and medication that a detained person had on them on arrival at the police station and any medication that they claim to need but do not have with them (Code C paras 9.15–9.17; Code H para 9.17; Code I paras 9.18–9.20).

- The responses received when attempting to rouse a person believed to be intoxicated, under Code C Annex H (Code C para 9.15(f)); under Code H Annex H (Code H para 9.17(f)); under Code I Annex G (Code I para 9.18(f)).
- Consultation with a healthcare professional about medication to be taken or applied in compliance with clinical directions prescribed before detention (Code C para 9.9; Code H para 9.11; Code I para 9.12).
- Times and reasons that the detained person is not in the custody of the custody officer, and the reason for any refusal to deliver a detainee out of that custody (Code C para 12.10; Code H para 12.11; Code I para 11.25).
- The use of any restraints, the reasons for it, and any arrangements for enhanced supervision (Code C para 8.11; Codes H and I para 8.12).
- The fact that a citizen of a Commonwealth or other foreign country has been informed of their rights under Code C section 7, and action taken to contact the High Commission, etc (Codes C, H and I para 7.5).
- The reminder that must be given under Code C para 15.4 before conducting a review or determining whether to extend detention (Code C para 15.12); under Code H para 14.6 (Code H para 14.14); under Code I para 13.4 (Code I para 13.13).
- The grounds for and extent of any delay in conducting a review (Code C para 15.13; Code H para 14.15).
- The outcome of each review and application for warrant of further detention (Code C para 15.16; Code H para 14.17; Code I para 13.6).
- Where a review officer terminates a telephone review or review conducted by video-conferencing and reverts to a review conducted in person, the reasons for doing so (Code C para 15.9C).

Custody records

2.114
- A note of any inspection of the original custody record under Codes C and H para 2.5; Code I para 2.4.
- The fact of and time of any refusal to sign a custody record (Code C para 2.7; Code H para 2.9; Code I para 2.8).

Legal advice

2.115
- The fact of and time of a request for legal advice, and action taken in response (Code C para 6.16; Code H para 6.18; Code I para 7.17).
- The grounds for delay in allowing access to legal advice (Code C Annex B para 13; Code H Annex B para 8; Code I Annex B para 9).
- The fact that an interview has been conducted in the absence of a solicitor, where the detainee has asked for legal advice, or the fact that a solicitor has been required to leave an interview (although this is to be noted in the interview record rather than the custody record) (Code C para 6.17; Code H para 6.19; Code I para 6.18).
- The signature of the detained person signifying whether or not they wish to receive legal advice at the time of initial detention (Codes C and H para 3.5(b); Code I para 3.6(b)).

- Any reasons given by the detained person for waiving their right to legal advice (Code C para 6.5; Code H para 6.4; Code I para 6.3).
- The fact of arrival at the police station of a solicitor wishing to see a detained person, and the decision of the detained person about whether they wish to see the solicitor (Code C para 6.15; Code H para 6.17; Code I para 6.16).
- The reminder that the detained person is entitled to legal advice, which must be given by the review officer before conducting a review or determining whether to extend detention (Code C para 15.12; Code H para 14.14; Code I para 13.13).
- Where a solicitor is initially instructed by a third party and attends the police station, the detained person's signature indicating whether they wish to see the solicitor (Code C Annex B para 4; Codes H and I Annex B para 5).
- Where the right to advice has been delayed, but the grounds for such delay expire within the relevant time limit, the fact that the detained person has been asked if they wish to exercise this right, and the detained person's endorsement about whether they then wish to receive legal advice (Code C Annex B para 6; Codes H and I Annex B para 7).
- The grounds for any action taken under Annex B (Code C Annex B para 13; Codes H and I Annex B para 9).
- The fact that a detained person is reminded of their right to legal advice before being asked to provide an intimate sample (Code D para 6.3(b)). There is no similar provision under the TA 2000 or the NSA 2023 or the respective codes.

Contact with others

2.116
- Details of requests by the detained person to have someone notified of their arrest; details of all letters, messages, telephone calls made or received and visits to the detained person; and refusal by a detained person to have information given to an enquirer (Codes C and I para 5.8; Code H para 5.9).
- The grounds for delaying intimation of arrest (Code C Annex B para 6; Codes H and I Annex B para 9).
- Where the right to intimation has been delayed, but the grounds for such delay expire within 36 hours, the fact that the detained person has been asked whether they wish to exercise this right (Code C Annex B para 6; Codes H and I Annex B para 7).
- The grounds for any action taken under Code C Annex B (Code C Annex B para 13; Codes H and I Annex B para 9).
- The fact that a citizen of a Commonwealth or other foreign country has been informed of their rights under Code C section 7 (Codes C, H and I para 7.5).

Interviews

2.117
- The grounds for commencing the interview of a suspect who has been allowed access to a solicitor before the solicitor arrives (although this is to be noted in the interview record rather than the custody record) (Code C para 6.17; Code H para 6.19; Code I para 6.18).

- Any decision to refuse access to, or to exclude from an interview, a probationary or accredited representative (Code C para 6.14; Code H para 6.16; Code I para 6.15).
- The grounds for interviewing a detained person under the urgent interview of vulnerable suspects provisions (urgent interviews of persons under the influence of drink or drugs; of children or mentally disordered or handicapped people in the absence of an appropriate adult; or of those with language or hearing difficulties in the absence of an interpreter) (Code C para 11.20; Code H para 11.13; Code I para 11.14).
- The reasons for not using an interview room and actions taken under Codes C and H para 12.5, or Code I para 11.19, in respect of a person who takes steps to prevent themself from being interviewed (Code C para 12.11; Code H para 12.12; Code I para 11.26).

Children and other vulnerable detainees

2.118
- Details of actions taken in respect of detainees who are deaf, a child, vulnerable or with a visual handicap (Code C para 3.20C; Code H para 3.23; Code I para 3.27).
- Where a child is kept in a cell, the reasons for this (Code C para 8.10; Codes H and I para 8.11).
- A child's decision not to have an appropriate adult present at an intimate search (although it is not specifically required that this should be in the custody record) (Code C Annex A para 5; Codes H and I Annex A para 6).
- Actions taken in relation to interpretation and translation (Codes C and H para 13.11; Code I para 12.16).
- The grounds for interviewing a detained person under Code C para 11.18, Code H para 11.11 or Code I para 11.12, which relates to urgent interviews of persons under the influence of drink or drugs, children or mentally vulnerable people in the absence of an appropriate adult, or those with language or hearing difficulties in the absence of an interpreter (Code C para 11.20; Code H para 11.13; Code I para 11.14).

Searches and samples

2.119
- Information relating to the taking of fingerprints, intimate and non-intimate samples, or impressions (PACE ss61(7), (7A), (8); 61A(5), (6); 62(7), (8); and 63(8B); and Code D para 6.10; TA 2000 Sch 8 para 11(3); NSA 2023 Sch 6 para 11(3)).
- Information relating to drug testing under PACE ss63B and 63C (PACE ss63B(5B) and 63C(4); Code C para 17.12).
- A child's decision not to have an appropriate adult present at an intimate search (although it is not specifically required that this should be in the custody record) (Code C Annex A para 5; Codes H and I Annex A para 6).
- If an intimate search is carried out, the parts of the person's body that were searched, who carried out the search, who was present, the reasons for and the results of the search, and if carried out by a police officer, the reason why it was impracticable for it to be carried out by a

medically-qualified person (Code C Annex A paras 7 and 8; Codes H and I Annex A paras 8 and 9).

- If a strip search is carried out, the reasons for this and the result (Code C Annex A para 12; Codes H and I Annex A para 13).

Identification procedures

2.120
- The reason why it is not practicable to hold a video identification or an identification parade requested by a suspect (Code D para 3.26).
- The refusal of a detained person to co-operate in an identification parade, group identification or video identification and, if relevant, the grounds for obtaining images in accordance with Code D para 3.20 (Code D para 3.27).
- The reason for taking fingerprints or footwear impressions without consent and of any force used (Code D paras 4.8A, 4.8 and 4.20).[151]
- The fact that the detained person has been told that their fingerprints or footwear impression may be the subject of a speculative search (Code D paras 4.8A and 4.21).
- Information regarding the search, examination or photographing of a person or of any identifying marks found on the person, and any force used (Code D paras 5.17 and 5.18).
- The reasons for taking a sample or impression and, where relevant, its destruction, and any force used (Code D paras 6.10 and 6.10A).
- The fact that a person has been informed that samples may be the subject of a speculative search (Code D para 6.10).
- The fact that a detained person has been reminded of their right to legal advice before being asked to provide an intimate sample (Code D para 6.11).
- A record of a warning under Code D para 6.3 that refusal to provide an intimate sample without good cause may harm the detained person's case if it comes to trial (Code D para 6.11).

Bail

2.121 Where a custody officer grants conditional bail, or varies conditions, the officer must enter a note of the reasons in the custody record and must give the bailed person a copy (BA 1976 s5A(3)).

Use of the custody record

2.122 The significance of the custody record was summed up by a custody officer who commented, 'If it's not in the custody record, it didn't happen'. It may be used by the police as a mechanism for legitimating events that occur during the period of detention. Equally it may be used by the lawyer in a number of ways that have potential benefit to the client.

151 Note that these recording provisions of Code D, and those in the remainder of this section, do not apply to persons detained under TA 2000 s41 or NSA 2023 s27. For the relevant recording requirements, see TA 2000 Sch 8 para 11(3) and NSA 2023 Sch 6 para 11(3).

2.123 The lawyer should carefully examine the custody record when first attending at the police station,[152] because it will provide valuable information on the police view of the history of the case. It will contain information that is relevant to assessing the legality of the arrest and detention, and which may be useful in any negotiations with the police, for example, the grounds on which detention was authorised. It will also contain information that may need to be checked with the client, for example, the address given, the reason for arrest, the time of the request for legal advice, and anything allegedly said by the suspect on arrest or subsequently. Furthermore, it will also contain information that is essential for the lawyer to carry out their duties, such as the time of arrest, the time of arrival at the police station and the time detention was authorised. Finally, it may contain information that should alert the lawyer to the need to make further enquiries, or the need to be cautious, for example, a deleted or amended entry, or a late entry which, in the circumstances, gives cause for suspicion (see further para 4.20 below). The lawyer should be mindful of the fact that important information, such as property taken from the client on being detained (see para 2.107 above), may be missing from the custody record. In some cases, especially where the investigating officer intends to use the strategy of phased disclosure (see para 4.30 below), the reason for arrest and/or detention that is recorded may be incomplete or misleading.

2.124 The custody record may be used by the lawyer during the period of detention. If significant events occur – if access to the client is denied, representations at review are made, representations about bail are made, or the client complains of unauthorised visits by police officers – the lawyer should press to have this noted on the custody record even if this is not formally required by PACE or the Codes of Practice. A written record of such an event may have a significant impact at any subsequent trial. Asking for something to be noted on the custody record may also be an important negotiating tactic. If, for example, access to a client is being denied, a demand that the lawyer's representations be entered in the record may lead the custody officer to reconsider the decision. The lawyer should keep their own record of such an event, whether or not it is entered in the custody record.

2.125 The custody record may be significant at any subsequent trial. Normally, a copy of the custody record should be requested if the client is charged, and should be carefully scrutinised. For example, the result of the risk assessment conducted under Code C paras 3.6–3.10 may cast doubt on the client's fitness for interview or, of course, may be of assistance to the prosecution. The record may show that a request for legal advice was not acted on – relevant if an application to exclude evidence of a confession is subsequently made. Similarly, the custody record may be important for what it does not contain. Absence of any record that the suspect was reminded of their right to legal advice at review may be critical in an application to exclude evidence. Likewise, absence of any record that the suspect was provided with meals or refreshments. In appropriate cases, prosecution witnesses may be cross-examined on the custody record.

152 See para 2.107 above regarding the lawyer's right to see the custody record.

Right to have someone informed of an arrest

2.126 PACE s56 confers a right, often known as the right of intimation, on a person arrested and detained to have a friend, relative or other person known to the arrested person or who is likely to take an interest in their welfare informed of the fact of the arrest as soon as practicable and at public expense. The right applies to any arrested person and not just those arrested for an offence, and may be exercised each time the person is taken to another police station (PACE s56(8); Code C para 5.3). A person detained under TA 2000 s41 or Sch 7 has a similar right (TA 2000 Sch 8 para 6; Code H para 5.3), as does a person detained under NSA 2023 s27(1) (NSA 2023 Sch 6 para 6; Code I para 5). If the person requested cannot be contacted, up to two alternatives may be nominated, and if they too cannot be contacted the custody officer has a discretion to allow further attempts (Codes C and H para 5.1; Code I para 5). If the detainee does not know anyone to contact, or contact cannot be made with a relative or friend specified, the custody officer should consider any local voluntary organisation that might be able to help (Code C NfG 5C; Codes H and I NfG 5D). If a friend, relative or other such person asks the police the whereabouts of the detained person, this information must be given, provided that the person in custody agrees and Annex B of the relevant code does not apply (Codes C and H para 5.5; Code I para 5.4). Furthermore, the person may receive visits at the discretion of the custody officer (Codes C and H para 5.4; Code I para 5.3), and NfG 5B of the relevant code indicates that visits should be allowed when possible.[153] The right of intimation under the respective provisions does not confer a right on the suspect to speak personally to the person contacted (although see para 2.128 below).

2.127 In the case of a person detained under PACE for an indictable offence (see para 2.23 above), the right of intimation as set out above may be delayed on the authority of an inspector or above for up to 36 hours, on the same grounds as access to legal advice can be delayed (see para 2.151 below) (PACE s56; Code C para 5.2 and Annex B). Where a person is detained under TA 2000 s41 or Sch 7, intimation may be delayed for up to 48 hours, on the same grounds as access to legal advice can be delayed (see para 2.156 below) (TA 2000 Sch 8 para 8; Code H para 5.2 and Annex B). Where a person is detained under NSA 2023 s27(1), intimation may be delayed for up to 48 hours, on the same grounds as access to legal advice may be delayed (see para 2.58 below) (NSA 2023 Sch 6 para 9).

2.128 In addition to the right of intimation, a person arrested and held in custody should be supplied with writing materials and allowed to speak on the telephone for a reasonable time to one person (Codes C and H para 5.6; Code I para 5.5). However, in the case of a person detained under PACE, this may be delayed or denied if the person is detained in respect of an indictable offence (see para 2.23 above) and an officer of the rank of inspector or above considers that sending a letter or making a telephone call may result in any of the consequences set out in Code C Annex B para 1 or 2 (interference with evidence connected to an indictable offence,

153 For persons detained under TA 2000 s41 and NSA 2023 s27, the guidance is more extensive. See Codes H and I NfG 5B and 5C respectively.

harm to other persons, alerting other suspects, hindering recovery of property obtained in consequence of the commission of such an offence, or hindering the recovery of the value of property that constitutes the benefit from criminal conduct under Proceeds of Crime Act (POCA) 2002 Part 2). Where a person is detained under TA 2000 Sch 7 or s41, access to writing materials, or to a telephone call, may be delayed or denied if it may lead to the consequences set out in Code H Annex B para 1 or 2 (the same consequences as under Code C, plus interference with information-gathering about acts of terrorism or alerting others). Where a person is detained under NSA 2023 s27(1), access to writing materials, or to a telephone call, may be delayed or denied on similar grounds (Code I Annex B paras 1 and 2). If communication is allowed under Code C or H para 5.6, or Code I para 5.5, the person must be told that the police can listen in to any telephone call or read any letter, and that information gained could be used in evidence (Codes C and H para 5.7; Code I para 5.6). Where appropriate, an interpreter may make the telephone call or write the letter on behalf of the detained person (Codes C, H and I NfG 5A).

Right to legal advice

Overview

2.129 All persons arrested and held in custody at a police station have a statutory right to consult a solicitor. This is in accordance with the rights guaranteed by ECHR Article 6(3)(c) as interpreted by the European Court of Human Rights (ECtHR) in *Salduz v Turkey*.[154] There is statutory provision for delaying access to a solicitor prior to charge provided certain conditions are satisfied, which may have the effect of denying the right altogether (see paras 2.151–2.159 below). 'Volunteers' also have a right to consult a solicitor. The Supreme Court has held that a person who suffers a significant curtailment of their freedom of action – for example, if they are detained following arrest whilst a search of premises is carried out – is entitled to legal assistance, but neither PACE nor the codes explicitly provide for this.[155] A person who is detained at a police station must be given a notice setting out their rights during detention.[156]

154 (App No 36391/02) (2008) 49 EHRR 421, ECtHR. Note that the right to legal advice 'belongs' to the suspect. PACE s58 does not confer a right on the solicitor to provide it (see *Rixon and Others v Chief Constable of Kent* (2000) Times, April 11, CA).

155 *Ambrose v Harris* [2011] UKSC 43.

156 Codes C and H para 3.2; Code I para 3.1. A copy of the respective notices are available at: www.gov.uk/government/publications/notice-of-rights-and-entitlements-english (Code C); www.gov.uk/government/publications/notice-of-rights-and-entitlements-english-pace-code-h/notice-of-rights-and-entitlements-english-pace-code-h-accessible-version (Code H); www.gov.uk/government/publications/notice-of-rights-and-entitlements-english-pace-code-i/notice-of-rights-and-entitlements-english-pace-code-i-accessible (Code I).

Volunteers

2.130 A 'volunteer' (see para 2.164 below) is entitled to consult a solicitor at any time and without hindrance. This is so whether the volunteer is at a police station (Code C NfG 1A) or elsewhere. However, a volunteer does not have to be told of this entitlement unless they are arrested (Code C para 3.21(a)) or cautioned (Code C para 3.21(b)). If arrested, the person must be taken before the custody officer, who must notify them of their rights in the same way as for other detained persons. If cautioned without being arrested, the officer who gives the caution must inform the person, among other things, that they are entitled to free and independent legal advice. The officer must also tell the person that they are entitled to speak to a solicitor on the telephone and must ask them if they wish to do so (Code C para 3.21A(b)).

Persons under arrest

2.131 A person who has been arrested, whether or not for an offence, and who is being held in custody in a police station or other premises is entitled to consult a solicitor privately at any time (PACE s58(1)). A person detained at a police station under TA 2000 Sch 7 or s41, or NSA 2023 s27(1), has the same right (TA 2000 Sch 8 para 7; NSA 2023 Sch 6 para 7. The police can only delay access to a solicitor in limited circumstances (see paras 2.151–2.159 below). Access can never lawfully be denied altogether, although it is possible for access to be delayed until the time that a person is charged.

Information about the right of access to a solicitor

2.132 Information must be given to a person about the right of access to a solicitor, and the fact that such advice is available free of charge:

(1) at the time that they are brought to a police station under arrest, or are arrested having initially attended voluntarily (Codes C and H para 3.1; Code I para 3);
(2) immediately before the beginning or re-commencement of any interview at a police station or other authorised place of detention (Code C para 11.2; Code H para 11.3; Code I para 11.2);
(3) before conducting a review of detention, or before determining whether to extend the maximum period of detention (Code C para 15.4); or where a person is detained under TA 2000 s41 or NSA 2023 s27(1), where a review officer authorises continued detention, and the person has not already exercised their right to consult a solicitor (TA 2000 Sch 8 para 27; NSA 2023 Sch 6 para 35);
(4) after charge or being informed that they may be prosecuted, where the police wish to bring to their attention any statement or the content of any interview, or where they wish to re-interview (Code C paras 16.4 and 16.5);
(5) before being asked to provide an intimate sample (Code D para 6.3);

(6) before an intimate drug search under PACE s55(1)(b) (Code C Annex A para 2B) or X-ray or ultrasound scan under PACE s55A(1) (Code C Annex K para 3);
(7) before being interviewed after charge (Code C para 16.5); and
(8) before any eye-witness identification procedure is conducted (Code D para 3.17).

Where appropriate, information should be provided regarding the availability of the duty solicitor.[157]

2.133 If a person, on being informed or reminded of their right to legal advice, declines to speak to a solicitor in person, the custody officer must point out that the right to legal advice includes the right to speak to a solicitor on the telephone. The officer must then ask the person whether they wish to speak to the solicitor. If the person declines, the officer must ask the reason why, and any answer must be recorded. However, once it is clear that the suspect does not wish to speak to a solicitor at all, the officer must cease to ask them the reasons for their decision (Code C para 6.5; Code H para 6.4; Code I para 6.3). No attempt should be made to dissuade a suspect from obtaining legal advice (Code C para 6.4; Code H para 6.3; Code I para 6.2), and no indication given (except in answer to a direct question) that a request for legal advice will have an impact on the length of detention (Codes C and H NfG 6ZA; Code I NfG 6A). It has been held that for waiver of the right to legal advice to be valid, it is normally sufficient that the person is told of the right, that they understand what the right is, and that the waiver is made freely and voluntarily. However, 'people who are of low intelligence or are vulnerable for other reasons . . . may need to be given more than the standard formulae'.[158] It may be assumed that a well-educated suspect with previous convictions could be expected to be well aware of the benefits of legal advice.[159] Failure to give adequate information about the right to legal advice may give cause for complaint, and may lead to exclusion of evidence at a subsequent trial (see chapter 13 below). Therefore, if relevant, the defence lawyer should carefully check the circumstances in which a suspect declined legal advice.

Children and others at risk

2.134 A child or vulnerable person has a personal right to seek legal advice, which must not be delayed pending arrival of an appropriate adult. The appropriate adult has an independent right to seek legal advice (Code C paras 3.19 and 6.5A; Code H paras 3.20 and 6.6; Code I paras 3.23 and 6.5). See further chapter 11 below.

157 See *R v Vernon* [1988] Crim LR 445, Crown Court; and *Beeres v Crown Prosecution Service (West Midlands)* [2014] EWHC 283 (Admin).

158 *McGowan v B* [2011] UKSC 54. This does not go as far as the ECtHR which, in *Pishchalnikov v Russia* (App No 7025/04) [2009] ECHR 1357, ECtHR, held that waiver of the right to legal advice 'must not only be voluntary, but must also constitute a knowing and intelligent relinquishment . . . it must be shown that [the suspect] could reasonably have foreseen what the consequences of his conduct would be' (para 77) (see para 13.55 below).

159 *R v Saunders* [2012] EWCA Crim 1380.

Police action when a request is made

2.135 Where a request is made for legal advice, the suspect must be permitted to consult a solicitor as soon as practicable, and the custody officer must act without delay to secure its provision (PACE s58(4); Code C para 6.5; Code H para 6.4; Code I para 6.3) (subject to the power to delay access to a lawyer – see paras 2.151, 2.156 and 2.158 below). It has been held that a delay of 22 minutes in attempting to contact a lawyer amounted to a breach of PACE s58(4).[160] Note that where a person is detained under TA 2000 s41 or NSA 2023 s27, a superintendent or above may give a direction under TA 2000 Sch 8 para 9 or NSA 2023 Sch 6 para 8, respectively, that the person cannot consult the nominated solicitor, but may consult another solicitor of their choice (and see Code H para 6.5 and Code I para 6.4).

2.136 The duties of the police where a request for legal advice is made are set out in Codes C and H NfG 6B, and Code I NfG 6C (as applicable) in similar terms. Whether or not the suspect intends to pay for legal advice privately rather than rely on legal aid, the police must contact the Defence Solicitor Call Centre (DSCC). If the suspect is to pay privately, the DSCC will contact the nominated solicitor, and the suspect must be given the opportunity to nominate alternatives if that solicitor is unavailable. If the suspect is to rely on legal aid, the DSCC will determine whether the case is covered by the Criminal Defence Direct (CDD) scheme and, if so, will direct the request to CDD. If it is not covered by the CDD scheme (which it will not be in the case of a person detained under TA 2000 s41 or NSA 2023 s27), the DSCC will attempt to contact the nominated solicitor (if the suspect has nominated a solicitor or firm) or, alternatively, the duty solicitor. See further paras 1.54–1.56 above. A police officer must not advise the suspect about any particular firm of solicitors (Codes C and H NfG 6B; Code I NfG 6C).

2.137 Once a request has been made by a suspect detained under PACE, they must not be interviewed or continue to be interviewed until they have received advice unless (Code C para 6.6):

(1) Code C Annex B applies, which refers to the grounds for delaying access to legal advice under PACE s58; or
(2) an officer of the rank of superintendent or above has reasonable grounds for believing that:
   - delay might lead to interference with, or harm to, evidence connected with an indictable offence; lead to interference or physical harm to another person; lead to alerting other people suspected of having committed an indictable offence but not yet arrested for it; hinder the recovery of property obtained in consequence of the commission of an indictable offence; or
   - the detained person has benefitted from their criminal conduct and recovery of the value of the property constituting the benefit will be hindered (in which case questioning must cease as soon as sufficient information to avert the risk has been obtained, unless other grounds for continuing the interview in the absence of legal advice apply (Code C para 6.7)); or

160 *Gearing v DPP* [2008] EWHC 1695 (Admin).

(3) the solicitor requested:
- cannot be contacted;
- has previously indicated that they do not want to be contacted; or
- having been contacted, declines to attend,

and the person has been told of but declines advice from a duty solicitor, provided starting or continuing the interview is authorised by an officer of the rank of inspector or above;[161] or

(4) the person who wants legal advice changes their mind, provided agreement to be interviewed without receiving legal advice is recorded in the interview record and it is authorised by an officer of the rank of inspector or above. The authorising officer must, before giving authority, enquire into the person's reasons for their change of mind, and the reasons given and the name of the authorising officer must be recorded (or confirmed) in the custody record and confirmed in the interview record. In addition, the authorising officer must ensure that the nominated solicitor is notified of the authorisation and of the time that the interview is expected to commence.

Where a person is interviewed in the absence of legal advice under (1) or (2) above, inferences from 'silence' cannot be drawn and the person should be cautioned in the terms set out in Code C Annex C para 2, rather than the 'normal' caution set out in Code C para 10.5. Evidence of such interviews is admissible at trial in the normal way.[162]

2.138 Where a request has been made by a person detained under TA 2000 s41, they must not be interviewed or continued to be interviewed until they have received advice, subject to the same conditions and exceptions as persons detained under PACE with the following modifications:

- the reference to Annex B is a reference to Code H Annex B; and
- in addition to the consequences that a superintendent or above may have reasonable grounds for believing in the case of a person detained under PACE, that a delay in interviewing the person might lead to: interference with the gathering of information about a person's involvement in foreign power threat activity; or making it more difficult by the alerting of a person to prevent foreign power threat activity or more difficult to secure a person's apprehension, prosecution or conviction in connection with the person's involvement in foreign power threat activity (Code H para 6.7).[163]

2.139 Where a request has been made by a person detained under NSA 2023 s27(1), they must not be interviewed or continued to be interviewed until they have received advice, subject to the same conditions and exceptions as apply to a person detained under TA 2000 s41 (Code I para 6.6). The reference to Annex B is a reference to Code I Annex B.

161 Note that in these circumstances, the prohibition on drawing inferences does not apply.

162 *R v Ibrahim and Others* [2008] EWCA Crim 880, confirmed in this respect by the ECtHR in *Ibrahim and Others v UK* (App Nos 50541/08, 50571/08, 50573/08, 40351/09) [2017] Crim LR 877. See further para 13.54 below.

163 It is unclear why Code H para 6.7 refers to foreign power threat activity whereas TA 2000 Sch 8 para 8(4) and Code H Annex B para 1 refer to acts of terrorism. This is probably an error in drafting.

2.140 Where a person detained for examination under TA 2000 Sch 7 (see para 1.61 above) asks for a solicitor, they may not be questioned until they have consulted a solicitor (or no longer wish to do so), unless the examining officer reasonably believes that postponing the questioning until then would be likely to prejudice determination of relevant matters.[164]

2.141 The rule that a person who has requested advice should not be interviewed until they have received it does not amount to a requirement that the lawyer must be allowed to be present at any police interview. The right in Codes C and I para 6.8 and Code H para 6.9 to have a solicitor present in interview is subject to the exceptions in Codes C and I para 6.6 and Code H para 6.7 (see para 2.137 above).[165] Therefore, if initial advice is given by the lawyer, either on the telephone or in person, the lawyer should make clear to the custody officer whether they wish to be present at any interview, and should ask that this be noted in the custody record. If this is not done, there is a danger that the police can argue that advice has been received (albeit on the telephone) and that an interview can thus proceed in the absence of a lawyer.[166] Since an interview may proceed in the absence of legal advice if the suspect changes their mind, any initial telephone advice to the person in custody should include a warning of this possibility (see further para 3.50 below).

2.142 The statutory drink/driving procedure under RTA 1988 s7 or Transport and Works Act 1992 s31 does not amount to an interview and, therefore, the suspect has no right to delay the procedure pending legal advice being received.[167]

2.143 If the police proceed with an interview contrary to the above provisions, this may provide grounds for complaint and/or for seeking exclusion of evidence subsequently obtained (see chapter 13 below).

'Arrested and held in custody'

2.144 The right to consult a solicitor under PACE s58(1) applies to persons arrested for an offence and also to persons arrested for other reasons, for example, for breach of bail conditions or under MHA 1983 s136. It has been held that the right to legal advice does not apply to persons arrested

164 TA 2000 Sch 7 para 7A(5); and see www.gov.uk/government/publications/code-of-practice-for-examining-officers-and-review-officers-under-schedule-7-to-the-terrorism-act-2000 para 50(a).

165 It was held in *R v Chief Constable of the Royal Ulster Constabulary ex p Begley* [1997] 4 All ER 833, HL (NI) that there is no common law right to have a solicitor present in a police interview. However, the ECtHR has held in a number of cases that the right to fair trial entails a right to have a lawyer present in interview. See *Sebalj v Croatia* (App No 4429/09) [2011] ECHR 1048; and *Mader v Croatia* (App No 56185/07) (2011) 21 September; and see para 13.10 below).

166 This would also have the effect of permitting inferences. See para 5.69 below.

167 See Code C para 11.1A; and *DPP v Billington and Others* [1988] 1 All ER 435, QBD; *DPP v Rous; DPP v D (A Minor)* (1992) 94 Cr App R 185, QBD; *Campbell v DPP* [2002] EWHC 1314 (Admin); *Kennedy v Crown Prosecution Service* [2002] EWHC 2297 (Admin); *Whitley v DPP* [2003] EWHC 2512 (Admin); *Crown Prosecution Service v Rice* [2004] EWHC 508 (Admin); *Myles v DPP* [2004] EWHC 594 (Admin); and *Gearing v DPP* [2008] EWHC 1695 (Admin). It was held in *Cowper v DPP* [2009] EWHC 2165 (Admin) that the introduction of the CDS Direct (now CDD) scheme made no difference.

and detained for breach of the peace (see para 2.27 above).[168] However, it is submitted that this is incorrect since PACE s58(1) grants the right to consult a solicitor to a person 'arrested and held in custody' and does not confine the right to persons arrested for an offence. While the right extends to persons held in custody at places other than a police station, it has been held that it applies only once detention has been authorised under PACE s37. Thus, the right did not apply to a suspect arrested and held in a hotel room.[169] However, denial of legal advice in such circumstances may be in breach of the right to a lawyer under ECHR Article 6(3)(c) (see para 2.129 above). Where detention has been authorised, the right to consult a solicitor under PACE s58 continues to apply even if the suspect is taken to other premises, for example, for a search to be conducted, or is removed to hospital because of ill-health. It also probably continues to apply after charge and first court appearance if the defendant continues to be in custody at a police station and the investigation is continuing.[170]

'Solicitor'

2.145 PACE, the TA 2000 and the NSA 2023 refer only to solicitors, but this is significantly modified by Codes C and I para 6.12 and Code H para 6.13, which define 'solicitor', for the purposes of the codes, as meaning a solicitor who holds a current practising certificate or an accredited or probationary representative included on the register of representatives maintained by the LAA. 'Solicitor' has the same meaning in Code D (Code D para 2.6), Code E (Code E para 1.5) and Code F (Code F para 1.5). By implication, 'solicitor' does not include a representative (who is neither accredited nor probationary) of a solicitor acting privately, although arguably a solicitor acting privately can send such a representative to advise at the police station if the client consents. Accredited and probationary representatives may be denied access to the police station on the authority of an officer of the rank of inspector or above who considers that their visit will hinder the investigation of crime (Code C para 6.12A; Code H para 6.14; Code I para 6.13; and see para 4.4 below).

'Privately'

2.146 All persons entitled to consult a solicitor are entitled to do so in private. Code C NfG 6J, and Codes H and I NfG 6I, describe the right to consult in private as fundamental, and state that if written or oral communications between the lawyer and their client are compromised by being overheard,

168 *R (Hicks) v Commissioner of Police of the Metropolis* [2014] EWCA Civ 3, following *Williamson v Chief Constable of the West Midlands* [2003] EWCA Civ 337.

169 *R v Kerawalla* [1991] Crim LR 451, CA, but see the critical commentary at p453. See also *Kirkup v DPP* [2003] EWHC 2354 (Admin). The Court of Appeal took an apparently contrary view in *R v Sanusi* [1992] Crim LR 43. In any event, arguably a person in such circumstances has a common law right to legal advice (see *R v Lemsatef* [1977] 2 All ER 835, CA; and *R v Chief Constable of South Wales ex p Merrick* [1994] 2 All ER 560, QBD). See also *Ambrose v Harris* [2011] UKSC 43 (note 153 above).

170 The section 58 right does not apply to a person who has been remanded in custody by magistrates, although the detainee then has a common law right to legal advice (*R v Chief Constable of South Wales ex p Merrick* [1994] 2 All ER 560, QBD).

listened to or read, the right is effectively denied. 'Privately' is not defined, and the police have sometimes argued that the right to consult a solicitor in private does not prevent the police from observing the lawyer and client, for example, through glass walls. However, it has been held in relation to lawyer/client consultations at court that '[t]he principle that the defendant is entitled to private and confidential discussions with his legal advisers, unsupervised *and unobserved* by police officers . . . is too elementary to require citation of authority' (emphasis added).[171] It is suggested that this principle also applies at the police station.

2.147 Telephone advice raises particular practical problems in terms of privacy, and this is exacerbated by the CDD scheme, under which publicly funded legal advice is limited to advice on the telephone in certain circumstances (see para 1.54 above). Code C NfG 6J, and Codes H and I NfG 6I, provide that where a person speaks to a solicitor on the telephone, this should be in private unless impracticable because of the design and layout of the custody area or the location of the telephones. This is arguably contrary to the statutory right to consult a solicitor, under which the right to consult privately is not qualified by reference to practicality. It has been held that absence of private facilities for consultations with a solicitor was not contrary to the applicant's ECHR Article 6 (right to a fair trial) rights, but it is suggested that this should be revisited in the light of the developing ECtHR case-law on the right to legal advice (see para 13.55 below).[172] Code C NfG 6J, and Codes H and I NfG 6I, state that the normal expectation is that private facilities will be available for both in-person and telephone consultations unless they are already in use.

2.148 Covert surveillance of private consultations between a lawyer and client at a police station are governed by the Regulation of Investigatory Powers Act (RIPA) 2000. It has been held that the power to conduct covert surveillance takes precedence over the right to legal advice in private, although it must be authorised under the RIPA 2000 as intrusive surveillance.[173] Even if properly authorised, use at trial of material obtained by such surveillance may breach the person's right to fair trial under ECHR Article 6. There is no obligation under the RIPA 2000 to inform either the suspect or their lawyer of such covert surveillance, either before or after the event.

'At any time'

2.149 A person entitled to consult a solicitor is entitled to do so 'at any time'. Subject to the power of the police to delay access to a solicitor under PACE s58, TA 2000 Sch 8 and NSA 2023 Sch 6 (see paras 2.151, 2.156 and 2.158

171 *Crown Prosecution Service v LR* [2010] EWCA Crim 924 at para 20.

172 *R (M (A Child)) v Commissioner of Police of the Metropolis* [2001] EWHC Admin 553, but see the critical commentary. See also R Pattenden and L Skinns, 'Choice, privacy and publicly funded legal advice at police stations' (2010) 73 *Modern Law Review* 3 at p349. For a report of a successful action for breach of statutory duty where the police insisted on being present when a suspect spoke to his solicitor on the telephone, see *Roques v Commissioner of Police of the Metropolis* September 1997 *Legal Action* 23.

173 *Re C's Application for Judicial Review; Re McE; Re M; Re C* [2009] UKHL 15. See Regulation of Investigatory Powers (Extension of Authorisation Provisions: Legal Consultations) Order 2010 SI No 461.

below), the right to consult a solicitor is not qualified in any way and may be exercised at any time.

2.150 The fact that a person is entitled to consult a solicitor at any time may assist a lawyer who is experiencing difficulty in speaking to their client either in person or on the telephone. PACE does not limit the right by any consideration of practicality or convenience. There may be difficulty, however, if the right to consult a solicitor at any time is used during the course of a police interview to prevent the interview from proceeding effectively (see further para 7.50 below).

Delaying access to advice – valid reasons

Grounds for delay – detention under PACE

2.151 Where an arrested person held in police custody exercises their right to consult a solicitor, the police may only delay access if:

- the person is detained in respect of an indictable offence (see para 2.23 above);
- the person has not been charged; and
- the delay is authorised by an officer of the rank of a superintendent or above (PACE s58(6); Code C Annex B).

Note, however, that in some circumstances an interview may proceed before advice has been received (see para 2.137 above). There is no power to delay access to a solicitor where a person is detained in respect of a summary-only offence, or where a person has been arrested otherwise than for an offence.

2.152 The maximum period of delay is 36 hours from the relevant time (see para 2.76 above), and the right may be delayed only for as long as is necessary (PACE s58(5); Code C Annex B para 6), which should be determined according to the reason why delay was authorised. If the grounds for delay cease to exist the person must, as soon as practicable, be asked if they wish to consult a solicitor, and appropriate action must then be taken. If the police seek a warrant of further detention under PACE s43, the person must be allowed access to a solicitor in reasonable time before the hearing, even if this is within the 36-hour period (Code C Annex B para 7).

2.153 Provided that the above conditions are satisfied, an officer of the rank of superintendent or above may authorise delay if they have reasonable grounds for believing that exercise of the right (PACE s58(8); Code C Annex B paras 1 and 2):

- will lead to interference with or harm to evidence connected with an indictable offence or interference with or physical injury to any person (PACE s58(8)(a));
- will lead to the alerting of other people suspected of having committed such an offence but not yet arrested for it (PACE s58(8)(b));
- will hinder the recovery of property obtained as a result of such an offence (PACE s58(8)(c)); or
- will hinder the recovery of the value of the property by which the person has benefited as a result of their criminal conduct (which is to be decided in accordance with POCA 2002 Part 2) (PACE s58(8A)).

2.154 The grounds for delaying access to advice under section 58 are strictly phrased, since the officer concerned must have reasonable grounds for believing that exercising the right to consult a solicitor *will* lead to one of the prohibited consequences. This is reinforced by Code C Annex B para 3 which provides:

> Authority to delay a detainee's right to consult privately with a solicitor may be given only if the authorising officer has reasonable grounds to believe the solicitor the detainee wants to consult will, inadvertently or otherwise, pass on a message from the detainee or act in some other way which will have any of the consequences specified under paragraphs 1 or 2.[174]

2.155 Code C Annex B NfG B3 makes it clear that a decision to delay access to a specific solicitor will be a rare occurrence, which will apply only when it can be shown that the suspect is capable of misleading that particular solicitor and there is more than a substantial risk that the suspect will succeed in causing information to be conveyed that will lead to one or more of the specified consequences. If a decision to delay access to a particular solicitor is made, the detainee must be allowed to choose another solicitor (Code C Annex B para 3). Thus, it will be unusual for the police to be able to justify delaying access to a particular solicitor and almost inconceivable that they could justifiably delay access to any solicitor.[175] It has been held that in order to comply with ECHR Article 6, delaying access to legal advice requires 'compelling reasons' and, even if justified, use of the interview in evidence may amount to a breach of the right to fair trial.[176]

Grounds for delay – detention under the Terrorism Act 2000

2.156 Where a person is detained for examination under TA 2000 Sch 7 (see para 1.61 above) or is detained following arrest under TA 2000 s41 (see para 2.58 above), access to a solicitor may only be delayed if the person has not been charged with an offence and delay is authorised by an officer of at least the rank of superintendent (TA 2000 Sch 8 para 8(1)(b); Code H para 6.4 and Annex B). Note that in some circumstances an interview may proceed before consultation with a solicitor has taken place (see paras 2.137–2.138 above). Where a person is detained for examination under TA 2000 Sch 7, the period of delay may be up to the maximum period of detention under that schedule (see para 1.61 above). Where a person is detained following arrest under section 41, the maximum period of delay is 48 hours from the time of arrest or, if they were detained under TA 2000 Sch 7 when they were arrested, from the time when their examination under that schedule began (TA 2000 s41(3) and Sch 8 para 8(2)). Any

174 A similar provision is to be found in Codes H and I Annex B para 4.

175 In *R v Samuel* [1988] QB 615, CA, the court said the authorising officer must believe that the relevant consequence 'will very probably happen'. However, in *Re McNamee and McDonnell LLP's Application for Judicial Review* [2014] NICA 13, the court suggested a lower test, that there was a real risk of the relevant consequence.

176 *Cadder v HM Advocate* [2010] UKSC 43, and see para 13.54 below. However, see *Ibrahim and Others v UK* (App Nos 50541/08, 50571/08, 50573/08, 40351/09) [2017] Crim LR 877, ECtHR, in which it was held that delaying access under TA 2000 Sch 8 satisfied the 'compelling reasons' requirement, and that on the facts admitting evidence obtained during interviews conducted in the absence of legal advice did not breach the right to fair trial.

authorised delay may only be for as long as is necessary, and if the grounds cease to exist the person must, as soon as practicable, be asked whether they wish to consult a solicitor (TA 2000 Sch 8 para 8(8); Code H Annex B para 7). If the police seek a warrant of further detention under Schedule 8 Part III, the detained person must be allowed access to a solicitor for a reasonable time before the hearing, even if this is within the 48-hour period (Code H Annex B para 8).

2.157 Delay in access to a solicitor may only be authorised if the officer has reasonable grounds for believing that exercise of the right at the time that the person desires to exercise it will (TA 2000 Sch 8 para 8(3)–(5); Code H Annex B paras 1 and 2):

- lead to interference with or harm to evidence of a serious offence;[177]
- lead to interference with or physical injury to any person;
- lead to the alerting of persons who are suspected of having committed a serious offence but who have not been arrested for it;
- hinder the recovery of property obtained as a result of a serious offence or in respect of which a forfeiture order could be made under TA 2000 s23 or 23A;
- lead to interference with the gathering of information about the commission, preparation or instigation of acts of terrorism;
- lead to the alerting of a person and thereby making it more difficult to prevent an act of terrorism;
- lead to the alerting of a person, thereby making it more difficult to secure that person's apprehension, prosecution, or conviction in connection with the commission, preparation or instigation of an act of terrorism; or
- hinder the recovery of the value of the property constituting a benefit from their criminal conduct (which is to be decided in accordance with POCA 2002 Part 2).

The grounds for delaying access to a solicitor are strictly phrased, although more extensive than under the equivalent provisions in PACE (see para 2.137 above).[178]

Grounds for delay – detention under the National Security Act 2023

2.158 Where a person is detained under NSA 2023 s27, access to a solicitor may only be delayed on the authorisation of a superintendent or above (NSA 2023 Sch 6 para 9(1)(b); Code I para 6.3 and Annex B). Note that in some circumstances an interview may be conducted before consultation with a solicitor has taken place (see para 2.139 above). The maximum period of delay is 48 hours from the time the person was arrested under NSA 2023 s27 or, if detained under a provision listed in NSA 2023 s27(4) when arrested under section 27, the time the person was detained under that

177 TA 2000 Sch 8 para 8(9) provides that a 'serious offence' is an indictable offence (see para 2.23 above) or any offence mentioned in TA 2000 s40(1)(a) or attempt or conspiracy to commit such an offence.

178 It was held in *Ibrahim and Others v UK* (App Nos 50541/08, 50571/08, 50573/08, 40351/09) [2017] Crim LR 877, ECtHR that interviews conducted in the absence of a lawyer under these provisions satisfied the 'compelling reasons' requirement and did not breach the applicants' right of access to a lawyer under ECHR Article 6(3)(c).

provision. Any authorised delay may only be for as long as the grounds for delay are satisfied, and if the grounds cease to apply, no further delay is permitted and the person must be asked if they wish to consult a solicitor (NSA 2023 Sch 6 para 9(8); Code I Annex B para 7). The detained person must be allowed to consult a solicitor for a reasonable time before any court hearing, even if this is within the 48-hour period (Code I Annex B para 8).

2.159 Delay in access to a solicitor may only be authorised if the officer has reasonable grounds for believing that exercise of the right at the time the person desires to exercise it will (NSA 2023 Sch 6 para 8(3) and (4); Code I Annex B para 9(3)(b) and (4)):

- lead to interference with or harm to evidence of an indictable offence;
- lead to interference with or physical injury to any person;
- lead to the alerting of persons who are suspected of having committed an indictable offence but who have not been arrested for it;
- lead to the hindering of the recovery of property obtained as a result of an indictable offence;
- lead to interference with the gathering of information about a person's involvement in foreign power threat activity;
- make it more difficult, by the alerting of a person, to prevent foreign power threat activity;
- make it more difficult, by the alerting of a person, to secure that person's apprehension, prosecution or conviction in connection with the person's involvement in foreign power threat activity; or
- hinder the recovery of the value of the property constituting a benefit from their criminal conduct (which is to be decided in accordance with POCA 2002 Part 2).

Representations against delaying access

2.160 The police are not under a duty to receive representations regarding the decision to delay access to a solicitor and, by its very nature, the decision will normally be taken without the solicitor knowing that the client has been arrested and detained. Evidence obtained following wrongful denial of access will not necessarily be excluded at trial (see paras 13.29, 13.38 and 13.55 below), so it is important that if a solicitor is aware that the decision has been made, or is being contemplated, they should make representations to the appropriate officer, which may relate to:

(1) whether the offence for which the person is detained is an indictable offence, or other relevant offence where a person is detained under the TA 2000;
(2) whether others are aware of the person's arrest because, if they are, the involvement of a lawyer is unlikely to have any adverse effect;[179]
(3) what grounds the officer has for believing that the lawyer concerned will conduct themself in such a way as to lead to one of the prohibited consequences;

179 See *R v Davison* [1988] Crim LR 442, where the court disapproved of delay in access to a solicitor after the defendant had spoken to his wife on the telephone from the police station.

(4) what grounds the officer has for believing that the suspect is capable of misleading the lawyer, and for believing that there is a substantial risk that the suspect will succeed in causing the lawyer to convey information that will lead to one or more of the specified consequences (ie those set out at para 2.151 or para 2.157 above); and
(5) whether the suspect has been asked whether they want to speak to the duty solicitor.

2.161 If these representations fail, the police should be asked to deliver a letter to the client explaining that the police are preventing access and advising the client to ask to speak to a duty solicitor. All representations, together with the time they were made and the responses given, should be carefully noted. In *R v Samuel*,[180] the solicitor who had sought access gave evidence of the times he had tried to speak to his client, and this almost certainly had an effect on the outcome.

Delaying access to advice – invalid reasons

2.162 The police sometimes use informal or unlawful methods to deter or prevent access to a solicitor. Some of these ploys are dealt with in greater length in chapters 3 and 4 below, but the following is a summary of the more common reasons given by the police for delaying or denying access.

(1) The lawyer may advise the person not to answer questions. Although in the past this was the reason for much of the reluctance of police officers to allow access to legal advice, it is specifically prohibited by Codes C and H Annex B para 4; Code I Annex B para 5.
(2) The lawyer was initially asked to attend by someone else and the suspect has not asked for them. In this case, the suspect must be informed of the lawyer's presence and must be asked to sign the custody record to signify whether they wish to see the lawyer (Codes C and H Annex B para 4; Code I Annex B para 5).
(3) The suspect has declined legal advice. Where a lawyer attends the police station, the suspect must, unless an interview in the absence of legal advice has been authorised (see paras 2.137, 2.138 and 2.139 above), be informed of the lawyer's arrival and must be asked whether they would like to see the lawyer. This is the case whether or not the suspect is then being interviewed, and even if the suspect has declined advice or, having initially requested it, subsequently agreed to being interviewed without it. The lawyer's attendance and the decision must be noted on the custody record, although it does not have to be signed by the suspect (Code C para 6.15; Code H para 6.17; Code I para 6.16). Strictly, this provision, and the one above, only applies where the lawyer actually attends the police station (as opposed to telephoning the police station) (see further para 3.20 below).
(4) There is a conflict of interests (see para 5.42 below). Codes C and H confirm that conflict is a question of professional ethics for the lawyer

180 [1988] QB 615, CA.

to decide, not the police,[181] although they provide that if waiting for a lawyer to give advice may lead to unreasonable delay to the interview of another, the provisions of Codes C and I para 6.6(b) or Code H para 6.7(b) (as applicable) may apply (see para 2.137 above) (Codes C and I NfG 6G; Code H NfG 6F).

(5) The suspect is a child or is vulnerable and the presence of an appropriate adult is awaited. All persons arrested and held in custody have a right to advice irrespective of age or other circumstances. If such a person requests advice, it must be acted on in the usual way (see para 2.135 above). This is explicitly set out in Code C para 6.5A; Code H para 6.6; and Code I para 6.5.

(6) An accredited or probationary representative has been denied access to the police station. In this case, the employing solicitor must be notified and given the opportunity to make alternative arrangements (Code C para 6.14; Code H para 6.16; Code I para 6.15).

(7) The lawyer has been excluded from interview for 'misconduct'. In this case, the suspect must be given the opportunity to consult another lawyer before the interview continues (Codes C and I para 6.10; Code H para 6.11).

2.163 If an invalid reason has been used to justify delaying or denying access to a lawyer, this may provide grounds for a complaint and/or grounds for any evidence subsequently obtained to be excluded at trial. It may also amount to a breach of the suspect's right of access to a lawyer under ECHR Article 6(3)(c). See further chapter 13 below.

Volunteers

2.164 A volunteer is a person who, for the purpose of assisting with an investigation, attends voluntarily at a police station or at any other place where a constable is present or accompanies a constable to a police station or any such other place without having been arrested (PACE s29). The term does not include a person being interviewed by someone other than a police officer unless the interview is in the presence of a constable. However, it is wide enough to include witnesses, victims and even appropriate adults. A volunteer is entitled to leave at any time unless and until arrested, and must be informed that they are under arrest if a decision is made to prevent them from leaving at will (PACE s29; Code C para 3.21). For arrest and detention of a person who attends at a police station as a volunteer, see paras 2.20 and 2.70 above.

2.165 A volunteer is entitled to legal advice at any time and to communicate with anyone outside the police station (Code C NfG 1A).[182] A volunteer must be informed of their right to consult a solicitor if they are cautioned, which they must be if there are grounds to suspect that they have committed an offence (Code C para 3.21A(b); and see para 2.130 above). If a volun-

181 Confirmed in *R (McDonagh) v Chief Constable of Leicestershire* [2013] EWHC 4690 (Admin).

182 There is no equivalent provision in Codes H and I since they specifically concern persons who are detained.

teer wants to consult a solicitor, it is the responsibility of the interviewer to arrange this by contacting the DSCC. Legal advice may be provided under the police station scheme if the volunteer attends at a police station, or elsewhere where a police constable is present, for the purpose of assisting with an investigation.[183] A person who is the subject of a non-police investigation may be entitled to legal aid under the free-standing legal advice and assistance scheme.[184] A witness is not entitled to legal aid unless there is a 'complicating factor'.[185]

2.166 Many of the provisions of PACE and the codes do not apply to volunteers, for example, those relating to review and those relating to treatment of detained persons (see para 1.60 above). However, Code C places responsibility on the interviewer to carry out a similar function to that of the custody officer in terms of providing information to a volunteer about their procedural rights, including the right to information concerning the suspected offence, the right to an interpreter and the right to consult a solicitor (Code C para 3.21A).[186] The provisions concerning appropriate adults for children and other vulnerable suspects who are volunteers are similar to those in respect of suspects who have been arrested and detained (Code C para 3.21(b)). Interviews of volunteers should be arranged for a time and location that enables the interview to be recorded using an authorised recording device (Code C para 3.21A(f); Codes E and F). However, a written record of an interview is permitted in certain specified circumstances (Code E para 2.3 and Annex). If a volunteer surrenders their electronic device for examination, then, for adults, it is necessary to consider Police, Crime, Sentencing and Courts Act 2022 s36. For children and the vulnerable, consider also whether the necessary authorisation under section 37 of the Act has been properly obtained.

183 LAA Standard Crime Contract (SCC) Specification 2022 paras 9.1 and 9.20 (draft SCC Specification 2025 paras 9.1 and 9.14).

184 SCC Specification 2022 paras 9.54–9.56 (draft SCC Specification 2025 paras 9.51–9.53).

185 SCC Specification 2022 paras 9.3 and 9.4 (draft SCC Specification 2025 paras 9.46 and 9.47).

186 See NPCC, *Voluntary Interview Guidance*, July 2024, available at: https://library.college.police.uk/docs/NPCC/Voluntary-interview-guidance-2024.pdf.

CHAPTER 3

Dealing with the initial call

continued

Introduction

3.1 The way in which the lawyer deals with the initial call concerning a person who has been arrested and detained will often determine whether the intervention will be successful, and whether the client will be satisfied with the lawyer's handling of their case. Generally, the first indication that a person has been arrested and wants legal advice will be a telephone call from the Defence Solicitor Call Centre (DSCC). Sometimes, however, the first contact will be made by a friend or relative, either by telephone or by calling at the office or, where the suspect is not under arrest, by the suspect themself. To some extent, different considerations apply depending on who makes the initial contact. This chapter is concerned with the initial call, whoever it comes from, and goes on to deal with the first contact with the police and the client.

3.2 As noted in para 1.35 above, careful recording of events is an important task for the defence lawyer and all staff that deal with a case, and the recording of some information is mandatory under the Legal Aid Agency's (LAA) Standard Crime Contract (SCC). This chapter makes extensive reference to information that should be sought, and advice that should be given by the defence lawyer, and this should always be recorded. Notwithstanding any local practice that might allow future access to a transcript of calls, interviews or copy of the custody record, it would be wrong and arguably negligent to fail to make an independent note.

Call from the Defence Solicitor Call Centre

3.3 Generally, where a suspect who is held in police custody requests legal advice to be paid for from public funds, the police are required to contact the DSCC. The DSCC then directs the request to Criminal Defence Direct (CDD) (if the case is covered by the CDD scheme), or to the nominated solicitor or firm, or to the duty solicitor (see paras 1.54–1.56 and 2.136 above).

Restrictions and obligations

3.4 No claim for payment for police station advice and assistance can be made under the police station scheme unless the initial instructions came from the DSCC. This is subject to limited exceptions:

(1) where a client attends a police station by prior agreement with the police (see para 3.14 below);
(2) where the instructions are received from a third party (see para 3.15 below); or
(3) where the lawyer is already at the police station when the client requests advice from them.[1]

1 SCC Specification 2022 paras 9.18–9.20 (draft SCC Specification 2025 paras 9.12–9.14).

In the case of (1) and (3), the solicitor must notify the DSCC within 48 hours, and in the case of (2), prior to speaking to the suspect or attending the police station. Where a case is covered by the CDD scheme, the fact that the suspect has refused advice from CDD does not enable a lawyer to provide advice and assistance under the police station scheme.[2] However, if CDD refers a case to the suspect's own solicitor, it ceases to be a CDD matter, and the normal rules regarding police station advice and assistance apply.[3]

3.5 In all cases under the police station scheme, payment relies on the sufficient benefit test having been satisfied. It is automatically satisfied in a case referred to the lawyer by the DSCC in respect of the initial advice, but after that the lawyer must consider whether, and what, further work is justified by reference to the test (see para 1.57 above).

3.6 The lawyer must record and keep on file details of the reference number provided by the DSCC, and the file must also contain a note of the time at which the call was accepted and the time at which first contact was made with the client.[4] Having been accepted, the case must be retained until the end of the investigation. However, a duty solicitor case may be handed back to the DSCC if:[5]

(1) the lawyer is unable to continue to act personally and there is no other suitable person in the firm able to act, and the lawyer is unable to instruct a suitable agent;
(2) the client removes or rescinds their instructions;
(3) the firm is unable to act because of legitimate concerns about a breach of the professional code of conduct; or
(4) the lawyer confirms that they will not make a claim under the police station scheme.

Duty solicitor cases

3.7 The Duty Solicitor Scheme Provisions are set out in the SCC section 6 (see para 1.49 above). The SCC section 9 sets out a number of obligations in duty solicitor cases regarding acceptance of cases and the time within which the client must be attended upon. If the duty solicitor is already at the police station when a person requests the duty solicitor, the solicitor must inform the DSCC when the solicitor accepts the request for advice.[6] A duty solicitor must inform a suspect that they are not obliged to instruct the duty solicitor.[7] If the suspect wants another solicitor to act, the duty solicitor must not act unless the named solicitor is unavailable and the suspect asks the duty solicitor to act on that occasion.[8]

2 SCC Specification 2022 para 9.12 (draft SCC Specification 2025 para 9.6).
3 SCC Specification 2022 para 9.13 (draft SCC Specification 2025 para 9.7).
4 SCC Specification 2022 paras 9.21 and 9.25 (draft SCC Specification 2025 paras 9.15 and 9.21).
5 SCC Specification 2022 paras 9.51–9.53 (draft SCC Specification 2025 paras 9.43–9.45).
6 SCC Specification 2022 para 9.47 (not included in draft SCC Specification 2025).
7 SCC Specification 2022 para 6.64 (draft SCC Specification 2025 para 6.63).
8 SCC Specification 2022 para 6.65 (draft SCC Specification 2025 para 6.64).

Use of representatives

3.8 The accreditation scheme for police station representatives is explained at para 1.46 above. Under the police station advice and assistance scheme (ie other than in privately funded cases), in own-solicitor cases the initial call from the DSCC can be taken, and advice and assistance provided (by telephone or in person), by accredited or probationary representatives who are registered with the LAA. In duty solicitor cases, accredited (but not probationary) representatives may be used to accept the initial call from the DSCC, and to provide advice and assistance (by telephone or in person). Probationary representatives are not permitted to provide advice in respect of indictable-only offences.[9] Non-duty solicitor staff may be used to receive calls from the DSCC in duty solicitor cases if the conditions in the SCC Specification 2022 para 9.50 (draft SCC Specification 2025 para 9.42) are satisfied.

Call from the suspect

3.9 The initial contact will rarely come from a suspect in police custody because Police and Criminal Evidence Act 1984 (PACE) Codes of Practice C and H provide that requests for legal advice are to be directed by the police to DSCC (Codes C and H note for guidance (NfG) 6B; Code I NfG 6C). The initial contact may be made by a person who has not been arrested but who is aware that the police are looking for them and/or wish to interview them, or by a person who is on police bail. In the former case, and subject to any conflicts, the lawyer should take initial instructions in a similar way to the instructions taken from a client who is in custody (see chapter 5 below), but there are also other considerations. Probably the most important question is whether the person should surrender themself to the police. This is a complex area of advice leading to a fact-specific decision in each case. At best, all the lawyer can do is identify the pros and cons, as well as matters that might create the optimal circumstances for any planned surrender. Ultimately this is a matter for them, and it would be a serious breach of professional duty for the lawyer to contact the police to indicate the person's whereabouts without their consent.

3.10 In such circumstances, the person should normally be advised that it is in their interests to attend the police station voluntarily, rather than by compulsion, since the police may agree to this being done by appointment at a mutually convenient time. Such an arrangement could be beneficial because the time would then be known in advance, it would enable the client to make any suitable domestic arrangements, and it would ensure that a lawyer could accompany the client to the police station. It may avoid an arrest at an inconvenient time or in embarrassing circumstances or, given the necessity requirement for arrest, avoid arrest (see para 2.18 above) or detention (see para 2.70 above) altogether. It would also give the lawyer the opportunity to try to discover more about the reasons why the

9 SCC Specification 2022 paras 9.26–9.28 and 9.34 (draft SCC Specification 2025 paras 9.23–9.25 and 9.29).

police wish to arrest and/or interview the person, including what evidence they have, thus enabling both the lawyer and their client to prepare more effectively in advance of any police interview. Care should be taken in contacting the police, since unless specifically agreed with the police, engaging in such a process does not prevent the police from continuing to try to locate the client with a view to arrest. If the police are not willing to come to an arrangement for attendance at the police station, it may be advisable for the lawyer to attend at the police station with the client as soon as possible. The client's voluntary attendance will still be relevant to the necessity of arrest or detention, particularly as the lawyer will be present to make representations to the custody sergeant regarding the necessity to arrest and whether detention should be authorised. Even if those representations are unsuccessful, voluntary attendance in anticipation of an arrest, may assist them in any subsequent bail application.

3.11 The lawyer should initially seek to confirm with the police that the attendance is to be treated as 'voluntary' as this will help to establish the safeguards set out in Code G NfG 2G.[10] If the client agrees to attend at the police station, they should be advised on what is likely to happen. Unless the police have indicated otherwise, the client should normally be advised that they may be arrested and detained on attendance at the police station. Even if the police have indicated that the attendance will be treated as voluntary, it is still advisable to inform the client about the possibility of arrest and detention on arrival. Among other things, the client must expect to be searched and have personal possessions removed (Codes C and H section 4). The lawyer should not take possession of a client's possessions in order to prevent them from being seized.[11] However, both the client and lawyer should be alive to documents and other material in possession of the client that are subject to legal professional privilege. For instance, a client's phone might contain emails to and from their lawyer or other documents created with a view to obtaining legal advice. The lawyer should clearly identify the presence of privileged material to the police so that the correct procedure can be followed.[12]

3.12 The client should be advised that they will be asked to give their name and address. If there are any problems with accommodation these should, if possible, be resolved before attending at the station so that this cannot be used as a reason for treating arrest as necessary or for withholding bail in the event of the client being charged. On detention, the client will be

10 'When the person attends the police station voluntarily for interview by arrangement as in Note 2F above, their arrest on arrival at the station prior to interview would only be justified if:
- new information coming to light after the arrangements were made indicates that from that time, voluntary attendance ceased to be a practicable alternative and the person's arrest became necessary; and
- it was not reasonably practicable for the person to be arrested before they attended the station' (Code G NfG 2G; and see para 2.20 above).

11 For example, in *R (S) v Chief Constable of the British Transport Police* [2013] EWHC 2189 (Admin), a solicitor who took possession of a client's mobile phone in circumstances where it was clear that the phone would form part of the police investigation was charged with conspiracy to pervert the course of public justice.

12 Criminal Justice and Police Act 2001 s54 creates an obligation on the police to separate and return legally privileged material without reviewing it.

informed of their rights, including the right to legal advice (Codes C and H section 3; Code I para 6), and they should be advised to confirm their wish to receive that advice. Finally, the client should be warned that although the police may be ready to proceed straight to an interview, they may, if arrested, be detained in a cell either before or after it. Many people are unaware of how long they can be detained in a police station, and advice should also be given on this.

3.13 Contact may be made by a person who has previously been arrested and then been granted 'street bail' (see para 2.48 above) or released without charge (see para 10.113 below). In these circumstances the lawyer should take initial instructions in a similar way to the instructions taken from a client who is in custody (see chapter 5), and should also ascertain the date on which, and the police station at which, the client is to surrender. Note that the police may vary the time and place for surrender, and may withdraw the requirement to surrender.

3.14 Where a person is advised in either of these circumstances, advice and assistance may be claimed as free-standing advice and assistance, although the means test will apply and there are limitations where the person has received advice and assistance in connection with the same matter in the previous six months.[13] If the lawyer attends the police station with the client, they may be paid under the police station advice and assistance scheme provided that the attendance is by prior agreement with the police, and that the lawyer informs the DSCC within 48 hours of the first attendance.[14]

Call from a third party

Overview

3.15 The initial contact may be from a relative, friend or acquaintance of the person who has been arrested. They may have been present at the arrest or may have heard about it from others. They may have been asked by the arrested person to contact a lawyer, or they may have done so on their own initiative. Whatever the situation, it must be remembered that it is the *suspect* who is the client, or potential client, and not the person who has contacted the lawyer. Nevertheless, that person may be a useful source of information. See checklist 1 at para 3.21 below for the information that should be sought from the third party.

3.16 If, as a result of the contact by the third party, advice is given to a client in police custody, payment may be claimed under the police station advice and assistance scheme, provided that the lawyer reports the matter to the DSCC prior to telephoning or attending the client.[15]

13 SCC Specification 2022 paras 9.113–9.115 and 9.125–9.131 (draft SCC Specification 2025 paras 9.117–9.119 and 9.124–9.126).

14 SCC Specification 2022 para 9.20(a) (draft SCC Specification 2025 para 9.14(a)).

15 SCC Specification 2022 para 9.20(b) (draft SCC Specification 2025 para 9.14(b)).

Instructions from a third party

3.17 It is well established that a third party can retain a lawyer on behalf of an arrested person,[16] subject to the lawyer being satisfied that the instructions arise from a genuine concern for the suspect's welfare, and subject to the instructions being confirmed by the suspect. Two common problems that may be encountered where instructions are received from a third party are dealt with below.

'The suspect has not asked for a solicitor'

3.18 Where the lawyer is initially contacted by a third party, the police may try to deter them from speaking to the suspect by maintaining that the suspect has not asked for a lawyer. Codes C and H Annex B para 4 and Code I Annex B para 5 provide that access to a solicitor may not be delayed on the ground that the solicitor 'was initially asked to attend the police station by someone else', provided that the suspect then wishes to see the solicitor. The suspect must be told that the lawyer has come to the police station and must be asked to sign the custody record to signify whether or not they wish to see the lawyer. This is reinforced by Code C para 6.15, Code H para 6.17 and Code I para 6.6, which provide that the detained person must be told of the arrival of the solicitor even if they have declined advice or, having initially asked for it, have agreed to be interviewed without it. In the past, where the suspect was being interviewed by police when the lawyer arrived, custody officers sometimes refused to interrupt the interview to inform the suspect of the lawyer's arrival. Code C para 6.15, Code H para 6.17 and Code I para 6.6 now provide that the suspect must be informed of the lawyer's arrival, whether or not they are being interviewed.

3.19 If the lawyer attends the police station and is refused access on the ground that the suspect has declined advice, the lawyer should consider asking the custody officer to pass a letter to the suspect. The lawyer should also consider asking to see the custody record to confirm that the refusal of legal advice has been recorded.

3.20 Strictly, Codes C and H Annex B para 4 and Code I Annex B para 5 are confined to the situation where a solicitor actually attends the police station in person, although it may also be of assistance in persuading the police to allow access on the telephone. At the very least, the lawyer should ask the custody officer to go to the suspect while the lawyer is on the telephone, to ask them whether or not they wish to speak to the lawyer. Any reply should be noted.[17]

16 *R v Jones* [1984] Crim LR 357, CA; and see Codes C and H Annex B para 4; also Code I Annex B para 5.

17 In *R v Chahal* [1992] Crim LR 124 the Court of Appeal upheld the trial judge's refusal to exclude admissions in circumstances where the police had failed to inform the suspect that a solicitor instructed by his family had telephoned the police station. In *R v Franklin* (1994) Times, June 16, CA, on the other hand, the court held that admissions should have been excluded. In this case, the solicitor actually attended the police station, and there were other relevant differences. Chahal was described as an experienced businessman whereas Franklin was described as a young unemployed man who had never previously been in a police station.

'The suspect has asked for another solicitor'

3.21 A further possibility is that the police will say that the suspect has instructed another lawyer. Code C para 6.15, Code H para 6.17 and Code I para 6.6 do not directly deal with this situation, although the wording implies that the suspect should, nevertheless, be informed of the lawyer's arrival. Clearly, the wishes of the suspect are paramount, although it may be advisable to contact the other lawyer to ensure that they have been instructed.

Checklist 1: Instructions from a third party

A full and accurate note must be taken of all information obtained and advice given, which should be timed and dated.

1 Date and time of call
2 Name of person taking the call

Details of the third party

3 Name
4 Address
5 Telephone number
6 Relationship to person arrested

Details of the arrested person

7 Name, age and date of birth
8 Address
9 Telephone number
10 Any aliases used
11 Any vulnerabilities, medication, etc
12 Whether the suspect requested legal advice

Details of the incident

13 Reason for the arrest
14 Time and place of arrest
15 Circumstances of the arrest
16 Involvement of the third party (if any)
17 Details of other persons arrested or suspected
18 Details of any other witnesses or relevant third parties
19 Is the third party aware of any search taking place

Details of the detention

20 Police station suspect taken to
21 Name(s) and/or contact details of officer(s) involved

Initial response/appraisal given and action taken

22 Information given to third party
23 Action taken in response to third party contact

Details of the third party

3.22 The name, address and telephone number of the third party should be obtained so that the suspect can be informed and so that, if instructed and permitted to do so, the lawyer can let the third party know whether access to the suspect has been secured (but see para 3.27 below). Details of the third party's relationship to the suspect may also assist in obtaining access.

Details of the arrested person

3.23 It is, of course, essential to obtain the name, address and telephone number of the arrested person and, if possible, their age and date of birth. Difficulties may arise if the arrested person uses one or more aliases, since the lawyer must avoid inadvertently alerting the police to this possibility. If the initial contact with the police station where the suspect is believed to be is met with the response that the person named is not there, it may be wise for another member of the firm to make a second enquiry referring to another name used by the suspect. Clearly, reference to both names in the same telephone conversation should be avoided. Such an approach, at this stage, is not unethical since it does not involve the lawyer in knowingly misleading the police. The third party may possess other important information about the arrested person, such as any vulnerability, medication, etc. It is also helpful to know whether the suspect asked the third party to instruct a lawyer, since if the suspect did, this should ease access.

Details of the incident

3.24 The third party can be an important source of information. They may have been present at the time of arrest and may know something of the apparent reasons for it and the circumstances surrounding it. They may also know whether anyone else has been arrested and/or details of any relevant witnesses.

3.25 Care is necessary if there is a possibility that the third party might be implicated in the alleged offence or that the police might believe this to be so. The third party should be questioned about this. The police will often ask how the lawyer has been instructed. Care ought to be taken in deciding how much information to give the police. The lawyer is under no obligation to inform the custody officer of the identity of the person from whom they have received initial instructions. Equally, if the third party is possibly implicated, the lawyer must be wary of telling them anything other than that the detained person has been contacted. In any event, if the suspect does instruct the lawyer, information should only be given to the third party if the suspect consents to such disclosure.

3.26 Care is also necessary where there is a possibility that the third party may be a witness in the case. The risk in these circumstances is that the lawyer may inadvertently introduce new information to the third party. If the lawyer has any reason to suspect that a third party has any involvement in a case, it is better to avoid sharing any information until the third party's position is clarified.

Advice and action taken

3.27 The lawyer may inform the third party of their appraisal in general terms and should also tell them what action is intended. However, in view of the duty of confidentiality, the lawyer should not offer to inform the third party of details about the client's case unless the client gives authority for such information to be given. If permission is given, then it should be clearly noted in the lawyer's file.

Finding the client

3.28 Apart from the use of an alias (see para 3.23 above), the lawyer may encounter other problems in finding the suspect. Where a person is arrested away from a police station, they will normally be taken to the local station, but there are a number of reasons why this may not happen, or may not happen immediately:

- The local station may not be a designated police station, and so the suspect may be taken to another police station which is designated.
- It may be that the suspect has been arrested for an offence allegedly committed in another police division, in which case the suspect may be taken to a police station in that division.
- Alternatively, the suspect may have been arrested in connection with an offence allegedly committed in another police force area. In this case, the suspect may be taken to a police station in that police force area, although they will normally be taken to a police station in the area of the arrest before transfer to the police force area where the interview is to take place.
- Finally, it may be that the suspect is not being detained at a police station at all – for example, where the arrest has been made by a His Majesty's Revenue and Customs (HMRC) officer, or the suspect is a member of the armed services detained by the services police.

Checklist 2 may help in finding the suspect.

Checklist 2: Finding the client

A full and accurate note should be kept of all information sought and obtained, including the date, time, and name and status of officers spoken to.

1 Contact the custody officer at the police station where it is believed that the suspect has been taken. Where an enquiry about the whereabouts of a suspect is made by a person with an interest in the suspect's welfare, that information must normally be given, provided the suspect agrees (Codes C and H para 5.5; Code I para 5.4).

2 If the custody officer is not willing to give the required information, it may be that a decision has been made to hold the suspect incommunicado under PACE s56, Terrorism Act (TA) 2000 Sch 8 para 8 or National Security Act (NSA) 2023 Sch 6 para 9 (see para 2.127 above). This presents a difficulty, since from the police point of view, disclosing to the lawyer that the person has been detained may defeat the purpose of the action they have taken. The lawyer may wish to give an undertaking not to disclose the whereabouts of the suspect to a third party. The lawyer should also ask whether a decision to delay access to legal advice under PACE s58, TA 2000 Sch 8 or NSA 2023 Sch 6 has been taken (see paras 2.151, 2.156 and 2.158 above), since if it has not, the police will be under a duty to inform the suspect of the lawyer's interest, although strictly only if the lawyer attends in person (see para 3.18 above). It is also possible that a custody officer may

not be willing to give the required information to a specific solicitor in circumstances where a superintendent has given a direction under TA 2000 Sch 8 para 9 (Code H para 6.5) or NSA 2023 Sch 6 para 8 (Code I para 6.4).

3 If the custody officer says that the person is not detained at that police station, they should be asked whether the person has been at that station and, if so, where they have been taken. If this still draws a blank, the custody officer should be asked whether they are aware of an arrest having taken place recently, whether they are expecting a suspect to be brought into the police station in the near future and/or how many people are in the queue waiting to be booked in. It may assist if the names of any officers involved in the arrest are known.

4 If this still does not work, it is worth asking the custody officer to check the custody records, since although they should be aware of who is, or has been, in custody, there may have been a recent change of shift or there may be a temporary custody officer. If this still does not work, the custody officer should be asked to inform the lawyer if and when the person is brought in. If the suspect is not located but there is still reason to believe that they are in custody, checks should be made at regular intervals.

5 If all of the above fail, the lawyer should consider telephoning other stations and going through the same process. Depending on the circumstances, the lawyer may also consider contacting HMRC offices or other police forces such as the British Transport Police.

Initial contact with the custody officer

Overview

3.29 The initial contact with the custody officer[18] provides the opportunity to gather important information, which will be needed in order for a decision to be made on how to proceed. In particular, it will help in deciding whether to attend the police station, and will help to indicate whether there are likely to be difficulties, such as a police decision to delay access to a lawyer. Sometimes a custody officer will say that they do not know much about the case and therefore cannot give details. Most of the information to be obtained at this stage should be in the custody record, but the custody officer may be reminded that, under PACE Part IV, legal responsibility for ensuring that the grounds for detention exist and continue to exist in respect of any person in police detention rests with the custody officer (see PACE ss34 and 37 in particular). Therefore, if the officer is not aware of crucial information about the case, the officer may be asked how

18 Reference is made here to the custody officer, but although certain duties under PACE are specifically assigned to a custody officer as defined in PACE (see para 3.32 above) in practice many functions associated with persons in police detention are carried out by detention officers or other civilian officers. If a delegated person cannot answer the question/deal with the query, insist on speaking to the custody officer as the responsibility is ultimately theirs.

they can satisfy these statutory duties. Although custody work may be carried out by detention officers or other civilians, the custody officer remains legally responsible (Code C para 1.15; Code H para 1.19; Code I para 1.19).

3.30 Checklist 3 below sets out the information that should be sought from the custody officer. The nature and extent of information to be obtained at this stage will vary depending on the circumstances of the case. However, it must be sufficient to enable the lawyer to make an informed decision on:

- whether and when to attend the police station (see para 3.55 below);
- whether there is, or is a risk of, a conflict of interests (see para 5.42 below);
- whether, given the nature of the case, the lawyer has the necessary knowledge and experience to be able to deal with the matter. It may be that the lawyer should do some preliminary research before attending the police station or should consider referring the case to someone else in the firm;
- whether anything has occurred that may be of particular legal or evidential significance; and
- what, if any, legal advice the client might require in advance of the lawyer's attendance at the police station.

Checklist 3: Obtaining information from the custody officer on the telephone

A full and accurate note must be taken of all information requested and obtained, and the source of that information, which should be timed and dated.

Details of the suspect

1 Name
2 Address
3 Date of birth and age
4 Gender
5 Whether a risk assessment has been conducted, and its outcome
6 Whether child/vulnerable/other special needs (for example, interpreter)
7 Identity of appropriate adult and whether contacted (if relevant)
8 Education, employment and professional background

Police and investigation details

9 Name of custody officer
10 Station where held and custody record number
11 Name and contact details of officer in the case (request that the custody officer passes the lawyer's details to the officer in the case)
12 Whether client arrested or a volunteer
13 Time and place of arrest
14 Name or shoulder badge number of arresting officer(s)
15 Time of arrival at station
16 Time detention authorised

17 Reason for and circumstances of arrest, and why arrest necessary
18 Details of alleged offence(s)
19 Whether an indictable offence
20 Any exceptional police procedure (delay in advice/delay in informing relative or friend/intimate body search/drug test/identification procedure)
21 Reason for detention
22 Time solicitor requested
23 Reason for delay in contacting solicitor (if relevant)
24 Reason for proceeding without solicitor (if relevant)
25 Whether interviewed yet (if so, why)
26 Whether and when interview likely to take place
27 Whether search made/proposed and/or samples taken/proposed, and result
28 Any request for PIN or encryption codes made and/or information provided
29 Any significant statement or silence
30 Any other person(s) arrested/sought by police

Charge/release (if relevant)

31 If charged:
- time of charge
- nature of charge(s)
- bailed/detained in custody

32 If bailed following charge:
- date/time/place of court appearance
- any conditions attached to bail
- reason for bail being considered necessary and proportionate

33 If not bailed:
- reason for refusing bail
- date/time/place of court appearance
- police/Crown Prosecution Service (CPS) attitude to bail from the court

34 If not charged:
- whether released unconditionally/reported for summons/bailed
- if reported for summons, what offence(s) anticipated

35 If released or bailed without charge:
- reason for police bail
- any conditions attached to bail
- date/time/place of surrender

Action

36 Arrange telephone access to client
37 Confirm with custody officer:
- expected time of arrival
- that the officer will contact the lawyer if plans change
- that the client will not be interviewed before the lawyer arrives
- that the above will be noted on the custody record
- whether the lawyer would like to be contacted on any review of detention

The suspect

Name and address, etc

3.31 The name and address, and date of birth and age, of the suspect should be confirmed, together with gender identity. For the risk assessment that must be conducted, see paras 4.24–4.26 below.

Children, or other vulnerable clients with additional needs

3.32 If the person in detention is a child, or mentally disordered or vulnerable, or has other additional needs (for example, language difficulties), special provisions will apply and particular care will be necessary (see chapter 11 below). On detaining a person, the custody officer must carry out a risk assessment as soon as practicable, and the results together with any action taken must be entered in the custody record (see para 4.25 below). If no specific risks have been identified, that must be noted in the custody record (Codes C and H para 3.8; Code I para 3.9).

Whether under the influence of drink or drugs

3.33 As noted above, when a suspect is booked in at the police station the custody officer must conduct a risk assessment and take appropriate action. If the lawyer is informed that the suspect is under the influence of drink or drugs, they must decide whether it is possible or necessary to speak to them on the telephone. Sometimes the custody officer will refuse to bring the suspect to the telephone for this reason.[19] There is no provision in PACE or the codes empowering the police to delay access to legal advice because the suspect is under the influence of drink or drugs, although clearly in certain situations it would be inappropriate for advice to be given over the telephone. On the other hand, as Codes C, H and I NfG 9C make clear, a person who appears to be drunk may in fact be ill, injured or suffering from the effects of drugs.

Police details

Names of officers concerned

3.34 The need to record the name of the custody officer and the police station concerned is self-evident.[20] It is also important to obtain the name and contact details of the officer in charge of the case. Although the custody officer may change at the end of a shift, the officer in charge is likely to remain the same throughout the investigation. In more serious cases there may well be a senior officer in charge of the case as a whole, with individual officers assigned to particular suspects. It is important to know whether this is the case and, if so, the names of both officers. It may be that any representations should be made to the officer in overall charge, since the more junior officer may not have the authority to make a partic-

19 Many police stations now have the capacity for the suspect to take a call from within their cell.

20 Should an officer refuse to provide their name, the lawyer should ask for and record the reason why and, alternatively, ask for their police or warrant number.

ular decision. A junior officer cannot be relied on to relay representations to the officer making the decision accurately or with the force with which the lawyer would wish to make them.

Status of the client

3.35 It is important to establish the status of the client, that is, whether they are under arrest or a volunteer, since this will determine whether they have an absolute right to legal advice and whether they are subject to a maximum period of detention. Where relevant, a check should be made on whether the client is detained under PACE, the TA 2000 or the NSA 2023 (see paras 2.56–2.59 above). If the client is a volunteer (see para 2.164 above), much of the information in the checklist will not be relevant unless they are subsequently arrested, but it will still be necessary to ascertain the name of the officer in the case, and details about interviews, searches, encryption codes, any voluntary samples or other voluntary requests anticipated during their attendance.

Time and place of arrest

3.36 Information about the time and place of arrest will help in assessing a number of things. If there is a significant lapse of time between the arrest and the time of arrival at the police station, an explanation should be sought. PACE s30 provides that, following an arrest away from a police station, the arrested person must be taken to a police station as soon as practicable (see para 2.48 above).[21] However, this is subject to a power of delay if the person's presence elsewhere is necessary to carry out 'such investigations as it is reasonable to carry out immediately' (PACE s30(10A)). This may include a search or taking the suspect to the scene of the alleged crime, but in any event PACE s30(11) provides that the reason for delay must be recorded when the suspect arrives at the police station. The lawyer will, therefore, want to know why the suspect was not taken to the police station immediately following arrest. The lawyer should enquire whether the suspect has made a 'significant statement or silence' (see para 5.116 below), and should ask whether they were interviewed before arriving at the police station. By Codes C and I para 11.1 and Code H para 11.2 this should not normally happen, although the codes do provide for exceptions (see para 4.46 below). If relevant, the lawyer should ask the custody officer to confirm that the suspect will not be asked to sign a pocket book or other document purporting to record an earlier statement or 'silence' other than in the presence of the lawyer.

Time of arrival at police station

3.37 The time of arrival at the police station will normally determine when the detention time limit expires, although it will differ if the suspect was arrested at the police station having attended voluntarily or was arrested in another police force area (see paras 2.76 and 2.83 above). A note should be made of the time of arrival at the police station, but it may be advisable for

21 A similar obligation applies where a person is arrested under TA 2000 s41 (TA 2000 Sch 8 para 1(4)), or under NSA 2023 s27 (NSA 2023 Sch 6 para 1(4)).

the lawyer subsequently to check that their calculation of the time that the detention time limit expires agrees with that of the custody officer.

Time detention was authorised

3.38 Where a person is detained under PACE, the time that detention was authorised will determine the timing of reviews (see para 2.86 above). Where a person is detained under TA 2000 s41 or NSA 2023 s27, the timing of reviews is governed by the time of arrest (see paras 2.97 and 2.101 above).

Reasons for arrest and detention

3.39 With regard to the reason(s) for arrest, it is necessary to find out both the initial reason for arrest and the offence for which the person has been detained. Normally the offence will be the same, but it may be that, having been arrested for one offence, the suspect is further arrested before arrival or while at the police station. Note that PACE s31 provides that where a person is at a police station having been arrested for an offence, if they would be liable to arrest for another offence when released, they must be arrested for that other offence (see para 2.35 above).

3.40 Ascertaining the reason for arrest will help in determining whether the arrest was lawful (see para 2.11 above). If the arrest was unlawful, the detention may be unlawful. The lawyer may wish to seek the suspect's release on this basis, but care will be needed since grounds for arrest may be 'discovered' even though such grounds were not considered at the time of arrest or, where relevant, the information required under PACE s28 may be given, rendering the arrest lawful (see para 2.47 above). In such a situation, therefore, it would be important to try to ascertain as much detail as possible about the ground for arrest before arguing that it was unlawful.

3.41 Ascertaining the offence in respect of which the suspect is detained is necessary in order to determine whether the suspect is being detained under PACE, the TA 2000 or the NSA 2023 and, if under PACE, whether they are being detained in respect of an indictable offence (see para 2.23 above), and also whether it is a recordable offence (see Code D NfG 4A for definition). This is important because the type of offence for which the suspect has been detained will determine what powers the police have. It will also enable the lawyer to decide whether they have sufficient knowledge or experience to deal with the case, and whether they need to check the law in relation to the offence(s).

3.42 A person arrested for an offence may only be detained in a police station without charge if the conditions under PACE s37(2) are satisfied. The custody officer will normally recite PACE s37(2) in whole or in part, although they should give the grounds for their belief rather than merely reciting the statutory authority for detention. Note that the grounds under PACE s37(2) relate only to those arrested for an offence. PACE s51 specifically provides that powers to detain in custody under the Immigration Act 1971, the TA 2000 and NSA 2023 s27 and Sch 6 are unaffected by PACE Part IV. Furthermore, the police also have certain powers to detain people other than in respect of an offence, for example, under Mental Health Act (MHA) 1983 s136 (removal to a place of safety), under Bail Act (BA) 1976 s7 (breach of bail conditions), under a warrant issued by a court (for example, for failure to surrender to custody following a grant of bail) or under a power of arrest in civil proceedings.[22] In such cases, PACE s37 does not apply, although the lawyer should ensure that proper grounds for the detention do exist. For powers to detain in a police station, see para 2.56 above.

Time of request for legal advice

3.43 The time that the suspect requested a lawyer may be relevant, particularly if the lawyer has been contacted some time after the original request was made. If this is the case, the lawyer should find out the reason for the delay. Where legal advice is requested, the custody officer must normally 'act without delay to secure the provision of such advice' (Code C para 6.5; Code H para 6.4; Code I para 6.3; and see para 2.135 above). Lawful delay under PACE, the NSA 2023 and the TA 2000 is dealt with at paras 2.149, 2.156 and 2.158 above, and is relatively unusual. It may be that the reason for delay is legitimate, or may not be the fault of the police – for example, it may result from the DSCC or from an inappropriate referral to CDD – but whatever the cause, prompt contact with the suspect is important since they may well have been adversely affected by, and are unlikely to know the reason for, the delay. A careful note should be made of the time the lawyer was first contacted, and a check should be made of whether the police have taken any significant step between the time that legal advice was requested and the time the lawyer was first contacted.

3.44 Generally, once a request to consult a solicitor has been made, the suspect cannot be interviewed, or continue to be interviewed, until they have consulted the solicitor (see para 2.137 above). If the custody officer maintains that one of the exceptions to the general rule did apply, they should be questioned about the reasons for this and the authorisation given, and a note made of the answers. If the suspect made admissions during any interview carried out under one of the exceptions, then whether the exception did in fact apply or whether, alternatively, the questioning went beyond that allowed for in the exceptions, will be relevant to the question of admissibility of evidence of the admissions at any subsequent trial (see para 4.37 below). Inferences cannot be drawn from 'silence' where a suspect who has requested legal advice is denied access to a lawyer before being interviewed (see para 5.69 below).

3.45 If a suspect changes their mind about wanting legal advice, an interview may be started or continued without delay if the Codes C and I para 6.6(d) or Code H para 6.7(d) conditions are satisfied; this process should be recorded in a suspect's custody record.

22 In all these cases, the person detained is entitled to consult a solicitor, since PACE s58 applies to all people arrested and held in custody, and not just those detained under Part IV. Where a person is detained under TA 2000 s41, the right to consult a solicitor is governed by TA 2000 Sch 8 para 7, and where detained under NSA 2023 s27, by Sch 6 para 7. See para 2.129 above.

Whether the client has been interviewed or questioned

3.46 It is important to find out whether the client has been interviewed. Such an interview may be entirely proper, since the suspect may not have requested legal advice until after the interview had taken place. Nevertheless, if the client has been interviewed, the lawyer should ask for information about the content of the interview, although such a request may be better directed to the officers who conducted the interview. It is also important to find out whether an interview is to be held and, if so, when this is likely to take place. The lawyer should ask whether the suspect has already made any 'significant statement or silence' (see para 5.116 below), whether or not in the context of a formal interview. Such a statement or silence may, or may not, be admitted at any subsequent trial and the lawyer will need to take account of it when advising the suspect.

Whether a search has been conducted

3.47 It is important to find out whether a search of the suspect's person, or of premises, has been conducted or is intended. Police powers of search are dealt with in chapter 6 below. At this stage, the lawyer should ascertain the power under which the search was carried out, or is intended to be carried out and, where appropriate, on whose authority. Note, in particular, that a search of property under PACE s32(2)(b) or s18 may only be conducted where the person has been arrested for an indictable offence (see para 2.23 above). The powers of entry, search and seizure under the TA 2000 are governed by sections 42–43A, and under the NSA 2023 are governed by section 57 and Schedule 11. Furthermore, where a search has already been carried out, the custody officer should be asked whether anything significant was found or seized, although this question may be better directed at the officer in charge of the case.[23] If a search of premises is intended, the lawyer must decide whether to be present.

Whether others are sought or have been arrested

3.48 The lawyer should ask whether any other person has been arrested or is sought by the police in connection with the offence for which the client has been arrested. If there is more than one person in custody, it may be that two or more of them will request the same lawyer to act for them. Conflict of interests is dealt with at para 5.42 below. If other people are being sought in respect of the offence, the lawyer must take care not to take any action that would hinder their arrest, either intentionally or unintentionally.

Charge or release

3.49 It is relatively uncommon for a lawyer to be contacted for the first time at the time of release or shortly after release from detention. If this does occur, a careful check on when legal advice was requested should be made and, if so, the time of the request and the reasons for delay in contacting

23 Property seized on the search should be marked up in the property sheet attached to the custody record.

the lawyer. In any event, it will be necessary to find out whether the suspect has been charged and, if so, what the charges are, whether they have been bailed from the police station (and any conditions that may have been imposed) and, if not, what the police/CPS attitude to bail from the court will be. Whether or not bailed, the lawyer should ascertain the time, date and place of the first court appearance, which may include appearance via video link from the police station. If the suspect has been released on bail without charge (see para 10.113 below), the time, date and place of surrender should be ascertained so that arrangements can be made for attendance by the lawyer.

Initial contact with the client

Timing

3.50 The lawyer should attempt to speak to the client as soon as possible. The SCC 2022 requires that the lawyer should endeavour to make first contact with the client (whether in person or on the telephone) within 45 minutes of first notification that they have been arrested and have requested advice.[24] A note of the time at which the call was accepted, and the time at which first contact was made with the client, must be noted in the lawyer's file. If contact is not made within 45 minutes, the reason for this must also be noted in the file.[25] It is important to do this, particularly since lawyers often experience difficulty in getting through on the telephone to the police station.

Confidentiality of the telephone conversation

3.51 Security and privacy should always be considered when speaking to a client on the telephone (see para 2.146 above). Many custody suites do not have facilities for truly private conversations to take place. This is, in part, due to the prevalence of CCTV and audio-recording equipment in police stations and carried by police officers, which can capture comments made by a suspect while on a telephone. It is of paramount importance that the lawyer very quickly controls the conversation. This is to prevent the client providing information or instructions without first understanding the issues concerning confidentiality. It is particularly important for clients who have not been previously arrested, who are, by this stage, typically scared and upset. If there is any doubt about confidentiality, the lawyer should advise their client not to speak other than to answer questions that should be capable of being answered by 'yes' or 'no', and which should not prompt any incriminating response. If the lawyer is concerned that the police might be listening in to the conversation covertly, the conversation should be kept to a minimum and a prompt visit made to the police station. In appropriate cases the client should be warned that the police may 'bug' their cell.

24 SCC Specification 2022 para 9.23 (draft SCC Specification 2025 para 9.18).

25 SCC Specification 2022 para 9.25 (draft SCC Specification 2025 para 9.21). The contract provides that the 45-minute target must be met in at least 80 per cent of matters (SCC Specification 2022 para 9.24; SCC Specification 2025 para 9.19).

Initial advice

3.52 Having spoken to the custody officer, the lawyer should normally speak to the client on the telephone immediately afterwards. By this stage, the client may have spent some time in custody and may be afraid, vulnerable, angry or just bored. In any of these states of mind, the client could be susceptible to an approach from the police to 'crack on with the interview' instead of waiting for the lawyer. Relying on the custody officer to pass on a message that the lawyer has telephoned and will be attending in person in due course is not adequate. The custody officer may forget, be too busy or may want the suspect to think that the lawyer has not been in contact. If a request to speak to the client on the telephone is resisted by the custody officer, they should be reminded that Codes C and H para 6.1, and Code I para 6, provide that, subject to the power to delay access to advice under PACE s58(8) and (8A), TA 2000 Sch 8 para 8 and NSA 2023 Sch 6 para 9, 'all detainees must be informed that they may at any time consult and communicate privately with a solicitor, whether in person, in writing or by telephone'. If told that the client is asleep then consider whether this falls within a reasonable rest period. If it is not. it may be necessary to insist on speaking to a client to avoid unreasonable delay in contact.

Initial advice by a duty solicitor

3.53 A duty solicitor (or an accredited representative[26]) is required to give initial advice to the suspect on the telephone unless they are already at or close to the police station and can advise the client in person without delay, or the police refuse to permit the suspect to speak to the duty solicitor on the telephone. The only exception to the obligation to speak to the suspect in person arises if they are incapable of speaking to the lawyer, for example, by reason of drunkenness or violent behaviour, or because an interpreter is required. In this case, the obligation is postponed, but the lawyer must make arrangements to provide initial advice as soon as the suspect is capable of speaking to them.[27] This will inevitably mean that the lawyer must rely on the custody officer to inform them when the suspect is in a fit state to speak, or is otherwise able to do so. It is advisable to ask that the custody record be endorsed with a request to this effect. For the obligation to inform the suspect that they are not obliged to use a duty solicitor, see para 3.7 above.

Objectives of the initial telephone contact

3.54 The objectives of the initial telephone contact with the client are set out in checklist 4 below. If the lawyer is not going to attend in person, the client should be given appropriate advice, which will depend on the reason for their detention and the proposed or likely action on the part of the police. Whether or not the lawyer intends to attend in person, the client should be reminded that they are entitled to legal advice at any time (under PACE s58(1); and Codes C and H para 6.1: Code I para 6), and that they can insist on being able to speak to the lawyer at any stage of the detention.

26 See para 3.8 above regarding the use of accredited representatives in duty solicitor cases.
27 SCC Specification 2022 paras 9.42–9.44 (draft SCC Specification 2025 paras 9.37–9.39).

Checklist 4: Initial telephone conversation with client

A full and accurate note should be taken of all information obtained and advice given, which should be timed and dated.

1 Confirm that the suspect does want legal advice, and does want it from the lawyer concerned (or the lawyer's firm).
2 Inform the client of the lawyer's status, and confirm that legal advice is free (unless the client has chosen to instruct the lawyer privately, in which case they should, nevertheless, be advised that they may be eligible for advice and assistance under the legal aid scheme).
3 If appropriate, inform the client of the lawyer's role and, in particular, that the lawyer's role is to act in the client's best interests.
4 Obtain initial information from the client, the client's understanding of the reason for the arrest, and any particular concerns or complaints that the client may have. The lawyer may at this stage be asked to contact a third party to inform them of the suspect's arrest. In principle, there is no reason why this should not be done, but care must be taken to ensure that this message is not used to pass on information to a person evading arrest, or which might result in evidence or proceeds not being recovered, or which might otherwise lead to interference with the course of justice. If in any doubt, the lawyer should agree to contact the third party only on the understanding that the lawyer will first tell the custody officer what is intended.
5 Decide whether, and when, to attend in person (see para 3.55 below).
6 Give initial advice to the client, including advice about whether it would be advisable for the lawyer to attend in person. If the lawyer does intend to attend, or to arrange for attendance, in person, usually they should advise the client not to answer police questions, and not to sign any documents, until they have received advice in person. However, in drink/driving cases the client should not normally be advised to refuse to give a sample pending arrival of the lawyer (see para 2.142 above). If attendance is to be delayed, the client should be warned of possible attempts by the police to persuade them to proceed with an interview in the absence of the lawyer and reminded of their continuing right to advice should this or any other issue arise about which they are unsure.

Deciding whether to attend

3.55 The decision whether to attend the police station in person can be difficult for a range of reasons, including the competing demands on the lawyer's time. Checklist 5 at para 3.61 below is designed to assist in making the appropriate decision, bearing in mind that the primary consideration is what is in the best interests of the client. The police are normally keen to persuade a suspect to talk, and the Court of Appeal has held that provided PACE and the Codes of Practice are observed, the police are entitled to try to obtain admissions from a suspect.[28] The presence of a lawyer at the

28 *R v Oliphant* [1992] Crim LR 40, CA.

police station and in the police interview may, therefore, be of critical importance.

Mandatory attendance

3.56 The starting-point for deciding whether to attend is the SCC,[29] which is binding on duty solicitors and own-solicitors providing services under the contract. In the absence of exceptional circumstances, once a case has been accepted attendance in person is mandatory:

(1) to provide advice and to attend all police interviews with the client where the client has been arrested in connection with an offence;
(2) at an identification parade, group identification or confrontation; and
(3) where the suspect complains of serious maltreatment by the police.

Attendance at a video identification is not mandatory under the contract, although it may be claimed for provided it is justified. The contract does not specify what constitutes exceptional circumstances, but may include where a client specifically instructs the lawyer not to attend. If they do arise, the lawyer must record on file the decision not to attend, including details of the exceptional circumstances and the reasons for the decision.

3.57 The provision of advocacy assistance at a warrant of further detention hearing is not mandatory, even for a duty solicitor. However, if the client is a services person requiring advocacy assistance within England and Wales at a custody hearing before a judicial officer under the Armed Forces Act 2006, the SCC[30] provides that a duty or own-solicitor must attend personally upon the client to provide advice and assistance, including advocacy assistance.

Discretionary attendance

3.58 Where attendance in person is not mandatory, a lawyer providing services under the SCC has a discretion to attend in person. Whether such attendance will be paid for under the contract will depend upon whether the sufficient benefit test is satisfied (see para 1.57 above) and whether the case falls within the restrictions on payment for attendance in person (see paras 1.54–1.56 above).

Clients under the influence of drink or drugs

3.59 A difficult problem arises where the lawyer is told by the custody officer that the suspect is unfit to be interviewed because they are drunk or suffering from the effects of drugs. An initial question is whether the suspect is really intoxicated through drink or drugs, or appears to be so as a result of causes other than alcohol or drugs. Codes C, Code H and I NfG 9C provide a reminder that a person who appears to be drunk or who is behaving abnormally may be ill or injured or may be suffering from the

29 SCC Specification 2022 paras 9.38–9.40 (draft SCC Specification 2025 paras 9.34–9.36),
30 SCC Specification 2022 para 9.58 (draft SCC Specification 2025 para 9.5).

effects of drugs. If there is any doubt, the police should call in a healthcare professional as a matter of urgency.

3.60 When a person is initially detained at a police station, the custody officer must conduct a structured risk assessment, which includes an assessment of whether the suspect is under the influence of alcohol or drugs (Codes C and H paras 3.5–3.10; Code I paras 3.7–3.12).[31] If the person is suspected of being under the influence of drink or drugs, or both, or of having swallowed drugs, or their level of consciousness causes concern, they must, subject to clinical directions, be visited and roused at least every half-hour and have their condition assessed in accordance with Code C and Code H Annex H; Code I para 9.3 and Annex G, and clinical treatment must be arranged if appropriate (Code C para 9.3; Code H para 9.4; Code I para 9.3). If a healthcare professional is called in, they must be asked for their opinion about the detainee's fitness for detention and fitness for interview, and the need for safeguards (Code C para 9.13; Code H para 9.15; Code I para 9.16). Therefore, if the lawyer has reason for doubting that the condition of the suspect is one of simple intoxication, they should press the custody officer to call in a healthcare professional, and attend in person if not satisfied with the response. A healthcare professional does not have to be called by the police if the suspect is simply intoxicated, but does have to be called (or in urgent cases, the suspect taken to hospital or to a medical practitioner) if the suspect:

- appears to be suffering from physical illness;
- is injured (unless a minor injury);
- appears to be suffering from a mental disorder; or
- otherwise appears to need medical attention (Code C para 9.5; Code H para 9.6; Code I para 9.7).

This obligation applies even if the suspect has not requested clinical attention and whether or not they have already received clinical attention elsewhere (Code C para 9.5A; Code H para 9.7; Code I para 9.8).

3.61 It would not normally be appropriate for the police to interview a suspect who is intoxicated. Before every interview, the custody officer must determine whether the suspect is fit to be interviewed, by reference to the factors set out in Code C, Code H Annex G and Code I para 11.17. Where necessary, the decision should be taken in consultation with the officer in charge of the investigation and with the healthcare professional (see further para 5.22 below). If the lawyer believes that their client is not fit to be interviewed, they should consider calling an independent medical practitioner. Code C para 9.8, Code H para 9.10 and Code I para 9.11 provide that a suspect is entitled to be examined by a medical practitioner of the suspect's own choice, although at the suspect's expense.[32]

31 See College of Policing, *Authorised professional practice: Detention and custody risk assessment*, available at: www.college.police.uk/app/detention-and-custody/detention-and-custody-risk-assessment.

32 Any cost may be claimable as a disbursement provided it is reasonably incurred. See para 5.24 below.

Checklist 5: Deciding whether to attend the police station

Always consider whether attendance is mandatory and, if not, whether the sufficient benefit test is satisfied. Consider whether professional obligations to the client require attendance even though payment may not be made under the SCC.

A full and accurate note must be taken of all information obtained, advice given, reason for not attending (where attendance is mandatory) and reason for attending (where attendance is not mandatory).

1 The lawyer should normally attend if:
   - the suspect has been arrested for an offence and is going to be interviewed;
   - the police are intending to conduct an identification procedure;
   - the client complains of serious maltreatment by the police;
   - the client is a child or a person at risk.

2 If 1 above does not apply, the lawyer should still consider attending if:
   - the client is apparently drunk, under the influence of drugs or complains of being seriously unwell (unless satisfied that the police have taken all appropriate action);
   - the alleged offence (or circumstances, if the client has been arrested for other than an offence) is serious or may have serious consequences;
   - there are important issues concerning searches of the person or property;
   - there are important issues concerning the taking of samples;
   - an interview has been conducted, but advice is necessary at the time of charge;*
   - the circumstances of the client indicate that attendance is necessary – for example, the client is unfamiliar with police processes, or the client is particularly upset or nervous;
   - detention is likely to be lengthy;
   - the lawyer is not satisfied that advice by telephone can be given with sufficient confidentiality;
   - the lawyer is not satisfied that they can adequately communicate with the client by telephone;
   - representations need to be made to the police, and these cannot adequately be made by telephone or email.

3 Attendance may not be necessary or justified where the client:
   - has been arrested for a road traffic offence (including excess alcohol);
   - has been arrested on warrant and no further offence is suspected;
   - has been arrested for breach of bail and no further offence is suspected;
   - has been arrested under a civil order or warrant.

* Which may be claimed for under the SCC.

Deciding when to attend

3.62 Having decided to attend, the lawyer must also decide when to attend. This will depend on a variety of factors including:

- how long the client has been at the police station;
- whether the client appears to be distressed and/or vulnerable; and
- when the police are intending to interview, conduct an identification procedure, etc.

The SCC[33] 2022 para 9.17 provides that where the time for a police interview or identification procedure has been fixed, the lawyer must attend in sufficient time to undertake reasonable steps that directly relate to the interview or identification procedure. This, of course, includes consultation with the client. The lawyer should discuss the decision whether and when to attend with the client, and should try to ensure that the client understands both the decision and the reasons for it. It is important to remember that the police may give the client the impression that delay in dealing with their case is the fault of the lawyer, which may make the client susceptible to proceeding to an interview without waiting for the lawyer to attend.

Informing the custody officer of the lawyer's intentions

3.63 The lawyer should inform the custody officer of their intentions regarding attendance. Where the lawyer has spoken to the client on the telephone, they should not ask the client to pass a message on to the police – the client may get it wrong or the custody officer may take no notice of what is said. If the lawyer is not intending to attend in person, it is a matter of courtesy to inform the custody officer so that the police can proceed to interview, if that is their intention. If the lawyer wishes to attend, they should inform the custody officer of the lawyer's intentions for a number of reasons.

3.64 First, the lawyer may wish to delay the visit until nearer the estimated time of a police interview. In this case, the lawyer will need to establish when the interview is likely to take place and to inform the custody officer that they intend to attend in person nearer the time. The custody officer should be asked to note this on the custody record and be asked to inform the lawyer of any change of plan. The client should be told of the lawyer's intentions, and if the delay is likely to be, or turns out to be, prolonged, the lawyer should consider attending to give initial advice in person. The longer the client is in custody, the more vulnerable they are likely to become, particularly to a suggestion by the police that the delay may be shortened if they agree to be interviewed in the lawyer's absence. Where the lawyer is acting as a rota duty solicitor and the interview (or identification procedure) is postponed to a time when the lawyer is no longer on duty (or, if as a panel duty solicitor, until a time when it is no longer convenient to act as duty solicitor), the lawyer is required to make arrange-

33 Draft SCC Specification 2025 para 9.11.

ments to ensure that the client continues to receive advice either by another duty solicitor or by acting as the client's own solicitor.[34]

3.65 Second, Code C para 6.6, Code H para 6.7 and Code I para 6.6 provide, subject to exceptions, that a person who wants legal advice may not be interviewed or continue to be interviewed until they have received such advice. Where a suspect has been given legal advice on the telephone and the custody officer is not aware that the lawyer intends to attend in person, the custody officer could argue that the interview can proceed in the lawyer's absence since the suspect has 'received' advice. By the same argument, despite the general prohibition on inferences being drawn from 'silence' where a suspect who has asked for legal advice is interviewed without having received it,[35] there is a risk that inferences could be drawn. However, this justification would be difficult to sustain if the police know that the lawyer intends to attend the police station.

3.66 Third, Code C para 6.6(b)(ii), Code H para 6.7(b)(ii) and Code I para 6.6(a) and Annex B provide that an interview can proceed in the absence of a lawyer, on the authority of an officer of the rank of superintendent or above, if waiting for the lawyer to arrive would cause unreasonable delay to the process of the investigation. However, Code C, Code H NfG 6A and Code I NfG 6B provide that if the lawyer says that they are on the way to the station or that they will set off immediately, it will not normally be appropriate to begin an interview before the lawyer arrives. Although the NfG states that the officer should ask the lawyer for an estimate of the time of arrival at the station, the lawyer should ensure that they inform the custody officer of the estimated time of arrival, whether or not they are asked.

3.67 Fourth, if the lawyer has other commitments that would result in their attendance being delayed, they should seek agreement with the custody officer that this will be acceptable. The effect of Code C para 6.6(b)(ii), Code H para 6.7(b)(ii) and NfG 6A, and Code I para 6.6(b) is that if the delay is unacceptable to the police, they should inform the lawyer how long they will be prepared to wait before commencing an interview so that alternative arrangements for the client to receive advice in person can be made. Again, the lawyer should speak to the client on the telephone so that they are made fully aware of any delay.

3.68 The custody officer should be asked to note on the custody record the decisions taken regarding attendance, and also to note, where relevant (as it usually will be), that the lawyer has requested that the client should not be interviewed or asked to sign any police document until the time of their attendance.

34 SCC Specification 2022 para 9.42(c) (draft SCC Specification 2025 para 9.37(c)).

35 Criminal Justice and Public Order Act 1994 ss34(2A), 36(4A) and 37(3A); and see paras 5.63, 5.69 below.

CHAPTER 4

Action on arrival at the police station

continued

Introduction

4.1 The action taken by a defence lawyer on arrival at the police station can significantly affect the whole case, and may determine whether it is successful from the defence point of view. A thorough, diligent and skilful approach may well improve the client's position, resulting in them being released without charge, police evidence being less strong than it otherwise would have been, or crucial evidence in mitigation being put forward at an early stage. While the lawyer will frequently encounter no particular difficulty with the police, they may be met with obstructiveness or prevarication, which may or may not be deliberate or legitimate. Some police officers regard the presence of a lawyer as a potential hindrance to their work, and research has identified informal ploys that attempt to keep lawyers away, or at least to try to minimise their impact.[1] Police behaviour of this kind, even if detected, will not necessarily result in the exclusion of any evidence obtained. However, even if the police are acting, and continue to act, entirely properly, an appropriately adversarial stance on the part of the defence lawyer will be the best way of protecting their client's interests.

4.2 This chapter deals first with problems in obtaining access to a client in police detention and suggests ways of dealing with them. It then goes on to deal with obtaining the information from the police that will be necessary for the lawyer to be able to advise their client properly. As always, the lawyer should keep a careful note of all relevant action taken and information obtained, together with relevant times. The quality of the records made at this stage will impact the ability of the lawyer and their client to rely them at a later stage.

Problems in obtaining access

Denial of access under PACE, the Terrorism Act 2000 and the National Security Act 2023

4.3 The powers of the police to delay access to a lawyer under Police and Criminal Evidence Act 1984 (PACE) s58, Terrorism Act (TA) 2000 Sch 8 and National Security Act (NSA) 2023 s27 and Sch 6, which are relatively rarely exercised, and guidance on what representations to make in this situation, are dealt with at paras 2.151–2.161 above.

Exclusion of representatives

4.4 Legal advisers who are not solicitors may be dealt with less favourably than solicitors by the police, who sometimes use the difference in status to undermine the advice given by them or to influence them into accepting a course of action that they would not otherwise wish to accept. It is important, therefore, to know precisely what different powers the police have in

1 See, for example, V Kemp, N Carr, H Kent, S Farrall, 'Examining the impact of PACE on the detention and questioning of child suspects' (University of Nottingham, 2023) para 9.2, available at: https://nottingham-repository.worktribe.com/output/21148005.

relation to non-solicitors compared with solicitors. It is also important to be clear about who does and does not qualify as a solicitor for the purposes of the PACE Codes of Practice (see para 2.145 above). Although probationary and accredited representatives come within the definition of 'solicitor' for the purposes of the Codes of Practice, they are subject to powers to exclude them from police stations that do not apply to solicitors (see para 4.6 below). The codes make no reference to representatives who are neither probationary nor accredited. While the Legal Aid Agency's (LAA's) Standard Crime Contract (SCC) 2022 (draft Standard Crime Contract 2025) does not permit payment for police station work carried out by such persons, there appears to be no reason in principle why a solicitor acting on a private basis could not use a representative who is not registered with the LAA. However, it may be argued that since PACE s58 specifically refers to the right to consult a solicitor, and Code C defines the meaning of the term 'solicitor' for the purposes of the code, the police would be entitled to refuse access to a non-solicitor who is neither a probationary nor an accredited representative.

4.5 While PACE s58, TA 2000 Sch 8 para 7(1) and NSA 2023 s27 and Sch 6 refer only to the right to consult a solicitor, a solicitor may send a probationary or accredited representative to the police station to provide advice on the solicitor's behalf (Code C para 6.12A; Code H para 6.14; Code I para 6.13). Generally, the additional powers police have to exclude a representative apply only at the stage of admission to the police station. Once admitted, they are to be dealt with as if they were a solicitor (Code C para 6.12A; Code H para 6.14; Code I para 6.13). For police tactics in respect of representatives during police interviews, see para 7.50 below.

4.6 The power to exclude a representative from the police station is governed by Code C para 6.12A, Codes H and I para 6.14,[2] which enable an officer of the rank of police inspector or above to refuse a representative admission to the station if the officer considers that such a visit will hinder the investigation of crime. This is a decision for individual officers, although they may receive guidance from senior officers.[3] Thus, senior officers could warn of the possible unsuitability of certain representatives, but it would be for individual inspectors to make a decision on exclusion in any particular case. Hindering the investigation of crime does not include giving proper advice to a detained person in accordance with Code C note for guidance (NfG) 6D, or Code H NfG 6C or Code I NfG 6D. It is unclear precisely what is meant by the phrase 'refuse admission to the station', but in practice it is likely to mean admission beyond the waiting area into the 'non-public' part of the station. In exercising their discretion to exclude, an officer should, in particular, take the following into account (Code C para 6.13; Code H para 6.15; Code I para 6.14):

(1) whether the identity and status of the representative has been established;

2 See para 2.127 above for additional powers to exclude a specific solicitor under the TA 2000 or NSA 2023.

3 *R v Chief Constable of Avon and Somerset ex p Robinson* [1989] 1 WLR 793, QBD.

(2) whether the representative is of suitable character to provide legal advice, which is unlikely if the representative has a relevant criminal record, unless for a minor offence and not of recent date;[4] and
(3) any other matters in any written letter of authorisation provided by the solicitor on whose behalf the representative is attending the station.

4.7 Code C para 6.13, Code H para 6.15 and Code I para 6.14 make no reference to the qualifications or experience of the representative, and lack of qualifications or experience are not grounds for exclusion. However, the SCC imposes requirements regarding suitability and supervision of non-solicitors conducting police station work. Similarly, the Solicitors Regulation Authority (SRA) Code of Conduct requires solicitors, and those they manage, only to undertake work that they are competent to carry out.[5] Lawyers employing representatives should ensure that they are competent and appropriately supervised, and should provide them with guidance on the types of case they are permitted to deal with, the circumstances in which they should seek advice or assistance from a solicitor, and the mechanisms for contacting a solicitor at short notice. Representatives must provide a written report to the conducting solicitor once the attendance at the police station has been concluded, and no later than the next working day (see para 1.48 above).

4.8 If the police decide to refuse access, they must inform the solicitor who employs the representative (as well as the suspect), and must give the solicitor the opportunity to make alternative arrangements (Code C para 6.14; Code H para 6.16; Code I para 6.15). The solicitor should seek reasons, preferably in writing, for the refusal of access and check that the decision was made by an officer of the appropriate rank. If necessary, the matter should be taken up at a more senior level, since if the representative is refused access on one occasion, there is a danger that they will be refused admission in the future. As a general rule, all solicitors and representatives attending the police station are well advised to have photographic ID demonstrating their role or other authorisation by the firm instructing them.

Acting for more than one client

4.9 Acting for more than one client in respect of the same or a connected allegation may present a conflict of interests, and the lawyer may have to make a difficult ethical decision about whether they can advise all or any of them. Guidance on what may amount to a conflict of interests, and how conflicts and potential conflicts should be dealt with, is given at para 5.42 below. The police will sometimes seek to deny a lawyer access to one or more suspects on the ground that there is a conflict of interests. Code C NfG 6G, Code H NfG 6F and Code I NfG 6G confirm that a solicitor may advise more than one client in an investigation and '[a]ny question of a

4 See *R v Chief Constable of Northumbria ex p Thompson* [2001] EWCA Civ 321, in which it was held that it was the responsibility of the employing solicitor, and not the police, to determine whether a representative was sufficiently independent.

5 SRA Code of Conduct paras 3.2, 3.3, 3.5 and 3.6.

conflict of interest is for the solicitor under their professional code of conduct'. It is, therefore, the lawyer's decision and not that of the police.

4.10 However, the NfGs go on to state that if waiting for the solicitor may lead to unreasonable delay, authority under Code C para 6.6(b), Code H para 6.7(b) or Code I para 6.6(b) may be given for an interview to proceed without the suspect having received advice. This will not be relevant if the same officers will be interviewing all suspects. However, the lawyer should check, particularly in more serious cases where a number of officers are involved in the investigation, when the interviews are to be conducted so that they can arrange for another lawyer to attend if necessary. Code C para 6.6(b), Code H para 6.7(b) and Code I para 6.6(b) enable the superintendent to give authority for the interview to proceed in the lawyer's absence only if 'awaiting their arrival' would cause unreasonable delay. It could be argued, therefore, that since the lawyer is at the station, albeit advising another suspect, the power to proceed in the absence of the lawyer does not apply.[6]

Child clients

4.11 Where the suspect is a child, the police may seek to delay a lawyer's arrival on the grounds that either the appropriate adult has not yet been contacted or that the appropriate adult has not asked for or confirmed the request for legal advice.[7] The right to legal advice under PACE s58, TA 2000 Sch 8 and NSA s27 and Sch 6 is not limited to adults and there is no authority for delaying access on the ground that the suspect is a child. The same applies to other vulnerable suspects. See further para 2.134 above and chapter 11 below.

'The suspect no longer wants a solicitor'

4.12 Having initially requested legal advice, a suspect may later change their mind and agree to proceed with a police interview without having received it or, having received it, without the presence of the lawyer in the interview. In order to ensure that a suspect's decision to proceed in the absence of legal advice is made voluntarily, Codes C and I para 6.6(d) and Code H para 6.7(d) provide that the following conditions must be satisfied:

(1) an officer of the rank of inspector or above speaks to the suspect to ask about their reasons for changing their mind, and makes or directs to be made reasonable efforts to ascertain the nominated lawyer's expected time of arrival and to inform them that the suspect has stated that they wish to change their mind;

(2) the suspect's reasons for changing their mind, and the outcome of the actions taken to contact the solicitor are recorded in the custody record;

6 In *R (McDonagh) v Chief Constable of Leicestershire* [2013] EWHC 4690 (Admin), the court held that an insistence by the custody officer that a police interview of a suspect must proceed before the solicitor could speak to a second suspect arrested in respect of the same matter, amounted to a breach of the first suspect's right to a lawyer.

7 Two police stations in London are currently piloting an 'opt out' rather than 'opt in' scheme for children as part of the Child First Custody Training & Research Pilot. See: www.london.gov.uk/programmes-strategies/mayors-office-policing-and-crime-mopac/mopac-funded-services/child-first-custody-training-and-research-pilot.

(3) the suspect confirms their decision to proceed in the absence of legal advice, or in the absence of the lawyer, by signing an entry in the custody record to this effect;
(4) the authorising officer, being satisfied that it is proper for the interview to proceed in these circumstances, records that authority in writing, and makes or directs to be made reasonable efforts to inform the lawyer that authority has been given and the time that the interview is expected to commence, and records this in the custody record; and
(5) at the commencement of the interview, the suspect is reminded of their continuing right to legal advice, is told that if the lawyer arrives before the end of the interview it will be interrupted to enable the suspect to consult with them if they wish, and the consent of the suspect to proceed with the interview is recorded in the interview record.[8]

4.13 If a lawyer arrives at the station to see a detained person, that person must, unless Annex B (of each relevant code) applies (ie access to a solicitor is delayed under PACE s58(8), TA 2000 Sch 8 para 8 or NSA 2023 Sch 6 para 9), be informed of the presence of the lawyer whether or not they are being interviewed, and must be asked whether they would like to see the lawyer (Code C para 6.15; Code H para 6.17; Code I para 6.16).[9] This applies whether or not the suspect has already declined advice or, having asked for it, has changed their mind. The fact of the lawyer's attendance and the decision of the suspect must be noted in the custody record.

4.14 Therefore, if on arrival at the station the lawyer is told that the client no longer wants to see them, the custody officer should be asked to confirm that the client has been informed of the lawyer's arrival and that they have been asked whether they wish to see them. The lawyer should consider asking the custody officer to hand a letter to the suspect, advising them to ask to see the lawyer. Strictly, there is no right to demand this, but it may help allay fears that the significance of the lawyer's visit has not been properly conveyed to the client. If the custody officer maintains that the client still does not wish to see the lawyer, the lawyer should consider asking to see the custody record to check that proceeding in the absence of legal advice has been properly authorised and recorded, and confirmed by the client.

'The interview has already started'

4.15 The custody officer may say that the client is being interviewed, and that they do not want to interrupt it. Code C para 6.15, Code H para 6.17 and Code I para 6.16 explicitly provide that, whether or not the client is being interviewed, the client must be told of the lawyer's arrival and asked whether they would like to see the lawyer.

4.16 Where the interview is interrupted and the client wants the lawyer to be present, the police may press for the interview to proceed without an

8 The fact that the detainee has changed their mind about wanting legal advice or (as the case may be) about wanting a solicitor present, and the reasons given for it together with the name of the officer who authorised the interview to go ahead should be recorded as part of the interview.

9 See paras 2.151 and 2.156 above.

opportunity being given to advise the client in private. This should be strongly resisted. The lawyer should insist on speaking to the client in private, an absolute right under PACE s58(1), TA 2000 Sch 8 para 7 and NSA 2023 Sch 6 para 7, before agreeing to the interview being re-commenced. In addition to the information the lawyer would usually seek to gather at the initial stage (see para 4.19 below), the client and the interviewing officer should be asked what has been said in the interview so far. If the interview has been electronically recorded, the lawyer should consider asking to listen to it. If it has been recorded in writing, a request should be made to see the written record. If the police seek to prevent the lawyer from seeing the client in private, the lawyer should normally make representations to the custody officer (or superior officer) and advise the client not to answer questions in the meantime.

'The suspect wants another solicitor'

4.17 On arrival at the police station, the lawyer may be told that the client has asked for another lawyer. This should not happen in a publicly funded case where the lawyer has been contacted by the Defence Solicitor Call Centre (DSCC) (see para 3.3 above), but may happen if the lawyer was instructed by a third party and has attended the police station. In this case, it will be advisable for the lawyer to contact the other lawyer to ensure that the instruction has been confirmed by the client. If the suspect has not yet seen the other lawyer, it will be advisable to try to see them to confirm the position. If the custody officer is not willing to allow this, the lawyer is faced with the problem that PACE s58 gives the right to legal advice to the suspect as opposed to giving the lawyer a right of access to give advice.[10] The police may treat it simply as a matter of competition between lawyers in which the suspect has the right to make the decision. On the other hand, in some cases the police may encourage the use of another lawyer if that lawyer is regarded as more compliant. In the absence of a right to see the suspect in the police station, there is little the lawyer can do other than to take it up with the suspect, and possibly the other lawyer, at a later stage, and keep a careful note of what is said and done.[11]

'The officer in the case is not here'

4.18 The custody officer may try to avoid taking responsibility for deciding whether to allow the lawyer access to the client by stating that the officer in the case is out, possibly conducting a search or interviewing witnesses, and that a decision on access cannot be made until the officer returns. PACE Part IV, especially section 39, firmly places legal responsibility for

10 *Rixon v Chief Constable of Kent* (2000) Times, April 11, CA.

11 *Criminal Bills Assessment Manual* (CBAM) – May 2025 para 5.11: '18. The LAA accepts that, in some circumstances, the solicitor will attend the Police Station in good faith having been contacted by the DSCC. Where a solicitor responds to a call from the DSCC but, for circumstances out of the solicitor's control, no attendance takes place, a Fixed Fee is still claimable. A note should be kept on the file detailing the particular circumstances. Reference should be made to the PoP DS 4', available at: www.gov.uk/guidance/legal-aid-points-of-principle-of-general-importance-pop.

the treatment of suspects on the custody officer. Furthermore, since access to a lawyer can only be delayed on the authority of an officer of the rank of superintendent or above under PACE s58(8), TA 2000 Sch 8 para 8, NSA Sch 6 para 7, if such authority has not been given the custody officer has no power to delay access. Related reasons for delay, including there being insufficient officers to supervise the consultation, are not permitted.

Obtaining information from the police

4.19 On arrival at the police station, the lawyer should normally:

- inform the custody officer of the lawyer's status;
- request sight of the full custody record and related documents, for example, property record or healthcare notes;[12]
- seek information from the custody officer; and
- seek information from the officer in charge of the case or interviewing officer.

This should normally be done before seeing the client, but if carrying out any of these functions is likely to involve any significant delay, the lawyer should have a preliminary consultation with the client.

Information from the custody record

4.20 A solicitor is entitled to consult the client's custody record as soon as is practicable after arrival at a police station, and at any other time while the client is detained. This is subject to a limited qualification, in that access must be arranged and agreed with the custody officer, and may not unreasonably interfere with the custody officer's duties (Codes C and I para 2.4; Code H para 2.5). Although custody records cannot be presumed to be accurate, they contain information that may be of great value to the defence lawyer.[13] A custody officer will often agree to provide a full printout of the custody record, especially as it frees up their desk if the record it taken away to be read as opposed to being painstakingly read from a screen at the custody counter. Given the circumstances, there is a danger that the lawyer may skim-read the record and miss important detail. The detainee's medical record is kept separate to the custody record. The police may insist on having the detainee's permission to share the health record with the lawyer. The records amount to sensitive personal information under

12 The detainee's medical record is kept separate to the custody record. The police may insist on having the detainee's permission to share the health record with the lawyer. The records amount to sensitive personal data under the GDPR and the Data Protection Act 2018. If necessary, the lawyer ought to obtain the detainee's permission in writing to prevent further queries should the police personnel change during the attendance.

13 For an explanation of what constitutes the custody record and what must be recorded in it, see para 2.106 above.

the UK GDPR[14] and the Data Protection Act 2018. If necessary, the lawyer ought to obtain the detainee's permission in writing to prevent further queries should the police personnel change during the attendance. The lawyer should ensure, therefore, that they take sufficient time to read it and take a careful and sufficiently private note of the relevant contents. This should be checked against what the lawyer has already been told, and against the relevant police powers, and it may prompt questions to the custody officer, the officer in the case and the client. Particular attention should be paid to the matters set out in checklist 6.

Checklist 6: Reading the custody record

A full and accurate note must be taken of all information obtained and further enquiries made, which should be timed and dated.

1 The custody record number
2 The name and address recorded for the suspect
3 The grounds and reasons for arrest
   - Is this the same as the information already given to the lawyer?
   - What is the statutory or common law authority for the arrest?
   - Why was arrest necessary?
   - Is the arrest lawful?
   - Is it an either-way offence?
   - Is it an indictable-only offence? This is relevant, in particular, to probationary representatives.
4 The age of the suspect
   - If the suspect is under 18 years, what action has been taken in respect of an appropriate adult?
   - Why was the arrest necessary (in light of the suspect's age)?
   - Why was the detention authorised (in light of the suspect's age)?
   - If there is a potential for remand, has the custody officer made enquiries as to local authority accommodation?
5 The time that a solicitor was requested
   - What time was this acted on by the police?
   - If there is a significant time lapse, why is this?
6 The time of arrest and the time of arrival at the police station
   - If there is a significant time difference, why is this?
7 The time detention was authorised and grounds for detention being authorised
   - Are the grounds for detention lawful?
   - Is there sufficient evidence to charge?
8 Whether documents or materials relevant to the lawfulness of the arrest or detention have been disclosed to the suspect, and the time of any such disclosure

14 Regulation (EU) 2016/679 of the European Parliament and of the Council of 27th April 2016 on the protection of natural persons with regard to the processing of personal data and on the free movement of such data (General Data Protection Regulation) as it forms part of the law of England and Wales, Scotland and Northern Ireland by virtue of section 3 of the European Union (Withdrawal) Act 2018).

9 The property found on the suspect, if recorded. This may give an important indication of evidence in relation to the offence for which the suspect has been arrested (for example, large sums of money, bunches of keys, self-sealing bags, etc), or of other offences about which the police may want to question the suspect

10 Any indication that the suspect is, or may be, neuro-divergent, has mental health difficulties or any other vulnerability, and the results of the risk assessment conducted by the custody officer
- If so, what action has been taken in respect of an appropriate adult?
- Has a healthcare professional been requested or called?
- Are you satisfied that your client does not require further medical care?

11 Any indication that the suspect is, or may be, unwell or otherwise unfit through drink or drugs
- If so, has a healthcare practitioner been requested or called?
- If a healthcare practitioner has already examined the client, what was the purpose of the examination and what was the result?
- Are you content that your client does not require further medical care?

12 Whether a property search has been authorised
- If so, on what authority and for what purpose?
- What, if anything, has been seized?

13 Whether the suspect has been asked to sign a police officer's notebook
- If so, why was the suspect asked to do so before the lawyer's arrival?
- What was in the officer's notebook?

14 Whether an interview has been conducted
- If so, why was an interview conducted at that stage?
- Was it conducted contrary to Code C para 6.6 or 11.1, Code H para 6.7 or 11.2, or Code I para 6.6 or para 11?
- What was said in the interview?

15 Any authorities given or decisions taken in respect of the taking of samples, fingerprints, photographs or drugs-testing
- Have these been conducted?
- What was the result?
- Why were they authorised/conducted before the arrival of the lawyer?

16 Have any requests been made of, or information provided by, the suspect (for example, for PIN numbers or encryption keys pursuant to the Regulation of Investigatory Powers Act 2000 or in respect of ID procedures)?
- What was the result?
- Why were they authorised/conducted before the arrival of the lawyer?

16 Actions taken in respect of the risk assessment required under Codes C and H para 3.6 and Code I para 3.7

17 Any unusual entries – for example, late entries, deleted entries

Information from the custody officer

4.21 Having seen the custody record, the lawyer should check with the custody officer whether there have been any changes in the information obtained earlier in the initial telephone call, request any further information in checklist 3 (see para 3.30 above) that was not obtained in the initial conversation, and raise any questions arising from the custody record. It will often be advisable to ask the custody officer what they know of the circumstances of the arrest and the evidence, since the custody officer may be more forthcoming than the officer in the case, and it may be instructive to compare this information with that subsequently given by the officer in the case. Furthermore, given the significance of previous convictions (see para 5.173 below), the custody officer should be asked for any information they have regarding the client's previous convictions. This is information that the custody officer is required to obtain as part of the risk assessment (see paras 4.24–4.26 below).

4.22 The custody officer is required to make available to the suspect or their lawyer any documents and materials that are essential to challenging the lawfulness of the suspect's arrest or detention. Documents and materials are essential for this purpose if they are 'capable of undermining the reasons and grounds which make the detainee's arrest and detention necessary' (Codes C and H para 3.4(b); Code I para 3.5). In making the decision as to disclosure, the custody officer should consult with the investigating officer 'who has the knowledge of the documents and materials in a particular case necessary to inform that decision'. The codes do not specify the documents and materials that should be considered for disclosure, but since the obligation concerns any that 'are capable' of undermining the lawfulness of the arrest or detention, they may include the arresting officer's pocket book, the pocket books or statements of other officers present at the arrest, and the crime report. Any offer by the suspect to attend the police station voluntarily, if made or recorded in writing, may also come within the definition of 'essential documents or materials'.[15] Arguably, the obligation extends to documents or materials that are relevant to the legality of (and not just the necessity for) the arrest, since if an arrest is not lawful, detention cannot be either lawful or necessary. Note that while it is for the custody officer to decide what to disclose, their obligation is to disclose documents that are capable of undermining the necessity of arrest or detention, which must include any documents which, viewed objectively, may do so. The lawyer should ask the custody officer whether they are in possession of, or have knowledge of, any such documents or materials, and whether they have consulted with the investigating officer in this regard, and to disclose any such documents or materials. If the custody officer indicates that there are no such materials, the lawyer should ask them what documents and materials they have considered in coming to that decision.[16]

15 See paras 2.20–2.21 above.

16 For a more extensive analysis of the disclosure obligations, see E Cape 'Transposing the EU Directive on the Right to Information: a firecracker or a damp squib?' [2015] Crim LR 48.

4.23 If a court-authorised search has been carried out, the solicitor should seek a copy of the warrant and the underlying material as this will be a valuable route to information. An ex parte application for a warrant requires the applicant to put their 'defence hat on' and draw to the court's attention those parts of the case that the defence would be likely to raise, had they been in court.[17] Any material that fell to be disclosed to the court in this exercise is highly likely to fall into the category of material which is essential to challenge the lawfulness of the suspect's arrest or detention. If a custody officer declines to disclose any material, an alternative route will be to ask the officer in the case (or senior investigating officer, as appropriate) to provide a copy of the information underlying the search warrant. While an officer is not obliged to provide this material (the formal application is made to the court[18]), any refusal will almost certainly only delay the disclosure given the consistent thread of authorities which make it plain that a person whose property has been the subject of a search order is entitled to see the information which persuaded the court to grant the order, save for public interest immunity (PII) considerations.[19]

4.24 The custody officer should be asked about the risk assessment that they must carry out in respect of all suspects when they are booked in at the police station (Codes C and H para 3.6; Code I para 3.7). If there are any indications that the suspect is injured, ill or suffering from the effects of alcohol or drugs, the lawyer should seek to ensure that appropriate action has been taken, and make suitable representations where necessary. This is important not only in relation to the general welfare of the client, and whether the client is fit to be detained and/or interviewed, but also because evidence shows that actions taken by the custody officer can be critical in preventing self-harm by suspects at risk while in police custody.[20] The lawyer should also ask whether there are any indications that the client might present a risk to the lawyer's own safety (see para 5.8 below).

4.25 The requirement to conduct a risk assessment means that the custody officer must consider whether a detainee is likely to present specific risks to custody staff or to themself. This includes a check on the police national computer, which must be done as soon as practicable. The risk assessment must be carried out in a structured way that clearly defines the categories of risk to be considered. The results of the risk assessment must be noted in the custody record, including, where relevant, that no specific risks have been identified. The content of the risk assessment, or any analysis of risk, does not have to be recorded in the custody record, but

17 See *Stanford International Bank Ltd v Director of the Serious Fraud Office* [2010] EWCA Civ 137.

18 Criminal Procedure Rules 2020 SI No 759 r5.7.

19 See *R (Haralambous) v Crown Court at St Albans* [2018] UKSC 1; *Commissioner of Police of the Metropolis v Bangs* [2014] EWHC 546 (Admin); *R (Cronin) v Sheffield Justices* [2002] EWHC 2568 (Admin); *R (Golfrate Property Management Ltd and Another) v Southwark Crown Court and Others* [2014] EWHC 840 (Admin); and *R (Austen) v Chief Constable of Wiltshire and South East Wiltshire Magistrates' Court* [2011] EWHC 3385 (Admin).

20 See generally College of Policing, *Authorised Professional Practice: Detention and custody*, available at: www.app.college.police.uk/app-content/detention-and-custody-2/response-arrest-and-detention/#detention-not-authorised.

information should not be withheld from the lawyer (or from an appropriate adult or interpreter), if to do so would put them at risk (Codes C and H para 3.8A; Code I para 3.10).

4.26 If a person is suspected of being intoxicated through drink or drugs, or their level of consciousness causes concern, they must (subject to clinical directions) be visited and roused at least every half hour, and have their condition assessed in accordance with Codes C and H para 9.5(b) and Annex H; Code H para 9.8 and Annex H; Code I para 9.3 and Annex G. If a suspect appears to be suffering from a physical illness or from a mental disorder, is injured or appears to need clinical attention, the custody officer must ensure that they receive appropriate clinical attention (Code C para 9.5; Code H para 9.6; Code I para 9.7). The custody officer must also consider the need for clinical attention where a suspect is suffering from the effects of alcohol or drugs (Code C para 9.5B; Code H para 9.8; Code I para 9.9 and NfG 9C). If a healthcare professional is called in, they must be asked for their opinion of any risks or problems that the police need to take into account when making decisions about detention, when to carry out an interview (if relevant), and the need for safeguards (Code C para 9.13; Code H para 9.15; Code I para 11.17). Before any interview, the custody officer must assess whether the detainee is fit to be interviewed (see para 5.22 below).

Information from the officer in the case

Introduction

4.27 In order to advise effectively, the lawyer should attempt to obtain a clear idea of what evidence the police have. Disclosure is governed by Code C para 11.1A,[21] which provides that before a suspect is interviewed they and, if represented, their lawyer must be given sufficient information to enable the suspect to understand the nature of the suspected offence and why they are suspected of committing it, in order to allow for the effective exercise of the rights of the defence.[22] This is modified in the case of a person arrested under TA 2000 s41, in which case the information must be sufficient to enable the suspect to understand the nature of their suspected involvement in the commission, preparation or instigation of acts of terrorism (Code H para 11.1). The same modification applies to persons arrested under NSA 2023 s27 (Code I para 11) suspected of foreign power threat activity, which may not be related to a specific offence and where it may more readily be asserted is based on sensitive information that cannot

21 The College of Policing APP on investigative interviewing includes a section on disclosure strategy: www.college.police.uk/app/investigation/investigative-interviewing/investigative-interviewing#disclosure-strategy.

22 Note that the College of Policing, *Authorised Professional Practice: Investigation: Investigative interviewing* (available at: www.college.police.uk/app/investigation/investigative-interviewing/investigative-interviewing#disclosure-strategy) states that unrepresented suspects should not be given a pre-interview briefing because they may not understand its evidential value. It does state that this must not be confused with the obligation to provide information about the suspected offence in accordance with Code C para 3.1.

be disclosed (Code I NfG 3F).[23] The information to be disclosed should normally include, as a minimum, a description of the facts relating to the suspected offence that are known to the officer, including the time and place in question (Code C NfG 11ZA; and see Code H NfG 11ZA for modifications in respect of persons arrested under TA 2000 s41, and Code I NfG 11A for modifications in respect of persons arrested under NSA 2023 s27). The disclosure obligation is subject to the limitation that it does not require the disclosure of details at a time that might prejudice the criminal investigation (Code C para 11.1A; Code H para 11.1; Code I para 11). The decision on what to disclose rests with the investigating officer. The officer should disclose the contents of a previous interview where this is necessary to enable the lawyer to advise their client about whether or not to consent to a caution.[24] In a case decided before the disclosure provisions were inserted into Codes C, H and I, it was held that the 'silence' provisions of the Criminal Justice and Public Order Act (CJPOA) 1994 do not impose any obligation on the police to give full disclosure before a police interview.[25] However, the codes now provide that the information to be disclosed must be sufficient to allow for the effective exercise of defence rights. One of those rights is the right to silence and, therefore, it is arguable that the information disclosed should be sufficient to enable the suspect to decide whether to exercise that right.[26]

4.28 The disclosure obligations give the investigating officer a great deal of discretion as to the information that they disclose.[27] The lawyer should normally seek as much information as possible about the suspected offence(s) for a number of reasons.

(1) Advice to the client is more likely to be correct, and effective, if it is based on full information.
(2) If the client is advised to answer police questions, it is necessary to consider what facts the client may rely on at trial and, therefore, what information the client should give to the police in interview.[28]

23 Code I para 11.1A is clear that the obligation to provide sufficient information applies whether or not the suspect is represented so that the suspect is clear about what they are said to have done and 'to help an innocent suspect clear the matter up more quickly'.

24 *DPP v Ara* [2001] EWHC Admin 493.

25 *R v Imran and Hussain* [1997] Crim LR 754, CA. See also *R v Nottle* [2004] EWCA Crim 599 and *R v Farrell* [2004] EWCA Crim 597. In *R v Thirlwell* [2002] EWCA Crim 2703, the Court of Appeal held that, where a person had been arrested on suspicion of murder, the police were under no obligation to disclose provisional medical evidence of the cause of death.

26 For a more extensive analysis of the disclosure obligations, see E Cape, 'Transposing the EU Directive on the Right to Information: a firecracker or a damp squib?' [2015] Crim LR 48.

27 A study of police disclosure conducted after the new disclosure obligations were introduced in 2014 found that while the police generally complied with their disclosure obligations, at least in relation to suspects who were represented by a lawyer, some police officers exaggerated the strength of the evidence. See D Sukumar, J Hodgson and K Wade, 'Behind closed doors: live observations of current police station disclosure practices and lawyer-client consultations' [2016] Crim LR 900.

28 See *R v Noor* [2021] EWCA Crim 1767, concerning the failure to provide facts central to the denial. Also, the initial reasoning of the Court of Appeal in *R v Baker* [2021] EWCA Crim 415.

(3) The courts have held that although a complete absence of information from the police may justify a failure to tell the police about facts that will be relied on at trial, a failure by the police to give all available information is unlikely to do so.[29] Furthermore, it has been held that an inference can be drawn in the following circumstances:
   - a suspect 'is expressly or by necessary implication invited to give his account of the matter which has given rise to the interview', the fact that they were not asked specific questions would not, in itself, prevent inferences from being drawn.[30]
   - Where the accused accepted presence and had 'lived through the events' so that the fact is one the accused could reasonably have been expected to mention.[31]
   - Where the recording of the interview was no longer available, the length of the interview is indicative of an adequate opportunity having been provided to raise facts relied on such that an inference can be drawn.[32]

(4) Intelligence-led policing, and techniques of targeting suspects, are likely to produce information that is not readily apparent, and may not be used as evidence at any trial, but which may be highly relevant to advising the client.

(5) Information may be obtained at the police station stage which, lawfully or not, may not subsequently be disclosed under the provisions of the Criminal Procedure and Investigations Act (CPIA) 1996; for instance, medical information regarding the complainant, or social media messages.

If the information obtained from the police is incorrect or misleading, it may provide grounds for the exclusion of evidence of a subsequent interview where the lawyer relied on that information as a basis for advising the client.[33]

4.29 The information that the lawyer is able to obtain will depend in part on the officer they are dealing with, but also on the lawyer's own negotiation strategy (see para 4.57 below). In a more serious case, the officer assigned to the client may not be the officer in charge of the case, and it may be advisable to try to speak to the latter since the officer dealing with a particular suspect may be under instructions to give limited information and may not know all of the relevant facts. Any information obtained should

29 See, in particular, *R v Condron* [1997] 1 WLR 827, CA; and *R v Argent* [1997] 2 Cr App R 27, CA.

30 See *R v Green* [2019] EWCA Crim 411, where the interviewing officer showed the suspect CCTV footage, made a series of factually inaccurate statements and asked the suspect whether there was anything that he would like to say. The suspect remained silent, on legal advice, but at trial raised the defence of self-defence. The trial judge permitted an inference to be drawn from silence, a decision upheld by the Court of Appeal.

31 *R v Black* [2020] EWCA Crim 915. See *R v Baker* [2021] EWCA Crim 415, where the court incorrectly elided the failure to mention facts later relied on with the 'failure to answer questions'.

32 *R v Harewood and Rehman* [2021] EWCA Crim 1936. See further para 5.70 below for further case-law concerning inferences from silence

33 *R v Mason* [1987] 3 All ER 481, CA; but see *R v Noor* [2021] EWCA Crim 1767.

be treated with caution, for it may be partial, incomplete or exaggerated (see further para 4.56 below).

4.30 The police may use a strategy of 'phased disclosure' (otherwise known as drip-feed, or managed disclosure), especially in more serious cases, by which the disclosure of information to the suspect and the lawyer is actively managed.[34] In some investigations, the police may appoint a 'disclosure officer'[35] whose function is to consider and advise the interviewing officers on what disclosure to make as the investigation and interviews progress. In some cases, the custody officer may be aware of the disclosure strategy, and may be working with the officers in the case to keep relevant information out of the custody record. One of the main purposes of a phased disclosure strategy is to preserve the element of surprise and to encourage the suspect to answer questions without being aware of the extent of the information known to the police, while disclosing enough information to persuade a court, if relevant, that inferences from silence should be drawn. Sometimes the fact that such a strategy is being employed is obvious, because the lawyer may be handed a written document headed something like 'Disclosure 1', but this is not always the case. If the lawyer suspects that the police are using a phased disclosure strategy, the lawyer should:[36]

- ask the police directly whether they are using a phased disclosure strategy;
- ask the police whether they have any evidence that they have not disclosed;
- note carefully what information is disclosed and at what time;
- keep a note of questions asked of the police and their responses, including any refusal to provide information;
- reconsider the advice whether to answer questions on each occasion that disclosure is made; and
- ask the police directly whether there will be downstream monitoring of the interview.

While complete lack of disclosure before an initial interview may be treated by a court as sufficient justification to prevent inferences from silence, the more information that is disclosed the less likely it will be that a court will accept this justification for failure to tell the police of relevant facts.

4.31 Sometimes an officer may give the lawyer certain information but then ask them to withhold it from the client. Lawyers have a general duty to

34 See College of Policing, *Authorised Professional Practice: Investigation: Investigative interviewing*, available at: www.app.college.police.uk/app-content/investigations/investigative-interviewing.

35 Not to be confused with a disclosure officer appointed for the purposes of the CPIA 1996.

36 See College of Policing, *Authorised Professional Practice: Investigation: Investigative interviewing* (note 34 above). This sets out the minimum standards that must be applied when an interview is to be downstream monitored. These include: a record being made on the suspect's custody record of the fact that the interview, or part of the interview, was remotely monitored; the names of the officers monitoring the interview; and the purpose of the monitoring.

pass on material information to their clients.[37] Therefore, if the officer seeks to prevent information from being passed on, normally the lawyer would have to inform the officer that they have no choice but to pass it on to the client. Alternatively, an officer may say that they will give information to the lawyer on condition that the lawyer does not tell the client. In this situation the lawyer should normally inform the officer that they cannot accept information on such a condition. However, there are exceptions to the general rule. First, the SRA recognises that a lawyer does not have to pass on information that could cause a person serious physical or mental injury.[38] Second, under the Proceeds of Crime Act (POCA) 2002, and other similar legislation, to make a disclosure that is likely to prejudice an investigation concerning the recovery of the proceeds of crime constitutes the offence of 'tipping off', although a lawyer normally has a defence if the disclosure was to a client in connection with the giving of legal advice.[39] Third, a client may give informed consent in writing to the lawyer withholding material information.[40] If in any doubt, the lawyer should contact the SRA professional ethics helpline or the Law Society Practice Advice Service.[41]

4.32 Generally, the lawyer should try to obtain or confirm the information in checklist 7 from the officer in the case, and compare it with information obtained from the custody officer and client. Some of the matters are dealt with in greater detail after the checklist.

Checklist 7: Information from the officer in the case

A full and accurate note must be taken of all information sought and obtained, together with relevant times.

1 The reason for and circumstances of the arrest, and reason why arrest was necessary
2 Details of the suspected offence(s) for which the client was originally arrested
3 Details of any other suspected offence(s) and whether the client has been, or is to be, re-arrested under PACE s31 in respect of such offences
4 Whether any other person has been arrested in connection with the offence(s), and whether that other person implicated the client
5 Whether any other person is being sought in connection with the offence(s)
6 Whether the client has been interviewed and, if so, why and what was said
7 Whether the client has made any admissions, or any significant statement or silence, outside the context of an interview

37 SRA Code of Conduct para 6.4.
38 SRA Code of Conduct para 6.4(c).
39 See, for example, POCA 2002 ss330–332; and see para 1.20 above.
40 SRA Code of Conduct para 6.4(b).
41 For contact details, see: www.sra.org.uk/contact-us and practiceadvice@lawsociety.org.uk

8 Whether any question has been put to the client under CJPOA 1994 s36 or 37 and any reply made
9 Details of the evidence the police have that allegedly implicates the client
10 Whether the investigating officer has brought to the custody officer's attention any Code C para 3.4(b), NfG 3ZA documents or material which appear to undermine the need to keep the suspect in custody.*
11 Whether a search of property has been conducted
  - If so, whether anything of evidential significance has been found
  - If not, whether and when it is proposed to carry out a search

  In both cases, the legal authority for the search should be ascertained and checked against the offence for which the client has been arrested
12 Whether it is intended to carry out any other procedure such as:
  - removal of clothing
  - an intimate or non-intimate search
  - taking an intimate or non-intimate sample
  - taking a handwriting sample
  - conducting an identification procedure

  and the reasons for and legal authority for such procedures
13 What other investigations are being conducted or are intended
14 Whether the client has any previous convictions or other forms of previous misconduct
15 The purpose of any forthcoming interview
16 Whether the officer has any other relevant information that has not been disclosed to the lawyer and, if relevant, whether a strategy of phased disclosure is being used
17 Is there additional evidence that will be put to the client in the interview, for example, documents/CCTV (implications for children and vulnerable clients)
18 Is the interview being audio and visually recorded
  - If visually recorded, why?
  - Will anyone be watching a live stream of the interview?
19 The officer's view of the client's fitness for interview and whether the client may come within the categories requiring an appropriate adult
20 Whether the officer has sufficient evidence to charge (if relevant), and what is likely to happen after the interview
21 (Where appropriate) the attitude of the officer to diversion from prosecution
22 Whether the officer is aware of any indications that the client may present a risk to the safety of the lawyer
23 Whether the officer has turned their mind to the question of bail and/or any concerns relating to bail or proposed bail conditions

* While Codes H and I have an equivalent to Code C para 3.4(b) (Code H para 3.4(b); Code I para 3.5), they do not have a direct equivalent to Code C NfG 3ZA. Instead, Code H (NfG 3G) and Code I (NfG 3F) recognise that there may be circumstances where the arrest has been based on sensitive information which cannot be disclosed.

The circumstances of the arrest

4.33 It is important to probe the reason for and the circumstances of the arrest, and the reasons why arrest was necessary, since this may disclose information about the true nature of the investigation, the legality of the arrest (see para 2.11 above), and of detention (see para 2.56 above), and information that may be relevant to and/or explain the attitude of the police to the client. For example, a client who resisted arrest, or who in some other way contested the authority of the police, is likely to be dealt with more harshly. It may also be important to question the officer about how the client came to be arrested. In many cases this will be obvious, but in others seeking to establish how or why the client came to be arrested may disclose the existence of evidence or information that has not been revealed, for example, the involvement of an informant or undercover officer, or some form of surveillance. See para 4.22 above regarding the documents and materials relevant to the lawfulness of arrest or detention that must be disclosed. Fuller information regarding the circumstances of the arrest enable the lawyer to reassess the lawfulness of the arrest and, where possible, initiate a further discussion with the custody sergeant about whether detention should continue to be authorised.

The suspected offence

4.34 It is important to confirm what the suspected offence(s) is (are).[42] This should lead the lawyer to consider:

(1) the category of the offence(s) – indictable-only, either-way or summary-only – that is relevant, for example, to the maximum period of pre-charge detention, whether the custody officer has power to charge and whether a probationary representative can act;
(2) what the police/prosecution will have to establish in order to prove the offence;
(3) what evidence the police appear to have, and/or what evidence they might seek, in order to prove the offence;
(4) whether the evidence that the police appear to have is sufficient to charge the client without conducting an interview (see para 2.64 above);
(5) whether the police may be considering, or may subsequently consider, whether to investigate the client for, or seek to charge the client with, other offences instead of or in addition to the offence(s) for which they have been arrested (for example, following an arrest for assault occasioning actual bodily harm the police may consider common assault or, on the other hand, wounding or grievous bodily harm);
(6) what defence(s) may be available to the client;
(7) whether a caution (simple or conditional) or a youth caution or diversion (in the case of a child[43]) may be considered; and
(8) what information should subsequently be sought from the client.

42 As noted at para 4.27 above, an arrest under NSA 2023 s27 and Sch 6 may be unrelated to a specific criminal offence.

43 See National Police Chiefs' Council, *Child Gravity Matrix 2025* (updated 2023), available at: www.npcc.police.uk, in particular the Disposal table at p15, which neatly sets out the eligibility requirements and impact of each disposal.

Other people arrested

4.35 If other people have been arrested in connection with the same offence(s), one question that arises is the significance of what they have told the police, particularly insofar as it may implicate the client. If a co-suspect, in the absence of the client, makes a confession in a police interview that also implicates the client, it is well established that evidence of this statement normally cannot be used by the prosecution as evidence against the client at a subsequent trial.[44] It may amount to evidence against the co-suspect, but not against the client. However, although evidence of the statement cannot be used at trial against the client, the co-suspect could give evidence against the client at a subsequent trial. This can happen if the co-suspect is not prosecuted or, having been prosecuted, the case is discontinued for some reason, or if prosecuted and the co-suspect pleads guilty before the trial of the client. In these circumstances, the co-suspect can be called as a prosecution witness. Alternatively, if the co-suspect is prosecuted and pleads not guilty, they can give evidence against the client when giving evidence on their own behalf.

4.36 At the police station, it will normally be impossible accurately to predict what will happen in respect of the co-suspect. However, it cannot be assumed that the fact that a co-suspect has implicated the client will necessarily have an adverse effect on the client at any trial.

Admissions or 'silences' already made by the client

Introduction

4.37 Whether evidence of a confession, or 'significant silence', made by the client before receiving advice from the lawyer is likely to be admitted at trial will be impossible to predict with certainty at the police station. However, it is important that the lawyer is aware of what may happen regarding any prior confession or 'silence' at the trial stage since this will affect the advice to be given to the client. The lawyer should consider:

- whether the client should have been cautioned and, if so, whether they were cautioned;
- whether the confession (or silence) was made in the context of an 'interview';
- whether, if it did come within the definition of an 'interview', it should have been conducted at that stage; and
- whether it was properly recorded.

In questioning the officer in the case, the lawyer will want to try to establish precisely what was said to the client by that, or any other, officer; the circumstances and purpose of such question(s); and the alleged response (if any) of the client. However, the lawyer should avoid alerting the officer

44 See, for example, *R v Rhodes* (1960) 44 Cr App R 23, CA. But note *R v Hayter* [2005] UKHL 6, in which it was held that where a co-defendant's guilt had been established by his own out-of-court confession, that finding of guilt could be used as evidence against the defendant. Note also *R v Nguyen* [2020] EWCA Crim 140, in which it was held that evidence of a co-defendant's interview may be admissible under Criminal Justice Act (CJA) 2003 s114(1)(d) (admissibility in the interest of justice).

to any actual or potential procedural errors (for example, a failure to caution) or requirements (for example, the obligation under Codes C and H para 11.4; Code I para 11.3 to put a significant statement or silence to a suspect at the beginning of an interview).

Admissions and confessions

4.38 The terms 'admission' and 'confession' can, in practice, be used interchangeably. Generally, evidence of a confession, such as evidence from the police officer who heard it or an electronic recording of it, will be admissible at trial (PACE s76(1)).[45] However, whether in a particular case a confession will be admitted will in part depend on whether it was made in the context of a police 'interview'. 'Confession' is defined, for the purpose of determining whether it is governed by PACE s76, as including 'any statement wholly or partly adverse to the person who made it, whether made to a person in authority or not' (PACE s82(1)). It includes direct or indirect statements by the suspect that they committed the offence, mixed statements such as 'I hit him, but it was in self-defence', and also statements that, although not amounting to a direct admission of involvement, are detrimental to the suspect in the light of other available evidence. However, a statement that is intended to be exculpatory or neutral at the time that it is made does not amount to a confession even if it is adverse by the time of the trial.[46] This means that such a statement is likely to be admissible at trial unless excluded under PACE s78 (see para 4.45 below).

'Interview' and the obligation to caution

4.39 'Interview' is defined as (Code C para 11.1A):

> [T]he questioning of a person regarding their involvement or suspected involvement in a criminal offence or offences which, under paragraph 10.1, must be carried out under caution . . . Procedures under the Road Traffic Act 1988, section 7 or the Transport and Works Act 1992, section 31 do not constitute interviewing for the purpose of this Code.[47]

A caution must be given where a person is questioned about their involvement or suspected involvement in an offence (or questioned further where the answers given to previous questions provide the grounds for suspicion)[48] if there are grounds to suspect them of that offence, and their answers or silence may be given in evidence (Codes C and H para 10.1; Code I para 10). Although the codes do not expressly say so, the courts have interpreted the provision so that a caution only has to be given where

45 Although this is subject to PACE s76(2), and the discretion to exclude prosecution evidence under section 78. See paras 13.25 and 13.33 below.

46 For example, a statement by the accused to the police that the accused was not present at the scene of a crime, which by the time of the trial the prosecution can prove, or the accused accepts, was false. See *R v Hasan* [2005] UKHL 22.

47 Where a person is arrested under TA 2000 s41, interview is defined as 'the questioning of a person arrested on suspicion of being a terrorist which, under *paragraph 10.1*, must be carried out under caution' (Code H para 11.1, original emphasis). Similar provisions under Code I para 11 replace the operative words with 'being involved in foreign power threat activity'.

48 For an example, see European Court of Human Rights (ECtHR), *Ibrahim and Others v UK* (App Nos 50541/08, 50571/08, 50573/08, 40351/09) [2017] Crim LR 877.

there are reasonable grounds for suspicion,[49] but whether there are grounds for suspicion must be viewed objectively.[50] An officer cannot ignore the possibility that an offence has been committed in an attempt to avoid compliance with the codes. Conversely, it is highly unlikely that questions put to a suspect without a caution would be excluded on the basis that an esoteric offence had potentially been committed.[51] Code C para 10.1 (but not Code H para 10.1 or Code I para 10) goes on to explain that a caution need not be administered if the questions are put for other purposes (see para 4.43 below). A request for a suspect's PIN or electronic key is akin to a key required to open a locked draw and is likely to fall within the exemptions of Code C para 10.1(c) (see also Code B para 6.12).[52] If a caution is not administered in circumstances where it is required, this may lead to exclusion of evidence obtained under PACE s76 or 78, but it may not, especially if the suspect's lawyer is present (see para 13.39 below). Further, the lawyer should carefully note any deficiency in the caution for future reference. For instance, whether the caution, as put, speaks to, for example, recent fabrication but the Crown Prosecution Service (CPS) subsequently seeks an inference for another reason. In these circumstances it is possible to argue that an inference should not arise because of the deficiency in the caution.[53]

4.40 Therefore, questions put to an arrested person about the offence for which they have been arrested, or any other offence of which they are suspected, will amount to an interview. Similarly, questions put to a person who has not been arrested about an offence of which they are suspected will also be an interview, provided that there are reasonable grounds for that suspicion. If an officer, without suspecting a person, puts questions to them about an offence and, as a result of the answers to those questions (or some other reason, such as evasiveness or refusal to answer), the officer forms a suspicion that the person is involved in an offence, the person must be cautioned before further questions are put to them about the offence, and such further questioning will amount to an interview.[54]

Was the confession made in an interview?

4.41 It is important to recognise that the definition of an interview given above is not confined to a formal police interview that takes place in an interview

49 See *R v James* [1996] Crim LR 650, CA. In *R v Miller* [2007] EWCA Crim 1891, it was held that a caution should have been given where, on finding a butterfly knife during a drug search, the officer asked the person why he had it with him. The contrary conclusion was drawn where questions were put to a TIE (trace, interview and elimination) individual, where there were conflicting accounts of his possible involvement and the police were not sure whether he was the person who was the last to be seen with the victim (*R v Shillibier* [2006] EWCA Crim 793). See also *Hughes v DPP* [2010] EWHC 515 (Admin).

50 *R v Williams* [2012] EWCA Crim 264.

51 *R v Shepherd* [2019] EWCA Crim 1062.

52 See the judgment of Mr Justice Turner in the Crown Court case of *R v AB and CD* [2025] EWCR 3.

53 *R v Baker* [2021] EWCA Crim 415.

54 See *R v Senior* [2004] EWCA Crim 454; *R v Perpont* [2004] EWCA Crim 2562; *Ridehalgh v DPP* [2005] EWHC 1100 (Admin); and *Sneyd v DPP* [2006] EWHC 560 (Admin).

room at a police station. Any 'questioning of a person regarding their involvement or suspected involvement in a criminal offence' which is required to be carried out under caution amounts to an interview, wherever it takes place,[55] even if it consists of only one question and answer.[56] This would include questions put by a custody officer if those questions concern involvement or suspected involvement in a criminal offence.[57] It has been held that a 'co-operation conversation' conducted by customs officers with a suspect, designed to encourage the suspect to provide information rather than for the purposes of gathering evidence against the suspect, was not an interview, although the inducement offered in return for co-operation meant that the conversation could not be used in evidence against the suspect.[58]

4.42 Questions put to a person in the street, in a police car or other place outside the police station can amount to an interview. Where a person has been cautioned (whether or not they have been arrested), or where a person ought to have been cautioned because there were reasonable grounds to suspect them of an offence, and they are questioned regarding involvement or suspected involvement in a criminal offence, such questioning will amount to an interview (Code C paras 10.1 and 11.1A). For example, questioning of a person in the street following their arrest for a drugs offence concerning three polythene wraps that they had been seen to throw away was held to amount to an interview.[59] Similarly, questions put to a person in a police car, following arrest for having an offensive weapon in a public place, about why the person was carrying a flick-knife, were held to amount to an interview.[60]

4.43 However, questions are necessary for a conversation to amount to an interview, so it will not be an interview if a suspect 'blurts out' a confession unprompted by any question, provided that the police do not then proceed to ask questions.[61] Questions put by a police officer during an undercover operation are not likely to amount to an interview, provided that the officer does not ask the questions for the sole purpose of gathering evidence rather than as part of the purpose of the transaction itself (see para 13.44

55 Thus, questioning that should have been carried out under caution ought to be treated as an interview even if, as a matter of fact, it was not carried out under caution.

56 See *R v Ward* (1994) 98 Cr App R 337, CA, where it was held that it was the nature of the question, rather than its length, that was relevant. For a useful illustration of this point, see *R v Miller* [1998] Crim LR 209, CA.

57 See *R v Oransaye* [1993] Crim LR 772, in which questioning by a custody officer about money found in the defendant's possession when being booked in was held to be an interview. Note that Code C para 3.4 specifically provides that a custody officer must not ask questions regarding a suspect's involvement in an offence, nor in respect of any comments made by the suspect in response to the arresting officer's account of the arrest or in response to the decision to detain, because of the danger that it will amount to an interview. See also *R v Weerdesteyn* [1995] 1 Cr App R 405, CA.

58 *R v de Silva* [2002] EWCA Crim 2673.

59 *R v Goddard* [1994] Crim LR 46, CA.

60 See *R v Hunt* [1992] Crim LR 582, CA; and see *R v Miller* [1998] Crim LR 209, CA at note 40 above which concerned similar facts.

61 See *R v Younis and Ahmed* [1990] Crim LR 425, CA; *R v Menard* [1995] 1 Cr App R 306, CA; and *R v Doyle* [2002] EWCA Crim 1176.

below).[62] Asking a person under arrest to account for an object, substance or mark or to account for their presence at the place where they were arrested will almost certainly amount to an interview (see paras 5.91 and 5.95 below).

4.44 Code C para 10.1 gives examples of questioning that would not require a caution and which, therefore, would not amount to an interview. These are questions:

- put solely to establish a person's identity or ownership of a vehicle;
- put to obtain information in accordance with any relevant statutory requirement, for example, under Road Traffic Act (RTA) 1988 s165 (which empowers a police constable to require certain people driving, or believed to have driven, motor vehicles to supply their name and address);[63]
- put in furtherance of the proper and effective conduct of a search (for example, questioning during a search about whether articles discovered belong to the suspect will not amount to an interview, but questioning that goes further, for example, about whether drugs found were intended to be supplied to others, would almost certainly amount to an interview);[64]
- seeking verification of a written record in accordance with Code C para 11.13 (see para 5.116 below).

In addition, questions put in examining a person in accordance with TA 2000 Sch 7 do not amount to an interview (see para 1.61 above).

4.45 If the conversation did not amount to an interview, evidence of any confession made will generally be admissible subject to the requirements regarding recording and verification (see para 4.51 below). If the conversation did amount to an interview, the next question in determining whether evidence of it is likely to be admitted at trial is whether it was permissible to conduct an interview at that stage.

Should an interview have been conducted?

4.46 Generally, once a decision to arrest a person has been made, the suspect must not be interviewed about the offence except at a police station or other authorised place of detention (Code C para 11.1; Code H para 11.2; Code I para 11.1). Note that this applies once a 'decision to arrest' has been made, as opposed to an arrest itself, so that it may be relevant to establish when a police officer made the decision to arrest, since the officer may not have acted on that decision immediately. Therefore, if a decision to arrest has been made, a person should not be interviewed at home, in the street or in the police car on the way to the station. The general prohibition on interviewing away from the police station is subject to an exception if delay would be likely to (Code C para 11.1; Code H para 11.2; Code I para 11.1):

62 See *R v Bryce* [1992] 4 All ER 567, CA; *R v Christou and Wright* [1992] QB 979, CA; *R v Edwards* [1997] Crim LR 348; and *R v Rajkuma* [2003] EWCA Crim 1955.

63 It has been held that the statutory 'drink-driving' procedure under the RTA 1988 is not an interview. See *DPP v Rous; DPP v D (A Minor)* [1991] Crim LR 911, QBD, also reported as *DPP v D (A Juvenile)*; *DPP v Rous* (1992) 94 Cr App R 185, QBD.

64 See Code B paras 6.12 and 6.12A; and *R v Langiert* [1991] Crim LR 777, CA; *R v Khan* [1993] Crim LR 54, CA; and *R v Raphaie* [1996] Crim LR 812, CA.

- lead to interference with or harm to evidence, or interference with or physical harm to other people, or serious loss of, or damage to, property; or
- lead to the alerting of other people suspected of committing an offence but not yet arrested for it; or
- hinder the recovery of property obtained in consequence of the commission of the offence.

If an interview is carried out under this exception, it must cease once the relevant risk has been averted or the necessary questions have been put in order to attempt to avert that risk.[65]

4.47 If the suspect was interviewed contrary to Code C para 11.1, Code H para 11.2 or Code I para 11.1, a court may exclude evidence of any confession or other adverse statement made during it (under PACE s76 or s78), although other factors will also be relevant, such as whether it was recorded, whether the suspect was given an opportunity to verify the record, whether the suspect was aware of their right to silence, and whether the suspect is a child or otherwise vulnerable. Evidence of an interview conducted under one of the exceptions outlined above will probably be admitted.[66] Note that the provisions on accounting for an object, substance or mark, etc, or for presence, under CJPOA 1994 ss36 and 37 do not authorise the police to interview a suspect away from the police station.

4.48 If it was permissible to conduct an interview away from the police station, a further question is whether the formalities in the relevant code have been complied with.

Have the interviewing requirements been complied with?

4.49 Certain requirements set out in Code C and Code H apply only to interviews conducted in police stations or other authorised place of detention (Code C para 11.2 and the whole of section 12; Code H para 11.3 and section 12; Code I para 11.2), but others apply to interviews wherever they are conducted. The requirements are dealt with more fully at para 7.5 below, but a number of points should be noted at this stage.

- Code C para 11.15 provides that while children and mentally vulnerable suspects should not be interviewed in the absence of an appropriate adult, this is subject to an exception where they are interviewed away from the police station under the provisions of Code C para 11.1 (see para 4.46 above) or in the police station under Code C para 11.18 (urgent interviews). Code H para 11.9 and Code I para 11.1 contain similar provisions. See further chapter 11 below.
- If a person is interviewed under caution without being arrested, they must be informed of their right of access to a solicitor (Code C para 3.21(b); and see para 2.164 above). If a person who has been arrested is

65 See para 2.123 above regarding the right to legal advice in such circumstances.

66 See *R v Ibrahim, Omar, Osman and Mohamed* [2008] EWCA Crim 880. This case concerned a 'safety' interview at a police station under TA 2000 Sch 8 paras 7–9, but the same principles are likely to apply to a 'safety' interview conducted away from a police station. The decision to admit evidence of the interviews was, in effect, confirmed in by the ECtHR Grand Chamber: *Ibrahim and Others v UK* (App Nos 50541/08, 50571/08, 50573/08, 40351/09) [2017] Crim LR 87.

interviewed before being taken to a police station, they should also be entitled to consult a solicitor and be informed of this right. This is not explicitly provided for in Code C or Code H, and it has been held that an arrested person is not entitled to legal advice under PACE s58 until detention has been authorised under PACE s37.[67] However, interviewing a person in such circumstances without giving them the right of access to a solicitor is likely to contravene their rights under European Convention on Human Rights (ECHR) Article 6(3)(c).

- Whether or not an interview takes place at a police station, the police must make an accurate record of it (Code C para 11.7).[68] If it is not practicable for the record to be made during the interview, it must be made as soon as practicable after the interview (Code C para 11.8).
- Whether or not the record is made during the interview, the suspect must, unless it is impracticable, be given the opportunity to read the interview record (unless it was electronically recorded, in which case the verification arrangements in Code E or F will apply) and to sign it as correct or to indicate the respects in which the suspect considers it inaccurate (Code C para 11.11).
- Voluntary interviews should be arranged for a time and place where they can be audio recorded and enable the safeguards and requirements of Code C paras 3.21–3.22B to be implemented. It would normally be reasonable to delay the interview to enable audio recording unless to do so would be likely to compromise the outcome of the interview or investigation (Code E NfG 2E).

4.50 At the beginning of an interview the interviewing officer must, following the caution, put to the suspect any significant statement or silence which occurred in the presence and hearing of a police officer or civilian interviewer before the start of the interview, and which has not been put to the suspect in the course of a previous interview (Codes C and H para 11.4; Code I para 11.3). This requirement applies whether or not the statement or silence occurred within the context of an interview (see para 4.39 above for definition). The recording and verification requirements noted above (if made in the context of an interview) and below (if not made in the context of an interview) would apply to such a statement or silence.

Recording and verifying 'non-interviews'

4.51 A record must be made of any comment (including unsolicited comments) made by a suspect outside the context of an interview which might be relevant to the suspected offence, and if practicable the suspect must be given an opportunity to read it and sign it as correct or indicate how they consider it to be inaccurate (Code C para 11.13; Code H para 11.8A; Code I para 11.8).[69] As with interviews conducted before arrival at the police

67 *R v Kerawalla* [1991] Crim LR 451, CA; and *Kirkup v DPP* [2003] EWHC 2354 (Admin).

68 Code H para 11.8 provides that interview records should be made in accordance with the Code of Practice issued under TA 2000 Sch 8 para 3 where the interview takes place at a designated place of detention.

69 This requirement is mandatory and applies irrespective of whether the suspect has been cautioned (*R (Karia) v Chief Constable of Hampshire* [2015] EWHC 4083 (Admin)).

station, Codes C and H para 11.4 and Code I para 11.3 provide that any such statement or silence must be put to the suspect at the beginning of any subsequent interview. See further para 5.116 below.

The effect of 'tainted' interviews on subsequent interviews

4.52 The foregoing sections deal with the question of the likely admissibility of a prior statement or silence and the effect that this might have on advice on whether to answer questions in a subsequent interview. This section deals with a further issue – whether an improperly conducted interview (or non-interview) might affect the admission in evidence of a subsequent interview that is properly conducted. The effect on a subsequent interview of an earlier 'tainted' interview will depend on how reliable or fair the subsequent interview is in the light of the tainted interview.

4.53 In order for a subsequent, properly conducted, interview to be excluded as a result of an earlier, inadmissible interview there must be a clear connection between them.[70] The courts will consider whether the arrangements for the second or subsequent interview gave the accused a sufficient opportunity to exercise an informed and independent choice about whether to repeat or retract what was said in the excluded interview or to say nothing.[71] In *R v McGovern*,[72] the Court of Appeal held that evidence of a confession made in a second interview should have been excluded because it was a direct consequence of a confession made in an initial interview held when access to a solicitor had been improperly denied. If the suspect receives advice from a lawyer before the subsequent interview, it is likely that a court will not regard it as being tainted by the first, and is likely to admit it in evidence. However, this may not be the result if the court takes the view that despite legal advice the suspect did not have the opportunity to make an informed and independent choice. Thus, in *McGovern* the Court of Appeal held that the second interview should have been excluded, despite the fact that the suspect received advice from a solicitor before, and during, that interview because the tainted interview was still operative, partly because the solicitor had not been told that the suspect had been denied access to a lawyer before the initial interview.[73]

4.54 In the cases cited in the previous paragraph, the accused had made admissions in the subsequent interviews. A question that appears to be undecided is whether inferences should be drawn where, in a second interview, the suspect remains silent. If the factors that rendered the initial interview inadmissible are still operative at the time of the subsequent interview, or if the suspect did not have the opportunity before the second interview of exercising an informed and independent choice, arguably no adverse inferences should be drawn.

70 *R v Gillard and Barrett* (1991) 92 Cr App R 61, CA. See also *Y v DPP* [1991] Crim LR 917, DC; *R v Geddis* (1992) Times, December 28, CA; *R v Conway* [1994] Crim LR 838, CA; *R v Glaves* [1993] Crim LR 685; and *R v Ahmed* [2003] EWCA Crim 3627.

71 *R v Neil* [1994] Crim LR 441, CA.

72 (1991) 92 Cr App R 228, CA.

73 For an example of where evidence of a second interview was excluded, where the first interview had been conducted in the absence of a caution, see *R v Webster* (2000) 12 December (unreported), CA.

Evidence implicating the suspect

4.55 The officer in the case should be asked for full information concerning the case, and a full note should be taken of their response. For the information regarding the suspected offence that must be disclosed prior to a police interview, see para 4.27 above. Taken together, Code C para 11.1A and NfG 11ZA (Code H para 11.1 and NfG 11ZA; Code I para 11 and NfG3F) require that normally the officer should provide the suspect and/or their lawyer with a description of the facts that is sufficient not only to enable the suspect to understand the nature of the suspected offence, but also why they are suspected of it, with the objective of ensuring that the suspect can exercise their procedural rights and that the right to fair trial is safeguarded. For example, if a suspect has been arrested for dwelling-house burglary, this would suggest that information such as that concerning possible eye-witnesses, biometric samples found at the premises and information linking property found in the suspect's possession with property taken from the premises, should be disclosed.[74]

4.56 Despite the disclosure obligations set out in Codes C, H and I, the officer in the case will frequently not disclose all relevant information in sufficient detail, and will usually need to be prompted. The lawyer should be careful to devote sufficient time to this since information obtained may be crucial to advising the client appropriately, and to the future conduct of the defence, and it may lead to the disclosure of information that might otherwise never be disclosed. The officer should be specifically asked whether they have any relevant information that they have not disclosed. The information that should be sought is set out in checklist 8.

Checklist 8: Summary of police evidence to be requested

A full and accurate note must be taken of all information sought and obtained, together with relevant times.

1 A history of the case, or 'case narrative', including whether and how the case was reported to the police or whether and why the police initiated the investigation, how the client came to be arrested and what happened on arrest, and what has happened in the case so far from the officer's point of view.
2 What investigations have been made at the crime scene (if relevant), including who has attended (arresting and other officers, scene of crime officers, forensic specialists, etc).
3 What relevant communications have taken place (for example, between members of the public and the police, and between police officers), what was said, and how this has been recorded. Where appropriate, the lawyer should ask to see or hear records made.

74 For a more detailed analysis of the disclosure provisions, see E Cape, 'Transposing the EU Directive on the Right to Information: a firecracker or a damp squib?' [2015] Crim LR 48 at p56.

4 Who has been interviewed in relation to the case, and who has made a statement. The lawyer should ask to see relevant statements, including those of any identifying witness. Where appropriate, a detailed note should be taken of descriptions given of relevant events and relevant people, especially possible suspects.
5 What searches have been conducted, samples taken, photographs or other recordings made. The lawyer should ask to see the product of such activities.
6 What relevant real evidence or objects the police have in their possession (for example, weapons, documents, clothing, CCTV recordings, etc). Again, where appropriate, the lawyer should ask to see such items.
7 What forensic examinations or tests have been conducted, and the results of such examinations or tests.
8 What other investigations, forensic tests, etc, are planned.
9 What information the officer has concerning the client's circumstances, including any previous convictions or other forms of previous misconduct.

Dealing with reluctance or refusal to disclose evidence

4.57 The police disclosure obligations are set out at para 4.55 above. Materials or documents relevant to the lawfulness of the arrest or detention may also be relevant (see para 4.22 above). In addition, if the police are intending to conduct an identification procedure, they should disclose the description of the suspect as first given by a potential witness (see para 8.9 below). Code C para 11.1A states that an interview 'is the questioning of a person regarding their involvement or suspected involvement in a criminal offence'.[75] The lawyer can argue, therefore, that they cannot properly advise the client in relation to that alleged involvement if the police are not willing to tell the lawyer about the evidence indicating the client's involvement.

4.58 If the officer refuses to provide information that is requested, the lawyer should consider what strategy to adopt. This will depend on the extent, and importance, of the information that the officer has refused to disclose. The lawyer should consider the following strategies.

- Persisting with the request for information. An officer who initially refuses to provide information may do so without thinking about why they are doing so, and faced with a tenacious lawyer may decide that refusal is not worth the aggravation.
- Telling the officer that the lawyer will stop the interview whenever the officer introduces evidence of which the lawyer has not been told or, where appropriate, allowed to see.
- Asking the officer to record the request for information, the information that has been disclosed in response (or the fact that no information was disclosed in response) and the time of the request and

75 See note 47 above concerning the definition of an interview for the purpose of the TA 2000 and NSA 2023.

response. Code C para 11.1A, Code H para 11.1 and Code I para 11 require the officer to record any information disclosed and the time of such disclosure, although there is no obligation to record the reasons for non-disclosure.
- Informing the officer that the lawyer will have no alternative but to advise the client not to answer questions at all.
- Informing the officer that the courts have held that inferences cannot be drawn if the police have disclosed insufficient information to enable the solicitor usefully to advise the client.[76]
- Making a formal complaint about the lack of disclosure. A complaint of this nature must be referred to an inspector to deal with (see Code C para 3.26; Code H para 3.24; Code I para 3.28[77]).
- Delaying the deployment of a prepared statement until the conclusion of an interview. If the statement has been dated and timed to show completion before the interview began, then there will be little risk of any adverse comment being made on the basis of recent fabrication.

4.59 Such strategies may lead the officer to disclose the relevant information. If they fail, the lawyer should consider advising the client not to answer questions in the police interview, and use the interview to obtain information about the allegation. In this case, the lawyer should explain at the commencement of the interview that in view of the lack of disclosure the lawyer is unable to give meaningful advice to the client or that the lawyer is now advising the client not to answer questions because the police have failed to disclose sufficient information (see further para 5.114 below). After the police interview, the lawyer can then advise the suspect whether to request a second interview during which the suspect will answer questions. There is no right to insist on a second interview. However, if a second interview is refused, the lawyer should advise the client whether to make a written statement either in the presence of a police officer or, if this is also refused, to the lawyer. Having taken a copy, the lawyer can then hand it to the police. This statement should include the preamble set out in Code C Annex D and a request should be made for the interviewing officer to add the statement to the file before any charging decision is made. A copy of this statement may also be sent directly to the CPS.[78] This may be advisable where, for example, the client has a defence which it is important to place on record at an early stage, but which the client should not divulge in detail until the full extent of the allegations are known, or

76 The extent to which officers are cognisant of what the courts have determined amounts to 'insufficient' information will vary and what is sufficient will vary in each case. See paras 5.87 and 5.111 below and the summary in para 4.28, point (3), above.

77 The right to complain stems from Directive 2012/13/EU on the right to information in criminal proceedings. If a complaint is made by or on behalf of a suspect that the information and (as the case may be) access to records and documents has not been provided as required, the matter shall be reported to an inspector to deal with as a complaint.

78 See Code for Crown Prosecutors para 3.4: 'although prosecutors primarily consider the evidence and information supplied by the police and other investigators, the suspect or those acting on their behalf may also submit evidence or information to the prosecutor, before or after charge, to help inform the prosecutor's decision. In appropriate cases, the prosecutor may invite the suspect or their representative to do so.'

where inferences from failure to give information to the police would be particularly damaging (see para 5.152 below).

The dangers of incomplete information

4.60 Any information that the officer gives concerning evidence against the client should be treated cautiously for a number of reasons. In some cases the information may be exaggerated in order to encourage the client to confess on the basis that the evidence is strong or overwhelming. It is common, for example, for the police to say that a suspect has been identified when in fact a witness has simply given a description which the police think fits the suspect. Whether the witness would pick out the suspect in an identification procedure is another matter altogether. Alternatively, the strength of the evidence may be underplayed by the officer in order to lull the suspect into a false sense of security so that they become careless. In particular, the officer may withhold some vital pieces of information from the lawyer in order to trap the suspect by introducing it during the interview, or in the hope that the suspect will assert facts that subsequently appear to be unsustainable in the light of that information. While the PEACE model of police interviewing does encourage the interviewing officer to consider the likely effect of giving insufficient information to the lawyer, it does not go so far as to encourage full disclosure.[79]

The evidential status of the information

4.61 Consideration must be given to whether any of the apparent evidence may be inadmissible or excluded at trial. For example, the evidence of a very young child may not be admissible, and a confession made by a co-defendant will normally not be admissible as evidence against the client (see para 4.35 above). Similarly, it may be that a potential witness may not be compellable as a witness and/or may be reluctant to give evidence (see para 5.55 below).

The purpose of the interview

4.62 It is important to ask the officer to explain the purpose of any intended police interview. In many cases, the officer may simply say that it is to give an opportunity to the suspect to give their version of events. This is unlikely to be the case. Since the police are engaged in an adversarial process, they are likely to view the interview as an opportunity to secure evidence that will be of use to them.[80] Occasionally, the police may genu-

79 See College of Policing, *Authorised Professional Practice: Investigation: Investigative interviewing* section 4 'PEACE framework', available at: www.app.college.police.uk/app-content/investigations/investigative-interviewing/#peace-framework. For an explanation of the PEACE model; see para 7.20 below.

80 While Principle 1 of the police investigative interviewing model states that the purpose of an interview is to obtain an accurate and reliable account, Principle 5 states that: 'Investigators should recognise the positive impact of an early admission', which has the following benefits for the police: 'gain valuable intelligence, increase detected offences rates, record a fuller picture of offending for possible use in future cases or to support applications for anti-social behaviour orders, or other restrictive orders'.

inely view the interview as an opportunity for the suspect to give an innocent explanation, but this is relatively unusual.

4.63 Establishing the purpose of the interview is important for a number of reasons:

(1) It will help to establish the nature of the questioning, the likely length of the interview and whether the police are considering questioning the suspect about matters other than those for which they have been arrested. In the latter case, it may be appropriate to try to negotiate separate interviews for separate matters.

(2) In those cases where there is likely to be more than one interview, the police may have different objectives in each interview, which may be part of a formal phased disclosure strategy (see para 4.30 above). The first interview may be used to establish the general response of the suspect – for example, whether the suspect admits the offence or whether they will be putting forward a particular defence – which will be useful to the police in determining what lines of enquiry to pursue. In a subsequent interview, the police interviewer may seek greater detail in respect of anything said by the suspect in the first interview, and may seek to exploit any inconsistencies between what the suspect says in the respective interviews, or between what the suspect has said and what any witnesses have said. The lawyer will need to consider appropriate strategies. The lawyer may, for example, want to consider using the first interview to put the police on notice of a particular defence or may want to use it as a way of gathering information about the police case. In any event, the lawyer should advise the client that anything said in the first interview may not only be of evidential significance, but may be used against them in a subsequent interview. Discrepancies and inconsistencies may be used by the police to try to undermine what the suspect says in the second or subsequent interview, or to seek to demonstrate that the suspect has lied.

(3) Probing the purpose of the interview may lead the officer to disclose information not previously disclosed, or may lead the officer to disclose that they believe that there is sufficient evidence to charge and/or that the police intend to charge the suspect irrespective of what is said in the interview. In these circumstances, the lawyer should consider what course of action to take. If the lawyer believes that an interview would be to the advantage of their client (for example, enabling the client to put forward a defence at an early stage), they should allow the interview to proceed. If, on the other hand, the lawyer is of the view that a police interview would not be to the client's advantage (for example, because the client is not going to answer questions and the lawyer wants to try to avoid adverse inferences at trial), there are two arguments for moving to a decision about charge without interview. The first involves making representations to the custody officer that since the officer in the case accepts that there is sufficient evidence to charge, PACE s37(7) requires the officer to proceed to make a decision about charge (see para 2.64 above). The second is that the combined effect of Code C para 11.6 (Code H para 11.7; Code I para 11.6) and Code C para 16.1 requires the officer to take the suspect to the custody officer for a decision about

charge (see para 10.9 below). In such circumstances, the lawyer should consider making representations to the custody officer that further detention without charge is unlawful and/or indicating at the beginning of the interview that the lawyer is advising the suspect not to answer questions because they believe that the interview is being conducted contrary to PACE s37(7) and/or the code provisions identified above (see further para 5.148 below).

Previous misconduct

4.64 The previous misconduct provisions under the CJA 2003 are explained at para 5.173 below. As a result of these provisions, the police may include questions about previous misconduct in interviews of suspects. In order to be able to advise the client appropriately, the officer in the case should normally be asked whether they intend to ask such questions, unless the lawyer has good reason to believe that this would prompt the officer to ask questions that the officer had not previously considered. The lawyer should ask:

- what information the police have about the client's previous convictions or other misconduct, including the source and extent of that information, and the precise details;
- what the specific purpose of the questions is; and
- under what 'gateway' of admissibility they are relevant.

The lawyer should also consider suggesting that such questions be asked in an interview separate from that dealing with the substantive offence(s).

What will happen after the interview?

4.65 The interviewing officer will often have a fairly firm idea of what will happen after the police interview. In most cases, especially in less serious cases, there is likely to be only one police interview, and the officer may well have decided that charge is likely to follow. Probing the officer for this information may also result in further information about the future course of the investigation, further police interviews, timescale, the likely attitude to bail, or the potential for a caution or other form of diversion from prosecution. It should also prompt the lawyer to consider whether they should initiate any action such as securing the attendance of a doctor or other expert, or interviewing witnesses. The lawyer will also want to consider whether formal pre-charge engagement will assist their client (see para 10.14 below).

CHAPTER 5

Advising the client

continued

Introduction

5.1 This chapter assumes that the lawyer has arrived at the police station, has successfully negotiated their way past the custody officer and is now seeing their client for the first time. This may not be the first time that the lawyer has spoken to the client. The client may be an existing or former client, and, in any event, the lawyer may have spoken to the client on the telephone before attending the police station.

5.2 The chapter deals with the following issues:

(1) The lawyer's role.
(2) The initial interview with the client:
- initial introduction;
- taking initial instructions; and
- assessing fitness to be interviewed.

(3) Issues arising from instructions received:
- admissions of guilt;
- suspicion of guilt;
- inconsistent instructions;
- an intention to mislead the police; and
- an intention to give a false identity.

(4) Conflicts of interests.
(5) Advising the client:
- advice on the legal position;
- the legal consequences of 'silence';
- advice on whether to answer police questions; and
- strategies for avoiding or minimising inferences.

(6) The relevance of previous misconduct.
(7) Preparing the client for the police interview.

The lawyer's role

5.3 Whether or not the client has been in police custody before, they are likely to be in a vulnerable state of mind, perhaps through fear or anxiety, or simply because they want to get out of the police station as soon as possible. In either case, the client may be less coherent than usual and is likely to be susceptible to pressure. Such considerations make it important for the lawyer to be absolutely clear about their role, sympathetic to the plight of their client, careful not to impose their views on the client, and willing to take appropriate action to ensure that the client's wishes and decisions are respected.

5.4 Although giving advice will sometimes simply involve the giving of information or outlining options, this will often be insufficient. The client may need careful guidance through the range of options open to them and sometimes may be unable to decide which option to follow. On occasions this will be directly expressed by the client in the form of a question to the lawyer such as, 'Well, what would you do?'. Strictly speaking, decisions should be made by the client, but it must be recognised that sometimes decisions are, in effect, made by the lawyer, whether directly or as a result of the way in which the options are presented to the client. Such a role places great responsibility on the lawyer, particularly where there is more than one appropriate course of action. Two things should be considered. First, having made clear to the client the possible consequences flowing from a particular decision, the lawyer may wish to write them down and ask the client to sign the record acknowledging that the consequences have been explained. Second, where the suspect is heavily reliant on the lawyer for advice to the point where the lawyer is making a decision, again this should be committed to writing and suitably endorsed by the client. In any event, the lawyer should make a careful note of the advice given and the reasons for that advice. This is especially important where the advice of the lawyer and/or the decision of the client may lead to a court considering whether to draw inferences under the Criminal Justice and Public Order Act (CJPOA) 1994. In recording the reasons for advice, the lawyer should be careful to note relevant factors such as the extent of the information disclosed by the police, the view taken by the lawyer of that information, and any factors affecting the physical or psychological state of the client.

5.5 Another responsibility resting upon the lawyer is to seek to ensure that any decision of the client is respected by the police. In chapter 7 below it will be seen, for example, that this may well lead to the lawyer intervening during the course of an interview. It may also mean that the lawyer will have to take action outside the context of the interview, particularly if the decision is likely to be unpopular with the police. For example, if the suspect decides that they do not want to give an intimate sample, or does not wish to give a handwriting sample, the lawyer will need to be vigilant to see that this decision is not undermined by the police. Since the lawyer will not be able to remain at the station throughout the period of detention, the suspect must be warned about action the police may take once the lawyer has left the station.

5.6 The lawyer, whether solicitor or representative, also needs to give consideration at this stage to the rules in the Solicitors Regulation Authority (SRA) Code of Conduct.[1] These provide that solicitors must clearly inform clients about their fees and when they are likely to change. If, as is usually the case, the lawyer is acting under the terms of the Legal Aid Agency's (LAA's) Standard Crime Contract (SCC) or is employed by the Public Defender Service (PDS), the issue of costs is usually straightforward since advice and assistance is available free and without reference to financial means to persons arrested and held in custody at a police station and to volunteers.[2] If, however, the lawyer intends to charge on a private basis, the lawyer should discuss with the client whether they may be eligible for legal aid and should apply for it, and must also give a clear

1 Available at: www.sra.org.uk/solicitors/standards-regulations/code-conduct-solicitors.

2 See para 1.54 above, and note the limitations imposed by the Criminal Defence Direct Scheme (at para 1.55 above) and the sufficient benefit rule (at para 1.57 above).

indication of fees and other charges. The SRA Code of Conduct also requires solicitors to inform clients in writing of the system for dealing with complaints. A suspect at a police station is not likely to be too concerned about the lawyer's complaints system, and it would be sufficient to give information about the complaints handling procedure in a letter to the client following charge and/or release.

Initial consultation

Overview

5.7 The initial consultation with the client is important for a number of reasons. It will present the lawyer with the opportunity to provide support and reassurance to the client, and to instil confidence in the lawyer's ability to deal with the case efficiently and effectively. The lawyer must ensure that the consultation is carried out in private (see para 2.146 above). If private facilities are not provided, the lawyer should make representations to a senior officer, and make a note of the details of any obstruction and of any representations made. If private facilities are still not granted, the lawyer should not proceed with the consultation, but should explain the situation to the client and advise them to say nothing until private facilities are provided.

5.8 The lawyer should take appropriate action to ensure their own safety. Enquires should have been made of the custody officer and the officer in the case to check whether there were any risk indicators of this kind (see para 4.24 above). If there were, the lawyer should discuss with the custody officer what action should be taken, for example, stationing an officer outside the consultation room. Home Office Circular 034/2007[3] states that lawyers 'should not expose themselves to unnecessary risk simply for the sake of expediency'. It also provides that police cells and secure visits rooms should not be offered for the purpose of a consultation other than as a last resort and provided arrangements are in place to deal with any identified risks that may affect the safety of the lawyer.[4] If necessary, the lawyer should insist on appropriate facilities and arrangements before proceeding with a consultation.

5.9 A suggested structure for the initial consultation is set out in checklist 9. For a checklist of information to be given and obtained, see checklist 10 in appendix 2. Generally, the consultation should be carried out in the order suggested.

3 *Safety of solicitors and accredited and probationary representatives working in custody suites at police stations*, available at: webarchive.nationalarchives.gov.uk/20130315044536/http://www.homeoffice.gov.uk/about-us/corporate-publications-strategy/home-office-circulars/circulars-2007/034-2007.

4 See Home Office Circular 034/2007.

Checklist 9: Structure of initial consultation

1. Explain who you are, your status, the fact that legal advice and assistance is free (or, if acting on a privately funded basis, set out your fees and also explain that free advice is available via the duty solicitor scheme), and how the consultation will be conducted.
2. Seek out any immediate preoccupations or specific needs – for example, medication, food – and take appropriate action.
3. Take client's background details. This may help the client to settle down and develop confidence in you, and enables you to assess the client. However, it may be more appropriate to do this later in the consultation, particularly if the client is known to you.
4. Tell the client what information you have obtained from the police, give an outline of what the prosecution would have to prove (if appropriate) and (where appropriate) an initial indication of the apparent strength of the police case.
5. Take the client's account of the relevant facts, including the circumstances of the arrest, the suspected offence(s) and whether the client has already said anything relevant to the police.
6. Give advice on the client's legal position.
7. Give advice on whether the client should answer questions in the police interview.
8. Give advice (as appropriate) on search, samples, identification procedures, etc.
9. Brief the client on the conduct of the police interview and your role during the interview.
10. Prepare the client for the police interview.

Initial introduction

5.10 On introducing themself, the lawyer should explain their status[5] and reassure the client that anything said is confidential and will not be passed to the police, or anyone else, without the client's permission. This is particularly important in the case of duty solicitors, since some suspects believe that they are associated with the police. In these circumstances, it is advisable to explain that the duty solicitor is a private or public defender service solicitor who happens to be on duty at that time. The lawyer should also make it clear whether they are a solicitor or a representative. There is evidence that some representatives do not do so. This not only amounts to a potential deception upon the client, but may prove counterproductive. One tactic sometimes adopted by the police to try to undermine legal advice that they do not like is to attack the credibility of the lawyer. If the client has been misled into believing that the lawyer is a solicitor, the client may well have their confidence shaken if a police officer points out that the

5 In duty solicitor cases, SCC Specification 2022 para 9.45 (draft SCC Specification 2025 para 9.40) provides that before advice is given, the client must be informed of the status of the duty solicitor or representative.

lawyer is 'only a clerk'. If, however, the lawyer has been clear about their status from the beginning, such a tactic is less likely to succeed.

5.11 The client should be reassured at an early stage that they are covered by the police station legal advice and assistance scheme and that they will not have to pay for work done in relation to detention at the police station (if this is the case). If the lawyer intends to charge privately, they must tell the client that they are entitled to legal aid and must give the client information about costs (see para 5.6 above). Although the Police and Criminal Evidence Act 1984 (PACE) Codes of Practice C, H and I provide that detained persons must be informed by the police that legal advice is free (Codes C and H para 3.1; Code I para 3(a)(i)) and this must be confirmed in writing (Codes C and H para 3.2; Code I para 3.1), evidence suggests that some suspects are still not aware that it is free.[6] Under Code C, volunteers should be treated with no less consideration than individuals under arrest and this includes their absolute right to legal advice. This is supported by the National Police Chiefs' Council's *Voluntary Interview Guidance* (July 2024).[7]

5.12 At this stage it may be very difficult to predict the future course of events. The client, however, is likely to want to know when the police are going to interview them, how long they will be in police custody, whether they are likely to be charged, whether they are likely to get bail from the police station or what sort of sentence they might receive. In less serious cases, some of this information may be known with some degree of certainty, and the officer in the case may have already given an indication. In other cases, while the lawyer may have some idea, accurate answers may simply not be possible. The lawyer may feel able to give some indication to the client, but this involves a difficult balancing act. An over-optimistic assessment may well result in a dissatisfied client, but if the lawyer is too pessimistic the client may feel unduly pressured into making unwarranted statements to the police. It will be possible, however, even in this kind of case, for the lawyer to give some useful information such as the likely length of detention without charge and the likely course of events while in police custody.

5.13 One issue that has presented difficulties is whether the lawyer can or should provide the client with any material benefit, such as money or food. The Law Society has stated that making a gift to a person with the intention of persuading them to become or remain a client is a breach of professional standards; and that the only form of gift that is acceptable is refreshments for immediate consumption in the presence of the lawyer.[8] Although this was stated some time ago, the same principles apply today. Refreshments of any sort should not be provided without the prior knowledge and consent of the custody officer.

6 Although the Notice of Right and Entitlements given to detained persons states that advice is free, there is evidence to suggest that many suspects did not understand this in earlier versions of the notice.

7 Available at: https://library.college.police.uk/docs/NPCC/Voluntary-interview-guidance-2024.pdf.

8 See (1994) LS Gaz 22 June p34.

Taking initial instructions

Overview

5.14 In order to advise the client, it is necessary to obtain information from them not only about the alleged offence(s), but also about:

- whether they have made any admissions or a significant statement or silence;
- the circumstances of the arrest; and
- the client's personal circumstances, including the client's criminal history (if any).

See further checklist 10 in appendix 2.

Preliminary matters

5.15 The initial consultation should commence with questions about any immediate preoccupations or worries that the client has (for example, concerns about medication, or who will collect the children from school), since they may prevent the client from paying adequate attention to the process, or from dealing with the situation appropriately. The lawyer should use this initial contact with the client to assess their physical and psychological state and to identify any particular problems, such as literacy difficulties or the effects of alcohol or drugs.[9] The lawyer should expect that this process may take some time, and any pressure from the police to proceed to the police interview quickly should be firmly resisted.

The alleged offence(s)

5.16 After the preliminary matters have been dealt with, the lawyer should tell the client what they have been told about the alleged offence(s) by the police. This helps the client to focus on the information that might be relevant. It often needs to be emphasised to the client, however, that this information may be incomplete and that, of course, it represents only one side of the story. The client can then be asked what they have to say about the allegation. In the first instance, it is usually appropriate to give the client freedom to tell the story in their own words and in terms of what they think is relevant, taking notes of their account. This having been done, the lawyer can then take the client back over the story, exploring in more detail those aspects that are most significant in terms of the elements of the alleged offence, possible defences and potential evidence. It is important at this stage to take a careful note of what the client says.

5.17 The importance of going through this kind of process cannot be overemphasised. The client cannot be expected to know what is legally or evidentially important about the case, but will have their own ideas about what is important. For example, a client arrested for assault may feel considerably aggrieved and may describe their actions as having been in self-

9 For guidance on factors relevant to fitness for interview, see Codes C and H Annex G and Code I Annex F; and for the observation list that the police must use where the suspect's condition causes concern, see Codes C and H Annex H and Code I Annex G.

defence. A more careful examination may show that while they were provoked, the provocation fell short of that which is required for the defence of self-defence to be successful. Furthermore, since explaining an event often involves a degree of interpretation of what happened and what the client felt during an event that may have only taken a few seconds or minutes, the way that the client explains what happened may determine the whole course of subsequent events and, most importantly, whether they are charged and subsequently convicted. In many cases, evidence of an offence is not simply 'out there' waiting to be collected. Rather, the police go through a process of constructing a case against the suspect, and the police interview is part of that 'construction' process. For this reason, the police interview may be crucial in determining not simply whether the client is ultimately found guilty, but in creating evidence that might not otherwise have existed. For example, suppose a person is found in possession of a baseball bat and is arrested for the offence of having an offensive weapon in a public place. A baseball bat is not offensive per se, but may be an offensive weapon if the person intended to use it for the purpose of causing injury. Therefore, whether an offence has been committed will depend on the person's state of mind, the primary evidence of which is likely to be what they say their intention was. If the person is asked whether they would have used it to defend themself if attacked, and the answer is in the affirmative, they have helped 'construct' the case against them. In such a case, the client will need to be closely questioned by the lawyer about their state of mind, and possible intentions, so that they can be advised about whether to answer questions in the police interview.

5.18 In seeking information about the alleged offence from the client, the lawyer must have in mind the key elements of the offence concerned. The identity of the offender, whether the physical acts involved in the offence were performed, and the necessary 'mental elements' are all relevant here and the lawyer needs to find out what the client has to say about them. Issues that may be relevant, such as self-defence, provocation and alibi, must also be explored. Similarly, the client may have knowledge of the potential evidence. Were there any witnesses, who were they and what connection do they have with the client or the victim? Are there any reasons why the evidence is likely to be unreliable or less convincing than it might otherwise seem? It is for the lawyer to pursue these issues, since the client may simply be unaware of their significance.

Admissions, statements or silence

5.19 Having explored the allegation with the client, the lawyer should ask them whether they have said anything of relevance to the police and, if so, what they said, from the time of their first contact with the police. The lawyer may have been told by the police that admissions or damaging statements have already been made and, if so, the lawyer will need to ask the client about them. If the police have not disclosed such information, the client should always be asked, and it is often helpful specifically to tell them that anything they have said may potentially be used in evidence. There is nothing worse than being told by a client that they had nothing to do with the offence and advising them to answer questions, only to find in interview that the police say that the client admitted the offence in the police car on the way to the station. Therefore, the client must be asked whether they remember saying anything to the police at any stage that might have a bearing on the question of guilt. Since any significant 'silence' (as well as statements) should be put to the client at the beginning of the police interview, and may lead to adverse inferences being drawn at trial, the client should also be asked whether any questions have been put to them by police officers (and possibly others, such as store detectives) and what, if any, reply they gave. In addition, the lawyer should check with the client what was found in their possession, either at the time of arrest or when booked in at the police station. If a search of property has been conducted, it is important to establish whether the client was made aware of anything being found during the search; and whether the client made any comments during the search, especially any comments that identify the owner of any property that was found.

Circumstances of the arrest

5.20 The lawyer should seek information from the client about the circumstances of the arrest. In particular, the client should be asked what information the police gave about the grounds and reasons for the arrest, and why arrest was necessary; what (if any) property was found at the time; whether anyone else was arrested; and whether there was any struggle or argument then or subsequently. The latter will be significant because it may determine the police attitude to the client, and may also lead the police to re-arrest and/or charge them in relation to the incident. Furthermore, in some cases it may not be obvious why the client was arrested, which may indicate the involvement of an informant or some kind of covert police operation. Where relevant, this should be discussed with the client, who should be asked whether they have any knowledge of what led to their arrest.

Client's personal circumstances

5.21 Finally, it is important during the initial consultation to obtain information about the client's personal circumstances, including whether they have previously been arrested for or convicted of an offence. This information is useful since it may give some indication of the client's familiarity with the interview process, which may affect the advice to be given. It may give an indication of whether the client is likely to be questioned about previous convictions in the police interview (see para 5.173 below), and will be relevant to the question of whether an out of court disposal is a realistic possibility if the offence is admitted. It will also give an early indication of whether there are likely to be problems regarding bail if the client is charged.

Assessing fitness to be interviewed

5.22 One objective of the initial consultation with the client is to assess their fitness to be interviewed by the police. The lawyer should have obtained information about the risk assessment that must be carried out by the custody officer and ascertained what action, if any, has been taken in respect of any risk identified (see para 4.24 above). The custody officer, where necessary in consultation with the officer in charge of the investigation and a healthcare professional, must assess whether a detainee is fit to be interviewed before any interview conducted at a police station (Codes C and H para 12.3; Code I para 11.17). According to the codes, fitness for interview involves two distinct sets of risks:

(1) the risk that conducting an interview could significantly harm the detainee's physical or mental state; and
(2) the risk that anything said by the detainee in an interview might be considered unreliable in subsequent court proceedings because of their physical or mental state.

Codes C and H Annex G and Code I Annex F set out guidance on how fitness is to be assessed, and provides that if a healthcare professional is consulted, they should:

- consider the functional ability of the suspect, and not simply give a medical diagnosis;
- advise on the need for an appropriate adult to be present;
- advise on whether re-assessment of fitness for interview will be necessary if the interview lasts beyond a specified time;
- advise on whether a specialist opinion is required; and
- be asked to quantify the risks involved in interviewing.

The circumstances in which a healthcare professional should be called in are set out in Code C paras 9.5–9.8, Code H paras 9.6–9.10 and Code I paras 9.7–9.10. The healthcare professional's determination and any advice or recommendation must be entered in the custody record (Codes C and H Annex G para 7; Code I Annex F para 7).

5.23 It is for the custody officer to decide, having regard to any information from the healthcare professional, whether to allow an interview to proceed, and to decide what safeguards are needed (Codes C and H Annex G para 8; Code I Annex F para 8). The custody officer must not allow a detainee to be interviewed if they consider that it would cause significant harm to the detainee's physical or mental state (Codes C and H para 12.3; Code I para 11.17). Suspects in any of the following categories must not be interviewed unless a superintendent or above considers that delay will lead to the consequences set out in Code C para 11.1(a)–(c), Code H para 11.2(a)–(c) or Code I para 11.1(a)–(c), and is satisfied that the interview would not significantly harm the person's physical or mental state:

(1) a child or person who is mentally disordered or otherwise mentally vulnerable (see chapter 11 below), if an appropriate adult is not present at the interview;
(2) any other person who at the time of the interview appears unable to:
   a) appreciate the significance of questions and their answers; or
   b) understand what is happening because of the effects of drink, drugs or any illness, ailment or condition;
(3) a person whom the custody officer has decided requires an interpreter, if an interpreter has not been arranged (Code C paras 11.18 and 12.3; Code H paras 11.11 and 12.3; Code I paras 11.12 and 12.6).

If a suspect within these categories is interviewed, the interview must cease once sufficient information has been obtained to avert the specified consequences (Code C paras 11.19 and 12.3; Code H paras 11.12 and 12.3; Code I paras 11.12 and 12.6), and a record must be made of the grounds for the decision to interview (Code C paras 11.20 and 12.3; Code H paras 11.13 and 12.3; Code I paras 11.14 and 12.6).

5.24 The lawyer should find out whether their client's fitness to be interviewed has been assessed and, if so, what the result was. However, it is the lawyer's responsibility to make their own assessment of the client's fitness for interview. The lawyer may have concerns about fitness that have not been identified by the custody officer or the healthcare professional. If the police insist on proceeding, the lawyer may wish to advise the client not to answer questions. However, there is a danger that in deciding whether inferences under the CJPOA 1994 can be drawn, a court would prefer the opinion of the healthcare practitioner to that of the lawyer,[10] so the lawyer should consider speaking to the healthcare professional to try to persuade them that the client is not fit to be interviewed. If the healthcare professional is not a doctor, the lawyer should consider asking the custody officer to call one in. If this fails, the lawyer should consider seeking an independent medical opinion. A suspect has a right to be examined by a doctor of their own choice at their expense (Code C para 9.8; Code H para 9.10). For lawyers acting under the SCC, the cost can be claimed under the contract provided it is incurred in the best interests of the client, is reasonably incurred and is reasonable.[11]

5.25 A comprehensive guide to assessment of clients at the police station was set out in *Police station skills for legal advisers: practical reference*.[12] It identified a number of tests that a lawyer can use to assess aspects of a client's condition such as memory, co-ordination and literacy. It also stated that in making an assessment, the lawyer should consider information obtained by:

- asking others who should or could know (for example, custody officer, relatives);
- listening to the way in which the client is talking (for example, slurring speech, talking very quickly or slowly, loss of control);
- finding out details of medication prescribed (whether or not taken);
- visual monitoring of the client (for example, to detect shaking, condition of the eyes, sweating); and
- conducting simple tests (for example, to assess memory, co-ordination, literacy).

To this list should be added:

- asking the client whether they have been taking any non-prescribed drugs and/or alcohol.

The lawyer should also take a careful note of their observations and the information gathered.

10 See *R v Condron* [1997] 1 Cr App R 185, CA.

11 SCC Specification 2022 para 5.38 (draft SCC Specification 2025 para 5.36).

12 E Shepherd, *Police station skills for legal advisers: practical reference* (Law Society, London, 2004) p306. This skills manual is now out of print.

5.26 A suspect who is unfit to be interviewed as a result of the effects of drink or drugs may become fit as the effects wear off. However, depending upon the nature of the disorder or vulnerability, a suspect who is vulnerable as a result of a mental health condition or mental disorder may not become fit for interview, or the risks may be appropriately dealt with by medication or a safeguard such as an appropriate adult. Therefore, the suspect's condition may not provide grounds for delaying an interview provided appropriate safeguards are implemented. If the lawyer believes that their client is or may be vulnerable as a result of a mental health condition or mental disorder but this has not been identified by the police, they should, subject to the instructions of the client, inform the custody officer. If the custody officer has any reason to suspect that a suspect may be vulnerable, in the absence of clear evidence to dispel that suspicion the suspect must be treated as such (Code C para 1.4; Code H para 1.10; Code I para 1.9; and see para 11.80 below).

5.27 A potentially more contentious problem arises if the lawyer believes that the client is not fit to be interviewed for other reasons. The client may be extremely tired, or may be distracted as a result of the arrest and detention, or may be preoccupied by worries such as a sick relative or care of their young child. In each case, the lawyer should seek to deal with the problem, since otherwise the client may be particularly prone to confessing falsely in order to get out of the stressful situation.[13] If the client is tired, the lawyer should direct the custody officer's attention to Code C para 12.2; Code H para 12.2; Code I para 11.16, which provide, subject to exceptions, that in any period of 24 hours the detained person must be allowed a continuous period of eight hours' rest, free from questioning. Although it states that this should usually be at night, it also provides that account must be taken of when the suspect last slept or rested.[14]

5.28 It is also worth noting the provisions for breaks in interview provided by Codes C and H para 12.8 and Code I para 11.22. If the client is suffering from serious stress as a result of the arrest and detention, the lawyer should consider trying to delay a police interview until the client has become calmer. If the police are reluctant to do this, the lawyer should consider advising the client to request a medical examination. If a suspect makes such a request, a healthcare professional must be called as soon as practicable to assess the suspect's clinical needs (Code C para 9.8; Code H para 9.10; Code I para 9.11). If the client is distracted for other reasons, it may be possible for them to be reassured, for example, that their child is being looked after by a person acceptable to them. In some circumstances it may be appropriate to suggest to the police that the client be released (on bail or otherwise) for a short period to enable arrangements to be made.

5.29 The lawyer should also be aware of other difficulties the client might face besides unfitness. The codes require special care to be taken in respect of those who are, or who appear to be, blind or seriously visually handicapped, deaf, unable to read, unable to speak or who have difficulty in

13 See further paras 5.131 and 7.39 below.

14 The custody officer's assessment is crucial. It has been held that the provision does not mean that every overnight detainee must be detained for a minimum of eight hours before interview so that they can rest or sleep (*Beeres v Crown Prosecution Service (West Midlands)* [2014] EWHC 283 (Admin)).

speaking because of a speech impediment (Code C para 1.6; Code H para 1.12; Code I para 1.11; and Codes C and H section 13; Code I section 12). Similarly, special provisions apply if the client has difficulty in speaking or understanding English (Codes C and H section 13; Code I section 12). See further chapter 11 below.

5.30 If the police decide to proceed despite the doubts and representations of the lawyer, the lawyer should consider asking for their representations regarding the condition or circumstances of the client to be entered on the custody record, and to make them again at the commencement of the interview, so that a contemporaneous record of them is made.

Issues arising from the instructions received

Overview

5.31 A number of issues may arise during the initial consultation that will require consideration or action before the police interview:

- admission of guilt;
- suspicion about guilt;
- inconsistent instructions;
- intention to mislead police;
- intention to give a false identity.

For guidance on the potential obligations on the lawyer to disclose information received from a client, especially in respect of terrorism and the proceeds of crime, see para 1.18 above.

Admission of guilt

5.32 The fact that a client tells the lawyer that they committed the offence does not necessarily mean that the client should be advised to answer police questions and admit their guilt. Even if the client is in fact guilty, the police may not have sufficient evidence to charge or successfully prosecute without a confession. This approach is well established, although it has come under concerted attack from both the government and some senior judges, who argue that times have changed and those who are guilty should have to assist the prosecution by admitting their guilt.[15] However, it accords with the privilege against self-incrimination and the presumption of innocence, and these are principles that defence lawyers should seek to uphold.

5.33 The client's belief that they committed an offence does not necessarily mean that they are guilty of it. There is ample evidence that some people confess to crimes they did not commit, and that they do so for a variety of reasons associated with their own circumstances or mental state, or the way in which the police interview them. In one case, for example, a suspect whose memory was adversely affected by drug addiction responded to police suggestions that they had evidence of her guilt by saying that she

15 See, for example, the judgments in *R v Howell* [2003] EWCA Crim 1; *R v Hoare and Pierce* [2004] EWCA Crim 784; and *R v Ferns* [2023] EWCA Crim 647.

must have done it.[16] However, a suspect's belief in their guilt may result from a mistaken understanding of the law. The suspect may, for example, believe that they are guilty of theft because they took something that belonged to another person. The layperson is likely to be unfamiliar with the concept of dishonesty as defined for the purposes of the Theft Act 1968, and be unaware of the requirement that there must be both a dishonest intention and an intention permanently to deprive.

5.34 The lawyer can play a crucial role in preventing false confessions. If the client says that they are guilty, they should be carefully questioned by the lawyer both in order to establish the facts and to establish their understanding of the law. It may then become clear that the client is not guilty or that they have a defence to the allegation, and must be advised accordingly.

Suspicion about guilt

5.35 Whether the client is guilty is for a court, and not the lawyer, to decide. This is not to say that the lawyer may not have very great suspicion of guilt. The instructions given by the client may sound highly improbable, or the client may simply refuse to tell the lawyer anything at all. In either case, the role of the lawyer is to act in the best interests of the client. In the case of instructions that do not appear credible, the lawyer should question the client, perhaps asking the kind of questions that are likely to be asked in the police interview. In the final analysis, the lawyer must advise on the basis of what the client tells them, whatever the lawyer's suspicions. These principles would also apply if the client had previously told the police that they are guilty, provided that the client now tells the lawyer that they are not guilty or gives instructions that indicate that they are not. The client should be advised, in appropriate terms, of the dangers of lying in the police interview. Demonstrable lies can be used to devastating effect by the prosecution at trial, and can also lead to inferences under CJPOA 1994 s34 (see para 5.70 below) and, where relevant, the client should be advised of this.

Inconsistent instructions

5.36 If the lawyer goes through the process of taking instructions as set out para 5.14 above, it may be that the client's story changes in a material way during the course of the consultation. This may be because the client's recollection has genuinely changed or is unclear or, of course, because the client has realised that there are gaps or inconsistencies in their story. The fact of inconsistent instructions is not, in itself, a reason for the lawyer to refuse to act. Only where it is clear that the client is attempting to put forward false evidence should the lawyer stop acting. It will normally be appropriate for the lawyer to question the client closely, but the lawyer must avoid assisting the client in concocting a defence. The lawyer's questions must be directed at establishing the instructions rather than to pointing out weaknesses so that the client can plug the gap.

16 *R v Brady* [2004] EWCA Crim 2230.

Intention to mislead police

5.37 It is a fundamental ethical rule that a lawyer must not, knowingly and actively, assist their client to mislead the police. This rule is derived from a number of sources. First, the SRA Code of Conduct provides that a solicitor acting in litigation must never deceive or knowingly or recklessly mislead the court, or be complicit in allowing the court to be misled.[17] While, at the police station stage, a lawyer may not be involved in deceiving or misleading a court directly, it is likely in many cases that a known deception at this stage would lead to a known deception of a court. In any event, the SRA Code of Conduct is wider than this and includes misleading 'others'. This rule applies as much to representatives as it does to the solicitors that employ them. Second, Criminal Law Act 1967 s4 provides that:

> Where a person has committed a relevant offence, any other person who, knowing or believing him to be guilty of an offence . . . does without lawful authority or reasonable excuse any act with intent to impede his apprehension or prosecution, shall be guilty of an offence.[18]

5.38 A number of practical considerations follow from this ethical rule.

(1) If a client tells the lawyer that they are guilty, or gives instructions that demonstrate their guilt, the lawyer should, subject to the matters considered at para 5.32 above, advise the client of the advantages and disadvantages of admitting guilt in the police interview (see para 5.142 below).

(2) If the client tells the lawyer that they intend to lie to the police, the lawyer should advise the client of the possible adverse consequences of doing so. If the client persists with this stated intention, the lawyer must withdraw. However, in doing so, the lawyer must be careful not to inform the police of the reason for withdrawal, because this would contravene the obligation of client confidentiality.

(3) The lawyer must advise the client on whether they should deal with the police interview by refusing to answer questions. It is perfectly proper for a lawyer to advise a client to make no comment in interview, even if they believe the client to be guilty. However, a further problem may arise here if the client, having accepted the advice not to answer police questions, starts to answer questions in the police interview in a way which the lawyer knows to be untrue. In such circumstances, it would normally be wrong for the lawyer to withdraw immediately, since this would be likely to have the effect of informing the police by implication that the suspect is not telling the truth (which would be a breach of confidence). However, at an appropriate moment, the lawyer should ask for a break in the interview to consult with their client. If the client persists with their false account, then the solicitor should withdraw (as above). A careful note should be taken of the reasons for, and circumstances of, the withdrawal.

17 SRA Code of Conduct para 1.4.

18 A 'relevant offence' is one for which sentence is fixed by law, or which carries at least five years' imprisonment (Criminal Law Act 1967 s4(1A)).

(4) Many lawyers will, at an early stage in the initial interview, advise the client that if they tell the lawyer that they are guilty, the lawyer will not be able to continue to act for them if they subsequently wish to deny the offence to the police. Opinions differ about whether this is appropriate. On the one hand, it is argued that it is a practical strategy designed to enable the lawyer to continue to act. On the other hand, since it may not be so much a statement of fact as an implied encouragement to lie to the lawyer (and, ultimately, to the court), it may be regarded as unethical. The authors favour the latter view and believe that the safer course is to ensure that the client fully understands the duty of confidentiality and the need for the client to be open and frank with their instructions. The professional obligation of the lawyer is to advise and assist the client in the client's best interests, and does not extend to assisting the client to present a false defence.

5.39 The principle of not knowingly misleading the police applies equally to the case of a client who tells the lawyer, or gives instructions that demonstrate, that they are innocent but that they intend to admit guilt to the police. In this case, the client should be informed of the disadvantages of such a course of action (particularly that it will be virtually impossible to convince a court that they are not guilty) and that the client risks prosecution for wasting police time or perverting the course of justice. If the client insists on proceeding on this basis, the lawyer should consider withdrawing, and must do so if they know that the client is admitting guilt in order to protect the person who did commit the offence.

Intention to give a false identity

5.40 A similar problem may arise where the client has given a false name to the police or pretends to be someone else. While it is the case that people can call themselves what they like, the lawyer must consider why the client has given the police a false or different name. If the purpose is to avoid the police finding out that the client has previous convictions or that they are wanted on warrant for another alleged crime, the lawyer must not assist the client in pursuing this deception.[19] The client should be advised of the likelihood of their true identity being established, for example, by fingerprints or other biometric data. The client should also be advised of other possible consequences, such as prosecution for wasting police time or perverting the course of justice.[20] If the client is not willing to disclose their true identity to the police, the lawyer should withdraw, but again must avoid disclosing the reason for withdrawal to the police.

5.41 The lawyer should also be cautious if the client, while not giving a false name, has given a false date of birth or address. The lawyer has to tread a careful path, which may be illustrated in the following way. If, within the knowledge of the lawyer, the client has given a false address for the purpose

19 SRA Code of Conduct para 1.4.

20 In *R v Sookoo* [2002] EWCA Crim 800, the Court of Appeal held that in the absence of aggravating features, giving a false identity to the police should be charged as wasting police time rather than perverting the course of justice, and imposed a three-month custodial sentence.

of supporting a false identity or to avoid their address being searched because there is stolen property there, the lawyer cannot continue to act if the client wishes to persist in the deception. If the client intends to refuse to answer questions about their address, the lawyer can continue to act. However, in practice, if the client has initially given an address to the police and subsequently refuses to answer questions in relation to their address, the police will suspect that it is false. Likewise with a name or date of birth. Thus, in most circumstances, either the client will have to agree to disclose their true name, address and date of birth or the lawyer will have to withdraw.

Conflicts of interests

Principles

5.42 A lawyer owes a number of important duties to a client:

(1) A solicitor must act in the best interests of each client.[21]
(2) A solicitor and their firm must keep the affairs of clients and former clients confidential except where disclosure is permitted or required by law, or by the client or former client.[22]
(3) A solicitor is under a duty (subject to important exceptions) to pass on to their client all relevant information that is relevant to the matter, irrespective of the source of the information.[23]

5.43 A conflict of interests arises whenever a solicitor or firm acts for more than one client in circumstances where one or more of the above duties conflicts with the other(s), or there is a significant risk that they may do so. At the police station, a lawyer must not normally act for two or more clients if there is a conflict, or a significant risk of a conflict, of interests between them.[24] If, having accepted instructions, a conflict arises between two or more clients, the lawyer must normally cease to act for both (all) clients, although they may continue to act for one of them provided that they are not in possession of relevant confidential information concerning the other client(s) which was obtained when acting for them.

Practice

5.44 The above principles can raise considerable practical difficulties when advising at the police station, particularly where more than one client, or potential client, is detained in respect of the same or a related matter. Although a pragmatic solution may often be found, the principles must always be observed. The following factors should be taken into account (and see checklist 11 below):

21 SRA Code of Conduct para 6.2.
22 SRA Code of Conduct para 6.3; and see para 1.16 above.
23 SRA Code of Conduct para 6.4; and see para 4.31 above.
24 SRA Code of Conduct paras 6.1–6.2.

(1) The issue of conflict is for the lawyer to resolve, not the police (see Code C note for guidance (NfG) 6G; Code H NfG 6F; Code I NfG 6G).[25]
(2) Firms must have a system for checking for actual or potential conflicts of interest, preferably one that can be used at short notice.
(3) Where two or more potential clients are arrested in respect of the same, or a connected, matter, the lawyer should always consider the potential for a conflict of interests before seeing the second or subsequent suspect. The risk of a conflict is especially high where the first client implicates the second while denying or minimising their own involvement. Information obtained from the police may also indicate a risk of conflict – for example, where two people have been arrested but the evidence suggests that only one could have been responsible.
(4) In principle, the lawyer is under a duty to provide each client with all relevant information, including what other clients have said. However, the duty of confidentiality always overrides the duty of disclosure.[26] Therefore, disclosure of information obtained from a client to a second or subsequent client would require permission of the client from whom the information had been obtained. The lawyer must approach this with extreme caution even if the first client is willing to give permission, since passing information from one client to another may assist them falsely to put forward the same story to the police. In some circumstances, this could amount to an offence such as that under Criminal Law Act 1967 s4 (see para 5.37 above).
(5) It is quite proper to give a second client relevant information that has been obtained from the police while acting for the first client, including information obtained during a police interview. Again, the lawyer must be alert to the danger of assisting the client to concoct a story. However, in certain, exceptional, circumstances information should not be passed on to the client (see para 4.31 above).
(6) If a conflict, or significant risk of a conflict, becomes apparent after seeing the second or subsequent client, the lawyer must consider whether they should withdraw from both (or all) cases. In the case of an actual conflict, generally the lawyer must withdraw from both (or all) cases. The critical question is whether the obligation to act in a client's best interests can be fulfilled having regard to whether the duty of full disclosure conflicts with the duty of confidentiality. However, if the lawyer concludes early on in an interview with the second client that there is likely to be a conflict, it may well be possible to withdraw from acting for that second client while continuing to act for the first.
(7) If the lawyer does have to withdraw from acting for a client, the duty of confidentiality requires that the lawyer does not disclose the reason for withdrawal either to the police or to another client.

25 In *R (McDonagh) v Chief Constable of Leicestershire* [2013] EWHC 4690 (Admin), the court decided that a refusal by the custody officer to allow a solicitor to consult with suspect 2 before they had interviewed suspect 1 (with the result that the solicitor, who tried to insist on seeing suspect 2, was required to leave the police station), amounted to a breach of the right of suspect 1 to a lawyer.

26 SRA Code of Conduct paras 6.2–6.3.

Checklist 11: Dealing with more than one client in respect of the same or a related offence

Keep a full and accurate note of what is said to the clients, and their responses, and consider asking the clients to endorse the notes.

1 Ask the investigating officer and/or custody officer to provide the name of other individuals under arrest.
2 Take instructions from Client 1 and tell them the names given to you by the investigating officer and/or custody officer. Tell them that you have also been asked to act for one of the other individuals under arrest and ask whether Client 1 is aware of any conflict or potential conflict of interests. If Client 1 says that there is, you cannot act for Client 2, although you should take action to ensure that Client 2 is able to secure access to legal advice.
3 If Client 1 says that they are aware of no conflict or potential conflict, consider for yourself whether the instructions given by Client 1 disclose a conflict or potential conflict, and if you conclude that they do, you cannot act for Client 2.
4 If you are satisfied that there is no conflict or potential conflict, advise Client 1 that if you receive information that is confidential to Client 1 but which is relevant to Client 2, you will have to disclose that information to Client 2, and will seek permission from Client 1 to disclose that information if the situation arises. If Client 1 does not agree to this, you cannot act for Client 2.
5 If Client 1 is content with this approach, see Client 2 and advise them that you are acting for Client 1, and that if there is a conflict or potential conflict of interests, you cannot act for Client 2. Ask Client 2 if they are aware of a conflict or a potential conflict with Client 1. If Client 2 says that there is, tell Client 2 that you cannot act for them, although you can take action to secure legal advice for them.
6 If Client 2 says that they are not aware of a conflict, or potential conflict, inform Client 2 that if they give you any information, or you subsequently receive information, that is relevant to Client 1 you will have to disclose it to Client 1. If Client 2 does not agree to this, you cannot act for Client 2.
7 If Client 2 is content with this, take instructions from Client 2. In view of the danger of concoction, do not give any information to Client 2 that you have obtained from Client 1 before you have taken instructions from them.
8 Consider whether the instructions obtained from Client 2 disclose a conflict or potential conflict of interests. If they do, you cannot continue to act for Client 2, and must also consider whether you can continue to act for Client 1 having regard to the principles set out in paras 5.42 and 5.43 above.
9 Continue to keep the issue of conflict of interests under review, and if a conflict of interests becomes apparent, consider whether you should cease to act for either or both clients.

5.45 A different form of conflict may arise if a client asks the lawyer to pass messages to a third party, either another suspect at the police station or someone outside of the police station. While a lawyer has a duty to act in the best interests of a client, this is obviously constrained by both ethical and legal rules. Many requests from a client detained in a police station to pass a message to someone outside the police station are perfectly legitimate. For example, a client may want a relative to be told about the client's arrest by the lawyer rather than by the police. However, the potential for abuse is self-evident. If the lawyer has any doubts about the purpose of a request, they should either refuse to accept the request or suggest that it only be passed on with the agreement of the custody officer. Lawyers must also be aware of the clear restrictions imposed by the Memorandum of Understanding between the National Police Chiefs' Council and the Law Society.[27]

Advising the client

Overview

5.46 Once the lawyer has taken initial instructions from the client and considered, where relevant, the client's fitness to be interviewed and any actual or potential conflict of interests, the lawyer must consider what advice to give concerning:

- the client's legal position (see para 5.50 below);
- the consequences of lying to the police (see para 5.48 below);
- whether the client should answer police questions (see para 5.105 below) or make a statement (see para 5.152 below);
- the relevance of previous convictions and other forms of misconduct (see para 5.173 below);
- whether to consent to fingerprints and photographs (see paras 6.3 and 6.11 below);
- whether to consent to, or ask for, an identification procedure (see paras 8.24–8.30 below);
- whether to consent to intimate or non-intimate samples (see paras 6.47 and 6.68 below); and
- whether to consent to search of the person (see paras 6.19 and 6.91 below) and property (see para 6.115 below).

5.47 The lawyer should try to ensure that the client understands not only what the advice is, but also the reasons why the advice is given. This is particularly important where the advice suggests a certain course of action as opposed simply to outlining the options open to the client. A careful note

27 National Police Chiefs' Council and The Law Society, *Memorandum of Understanding Electronic Communication Devices being taken into Custody Suites by Solicitors* (July 2025) para 5.1(F), available at: www.npcc.police.uk/SysSiteAssets/media/downloads/publications/publications-log/criminal-justice/2025/mobile-telephones-and-laptops-being-taken-into-custody-suites-by-solicitors-and-their-usage.pdf.

of the advice given, and the reasons for the advice, must be taken.[28] The lawyer should consider whether to ask the client to sign a statement that the client has received and understood the advice. This may be particularly important if the advice is not to answer police questions, or if the client does not want to accept the advice given by the lawyer.

5.48 Where appropriate, it is important that the lawyer explains to the client the possible consequences of lying in a police interview. This, of course, has to be approached with suitable diplomacy, but there are many occasions when the client's version of events sounds inherently improbable or lacks credibility for some other reason (see para 5.37 above). While it would not normally be appropriate for the lawyer to tell the client that they do not believe the client's version of events, it is possible to impress on the client the dangers of not telling the truth without directly indicating that the lawyer thinks the client is lying. Of course, lying will not necessarily have adverse consequences for the client. However, if the client is prosecuted and pleads not guilty and the prosecution is able to establish that the client did lie to the police, or if the defence put forward at trial is significantly different to that put forward in the police interview, this may be used not only to attack the defendant's credibility but also as evidence supportive of guilt. Furthermore, if the defence at trial differs from that put forward to the police, inferences may be drawn under CJPOA 1994 s34 since the defendant will be relying on facts at trial not mentioned to the police on being questioned.[29]

5.49 In order to be able to give effective advice to a client, especially as to what strategy to adopt in the police interview, the lawyer requires a good understanding of the client's legal position, the potential implications of the client's previous misconduct, and the legal consequences of failure to answer questions and, more specifically, the consequences of failure to tell the police about matters that may become relevant at trial. Thus, the remainder of the chapter is structured as follows:

- advising the client on their legal position;
- the legal consequences of 'silence';
- advice on whether to answer police questions;
- strategies to avoid or minimise adverse inferences;

and finally:

- the relevance of previous misconduct; and
- preparing the client for interview.

28 The result of a series of cases addressing the right to silence is that the prosecution is likely to have a wide range of circumstances in which they can seek a section 34 direction, and the onus will increasingly be on the defence to have a complete understanding of the decisions made at the interview stage. More than ever, this will require a clear note to be taken during the attendance for interview, including: the timing and content of pre-interview disclosure; the pre-interview advice; and how the interview developed. See, *R v Oni* [2025] EWCA Crim 12; *R v Green* [2019] EWCA Crim 411; *R v Black* [2020] EWCA Crim 915; and *R v Harewood and Rehman* [2021] EWCA Crim 1936.

29 See *R v Hackett* [2011] EWCA Crim 380; *R v Spottiswood* [2019] EWCA Crim 949; and *R v Bhatti* [2025] EWCA Crim 8 for a consideration of whether a section 34 direction or a *Lucas* direction (see *R v Lucas* [1981] QB 720, CA) would be appropriate.

Advice on the client's legal position

5.50 Before considering and giving advice to the client on what strategy to adopt in relation to the police interview, the lawyer should consider, and advise the client on, their legal position. This involves consideration of:

(1) the offence or offences of which the client is suspected;
(2) any additional offences that may be founded on the facts;
(3) the apparent strength of the evidence in relation to that offence or those offences;
(4) the defences that may be available; and
(5) police powers and the possible outcomes of detention at the police station.

The suspected offence(s)

5.51 The lawyer should consider the offence or offences that the client has been arrested for, and also other offences that may be suggested by the police and/or by the evidence. This involves considering what the prosecution would have to prove, both in terms of the actus reus (the act or omission) and the mens rea (the mental element). The lawyer should be familiar with the elements of the offences that are frequently encountered, but if in any doubt they should check them before giving advice. It is important that the lawyer does not ignore this or guess what the relevant elements of the offence(s) are, since otherwise the advice given may well be incorrect. Establishing the elements of the alleged offence(s) is an essential step before going on to consider the strength of the evidence in respect of those elements.

The strength of the evidence

Overview

5.52 Advising on the strength of the prosecution evidence is often difficult because the lawyer cannot be sure that they have been given full information about the evidence the police have, the police may have exaggerated or minimised it, there is often uncertainty about what other evidence the police are seeking or may obtain, and it may not be possible to predict with any certainty whether the evidence would be admitted by a court. The lawyer should consider the following factors:

(1) What is known about evidence from witnesses – have they been interviewed; has the lawyer seen their witness statements; what is the status of such witnesses (for example, are they likely to be co-defendants)?
(2) What other forms of evidence are there – do the police have evidence resulting from searches or samples, or from speculative searches of fingerprint, DNA and other databases; what evidence do they have from a scene-of-crime investigation; do the police have documentary evidence?
(3) What other evidence is the police likely to seek or obtain in a case of this nature – which witnesses are the police likely to interview; what searches are they likely to conduct; what samples are they likely to take; what other forms of evidence are they likely to seek (for example,

bank records, communication records such as those relating to telephone or computer use); what forensic examinations are they likely to conduct?

(4) What evidence would the lawyer expect in a case of this nature – are the police likely to have relied on information from an informant; are they likely to have conducted some form of surveillance; what kind of police records are likely to exist (for example, crime reports, communications, information from databases)?[30]

(5) Is the evidence likely to be admitted at trial and what is its likely effect?

5.53 Evidential rules that may affect the strength of the police case primarily concern corroboration; competence and compellability; and admissibility. It is often difficult at the police station stage to assess with any certainty how evidential rules will apply to a particular case at the trial stage, but they do need to be considered in formulating advice to be given to the client.

Corroboration

5.54 The general rule is that a defendant can be convicted on the basis of any admissible evidence (for example, a confession) even though it is not corroborated (ie supported) by other evidence, provided that the court is nevertheless satisfied of guilt beyond reasonable doubt. There are a few, relatively unusual, exceptions where a person cannot be convicted in the absence of corroborating evidence.[31] Of more practical importance are cases where the court must be warned of the dangers of convicting a person on the basis of certain evidence that is not supported by other evidence. The most important of these are:

- the evidence of a mental health patient of bad character;[32]
- confessions by mentally handicapped persons made in the absence of an independent person;[33] and
- the evidence of an identification witness.[34]

The requirement that a judge give a corroboration warning in respect of the evidence of an accomplice and the evidence of the complainant of a sexual offence was abolished by CJPOA 1994 s32, but a warning may still be given if the judge concludes that an accomplice may have a motive for falsely incriminating the accused or exaggerating the accused's role in the offence.[35] In any case where the prosecution case is likely to rest wholly or mainly on such evidence, the lawyer must carefully consider whether evid-

30 For official police guidance on the investigation process, see College of Policing, *Authorised Professional Practice: Investigation*, available at: www.app.college.police.uk/app-content/investigations.

31 See, for example, Perjury Act 1911 s13; Road Traffic Regulation Act 1984 s89(2); and Criminal Attempts Act 1981 s2(2)(g).

32 See *R v Spencer* [1987] AC 128, HL.

33 By PACE s77 a judge in a trial on indictment must warn the jury of the special need for caution before convicting a person on the basis of their confession if the case depends wholly or mainly on the confession, the accused is mentally handicapped, and the confession was not made in the presence of an independent person.

34 When the Turnbull guidelines apply. See *R v Turnbull* [1977] QB 224, CA.

35 See *R v Makanjuola* [1995] 1 WLR 1348, CA.

ence derived from the police interview with the suspect might provide the supporting evidence.

Competence and compellability

5.55 Some potential witnesses are not able to give evidence for the prosecution (ie they are not competent), and others may be competent but cannot be required to give evidence for the prosecution (ie they are not compellable). A co-defendant is not competent to give evidence for the prosecution unless they cease to be a co-defendant for these purposes, usually by the prosecution deciding not to proceed against them, by securing separate trials or by the co-defendant pleading guilty before the trial. Note, however, that a co-defendant can give evidence on their own behalf that may implicate the client. Other witnesses who may not be competent to give evidence are those who are mentally ill and very young children. The most important example of a competent witness who nevertheless cannot be compelled to give evidence for the prosecution is the defendant's spouse or civil partner. However, the spouse or civil partner is compellable where the defendant is accused of assault on or injury or threat of injury to the spouse or civil partner, or assault or a sexual offence on a person under 16 years.[36]

5.56 Therefore, if significant evidence is likely to come from a witness who is not, or may not be, competent or compellable, refusal to answer police questions may be appropriate at this stage. This may also be the case if, despite the witness being technically competent and compellable, they are likely to be reluctant or unwilling to give evidence despite any adverse consequences; for example, close friends or relatives of the accused, and members of certain religious sects.

Rules on admissibility

5.57 Certain evidence may not be admissible at trial:

- The admissibility of evidence of the defendant's own confession or admissions is discussed at para 4.38 above and paras 13.25 and 13.33 below.
- Evidence of a confession by a co-suspect that implicates the defendant is normally not admissible against the latter (see para 4.35 above).
- The admissibility of identification evidence is dealt with in chapter 8 and para 13.41 below.
- The evidential rules concerning previous misconduct are dealt with at para 5.173 below.
- The court has a discretion under PACE s78(1) to exclude any prosecution evidence if it would have such an adverse effect on the fairness of the proceedings that it ought not be admitted (see para 13.33 below).

Available defences

5.58 Defences are broadly of two types:

36 See, in particular, PACE 1984 s80 (spouses and civil partners); and Youth Justice and Criminal Evidence Act (YJCEA) 1999 ss53–56 (other limitations on competence and compellability).

(1) The first type essentially consists of the assertion that the prosecution cannot prove the elements of the offence beyond reasonable doubt. This includes defences that consist of the accused asserting that they were not present at the time of the offence, that identity cannot be established or that they did not have the requisite mens rea (see para 5.51 above).

(2) The second type, often described as positive or assertive defences, are those where the accused claims a defence based upon a common law or statutory rule. An example is the defence of self-defence – the accused accepts that they did assault the complainant but the circumstances were such that this was legally justified (as a result of the rule that permits a person to use reasonable force to defend themself against attack).[37] Generally, the accused bears an evidential burden in respect of an assertive defence. This means that in order to make the defence a live issue at trial, the accused must adduce sufficient evidence to satisfy the judge that it should be treated as a potential defence. Once the accused has done so, the accused must be found not guilty unless the prosecution can disprove the defence beyond reasonable doubt.

5.59 The lawyer must consider what defences may be available to the client. This involves careful consideration of:

- whether there is a specific common law or statutory defence;[38]
- the type and elements of the defence;
- whether there is evidence (or whether evidence is likely to be available) to establish the defence; and
- where the burden of proof lies.

With regard to the latter, the general rule is that the legal (or persuasive) burden of proof rests with the prosecution – in order to secure a conviction, the prosecution must prove beyond reasonable doubt all the elements of the offence and, in effect, disprove the defence. For example, in a prosecution for assault in which the accused satisfied the evidential burden in respect of the defence of self-defence, the prosecution must prove the elements of assault and demonstrate beyond reasonable doubt that the accused did not act in self-defence. If the court concludes that the accused may have acted in self-defence, it must acquit the accused.

5.60 However, there are both common law rules and statutory defences that have the effect of placing the legal burden of proving a defence (on a balance of probabilities) on the accused in the case of certain offences (sometimes described as reverse-onus clauses or defences). In such cases, if the prosecution can prove the elements of the offence beyond reasonable doubt, it will succeed unless the accused can persuade the court that the defence is more likely than not to be true. For example, in a prosecution under Criminal Justice Act (CJA) 1988 s139 (possession of a bladed

37 See, in particular, Criminal Justice and Immigration Act 2008 s76 regarding reasonable force for the purposes of self-defence.

38 Especially in respect of offences with which the lawyer is not familiar. The Court of Appeal has been critical of defence lawyers acting in relation to immigration document offences who have not advised their clients in respect of the statutory defences available. Lawyers must also be aware of circumstances which may engage a modern slavery defence (see para 11.131 below).

article in a public place), if the prosecution can prove beyond reasonable doubt that the accused did have a bladed article in a public place, it will succeed unless the accused can satisfy the court that it was more likely than not that they had a good reason or lawful authority.

5.61 In some cases where the legal burden of proof is apparently imposed on the accused, the courts have concluded, as a result of the Human Rights Act (HRA) 1998 and European Convention on Human Rights (ECHR) Article 6 (right to a fair trial), that it amounts only to an evidential and not a legal burden. Determining where the burden of proof lies may be relevant to the advice to be given on the appropriate strategy to adopt in the police interview, particularly because inferences from silence may be more damaging where a legal burden, as opposed to an evidential burden, of proof is placed on the accused. Some examples of cases where the courts have determined the nature of the burden on the accused are set out below.

(1) Cases where the courts have held that a legal burden on the accused to establish a defence does not infringe ECHR Article 6:
   - Health and Safety at Work etc Act 1974 s40 (proving that it was not reasonably practicable to do more than was in fact done to satisfy the duty of care under sections 3 and 33);[39]
   - CJA 1988 s139 (proving that the accused had a good reason or lawful authority for having a bladed article in a public place);[40]
   - Road Traffic Act (RTA) 1988 s5 (establishing that at the time the accused is alleged to have committed the offence of driving or being in charge of a motor vehicle, there was no likelihood of them driving while the proportion of alcohol in their breath, blood or urine exceeded the prescribed limit);[41]
   - Road Traffic Offenders Act 1988 s15 (proving that the accused had consumed alcohol after the offence and before providing a specimen);[42]
   - Road Traffic Offenders Act 1988 s37(3) (proving that the accused had a provisional licence and that they were driving in accordance with its conditions);[43] and
   - Firearms Act 1982 s1 (proving that the accused did not know or have reason to suspect that an imitation firearm was readily convertible).[44]

(2) Cases where the courts have held that a burden should be treated as an evidential and not legal burden:
   - Terrorism Act (TA) 2000 s11(2) (proving that an organisation that the accused belongs or professes to belong to was not proscribed when they belonged to it and that they had not taken part in its activities while it was proscribed);[45] and

39 *Davies v Health and Safety Executive* [2002] EWCA Crim 2949.

40 *L (A Juvenile) v DPP* [2001] EWHC Admin 882; and *R v Matthews* [2003] EWCA Crim 813.

41 *Parker v DPP* (2001) 165 JP 213, DC; *Sheldrake v DPP* [2004] UKHL 43.

42 *R v Drummond* [2002] EWCA Crim 527.

43 *DPP v Barker* [2004] EWHC 2502 (Admin).

44 *R v Williams* [2012] EWCA Crim 2162.

45 *Sheldrake v DPP sub nom Attorney General's Reference (No 4 of 2004)* [2004] UKHL 43.

- Misuse of Drugs Act 1971 s28(2) and (3)(b)(i) (proving that the accused did not believe, suspect or have reason to suspect that the substance was a controlled drug contrary to section 5(3)).[46]

Powers of the police and possible outcomes

5.62 Depending upon the circumstances, it may be appropriate to consider and to advise the client about:

- the powers that the police have to gather evidence (for example, searches, samples, fingerprints, photographs);
- the powers that the police have to require the disclosure of encryption keys (for example, passwords) under Regulation of Investigatory Powers Act 2000 Part III (see para 6.121 below);
- the length of time the police can detain without charge;
- the powers of the police to detain or release following charge;
- the powers of the police to release, and the likelihood of them releasing, without charge (with or without bail);
- the possibility of diversion from prosecution, such as simple or conditional caution; and
- possible sentences, and possible sentence-discount resulting from an admission.

The lawyer should also consider, where appropriate, asking the police to pursue a particular line of enquiry. Under the Criminal Procedure and Investigations Act (CPIA) 1996 Code of Practice 'the investigator should pursue all reasonable lines of inquiry, whether these point towards or away from the suspect'.[47] Therefore, if the instructions from the client suggest that their case would be assisted if the police pursue particular enquiries, an explicit request to do so should be made. The lawyer should make a careful note of both the request and the police response.[48] The lawyer should also consider whether pre-charge engagement[49] is an appropriate step (see para 10.14 below). Pre-charge engagement may be an appropriate route to explore potential lines of enquiry raised by the defence or the police. The (non-exhaustive) examples of pre-charge engagement include a suspect providing an encryption key (for example, the password for a mobile phone) or identifying potential witnesses. It is possible for pre-charge disclosure to take place to make sure that the process is fair and that the suspect is not misled as to the strength of the prosecution case.

46 *R v Lambert* [2001] UKHL 37.

47 Ministry of Justice, Criminal Procedure and Investigations Act 1996 (section 23(1)): Code of Practice (2015) para 3.5, available at: www.gov.uk/government/uploads/system/uploads/attachment_data/file/447967/code-of-practice-approved.pdf. See also PACE Code G NfG 2B.

48 In *Morris v DPP* [2014] EWHC 105 (Admin), the court accepted that the police were under a duty to contact witnesses identified by the accused, who had been arrested on suspicion of assault and who was asserting self-defence. On the facts, the court did not find the trial to have been unfair, but this underlines the importance of the lawyer, where appropriate, making a specific request that the police should pursue particular enquiries.

49 Attorney General's Guidelines on Disclosure (2024) annex B, available at: www.gov.uk/government/publications/attorney-generals-guidelines-on-disclosure.

The legal consequences of 'silence'

Overview

5.63 Before the CJPOA 1994, the 'right to silence' was regarded as a well-entrenched principle of law, although it was by no means uncontested. Despite the fact that the Royal Commission on Criminal Justice recommended that there be no change to the common law position, believing that the possibility of an increase in the conviction of the guilty was outweighed by the risk of more convictions of the innocent,[50] shortly after its report was published the government announced its intention to 'abolish' the right to silence. Thus, CJPOA 1994 ss34, 36 and 37 came into force on 10 April 1995.[51] These three sections are examined below (see para 5.70 below onwards), but a number of contextual matters should be noted.

5.64 The right to silence was not, strictly, abolished. Silence, or refusal to answer police questions, remains a viable, and indeed, appropriate option in many cases. Rather, the primary issue is the use that the prosecution can make of such silence or refusal at any trial. Additionally, in the absence of information, the police may not pursue lines of enquiry which would otherwise have been pursued.[52] Furthermore, a defendant cannot be convicted (or have a case to answer, or have a case transferred to the Crown Court) solely on the basis of an inference drawn from silence.[53] There must be some other evidence tending to show that the person is guilty.

5.65 Quite separately from the CJPOA 1994, there are a number of statutory and other obligations on persons to provide information or otherwise co-operate in connection with the investigation of crime, in respect of which failure or refusal may amount to an offence or have other adverse consequences. These include the following.

(1) Refusal to give an intimate sample may result in adverse inferences (see para 6.50 below).
(2) Failure to submit to a drugs test may amount to an offence (see para 6.83 below).
(3) In some circumstances, failure to provide information is a criminal offence. YJCEA 1999 s59 and Sch 3 prohibit the use of information obtained as a result of compulsory disclosure under a number of statutory powers, mostly concerning financial investigations, as evidence against the person from whom it was obtained.[54] However, the

50 *Report of the Royal Commission on Criminal Justice* (1993) p54, available at: www.gov.uk/government/publications/report-of-the-royal-commission-on-criminal-justice.

51 CJPOA 1994 s35 also enables a court to draw inferences from the failure of a defendant to give evidence at their trial, but is not dealt with further here. The provisions are applied to courts martial and other related proceedings by CJPOA 1994 s39 and the Criminal Justice and Public Order Act 1994 (Application to the Armed Forces) Order 2009 SI No 990.

52 See, *R (Damji) v Crown Court at Wood Green* [2025] EWHC 258 (Admin), where it was held that the suspect's prepared statement was insufficiently detailed to require the police to have taken step to obtain and disclose IP addresses, etc until the point when further detail was given via the defence statement.

53 See CJPOA 1994 s38(3).

54 Insolvency Act 1986; Company Directors Disqualification Act 1986; Building Societies Act 1986; Criminal Justice Act 1987; Companies Act 1989; Friendly Societies Act 1992; Theft Act 1968.

evidential use of information obtained from some forms of compulsory questioning has not been treated as breaching ECHR Article 6(1). In particular, it has been held that compulsory questioning under RTA 1988 s172, requiring the registered keeper of a motor vehicle to supply information identifying the driver of a vehicle, does not breach Article 6(1).[55]

(4) The Proceeds of Crime Act (POCA) 2002 imposes potentially extensive obligations to disclose to the authorities knowledge or suspicion that a person is in some way dealing with criminal property, and failure to do so may amount to a criminal offence (see para 1.20 above).

5.66 The common law position continues to apply where the statutory provisions do not apply or the conditions for drawing inferences are not satisfied, for example, where questioning was not conducted under caution (see para 5.76 below).[56] The common law position generally is that failure or refusal to answer questions does not amount to evidence against the person concerned, unless it can be said that the defendant was on 'equal terms' with the questioner. Therefore, where the CJPOA 1994 conditions are not satisfied, failure to answer questions put by a police officer, or someone in a similar position, is unlikely to lead to adverse inferences being drawn at any trial.[57] However, failure to answer some questions where other questions are answered can have an adverse effect on the defendant at trial. In some situations, the questions not answered should be edited out so that the jury or magistrates do not hear them. However, this will not always achieve the desired result. Although a jury should be told that in circumstances where CJPOA 1994 ss34, 36 and 37 do not apply a suspect need not answer questions, a jury or bench is likely to make its own judgment about why certain questions have not been answered.[58]

5.67 The European Court of Human Rights (ECtHR) has held that CJPOA 1994 s34 does not, per se, contravene ECHR Article 6(1). In *Condron v UK*,[59] the court held that while it would be incompatible with Article 6 to base a conviction solely or mainly on the accused's silence, silence could be taken into account in assessing the persuasiveness of the prosecution evidence where the situation clearly called for an explanation from the accused. While the courts must be cautious in invoking silence against the accused, whether it breaches Article 6 depends upon the circumstances, having regard to:

55 See *Stott (Procurator Fiscal) and Another v Brown* [2001] 2 All ER 97, PC (Scotland); *DPP v Wilson* [2001] EWHC Admin 198; and *Charlebois v DPP* [2003] EWHC 54 (Admin). In *O'Halloran and Francis v UK* (App Nos 15809/02, 25624/02) [2007] Crim LR 897, the ECtHR confirmed that this did not breach ECHR Art 6(1). See also *R v Hertfordshire CC ex p Green Environmental Industries Ltd* [2000] 2 AC 412, HL, concerning a notice issued under Environmental Protection Act 1990 s71(2).

56 Confirmed in *R v Johnson; R v Hind* [2005] EWCA Crim 971.

57 See, for example, *R v Gilbert* (1978) 66 Cr App R 237, CA; *R v Raviraj* (1987) 85 Cr App R 93, CA; *R v Hubbard* [1991] Crim LR 449, CA; *R v Forbes* [1992] Crim LR 593, CA; and *R v Chandler* [1976] 3 All ER 105, CA.

58 See *R v Mann* (1972) 56 Cr App R 750, CA; *R v Henry* [1990] Crim LR 574, CA; and *R v Welch* [1992] Crim LR 368, CA.

59 App No 35718/97 (2001) 31 EHRR 1, ECtHR.

- the situations in which an inference can be drawn;
- the weight attached to inferences by the court in its assessment of the evidence; and
- the degree of compulsion inherent in the situation.

The fact that the accused was advised by a lawyer to remain silent must be given appropriate weight by the court, but it does not prevent inferences from being drawn (see further para 5.99 below).[60]

5.68 Different courts and judges have drawn very different conclusions as to the purpose of the silence provisions in the CJPOA 1994 which, in addition to the differing reactions of juries and magistrates, make it difficult to predict with any degree of accuracy whether, and what, inferences will be drawn. One line of cases, exemplified by *R v Howell*[61] and *R v Hoare and Pierce*,[62] reflects the view that suspects are under an obligation to put forward their defence from the time of their first interview following arrest, and that the silence provisions are designed to enforce this. Thus Auld LJ said in *Hoare and Pierce*:

> [CJPOA 1994 s34] is concerned with flushing out innocence at an early stage or supporting other evidence of guilt at a later stage, not simply with whether a guilty defendant is entitled, or genuinely or reasonably believes that he is entitled, to rely on legal rights of which his solicitor has advised him.[63]

Another line of cases, of which *R v Brizzalari*[64] and *R v Beckles*[65] are leading examples, view the silence provisions as being directed at non-disclosure of positive defences and ambush defences. In *Brizzalari*, Hedley J, giving the judgment for the court, said:

> . . . the mischief at which [CJPOA 1994 s34] was primarily directed was the positive defence following a 'no comment' interview and/or the 'ambush' defence . . . [and] we would counsel against the further complicating of trials and summings-up by invoking this statute unless the merits of the individual case require that it should be done.[66]

In *Beckles*, Woolf LCJ doubted whether the silence provisions should have been invoked in circumstances where the accused had told the police the substance of his defence on being arrested. He went on to say:

> This last point, coupled with the fact that he had made it clear that he was prepared to give evidence as to the advice he had received (albeit that this was not pursued by the advocates), suggest that a [CJPOA 1994] section 34 direction may not have been appropriate in this case at all, because the evidence before the jury was consistent with the Appellant having acted genuinely on the advice of his solicitor. His being silent could not result in the prosecution being ambushed or taken by surprise.[67]

60 See also the ECtHR cases of *Murray v UK* (App No 18731/91) (1996) 22 EHRR 29; *Averill v UK* (App No 36408/97) (2001) 31 EHRR 36; and *Beckles v UK* (App No 44652/98) (2003) 36 EHRR 13. In fact, the Court of Appeal has given little weight to the fact that silence was on legal advice.

61 [2003] EWCA Crim 1.

62 [2004] EWCA Crim 784. See also *R v Essa* [2009] EWCA Crim 43.

63 [2004] EWCA Crim 784 at para 54.

64 [2004] EWCA Crim 310. See also *R v Johnson* [2005] EWCA Crim 3540.

65 [2004] EWCA Crim 2766.

66 [2004] EWCA Crim 310 at para 57.

67 [2004] EWCA Crim 2766 at para 51.

5.69 Finally, inferences cannot be drawn under CJPOA 1994 ss34, 36 and 37 if the accused was at an authorised place of detention[68] at the time of failure to mention facts subsequently relied upon, and they had not been allowed an opportunity to consult a lawyer before being questioned, charged or informed that they may be prosecuted (CJPOA 1994 ss34(2A), 36(4A) and 37(3A)). Therefore, inferences under these provisions cannot be drawn if access to legal advice is delayed under PACE s58(8), TA 2000 Sch 8 para 8 or NSA 2023 Sch 6 para 9, or if a superintendent or above authorises an interview to proceed under PACE Code C para 6.6(b) without the suspect having received legal advice (see paras 2.137 and 2.151 above). In such circumstances, the suspect must be given a different caution which makes no reference to adverse consequences of silence (see Codes C and H Annex C para 2; Code I Annex C para 2). Where the lawyer nominated by the suspect cannot be contacted or refuses to come to the police station, and the suspect refuses the services of a duty solicitor, the prohibition on inferences from failure to mention relevant facts in a subsequent interview does not apply (see Codes C, H and I Annex C). One question arising from these provisions, for which there is no clear answer, is whether the restriction on drawing inferences would apply where, although a lawyer was not present at the interview, the suspect had received legal advice on the telephone. For this reason, as noted in para 3.65 above, it is very important for the lawyer, when giving initial telephone advice, to ensure that the custody officer is aware that they intend to attend the police station in person, and to agree the arrangements for the visit.

Criminal Justice and Public Order Act 1994 s34

Introduction

5.70 CJPOA 1994 s34 is directed at enabling a court to draw inferences where a defendant relies on facts in their defence that they did not tell the police about at the time they were being questioned under caution or charged. It is important to note that it is not silence, or failure to answer a question or questions, per se, that may have adverse consequences.[69] Rather, it is the *failure to mention facts that are subsequently relied on in that person's defence.* This includes facts that a suspect could 'reasonably' be expected to volunteer irrespective of questions asked,[70] particularly when the suspect could be expected to raise the fact having lived through the events.[71] Examples include: if a defendant relies at trial on an alibi defence but did not tell the police about the alibi when being questioned or when charged then, assuming that all of the conditions are satisfied, the court may draw

68 'Authorised place of detention' means a police station or any other place prescribed for the purpose of that provision by order made by the secretary of state (CJPOA 1994 s38(2A)).

69 See *T v DPP* [2007] EWHC 1793 (Admin), in which the magistrates' court wrongly drew inferences from a failure to answer police questions; see also *R v Green* [2019] EWCA Crim 411, which makes it clear that specific questions are not necessary in order to trigger the inference provisions of CJPOA 1994 s34, and raising a defence of self-defence (or defence of another or of property) for the first time at trial will always present a significant risk of adverse inferences.

70 *R v Harewood and Rehman* [2021] EWCA Crim 1936.

71 *R v Black* [2020] EWCA Crim 915.

'proper' inferences from that failure. Inferences also may be drawn even though the defendant answered all questions put to them by the police. This may happen if the defendant lied during the police interview or gave evasive answers.[72] Furthermore, an inference may be permissible where a suspect fails to mention a hypothesis relied upon at trial.[73]

5.71 In order to take proper account of CJPOA 1994 s34 when formulating advice at the police station, it is necessary to be clear about the circumstances in which the section will apply, and its relationship to other relevant aspects of law, especially PACE and the Codes of Practice. CJPOA 1994 s34 enables a court to draw 'proper' inferences where evidence is given that the accused:

- at any time before they were charged with the offence, on being questioned under caution by a constable trying to discover whether or by whom the offence had been committed, failed to mention any fact relied on in their defence in those proceedings; or
- on being charged with the offence or officially informed that they might be prosecuted for it (which includes reporting with a view to prosecution or a caution), failed to mention any such fact, being a fact which in the circumstances existing at the time they could reasonably have been expected to mention (CJPOA 1994 s34(1)).

Inferences cannot be drawn where the accused was at an authorised place of detention (for example, a police station) at the time of the failure to mention facts subsequently relied upon, and they had not been allowed an opportunity to consult a solicitor before being questioned, charged or informed that they may be prosecuted (see para 5.69 above). Where the conditions for drawing inferences are satisfied, inferences may be drawn in deciding whether to transfer a case to the Crown Court, in determining whether there is a case to answer and in determining guilt (CJPOA 1994 s34(2)).[74]

In what circumstances can an inference be drawn?

5.72 An inference from 'silence' under CJPOA 1994 s34 may only be drawn where all of the conditions set out in section 34(1) have been satisfied, as follows (explained below):[75]

- there must be proceedings for an offence;
- the failure to mention facts must occur no later than charge;
- the failure must occur during questions under caution or at charge;
- the questioning must be directed to trying to discover whether or by whom the alleged offence was committed;
- the fact not mentioned is relied on by the defence at trial; and
- the accused could reasonably have been expected to mention the fact.

72 Although in such cases, at trial the judge should normally give a CJPOA 1994 s34 direction or a *Lucas* direction concerning lies, and not both (*R v Rana* [2007] EWCA Crim 2261).

73 See *R v Lewis* [2018] EWCA Crim 1101.

74 Inferences can also be taken into account in deciding whether to grant an application under Crime and Disorder Act (CDA) 1998 Sch 3 para 2 (application to dismiss a charge sent for trial under CDA 1998 s51) (CJPOA 1994 s34(2)(b)).

75 *R v Argent* [1997] 2 Cr App R 27, CA.

There must be proceedings for an offence

5.73 CJPOA 1994 s34 only applies in criminal proceedings. It does not apply, for example, to proceedings for disqualification of a company director.[76]

The failure to mention facts must occur no later than charge

5.74 The failure to mention a fact must occur when the suspect is being questioned under caution or when they are charged or informed that they might be prosecuted. The wording of the section is such that a court could draw an inference from failure to mention a fact on being questioned even though the suspect did subsequently mention it on being charged. This could be important, for example, where a suspect gives a 'no comment' interview but makes, or hands in, a statement at charge. While handing in a statement at that stage may prevent an inference that the defence was fabricated after charge, it may not prevent an inference that the defendant was not prepared at an early stage to subject their defence to scrutiny in a police interview (see further para 5.88 below). Conversely, inferences from failure to mention a relevant fact at the time of charge could be drawn where, for example, a statement is handed in at the beginning of a police interview, but evidence is disclosed by the police during the interview that has not been taken into account in the statement (see para 5.76 below). However, some cases have suggested that inferences should not be drawn where the accused did give information to the police about their defence before being formally interviewed, and before obtaining legal advice, even though they then remained silent in interview.[77]

5.75 Failure to mention a fact after charge cannot lead to inferences being drawn. This would be significant where the relevance of a particular fact (for example, that the suspect was present at a certain place at a particular time) only became apparent after charge.[78] Note, however, that the fact that a person has been charged with one offence does not prevent inferences being drawn from failure to mention a fact in respect of an offence for which the person has not yet been charged.

The failure must occur during questions under caution or at charge

5.76 The failure to mention relevant facts must occur 'on being questioned under caution' (CJPOA 1994 s34(1)(a)) or 'on being charged' (or on officially being informed that the person might be prosecuted) (CJPOA 1994 s34(1)(b)). If a defendant did not mention relevant facts in the police interview, the prosecution is likely to concentrate on inferences under section 34(1)(a). If, on the other hand, the defendant did mention relevant facts during the police interview, there will usually be no conceivable 'proper

76 See *R v Secretary of State for Trade and Industry ex p McCormick* (1998) Times, February 10, CA. See also *Secretary of State for Trade and Industry v Crane and Another* (2001) Times, June 4, ChD.

77 *R v Beckles* [2004] EWCA Crim 2766; and *R v Johnson* [2005] EWCA Crim 3540.

78 See *R v Nickolson* [1999] Crim LR 61, CA, where the defendant did not give an explanation of how the victim's nightdress had come to have a semen stain on it in circumstances where the police had not known, at the time of the police interview, that this was the case, and had therefore not questioned him about it. In order for inferences to be drawn, the prosecution would have to prove that the defendant knew of the relevant facts at the time of interview or charge (*R v MB (Appeal Against Conviction)* [2000] Crim LR 181, CA).

inference' to be drawn from the fact that the defendant did not repeat those facts on being charged. The only exception to this might be where the defendant had not been questioned, where the questioning had been defective in that a caution had not been administered (see below), or where the accused did mention relevant facts in the interview, but the police subsequently made further disclosure. In *R v Dervish*,[79] inferences were drawn under section 34(1)(b) where evidence was disclosed by the police during the interview which had not been taken into account in the statement that the accused had handed in. The court observed that the accused could have made a statement at the time of charge in respect of that information, which would have prevented inferences under this subsection. Alternatively, following further disclosure by the police, a supplementary statement could be handed in by the suspect. Apart from these exceptions, in most circumstances it would be arguable that it would not be reasonable to have expected the defendant to have mentioned relevant facts at the charge stage (see para 5.87 below).

5.77 CJPOA 1994 s34(1)(a) only applies in respect of questioning under caution. Therefore, if no caution is administered, through inadvertence or otherwise, no inference can be drawn from failure to mention a fact in response to such questioning. A number of issues arise in this connection.

(1) **Was the person properly cautioned?** The caution which must normally be given prior to police questioning is (Code C para 10.5; Code H para 10.4; Code I para 10.3.):

> You do not have to say anything. But it may harm your defence if you do not mention when questioned something which you later rely on in Court. Anything you do say may be given in evidence.

The caution on being charged, set out at Code C para 16.2, is almost identical. For the caution to be given where a person is questioned in circumstances where inferences cannot be drawn, see para 5.69 above. Minor variations in the wording of the caution will not constitute a breach provided that the sense of the caution is preserved (Code C para 10.7; Code H para 10.6; Code I para 10.5).[80]

(2) **Should a caution have been administered?** A person must be cautioned, where there are grounds to suspect them of an offence,[81] before any questions are put to them regarding their involvement or suspected involvement in that offence if their answers or silence could be given in evidence in a criminal prosecution (Codes C and H para 10.1; Code I para 10; and see paras 4.39 and 4.44 above). If there is any break in questioning, the interviewing officer must ensure that the person is

79 [2001] EWCA Crim 2789.

80 See *R v Saunders* [1988] Crim LR 521.

81 It can be challenging to identify the precise point at which, on an objective assessment, an officer has sufficient grounds to suspect an individual of committing an offence. See, for example, *R v Shepherd* [2019] EWCA Crim 1062, where the initial questioning (at the scene) was to find out what had happened before the officers had identified Mr Shepherd as a suspect; see also *R v Leivers* [2023] EWCA Crim 1469, where the police's initial questioning (at the scene) was found to have occurred at an '. . . investigative stage, where the police were seeking an understanding of what happened'.

aware that they are still under caution (Code C para 10.8; Code H para 10.7; Code I para 10.6). Furthermore, a person must normally be cautioned on being arrested (Code C para 10.4; Code H para 10.3; Code I para 10.3).

(3) **Did the questioning amount to an interview?** Most questioning in circumstances where a person has been cautioned is likely to constitute an interview (see para 4.39 above).

(4) **Should an interview have been conducted?** Where a decision to arrest a person has been made, the person should not normally be interviewed except at a police station (see para 4.46 above). Evidence of an interview conducted contrary to Code C, H or I may be excluded at trial by virtue of PACE s76 (if it led to a confession) or s78 (if it led to a confession or other evidence the prosecution wishes to use, including inferences from 'silence').[82]

5.78 Any alleged 'significant statement or silence' made before the lawyer reached the police station should be considered in the light of the discussion above. Evidence of such a statement or silence may be excluded at trial if it was obtained in breach of the cautioning or interviewing provisions, and this will therefore affect the advice to be given regarding police interviews at the police station. Alternatively, it could be argued that even if the evidence is not excluded, a defendant could not reasonably be expected to have mentioned a fact in the context of an interview conducted contrary to Code C. See further para 5.87 below.

The questioning must be directed to trying to discover whether or by whom the alleged offence was committed

5.79 Although CJPOA 1994 s34(1)(a) refers to questioning by a constable,[83] section 34 also applies in relation to questioning by other persons charged with the duty of investigating offences or charging offenders (CJPOA 1994 s34(4)). This is the same wording as is used in PACE s67(9), which concerns the application of the Codes of Practice (see paras 1.68–1.71 above). If questioning is carried out by a person charged with the duty of investigating offences or charging offenders and a caution is administered, inferences are possible if the other conditions of section 34 are satisfied. If a caution is not administered, or if the questioning is by a person who does not come within section 34(4), no inferences are possible under section 34, and the common law rules apply (see para 5.66 above).

5.80 In order for the inference provisions of CJPOA 1994 s34(1)(a) to apply, the questioning must be directed at trying to discover whether or by whom the offence had been committed. This has been considered by the Court of Appeal in a number of cases, with differing results. In *R v Pointer*,[84] the

82 See, for example, *R v Weekes* (1993) 97 Cr App R 222, CA; and *R v Oransaye* [1993] Crim LR 772, CA; and see generally paras 13.25 and 13.33 below.

83 'Constable' includes police officers of all ranks, and also includes constables of forces whose powers are limited by reference to their purpose, or their geographical area, such as British Transport Police or Ministry of Defence Police, although probably only when acting within their jurisdiction. A designated civilian officer (see para 2.54 above) is not a constable but, depending on the terms of their designation, may be a person charged with the duty of investigating offences.

84 [1997] Crim LR 676, CA.

police had conducted an undercover operation in which, the prosecution alleged, undercover officers purchased, or tried to purchase, unlawful drugs from the appellant. The court held that since the interviewing officer believed that he had sufficient evidence for a successful prosecution before the interview, he could not have been trying to discover whether or by whom an offence had been committed, and therefore the section 34 conditions had not been satisfied. However, in *R v Elliot*,[85] the court reviewed the authorities and concluded that even where the interviewing officer believed that there was sufficient evidence to justify charging the suspect, Code C paras 11.4 and 16.1 (of the version of Code C applicable at the time) did not prevent the officer from interviewing the suspect since it would give the opportunity for an innocent explanation or a defence to be proffered. For the same reason, the condition that questioning be directed to trying to discover whether or by whom the offence had been committed was satisfied. This interpretation is reinforced by para 11.6 of the current Code C, which permits questioning to continue until the officer in charge of the investigation is satisfied that all the questions they consider relevant to obtaining accurate and reliable information have been put to the suspect.[86] It would seem, therefore, that if the police have already made up their mind to charge the suspect before the interview commences, inferences should not be drawn, but that if they still have an open mind despite the fact that there is sufficient evidence to charge, inferences can be drawn.

The fact not mentioned is relied on by the defence at trial

5.81 According to the Court of Appeal in *R v Argent*,[87] this part of CJPOA 1994 s34(1) involves two questions of fact: (a) Is there some fact which the defendant has relied on in their defence? and (b) Did the defendant fail to mention it when they were being questioned or on being charged?

'Relied on in their defence'

5.82 The lawyer at the police station has to consider what facts are likely to be relevant at trial, and what matters the defendant may seek to rely on. In any particular case, this will depend on what information has been gained from the police and the client (and any other source), the substantive criminal law and any relevant rules of evidence. This is an important task, and one that is not made easier by the elastic interpretation given to the expression 'any fact relied on in his defence' by the Court of Appeal in *Argent*. A 'fact' is not limited to events or acts, but can be an assertion that 'something is actually the case', as where a person accused of conspiracy gives in evidence an explanation for their association with their alleged co-conspirators.[88]

5.83 Clearly, a fact is relied on by the accused if they give or call evidence about that fact. However, it has been held that a defendant may be treated

85 [2002] EWCA Crim 931. See also *R v Hoare and Pierce* [2004] EWCA Crim 784.

86 Note that there is some inconsistency between Code C para 11.6 and para 16.1, and that it may also be arguable that if the custody officer is aware that there is sufficient evidence to charge, continued detention is unlawful. See para 2.64 above and para 10.9 below.

87 [1997] 2 Cr App R 27, CA.

88 *R v Milford* [2001] Crim LR 330, CA.

as having relied on a fact even if they do not give or call evidence. Merely putting the prosecution to proof is unlikely to be treated as relying on a fact, but cross-examination of prosecution witnesses which involves asserting the existence of facts may well be so treated.[89] Offering a hypothesis about facts put in evidence by the prosecution has been held not to amount to relying on a fact,[90] although the Court of Appeal has more recently appeared to have taken a different view[91] (see para 5.70 above). Making a bare admission in cross-examination has been held not to amount to relying on a fact.[92]

5.84 Note that even if an inference cannot be drawn under section 34 because it cannot be said that the defendant relied on a fact, an inference may in some circumstances still be drawn under CJPOA 1994 s36 or 37 (see para 5.90 below).

'Failed to mention any fact'

5.85 Whether a suspect did mention a fact to the police may be disputed, and will be for the court to decide on hearing evidence. It has been suggested that in some circumstances, a police officer might maintain that a suspect had not mentioned a fact when in fact the suspect had done so, since this could lead a court to draw adverse inferences. If the alleged 'silence' occurred before the suspect arrived at the police station, the failure to answer questions would have to be put to the suspect at the beginning of the interview in the police station (see para 5.116 below).

5.86 The courts have accepted that a defendant does mention a fact if they make a statement setting out the fact to the police at the time of questioning or charge.[93] This is also the case if the defendant orally asserts facts to the police in interview but does not answer questions.[94] See further para 5.152 below.

The accused could reasonably have been expected to mention the fact

5.87 CJPOA 1994 s34(1) refers to facts that the defendant could reasonably have been expected to mention in the circumstances existing at the time and, therefore, requires the court to assess reasonableness in the light of those circumstances, rather than with the benefit of hindsight. It would seem that the test of reasonableness is a mixed subjective/objective test. The court must have regard to 'the actual accused with such qualities, apprehensions, knowledge and advice as he is shown to have had at the time',[95] but it is a matter for the jury 'in the exercise of their collective common-sense'.[96] Ultimately, what is reasonable depends upon what is expected of suspects in an adversarial system, and on the purpose of

89 See *R v Bowers* [1998] Crim LR 817, CA; *R v Moshaid* [1998] Crim LR 420, CA; *R v Reader, Connor and Hart* (1998) 7 April (unreported); and *R v Webber* [2004] UKHL 1.

90 *R v Nickolson* [1999] Crim LR 61, CA.

91 See *R v Lewis* [2018] EWCA Crim 1101.

92 See *R v Betts and Hall* [2001] EWCA Crim 224; and *R v Milford* [2001] Crim LR 330, CA.

93 *R v McGarry* [1999] 1 WLR 1500, CA. See also *R v Ali* [2001] EWCA Crim 863 and *R v Knight* [2003] EWCA Crim 1977.

94 *R v Ashton* [2002] EWCA Crim 2782.

95 *R v Argent* [1997] 2 Cr App R 27, CA.

96 *R v Hoare and Pierce* [2004] EWCA Crim 784.

section 34, and as noted at para 5.68 above, the courts have disagreed on this. In this context, there can be no absolute rules about what is, or is not, reasonable, but a number of factors must be taken into account, including the three observations made in the case of *R v Harewood and Rehman*,[97] which were: (1) there is no requirement that the unmentioned fact must be one about which the accused has specifically been asked a question; (2) the test is simply whether the fact is one that the accused could reasonably have been expected to mention; and (3) the circumstances that the jury is to take into account when determining whether the accused could reasonably have been expected to mention the fact in question include the length of the questioning and the relevant significance of the unmentioned fact to any account given in interview. A jury is entitled to infer that if the interview lasted a considerable period, the questions are likely to have descended to a commensurate level of detail. A jury is also entitled to infer that if the accused has provided a prepared statement, questions will, at least in part, have been directed at the contents of that statement.[98]

(1) **Understanding of the caution:** It is unlikely to be reasonable to expect a person to have mentioned a fact if they genuinely could not understand the caution, or any explanation given by the police officer under Code C NfG 10D.[99] If the relevant caution was given in the absence of the lawyer, it is important to find out precisely what the officer did say, whether the officer gave an adequate explanation of its meaning and whether the client understood it. An argument that the defendant did not understand the caution is likely to be unsuccessful if the defendant was in receipt of legal advice at the time. Nevertheless, many suspects, especially those who are vulnerable as a result of a mental health condition or mental disorder, have great difficulty in understanding, or may not be able to understand at all, the meaning and significance of the caution. If the lawyer is concerned that the client does not understand the caution, they should tell the interviewing officer at the commencement of the police interview. This may subsequently help to persuade a court that inferences under CJPOA 1994 s34 should not be drawn.[100]
(2) **Legal advice:** See para 5.99 below.
(3) **Age, health and mental disorder:** In deciding whether it is reasonable for a defendant to have mentioned a fact subsequently relied upon at trial, the court should take account of the age of the defendant, and whether they are vulnerable as a result of a mental health condition or mental disorder, or unable to understand the significance of failure to mention a fact for some other reason, such as substance abuse, bereavement, severe stress, etc. It should be noted that Codes C and H

97 [2021] EWCA Crim 1936.

98 *R v Harewood and Rehman* [2021] EWCA Crim 1936.

99 Which requires the officer giving the caution to explain it in their own words if the suspect does not understand it.

100 Although see *R v V* [2005] EWCA Crim 581, in which it was held that the judge was right to leave inferences to the jury even though the defendant's solicitor gave evidence that he advised silence because he believed that his client was unable to understand the caution, and the defendant gave evidence that he did not understand it.

NfG 11C and Code I NfG 11D state that children and vulnerable people may be particularly prone to providing information that is unreliable, misleading or self-incriminating. By analogy, it could also be argued that they may be particularly prone to failing to recognise that a particular fact is, or may be, relevant to their defence. In *R v Howell*,[101] the court indicated that mental vulnerability, confusion, intoxication and shock could mean that it would not be reasonable to expect the defendant to have mentioned facts, although the fact that they were suffering from the effects of drugs or alcohol has not prevented courts from drawing inferences from silence in a number of cases.[102] It is important in such cases for the lawyer to try to obtain medical evidence at the time of the suspect's unfitness to be interviewed (see para 5.22 above).

(4) **Inadmissible evidence:** It can be argued that it would not be reasonable for a defendant to mention a fact in response to information given, or material provided, by the police that is itself inadmissible. For example, if a suspect is shown, or informed of, a statement of a co-suspect that implicates them, it is arguable that it would not be reasonable to expect them to have mentioned a fact in response since the statement itself would be inadmissible at trial as evidence against them.

(5) **Unfair or unlawful police conduct:** If prosecution evidence (including failure to mention a fact) is obtained as a result of unfair or unlawful police conduct, the defence lawyer should argue for its exclusion at trial under PACE s76 or 78 (see paras 13.25 and 13.33 below). However, even if such evidence is not excluded, it may be argued that it would not be reasonable to expect a defendant to have mentioned a fact in the context of such police behaviour.[103]

(6) **Complexity of the evidence or age of the allegation:** The Court of Appeal has held that a lawyer could be regarded as having a good reason for advising a client not to answer questions where the material in the hands of the police is complex, or relates to incidents so long ago that no sensible immediate response is feasible.[104] It would follow that it would not be reasonable to expect the suspect to mention facts in such circumstances. However, it may become reasonable if the police give the suspect sufficient time or sufficient notice of the allegation to enable a sensible response to be made. Similarly, it may be considered reasonable if the suspect had lived through the events.[105]

(7) **The apparent strength of the police case:** It is arguably not reasonable to expect a suspect to respond to police questioning where the evidence in the hands of the police is so weak as not to deserve an explanation. In *R v Argent*,[106] the trial judge excluded evidence of the first police interview where the defendant had been arrested on the basis of one

101 [2003] EWCA Crim 1.

102 See, for example, *R v Condron* [1997] 1 Cr App R 185, CA; and *R v Kavanagh* (1997) 7 February (unreported).

103 See cases such as *R v Paris, Abdullahi and Miller* (1993) 97 Cr App R 99, CA; and *R v Glaves* [1993] Crim LR 685, CA.

104 *R v Roble* [1997] Crim LR 449, CA. See also *R v Howell* [2003] EWCA Crim 1.

105 *R v Black* [2020] EWCA Crim 915.

106 [1997] Crim LR 346, CA.

anonymous telephone call. The Court of Appeal took the view that the judge had probably gone too far in excluding the evidence for this reason, but it certainly would have been arguable that it would not have been reasonable to expect the suspect to have answered police questions at that stage. Similarly, in *R v McGarry*,[107] where the police had arrested the defendant on a 'fishing expedition', the prosecution did not seek to rely on inferences from his failure to answer police questions, and this was not criticised by either the trial judge or the Court of Appeal. Conversely, if the prosecution evidence is, or is likely to be, strong a court is likely to take the view that this is a situation calling for an explanation from the suspect.[108]

What inferences may be drawn?

5.88 If the conditions for an inference to be drawn are satisfied, a jury must be directed that they must only draw an inference where they are satisfied that the accused had no innocent explanation or none that would stand up to scrutiny.[109] Having decided to draw an inference, the jury or court must decide what inference to draw, and the only guidance from CJPOA 1994 s34 itself is that the inference must be 'proper'. The Judicial College states that possible inferences include:[110]

- the fact now relied on is true but the defendant, for reasons of their own, chose not to reveal it;
- the fact now relied on is irrelevant;
- the fact now relied on is of more recent invention;
- the defendant's present answer to the prosecution case is fabricated; and
- the defendant is guilty.

What inference is drawn is very much dependent on the facts, and on the particular jury (or magistrates or district judge), and it is possible that no inference is drawn even though the conditions for doing so are satisfied.

5.89 The damage that inferences may do to a defence put forward at trial will depend on a number of factors, in particular, the strength of the other evidence presented at trial. Inferences may, of course, be crucial. A defence of self-defence, for example, may be considerably undermined even if the prosecution evidence consists primarily of the evidence of the complainant. It must be remembered, however, that answering police questions may also damage the defence if, for example, alibi witnesses named to the police do not give evidence for the defence or inconsistencies are exploited by the prosecution. See further para 5.105 below.

107 [1998] 3 All ER 805, CA.

108 See, for example, *Condron v UK* (App No 35718/97) (2001) 31 EHRR 1, ECtHR; and *R v Howell* [2003] EWCA Crim 1.

109 *R v Betts and Hall* [2001] EWCA Crim 224; and see Judicial Studies Board, *Crown Court Bench Book: Directing the jury* (London, 2010) p264.

110 Judicial College, *The Crown Court Compendium: Part 1: Jury and trial management and summing up* (2024) 17-1 para 16, available at: www.judiciary.uk/wp-content/uploads/2024/09/Crown-Court-Compendium-Part-I-July-2024.pdf. It must be doubted whether it is legitimate for a direct inference of guilt to be drawn.

Criminal Justice and Public Order Act 1994 ss36 and 37

Overview

5.90 CJPOA 1994 ss36 and 37 enable a court to draw inferences from the failure of a defendant, following their arrest, to account for an object, substance or mark, etc, or to account for their presence at a place at or about the time a crime was committed. In some cases, a defendant may be at risk of inferences under either or both of these sections and under CJPOA 1994 s34. There are many similarities between the three sections, including the fact that inferences cannot be drawn where the accused was at an authorised place of detention when asked to account and had not been given an opportunity to consult a lawyer.[111] Before examining the provisions in detail, it is worth noting the major differences between them.

- Section 34 applies where the suspect has been cautioned, but not necessarily arrested,[112] whereas sections 36 and 37 only apply where the suspect has been arrested.
- Sections 36 and 37 apply whether or not a fact is relied upon in a person's defence, whereas section 34 applies only in respect of failure to mention a fact relied upon in the person's defence.
- Section 34 applies to questioning by police constables and others having a duty to investigate offences or charge offenders, whereas sections 36 and 37 apply only to questions put by police constables, designated civilian investigating officers (see para 2.54 above) and His Majesty's Revenue and Customs (HMRC) officers (sections 36(1), (5) and 37(1), (4)).
- Under sections 36 and 37, inferences may not be drawn unless the constable or officer has explained why the substance, etc, or the presence of the suspect, is attributable to the suspect's participation in the offence (sections 36(1) and 37(1)), and the effect of failure or refusal (sections 36(4) and 37(3)), whereas under section 34 only a caution is required.

Criminal Justice and Public Order Act 1994 s36

The conditions for drawing an inference

5.91 CJPOA 1994 s36(1) provides that a court can draw proper inferences where:

(a) a person is arrested by a constable, and there is–
  (i) on his person; or
  (ii) in or on his clothing or footwear; or
  (iii) otherwise in his possession; or
  (iv) in any place in which he is at the time of his arrest,
  any object, substance or mark, or there is any mark on any such object; and
(b) that or another constable investigating the offence reasonably believes that the presence of the object, substance or mark may be attributable to

111 CJPOA 1994 ss36(4A) and 37(3A); and see para 5.69 above.

112 Although generally, where a person under arrest has been cautioned, they should not normally be interviewed except at a police station. See para 4.46 above.

the participation of the person arrested in the commission of an offence specified by the constable; and

(c) the constable informs the person arrested that he so believes, and requests him to account for the presence of the object, substance or mark; and

(d) the person fails or refuses to do so.

For what purposes can an inference be drawn?

5.92 Inferences under CJPOA 1994 s36 can be drawn for the same purposes as under CJPOA 1994 s34 (see para 5.71 above). However, since the power to draw inferences under section 36 arises where there has been a failure to account (whereas under section 34 it only arises where the defendant has relied on a fact not previously mentioned), it is quite clear that an inference can be drawn in determining whether to commit for trial, and in determining whether the defendant has a case to answer, irrespective of any defence that might be put forward.

In what circumstances can an inference be drawn?

5.93 In addition to the legal advice requirement (see para 5.66 above), an inference from 'silence' under CJPOA 1994 s36 will only be possible where all of the conditions set out in section 36(1) and (4) are satisfied.

(1) **Arrest:** The defendant must have been arrested by a constable (or HMRC officer), although not necessarily for the offence in respect of which the constable has the necessary belief.[113] It is likely that the arrest must be a lawful arrest, so that failing to account following an unlawful arrest should not lead to inferences being drawn (see para 2.11 above).

(2) **Presence of an object, substance or mark:** There must, as a matter of fact rather than belief, be an object, substance or mark on the suspect's person, in or on their clothing, in their possession, or in any place in which they were at the time of arrest. Inferences will not be possible if the object, etc, was found elsewhere.[114] The reference to clothing or footwear in CJPOA 1994 s36(1)(a)(ii) includes its condition as well as any object, substance or mark in or on it (CJPOA 1994 s36(3)).

(3) **Reasonable belief by the constable:** The constable (or designated civilian or HMRC officer) conducting the interview, or another constable investigating the offence, must have a reasonable belief that the presence of the object, etc, may be attributable to the participation of the arrested person in the commission of an offence specified by the constable (not necessarily the offence for which the person was arrested). The term 'reasonable' has, in relation to arrest, been held to require that the officer actually held the requisite belief and that the belief was reasonable according to the standards of the ordinary person (see para 2.15 above). If the prosecution cannot establish that the belief was reasonable, or that the officer specified the relevant offence, inferences could not be drawn under CJPOA 1994 s36.

113 However, in this case if the person is at a police station the person should normally have been re-arrested by virtue of PACE s31 before the request is put to the person.

114 For example, in possession of the complainant. *See R v Abbas and Another* [2010] All ER (D) 79 (Jan).

(4) **Request to account for the presence of the object, etc:** CJPOA 1994 s36(1)(c) requires that the officer informs the arrested person of their relevant belief and requests the suspect to account for the presence of the object, substance or mark. This is supplemented by section 36(4), which provides that inferences cannot be drawn unless the accused was told in ordinary language by the constable when making the request what the effect would be if the accused failed or refused to comply with the request. These requirements are set out in, and extended by, Code C para 10.11 and Code H para 10.10, which provide that, in order for an inference to be drawn, the constable must inform the suspect in ordinary language:
- what offence the constable is investigating;
- what fact the constable is asking the suspect to account for;
- that the constable believes this fact may be due to the suspect taking part in the commission of the offence in question;
- that a court may draw a proper inference if the suspect fails or refuses to account for the fact about which they are being questioned; and
- that a record is being made of the interview and that it may be given in evidence if the suspect is brought to trial.

Unlike with the caution under Code C para 10.5, Code H para 10.4 and Code I para 10.3, there is no set form of words, and it may be relevant to ascertain precisely what was said by the police officer, and whether the client understood what was said to them. Although the CJPOA 1994 does not explicitly provide that section 36 only applies to the situation where a suspect is asked to account in an interview at a police station or other authorised place of detention, this is clearly implied by the first sentence of Code C para 10.10, Code H para 10.9 and Code I para 10.7. The drafting of section 36 means that while the belief as to the relevance of the object, substance or mark etc, may be held either by the officer conducting the interview or another officer, inferences may only be drawn when the request to account is made by the officer who arrested the suspect.

(5) **Failure or refusal to account for the object:** Unlike under CJPOA 1994 s34, there is no reasonableness requirement. Simple failure or refusal to account for the object, etc, reasonable or otherwise, will enable the court to draw inferences.[115] However, the court may take into account the reason for failure or refusal to account in deciding what inference is proper. Whether a person 'refused' to account will usually be a fairly clear-cut question of fact. 'Failure' to account may be more difficult to determine, especially where the suspect has given a partial account, and raises similar issues to those in respect of section 34 (see para 5.87 above). It has been held that the presence of heroin and a substantial amount of money in a safe found at the accused's premises was not 'accounted' for by a bare statement that the accused was a heroin user.[116]

115 Although it can be argued that the approach of the ECtHR to CJPOA 1994 s34 in *Condron v UK* (App No 35718/97) (2001) 31 EHRR 1 would require a court to give due weight to the fact that a failure or refusal to account had been as a result of legal advice.

116 *R v Compton and Others* [2002] EWCA Crim 2835.

What inferences may be drawn?

5.94 If the conditions for an inference to be drawn are satisfied, a jury should be directed that they must only draw an inference where they are satisfied that the accused had no innocent explanation or none that would stand up to scrutiny (see para 5.88 above). As noted above, although there is no reasonableness requirement under section 36, a court should take into account the reasonableness of the failure or refusal to account in deciding what inference is proper. The Judicial College suggests that the normal inference to be drawn is that the explanation provided at trial was made up after the interview and is not true.[117]

Criminal Justice and Public Order Act 1994 s37

The conditions for drawing an inference

5.95 CJPOA 1994 s37(1) provides that a court may draw proper inferences where:

> (a) a person arrested by a constable was found by him at a place at or about the time the offence for which he was arrested is alleged to have been committed; and
> (b) that or another constable investigating the offence reasonably believes that the presence of the person at that place and at that time may be attributable to his participation in the commission of the offence; and
> (c) the constable informs the person that he so believes, and requests him to account for that presence; and
> (d) the person fails or refuses to do so.

For what purpose can an inference be drawn?

5.96 Inferences under CJPOA 1994 s37 can be drawn for the same purposes as under section 36 (see para 5.92 above).

In what circumstances can an inference be drawn?

5.97 In addition to the legal advice requirement (see para 5.66 above), an inference from 'silence' under CJPOA 1994 s37 will only be possible where all of the conditions set out in section 37(1) and (3) are satisfied.

(1) **Arrest:** The condition is the same as for section 36 (see para 5.93), except that under section 37 the arrest must be for the offence in respect of which the suspect is being asked to account.

(2) **At a place at or about the time the offence was committed:** 'Place' is defined to include any building or part of a building, any vehicle, vessel, aircraft or hovercraft, and any other place whatsoever (CJPOA 1994 s38(1)). It is likely that the reference to 'place' is a reference to any place, and not necessarily the place where the alleged offence was committed, provided that the person was found there at or about the time the offence was allegedly committed (and provided the person's presence may be attributable to their participation in the alleged offence (see point (3) below)). The expression 'at or about the time' the offence was committed clearly leaves room for interpretation and will, in part, depend on the circumstances of the alleged offence.

117 Judicial College, *The Crown Court Compendium: Part 1: Jury and trial management and summing up* (2024) 17-2 para 12.

The section refers to a person being found by the constable who arrested the person at the relevant time and place. Therefore, it will not apply where a person is asked to account for their presence at a place where they were seen by some other person (for example, a store detective). However, such a failure to account may come within CJPOA 1994 s34 if the conditions for the drawing of an inference under that section are satisfied. Furthermore, inferences may be drawn at common law from unexplained presence at a particular place at a particular time.[118]

(3) **Reasonable belief by the constable:** The issues are similar to those in respect of CJPOA 1994 s36 (see para 5.93 above), except that the belief must be in relation to the offence for which the person was arrested.
(4) **Request to account for presence, etc:** The issues are similar to those in respect of CJPOA 1994 s36 (see para 5.93 above).
(5) **Failure or refusal to account:** The issues are similar to those in respect of CJPOA 1994 s36 (see para 5.93 above).

What inferences may be drawn?

5.98 The inferences that may be drawn are the same as for CJPOA 1994 s36 (see para 5.94 above).

Legal advice and waiver of privilege

Legal advice

5.99 The mere assertion by the accused that they were advised by their lawyer not to answer questions is unlikely to be sufficient to prevent inferences from being drawn.[119] In *Condron v UK*,[120] the ECtHR treated the presence of a solicitor during the police interview as an important safeguard against any compulsion to speak. It followed that 'the very fact that an accused is advised by his lawyer to maintain his silence must . . . be given appropriate weight by the domestic court', and therefore the jury should not have been left to draw an adverse inference notwithstanding that it may have been satisfied that the explanation given by the accused (that the accused was relying on legal advice) may have been plausible. This was followed by *R v Betts and Hall*,[121] in which the Court of Appeal held that if the fact of legal advice is a plausible reason for not mentioning relevant facts, then inferences must not be drawn.

5.100 However, the argument that inferences should not be drawn where the accused relied on the advice of their lawyer to remain silent presented the courts with a dilemma, summed up by Woolf LCJ in *R v Beckles*:

> Where the reason put forward by a defendant for not answering questions is that he is acting on legal advice, the position is singularly delicate. On the one hand the Courts have not unreasonably wanted to avoid defendants driving a coach and horses through section 34 and by so doing defeating the statutory objective. Such an explanation is very easy for a defendant to

118 See *R v Morgan* [1993] Crim LR 870, CA.
119 *R v Condron* [1997] 1 Cr App R 185, CA; and *R v Argent* [1997] 2 Cr App R 27, CA.
120 App No 35718/97 (2001) 31 EHRR 1, ECtHR.
121 [2001] EWCA Crim 224.

> advance and difficult to investigate because of legal professional privilege. On the other hand, it is of the greatest importance that defendants should be able to be advised by their lawyer without their having to reveal the terms of that advice if they act in accordance with that advice.[122]

In this context, the cases following *R v Betts and Hall* and the Judicial College Crown Court Compendium fail to stress the importance of legal advice in determining whether inferences should be drawn.[123]

5.101 An indication of the approach that will be taken by the courts to a defendant who adduces evidence that the reason why they remained silent, or did not tell the police about facts they relied on at trial, was because of the legal advice they were given, is provided by the Crown Court Compendium, which states that in such circumstances the jury should be directed that:

(1) if they decide that accused was, or may have been, so advised this is an important matter for them to consider but it does not automatically prevent them from drawing any conclusion against them from their silence, because a person who is given legal advice can choose whether to follow it or not and was made aware at the time of the interview that their defence might be harmed if they did not mention facts on which they later relied at trial;
(2) in deciding whether, despite having been advised to remain silent, the accused could reasonably have been expected to mention the facts on which they now rely, they should take account of such things as the accused's age, maturity, the complexity of the facts on which they now rely and any evidence about the reason for the advice being given;
(3) if they find that the accused had a good defence but chose to say nothing on their solicitor's advice, they should not draw any conclusion against the accused; and
(4) if they are sure that the real reason for the accused's silence was that they had no defence to put forward and merely hid behind the legal advice which they had been given, they would be entitled to draw a conclusion against the accused.[124]

Unfortunately, while reflecting relevant case-law, this is both contradictory and confusing. If a jury concludes that an accused has a good defence, then an adverse inference would be irrelevant. On the other hand, while point (4) suggests that a jury should only consider inferences once they have decided that the real reason for silence was that the accused had no defence (which, if followed by the jury would mean, again, that an adverse inference would be irrelevant), the danger is that a jury may infer that the accused had no defence from the evidence that they relied on legal advice.

5.102 The defence lawyer is, therefore, placed in considerable difficulty in formulating advice to a client as to whether or not they should remain

122 [2004] EWCA Crim 2766 at para 43.

123 In *R v Sakyi* [2014] EWCA Crim 1784, the court rejected an analogy put forward by defence counsel that advice from a solicitor should be equated with advice from a doctor. See also *R v Karapetyan* [2013] EWCA Crim 74.

124 Judicial College, *The Crown Court Compendium: Part 1: Jury and trial management and summing up* (2024) 17-1 para 30.

silent. The Court of Appeal has clearly attempted to persuade lawyers that they must only advise silence for reasons that would be approved of by the court.[125] However, the courts have not been entirely consistent in determining what are 'good' reasons for advice and, in any event, the obligation of the lawyer is to advise the client in their best interests, which may well lead to silence being advised for reasons that would not be approved of by a court. Nevertheless, the lawyer must always be clear in their own mind why they are advising a particular course of action, such as silence, and should both explain the rationale to the client and keep a careful record. The client should not be left with the impression that advice to remain silent will necessarily prevent inferences from being drawn.

Waiver of privilege

5.103 As noted above, the lawyer's reasons for advising a client to remain silent may be relevant to the question whether a court should draw inferences from silence. However, if either the accused or their lawyer explains the grounds or reasons for the advice, this is likely to amount to a waiver of privilege. Confidential communications between a lawyer and their client concerning legal advice are usually legally privileged, meaning that neither can be required to disclose to the prosecution, or to the court, the content of those consultations.[126] If privilege is waived, this enables the accused (or their lawyer if they give evidence) to be cross-examined about what was said and this, of course, may be damaging to the interests of the accused. The following principles can be drawn from the relevant cases.

- If the accused simply gives evidence that they were advised to remain silent, this will not amount to a waiver of privilege.[127]
- If the accused, or their lawyer, tells the police during the police interview (or at any other time), or gives evidence of, the grounds or reasons for the advice, this will almost certainly amount to a waiver of privilege.[128] Note that a lawyer's opening statement in a police interview can be adduced in evidence by the prosecution at trial.[129]
- If privilege is waived, the accused (and their lawyer if giving evidence) may be asked what else was said in the consultation, including whether there were any other reasons for advice to remain silent, although this is not necessarily the case.[130]

5.104 Normally, therefore, the solicitor should not tell the police, nor state in the police interview, the reason(s) for advice given to the client. This is the case even if the reasons given for the advice do not refer to anything said by the client to the lawyer. For example, where a lawyer told the police that

125 See, for example, *R v Howell* [2003] EWCA Crim 1; *R v Hoare and Pierce* [2004] EWCA Crim 784.

126 See para 1.16 above and *R v Derby Magistrates' Court ex p B* [1996] AC 487, HL.

127 *R v Condron* [1997] 1 WLR 827, CA.

128 *R v Bowden* [1999] 1 WLR 823, CA; *R v Loizou* [2006] EWCA Crim 1719; *R v Seaton* [2010] EWCA Crim 1980.

129 *R v Fitzgerald* (1998) 6 June (unreported) CA.

130 In *R v Seaton* [2010] EWCA Crim 1980, the court said that waiver may well not open up everything said to cross-examination, and that the test is 'fairness and/or the avoidance of a misleading impression' (at para 43(d)).

he had advised his client not to answer questions because he had not been given sufficient information by the police, and that he understood that there was forensic evidence and possibly relevant CCTV footage, this was held to amount to a waiver of privilege.[131] Although there is no specific authority on the point, it should not amount to a waiver of privilege for the lawyer to tell the police that they have advised their client not to answer questions and, separately and without reference to the advice, to inform them of facts relevant to that decision, for example, a belief on the part of the lawyer that the detention or interview is unlawful or contrary to Code C or H. Similarly, it should not amount to a waiver of privilege if the solicitor advises their client in the police interview not to answer questions, provided that no reference is made to information obtained or advice given during a privileged conversation with the client. Thus, 'I now advise my client not to answer questions because you have given me no disclosure' or 'In view of the lack of disclosure I am unable to advise my client' should not amount to a waiver. On the other hand, saying 'I now advise my client not to answer questions because my client has told me that he does not want to name the person who is in fact responsible for the offence' will amount to a waiver.

Advice on whether to answer police questions

Overview

5.105 Advising a client on whether to answer police questions is normally the most important, and the most difficult, task for the lawyer at the police station. Anything said by a suspect in the context of a police interview at which their lawyer was present will almost certainly be admitted at trial. On the other hand, things that are not said in the interview may, as a result of CJPOA 1994 ss34, 36 and 37, have a critical impact on both the decision whether to initiate criminal proceedings and on the outcome of any trial. Furthermore, the lawyer has to give advice in circumstances where they normally have limited information, and are uncertain about both the possible prosecution evidence and about the position of the client. Providing an account in interview can be considered 'good evidence' of a suspect's ability to participate in the trial process if it demonstrates that they understand the allegation made against them and that they can develop their account when questioned by the police. A coherent account will suggest an ability to engage with a process akin to a trial. In contrast, a written statement prepared by a solicitor may simply show that a suspect was able to give basic instructions in relation to the allegation rather than demonstrating an ability to engage satisfactorily in the trial process.[132]

5.106 Advice should always be given on the basis of a considered balancing of the risks of answering questions set against the risks of not answering questions, having regard to the fact that the burden of proving guilt rests on the prosecution (subject to the exceptions noted at para 5.60 above). The client should, as far as possible, be made aware of the possible benefits and

131 *R v Hall-Chung* [2007] EWCA Crim 3429.

132 *TI v Bromley Youth Court* [2020] EWHC 1204 (Admin).

risks of any course of action considered, but where appropriate the lawyer should give positive advice and, if necessary, in strong terms. Despite the fact that the Court of Appeal has attempted to limit the circumstances in which a lawyer advises a client to remain silent (see para 5.101 above), the lawyer's professional obligation is to advise a client in the client's best interests.

5.107 This is particularly important in the context of CJPOA 1994 ss34, 36 and 37. While a client must be informed of the possible consequences of failure to mention a fact or failure to account, and the fact that legal advice to remain silent will not necessarily prevent inferences from being drawn, the lawyer must seek to minimise any adverse consequences. If the lawyer considers that a particular course of action is in the interests of the client, it is the lawyer's duty to give such advice, and to act in a manner designed both to ensure that any decision of the client is respected and (as far as legitimately possible) that inferences will not be drawn or that they will not be adverse to the client. It is important to recognise that many clients at the police station are not in a position to make a decision without considerable guidance from their lawyer. This may be because of factors such as age, mental capacity or their psychological state, but it may also be because of the pressures resulting from arrest and detention. The lawyer is the legal expert and, as with any professional, should expect to give (and should be expected to give) such guidance and protection.

5.108 In considering, and giving, advice about whether to answer questions in interview, the lawyer should, in particular:

- consider the possible impact of all three sections of the CJPOA 1994 (ie sections 34, 36 and 37) and whether the pre-conditions for drawing inferences are likely to be satisfied;
- consider whether the client has allegedly made a 'significant statement or silence' at any prior time, and what impact this may have (see para 5.116 below);
- remember that one consequence of a client not answering questions in the police interview is that the police may not have sufficient evidence to charge them with any offence;
- consider how to avoid, or minimise, the impact of inferences at trial, including what should be said by the lawyer in any opening statement in the police interview (see paras 5.146–5.172 and 7.47 below); and
- take a careful note of the advice given to the client and the reasons for that advice.

5.109 The major factors, in addition to the possible adverse consequences of 'silence', that should be considered in formulating advice to the client regarding the police interview are set out below:

- the police case;
- the legality of arrest, detention and questioning;
- prior comments and silences of the client;
- the likely fairness of the interview;
- the state of the client;
- the client's case;
- specific reasons for not answering questions; and
- advantages of admitting guilt.

The weight to be attached to each of these factors will vary, depending on the circumstances of the case, and the strategies that may be available to prevent or minimise inferences.

The police case

5.110 Seeking information from the police about the evidence in their possession is dealt with in chapter 4 above. The lawyer must be cautious in making judgments about the police case because it may have been exaggerated or, on the other hand, crucial information may have been withheld (see para 4.60 above).[133]

5.111 The police are only under a limited obligation to provide disclosure prior to interview (see para 4.27 above). In *R v Argent*,[134] the appellant argued that the police had not given the solicitor sufficient information to enable him to advise his client. The police had provided limited disclosure, and the Court of Appeal took the view that the appellant could have given basic information to the police, such as the fact that he had left the scene before the incident occurred and was not involved in any violence, even if he had not received full disclosure from the police. In *R v Howell*,[135] it was held that the fact that the police did not have a written statement from the complainant did not amount to a 'good' reason for advising the client to remain silent. However, in such circumstances the lawyer will need to consider why there is no written statement, and what other evidence has been disclosed. The Court of Appeal also stated in *Howell* that a belief that the complainant may withdraw the complaint was not a 'good' reason for silence. Whether a 'withdrawal' of a complaint will, in practice, prevent a prosecution will depend upon the nature and seriousness of the allegation and the other evidence in the case. In many circumstances, such a belief may justify advice to remain silent, although the suspect must be advised that if the complainant does not withdraw the complaint or the prosecution proceeds on the basis of other evidence, inferences are likely to be drawn.

5.112 The lawyer must carefully consider how far it is appropriate to press the police to supply information about the evidence in advance of the interview. Pressing too hard may result in information being given that would make it difficult to justify the client not answering questions for this reason. However, failure to seek information from the police may result in the interviewing officer responding to an opening statement by an offer of more information. In terms of the impression it may make on a court in considering inferences to be drawn, failure to answer questions following an offer of further information is likely to have an adverse effect on the client's case. In most circumstances, the lawyer should seek as much information as possible from the police.

133 In *R v Farrell* [2004] EWCA Crim 597 it was held that it was not necessarily wrong for the police to hold back information before interviewing a suspect because disclosing it might handicap legitimate police enquiries. However, this must now be considered in the light of the disclosure requirements set out in Code C para 11.1A and NfG 11ZA.

134 [1997] 2 Cr App R 27, CA.

135 [2003] EWCA Crim 1.

5.113 Having assessed the information obtained from the client and the police, and having considered the likely admissibility of the potential evidence (see paras 5.52–5.57 above), the lawyer will be in a position to make a preliminary assessment of the strength or weakness of the police case. Where the evidence of guilt is, or is likely to be, strong, a court is likely to take the view that this is a situation calling for an explanation from the suspect. In such circumstances, adverse inferences flowing from silence may not add very much to the prosecution case, although they are likely to damage a positive defence put forward at trial. Therefore, if the client is to be advised to remain silent in the police interview, the lawyer should consider what strategies might be adopted that would minimise the effect of inferences. In particular, regard should be had to whether there is already sufficient evidence to charge (see para 2.64 above) or whether the interviewing officer believes that there is already sufficient evidence to establish the guilt of the suspect (see para 5.80 above and para 10.9 below), and also whether to make a prepared statement (see para 5.152 below). If the lawyer does succeed in persuading the police not to interview, the lawyer must still consider whether the client should state any facts on being charged to avoid inferences being drawn under CJPOA 1994 s34(1)(b) (see para 5.76 above).

5.114 If the police have disclosed little or no information about the accusation, or it appears uncertain (for example, there is uncertainty about relevant dates or times), or the evidence is weak, answering questions will often be inadvisable (see para 5.87 above) – although given the danger of inferences, the lawyer should consider whether a statement should be handed in. If a prepared statement is to be handed in, it requires careful drafting. To protect against a section 34 direction, a statement must at least set up the line of reasoning upon which a suspect later relies (see para 5.152 below).[136]

Legality of arrest, detention and questioning

5.115 The lawyer should carefully consider the legality of the arrest (see para 2.11 above) and the legality of the detention (see para 2.56 above). If the arrest or detention is unlawful, a court may be persuaded that evidence of the interview should not be admitted (see paras 13.25 and 13.33 below), so that the prosecution would be unable to establish that the accused failed to mention relevant facts, etc. Alternatively, even if the interview is admitted, the court may be persuaded that it would not be reasonable to expect the accused to have mentioned facts on which they rely at trial. Where the lawyer believes that the client's detention is unlawful, but that belief is not subsequently upheld by a court, the fact that advice to remain silent is based upon that belief should be taken into account by the court in determining whether the accused acted reasonably in failing to mention relevant facts, but it does not necessarily render silence reasonable.[137] The lawyer should normally make representations as to the unlawfulness of arrest or detention to the officer in charge of the investigation and/or the custody officer, and should always keep a careful record of the reasoning, repres-

136 *R v Johnson* [2017] EWCA Crim 191.
137 *R v Hoare and Pierce* [2004] EWCA Crim 784.

entations and responses. As noted at para 7.70 below, the police are given a great deal of latitude in determining when interviewing should cease, and it will be difficult to argue that an interview breaches Code C para 11.6, Code H para 11.7 or Code I para 11.6 unless it is clear that the police have decided to charge whatever is said in interview[138] or they have asked all relevant questions of the suspect (see para 5.148 below).

Prior statements and silences of the client

Introduction

5.116 An important consideration in formulating advice concerning the police interview is whether the client has, or is alleged by the police to have, made a significant statement or silence at some prior stage.

- A 'significant statement' is defined by Code C para 11.4A, Code H para 11.5 and Code I para 11.4 as 'one which appears capable of being used in evidence against the suspect, in particular a direct admission of guilt'.[139] It does not include anything said by the suspect as part of the conduct constituting the alleged offence.[140]
- A 'significant silence' is defined as 'a failure or refusal to answer a question or answer satisfactorily when under caution, which might, allowing for the restriction on drawing adverse inferences from silence . . . give rise to an inference under the Criminal Justice and Public Order Act 1994, Part III' (Code C para 11.4A; Code H para 11.5; Code I para 11.4; and see para 5.63 above).

Where there has been a significant statement or silence that occurred in the presence and hearing of a police officer or other police staff before the start of the interview, and which has not been put to the suspect in the course of a previous interview, the interviewing officer must, at the beginning of an interview, ask the suspect whether they confirm or deny the statement or silence and whether they wish to add anything to it (Codes C and H para 11.4; Code I para 11.3). A written record should have been made of any interview, whether or not conducted at a police station (Code C para 11.7(a)).[141] Furthermore, a written record should have been made of any relevant comments made by the suspect outside an interview,

138 In *R v Howell* [2003] EWCA Crim 1, the Court of Appeal said that the fact that the lawyer believed that the suspect would be charged in any event was not a 'good' reason for advice to remain silent. Nevertheless, in practice it may be appropriate for the lawyer to advise silence in such circumstances, but the argument that inferences should not be drawn will be stronger if there is evidence that the police have already decided to charge, for example, a statement to that effect by the officer in the case or the custody officer.

139 Note that an exculpatory statement that could be used at trial to show that the suspect was lying would also amount to a significant statement (*R v Park* (1994) 99 Cr App R 270, CA).

140 For example, as part of conduct amounting to disorderly conduct contrary to Public Order Act 1986 s5 (*DPP v Lawrence* [2007] EWHC 2154 (Admin)).

141 Code H para 11.8 provides that interview records should be made in accordance with the Code of Practice issued under TA 2000 Sch 8 para 3 where the interview takes place at a designated place of detention. Code I para 11.7 provides that interview records should be made in accordance with the Code of Practice issued under NSA 2023 Sch 6 para 3.

solicited or not (Code C para 11.13), although under Code C there is no obligation on an officer to record a significant silence or, as important, the questions that led to the silence. Note that the obligation to put a significant statement or silence to a suspect applies whether it occurred before arrival at the police station or at the police station but outside the context of an interview.

5.117 Where there is an alleged significant statement or silence, the lawyer must consider:

- what comment, if any, the client should make in respect of the significant statement or silence;
- what impact the alleged significant statement or silence has on the decision whether the client should answer questions in the interview; and
- in the case of a significant silence, whether the client should answer any question(s) which allegedly resulted in the silence if they are repeated in the police interview.

To a certain extent, significant statements raise different considerations to significant silences, so they are each dealt with separately below.

Significant statements

5.118 If the client denies having made the alleged statement, they should normally be advised to say so, even if they are not going to answer questions generally in the interview. If a defendant relies at trial on an assertion that they did not make such a statement, a failure to make the denial at this stage would almost certainly lead to adverse inferences being drawn under CJPOA 1994 s34. If the lawyer is concerned that the client would find it difficult to comment on the alleged statement and then remain silent for the rest of the interview, there is no reason why the lawyer should not indicate to the police that the client does not accept that the statement was made, or include a denial in a prepared statement. A comment on an alleged statement or silence would normally be appropriate even if the lawyer believes that it was made in the context of an interview that should not have been conducted (see para 4.46 above), although this should also normally be indicated. If the officer, in accordance with the requirement under Code C para 11.11 or 11.13, asks the client to verify the written record of the alleged statement, an endorsement should be made in similar terms.

5.119 If the statement that is denied was allegedly made in response to a question put by the police officer, the officer may repeat the question in the interview in the hope that, even if evidence of the original question and response is excluded, either the suspect will now answer it or, if not, the court could be asked to draw inferences from failure to do so. Therefore, the client will need advice on how to respond.

5.120 It may help to illustrate this process with an example. Suppose the police allege that, following an arrest for having an offensive weapon in a public place, they asked the suspect in the street why they were carrying the weapon, and that the suspect responded by saying that they had it for protection. In instructions to the lawyer, the suspect denies having said this. The alleged conversation is almost certainly an interview within

Code C para 11.1A and, in view of Code C para 11.1, almost certainly should not have been conducted at that time. Evidence of such an unlawfully conducted interview may be excluded by a court under PACE s78, although since section 78 is discretionary it is possible that the court will not exclude the evidence. It was suggested above that when the conversation is put to the client in interview, their alleged statement should be denied and, normally, the illegality of the interview asserted. This response will, if anything, bolster an argument in court that evidence of the conversation should be excluded. However, if the court does not exclude it, the client can deny having responded in the manner alleged, and will then be able to point to their consistent denial at the interview in the police station. Of course, the interviewing officer could simply repeat the question in the interview, but the officer is likely to do so in any event.

5.121 If the client accepts that they did say what the police allege they said, the first issue to be considered is whether the statement was made in the context of an interview that should not have been conducted (see para 4.46 above). If it was made in that context, it would normally be advisable for the client to make no comment when the significant statement is put to them, but for the lawyer to indicate that they believe the street interview to have been unlawfully conducted. If at trial the court cannot be persuaded to exclude evidence of the street interview, and if the client then relies in their defence on the fact that it was not true, arguably an inference should not be drawn from their failure to mention this in interview since, in view of the lawyer's advice that the street interview was unlawful, it would not be reasonable to expect the defendant to have mentioned it. This is likely to be better than the client, in the police station interview, admitting making the statement but denying its truth, since it would then be more difficult to seek exclusion of the original statement.

5.122 If the statement was not made in the context of an unlawfully conducted interview, a critical factor will be whether the client accepts the statement as being true. If the client accepts that they said it but denies that it was true, it will normally be appropriate to state this, since otherwise it will be difficult to challenge it at trial. If, however, the client admits that they made the statement and accepts that it is true, then clearly the client should not comment upon it unless they intend to admit the offence or wish to argue that the statement is consistent with innocence.

5.123 The impact that the prior statement has on the decision whether to answer questions generally in the police interview will depend, in part, on whether that statement is likely to be admitted in evidence at trial, the nature of the statement and the strength of the other evidence. Certainly, if the prior statement is not likely to be admitted at trial, and there is little or no other evidence, the client should not normally answer questions in interview unless the client wishes to admit the offence.

Significant silences

5.124 A significant silence is likely to be a failure or refusal to answer a specific question or questions put to the client before arriving at the police station or outside the context of the formal police interview. However, Code C para 11.4A, Code H para 11.5 and Code I para 11.4 also include a failure to answer a question satisfactorily. CJPOA 1994 ss36 and 37 refer to failure to 'account' (for an object, substance or mark, or for presence at or about the time of an offence), which could include a failure to answer satisfactorily.[142] However, whether an answer is 'satisfactory' is a matter of degree and perspective, since a satisfactory answer from the defence point of view may not be one that a police officer finds satisfactory. In this case, when the alleged significant silence is put to the suspect in the police interview, the lawyer may wish to point out that they do not regard the answer given as unsatisfactory and therefore that there is no significant silence.

5.125 The potential areas of dispute include both the question(s) put to the client and the client's alleged failure or refusal to answer, or failure to answer satisfactorily. If the client denies that a question (or questions) was put to them, this should normally be asserted by the client, or by the lawyer on the client's behalf, in order to try to avoid adverse inferences at trial. This is the case even if the question should not have been put because it would have amounted to an unlawful interview. However, in such circumstances the lawyer should also consider stating that in their view the interview was unlawful. The officer may, of course, repeat the question in the interview, and the client will require advice on whether to answer it at this stage.

5.126 If the client accepts that they were asked the question, but maintains that they did answer it, whether the client should now assert this will depend on whether the alleged answer was incriminating (which is unlikely, as otherwise the officer would want to use the answer as evidence against the suspect) and whether the conversation amounted to an interview that should not have been conducted by virtue of Code C para 11.1, Code H para 11.2 or Code I para 11.1. As stated at para 5.93 above, most questions consisting of a request to account for a substance, etc, or presence, put following an arrest but before arrival at the police station, will amount to an interview that should not have been conducted at that stage, although there can be circumstances where questions will be considered to be the police seeking an understanding of what happened.[143] The lawyer must also consider whether, if it is a situation where CJPOA 1994 s36 or 37 may apply, the requirements of those sections and the requirements of Code C para 10.11 or Code H para 10.10 have been satisfied (see paras 5.91 and 5.95 above). If the client did answer the question in a way that was, and is, consistent with innocence, it will normally be advisable for them to so assert at this stage, even if the question was originally asked in the context of an unlawfully conducted interview. If the answer was incriminating, clearly it should not now be asserted. If, however, the question was asked in the context of an unlawfully conducted interview or did not comply with the relevant requirements (see above), the lawyer should normally make this clear in order to try to avoid adverse inferences being

142 In *R v Compton* [2002] EWCA Crim 2835 it was held, where the drugs and a large amount of money were found near to the accused, that they were not accounted for by a mere statement by the accused that he was a heroin user.

143 In *R v Leivers* [2023] EWCA Crim 1469, officers arrived at a scene that was 'confused and chaotic'. Their questions to the suspects were at an investigative phase and were an attempt to find out what had happened, and the answers to those un-cautioned questions contained admissions, but were admissible and not in breach of Code C.

drawn from the alleged failure to answer the question.[144] In either case, the client will need advice on how to respond if the question is repeated in the interview.

5.127 If the police version of the question(s) and the failure or refusal to answer is accepted by the client, it must first be considered whether they should now answer the question and explain why it was not answered before. If the client is to answer questions in the police interview, it will normally be advisable for them to comment on and, if possible, explain their previous failure to answer the question in order to try to avoid an adverse inference being drawn from their prior silence. If the conversation amounted to an unlawfully conducted interview or if the relevant requirements were not satisfied (see above), the lawyer should make this clear, in order to try to prevent an adverse inference being drawn from the original failure to answer. If the client is not going to answer questions in the police interview, it will not normally be appropriate to comment on the prior silence. Even if the prior silence was in the context of an unlawfully conducted interview, there is probably little advantage in pointing this out at this stage since it will only put the officer on notice and give the officer a reminder to rectify it in the interview.

Likely fairness of the interview

5.128 Whether the police interview is likely to be conducted in a fair manner may be difficult to judge, but relevant factors will include:

- prior knowledge of the officer(s) who will be interviewing the suspect; and
- the nature and circumstances of the alleged offence.

Certain police officers have a reputation for being aggressive in interview or for resorting to underhand tactics, despite the presence of a lawyer. Experienced lawyers will build up their own knowledge of officers in the police stations with whom they are familiar, and defence lawyers should be encouraged to share this information with each other. Such knowledge of the officers concerned will be a factor to be taken into account, together with the other factors identified. Likewise, the nature and circumstances of the alleged offence may have an impact on the way in which the police interview is likely to be conducted. This will be particularly so if the allegation is of assault on a police officer, or it is a serious offence where the police may be under some pressure to achieve a 'result'. In these circumstances, the lawyer must be careful to avoid undue pressure being placed upon the client, and advising the client not to answer questions may be one way of achieving this. It may also be the case that an interview that starts off being conducted fairly degenerates so that it becomes unfair.

5.129 In such circumstances, the lawyer may consider making a statement such as:

> I am now advising my client not to answer further questions, since your style of interviewing is such that my client is unnecessarily distressed [or] is

144 Although probably only in very general terms, in order not to alert the officer to problems that may be rectified by repeating the question in the proper form in the interview.

> unable properly to explain their position [or] is being intimidated. I want the interview to be halted to enable me to consult with my client in private.

If this is done during the course of the police interview, it should not amount to a waiver of privilege since there is no reference to a privileged conversation (see para 5.103 above). Having made the statement, the lawyer should normally then have a private consultation with the client to explain the reasons for the intervention. On resumption of the interview, the lawyer should then state that they have advised the client not to answer further questions, without giving reasons for that advice.

5.130 Another way in which the interview process might be unfair is if the nature of the questioning is likely to relate to memory of fine detail, particularly where the client has not had an opportunity to refresh their memory, for example, by looking at documents (see para 5.87 above). In these circumstances it may be advisable for the client not to answer questions at least until they have had the opportunity to refresh their memory or to examine the documents concerned. The opening statement in such circumstances should not normally include reasons for the advice, but the lawyer should separately make representations to the officer concerned, for example, that time should be allowed to examine relevant documents.

State of the client

5.131 The question of whether a suspect is fit to be interviewed is dealt with at para 5.22 above. The question here is whether, assuming that they are fit to be interviewed, the client is in a position to be able to deal with the interview either by answering questions or by not doing so. This is very much a matter for the judgment of the lawyer and, where appropriate, should be discussed with the client. Some people would be unable to deal with the pressure inherent in an interview where they are not answering questions. Others might find this relatively easy, whereas they may not be able to answer police questions without becoming belligerent or careless. It is perfectly legitimate for a guilty suspect to refuse to answer questions, and this may be their only option if they wish the lawyer to remain in the interview but have already told the lawyer that they are guilty (see para 5.32 above). Conversely, a client who has asserted their innocence may be best advised not to answer questions if they are likely to become confused or to falsely confess. Although false confessions probably occur more often in the absence of a lawyer, research suggests that certain types of people, or people in certain types of situations, are particularly prone to false confessions.

5.132 The forensic psychologist Gisli Gudjonsson has suggested a number of factors that tend to make a suspect vulnerable to falsely confessing:[145]

- an inability to handle interrogation pressure;
- unfamiliarity with police procedures and the process of detention and interrogation;

145 G Gudjonsson, 'Interrogation and false confessions: vulnerability factors' (1992) 47 *British Journal of Hospital Medicine* 8; and see generally, G Gudjonsson, *The psychology of interrogations and confessions: a handbook* (Wiley, Chichester, 2003).

- specific fears – such as a fear of a police officer, or a fear of being locked up;
- physical discomfort, pain or exhaustion;
- a mental state that interferes with the suspect's ability to make a rational decision, such as extreme anxiety, depression or bereavement;
- a failure to consider seriously enough the long-term consequences of making a false confession;
- a propensity to tell lies to escape from stress;[146]
- an inability to recall events, or lack of confidence in one's ability to do so, which may be specifically related to alcohol or drug abuse, or other interference with the functioning of the brain such as a head injury or emotional trauma;
- an inability to detect discrepancies between what the suspect observed and what they have subsequently been told, whether by the police or others; and
- factors associated with mental states such as severe anxiety or confusion, or feelings of guilt or bereavement.

Furthermore, if the suspect is likely to become aggressive, or overly cynical or sarcastic, the lawyer should remember that at trial this may look or sound like evidence of guilt.

5.133 However, the state of the client and their fitness for interview must be approached with some caution by the lawyer. The Court of Appeal in *R v Argent*[147] said that in considering reasonableness, the circumstances of the suspect must be taken into account (see para 5.87 above). However, in a number of cases, the fact that the suspect was suffering from the effects of drugs was not sufficient to remove the issue of inferences from the jury, particularly where the forensic medical examiner had certified the suspect fit to be interviewed.[148] In formulating advice, the lawyer must consider whether answering questions will present a greater danger than the possibility of inferences. Consideration should also be given to obtaining a second medical opinion (see para 5.24 above).

5.134 Given the dangers of waiver of privilege (see para 5.103 above), it will normally be better not to explain the reasons for the advice given to the client in the opening statement, but to make appropriate representations to the relevant officer outside of the police interview. For example, the lawyer may suggest a postponement of the interview and, if relevant, a temporary release (whether on or without bail), to enable the problem to be sorted out.

The client's case

5.135 Where the instructions obtained from the client and/or the lawyer's assessment of the legal position demonstrate that the client has a defence,

146 In *R v Brine* [1992] Crim LR 122, CA, it was accepted that a confession should have been excluded where a propensity to lie under pressure resulted from mild paranoid psychosis.

147 [1997] 2 Cr App R 27, CA.

148 See *R v Condron* [1997] 1 Cr App R 185, CA; and *R v Kavanagh* (1997) 7 February (unreported).

the lawyer must consider the dangers of not putting it forward in interview, particularly in terms of the potential damage from inferences and the general impact on credibility from failing to put forward a defence at the investigative stage. If putting forward the defence in police interview is appropriate, the lawyer should go on to consider what strategy (for example, answering questions or making a prepared statement) would be most appropriate. See further para 5.146 below.

5.136 If the client has a specific defence, there will be advantages to this being placed on record at an early stage, either in the hope that the police will decide not to prosecute or with a view to strengthening that defence for the purposes of a trial. Furthermore, failure to mention a specific defence at this stage is likely to lead to adverse inferences being drawn if that defence is subsequently relied on at trial. The two most obvious defences in this category are those of alibi and self-defence, but there is a need for caution in respect of both. Potential alibi witnesses have an unfortunate propensity to fail to confirm the suspect's whereabouts at the crucial time, or to be unwilling to become involved at all. The problem in formulating advice is this. On the one hand, it would sound very convincing at trial for the defendant to be able to say that they gave the names and addresses of their alibi witness(es) at the earliest opportunity. On the other hand, if the police do go to see a potential alibi witness while the suspect is still in custody, the witness may very well be unco-operative because of their own view of or relationship with the police, or may simply not support the version of events given by the suspect.

5.137 One possibility is for the lawyer to visit the witness before their details are given to the police. In this case, the lawyer must be careful to find out what the witness has to say, and whether the witness would be willing to confirm this to the police, and at all costs must avoid passing on information that the client has given to the lawyer. Interviewing a witness in these circumstances is not within the scope of police station attendance under the SCC but could be paid for as free-standing legal advice and assistance, provided the witness satisfies the means test.[149] Another possibility is for the client to indicate the fact, and general nature of, the alibi without specifying the detail. This may be done in the form of a written statement rather than by answering questions. However, this may not prevent inferences from being drawn at trial.[150] Alternatively, the lawyer may take a full statement from the client regarding the alibi, and reserve its use for trial should it become necessary (see further para 5.168 below). Note that if the client does answer questions regarding an alibi in the police interview, or a statement is handed to the police outlining the alibi, this could be used against the client if the defence at trial differs.

149 See SCC Specification 2022 para 9.138 (draft SCC Specification 2025 para 9.134), although para 9.141 (draft SCC Specification 2025 para 9.137) provides that advice and assistance to a witness may only be provided under the scheme if there is a complicating factor.

150 In *R v Lewis* [2003] EWCA Crim 223, it was held that the fact that the accused had, in general terms, told the police in his first interview of his alibi of which he gave evidence at trial, did not prevent inferences from being drawn from failure to mention facts in support of the alibi. However, the police had, in a second interview, asked him detailed questions about his alibi and, had they not done so, the court may have taken a different view.

5.138 With regard to the defence of 'self-defence', the client's understanding of it may well be at variance with its legal meaning. Broadly, the force used must be reasonable in the sense that it was proportional to the threat as perceived by the defendant.[151] Although putting the defence forward at the earliest opportunity can be advantageous, the lawyer should gather as much information as possible from the police including, if possible, sight of the witness statements and any CCTV record. The lawyer should also question the client carefully to ensure that their version of events does indeed constitute a legal defence. Advancing self-defence may also confirm the client's presence at a scene or involvement with an incident. If there is serious doubt resulting from lack of information from the police, or from the version of events given by the client, the lawyer may conclude that the possible adverse consequences of an interview in which the client answers police questions may be worse than adverse inferences which may be drawn at trial under CJPOA 1994 s34. This is particularly so given the confusing evidence that often surrounds a fight and the tendency of the police to treat the original complainant as the innocent party. As with an alibi defence, the lawyer should consider what strategy to adopt to try to avoid or minimise adverse inferences (see further para 5.146 below).

5.139 In those cases where the burden of proof in establishing a defence is on the accused (see para 5.60 above), inferences resulting from failure to mention the facts on which the defence is based in the police interview (by answering questions or by making a prepared statement) are likely to be particularly damaging.

5.140 Note that in view of the previous misconduct provisions of the Criminal Justice Act (CJA) 2003, special care is needed in putting forward a defence in the police interview that involves an assertion of good character, or in casting imputations on the character of another person (see para 5.173 below).

Specific reasons for not answering questions

5.141 In addition to the other factors dealt with here, there are some specific reasons why a client may not wish to answer police questions despite being innocent. These include:

- a desire to protect others;
- fear of reprisals; and
- embarrassment about the allegations.

In each case, the client should be advised of the potential adverse consequences of failure to answer questions, which may include a police assumption that the client is guilty, as well as the possibility of adverse inferences being drawn at trial. Nevertheless, the lawyer or, more likely, the client may still believe that answering questions would have worse consequences than not doing so. In these circumstances it may be difficult for the lawyer to protect the client against adverse inferences being drawn. If the lawyer informs the police that they have advised the client not to answer questions because, for example, the fear of reprisals outweighs the danger of inferences, this is likely to amount to a waiver of privilege

151 See Criminal Justice and Immigration Act 2008 s76; and PACE Code G NfG 2A.

(see para 5.99 above). The best course of action may be for a prepared statement to be drafted which is not handed in to the police, although this may not have the effect of preventing inferences from being drawn (see para 5.168 below).

Advantages of admitting guilt

5.142 If, having regard to the relevant law, the client's instructions indicate that they are guilty of the alleged offence(s), the lawyer should consider the strength of the police evidence. A guilty client may feel it important to admit guilt to the police and this is, of course, the client's decision, but the lawyer's function is to advise the client whether from a legal point of view it is in their best interests to do so. If the evidence of the client's guilt is weak or there are particular difficulties of the kind discussed at paras 5.52–5.57 above, the client must be advised that one of the options is to refuse to answer questions and to wait to see whether the prosecution can prove its case. Refusing to answer questions at the police station will not normally irrevocably determine the subsequent course of the client's approach to the case (except that it may prevent an out-of-court disposal), whereas a confession at this stage will make it very difficult, if not impossible, for the client to plead not guilty at trial even if the prosecution case turns out to be weak or seriously flawed.

5.143 If the prosecution evidence does appear to be strong, there may be advantages to the client admitting guilt at the interview. CJA 2003 s144 requires a court to take into account the stage of the proceedings at which an offender indicated their intention to plead guilty and the circumstances in which the indication is given. The sentencing guidelines provide that the maximum discount (of one-third) should normally be given where an accused indicated a guilty plea at the first stage of proceedings, and that the first stage is normally the first hearing at which a plea or indication of plea is sought and recorded.[152] Therefore, indicating a willingness to plead guilty at the police station (rather than at the first court hearing) will make no difference to sentence discount, although an admission of guilt may mitigate the sentence where, for example, it leads to:[153]

- a demonstration of remorse;
- the curtailment of an otherwise lengthy and costly investigation;
- the recovery of property that otherwise would not have been recovered;
- a significant reduction in the risk to, or suffering experienced by, a victim;

152 See Sentencing Guidelines Council, *Reduction in sentence for a guilty plea – first hearing on or after 1 June 2017*, available at: www.sentencingcouncil.org.uk/overarching-guides/magistrates-court/item/reduction-in-sentence-for-a-guilty-plea-first-hearing-on-or-after-1-june-2017. See also the Northern Ireland case of *R v Maughan* [2022] UKSC 13, which held that: '. . . the police investigation by way of questioning is concerned with confirming or dispelling a suspicion that an offence has been committed. The offence which is the subject of proceedings only crystallises at the moment of charge, summons or, unusually, presentation of an indictment, in other words after the police interview.' (para 37).

153 See Sentencing Guidelines Council, *Reduction in sentence for a guilty plea – first hearing on or after 1 June 2017.*

- the arrest of other suspects;
- the release of other persons suspected of the crime;
- the police accepting that the suspect played a minor role in the crime; or
- a charge for a less serious offence than might have been warranted by the circumstances.

Even if one or more of these factors applies, the client should be made aware that the impact on sentence of an admission of guilt is uncertain.

5.144 In addition to the factors relevant to sentence listed above, admission of the offence in interview could have two other possible advantages for the client. First, it might assist with a subsequent bail application, particularly where property has been recovered. The fact of co-operation with the police may, in particular, persuade the custody officer or a court that there are no substantial grounds for believing that the suspect would interfere with witnesses or the course of justice if released on bail. However, again the client should be warned that this could not be guaranteed, and that this uncertain advantage might be outweighed by other more certain disadvantages. Second, admission of guilt might be advisable where it may lead to the police or prosecutor proceeding by way of an out-of-court disposal, rather than prosecution. Even here, the lawyer would have to weigh up the likelihood of diversion from prosecution against the possibility of an acquittal in the absence of an admission. See further paras 10.58, 10.77, 11.44 and 11.56 below.

5.145 A further area of difficulty relates to offences to be taken into consideration (TICs). Over the years the practice has developed of defendants accused of a number of crimes asking the court to take into account offences with which they have not been charged for the purpose of sentencing. The advantage to the defendant is that they are likely to receive a lesser sentence than if they were separately charged with each of the offences.[154] For the police it improves their clear-up rate with very little effort. The problem at the police station stage is that whatever the interviewing officer says about treating offences as TICs, this cannot be guaranteed, and once the client has admitted the offences there is nothing to stop the police from charging the client with all the offences. Therefore, the client must be warned of this possibility. Furthermore, TICs can tip the balance so that a court can impose a custodial or a community sentence where it would not have had the power to do so in the absence of a TIC.[155] Although the matter will often be difficult to judge at the police station stage, if there is any reason to suggest that a TIC may tip the balance in this way, the client should be advised of this danger.

154 In *R v Miles* [2006] EWCA Crim 256, it was stated that TICs will often add nothing, or relatively little, to the sentence for the substantive offence(s), but may do so if, for example, they show a pattern of criminal behaviour that suggests careful planning or deliberate criminality, offences committed on bail or a return to crime immediately after being given a non-custodial sentence.

155 CJA 2003 ss148(2) and 153(2). TICs count as an 'associated offence' for the purposes of assessing seriousness.

Strategies to avoid or minimise adverse inferences

Introduction

5.146 In considering the appropriate advice as to whether a client should answer questions in the police interview, the lawyer should consider the various strategies that may have the effect of avoiding or minimising adverse inferences under the CJPOA 1994. They are also, of course, relevant once a decision has been made that the client will not answer questions. A distinction should be made between strategies that may avoid inferences altogether and strategies that, while not avoiding inferences, may lead to inferences that are less damaging to the defence than they might otherwise have been. Of course, no strategy can be guaranteed to be successful, and the client must be made aware of the risks attached to any suggested course of action. The strategies that are available or appropriate in any particular case will depend on all the circumstances, including both the instructions obtained from the client and the degree of confidence that the lawyer has in those instructions.

Strategies that may avoid inferences

5.147 Strategies to avoid adverse inferences will be relevant if the lawyer considers that:

- one or more of the conditions necessary for inferences to be drawn under CJPOA 1994 s34, 36 or 37 are not, or will not be, satisfied; or
- factors exist which may lead to evidence of the police interview(s) not being admitted.

The lawyer should consider the following strategies, explained below:

- arguing no power to detain or interview;
- making a prepared statement;
- answering some questions and not others; and
- refusal to be interviewed.

Arguing no power to detain or interview

5.148 If the lawyer is aware that the police case is apparently strong, it may be appropriate to make representations to the interviewing officer, or the custody officer, that an interview should not be conducted. While such representations are unlikely to succeed, the fact that such representations are made may assist in avoiding adverse inferences at trial. There is some difficulty with this argument in view of the line of cases starting with *R v McGuinness*.[156] However, there are two reasons why, if a person is interviewed in such circumstances, evidence of the interview may be excluded under PACE s78, with the result that inferences could not be drawn under CJPOA 1994 s34(1)(a).

5.149 First, if the custody officer is aware that there is sufficient evidence to charge, PACE s37(7) requires the officer to charge or release without delay. The meaning of 'sufficient evidence to charge' is dealt with at para

156 [1999] Crim LR 318, CA; and see para 2.64 above and para 10.7 below.

10.9 below. Detention for the purposes of interviewing the suspect in such circumstances is, arguably, unlawful.

5.150 Second, if the police intend to charge, whatever is said in interview, the custody officer should proceed to deal with them under PACE s37(7), and if they do not do so detention is, again, arguably unlawful.[157] Furthermore, if an interview is conducted in such circumstances, it can be argued that inferences should not be drawn under CJPOA 1994 s34(1)(a) since the officer would not be trying to discover whether or by whom the offence was committed (see para 5.79 above). If appropriate, the lawyer should consider:

- informing the custody officer of the evidence showing that there is sufficient evidence to charge; and/or
- asking the officer in the case questions such as whether they believe that there is sufficient evidence to charge; whether they believe that the client is guilty of the offence; what other evidence they would expect to obtain; and what they intend to do after the interview.

5.151 Note, however, that if an interview is successfully avoided, this would not prevent inferences from being drawn under CJPOA 1994 s34(1)(b), and the lawyer should consider whether to advise the client to make an oral statement, or to offer a prepared statement, at charge.

Making a prepared statement

5.152 The use of prepared statements as a way of potentially avoiding adverse inferences under the CJPOA 1994 is now well established,[158] but the strategy needs to be approached with care. Although the early cases on prepared statements adopted a fairly liberal approach, especially as to how much information had to be included to avoid inferences, the subsequent approach of the courts has been to limit their utility from the defence point of view. The reason why a prepared statement may avoid adverse inferences is that an inference can only be drawn where a fact is relied on at trial that was not mentioned to the police in interview or at charge (CJPOA 1994 s34), or where an accused refuses or fails to account (CJPOA 1994 ss36 and 37). Mentioning facts, or providing an account, in a prepared statement is treated in the same way as if the information had been provided in response to police questions. Inferences under the CJPOA 1994 may be drawn from failure or refusal to provide the information specified in those sections, not from failure to answer police questions.[159] Furthermore, as the Court of Appeal said in *R v Knight*:

> . . . the aim of s34(1)(a) does not distinctly include police cross-examination of a suspect upon his account over and above the disclosure of that account. Had that been intended, it seems to us that parliament would have used significantly different language.[160]

157 See *R v Dervish* [2001] EWCA Crim 2789, in which it was held that where it was established that the police intended to charge irrespective of what was said in interview, the interview was conducted in breach of (former versions of) Code C paras 11.4 and 16.1.

158 See *R v McGarry* [1998] 3 All ER 805, CA; *R v Ali* [2001] EWCA Crim 863; and *R v Knight* [2003] EWCA Crim 1977.

159 *R v Knight* [2003] EWCA Crim 1977; and *T v DPP* [2007] EWHC 1793 (Admin).

160 [2003] EWCA Crim 1977 at para 11.

Therefore, once a statement has been given by the suspect, while the police may seek to question them on it,[161] the suspect is under no obligation to answer such questions.

5.153 The strategy of making a prepared statement should be considered where there are good reasons for informing the police of facts that are likely to be relied on by the defence at trial (or for providing an account), but there are reasons why the client should not be subjected to the risks associated with police questioning – for example, because:

- the client is nervous;
- the client may not respond well to police questioning;
- the facts are complicated; or
- police disclosure has been limited or partial.

In considering whether and how to use a prepared statement, the following factors should be considered, explained below:

- the implications of making a statement;
- how much information to include in the statement;
- when to submit a statement; and
- handing in or reading out a statement.

The implications of making a statement

5.154 While a prepared statement may avoid inferences at trial, it will have the effect of 'fixing' the suspect with the defence. If the defence advanced at trial differs in a significant way from the statement, the prosecution is likely to use this against the accused.[162] The defendant may then try to 'blame' the lawyer for the 'inaccuracies' in the statement, although this is unlikely to be successful.[163] A prepared statement will give the police and prosecution early warning of the defence, which may be used as the basis for asking further questions in interview or for gathering further evidence, and may lead the police or prosecution to adjust their case against the accused accordingly. Furthermore, the statement may give the police sufficient evidence to charge, and may enable the prosecution to establish a prima facie case in circumstances where otherwise this may not have been possible. For example, if the client is suspected of assault, and there is a question about whether the police can establish identity, handing in a statement putting forward self-defence will provide the necessary evidence of identity. The lawyer will have to balance the disadvantages of this against those that follow from the use of any other strategy.[164]

5.155 It is important, therefore, that the lawyer explains to the client the implications of making a prepared statement, ensures that the statement accurately reflects the client's instructions and that the client reads the statement (or has it read to them) before it is given to the police. It is also

161 College of Policing, *Authorised Professional Practice: Investigative interviewing* states that on receipt of a prepared statement the investigator should consider suspending the interview to consider the contents of the statement, and that the investigator is still entitled to question the suspect about it or about other matters.

162 See, for example, *R v Alagaratnam* [2010] EWCA Crim 1506.

163 See, for example, *R v Seaton* [2010] EWCA Crim 1980.

164 See *TI v Bromley Youth Court* [2020] EWHC 1204 (Admin) at para 5.105 above.

advisable for the statement to include a declaration, signed by the client, such as:

> This is my statement. I have read the statement [The statement has been read to me], and I agree with its contents. I have not been told what to say.

How much information to include in the statement

5.156 In the early case of *R v McGarry*,[165] the court accepted that a statement that contained the key elements of the defence, without setting out full details, was sufficient to avoid inferences. The cases decided since then have tended to emphasise that while a prepared statement prevents inferences in respect of facts set out in the statement, it does not prevent inferences from being drawn from failure to mention facts in the statement that are subsequently relied on at trial. For example, in *R v Lewis*,[166] the fact that basic information regarding an alibi had been given to the police in interview did not prevent inferences from being drawn from failure to mention various details concerning the alibi that were subsequently relied on at trial.[167] Similarly, in *Damji*, referencing the overriding objective in criminal proceedings, the Administrative Court was critical of the 'forensic stance' adopted during an interview under caution where there was a 'very carefully worded' statement 'not designed to illuminate'.[168] The Court of Appeal came to a different conclusion in *R v McKnight*, in which it concluded that it was 'highly arguable that no adverse inference direction should have been given' in circumstances where, although the account provided in evidence at trial was fuller than that given in the statement, the substance of what the defendant said in evidence did not vary from the earlier prepared statement.[169] However, the Judicial College, in the Crown Court Compendium, has chosen to adopt the more restrictive interpretation:

> If a prepared statement is submitted by or on behalf of D in lieu of answers to questions posed in interview, no inference is available unless D later relies on facts which do not appear in the prepared statement.[170]

5.157 Therefore, care must be taken to anticipate the facts that are likely to be relied upon at trial,[171] and also to respond to any request to account under CJPOA 1994 s36 or 37 (see para 5.90 above), and to deal with these in the statement. If there is more than one interview, or the police are using a

165 [1998] 3 All ER 805, CA.

166 [2003] EWCA Crim 223.

167 See also *R v Ali* [2001] EWCA Crim 863; *R v Knight* [2003] EWCA Crim 1977; *R v Turner* [2003] EWCA Crim 3108; and *R v Mohammad* [2009] EWCA Crim 1871.

168 *R (Damji) v Crown Court at Wood Green* [2025] EWHC 258 (Admin).

169 [2013] EWCA Crim 937. See also *R v Johnson* [2017] EWCA Crim 191, in which the court held that a section 34 direction should not have been given where, although the accused had not mentioned every fact relied on at trial, he had 'set up the line of reasoning upon which he later relied' (para 28).

170 Judicial College, *Crown Court Compendium Part I: Jury and trial management and summing up* (2024) 17-1 para 5.

171 See, for example, *R v Noor* [2021] EWCA Crim 1767, where the suspect was questioned about whether the complainant had fallen asleep or had to be roused awake. The prosecution case was that the complainant had fallen asleep, but the adverse inference was drawn from the suspect's failure to mention when questioned that he had attempted to wake up the complainant (as this might have explained a 15-minute period of time).

strategy of 'phased disclosure' (see para 4.30 above), the statement should be reviewed in the light of any information disclosed by the police during the course of a prior interview, or between interviews, and consideration given to handing in a supplementary statement.

5.158 Provided that the facts subsequently relied upon at trial are adequately covered, a statement handed to the police during a police interview should have the effect of avoiding inferences under CJPOA 1994 s34(1)(a), or under s36 or 37. Similarly, a statement that sets up the line of reasoning upon which a suspect later relies may avoid a section 34 inference.[172] However, a statement submitted during an interview will not necessarily prevent inferences being drawn under section 34(1)(b). Normally, the courts appear reluctant to draw inferences under section 34(1)(b), especially where facts have been disclosed in interview, but it could be relevant if information is disclosed by the police in the interview that is not adequately covered in the prepared statement (see para 5.76 above). In these circumstances, the lawyer should consider whether a supplementary statement should be provided.

When to submit a statement

5.159 Careful thought must be given to when a prepared statement should be made to the police. It follows from the wording of CJPOA 1994 s34(1)(a) that in order to avoid inferences under that subsection, the statement must be handed in or read out during the interview. If a prepared statement is given to, or read out to, the police at the beginning of an interview, information may be disclosed by the police during the interview that renders the statement inadequate. On the other hand, waiting until the end of the interview may mean that the opportunity to hand it in or read it out during the interview is lost. In a straightforward case, where the lawyer is satisfied that the police have made adequate disclosure, it will normally be appropriate to submit the statement at the beginning of the interview. However, in a more complex case or where the police have given no, or limited, disclosure (or the lawyer is not confident that the disclosure provided is sufficiently complete), it may be better to provide the statement towards the end of the interview. In this case, before the interview ends, the lawyer should tell the police that before it is concluded they wish to have a private consultation with the client. The statement should then be drafted in consultation with the client, and provided to the police at the resumed interview. If the police try to end the interview before the statement is submitted, the interviewing officer should be reminded that under Code C para 11.6 they are, in effect, obliged to give a suspect the opportunity to give an innocent explanation.

Handing in or reading out a statement

5.160 It has been held that an oral statement of facts by the suspect, who then refuses to answer questions, amounts to mentioning facts for the purpose

172 See *R v Johnson* [2017] EWCA Crim 191; however, cf *R (Damji) v Crown Court at Wood Green* [2025] EWHC 258 (Admin), where the court found a prepared statement to be, '. . . very carefully worded and not designed to illuminate'. In that case, the statement was not sufficient to trigger disclosure obligations and the court observed that the 'forensic stance' adopted was the claimant's right, but was not without its consequences.

of CJPOA 1994 s34.[173] Unless the client is particularly confident, it would normally be more advisable for the lawyer to read out the statement, or to hand a copy to the interviewer. In the latter case, the lawyer should, before giving the statement to the officer, ask them to confirm that they will copy it and return the original to the lawyer. If the officer is unwilling to do this, the lawyer should reconsider whether they should read it out rather than hand it over, but if they do decide to hand it over, they should ensure that they have a copy before doing so.[174] If, before reading out or handing in a prepared statement, the lawyer considers that it omits relevant information or includes information that should not be disclosed to the police, the statement should be re-drafted during a private consultation with the client. Unused prepared statements should be covered by legal professional privilege. The police have no right to seize a prepared statement (see para 1.20 above).[175] If the interviewing officer makes a serious attempt to seize the statement, the lawyer should ask to speak to a senior officer and, as a last resort, should ask that the statement be placed in a sealed envelope with the condition that it only be opened on the order of a court.

Answering some questions and not others

5.161 Generally, a client should be advised to answer either all questions or none. Answering only some questions is not normally an appropriate strategy because of the potential adverse effects on credibility of the defence at trial (see para 5.66 above). Where a client is advised to answer police questions, but the client indicates that they are not willing to answer questions concerning certain matters (assuming that they are relevant and proper questions), it may be more advisable to submit a prepared statement covering the relevant facts.

Refusal to be interviewed

5.162 It would not normally be appropriate to advise a client to refuse to be interviewed unless the lawyer is strongly of the view that the client is not fit to be interviewed (see para 5.22 above). However, clients do occasionally decide for themselves that they are not prepared to leave their cell for the purpose of an interview, and the police should not use force to take them to an interview room.[176] Such a refusal may have the effect of preventing an interview from taking place, although Codes C and H para 12.5 state that in these circumstances, the suspect should be cautioned and told that their failure or refusal to co-operate may not prevent an interview taking

173 See, for example, *R v Ashton and Others* [2002] EWCA Crim 2782.

174 For example, by saving an electronic copy of the statement or, where the statement has been hand-written, by taking a photograph of it.

175 The Association of Chief Police Officers' (ACPO's) *ACPO position statement: dealing with prepared statements in investigative interviews with suspects* (undated, available at: https://library.college.police.uk/docs/APPREF/ACPO-Position-Statement-Prepared-Statements.pdf) confirms that the police have no right to seize a prepared statement, and states that the interviewing officer should copy the statement and return the original to the lawyer. However, this is not repeated in the College of Policing's *APP (Authorised Professional Practice)*, available at: www.college.police.uk/app.

176 Code C para 12.5A, which deals with such circumstances, does not suggest that the police can use force. This is supported by *R v Jones and Nelson* (1999) Times, April 21, CA, which found that the use of force on a suspect to enable a confrontation to take place was unlawful.

place in the cell and that evidence of such an interview may be given in evidence. If an interview does take place in the cell, the normal principles regarding inferences from silence apply. If an interview does not take place, inferences cannot be drawn under CJPOA 1994 s34(1)(a),[177] but may still be possible under section 34(1)(b).

Strategies to minimise inferences

5.163 If the circumstances are such that it will not be possible to prevent the prospect of inferences under the CJPOA 1994, the lawyer should consider what action may be taken at the police station stage which could help persuade a court that:

- the suspect could not reasonably have been expected to mention facts to the police that are relied upon at trial; or
- any inference to be drawn should be less damaging than it might otherwise have been.

The lawyer should consider the following strategies, explained below:

- telling the police about the reasons for the advice;
- asking whether the interviewing officer has disclosed all available evidence;
- stating that the client does not understand the caution;
- taking a statement that is not handed to the police; and
- handing in a statement in interview or at charge.

Telling the police about the reasons for the advice

5.164 Explaining, in the police interview, the grounds for advice to remain silent can, in principle, help to minimise the risk of inferences since it has been held in a number of cases that 'good' reasons for advice to remain silent may persuade a court that it is not reasonable to expect the accused to have mentioned relevant facts. However, this will almost certainly amount to a waiver of privilege and, furthermore, any explanation given may be used against the accused if the defence at trial is incompatible with the explanation given.[178] In some circumstances it may be appropriate to give advice not to answer questions in the police interview, and provided no reference is made to a privileged conversation in so doing, privilege should not be regarded as having been waived. Alternatively, it may be possible to separate the advice from the reasons for it, for example, by making representations to the officer in the case or the custody officer as to the relevant issue and, in the interview, simply stating that the client has been advised not to answer questions. In circumstances where there has been no, or very limited disclosure, by the police, informing the interviewing officer that given the lack of disclosure the lawyer has not been able to give sensible advice to the client will not amount to a waiver of privilege. See further para 5.99 above.

5.165 In view of the dangers of waiver of privilege, the lawyer should only give an explanation of the reasons for the advice if:

177 *R v Johnson; R v Hind* [2005] EWCA Crim 971.

178 *R v Fitzgerald* (1998) 6 June (unreported), CA.

- the lawyer is confident that any defence disclosed by the explanation will be consistent with any defence put forward at trial;
- waiver of privilege would not lead to disclosure of information that would be adverse to the client; and
- the lawyer is confident that the client understands the consequences of the waiver and provides their informed consent.[179]

However, even if these conditions are satisfied, careful consideration should be given to whether to give reasons for the advice in interview since it is not always possible to predict whether waiver of privilege may have a damaging effect on the client's case.[180] It may be better for the lawyer to take a careful note of the advice given, the reasons for it, and the time and date the advice was given (which the lawyer should do in any event). If, at trial, it is apparent that waiver of privilege will not cause difficulty for the client, the lawyer could then give evidence of the reasons for the advice given, and use the note to refresh their memory.

Asking whether the interviewing officer has disclosed all available evidence

5.166 Asking the officer whether they have disclosed all relevant information (see para 4.27 above) may lead them to disclose further information, in which case the lawyer will want a further private consultation in order to reconsider their advice to the client regarding the interview strategy. If the officer says that there is information that has not been disclosed, but refuses to give further information, the lawyer may use the interview as a means of discovering that further information. The lawyer should then re-consider their advice, and consider whether to ask for a further police interview at which the client answers questions or submits a prepared statement.

Stating that the client does not understand the caution

5.167 This strategy is only appropriate if the client genuinely does not understand the implications of the caution, for example, if the client is very young or has limited intellectual capacity. If it appears to the interviewing officer that the suspect does not understand the caution given, the officer must explain it in their own words (Code C NfG 10D; Code H NfG 10C; Code I NfG 10C), and the lawyer should check that the explanation given accurately reflects the caution. Research has shown not only that the caution is too complex for most suspects to understand, but that many police officers do not understand it either. The lawyer should also prepare the client so that they do not agree that they understand the explanation of the caution given unless they genuinely do so.[181]

179 It is advisable for this to be recorded in writing.

180 In *R v Bowden* [1999] 1 WLR 823, CA damage was caused to the defendant's case because waiver of privilege enabled the prosecution to cross-examine him about what he had not said to his solicitor at the police station, ie that his mother had paid for a holiday which the prosecution alleged had been paid for out of the proceeds of a robbery.

181 A defendant's lack of understanding of the caution may still not prevent inferences from being left to the jury. See *R v V* [2005] EWCA Crim 581.

Taking a statement that is not handed to the police

5.168 This strategy was, in effect, suggested by the Court of Appeal in *R v Condron*,[182] in which it held that an inference that a defence had been fabricated could be avoided if the accused adduced evidence that information about the defence had been given to a solicitor at or about the time of the police interview.[183] Crucially, it held that doing so would not amount to a waiver of privilege (see para 5.103 above). Such a strategy would not necessarily prevent any inference from being drawn, since it has been made clear in subsequent cases that other inferences are possible: that the accused had fabricated the defence before the police interview but was not sufficiently confident of it to expose it to police questioning, or that the accused had not thought up all of the details of the defence at the time of the police interview.[184] Nevertheless, it provides a useful means of trying to limit inferences in circumstances where they could not be avoided altogether.

5.169 While it may still be the best available strategy in any particular circumstances, more recent cases have limited its usefulness. First, in *R v Seaton*,[185] the Court of Appeal held that if a defendant gives evidence that they provided their lawyer with an account of their defence at the police station, this will normally amount to a waiver of privilege. Second, if at trial the prosecution avoids alleging recent fabrication, as in *R v Howell*,[186] the accused may not be able to adduce evidence of the statement made to the lawyer since it will amount to a previous consistent statement.[187]

5.170 Nevertheless, taking a statement that is not handed in to the police may be an appropriate strategy where the lawyer takes the view that a statement should not be handed in because of doubts about the instructions received or about information that has not been disclosed by the police, and that these considerations outweigh the advantages of other strategies, particularly that of making a prepared statement. The lawyer should take as full a statement as possible from the client and ensure that it is checked and signed by the client. The lawyer should also anticipate whether the client is likely to be asked to account under CJPOA 1994 s36 or 37 (see para 5.90 above) and include relevant information in the statement. The client should be advised of the implications of using this strategy, in particular, that a court may subsequently see the statement and that it may not have the effect of preventing damaging inferences.

182 [1997] 1 WLR 827, CA.

183 This may amount to hearsay evidence, normally requiring notice of intention to adduce. See the analysis in E Cape, 'Police station law and practice update' October 2009 *Legal Action* 12.

184 See *R v Daniel* [1998] Crim LR 818, CA; *R v Randall* (1998) 3 April (unreported), CA; and *R v Beckles and Montague* [1999] Crim LR 148, CA; and see para 5.88 above.

185 [2010] EWCA Crim 1980.

186 [2003] EWCA Crim 1.

187 However, see *R v Athwal and Others* [2009] EWCA Crim 789, in which it was held that a previous consistent statement is admissible hearsay (subject to the power of the judge to exclude it) by virtue of CJA 2003 s120(2).

Handing in a statement in interview or at charge

5.171 Handing in a statement during a police interview was described at para 5.152 above as a strategy designed to prevent inferences from being drawn. As explained, however, this may fail if the defence put forward at trial goes beyond the facts set out in the statement. In these circumstances, while not preventing inferences, such a statement may minimise the inferences drawn in the same way as a statement that is not handed to the police. The lawyer should also anticipate whether the client is likely to be asked to account under CJPOA 1994 s36 or 37 (see para 5.90 above) and include relevant information in the statement.

5.172 Alternatively, a prepared statement may be submitted at charge. This may be particularly useful if the lawyer believes that the police will not have enough evidence to charge. As noted at para 5.154 above, a statement given to the police during the interview may give them enough evidence to charge. Thus, the lawyer may consider advising a 'no comment' interview, and submitting a statement only if the police do decide to charge. The police can only interview after charge for limited reasons, such as clearing up an ambiguity in the statement (Code C para 16.5), and inferences cannot be drawn from failure to mention facts after charge. However, while inferences cannot be drawn under CJPOA 1994 s34(1)(b) (assuming that the defence put forward at trial is consistent with the statement), inferences can be drawn under CJPOA 1994 s34(1)(a), and these may damage the client's defence.

The relevance of previous misconduct

5.173 The previous misconduct provisions of CJA 2003 ss98–113 mean that what the suspect says in a police interview, or in a statement handed in to the police, may allow the prosecution to introduce evidence of 'bad character' or to cross-examine them as to 'bad character' at trial. If such evidence is admitted, it may be used to show that they had the propensity to commit the offence of which they are accused and/or to attack the credibility of their evidence. As a result of these provisions, questions relating to 'bad character' may be introduced into police interviews. The provisions are complex, and a full guide to them is not provided here. However, in advising clients at police stations, lawyers should be particularly aware of the following.

5.174 Evidence of a defendant's 'bad character' is admissible if (CJA 2003 s101(1)):

(a) all parties to the proceedings agree to the evidence being admissible,
(b) the evidence is adduced by the defendant himself, or is given in answer to a question asked by him in cross-examination and intended to elicit it,
(c) it is important explanatory evidence,
(d) it is relevant to an important matter in issue between the defendant and the prosecution,
(e) it has substantial probative value in relation to an important matter in issue between the defendant and the co-defendant,
(f) it is evidence to correct a false impression given by the defendant, or
(g) the defendant has made an attack on another person's character.

These are known as the character 'gateways', and gateways (c)–(g) are further defined in CJA 2003 ss102–106. Broadly, if one or more of the gateways is satisfied, evidence of previous misconduct of the accused will be admissible and/or the accused can be cross-examined on it. Where evidence of previous misconduct is admissible under gateways (d) and (g), the court must not admit that evidence if it appears to the court that to admit it would have such an adverse effect on the fairness of the proceedings that the court ought not to admit it (CJA 2002 s101(3)). There is no similar provision in respect of the other gateways, although the court has a general discretion to exclude prosecution evidence under PACE s78 (see para 13.42 below).

5.175 'Bad character' is widely defined to mean evidence of, or of a disposition towards, misconduct of the accused (CJA 2003 s98); and 'misconduct' means the commission of an offence or other reprehensible behaviour (CJA 2003 s112(1)). Clearly, previous convictions come within the definition, but so too could previous arrests, cautions,[188] unproven allegations or the use of unlawful drugs.[189] It could also include conduct that, while reprehensible, is not criminal, such as misconduct at work.

5.176 Information given by a suspect in a police interview could be used by the prosecution to establish previous misconduct. The police could, of course, simply ask the accused whether they have previous convictions. They are likely to be in possession of such information already, but may not know about other forms of previous misconduct. They may wish to question the suspect about the circumstances of any previous convictions. In *R v Hanson, Gilmore and Pickstone*,[190] it was held that in order to decide on admissibility it will sometimes be necessary to look beyond the mere fact of conviction to the surrounding circumstances, for example, to see if there was a similar pattern of behaviour. If the suspect answers such questions, the prosecution may be able to adduce evidence of previous misconduct in circumstances where they otherwise would not be able to do so. Furthermore, even in the absence of a direct question, a suspect could disclose information that amounts to an admission of previous misconduct. For example, if a suspect tells the police that they are a drug addict, this may be admitted if it is relevant to an important matter in issue between the accused and the prosecution.[191] Therefore, where a suspect is answering police questions, or hands in a statement, the lawyer must care-

188 *R v Olu, Wilson and Brooks* [2010] EWCA Crim 2975, although it was held in that case that an accused could, for the purpose of the misconduct provisions, adduce evidence that the accused was not guilty of the offence.

189 *R v Highton, Van Nguyen and Carp* [2005] EWCA Crim 1985.

190 [2005] EWCA Crim 824. See also *R v Humphris* [2005] EWCA Crim 2030; and *R v Ainscough* [2006] EWCA Crim 694.

191 For example, in *R v Highton, Van Nguyen and Carp* [2005] EWCA Crim 1985, in a prosecution for cultivating cannabis, the prosecution sought to admit evidence of an admission by one of the accused in interview that he was a heroin addict in order to demonstrate that he must have known that the plants being cultivated were cannabis. On the facts, the Court of Appeal held that the evidence should not have been admitted (since the accused accepted that he knew it must have been an unlawful drug), but it is clear that in principle such evidence could have been admitted.

fully consider whether any admission of previous bad character is necessary.

5.177 Two of the character gateways specifically refer to things said or done by a suspect at a police station (CJA 2003 s101(2)(f) and (7)(g)), so that what a suspect says in a police interview (or in a prepared statement) may have the effect of opening the gateway to the introduction of previous misconduct. The first of these two gateways, contained in CJA 2003 s101(1)(f), permits the prosecution to adduce evidence to correct a false impression given by the defendant. A defendant gives a false impression if they are 'responsible for the making of an express or implied assertion which is apt to give the court or jury a false or misleading impression' about themself (CJA 2003 s105(1)(a)). There is a number of ways in which a defendant may make such an assertion, and one is if they make the assertion on being interviewed by the police, or on being charged (or officially informed that they may be prosecuted), and evidence of the assertion is given in the proceedings (CJA 2003 s105(2)(b)). Thus the conditions are only satisfied if evidence of the assertion is given at trial, but once the assertion has been made by the suspect in the police interview, they have no control over whether the prosecution will seek to use it, and (assuming the other conditions are satisfied) the court has no specific power to prevent them from doing so.[192]

5.178 The scope of this provision is potentially very wide. Clearly a suspect gives a false impression if they wrongly tell the police that they have no previous convictions.[193] A suspect may also do so if they wrongly tell the police that they have never been arrested for a similar offence before. The false impression need not relate to previous contact with the police or the courts. An assertion by a suspect that they have a good work record, or a high reputation in the community, when this is demonstrably false, can satisfy the conditions.[194] Again, therefore, if a client is answering police questions, or handing in a statement, they must be advised about the dangers of making such assertions. If a suspect is to refer to past behaviour which may be caught by CJA 2003 s101, it is important to consider precisely what express of implied assertion is being made.[195]

5.179 The second of the two gateways that specifically refers to what may be said or done at a police station is CJA 2003 s101(1)(g), which enables evidence of the defendant's bad character to be adduced where the defendant

192 CJA 2003 s101(3) does not apply, although the court does have a discretion to exclude any prosecution evidence under PACE s78.

193 As in *R v Ullah* [2006] EWCA Crim 2003.

194 In *R v Weir and Others* [2005] EWCA Crim 2866, seeking to demonstrate that the accused had a good reputation as a priest was held to satisfy CJA 2003 s101(1)(f). See also *R v Renda and Others* [2005] EWCA Crim 2826; and *R v Chable* [2009] EWCA Crim 496.

195 In *R v Khan* [2020] EWCA Crim 163, the suspect asserted that they had never sold drugs in a hostel. At trial, the Crown successfully applied to admit into evidence Mr Khan's previous conviction for supplying class A drugs to correct a false impression (CJA 2003 s101(f)). The Court of Appeal quashed the conviction and noted that Mr Khan's previous conviction has come about in very different circumstances, that his denial had been to supplying class A drugs in the hostel, and that the interview could have been edited under CJA 2003 s105(6) to remove references to any more general implied assertion that he was not the sort of person who supplied drugs, so as to correct any false impression.

has made an attack on another person's character. Attacking another person's character means giving evidence that the other person has committed an offence or has behaved, or is disposed to behave, in a reprehensible way (CJA 2003 s106(2)). There is a number of ways in which a defendant may make such an attack, including if they make it on being interviewed by the police or on being charged (or officially informed that the defendant may be prosecuted), and evidence of the attack is given in the proceedings (CJA 2003 s106(1)(c)). As with giving a false impression, having made an attack, a suspect has no control over whether the prosecution will seek to use it against them at trial, although CJA 2003 s101(3) does apply (see para 5.174 above).[196]

5.180 The potential adverse effects of CJA 2003 s101(1)(g) are much wider than those of section 101(1)(f). The conditions may be satisfied if the suspect asserts that a co-suspect or, indeed, any other person committed the offence of which they are suspected, and this is so even if that other person is not named. The conditions could also be satisfied if the suspect accuses the police of misconduct, for example, that the police assaulted them during the course of arrest. The provisions create particular difficulty where the suspect seeks to place blame on the victim or complainant. For example, where a person has been arrested for assault, an assertion that they acted in self-defence will almost inevitably involve an assertion that the complainant assaulted them or, at least, acted in a reprehensible manner.[197]

5.181 In some cases, if the suspect is to answer questions or hand in a statement, there will be no alternative but to provide information that may mean that the conditions for admission of evidence of bad character are satisfied. It will normally not be possible to put forward a defence of self-defence without casting imputations on the complainant, and a defence to assault on police may inevitably mean that the suspect alleges that the police assaulted them. Since, if such a defence is put forward at a trial, the gateway will be opened anyway, it will often be better to assert the defence in the police interview because otherwise inferences under CJPOA 1994 s34 may be even more damaging. However, the various courses of action must be carefully thought through, and the client advised of the potential consequences. Where appropriate, the client should be advised not to make unwarranted or unnecessary allegations or comments.[198]

5.182 Guidance on preparing for an interview where questions about previous bad character may be asked is given at para 4.64 above, but the question remains whether a client should be advised to answer questions about

196 It was held in *R v Nelson* [2006] EWCA Crim 3412 that the prosecution should not be permitted to adduce evidence of an attack on the character of a person (who did not appear as a witness) where it was irrelevant to the facts in issue. It was not proper, said the court, 'for the prosecution to seek to get such comments before a jury simply to provide a basis for satisfying gateway [CJA 2003 s101(1)(g)]'.

197 *R v Lamaletie and Royce* [2008] EWCA Crim 314. See also *R v O* [2009] EWCA Crim 2235.

198 In *R v Renda and Others* [2005] EWCA Crim 2826, during the course of the police interview one of the appellants, who had been arrested for rape, described the complainant as 'a slag' who had had sex with most of the men in the pub. It was held that this was enough to satisfy the CJA 2003 s101(1)(g) conditions so that the prosecution could introduce evidence of his previous bad character.

character if they are put to them by the police. In some circumstances it may be to the client's advantage to answer questions about previous bad character, or to deal with it in a prepared statement, particularly where this would demonstrate that there is no particular connection between the previous bad character and the client's credibility or the client's propensity to commit the offence of which they are now suspected. However, there will often be no advantage to the client answering such questions even if they do answer questions about the suspected offence. Although the issue has not yet been addressed by the courts, it is unlikely in most circumstances that inferences could be drawn from a failure or refusal to answer questions about previous misconduct.

Preparing the client for interview

5.183 The police interview is almost certainly the most crucial event during the period of a person's detention at a police station. Having listened carefully to what the client has to say, and having advised them on their position and the approach that should be taken, the lawyer must then prepare them for the coming event. The client may never have been through a police interview before, but even if they have, time spent at this stage on preparing them for interview may make the difference between the interview proceeding in accordance with the advice given and complete disaster. Quite literally, it may make the difference between a conviction and an acquittal.

5.184 It is important that the client understands what to expect during a police interview, and the lawyer should explain in general terms how the interview is likely to be conducted. This will include:

- who is likely to be present;
- how the room will be arranged;
- where the lawyer will be;
- how long it may last; and
- what may happen at the end of the interview.

Of course, some of this may not be known, but the client should be given the best indication possible. Most interviews are electronically recorded, so the lawyer should explain how this will be done, and what will happen to the record of the interview. If the interview is to be visually recorded, the client should be advised of the potential impact of visual cues. If it is not to be electronically recorded, the system of contemporaneous recording that is likely to be used should be explained. The purpose and content of an opening statement to be made by the lawyer should be discussed with the client.

5.185 The client should also be advised how to behave during the interview. The client's general demeanour will be important, particularly if the interview is to be visually recorded. If the client is to answer questions, they should be advised to try to avoid sarcastic comments, 'clever' answers and, above all, losing their temper. All of these would be likely to come over very badly, particularly if a court were subsequently to hear or see the recording of the interview. It may help to remind the client that the police may use tactics precisely in order to encourage them to make off-hand remarks or to lose their temper. The lawyer should tell the client that they are entitled to ask for legal advice in private at any time during the course of the interview. Although the police may not like this, PACE s58(1), TA 2000 Sch 8 para 7 and NSA 2023 Sch 6 para 7 are absolutely clear that the suspect is entitled to 'consult a solicitor privately *at any time*' (emphasis added) (see para 2.149 above). Conversely, the client cannot expect the lawyer to prompt them or to answer questions on their behalf.

5.186 It should also be made clear to the client that anything they say within the hearing of the police may be used as evidence. Some people believe that it is only what they say during the course of the interview that is important in this respect, and that once the recording device is switched off, they can make admissions with impunity. This belief may be encouraged by the police. This is clearly not the case. Code C para 11.13 explicitly refers to comments made by a suspected person, including unsolicited comments, outside the context of an interview, which may be relevant to the offence. There have been a number of reported cases where alleged 'off the record' remarks have resulted in conviction, even though the police breached the recording requirements.[199] There have also been instances where the police have set up situations enabling them covertly to record conversations between suspects.[200] Therefore, the client should be left in no doubt that there is no such thing as an 'off the record' conversation with a police officer, and that they need to be cautious about any conversation with co-suspects or others.

5.187 The client should be prepared for interviewing tactics that might be employed by the police, and the lawyer should explain the purpose behind them. How to deal with these tactics during the course of the interview is covered in chapter 7 below, but such tactics are less likely to be successful if the client is prepared for them. Attempts to undermine advice and to drive a wedge between lawyer and client are not uncommon, as are trick questions and questions designed to put pressure on the suspect, and they are not necessarily contrary to the provisions of Codes C or H. The client must also be advised how to respond to:

- any request by the police under Code C or H para 11.4, or Code I para 11.3 to comment on any earlier significant statement or silence (see para 5.116 above);
- any specific request to account for an object, etc, or presence under CJPOA 1994 ss36 and 37 (see para 5.90 above); and
- any questions about previous misconduct (see para 5.173 above).

5.188 If the client has decided not to answer police questions, they should be given practical advice on how to do this, and should be prepared for tactics

199 See, in particular, *R v Dunn* (1990) 91 Cr App R 237, CA, where evidence of the comments was admitted despite breaches of the codes and despite denials of the comments by both the defendant and his co-accused and their lawyer, who was present.

200 For example, in *R v Plunkett and Plunkett* [2013] EWCA Crim 261, the accused were deliberately left in a police van outside the police station for a period of time in order that their conversations could be covertly recorded. In *R v Bond* [2020] EWCA Crim 1596, the trial judge was correct to admit into evidence a covert audio recording of two defendants speaking in a police van following their arrest.

designed to encourage them to talk. Many people find it difficult, if not impossible, simply to sit and say nothing when faced with a series of questions. For this reason, the client may be best advised to say 'no comment' to each question, although they can confirm their name and address at the outset. It may also be advisable to warn the client that they may feel a strong impulse to say something and that, if necessary, they should ask to speak to the lawyer in private.

5.189 One way in which the police try to encourage suspects to talk is to start by asking some seemingly innocuous questions, or by trying to engage the suspect in seemingly friendly or light-hearted conversation. Furthermore, some police forces have prepared scripts for use when faced with a 'no comment' interview, referring to their desire to give the suspect an opportunity to tell their side of the story. Other tactics include seeking to undermine the advice given by the lawyer by commenting on the lawyer's status (particularly if they are a representative), by referring to the view expressed by some judges that suspects do not have to follow their lawyer's advice, or by referring to the supposed views of the Law Society. As stated earlier, informing the client of such possibilities will probably reduce their likely effectiveness. Finally, the 'right to silence' provisions of the CJPOA 1994 are likely to be used by some officers to try to persuade the client to talk. The caution may, in effect, be used as a threat. Despite the inferences that may follow from failure to answer questions, the aim of some police officers is still to get the suspect to talk. The certainty of a confession is better, from the police point of view, to the unknown effects of an inference. The client must be fully prepared for such tactics.

5.190 Another tactic, although not necessarily deliberately employed by the interviewing officer, is to ask during the course of the interview whether the client is willing to take part in an identification procedure. While this is unlikely to affect the admissibility of the interview, it may be better, during an interview in which the client is exercising their right to silence, for them to refrain from answering such a question since, having answered one question, it may be more difficult for them to revert to not answering subsequent questions. One method of dealing with this is for the lawyer to indicate on the client's behalf whether they would be willing to participate.

5.191 By this stage, the client should be fully prepared, or as prepared as they will ever be, for the interview with the police, but it may be advisable to deal with a few final matters:

(1) The client should be given the opportunity to ask the lawyer any questions. The client may have a remaining concern that they have not yet had the opportunity of raising.
(2) The client should be told (where appropriate) that there may be subsequent police interviews and, particularly if it is to be a 'no comment' interview, that they should be wary of the police subsequently coming to see them in the absence of the lawyer (see paras 7.75 and 10.153 below).
(3) The client should be reminded that they may interrupt the interview at any stage in order to consult with the lawyer in private.

CHAPTER 6

Fingerprints, photographs, samples, drug-testing and searches

continued

Introduction

6.1 This chapter deals with the police powers under the Police and Criminal Evidence Act 1984 (PACE), the Terrorism Act (TA) 2000 and the National Security Act (NSA) 2023 to:

- take fingerprints;
- take photographs;
- conduct searches and examinations to establish identity; and
- take footwear impressions,

as well as police powers to:

- take samples and skin impressions, including:
  - intimate samples (including dental impressions);
  - non-intimate samples and skin impressions;
  - handwriting samples; and
  - samples in road traffic cases;
- conduct drug-testing procedures; and
- conduct searches, including search of the person and search of premises.

It does not cover search warrants and orders under PACE ss8 and 9, or other legislation. Identification procedures are dealt with in chapter 8 below.

Fingerprints, photographs, establishing identity and footwear impressions

Introduction

6.2 The powers of the police to take, use and retain biometric samples and impressions, footwear impressions and photographs, both with or without consent, are extensive. Some powers apply in respect of suspects in police detention,[1] but others may be exercised in respect of people who are not in police detention, although there are extensive powers to require a person to attend a police station for the purposes of taking biometric samples, with a power of arrest in default. In addition to the statutory provisions contained in PACE, the powers are also governed by PACE Code of Practice D. Code D applies to persons arrested and/or detained under TA 2000 s41 and Sch 7, Counter-Terrorism and Border Security Act (C-TBSA) 2019 Sch 3, and NSA 2023 s27, except those provisions relating to photographs, fingerprints, skin impressions, body samples and impressions of people (Code D para 2.17). The taking of fingerprints and photographs is routinely carried out by the police, partly for evidential purposes but also to enable them to conduct speculative searches and to populate their databases. Therefore, a lawyer should advise the client about these powers in the initial contact so that they are aware that their fingerprints and a photograph will be taken, and the use that may be made of them.

1 The provisions refer to a person who is 'detained at a police station', which is likely to be a reference to a person who is in police detention (see para 1.58 above).

Fingerprints

Power to take fingerprints under PACE

6.3 'Fingerprints' are defined as any record, produced by any method, of the skin pattern and other physical characteristics or features of a person's fingers or palms (PACE s65(1)). The police can always take a person's fingerprints if 'appropriate consent' is given, although in the case of a person at a police station (not necessarily in police detention), such consent must be in writing (PACE s61(2); Code D para 4.2). 'Appropriate consent', in the case of a person aged 18 years or over, is the consent of that person; for a child under 14 years it is the consent of a parent or guardian;[2] and for a child aged 14 years or more it means the consent of both the child and a parent or guardian (PACE s65(1); Code D para 2.12). PACE s65 and Code D refer to the parent or guardian rather than the appropriate adult, and Code D note for guidance (NfG) 2A indicates that if a parent or guardian is not present (for example, because another person is acting as appropriate adult), consent can be given by telephone, but they must be given full information and must be allowed to speak to the child and the appropriate adult if they wish. The consent of a mentally disordered or mentally vulnerable person[3] must be given in the presence of the appropriate adult (Code D para 2.12). In both cases, the fingerprints should be taken in the presence of the appropriate adult (Code D para 2.15).

6.4 Fingerprints can be taken without consent in the following circumstances:

(1) The fingerprints of a person detained at a police station in consequence of arrest for a recordable offence[4] may be taken without consent, provided that they have not had their fingerprints taken in the course of the investigation of that offence by the police (PACE s61(3); Code D para 4.3(a)). The latter proviso does not apply if the fingerprints taken on a previous occasion do not constitute a complete set of fingerprints or some or all of them are not of sufficient quality to allow for satisfactory analysis, comparison or matching (PACE s61(3A)). Authorisation by a senior officer is not required.

(2) The fingerprints of a person detained at a police station may be taken without consent if the person has been charged with a recordable offence, or informed that they will be reported for such an offence,[5] and the person's fingerprints have not been taken during the course of the investigation (PACE s61(4); Code D para 4.3(b)). This is subject to the same exception to the proviso as in (1) above. The fingerprints of a person not detained at a police station may be taken without consent if they have been charged with a recordable offence (or informed that

2 Or local authority or voluntary organisation if the child is in their care (Code D NfG 2A).

3 Code D continues to refer to a 'mentally disordered or mentally vulnerable person', although the current version of Code C now refers to a 'vulnerable person', defined in Code C para 1.13(d). See further para 11.80 below.

4 Regulations governing recordable offences are issued under PACE s27(4). All imprisonable offences are recordable offences, as are a small number of non-imprisonable offences. See Code D NfG 4A for an explanation.

5 With a view to written charge or caution.

they will be reported for such an offence), and they have not had their fingerprints taken in the course of the police investigation; or they have had their fingerprints taken but either the exception to the proviso in (1) above applies, or the investigation was discontinued but subsequently resumed and before that resumption, their fingerprints were destroyed pursuant to PACE s63D(3) (PACE s61(5B); Code D para 4.3(cb)). Authorisation is not required.

(3) The fingerprints of a person who has answered to bail at court or a police station may be taken without consent at the court or police station on the authorisation of the court or of an inspector or above, which may be given if the person answering to bail has answered it for a person whose fingerprints have been taken and there are reasonable grounds to believe that they are not the same person, or the person who has answered to bail claims to be a different person from the person whose fingerprints were taken on a previous occasion (PACE s61(4A) and (4B); Code D para 4.3(c)). Authorisation may be given orally or in writing, but if given orally, must be confirmed in writing as soon as is practicable (PACE s61(5)).

(4) A person's fingerprints can be taken without consent if they have been arrested for a recordable offence and released and, in the case of a person who is on bail, they have not had their fingerprints taken in the course of the police investigation; or they have had their fingerprints taken but the exception to the proviso in (1) above applies (PACE s61(5A); Code D para 4.3(ca)). Authorisation is not required.

(5) A person's fingerprints can be taken without consent if they have been convicted of a recordable offence, or have been cautioned in respect of a recordable offence and admitted the offence at the time of the caution (PACE s61(6)). This is subject to the condition that the person has not had their fingerprints taken since the conviction or caution, or they have but the exception to the proviso mentioned in (1) above is satisfied. Authorisation by an inspector or above is required, which may only be given if satisfied that taking the fingerprints is necessary to assist in the prevention or detection of crime (PACE s61(6)–(6ZC); Code D para 4.3(d)).

(6) A person's fingerprints may be taken without consent if a constable reasonably believes that the person is committing or attempting to commit, or has committed or attempted to commit, an offence and the name of the person is unknown to and cannot readily be ascertained by the constable, or the constable has reasonable grounds for doubting whether the name given by the person is their real name (PACE s61(6A) and (6B); Code D para 4.3(e)). Note that this power can be exercised without the person being arrested, and in respect of any offence, not necessarily a recordable offence.

In addition, there are powers to take fingerprints from a person who has been convicted of an offence in a foreign jurisdiction, provided certain conditions are satisfied (PACE s61(6D)–(6G); Code D para 4.3(f)). For powers to require a person to attend a police station to have their fingerprints taken, with arrest in default, see PACE s63A(4) and Sch 2A; and Code D para 4.4. If a person is required to attend a police station to have their fingerprints taken, it is important to check that the date of attendance is within the time limits set out in PACE Sch 2A.

6.5 Where fingerprints are taken without consent under PACE s61, before they are taken the person must be informed of the reason for taking the fingerprints; the power under which they are taken; and, where authorisation is necessary, that authorisation has been given (PACE s61(7); Code D para 4.7). In the case of a person detained at a police station, the fact that this information has been given must be noted in the custody record (PACE s61(8); Code D para 4.8A). Where fingerprints are taken (with or without consent) at a police station, or other place in the case of powers under section 61(4A) or (6A), the person must be told that their fingerprints may be made the subject of a speculative search, and this must be recorded as soon as is practicable (PACE s61(7A); Code D para 4.8A)). If fingerprints are taken without consent, a police constable or designated civilian who is designated with a power to take fingerprints may use reasonable force in order to take them (PACE s117; Police Reform Act (PRA) 2002 s38(8)). If force is used, a record must be made of the circumstances and of those present (Code D para 4.8).

Power to take fingerprints under the Terrorism Act 2000

6.6 Where a person is detained for examination under TA 2000 Sch 7 or on suspicion of being a terrorist under TA 2000 s41, fingerprints may be taken by a constable with appropriate consent[6] or, where the person is detained at a police station, on the authority of a superintendent or above, or if the person has been convicted of a recordable offence (TA 2000 Sch 8 para 10(4)). Where authorisation is required to take fingerprints from a person arrested under TA 2000 s41, it may be given if the officer reasonably suspects the person has been involved in a terrorist offence mentioned in TA 2000 s40(1)(a), and reasonably believes that fingerprints will tend to confirm or disprove the person's involvement. In any other case, authorisation may only be given if the officer is satisfied that the taking of the fingerprints is necessary in order to assist in determining whether the person falls within TA 2000 s40(1)(b) (ie is or has been concerned in the commission, preparation or instigation of acts of terrorism). If authorisation is given orally, it must be confirmed in writing as soon as is reasonably practicable (TA 2000 Sch 8 para 10(7)). For the information that must be given to a person before fingerprints are taken, see TA 2000 Sch 8 para 11. Note that the provisions concerning fingerprints in Code D do not apply to a person detained for examination under TA 2000 Sch 7 or arrested under TA 2000 s41, and there are no equivalent provisions in Code H.

Power to take fingerprints under the National Security Act 2023

6.7 Where a person is arrested and detained under NSA 2023 s27, fingerprints may be taken by a constable with appropriate consent[7] or, where the

6 Which has the same meaning as under PACE s65 (TA 2000 Sch 8 para 15(1)) (see para 6.3 above).

7 Which has the same meaning as under PACE s65 (NSA 2023 Sch 6 para 14(1)) (see para 6.3 above).

person is detained at a police station, on the authority of a superintendent or above, or if the person has been convicted of a recordable offence (NSA 2023 Sch 6 para 10(2) and (4)). Where authorisation is required to take fingerprints from a person arrested under NSA 2023 s27, it may be given if the officer reasonably suspects the person has been involved in foreign power threat activity and the fingerprints will tend to confirm or disprove involvement; or, where the person has refused to identify themself or the officer has reasonable grounds for suspecting that the person is not who they claim to be, the officer is satisfied that fingerprints will help to determine the person's identity (NSA 2023 Sch 6 para 10(6) and (7)). Note that the provisions concerning fingerprints in Code D do not apply to a person arrested and detained under NSA 2023 s27, and there are no equivalent provisions in Code I.

Speculative searches, retention and destruction

6.8 Where fingerprints have been taken under any of the powers set out in para 6.4 above (other than under PACE s61(4A)), they may be checked against other fingerprints held by or on behalf of a relevant law enforcement authority[8] or held in connection with or as a result of an investigation of an offence (a 'speculative search') (PACE s63A).[9] Where fingerprints are taken under other powers, or with consent, they may be the subject of a speculative search only if the person consents in writing (PACE s63A(1C)), but once consent has been given it cannot be withdrawn (PACE s63A(1D)).

6.9 Provisions governing retention and destruction of fingerprints taken under PACE are set out in PACE ss63D–63U, and Code D Annex F contains a useful table setting out retention periods. Provisions governing retention and destruction of fingerprints taken under the TA 2000 are set out in TA 2000 Sch 8 paras 20A–20J. Provisions governing retention and destruction of fingerprints taken under the NSA 2023 are set out in NSA 2023 Sch 6 Part 4. Guidance on the deletion of biometric records has been issued by the Home Office.[10]

Advising on fingerprints

6.10 It will be evident from the above that the police have very extensive powers to take fingerprints without consent. In the case of a client who is in police detention following arrest under PACE, the only real limitation on the police power to take their fingerprints is that the offence for which the client has been arrested must be a recordable offence. Having checked that it is, the client should be advised that resistance is pointless and could result in a charge of obstruction or assault on a police officer (or

8 For definition, see PACE s63A(1A) and (1B).

9 For a case reviewing the nature of fingerprint evidence and the standards to be applied, see *R v Smith* [2011] EWCA Crim 1296.

10 *Guidance: Record deletion* (2023), available at: www.gov.uk/government/publications/dna-early-deletion-guidance-and-application-form/guidance-record-deletion-accessible.

designated civilian)[11] in the execution of their duty. Similar considerations apply where a client is detained under the TA 2000 or the NSA 2023.

Photographs

Power to take photographs under PACE

6.11 The police have extensive statutory powers to photograph persons detained at a police station with or without their consent, which are summarised in Code D paras 5.12–5.16. PACE s64A(1) provides that a person detained at a police station (see para 6.2 above) may be photographed with appropriate consent (see para 6.3 above), or without appropriate consent if it is withheld or it is not practicable to obtain it. There are no other pre-conditions for the exercise of this power. Furthermore, a person who is not at a police station may be photographed with appropriate consent, or without appropriate consent if it is withheld or it is not practicable to obtain it, where the person has been:

- arrested by a constable for an offence;
- taken into custody by a constable after being arrested for an offence by a person other than a constable;
- made subject to a requirement to wait with a community support officer or volunteer under PRA 2002 Sch 3B para 7;
- given a direction by a constable under the Anti-social Behaviour, Crime and Policing Act 2014 s35;
- given a penalty notice by a constable under Criminal Justice and Police Act (CJPA) 2001 Part 1 Chapter 1; or a penalty notice by a constable under Education Act 1996 s444A; or a fixed penalty notice by a constable in uniform under Road Traffic Offenders Act 1988 s54;
- given a fixed penalty offence notice by a community support officer or volunteer who is authorised to give the notice by virtue of a designation under PRA 2002 s38;
- given a notice in relation to a relevant fixed penalty offence (within the meaning of PRA 2002 Sch 5 para 1) by an accredited person by virtue of accreditation specifying that Schedule 5 para 1 applies to them; or
- given a notice in relation to a relevant fixed penalty offence (within the meaning of PRA 2002 Sch 5A) by an accredited inspector by virtue of an accreditation specifying that Schedule 5A para 1 applies to them (PACE s64A(1A) and (1B)).[12]

Code D NfG 5E gives examples of when it would not be practicable to obtain consent, including that the person is drunk or otherwise unfit to give consent, that there are reasonable grounds to suspect that if the person became aware that a photograph was to be taken they would take steps to prevent this, that in order to take a suitable photograph it is necessary to take it covertly, and, in the case of a child, that their parent or

11 PRA 2002 s46(1) makes it an offence to assault a designated person in the execution of their duty.

12 For further circumstances in which a photograph may be taken without consent, see PACE s64A(1C)–(1M).

guardian cannot be contacted in sufficient time to allow the photograph to be taken. The power under PACE s64A(1) is in addition to the power to photograph any identifying mark found in an examination under PACE s54A (see para 6.21 below). Code D para 5.19 provides that the powers to take photographs of detained persons also apply to volunteers, but force may not be used (Code D para 5.21).

6.12 The photograph must be taken by a constable (PACE s64A(3)), and reasonable force can be used (PACE s117; and see Code D NfG 5F). The person may be required to remove any item or substance worn on or over the whole or part of the face or head, and the constable or designated civilian may remove it themself if the requirement is not complied with (PACE s64A(2)). The term 'photograph' includes any process by means of which a visual image may be produced and includes both still and moving images (PACE s64A(6) and (6A)). Where a person is to be photographed under this power, they must be told the purpose of the photograph, and the purposes for which the photograph may be used, disclosed or retained (Code D para 5.16). This information must be given before the photograph is taken, unless it is taken covertly or is copied from an image taken at any time from a camera system installed in the police station. The documentation requirements are set out in Code D paras 5.17 and 5.18.

Power to take photographs under the Terrorism Act 2000

6.13 The power to photograph a person detained under TA 2000 Sch 7 or s41 is even more extensive than under PACE. An authorised person (including a constable and an examining officer) may take any steps that are reasonably necessary for photographing a detained person (TA 2000 Sch 8 para 2). No authorisation is necessary.

Power to take photographs under the National Security Act 2023

6.14 The power to photograph a person arrested and detained under NSA 2023 s27 is the same as under the TA 2000 (NSA 2023 Sch 6 para 2).

Retention, use and destruction

6.15 Where a photograph is taken under PACE s64A, it may be used by, or disclosed to, any person for any purpose related to the prevention or detection of crime, the investigation of an offence, the conduct of a prosecution or the enforcement of a sentence (PACE s64A(4)(a)). 'Crime' includes conduct that constitutes a criminal offence in any part of the UK or any other country, and conduct that would be a crime if it took place in the UK (PACE s64A(5)(a)). References to an investigation and to a prosecution include any criminal investigation outside the UK and to a prosecution brought outside of the UK (PACE s64A(5)(b)).

6.16 Photographs taken under PACE s64A do not have to be destroyed, but may only be used for a purpose set out in PACE s64A(4)(a) (PACE s64A(4)(b)). A photograph of a volunteer must, subject to any retention requirement under the Criminal Procedure and Investigations Act 1996, be destroyed (together with any negatives and copies) unless they are charged or informed that they may be prosecuted for a recordable offence, prosecuted or cautioned for a recordable offence, or they have given written consent to retention (Code D para 5.22). Where the destruction obligation applies, the person must be given an opportunity to witness the destruction or be given a certificate confirming the destruction (Code D para 5.23).

6.17 There are no equivalent provisions regarding use, disclosure or destruction of photographs taken under the TA 2000 or the NSA 2023.

Advising on photographs

6.18 It will be seen from the above that the police have extensive powers to take photographs with or without consent, and there is no requirement that the offence concerned be a recordable offence. The client should be advised that resistance could result in a charge of obstruction or assault on a police officer (or designated civilian[13]) in the execution of the officer's duty. There is no reference in PACE s64A to the parts of the body that may be photographed, although the reference to removal of a face or head covering in PACE s64A(2) implies that, although a photograph could be taken of more than merely a person's face or head, they could not be required to remove other forms of clothing to facilitate the taking of a photograph. However, the police do have powers to photograph other parts of the body under PACE s54A, although only in respect of a person who is detained in a police station (see para 6.19 below). A client who is a volunteer should be advised of the destruction and use provisions, and should be advised that if they give consent it is likely that it cannot subsequently be withdrawn.[14] The power to take photographs of a detained person under the TA 2000 and the NSA 2023 appears to be limited only by what an authorised person regards as 'reasonably necessary'.

Search and examination to ascertain identity

Power to search and examine under PACE

6.19 An inspector or above may authorise a person detained in a police station (see para 6.2 above) to be searched or examined, or both:

- for the purpose of ascertaining whether the person has any mark that would tend to identify them as a person involved in the commission of an offence (PACE s54A(1)(a)); or
- for the purpose of facilitating the ascertainment of the person's identity (PACE s54A(1)(b)).

A 'mark' includes features (for example, moles, scars, tattoos) and injuries, and a mark is an 'identifying mark' if its existence facilitates the ascertainment of the person's identity or their identification as a person involved in the commission of an offence (PACE s54A(12)). Establishing a person's

13 PRA 2002 s46(1) makes it an offence to assault a designated person in the execution of their duty.

14 Although unlike with fingerprints, there is no statutory provision to this effect (see para 6.8 above).

identity includes showing that they are not a particular person (PACE s54A(11)(a)). A person taken to a police station in order to be searched under a stop and search power (see para 2.2 above) is not a person detained at a police station for these purposes (Code D para 5.1).

6.20 Authorisation may only be given for a search or examination under PACE s54A(1)(a) if appropriate consent (see para 6.3 above) has been withheld or it is not practicable to obtain such consent (PACE s54A(2)). Code D NfG 5D gives examples of when it would not be practicable to obtain consent, including:

- that the person is drunk or otherwise unfit to give consent;
- that there are reasonable grounds to suspect that if the person became aware that a search or examination was to be conducted they would take steps to prevent this; and
- in the case of a child, that their parent or guardian cannot be contacted in sufficient time to allow the search or examination to be carried out or the photograph to be taken.

Authorisation may only be given under PACE s54A(1)(b) if the person has refused to identify themself, or the officer has reasonable grounds for suspecting that the person is not who they claim to be (PACE s54A(3)). Authorisation may be given orally or in writing, but if given orally must be confirmed in writing as soon as is practicable (PACE s54A(4)). Code D para 5.19 provides that the powers to search or examine detained persons also apply to volunteers, but force may not be used (Code D para 5.21). Where a person is to be searched, examined or photographed under PACE s54A, they must be told (Code D para 5.16):

- the purpose of the search, examination or photograph;
- the grounds on which authority has been given; and
- the purposes for which any photograph taken may be used, disclosed or retained.

This information must be given before the search, examination or photograph unless the photograph is to be taken covertly. The documentation requirements are set out in Code D paras 5.17 and 5.18.

6.21 Any identifying mark found on a search or examination under PACE s54A can be photographed, either with the appropriate consent (see para 6.3 above), or without it if consent is withheld or it is not practicable to obtain it (PACE s54A(5); and see Code D NfG 5D). A photograph includes any process by means of which a visual image may be produced (PACE s54A(11)(b)). A search or examination may only be conducted, or a photograph taken, by a constable or designated civilian officer of the same sex as the person searched, examined or photographed, and reasonable force may be used (PACE s54A(6) and (7)). If there is doubt about whether a person is to be treated as male or female for this purpose, their gender must be established and recorded in accordance with Code C Annex L (Code C para 1.13(c)). An intimate search (see para 6.101 below) cannot be conducted under PACE s54A, and if the search or examination involves the removal of more than outer clothing it must be treated as a strip search and conducted in accordance with Code C Annex A para 11 (Code D para 5.10; and see para 6.98 below).

Power to search and examine under the TA 2000

6.22 The power to search and examine a person detained under TA 2000 Sch 7 or s41 is more extensive, and less regulated, than under PACE. An authorised person (including a constable or an examining officer) may take any steps that are reasonably necessary for the purpose of identifying a detained person (TA 2000 Sch 8 para 2). No authorisation is necessary.

Power to search and examine under the NSA 2023

6.23 The power to search and examine a person detained under NSA 2023 s27 is almost identical to that under the TA 2000. A constable, or other authorised person may take any steps that are reasonably necessary for the purpose of identifying a detained person (NSA 2023 Sch 6 para 2). No authorisation is necessary.

Retention, use and destruction

6.24 The provisions on retention, use and destruction of photographs taken under PACE s54A are the same as those under PACE s64A (see para 6.15 above). There are no equivalent provisions regarding use, disclosure or destruction of photographs taken under the TA 2000 or the NSA 2023.

Advising on search and examination to establish identity

6.25 Although PACE s54A gives the police extensive powers to search and examine detained persons, the lawyer should carefully consider whether the conditions set out in PACE s54A(1)–(3) are satisfied. Note that there is no requirement that the offence concerned be a recordable offence. Where the conditions are satisfied, the client should be advised that refusal of consent will not prevent a search or examination from taking place, and that resistance could result in a charge of obstruction or assault on a police officer (or designated civilian[15]) in the execution of their duty. A client who is a volunteer should be advised of the destruction and use provisions, and should be advised that if they give consent it is likely that it cannot be subsequently withdrawn.[16] The power to search and examine under the TA 2000 and the NSA 2023 appears to be limited only by what the constable or authorised person regards as 'reasonably necessary'.

Footwear impressions

Power to take footwear impressions under PACE

6.26 The police can take a footwear impression from a person if appropriate consent (see para 6.3 above) is given, which, if the person is at a police station when consent is given, must be in writing (PACE s61A(1), (2); Code D para 4.16). A footwear impression can be taken without appropriate consent if (PACE s61A(3)):

15 PRA 2002 s46(1) makes it an offence to assault a designated person in the execution of their duty.

16 Although unlike with fingerprints, there is no statutory provision to this effect (see para 6.8 above).

- the person is detained at a police station (see para 6.2 above) in consequence of an arrest for a recordable offence, or has been charged with, or informed that they will be reported for, a recordable offence;[17] and
- the person has not had an impression taken of their footwear in the course of the investigation of that offence by the police.

In relation to the latter, if the person has already had an impression taken of their footwear in the course of the investigation, a further impression may be taken if the previous impression was incomplete or is not of sufficient quality to allow for satisfactory analysis, comparison or matching (PACE s61A(4)). The power to take an impression may be exercised by any police constable (PACE s61A(7)). The meaning of 'impression of footwear' is not defined.

6.27 Before an impression is taken, whether with or without consent, the person must be informed of the reason the impression is to be taken, and that it may be retained and made the subject of a speculative search, unless destruction is required (PACE s61A(5); Code D para 4.19 and Annex F Part (a)). Where the person is detained at a police station, this must be recorded in the custody record (Code D paras 4.20–4.21).

Power to take footwear impressions under the TA 2000

6.28 There is no explicit power to take a footwear impression from a person arrested and/or detained under TA 2000 s41 or Sch 7. The power to take a footwear impression without consent under PACE is limited to persons detained in consequence of an arrest for a recordable offence, and a person detained under the TA 2000 is not regarded as having been arrested for an offence. In any event, PACE s61A(8) explicitly excludes persons arrested under the terrorism provisions from exercise of the power under section 61A. Code D does not apply (Code D para 2.17(iii)), and Code H contains no provisions regarding footwear impressions. It may be argued that a power to take a footwear impression is granted by TA 2000 Sch 8 para 2(1), that is, for the purpose of measuring or identifying a detained person, but that would depend upon the purpose for which it is proposed to take a footwear impression.[18]

Power to take footwear impressions under the NSA 2023

6.29 There is no explicit power to take a footwear impression from a person arrested and detained under NSA 2023 s27. The power to take a footwear impression without consent under PACE is limited to persons detained in consequence of an arrest for a recordable offence, and a person detained under the NSA 2023 is not regarded as having been arrested for an offence.[19]

17 See note 4 above.

18 The same argument would apply where a person is detained for examination under the C-TBSA 2019 since neither Schedule 3 nor the code of practice include provisions regarding footwear impressions.

19 Note that PACE s61A(8) does not specifically exclude persons arrested and detained under NSA 2023 s27, but since a person arrested under section 27 is not regarded as being arrested for an offence, it would seem that the PACE power would not apply in any event.

Code D does not apply (Code D para 2.17(iii)), and Code I contains no provisions regarding footwear impressions. It may be argued that a power to take a footwear impression is granted by NSA 2023 Sch 6 para 2(1), that is, for the purpose of measuring or identifying a detained person, but that would depend upon the purpose for which it is proposed to take a footwear impression.

Speculative searches, retention and destruction

6.30 The provisions regarding footwear impressions taken under PACE s61A are the same as for fingerprints (see paras 6.8 and 6.9 above).[20] There are no equivalent provisions regarding retention or destruction of footwear impressions taken under the TA 2000 or the NSA 2023.

Advising on footwear impressions

6.31 The position is essentially the same as for fingerprints (see para 6.10 above), subject to the limitations noted above in respect of persons arrested and/or detained under the TA 2000 or the NSA 2023.

Samples and skin impressions

6.32 Four kinds of sample are dealt with in this section:

(1) intimate samples (including dental impressions);
(2) non-intimate samples and skin impressions;
(3) handwriting samples; and
(4) samples in road traffic cases.

Intimate samples

Introduction

6.33 The power to take intimate samples is governed by PACE s62 and Code D section 6. An 'intimate sample' is defined as (PACE s65(1)):

- a sample of blood, semen or any other tissue fluid, urine or pubic hair;
- a dental impression; or
- a swab taken from any part of a person's genitals (including pubic hair) or from a person's body orifice other than the mouth.

However, despite the reference to urine and blood samples, the taking of such samples under the Road Traffic Act (RTA) 1988 or the Transport and Works Act 1992 is unaffected by this section (PACE s62(11); and see para 6.72 below). The powers under PACE s62 and the Code D provisions do not apply to a person arrested and/or detained under the terrorism provisions (including TA 2000 Sch 7 and s41), C-TBSA 2019 Sch 3 or NSA 2023 s27 (PACE s62 (12)–(14), and see paras 6.41 and 6.44 below).

20 It was held in *R v T* [2010] EWCA Crim 2439 that current statistical data do not provide a sufficiently reliable basis for an expert to express an opinion based on the use of mathematical formulae. However, given the time that has passed since the judgment, the issue may be revisited if there have been significant developments in the data.

Power to take intimate samples under PACE

6.34 An intimate sample may only be taken if all of the following three conditions are satisfied:

(1) Authorisation is given by an officer of the rank of inspector or above under PACE s62(1)(a), (1A)(a) or (2A)(b). Authorisation may be given orally or in writing, but if given orally, must be confirmed in writing as soon as is practicable (PACE s62(3)). Authorisation may only be given if:
  - in the case of a person in police detention (see para 1.58 above), the officer has reasonable grounds for suspecting their involvement in a recordable offence[21] and for believing that the sample will tend to confirm or disprove involvement (PACE s62(1) and (2));
  - in the case of a person who is not in police detention but from whom, in the course of investigation of an offence,[22] two or more non-intimate samples suitable for the same means of analysis have been taken which proved to be insufficient, the officer has reasonable grounds for suspecting the person's involvement in a recordable offence and for believing that the sample will tend to confirm or disprove involvement (PACE s62(1A) and (2));[23] and
  - in the case of any person,[24] two or more non-intimate samples suitable for the same means of analysis have been taken under PACE s63(3E) (persons convicted of offences outside England and Wales) which have proved insufficient (PACE s62(2A)).

(2) Appropriate consent (see para 6.3 above) is given (PACE s62(1)(b), (1A)(b) or (2A)(c)). The consent requirement means that an intimate sample may never be taken in the absence of consent, although refusal may result in adverse inferences (see para 6.50 below).

(3) Before the sample is taken, the person is informed of the reason for taking the sample, the fact that authorisation has been given and the provision under which it was given, and, if the sample is taken at a police station, the fact that it may be the subject of a speculative search (PACE s62(5) and (6)). Although not a statutory requirement, the person should, in addition, be cautioned (see para 6.37 below).

6.35 Where the conditions for taking an intimate sample are satisfied, the sample may be taken in any prison or other institution to which the Prison Act 1952 applies (PACE s63A(3)). This would seem to be confined to powers under PACE s62(1A) or (2A), since the powers under section 62(1) can only be exercised if the person is in police detention (see para 1.58 above). Powers to require a person to attend a police station for the purpose of taking an intimate sample are governed by PACE s63A(4) and Sch 2A

21 See note 4 above.

22 Note that the words 'an offence' are used rather than 'the offence', which implies that the non-intimate samples may have been taken in respect of an offence other than that for which an intimate sample is required (see note 36 below).

23 An insufficient sample is one that is insufficient with regard to quantity or quality, or as a result of loss, damage or use, has become insufficient or unavailable. See PACE s65(1) and (2); and Code D para 6.2(b) and NfG 6B.

24 There is no reference in this subsection to whether or not the person is in police detention, so presumably it applies whether or not the person is in police detention.

(and see Code D para 6.2A). These provisions only grant powers to require a person to attend a police station, and do not confer any extra powers to take an intimate sample. Therefore, even if the person is required to attend for the purpose of taking an intimate sample, or is arrested in default, a sample cannot be taken unless the relevant conditions are satisfied and appropriate consent is given.

6.36 An intimate sample – other than a sample of urine (which may be taken by a police officer) or a dental impression (which can only be taken by a registered dentist) – may only be taken by a registered medical practitioner or registered healthcare professional (PACE s62(9) and (9A)).

6.37 PACE s62(10) provides that where a person refuses without good cause to consent to an intimate sample, a court may draw 'proper' inferences (see para 6.50 below). Before an intimate sample is requested, the person must be cautioned in the following terms (Code D para 6.3 and NfG 6D):

> You do not have to provide this sample/allow this swab or impression to be taken, but I must warn you that if you refuse without good cause, your refusal may harm your case if it comes to trial.

6.38 If the suspect is in police detention and not legally represented, they must be reminded of their entitlement to free legal advice, or if the sample is being taken under PACE s62(1A) (see para 6.34 above) and the person is attending the police station voluntarily, the right to free legal advice must be explained (Code D para 6.3). If the person has been arrested under the provisions in PACE Sch 2A (see para 6.35 above), then although they are not in police detention, they are entitled to legal advice under PACE s58 since they are a 'person arrested and held in custody'. A record must be made of the authorisation, the grounds for giving that authorisation, the fact of consent, the reminder of the right to legal advice, and the fact that a speculative search may be conducted and, where the person is detained at a police station, the record must be made in the custody record (PACE s62(7), (8); Code D paras 6.3, 6.10 and 6.11).

Speculative searches

6.39 The power is the same as for fingerprints (see para 6.8 above).

Retention, use and destruction

6.40 The provisions are the same as for fingerprints (see paras 6.8 and 6.9 above).

Power to take intimate samples under the Terrorism Act 2000[25]

6.41 An intimate sample can be taken from a person who is detained under the 2000 Sch 7 or s41 if they are detained in a police station, appropriate consent[26] is given in writing, and it is authorised by a superintendent or

25 Note that there are no powers to take an intimate sample from a person detained under C-TBSA 2019 Sch 3.

26 Which by TA 2000 Sch 8 para 15 has the same meaning as under PACE. See para 6.3 above.

above. Code D does not apply (Code D para 2.17(iii)), and the taking of intimate samples is not covered in Code H. A superintendent may only give authority if:

- in the case of a person detained under TA 2000 s41, the officer reasonably suspects that the person has been involved in an offence under the provisions mentioned in TA 2000 s40(1)(a) and the officer reasonably believes that the sample will tend to confirm or disprove the person's involvement; or
- in any case, the officer is satisfied that the taking of the sample is necessary in order to assist in determining whether the person falls within TA 2000 s40(1)(b) (ie is or has been concerned in the commission, preparation or instigation of acts of terrorism) (TA 2000 Sch 8 para 10(5) and (6)).

Where two or more non-intimate samples suitable for the same means of analysis have been taken from a person under TA 2000 Sch 8 para 10, and those samples have proved insufficient and the person has been released from detention, an intimate sample can be taken if appropriate consent is given and it is authorised by a superintendent or above. The superintendent must be satisfied that taking a sample is necessary for the same reasons as under TA 2000 Sch 8 para 10(6).

6.42 An intimate sample, other than a sample of urine (which may be taken by a police constable) or a dental impression (which can only be taken by a registered dentist), may only be taken by a registered medical practitioner (TA 2000 Sch 8 para 13(2) and (3)). Refusal without good cause to provide a sample can result in inferences being drawn (TA 2000 Sch 8 para 13(1)). For the information that must be given to the person before samples are taken, see TA 2000 Sch 8 para 11.

6.43 Speculative searches, and the retention, use and destruction of intimate samples and the data derived from them, are governed by TA 2000 Sch 8 paras 20A–20J.

Power to take intimate samples under the National Security Act 2023

6.44 An intimate sample can be taken from a person who is detained under NSA 2023 s27 only if they are detained at a police station, appropriate consent is given in writing and it is authorised by a superintendent or above. A superintendent may only give authority if they reasonably suspect that the detained person has been involved in foreign power threat activity, and reasonably believes that the sample will tend to confirm or disprove the person's involvement (NSA 2023 Sch 6 para 10(5) and (6)). Code D does not apply, and the taking of intimate samples is not covered by Code I.

6.45 The provisions governing the persons who may take an intimate sample (NSA 2023 Sch 6 paras 10(5) and 13), the taking of an intimate sample where non-intimate samples have proved insufficient (Sch 6 para 12), and inferences following a refusal of consent (Sch 6 para 13), are similar to those under the TA 2000. For the information that must be given to the detained person before a sample is taken, see NSA 2023 Sch 6 para 11.

6.46 Speculative searches, and the retention, use and destruction of intimate samples and the data derived from them, are governed by NSA 2023 Sch 6 Part 4.

Advising on intimate samples

6.47 In advising the client, the lawyer must consider all of the conditions set out in para 6.34 above (samples under PACE), para 6.41 above (samples under the TA 2000) or para 6.44 above (samples under the NSA 2023). With regard to authorisation under PACE s62(2), the lawyer should first consider whether the offence suspected is a recordable offence,[27] and whether a sample will tend to confirm or disprove involvement. The officer should be asked whether the police are in possession of any forensic samples and the nature of such samples. If they do not possess them, it may be argued that the taking of an intimate sample cannot fulfil this requirement. If this is the case, the lawyer may consider advising the suspect to withhold consent (but see para 6.50 below). Similarly, the lawyer must consider whether the nature of the alleged offence is such that an intimate sample is likely to have probative effect. For example, in an allegation of rape, a sample of semen will not tend to confirm or disprove the allegation if the client has admitted intercourse at the relevant time. If authority has already been given, the lawyer should ask to see the written authority (if given in writing, see paras 6.34 and 6.41 above), and should check the grounds on which authority has been given.

6.48 Where the person has been requested to return to the police station or is arrested under PACE Sch 2A, consideration must be given to whether the police have the power to take an intimate sample since, even if the suspect consents, it can only be taken if the conditions set out in para 6.34 above are satisfied. If the person attends voluntarily in response to a request, or is arrested under PACE Sch 2A, a sample cannot be taken under PACE s62(1) because the person is not in police detention since they have not been arrested for an offence. If the person attends voluntarily and is then arrested, it could be argued by the police that the person is then in police detention, since PACE s118(2)(b) (arrest after attending voluntarily) does not refer to arrest for an offence. However, the structure of PACE s118(2) clearly implies that section 118(2)(b) refers to arrest for an offence, and normally arrest for an offence would not be justified in these circumstances.

6.49 If the only available power to take an intimate sample is under PACE s62(1A) or (2A), TA 2000 Sch 8 para 12, or NSA 2023 Sch 6 para 12, it must be remembered that these provisions require that the police have previously taken at least two non-intimate samples. Therefore, if the police originally took an intimate sample, or only one non-intimate sample, that has proved insufficient, they have no power to take an intimate sample. The police may be able to rectify this by their power to take non-intimate samples under PACE s63(3A) which, if the sample then proved insufficient, may enable an intimate sample to be taken under PACE s62(1A). The police cannot short-circuit this by simply asking the person to consent

27 See note 4 above.

to an intimate sample, since the conditions in PACE s62 (or TA 2000 Sch 8 para 12 or NSA 2023 Sch 6 para 12, as relevant) must always be satisfied. In relation to the power to take an intimate sample under PACE Code D NfG 6C provides that nothing in Code D para 6.2 prevents intimate samples being taken with consent for elimination purposes. The meaning of this is not defined, but is likely to refer to a sample taken in order to establish that the person is not a suspect, as opposed to seeking to establish that a suspect is, or may be, guilty. This is unlikely to be the case where the person has been required to attend or has been arrested under PACE Sch 2A. Note that as a result of the definition of 'insufficient' in PACE s65(1) and (2), the powers under PACE s63A will be available if the sample had been lost, damaged or destroyed.

6.50 If authority is given for the taking of an intimate sample and the lawyer is satisfied that the statutory conditions are satisfied, the client will require advice on whether to give consent. PACE s62(10), TA 2000 Sch 8 para 13 and NSA 2023 Sch 6 para 13 provide that if consent is refused without good cause, the court or jury in subsequent proceedings may draw such inferences from the refusal as appear proper. Before being asked to provide an intimate sample, the person must be warned that refusal may be so treated (Code D para 6.3 and NfG 6D), although there is no similar provision in relation to the TA 2000 or the NSA 2023. It is difficult to predict accurately how a refusal to give consent to a sample being taken will be interpreted at the trial stage, and a client should always be warned of the dangers of refusal. Three factors need to be considered.

6.51 The first factor is relevant if the refusal is based on legal advice. What inferences can a court or jury properly draw if the evidence is that the refusal resulted from the advice given by the lawyer? Unlike inferences under Criminal Justice and Public Order Act (CJPOA) 1994 s34, there is no reasonableness requirement, but PACE s62(10) only permits inferences if consent was refused without good cause. It can be argued that legal advice not to consent should amount to good cause. Even if it does not, it may be argued that refusal to give consent on advice should not be taken as an indication of guilt. In the case of a child, refusal to give consent by a parent or guardian may also present difficulties to a court in determining whether and what inference to draw. On the other hand, irrespective of the strict legal provisions regarding inferences, if a jury or court is made aware that consent was refused, it may well lead them to place less credibility on the defence put forward at trial.

6.52 The second factor concerns the question of what other evidence the police have, or might secure. It will often not be easy to assess this for the reasons discussed at para 4.27 above. However, if there is no other evidence, or that other evidence is weak, a refusal may not in itself add very much to the overall weight of evidence. For example, if the case involves identification, and the client has not been picked out in an identification procedure and there is no other evidence, not only may there be no other evidence to be corroborated by the fact of refusal to allow a sample to be taken, but allowing a sample to be taken may actually provide the police with the evidence they need to be able to prosecute the client successfully. It is not improper for a lawyer who knows the client to be guilty to advise them to refuse consent for a sample to be taken. However, it should be noted that if the police are seeking an intimate sample for the purposes of DNA analysis, as is often the case, they are likely to be able to achieve the same result by taking a non-intimate sample, which they may take whether or not the suspect consents (see para 6.58 below). If this is the case, the suspect would be at risk of inferences being drawn without any advantage resulting from refusal to consent.

6.53 The third factor concerns the feelings of the client and is related to the question of whether an accused has 'good cause' to refuse consent. The client may be embarrassed, worried about being roughly treated, scared of needles or have religious objections. With regard to embarrassment or a fear of rough treatment, a number of provisions in the legislation and codes may be relevant. Intimate samples other than of urine may only be taken by a medical or dental practitioner, as appropriate (see para 6.42 above). In PACE cases, where the taking of a sample requires the removal of clothing in circumstances likely to cause embarrassment to the person, no person of the opposite sex other than a medical practitioner or nurse may be present (unless, in the case of a child or a mentally vulnerable person, they specifically request the presence of a particular adult of the opposite sex who is readily available), nor may anyone whose presence is unnecessary (Code D para 6.9). In most cases this will mean that no more than one police officer, or possibly two if necessary in the interests of security, should be present. There are no equivalent provisions in TA 2000 Sch 8 or NSA 2023 Sch 6, or Code H or I, although it is submitted that the same restrictions should apply.

6.54 In the case of a child, removal of clothing in these circumstances may only take place in the absence of the appropriate adult if the child requests this in the presence of the appropriate adult and the appropriate adult agrees (Code D para 6.9). This would seem to mean that a child could insist on a particular adult of the opposite sex being present (provided the adult is readily available) and/or that the appropriate adult should not be present. For example, a child in the care of a local authority might want a parent to be present rather than the social worker who is acting as appropriate adult. It appears to be an anomaly that a child could insist on the presence of a parent if the parent is of the opposite sex, but not if they are both of the same sex. In respect of persons detained under TA 2000 s41 or NSA 2023 s27, Codes H and I Annex A para 6 contain similar provisions regarding intimate or strip searches of a child, and whilst there is no similar provision regarding the taking of an intimate sample, arguably the same approach should be adopted.

6.55 In the case of a mentally disordered or mentally vulnerable person,[28] it would seem that the appropriate adult should be present, since Code D para 2.15 provides that an appropriate adult must be present for any procedure involving the 'participation of a suspect' who is mentally disordered or otherwise mentally vulnerable. Code C Annex A para 12 and Codes H and I Annex A para 6 provide that an intimate search of such a person should only be carried out in the presence of an appropriate adult of the same sex, unless the person specifically requests otherwise. Whilst

28 See note 3 above.

there is no similar provision regarding the taking of an intimate sample, arguably the same approach should be adopted.

6.56 Given the above provisions, it is unlikely that embarrassment or fear of the way in which the person might be treated would amount to good cause for the purposes of PACE s62(10), TA 2000 Sch 8 para 13 or NSA 2023 Sch 6 para 13, particularly if the client has received legal advice. With regard to other reasons for refusal of consent, the difficulty for the lawyer in advising the client is that it would be impossible accurately to predict how a court would view the refusal. There are no reported cases on this point, although it may be instructive to consider decisions made under RTA 1988 s7 and its predecessors, which provide for the defence of 'reasonable excuse' to a prosecution for failure to provide a specimen. It was held in *Kemp v Chief Constable of Kent*[29] that the question of whether circumstances were capable of amounting to a reasonable excuse was a question of law, whereas whether those circumstances did in fact provide a reasonable excuse was a matter of fact. Generally, the excuse must arise out of a physical or mental inability to provide a specimen, or a substantial risk to health resulting from providing a specimen.[30] It has been held that a fear of AIDS is not a reasonable excuse, but that a medically recognised phobia may be.[31] If a client puts forward such reasons for wanting to refuse consent, they should be carefully questioned in order to try to determine the basis for the view, and an accurate note taken of what the client says. It may also be advisable, subject to agreement of the client, to inform the police of the reasons and ask that they be noted on the custody record. In any event, the lawyer should warn the client that a court may not accept that the reasons for refusing consent amount to good cause.

Non-intimate samples and skin impressions

Introduction

6.57 Non-intimate samples and skin impressions are governed by PACE s63 and Code D section 6. A 'non-intimate sample' is defined as (PACE s65(1)):

- a sample of hair other than pubic hair;[32]
- a sample taken from a nail or under a nail;
- a swab taken from any part of the body other than a part from which a swab taken would be an intimate sample (see para 6.33 above);
- saliva; or
- a skin impression.

29 [1987] RTR 66, DC.

30 *R v Lennard* [1973] 1 WLR 483, CA.

31 See *DPP v Fountain* [1988] Crim LR 123, QBD; and *De Freitas v DPP* [1993] RTR 98, DC, respectively.

32 Note that a plucked hair, as well as a cut hair, is a non-intimate sample (unless it is a pubic hair) (Code D para 6.1(b)). Where hair samples are taken for the purpose of DNA analysis (as opposed to, for example, making a visual match), the suspect must be permitted, within reason, to choose the part of the body from where the hairs are to be taken (Code D NfG 6A).

A 'skin impression' is defined as any record, other than a fingerprint, of the skin pattern and other physical characteristics or features of the whole or any part of a person's foot or any other part or their body (PACE s65(1)). The definition is such that it includes ear impressions.[33] Although PACE s63 is headed 'Other samples', it is confined to non-intimate samples as defined by PACE s65, and does not cover non-body samples such as handwriting. The power under PACE s63 and the Code D provisions do not apply to a person arrested and/or detained under the terrorism provisions (including TA 2000 Sch 7 and s41), C-TBSA 2019 Sch 3 or NSA 2023 s27 (PACE s63(10) and (10A)); and see paras 6.64 and 6.66 below).

Power to take non-intimate samples under PACE

6.58 The major difference between the powers to take intimate and non-intimate samples concerns the question of consent. Unlike intimate samples, a non-intimate sample may always be taken with appropriate consent (see para 6.3 above) in writing (PACE s63(1), (2); Code D para 6.5). If consent is given, the offence concerned does not have to be a recordable offence. If appropriate consent is not given, a non-intimate sample can be taken:

(1) From a person in police detention (see para 1.58 above) in consequence of their arrest for a recordable offence,[34] provided that the person has not had a non-intimate sample of the same type and from the same part of the body taken from them in the course of investigation of the offence, or has had such a sample taken but it proved insufficient (PACE s63(2A)–(2C)).[35] No authorisation is required.

(2) From a person who is being held in custody by the police on the authority of a court, and an inspector or above authorises it to be taken (PACE s63(3)). Authorisation may only be granted if the officer has reasonable grounds:
- for suspecting the person's involvement in a recordable offence; and
- for believing that the sample will tend to confirm or disprove that involvement (PACE s63(4)).

Authorisation cannot be given for a non-intimate sample consisting of a skin impression if a skin impression of the same part of the body has already been taken from the person in the course of the investigation of the offence, and the impression taken has not proved insufficient (PACE s63(5A)). Authorisation under PACE s63(4) maybe given orally or in writing, but if orally, must be confirmed in writing as soon as practicable (PACE s63(5)).

(3) From a person who has been arrested for a recordable offence and released and:

33 The scientific analysis of ear impressions has caused significant difficulty. See *R v Dallagher* [2002] EWCA Crim 1903; and *R v Kempster* [2008] EWCA Crim 975, in which the science was reviewed.

34 See note 4 above.

35 For the meaning of 'insufficient' see note 23 above.

- in the case of a person who is on bail, they have not had a non-intimate sample of the same type and from the same part of the body taken in the course of the investigation of the offence, or
- in any case, the person has had a non-intimate sample taken in the course of that investigation but it was not suitable for the same means of analysis or it proved insufficient (PACE s63(3ZA)),

no authorisation is required.

(4) From a person who has been charged with a recordable offence or informed that they will be reported for such an offence (with a view to a written charge or caution), and either they have not had a non-intimate sample taken in the course of investigation of the offence or they have had a non-intimate sample taken but either it was not suitable for the same means of analysis or, though so suitable, the sample proved insufficient (PACE s63(3A)).[36] No authorisation is required.

(5) From a person who has been convicted of a recordable offence, or cautioned for a recordable offence which, at the time of the caution, the person had admitted, or been reprimanded or warned for a recordable offence (PACE s63(3B)). The power to take a non-intimate sample under this provision only applies if a non-intimate sample has not been taken from the person since the person was convicted or cautioned, or it has been taken but was not suitable for the same means of analysis or it proved insufficient (PACE s63(3BA)). Authorisation is required from an inspector or above, who may only give authorisation if satisfied that it is necessary to assist in the prevention or detection of crime (PACE s63(3BB) and (3BC)).

(6) From a person who is imprisoned or detained following an acquittal on grounds of insanity or a finding of unfitness to plead (or similar) (PACE s63(3C)).

In addition, there are powers to take a non-intimate sample from a person who has been convicted of an offence in a foreign jurisdiction, provided certain conditions are satisfied (PACE s63(3E)–(3H)).

6.59 Where the conditions for taking a non-intimate sample are satisfied, it may be taken in any prison or other institution to which the Prison Act 1952 applies (PACE s63A(3)). However, this would not apply to the powers described in (1) or (2) above since for these powers to be exercised the person must either be in police detention or held in custody by the police on the authority of a court, and this would usually exclude detention in a prison. Where the power to take a non-intimate sample is provided by PACE s63(3B) in respect of a person who is detained under Mental Health Act 1983 Part III pursuant to a hospital order, interim hospital order or transfer direction imposed following conviction for a recordable offence, or by PACE s63(3C), the sample may be taken in the hospital where the person is detained (PACE s63A(3A)). Where the power to take a non-intimate sample is provided by PACE s63(3B) in respect of a person detained in pursuance of directions of the secretary of state under Powers

36 Note that it refers to whether samples have been taken in the investigation of 'the' offence, ie the one for which the person has been charged or informed that he or she will be reported. Contrast this with the power to take an intimate sample under PACE s62(1A) (see note 22 above).

of Criminal Courts (Sentencing) Act 2000 s92, the sample may be taken at the place where the person is detained (PACE s63A(3B)).

6.60 Where a non-intimate sample is taken without appropriate consent, before the sample is taken the person must be informed of the reason for taking the sample, the power under which it is to be taken and, where authorisation is required, the fact that it has been given (PACE s63(6)). If the person is at a police station, whether with or without appropriate consent, the person must be told that the sample may be the subject of a speculative search (PACE s63(8B)). In each case, the relevant matters must be recorded, and if at a police station, the record must be made in the custody record (PACE s63(8), (8B), (9)). Since a non-intimate sample can be taken without consent, there is no provision for the person to be warned of the evidential consequences of failure to consent. A non-intimate sample may be taken by a constable (PACE s63(9ZA)), or a community support officer or volunteer who is authorised to take a non-intimate sample by virtue of a designation under PRA 2002 s38.

6.61 Powers to require a person to attend a police station for the purpose of taking a non-intimate sample are governed by PACE s63A(4) and Sch 2A (and see Code D para 6.6A). If a person is required to attend a police station for a non-intimate sample to be taken, it is important to check that the date of attendance is within the time limits set out in Schedule 2A. The power to take a non-intimate sample under PACE s63(2A)–(2C) would not apply to a person who voluntarily attended the police station or who was arrested in default; the person is not in police detention since they have not been arrested for an offence. However, many of the other powers to take a non-intimate sample set out in para 6.58 above would apply to such a person.

Speculative searches

6.62 The power is the same as for fingerprints (see para 6.8 above).

Retention, use and destruction

6.63 The provisions are the same as for fingerprints (see paras 6.8 and 6.9 above).

Power to take non-intimate samples under the Terrorism Act 2000

6.64 Where a person is detained under TA 2000 Sch 7 or s41, a non-intimate sample may be taken by a constable with appropriate consent in writing, on the authority of a superintendent or above, or if the person has been convicted of a recordable offence on or after 10 April 1995 (TA 2000 Sch 8 para 10(3) and (4)). Where authorisation is required, a superintendent may only give it if:

- in the case of a person detained under TA 2000 s41, the officer reasonably suspects that the person has been involved in an offence under the provisions mentioned in TA 2000 s40(1)(a) and the officer reasonably believes that the sample will tend to confirm or disprove the person's involvement; or
- in any case, the officer is satisfied that the taking of the sample is necessary in order to assist in determining whether the person falls

within TA 2000 s40(1)(b) (ie is or has been concerned in the commission, preparation or instigation of acts of terrorism) (TA 2000 Sch 8 para 10(5) and (6)).

6.65 For retention, use and destruction of samples taken under these provisions, and the power to conduct speculative searches, see TA 2000 Sch 8 paras 20A–20J. For the information that must be given to the person before samples are taken, see TA 2000 Sch 8 para 11.

Power to take non-intimate samples under the National Security Act 2023

6.66 Where a person is detained under NSA 2023 s27, a non-intimate sample may be taken by a constable with appropriate consent in writing, on the authority of a superintendent or above, or if the person has been convicted of a recordable offence on or after 10 April 1995 (NSA 2023 Sch 6 para 10(3) and (4)). Where authorisation is required, a superintendent may only give it if the officer:

- reasonably suspects that the person has been involved in a foreign power threat activity; and
- reasonably believes that the sample will tend to confirm or disprove the person's involvement (NSA 2023 Sch 6 para 10(4) and (6)).

6.67 For retention, use and destruction of samples taken under these provisions, and the power to conduct speculative searches, see NSA 2023 Sch 6 paras 19–28. For the information that must be given to the person before samples are taken, see NSA 2023 Sch 6 para 11.

Advising on non-intimate samples

6.68 The police have extensive powers to take non-intimate samples, although in most cases involving persons detained under PACE the power can only be exercised in relation to a recordable offence, and a number of the powers require authorisation. Having checked the power under which the police intend to proceed, and that the relevant conditions are satisfied, the lawyer should normally advise the client that they have little alternative but to submit to the sample being taken. There is no provision in the legislation governing non-intimate samples for a court to draw adverse inferences from a refusal to allow a sample to be taken (as there is for intimate samples), but if the conditions for taking a sample are satisfied and the suspect does not co-operate, reasonable force may be used in order to obtain the sample (PACE s117; PRA 2002 s38(8); TA 2000 s114; NSA 2023 s28). Furthermore, resistance could result in a charge of obstruction of or assault on a police constable (or designated civilian) in the execution of their duty.

Handwriting samples

6.69 PACE, the TA 2000 and the NSA 2023 do not deal with handwriting samples.[37] The use of disputed handwriting as evidence is governed by

37 Although PACE s76(4) permits part of an excluded confession to be admitted to establish that an accused writes in a particular way.

Criminal Procedure Act 1865 s8, which permits evidence of handwriting to be admitted at trial, but the taking of handwriting samples is not regulated. This lack of statutory authority creates difficulty for the lawyer in advising the client whether to co-operate in the taking of such samples. In particular, it is unclear whether a refusal to co-operate can lead to adverse inference being drawn at trial.

6.70 It was seen in the section on advising clients whether to answer police questions (see para 5.66 above) that at common law, the failure of a person to answer police questions could not be used as evidence against them at trial. There is a strong argument that the question of samples[38] is analogous with silence, that is, a person cannot be required to incriminate themself, whether by words or actions. The initial difficulty with this argument lies in the case of *R v Smith*,[39] in which the analogy was rejected in relation to a hair sample, and it was held that a suspect's refusal to allow the police to take a sample of his hair was evidence capable of amounting to corroboration. It has been suggested that this case is authority for the proposition that refusal, in the presence of a solicitor, of a police request for a sample, handwriting or participation in an identification procedure may be capable of amounting to corroboration.[40] However, *Smith* was decided before PACE came into force. The particular facts of the case would now be covered by PACE s63, and reasonable force could have been used to take the sample since the accused was suspected of involvement in robbery, a recordable offence. More importantly, it could be argued that since that case, parliament has considered the question and chosen not to provide for inferences to be drawn other than in the case of intimate samples under PACE s62, the TA 2000 and the NSA 2023. If it were the general common law position that refusal to allow a sample to be taken could result in adverse inferences at trial, there would have been no need for these special statutory provisions.

6.71 However, it has to be accepted that the position is uncertain as there is no reported case on the point since PACE came into force. In terms of advising a client faced with a request for a handwriting sample, the advice should be that there may be some danger in refusing to co-operate, but that the dangers are likely to be minimal. Even if adverse inferences could be drawn at trial, such a danger may well be outweighed by the danger of providing the sample. This is particularly so in the case of handwriting, since forensic handwriting analysis cannot be regarded as an exact science. Furthermore, one way of reducing any danger of adverse inferences is for the lawyer to ensure that they advise the suspect before responding to the request, and that if the suspect decides to refuse to co-operate, they should say that they are not willing to provide the sample on legal advice. In this way, the primary inference to be drawn should be that the suspect was acting on advice.[41] The lawyer should keep a careful note of the advice, and of the reasoning behind it, since this may become relevant at trial.

38 Except intimate samples, which are governed by PACE s62(10).

39 (1985) 81 Cr App R 286, CA.

40 Law Society, *Advising a suspect in the police station* (1991) p25.

41 However, see the discussion regarding the impact of legal advice on inferences under CJPOA 1994 s34 at para 5.99 above.

Road Traffic Act 1988 samples

6.72 As was noted at para 6.33 above, blood and urine samples taken for the purpose of the drink/drug driving procedures under the RTA 1988 are excluded from the PACE provisions relating to intimate samples by PACE s62(11). Samples of breath would not come under either PACE s62 or 63 in any event.

6.73 The major question that arises at the police station is whether the suspect should be advised to provide a sample. Failure without reasonable excuse to provide a sample is an offence under RTA 1988 s7(6), on conviction for which the defendant will usually be disqualified from driving. It has been held that it is not a reasonable excuse to refuse to give a sample until the person has consulted a solicitor, although the person should be permitted to consult a solicitor briefly if the solicitor is immediately available.[42] Medical reasons for not giving a sample will not normally amount to a reasonable excuse unless the act of giving a sample, or attempting to give a sample, would be injurious to health (see para 6.56 above). For this reason, even if the lawyer suspects that the procedure may be unlawful, they should advise the suspect that failure to provide a specimen is likely to lead to prosecution and disqualification.

6.74 The current prescribed limits[43] are 35 mg of alcohol in 100 ml of breath; 80 mg of alcohol in 100 ml of blood; and 107 mg of alcohol in 100 ml of urine. The sample taken at the police station will normally be of breath. However, a constable may require a sample of blood or urine rather than of breath if:

(1) the constable has reasonable cause to believe that for medical reasons a specimen of breath cannot be provided or should not be required; or
(2) at the time of the request a device for taking a breath sample is not available or it is not practicable to use such a device (for example, it is broken);
(3) the constable who required the specimens of breath has reasonable cause to believe that the device has not produced a reliable indication of the proportion of alcohol in the breath;
(4) as a result of the administration of a preliminary drug test, the constable making the requirement has reasonable cause to believe that the person required to provide a specimen of blood or urine has a drug in their body; or
(5) the suspected offence is one under RTA 1988 s3A, 4 or 5A, and the constable has been advised by a medical practitioner or registered health care professional that the condition of the suspect might be due to some drug (RTA 1988 s7(3)).

6.75 In these circumstances, it is for the officer to decide whether the sample should be of blood or of urine, unless they have been advised by a medical

42 See *Kennedy v Crown Prosecution Service* [2002] EWHC 2297 (Admin); and *Whitley v DPP* [2003] EWHC 2512 (Admin); and cases cited at para 2.142 above.

43 For specified drugs, the current limits (microgrammes per litre of blood) are set out in the Drug Driving (Specified Limits) (England and Wales) Regulations 2014 SI No 2868 and the Drug Driving (Specified Limits) (England and Wales) (Amendment) Regulations 2015 SI No 911.

practitioner that for medical reasons a specimen of blood cannot or should not be taken (RTA 1988 s7(4)). However, the officer should give the suspect the opportunity to express a preference before they decide which form of sample to require.[44] Therefore, if the suspect does not wish to give a blood sample, they should say so at this stage, and if there is a medical reason for the suspect's preference, this should be made known to the doctor who is called to take a blood sample.

Drug-testing for class A drugs

Power to test for class A drugs

6.76 The power to test people in police detention (see para 1.58 above) for class A drugs is governed by PACE ss63B and 63C and Code C section 17. The powers are not available in all police stations, and in some stations they are only available in respect of suspects who have attained the age of 18 years, whereas in others drug-testing following charge (but not before charge) is possible in respect of suspects who are between the ages of 14 and 17 years.[45]

6.77 Where a person is in police detention (in a police station in which the powers are available) a sample of urine or a non-intimate sample may be taken from them for the purpose of ascertaining whether they have any specified class A drug in their body, provided that they have been brought before a custody officer (PACE s63B(5D)) and the conditions set out below are satisfied. The conditions are:

- either the arrest condition or the charge condition is met;
- both the *age condition* and the *request condition* are met; and
- the *notification condition* is met in relation to the arrest condition, the charge condition or the age condition (as relevant) (PACE s63B(1)).

6.78 The *arrest condition* is satisfied if the suspect has been arrested for, but not charged with, a trigger offence or any offence where an inspector or above, having reasonable grounds for suspecting that the misuse by that person of any specified class A drug caused or contributed to the offence, authorises a sample to be taken (PACE s63B(1A)). The *charge condition* is satisfied if the suspect has been charged with a trigger offence or any offence where an inspector or above, having reasonable grounds for suspecting that the misuse by that person of any specified class A drug caused or contributed to the offence, authorises a sample to be taken (PACE s63B(2)). If a sample is taken in respect of which the arrest condition was satisfied, no further sample can be taken under PACE s63B during the same continuous period of detention unless the suspect remains in police detention in respect of another offence, in respect of which the arrest condition is satisfied (PACE s63B(5B), (5C); Code D para 17.9). A 'specified class A drug' and 'trigger offence' have the same meanings as in the

44 *DPP v Warren* [1992] Crim LR 200, QBD.
45 See PACE s63B(4A) and (4B); and Code C NfG 17F.

Criminal Justice and Court Services Act 2000 Part III, and the trigger offences are set out in Code C NfG 17E.

6.79 The *age condition* is, where the arrest condition is met, that the person has attained the age of 18, and where the charge condition is met, that the person has attained the age of 14 (PACE s63B(3)). The *request condition* is simply that a police officer has requested the suspect to give the sample (PACE s63B(4)). Before requesting a sample, the suspect must be warned that failure without good cause to provide the sample requested renders them liable to prosecution (PACE s63B(5); Code C NfG 17A). Failure without good cause to provide a sample is an offence punishable, on summary conviction, with up to three months' imprisonment and/or a fine not exceeding level 4 (PACE ss63B(8) and 63C(1)). If the suspect does refuse to provide a sample, the police cannot use force to obtain one (Code C para 17.14). The suspect must also be told the purpose of taking the sample, that authorisation has been given (where required), and of their right to have someone informed of their arrest, to legal advice and to consult the codes of practice (Code C para 17.6). Where the suspect has not attained the age of 18 years, the making of the request, the warning that refusal may amount to an offence, and the taking of a sample must be in the presence of an appropriate adult (PACE s63B(5A); Code C para 17.7). The *notification condition* is that the relevant chief officer has been notified by the secretary of state that appropriate arrangements have been made for the police area as a whole, or for the particular police station in which the suspect is in police detention (PACE s63B(4A)).

6.80 The authorisation (where authorisation is required) and grounds for suspicion, the warning as to the consequences of refusal and the time at which the sample is given, must be recorded in the custody record (PACE s63C(3) and (4); Code C para 17.2). Where a suspect aged 18 years or older has tested positive for a specified class A drug under PACE s63B the police may, before they are released, impose a requirement that they attend an initial assessment of their drug misuse and to remain for the duration of the assessment, and also to attend a follow-up assessment. Where the suspect is tested before charge, the requirement can be imposed even if they are not subsequently charged with an offence. Failure to attend or to remain at the assessment, or to attend a follow up assessment, is an offence carrying imprisonment up to 51 weeks and/or a fine not exceeding level 4 (Drugs Act (DA) 2005 ss12(3), (4) and 14(3), (4)). When such a requirement is imposed, the suspect must be told of the time and place for the assessment and be warned that failure without good cause to attend and to remain renders them liable to prosecution (DA 2005 ss11(2), (3) and 13(4), (5); Code C para 17.18). The suspect must also be given a written notice containing this information (Code C para 17.19) and the process must be entered in the custody record (Code C para 17.20).

6.81 Where the arrest condition is met, a suspect can be detained for up to 24 hours from the relevant time (see para 2.76 above) in order for a sample to be taken, even though the custody officer would otherwise have decided that the suspect should be released on bail under PACE s37(2) (bail without charge), or under PACE s37(7)(a) (release without charge and on bail with a view to a Crown prosecutor making the charge decision) or under PACE s37(7)(b) (release without charge and on bail but not for that purpose) (PACE s37(8A) and (8B); Code C para 17.10). Where the arrest condition (but not the charge condition) is satisfied in respect of one offence (offence 1) and the suspect's release would be required before a sample could be taken but for the suspect's continued detention in respect of an offence that does not satisfy the arrest condition (offence 2), the suspect may have a sample taken while they continue to be detained provided that it is taken within 24 hours of their arrest for offence 1 (PACE s63B(5C); Code C para 17.10). Thus, if a person is charged with an offence that did satisfy the arrest condition, and a sample could not be taken before they were charged, but they continue to be detained in respect of an offence that does not satisfy the arrest condition, a sample may be taken during that period of further detention, provided that it is taken within 24 hours of the arrest for the first offence. Where a sample may be taken from a person under PACE s63B, but they are charged before a sample is taken and the custody officer would otherwise release them on bail under PACE s38, the custody officer may authorise their detention for up to six hours from the time of charge in order for a sample to be taken (PACE s38(1)(a)(iiia), (2); Code C para 17.10).

6.82 A sample taken under PACE s63B cannot be used for any purpose other than to ascertain whether the person concerned has a specified class A drug present in their body (Code C para 17.16(a)). Although it must be retained until the person has made their first appearance at court (Code C para 17.16(b)), it cannot be used for the purpose of prosecuting them for an offence, other than those offences mentioned below. Information obtained from a sample taken under these powers may be disclosed for any of the following purposes:

- informing a decision as to bail, whether by the police or by a court;
- informing a decision about the imposition of a conditional caution;
- informing any decision about the supervision of the person in police detention, in custody or on bail;
- following conviction, informing any decision about sentence, and any decision about supervision or release;
- a drugs assessment that the suspect is required to attend by the police by virtue of DA 2005 s9(2) (initial assessment) or s10(2) (follow-up assessment);
- prosecution under DA 2005 s12(3) (for failure to attend or remain at an initial assessment) or s14(3) (for failure to attend or remain at a follow-up assessment); and
- ensuring that appropriate advice and treatment is made available to the person concerned (PACE s63B(7)).

Advising on drug-testing

6.83 Where the conditions for drug-testing under PACE s63B are satisfied, the lawyer should advise the client about the drug-testing process and the possible consequences of failure to comply. Force cannot be used to drug-test under PACE s63B, but the client may commit an offence if they do not permit a sample to be taken, and if they are charged with such an offence, this may in itself adversely affect the prospects of bail following charge. If a sample is taken and the test is positive for a specified class A drug (heroin, cocaine and crack cocaine), the suspect can be required to attend an initial assessment. If the suspect is unwilling to attend or otherwise to co-operate with a drugs assessment, or to attend a follow-up assessment, they must be advised that this may amount to an offence and may also mean that bail is not granted, either by the police or by a court.[46]

Search of the person and property

Search of the person away from the police station

Power to search the person

6.84 Police powers of search of the person are complex and various, and this book does not attempt to provide a comprehensive treatment of such powers. The police have power to search a person who has not been arrested without that person's consent under a number of statutes, including PACE Part I; CJPOA 1994 s60; TA 2000 ss43 and 44; and Misuse of Drugs Act (MDA) 1971 s23 (see para 2.2 above).

6.85 Where a person is arrested other than at a police station, they may be searched if the officer has reasonable grounds for believing that they may present a danger to themself or others (PACE s32(1)). In addition, a person may be searched for anything that might be used to assist them in escaping from lawful custody or that might be evidence relating to an offence (PACE s32(2)(a)). The officer must have reasonable grounds for believing that the person may have such an item concealed on them. Any item found in such a search may be seized by the officer if they have reasonable grounds for believing that the person searched might use it to cause physical injury to themself or others (PACE s32(8)), or (providing it is not an article subject to legal privilege) has reasonable grounds for believing that the person might use it to assist them to escape, or that it is evidence of an offence, or has been obtained in consequence of the commission of an offence (PACE s32(9)). It was held in *Tomlinson v DPP*[47] that whether an officer had reasonable grounds for a search was a two-stage question. The first question is whether the officer had grounds from a subjective point of view – ie did the officer believe there were grounds for a search? If the answer is 'no', the search is unlawful. If the answer is 'yes', the second question is whether the belief was reasonable from an objective point of view – that is, would a reasonable person in possession of the same information as the officer have had such a belief? Only if both questions can be answered in the affirmative will the search be lawful.

6.86 The power of search under PACE s32 applies to persons arrested under TA 2000 s41 and under NSA 2023 s27 since the power under section 32 applies where a person has been arrested, irrespective of whether they have been arrested for an offence. However, in the case of a person

46 See Bail Act (BA) 1976 s3(6C)–(6E) and Sch 1 Part I para 6.

47 May 1992 *Legal Action* 21, QBD.

arrested under TA 2000 s41, PACE s32(10) states that nothing in the section affects the power of search conferred by TA 2000 s43. TA 2000 s43(2) grants a power to search a person arrested under section 41 to discover whether they have in their possession anything which may constitute evidence that they are a terrorist.

6.87 A search under PACE s32 must only be conducted to the extent that is reasonably required for the purpose of discovering the thing or evidence concerned (PACE s32(3)). It does not enable the officer to require the person to remove any of their clothing (other than an outer coat, jacket or gloves) in public,[48] but it does enable the officer to search the person's mouth which, it would seem, could be in public and using reasonable force if the person refuses the request (PACE s32(4)). It appears that the power of search under PACE s32(1) applies whether or not the arrest was for an offence, and unlike search of premises under PACE s32(2)(b) (see para 6.114 below) there is no requirement that the arrest be for an indictable offence.

Advising on search of the person

6.88 Following a search it may be alleged that the suspect had items of evidential value on them when arrested. The lawyer should, therefore, check with the custody officer and the arresting officer or officer in charge of the case on arrival at the police station to see whether they say that any such item has been found. Instructions should then be taken from the suspect to find out, among other things, whether they accept that the item was found in their possession and, if so, how the item came to be there. The lawyer will also need to consider whether the search was lawful, since this may affect the advice to be given, particularly in relation to whether the client should answer questions in interview.

6.89 In practice, it will be very difficult to make an accurate assessment at this stage of whether the search was lawful, and even more difficult to predict whether any unlawfulness would result in a court refusing to admit evidence obtained from such a search. The common law position is that the fact that an item was found as a result of an unlawful search will not render evidence of it having been found inadmissible at trial.[49] The common law rule is subject to PACE s78, which gives a discretion to a court to refuse to admit prosecution evidence if it appears, having regard to all the circumstances including the circumstances in which the evidence was obtained, that the admission of such evidence would have such an adverse effect on the fairness of the proceedings that it ought not to be admitted. Although there have been no reported cases on the admission of evidence obtained by an illegal search under PACE s32, it is likely that evidence would be admitted despite the fact that it was obtained in an unlawful search unless, perhaps, it could be shown that the police knew

48 Although note the power under CJPOA 1994 s60AA to remove items that conceal identity (see para 2.6 above).

49 See *Kuruma v R* [1955] 1 All ER 236, PC (Eastern Africa); and *Jeffrey v Black* [1978] 1 All ER 555, DC.

that they were acting unlawfully.[50] In consequence, it is likely that even if the lawyer believes that a search may have been unlawful, this will have little effect on the advice to be given regarding whether to answer police questions. The lawyer should consider advising the client regarding any civil claim that the client may have and about whether a complaint is appropriate (see chapter 13 below).

6.90 For the power of the police to require a suspect to disclose the PIN or other code necessary to gain access to data held on a mobile telephone, computer or other password-protected or encrypted electronic device found in the course of a search, see para 6.121 below.

Search of the person at the police station after arrest

Power to search at the police station

6.91 This section deals with searches carried out at the police station, other than intimate searches, which are dealt with at para 6.101 below. Where a person is taken to a police station having been arrested (whether or not for an offence) elsewhere or after being committed to custody by an order or sentence of a court, or is arrested (whether or not for an offence) at the police station,[51] the custody officer is under a duty to ascertain everything the person has with them (PACE s54(1); Codes C and H para 4.1; Code I para 4). In order to do so, the person may be searched if the custody officer considers this is necessary in order to ascertain what property they have, but only to the extent that the custody officer considers necessary for that purpose (PACE s54(6); Codes C and H para 4.1; Code I para 4). Furthermore, a person who is in police detention (see para 1.58 above) may be searched at any time in order to ascertain whether they have with them anything that could be used to cause physical injury to themself or others, to damage property, to interfere with evidence, or to assist the person to escape (PACE s54(6A)).[52] An intimate search cannot be carried out under this provision (PACE s54(7)), but a strip search can be conducted if the custody officer considers it to be necessary in order to remove an article that the detained person would not be allowed to keep and the officer reasonably considers that the person might have concealed such an article (Code C Annex A para 10; Codes H and I Annex A para 11; and see para 6.98 below).[53]

50 See *R v Wright* [1994] Crim LR 55, CA (unlawful search purportedly conducted under PACE s18); and *Khan v UK* (App No 35394/97) [2000] Crim LR 684, ECtHR (which suggested that evidence would not be excluded even if it amounted to a breach of the right to private life under European Convention on Human Rights Article 8). However, note *R v Olden* [2007] EWCA Crim 726, in which it was held that evidence seized in an unlawful property search should have been excluded.

51 Or is detained at a police station having answered to police bail, or having been arrested under PACE s46A having failed to answer to police bail (PACE s54(1)(b)).

52 It was held in *Pile v Chief Constable of Merseyside* [2020] EWHC 2472 (QB) that removal of clothing that had been soiled by a heavily intoxicated detainee did not amount to a search under PACE s54.

53 It was held in *Davies v Chief Constable of Merseyside* [2015] EWCA Civ 114 that the provisions of Code C Annex A regarding strip searches (see para 6.98 below) do apply where the police remove a suspect's clothing on the grounds that the suspect may use them to cause injury to themself or others.

6.92 The officer can seize and retain anything found in such a search, subject to the proviso that clothes and personal effects can only be seized if the officer:

(1) believes[54] that the person from whom they are seized may use them to:
- cause physical injury to themself or others;
- damage property;
- interfere with evidence; or
- assist the person to escape; or

(2) has reasonable grounds for believing that they may be evidence relating to an offence (PACE s54(3), (4), (6B), (6C); Codes C and H para 4.2; Code I para 4.1).

'Personal effects' are defined as those items which a person may lawfully need or use or refer to while in detention, but not cash or other items of value (Codes C and H para 4.3; Code I para 4.2). Therefore, a suspect should normally be allowed to keep their watch, glasses and belt. Generally, the suspect must be told of the reason for seizure unless they are violent or likely to become violent, or are incapable of understanding what is said to them (PACE s54(5); Codes C and H para 4.2; Code I para 4.1).

6.93 A search can only be carried out by a police constable or civilian detention officer[55] of the same sex as the suspect (PACE s54(8) and (9)). If there is doubt about whether a person is to be treated as male or female for this purpose, their gender must be established and recorded in accordance with Code C Annex L (Code C para 1.13(c); or Code H or I Annex H (Codes H and I para 1.17(c)). It is for the custody officer to decide whether to record any or all of the things that the person had with them, and if the officer does make a record it does not have to be in the custody record (PACE s54(2) and (2A); Codes C, H and I para 4.4; and see para 2.107 above). However, if the person is not allowed to keep any article of clothing or personal effects, the reason must be recorded (Codes C, H and I para 4.5), although it appears that this does not have to be in the custody record.

6.94 In addition to the power of search under PACE s54, section 54B gives the power to any police officer to search, at any time, a person who is in a police station to answer to live link bail (see para 10.136 below), and any article in the possession of such a person (PACE s54B(1)). The officer may seize and retain, or cause to be seized and retained, anything in the possession of the person that they believe ought to be seized on the grounds that it may jeopardise the maintenance of order in the police station, may put the safety of any person at the police station at risk, or may be evidence of, or in relation to, an offence (PACE s54B(2) and (3)). Such a search must be carried out by an officer of the same sex as the person being searched, and an intimate search cannot be conducted under this section.

6.95 For the power of the police to require a suspect to disclose the PIN or other code necessary to gain access to data held on a mobile telephone, computer or other password-protected or encrypted electronic device found in the course of a search, see para 6.121 below.

54 There is no requirement that the belief be reasonable (*Chief Constable of Essex v Carter* [2025] EWCA Civ 367).

55 PRA 2002 Sch 4 para 26, which grants powers of search and seizure under PACE s54.

Advising on search at the police station

6.96 A search will normally already have been carried out before the lawyer arrives at the police station and, therefore, their scope for intervention is limited. The lawyer should ask whether a record was made of anything found on the suspect and, if so, whether it was made in the custody record, and should ask to see the record.[56] This is important, since the property that the person had with them at the time of the search may be the subject of questions in the police interview (for example, money, keys, mobile telephone, etc). Since the power to search on arrival at the station is very broad, it is unlikely to have been unlawful (but see the discussion on strip searches at para 6.97 below). However, it is worth noting that Codes C, H and I NfG 4A emphasise that PACE s54 does not require every detained person to be searched and, in particular, that a search may not be necessary if it is clear that the person will only be detained for a short period and is not to be placed in a cell.

6.97 Exceptionally, the police may wish to carry out a search while the lawyer is at the police station, for example, where they accompanied their client to the station, or where the police are exercising their power to search under PACE s54(6A). Generally, since the search is likely to be lawful, the client should be advised to co-operate. The police are entitled to use reasonable force in order to carry out the search (PACE s117). The lawyer should insist on being present if the client so wishes, which the client is entitled to demand since PACE s58(1) provides that a person arrested and held in custody is entitled to consult a solicitor at any time.

Strip searches

6.98 A strip search is a search that is not an intimate search, but which involves the removal of more than outer clothing (ie coat, gloves, scarf, shoes and socks, etc) (Code C Annex A para 9; Codes H and I Annex A para 10). It was recognised in the pre-PACE case of *Lindley v Rutter*[57] that strip searches 'involve an affront to the dignity and privacy of the individual', and Donaldson LJ said that removal of a brassiere would require considerable justification. A police officer carrying out a strip search must be of the same sex as the suspect (Code C Annex A para 11A; Codes H and I Annex A para 12(a)). If there is doubt about whether a person is to be treated as male or female for this purpose, their gender must be established and recorded in accordance with Code C Annex L, Code H Annex I and Code I Annex H. If a strip search is carried out, the reasons for the search and its result must be recorded (Code C Annex A para 12; Codes H and I Annex A para 13). For strip searches of a child, see para 11.70 below.

6.99 It was seen earlier that a strip search can be carried out if the custody officer considers it to be necessary to remove an article that the detained person would not be allowed to keep (see para 6.91 above), and it is likely that this refers to the items specified in PACE s54(4) (see para 6.92 above).

56 If a record made is not in the custody record the lawyer has no right to see it, but as noted in para 2.107 above it is difficult to see what legitimate reason there could be to refuse such a request.

57 [1981] QB 128, DC.

In addition, the officer must reasonably consider that the person might have concealed such an article (Code C Annex A para 10; Codes H and I Annex A para 11). The lawyer should, therefore, ask the officer to justify the decision to carry out a strip search in terms of what it is the officer expects to find and on what grounds the officer believes the person to be in possession of such items. If the lawyer forms the view that the strip search is or may be unlawful, they should make appropriate representations, including an indication that the client will be advised about the possibility of taking civil action for assault, and ask that they be noted on the custody record. However, if the officer insists on carrying out the search, the client should normally be advised that while they should not consent to the search, they should not actively resist it. Active resistance could result in a successful prosecution for obstruction or assault if a court were subsequently to find that the search was lawful. Subject to the client's wishes, the lawyer should insist on being present, although if not of the same sex as the client, the lawyer should arrange for the attendance of a lawyer who is of the same sex.

6.100 Note that a search or examination to ascertain identity under PACE s54A (see para 6.19 above) that involves the removal of more than outer clothing must be conducted in accordance with Code C Annex A para 11 or Codes H and I Annex A para 12 (Code D para 5.10).

Intimate searches, X-rays and ultrasound scans

Power to carry out an intimate search

6.101 An 'intimate search' is defined as a search that consists of the physical examination of a person's body orifices other than the mouth (PACE s65(1)). 'Body orifice' is not defined, but consists of ears, nose, anus and vagina. Physical insertion into a body orifice would amount to an intimate search, as would any application of force to an orifice or its immediate surroundings, such as the removal of something within an orifice.[58] The definition of an intimate search is not co-extensive with those parts of a body from which an intimate sample may be taken, since an intimate sample includes the taking of samples from parts of the body other than orifices.

6.102 An intimate search can only be carried out if an officer of the rank of inspector or above authorises it, for which purpose the officer must have reasonable grounds for believing that:

(1) a person who has been arrested and is in police detention (see para 1.58 above) may have concealed on them anything which:
- the person could use to cause physical injury to themself or others; and
- the person might use it for this purpose while in police detention or in the custody of a court (PACE s55(1)(a)); or

58 See Code C Annex A para 11(e) and Codes H and I Annex A para 12(e), which also imply that touching an orifice in these circumstances would amount to an intimate search. Requiring a suspect to touch their own genitals or make an insertion into their own body orifice would also amount to an intimate search (*R v Hughes* [1994] 1 WLR 876, CA; *Owens v Chief Constable of Merseyside* [2021] EWHC 3119 (QB)).

(2) such a person:
- may have a class A drug concealed on them; and
- was in possession of it with the appropriate criminal intent (see para 6.106 below) before the person's arrest (PACE s55(1)(b)).

Codes C, H and I Annex A NfG A1 and A2 provide that the authorising officer must first try to obtain the relevant article by seeking to persuade the detainee to hand it over and, if this fails, the officer must review all relevant factors before authorising an intimate search.

6.103 Authorisation may be given orally or in writing, but if given orally it must be confirmed in writing as soon as practicable (PACE s55(3)). Note that there is no requirement that the person be suspected of involvement in a recordable offence,[59] although the conditions for conducting a search under PACE s55(1)(b) would inevitably involve suspicion of a recordable offence. In order for authorisation to be given, the officer must have reasonable grounds for believing that the item cannot be found without the person being intimately searched (PACE s55(2)). It will be seen that the circumstances in which an intimate search may be carried out are extremely limited, and are probably infrequently used.

6.104 Consent is not required for a search under PACE s55(1)(a), but appropriate consent (see para 6.3 above) in writing is required for a search under PACE s55(1)(b) (a drug offence search). If consent to a search under PACE s55(1)(b) (but not under PACE s55(1)(a)) is refused without good cause, proper inferences can be drawn (PACE s55(13A); and see para 5.88 above). Assuming that the requirements of CJPOA 1994 s36 have been satisfied (see para 5.91 above), an inference could be drawn from failure or refusal to account for an object or substance found in an intimate search, since the object is likely to be regarded either as 'on his person' (CJPOA 1994 s36(1)(a)(i)) or 'otherwise in his possession' (CJPOA 1994 s36(1)(a)(iii)). An intimate search must not be carried out in conducting a search or examination under PACE s54A (search or examination to establish identity).

6.105 Anything found in an intimate search may be seized and retained if the custody officer:

(1) believes that the person from whom it is seized may use it to:
- cause physical injury to themself or others;
- damage property;
- interfere with evidence; or
- assist them to escape; or

(2) has reasonable grounds for believing that it may be evidence relating to an offence (PACE s55(12)).

The power to seize and retain the item applies even if the item found was not the item or in the same class of items for which the intimate search was carried out.

Power to take an X-ray or ultrasound scan

6.106 An X-ray and/or ultrasound scan can be taken where an inspector or above authorises it, for which purpose the officer must have reasonable grounds

59 See note 4 above.

for believing that a person who has been arrested and who is in police detention (see para 1.58 above):

(1) may have swallowed a class A drug; and
(2) was in possession of it with the appropriate criminal intent (see para 6.106 below) before their arrest (PACE s55A(1)).

The power can only be exercised with the appropriate consent (see para 6.3 above), but refusal of consent may result in proper inferences (PACE s55A(9); and see para 5.88 above).

Advising on intimate searches, X-rays and ultrasound scans

6.107 Although an authorising officer is not under a specific duty to receive representations from the lawyer, the lawyer should seek to establish what grounds the officer has for the belief that the grounds are satisfied. Since the officer must have reasonable grounds for the belief that the person has concealed or swallowed a relevant item, the officer must be capable of stating what those grounds are. Clearly, a simple recitation of the statutory grounds is not sufficient, since the officer must be able to articulate the basis on which they believe the grounds to be satisfied. The basis for the belief does not have to consist of evidence that would necessarily be admissible in court, but it would have to give cause for more than mere suspicion or even reasonable suspicion.

6.108 As noted above, the powers can only be exercised if the authorising officer has reasonable grounds for the belief. In the case of an intimate search, the reasonableness of the belief relates not only to the grounds for the search but also to whether an intimate search is the only way of finding out whether the person is secreting the item concerned. If the officer is reluctant to state the basis for the belief, the lawyer could argue that the officer cannot reasonably believe that an intimate search is the only way of finding the item (and that, therefore, the search would be unlawful), since if the officer were to say what it is they are looking for and why they believe it to be concealed, the lawyer could advise the client to produce it (if, indeed, the client has concealed the item). Furthermore, if it is likely that the item would be naturally expelled within a reasonable period of time, the officer cannot be satisfied that it cannot be found without an intimate search, although in these circumstances an X-ray or ultrasound scan could be carried out.

6.109 For the purposes of a search under PACE s55(1)(b), 'class A drug' has the meaning assigned to it by MDA 1971 s2(1)(b) (PACE s55(17)). The officer must believe that the person was in possession of it 'with the appropriate criminal intent before the arrest', which means an intent to commit an offence under:

- MDA 1971 s5(3) (possession of controlled drugs with intent to supply another); or
- Customs and Excise Management Act 1979 s68(2) (exportation, etc, with intent to evade a prohibition or restriction) (PACE s55(17)).

This ground is, therefore, very restrictive, and a mere belief that the person is a known drug-user or drug-dealer would not be sufficient to warrant authorisation being given. The officer would have to have reasonable grounds for believing that the person had the concealed drugs on them, or had swallowed them, and that the person was intending to supply or export those drugs.

6.110 If authorisation is given for an intimate search under PACE s55(1)(a) (but not under PACE s55(1)(b) or an X-ray or scan under PACE s55A), the police can use reasonable force in order to carry out the search (PACE s117). Whereas a search under PACE s55(1)(b), or an X-ray or ultrasound scan under PACE s55A, can only be conducted by a suitably qualified person, that is, a registered medical practitioner or a registered nurse (PACE s55(4) and (17) and s55A(4) and (10)), a search under PACE s55(1)(a) can be carried out by a constable if an inspector or above considers that it is not practicable for it to be carried out by a suitably qualified person. If the search is to be carried out by a suitably qualified person, they could not lawfully use force and it would seem that the wording of PACE s117 is such that an officer present at such a search could not use force themself since the officer would not be carrying out the search. This is only relevant to a search under PACE s55(1)(a) since searches under PACE s55(1)(b) and X-rays or scans can only be conducted with the appropriate consent.[60] If it is clear that the police intend to carry out such a search, the lawyer should advise the client to indicate that they do not consent to the search, but to offer no resistance, for to do so could result in a charge of obstruction or assault. If the search is unlawful, a court may not admit evidence of anything so obtained. Although it was suggested in the discussion at para 6.89 above that unlawfulness of a search will usually not render inadmissible evidence found as a result, it may be that a court would exclude evidence under PACE s78 if it was obtained when the police were clearly put on notice that such a search was unlawful. The argument is stronger given the gross intrusion of privacy that such a search would constitute. The lawyer should also signpost the client to advice about whether the client whether a civil action against the police for assault, or complaint, would be appropriate.

6.111 If a search under PACE s55(1)(a) is not to be carried out by a suitably qualified person, it must be carried out by a police constable of the same sex as the suspect (PACE s55(5), (6), (7); Code C Annex A para 6; Codes H and I Annex A para 7). A police officer carrying out a strip search must be of the same sex as the suspect (Code C Annex A para 11(a); Codes H and I Annex A para 12(a)). If there is doubt about whether a person is to be treated as male or female for this purpose, their gender must be established and recorded in accordance with Code C Annex L, Code H Annex I or Code I Annex H. Whether it is impracticable for the purposes of section 55(5) would depend on the circumstances of the case, but Code C Annex A para 3A, and Codes H and I Annex A para 5, provide that a search by a person other than a medical practitioner or nurse must only be considered as a matter of last resort and when the authorising officer is satisfied that the risks associated with allowing the item to remain with the detainee outweigh the risks associated with removing it. Furthermore, Codes C, H

60 Although it could still be relevant if the suspect is under 14 years of age where their parent or guardian consents but the suspect does not.

and I Annex A NfG A4 provide that a search in these circumstances must only be used if other approaches have failed, and the authorising officer is satisfied that the detainee might use the article to cause physical injury to themself or to another and that the injury likely to be caused is sufficiently severe to justify it being carried out by a non-medically qualified person. If the authorising officer has any doubts, they should seek the advice of a superintendent or above (Codes C, H and I Annex A NfG A5). An intimate search carried out under PACE s55(1)(a) may only take place at a hospital, surgery, other medical premises or a police station (PACE s55(8); Code C Annex A para 4).[61]

6.112 If the intimate search is to be carried out under PACE s55(1)(b), or an X-ray or ultrasound scan is to be taken under PACE s55A(1), it must be carried out by a registered medical practitioner or registered nurse, and cannot be carried out by a police officer, or community support officer or volunteer (PACE ss55(4) and 55A(4); Code C Annex A para 4). There is no requirement that the medical practitioner or nurse be of the same sex. A drug search, X-ray or ultrasound scan may only be carried out in the same premises as for a search under PACE s55(1)(a), except that it cannot be carried out in a police station (PACE ss55(9) and 55A(4); Code C Annex A para 4).

6.113 If the detainee is a child or a vulnerable person, and the intimate search is carried out at a police station, it may only be carried out in the presence of an appropriate adult of the same sex, unless the detainee specifically requests the presence of a particular adult of the opposite sex who is readily available. In the case of a child, the search may only take place in the absence of an appropriate adult if the child makes this request in the presence of the appropriate adult and the appropriate adult agrees (Code C Annex A para 5; Codes H and I Annex A para 6). Subject to the above provision, no person of the opposite sex may be present at the search, and no one else should be present whose presence is unnecessary (Code C Annex A para 6; Codes H and I Annex A para 7). Generally, therefore, only those police officers who are carrying out the search (where this is permitted) and the minimum number of officers necessary for the purposes of security, should be present.

6.114 Subject to the wishes of the client, the lawyer should insist on being present. Such presence can be justified by virtue of PACE s58(1) (or TA 2000 Sch 8 para 7 or NSA 2023 Sch 6 para 7, as relevant), which provides that a person arrested and held in custody is entitled to consult a solicitor at any time. This would apply, in the case of a detention under PACE, even if the search is carried out away from the police station, since PACE s58 refers to the person being held in custody 'in a police station or other premises'. If the lawyer is of the opposite sex to the client then, by virtue of Code C Annex A para 6 (Codes H and I Annex A para 7), the lawyer will have to arrange for the presence of a lawyer of the same sex. Arguably, in the case of a child or vulnerable person who is searched at a police station (where this is permitted), a lawyer of the opposite sex could be present if the person specifically requests the presence of the lawyer (Code C Annex A

61 This is not explicitly stated in Codes H and I, but is a condition set out in PACE s55(8), which would apply where a person is arrested and detained under the TA 2000 or the NSA 2023.

para 5; Codes H and I Annex A para 6), although this would not normally be appropriate.

Search of premises

Introduction

6.115 The powers of the police to enter and search premises are both extensive and various. An entry on to and search of premises is always permissible with the consent of a person entitled to grant entry, although consent should be obtained in writing if practicable (Code B section 5). The police may enter and search premises without consent on the authority of a warrant from a court, or without a warrant under a number of statutory powers including PACE ss17, 18 and 32 and under numerous other statutes. This section is confined to the powers to search premises at the time of arrest under PACE s32, and after arrest under PACE s18.

6.116 Generally, powers of search and seizure under PACE are limited to police constables, but they may be carried out by community support officers or volunteers designated for this purpose (PRA 2002 s38(6B) and Sch 3B). However, any power that includes a power to use force to enter any premises is only exercisable by a designated person if they are in the company, and under the supervision, of a constable, or the entry is for the purpose of saving life or limb or preventing serious damage to property (PRA 2002 s38(9)).

Search of premises on arrest

6.117 Where a person is arrested at a place other than a police station, a constable has power to enter and search any premises in which the arrested person was when they were arrested or immediately before they were arrested, for evidence relating to the offence for which they had been arrested (PACE s32(2)(b)). This power is only available where the person is arrested for an indictable offence (see para 2.23 above). 'Premises' are defined as including any vehicle, vessel, aircraft, hovercraft, offshore installation, renewable energy installation, tent or moveable structure (PACE s23). Where the premises concerned consist of two or more separate dwellings (for example, a multi-occupied house), the power to search is limited to any dwelling in which the arrest took place or in which the person arrested was immediately before their arrest, and any parts of the premises which the occupier of any such dwelling uses in common with the occupiers of any other dwellings comprised in the premises (PACE s32(7)). Where the premises consist of self-contained dwellings, it is clear that the search must be confined to the dwelling occupied by the arrested person, together with any common parts such as stairways and corridors. If the premises consist of shared accommodation, where each occupier has their own room, perhaps with shared use of some rooms such as kitchen, living room and toilet, the police should not enter those rooms exclusively occupied by the other flat-sharers.[62] The power of search applies whether or not

62 See *Thomas v DPP* [2009] EWHC 3906 (Admin), a case concerning entry and search under PACE s17(1)(b).

the person arrested owns, controls or occupies the premises. Therefore, if the person is arrested at a friend's house, the police would have power to search it provided the other conditions are satisfied.

6.118 PACE s32(2)(b) refers to the premises where the person was at the time of arrest 'or immediately before he was arrested'. Where the person is arrested in premises, this will present no problem, but 'immediately before' requires interpretation. It has been held that, in contrast to a search under PACE s18, section 32 is an immediate power and the police cannot return to search the premises several hours after the arrest.[63] It is probable that once a person has been taken to a police station, a section 32 search cannot be carried out, although a section 18 search may be possible (see para 6.118 below).

6.119 In order to carry out such a search, the officer must have reasonable grounds for believing that there is evidence for which a search is permitted on the premises (PACE s32(6)). Furthermore, the power to search is only a power to search to the extent that is reasonably required for the purpose of discovering any such evidence (PACE s32(3)). Therefore, the nature of the search must relate to the kind of evidence the officer believes to be on the premises, having regard to the offence for which the person has been arrested. For example, an arrest on suspicion of a recent burglary could justify a search of the premises for the items stolen. On the other hand, if the person is arrested for an assault, a search would be hard to justify except, perhaps, to look for any weapon used. Furthermore, once found, no further search would be justified.

6.120 The police may use reasonable force to carry out the entry and search (PACE s117). There are no specific powers of seizure under PACE s32(2)(b), but PACE s19 provides that a constable who is lawfully on any premises has power:

(1) to seize anything that is on the premises if the constable has reasonable grounds to believe that it has been obtained in consequence of the commission of an offence, or that it is evidence in relation to an offence, and that it is necessary to seize it in order to prevent it being concealed, lost, altered or destroyed (PACE s19(2) and (3)); and
(2) where the constable has similar reasonable grounds, to require that information that is stored in any electronic form and is accessible from the premises be produced in a form in which it can be taken away and which is in a visible and legible form or in a form (such as a disk or memory stick) from which a visible and legible version can be produced (PACE s19(4)).

The power of seizure under PACE s19(2) and (3) includes the premises themselves if they are readily moveable, for example, a car or caravan. However, it does not extend to seizing things that are not on the premises, such as a car parked in a car park adjacent to the premises.[64] Items that the constable has reasonable grounds for believing to be subject to legal

63 *R v Badham* [1987] Crim LR 202, Crown Court (Wood Green). In *Hewitson v Chief Constable of Dorset* [2003] EWHC 3296 (QB), it was indicated that a gap of two hours and 10 minutes between the arrest and the search was too long for a search to be carried out under PACE s32.

64 *Wood v North Avon Magistrates' Court* [2009] EWHC 3614 (Admin).

professional privilege must not be seized (PACE s19(6)). However, this must be interpreted by reference to CJPA 2001 s50. This enables a constable to seize the whole or part of a suspect item so as to remove it from the premises for the purpose of determining whether it falls within the power, provided that it is not reasonably practicable to do this on the premises. Note the procedural requirements governing section 32 searches in Code B sections 6–9.

6.121 Note that Regulation of Investigatory Powers Act (RIPA) 2000 s49 provides that where the police have come into the possession of information protected by a password, etc (a 'key') by exercising a statutory power to seize, detain, inspect, search or otherwise to interfere with documents or other property, a person with 'appropriate permission' may give written notice to a person who they have reasonable grounds to believe has possession of that key to disclose it. Section 49 contains a number of detailed pre-conditions for exercise of the power. 'Appropriate permission' requires authorisation by an officer of at least the rank of superintendent.[65] Knowing failure by the person to provide the key in accordance with the disclosure notice is an offence, with a maximum penalty following conviction on indictment of two years' imprisonment (or five years in a national security or child indecency case), or six months following summary conviction (section 52). The precise powers regarding extraction of data from the device depend upon whether or not the device is connected to a telecommunication system at the time of extraction,[66] but for practical purposes, this does not affect the advice to be given at the police station. In *KNZ v Commissioner of Police of the Metropolis*,[67] the Investigatory Powers Tribunal considered the correct approach to RIPA 2000 s49. Other statutory police powers may be considered by analogy and the analogy with the power of arrest (PACE s24) (see paras 2.13–2.23 above) is a good one:

> 46. [T]he lawfulness of a notice given under s. 49 depends on two things. First, the person who gives the notice must believe that the preconditions in sub-paragraphs (a)–(d) are met. Second, in the case of each precondition, the belief must be reasonable. The first requires a focus on the subjective belief of the authorising officer. The second requires the court to consider whether, on the facts known to the person giving the notice, the belief was reasonable.

The lawfulness of a section 49 notice cannot be established by ex post facto reference to reasons that were not those that the person giving the notice had at the time. Preventing and detecting crime (RIPA 2000 s81(5)) has a broad formulation and a section 49 notice is likely to be issued at a relatively early stage of an investigation, so while there must be a 'reasonable foundation' for the enquiry (as per *R v CB*[68]):

> 53. . . . It is sufficient that there is reason to think that the information to be downloaded from the device will cast relevant light on the elements of the

65 The law is usefully summarised in Home Office, *Code of Practice for investigation of protected electronic information* (2018), available at: www.gov.uk/government/publications/code-of-practice-for-investigation-of-protected-electronic-information.

66 See *Hill v Metropolitan Police Service and Independent Office for Police Conduct* [2022] UKIP Trib 6; and *KFJ v Surrey Police* [2022] UKIP Trib 7.

67 [2025] UKIP Trib 4.

68 [2020] EWCA Crim 790.

alleged offence so as to assist in confirming or undermining one or more of those elements.

The section 49(2)(d) requirement that the officer giving the notice believes, on reasonable grounds, that it is 'not reasonably practicable' to obtain the information sought by other means should not be elevated into a requirement to show that it would be completely impossible to do so.

Search of premises after arrest

6.122 A police constable, or a community support officer or volunteer designated for this purpose (PRA 2002 s38(6B) and Sch 3B),[69] can enter and search any premises occupied or controlled by a person who is under arrest[70] for an indictable offence (see para 2.23 above) provided that they have reasonable grounds for suspecting that there is on the premises evidence, other than items subject to legal privilege, relating to that offence or to some other indictable offence which is connected with or similar to that offence (PACE s18(1)). The power to search is only a power to search to the extent that is reasonably necessary for the purpose of discovering such evidence (PACE s18(3)).

6.123 Generally, an entry and search under PACE s18 can be carried out only if it is authorised in writing by an officer of the rank of inspector or above (PACE s18(4)). However, a constable can conduct a search without authorisation and before taking the arrested person to the police station, or before releasing the person following arrest (see para 2.48 above), if the presence of that person at a place other than a police station is necessary for the effective investigation of the offence (PACE s18(5) and (5A)). In such a case, the officer must inform an inspector or above of the search as soon as is practicable afterwards (PACE s18(6)). It would be possible, provided that the various conditions were satisfied, for both a section 32 search and a section 18 search to be carried out before an arrested person is taken to a police station – for example, where the person is arrested at a friend's house, and a search is conducted there and at the suspect's own home. However, neither power of search is available unless the person is arrested for an indictable offence, and thus where a person is arrested for a summary-only offence the police do not have power to enter and search premises for evidence.[71]

6.124 Even if authorised under PACE s18(4), section 18 powers cannot be exercised unless the officer conducting the search has reasonable grounds for suspecting that there is evidence on the premises relating to that offence or to some other indictable offence which is connected with or

69 A power to use force to enter any premises is only exercisable by a designated person if they are in the company, and under the supervision, of a constable, or the entry is for the purpose of saving life or limb or preventing serious damage to property (PRA 2002 s38(9)).

70 The premises must as a fact, or perhaps as a matter of mixed fact and law, be occupied or controlled by the person under arrest: reasonable suspicion that the person occupies or controls them is not enough (*Khan v Commissioner of Police of the Metropolis* [2008] EWCA Civ 723; and see Code B para 4.3).

71 Although the police do have certain powers of entry and search under PACE s17, for example, to effect an arrest in respect of certain specified offences that are not indictable offences.

similar to that offence (PACE s18(1)). 'Reasonable grounds for suspecting' implies a mixed subjective/objective test.[72] The evidence concerned must relate to the offence for which the person has been arrested or to some other indictable offence which is 'connected with or similar to' the offence for which the person has been arrested. For example, if a person has been arrested for burglary of a dwelling-house that is situated in a road where there have been a number of other burglaries within the previous few days, all with the same method of entry, this could justify a search for property stolen from the other dwellings, since they could be said to be 'connected'. However, the officer must have reasonable grounds for suspecting the presence of such evidence, and a search of premises occupied by a person arrested when attempting to burgle a dwelling-house would not be justified simply because the police believe that the person may have committed other burglaries.

6.125 A search under PACE s18 extends to premises occupied or controlled by the arrested person. 'Premises' has the same meaning as for section 32 searches (see para 6.117 above). The meaning of 'occupied or controlled' is not defined in PACE. 'Occupied' denotes at least some degree of permanency and would not include premises that were simply being visited by the arrested person at the time of their arrest, but would include temporary accommodation occupied by the arrested person, such as a hotel room.[73] 'Controlled' would include management as well as ownership, for example, a shop owned or managed by the arrested person. While it is clear that a section 18 search could be carried out at residential premises rented by an arrested tenant, the question arises whether those premises could be searched if the person arrested was the landlord. It is certainly arguable that the landlord does not 'control' the premises, since generally the landlord will have no right to enter the premises without permission of the tenant. The position is less clear if the premises are let on some form of licence, and a hotel room would almost certainly be regarded as 'controlled' by the hotel owner or manager. There is no similar provision in section 18 to that in PACE s32(7) regarding premises consisting of two or more separate dwellings (see para 6.117 above), although it is likely that the same principles would apply.

6.126 A constable may use reasonable force to carry out an entry and search under section 18 (PACE s117). The officer may seize and retain anything for which they may search under section 18(1), and in addition, the powers of seizure under PACE s19 and the power to demand access to password protected information apply (see paras 6.120 and 6.121 above). Note the procedural requirements governing section 18 searches in Code B sections 6–9.

72 See, in relation to arrest, para 2.15 above.

73 In *R (AB and CD) v Huddersfield Magistrates' Court and Chief Constable of West Yorkshire* [2014] EWHC 1089 (Admin), it was held that the arrested person's occupation of the premises must be such as to support the belief that it would have caused or contributed to the presence of the evidence.

Advising on search of premises

6.127 A client at the police station may require legal advice on a number of aspects relating to search of premises. If a search has already been carried out (particularly if it was carried out at the time of the arrest), or if it was carried out with some degree of force or if damage was done on gaining entry, the client may well feel angry and believe that the search must have been unlawful. With regard to damage, Code B para 6.13 provides that before leaving premises entered by force, the officer in charge must satisfy themself that the premises are secure. If the client is concerned about this, the lawyer could ascertain what arrangements were made and consider whether they are satisfactory. The lawyer may also seek to check that the damage has been recorded on the record of the search (see Code B para 8.1).

6.128 The legality of the search may have a bearing on whether any evidence obtained is likely to be admissible at trial. This, in turn, may affect the advice the lawyer gives to the client at the police station, particularly regarding whether they should answer police questions. An arrest carried out in order to conduct a section 18 search, in circumstances where the police believe that a search warrant would not be granted, may be unlawful.[74] However, it has been held that where the conditions for both an arrest followed by a search and a search warrant are satisfied, the police have a choice as to which procedure to use.[75] The effect of the illegality of search of the person is discussed at para 6.89 above and similar principles apply to search of premises. Answering questions regarding any item found in such a search may render pointless any application to exclude evidence of the item being found. However, a failure to answer questions may lead to inferences under CJPOA 1994 ss34 and 36, and it is unlikely that a court would direct that inferences should not be drawn merely on the basis that a search was believed to be unlawful. Advice may also be necessary regarding a possible formal complaint or civil action in respect of an illegal search (see chapter 13 below).

6.129 It was suggested at para 4.37 above that the lawyer should establish at an early stage whether the client has already made any comment or admissions. This is particularly important if a search of premises was carried out at which the client was present, since anything allegedly said may form the basis for questions in the police interview and may, subject to what is said below, be used in evidence at trial. As with other comments allegedly made by the suspect outside the context of an interview at the police station, the lawyer must make an assessment of whether evidence of such statements is likely to be admissible at trial since this will affect the advice to be given, particularly with regard to whether the client should answer police questions in interview.

6.130 Generally, once a decision has been made to arrest a person, they must not be interviewed except at a police station (Code C para 11.1; Code H para 11.2; and see para 4.46 above). If an interview is conducted contrary to this provision, it may be possible to exclude evidence of the interview at

74 *R (TL) v Chief Constable of Surrey* [2017] EWHC 129 (Admin); see also *ST v Chief Constable of Nottinghamshire* [2022] EWHC 1280 (QB).

75 *R (Singh) v National Crime Agency* [2018] EWHC 1119 (Admin).

trial under PACE s76 or 78. Questioning will not amount to an interview if the questions are put only as part of the proper and effective conduct of a search.[76] The police should confine questions to whether any article they discover is property claimed by the suspect and, if so, whether it is property that could amount to evidence of an offence. The police must not use a search to ask questions on unconnected matters.[77]

6.131 If a conversation during the search did not amount to an interview, it is not covered by the prohibition in Code C para 11.1, and evidence of what was said is likely to be admitted at trial, although as with any relevant comment, a written record should be made and where practicable the suspect must be given an opportunity to verify the record (Code C para 11.13). If this is not done, a court may refuse to admit evidence of the conversation, whether or not it amounted to an interview. As with items found during a search, it may be advisable for the client not to answer questions in interview if the lawyer has reason to believe that anything said during the course of the search may not be admitted at trial (see para 6.128 above).[78]

6.132 If the police are proposing to carry out a search of premises, the lawyer should consider its legality. It is likely that a proposed search at this stage would be under PACE s18, and the lawyer should consider, in particular:

- whether the client is under arrest for an indictable offence;
- whether the premises to be searched are occupied or controlled by the client;
- whether there are reasonable grounds for suspecting that there is on those premises evidence relating to the offence for which the person is under arrest, or some other connected or similar indictable offence; and
- whether the search has been properly authorised.

6.133 If the lawyer believes the search to be unlawful, they should make representations to the authorising officer to this effect. Whether or not it is likely to be lawful, if authorisation for a search is given the lawyer should check (if appropriate) whether the client has a key in their possession or whether someone else can provide access, in order to avoid unnecessary damage caused by a forced entrance. The lawyer should also consider whether they should attend at the search. Neither PACE nor Code B require that either the suspect or their lawyer be given the opportunity to attend, although Code B para 6.11 states that if the occupier wishes a friend, neighbour or

76 An 'interview' is defined by Code C para 11.1A as questioning of a person regarding their involvement or suspected involvement in an offence and which by virtue of Code C para 10.1 is required to be carried out under caution. Paragraph 10.1 provides that a caution is not necessary where questions are put in the furtherance of the proper and effective conduct of a search. See also Code B paras 6.12 and 6.12A; and para 4.39 above.

77 *R v Langiert* [1991] Crim LR 777, CA, although in this case the evidence was not in fact excluded. See also *R v Khan* [1993] Crim LR 54, CA; *R v Joseph* [1993] Crim LR 206, CA; and *R v Raphaie* [1996] Crim LR 812, CA.

78 See, for example, *R v Chung* (1991) 92 Cr App R 314, CA and *R v Williams* [1989] Crim LR 66, Crown Court (Inner London) (where evidence of questioning during a search was excluded); and *R v White* [1991] Crim LR 779, CA and *R v Courtney* [1995] Crim LR 63, CA (where it was not).

other person to witness the search, this must be allowed unless the officer in charge has reasonable grounds for believing that this would seriously hinder the investigation or endanger the officers concerned or other people, and provided it does not cause unreasonable delay. Therefore, if the client is the occupier, arguably the lawyer can insist on being present.

CHAPTER 7

The police interview

continued

Introduction

7.1 The police interview is without doubt the most crucial event during the course of a person's detention in a police station. As McConville et al pointed out many years ago, 'interrogation is the central investigative strategy', and this is still true.[1] This is not surprising, since if the police can obtain a confession during an interview, it reduces the investigative work they have to do and makes a successful prosecution more likely. Even where the police have carried out extensive investigations before arrest or interview, emphasis is still likely to be placed on the interview.

7.2 At the same time, it has come to be recognised that police interviews can produce false evidence, either because suspects falsely confess or because the police falsely maintain that the suspect has confessed.[2] A series of notorious miscarriages of justice in the 1970s and 1980s – such as the 'Guildford Four', the 'Birmingham Six', the 'Tottenham Three', Judith Ward, the Darvell brothers, Stefan Kiszko, David McKenzie, the 'Cardiff Three' and cases involving the West Midlands Serious Crime Squad – all involved false confession evidence of one type or other. While many of these cases were originally investigated prior to the introduction of the Police and Criminal Evidence Act 1984 (PACE), there is plenty of evidence that the problem has not gone away.[3] Moreover, it has also been established that certain psychological conditions, or certain external factors, can mean that some suspects falsely confess even if the police conduct themselves properly.[4]

7.3 Although most of the cases referred to above involved confessions made in the absence of a lawyer, there is evidence that even if a lawyer is present a suspect may still make a false confession, particularly if the lawyer is too passive. This is graphically illustrated by the case of *R v Paris, Abdullahi and Miller*[5] (the 'Cardiff Three' case), in which Miller finally (falsely) confessed to murder during 13 hours of interviews conducted over a four-day period in the presence of his lawyer. In allowing the appeal, the Court of Appeal held that Miller's confession should have been excluded under PACE s76(2) because the police adopted hostile and intimidating techniques amounting to oppression The solicitor should, said the court, have intervened when improper questions were put, and to the extent that he did not, may have helped lead the police to believe that they were doing nothing wrong.[6]

1 M McConville, A Sanders, and R Leng, *The case for the prosecution* (Routledge, London, 1991) p57.

2 See, for example, the Royal Commission on Criminal Justice, *Report* (HMSO, London, 1993) p57.

3 See, for example, *R v Ridley* (1999) 17 December (unreported), CA; *R v Smith* [2003] EWCA Crim 927; *R v Brady* [2004] EWCA Crim 2230; and *R v Campbell* [2024] EWCA Crim 1036.

4 See G Gudjonsson, *The psychology of interrogations and confession: a handbook* (Wiley, Chichester, 2003); and paras 7.40–7.45 below.

5 (1993) 97 Cr App R 99, CA. It was not until July 2003 that the real murderer was finally convicted.

6 See also *R v Glaves* [1993] Crim LR 685, in which the Court of Appeal commented: 'It behoved the solicitor representing the appellant to ensure that there was somebody present who would interfere if questioning apparently went too far.'

7.4 This chapter explains the formal requirements applicable to police interviews and examines the police objectives in interview. It goes on to deal with the role and objectives of the defence lawyer in the police interview, including the circumstances in which the lawyer should intervene. It also includes an overview of questioning at a port or border under the Terrorism Act (TA) 2000 or the National Security Act (NSA) 2023. Note that Police Reform Act (PRA) 2002 Part 4 enables interviewing to be conducted by a designated policing support officer (see para 2.54 above).

Formal requirements of police interviews

Introduction

7.5 The meaning of the term 'interview' is set out at para 4.39 above. An interview at a police station at which a lawyer is present will undoubtedly come within the definition.[7] A number of formalities must normally be complied with. These are listed in the box below and are thereafter dealt with more fully. An important first step is to identify which power of detention is being used (PACE Parts IV and V; TA 2000 Part V and Sch 8; or NSA 2023 Part 1 and Sch 6). For the information that must be disclosed by the police before an interview, see para 4.27 above. Note that where an interview is conducted by an officer who is not at the police station using live link, they are under the same obligations as those that apply to an officer conducting an interview face to face.[8]

The formal requirements of police interviews

1. The suspect must be cautioned.
2. The suspect must be reminded of their right to legal advice.
3. The interview must normally be recorded contemporaneously.
4. At the beginning of the interview, the police interviewer must put to the suspect any significant statement or silence that occurred before the interview commenced.

Cautioning

7.6 A person who is suspected of an offence must be cautioned before being questioned for the purpose of obtaining evidence (PACE Code C para 10.1A; Code H para 10.1; Code I para 10; and see para 4.39 above), and must be reminded of the caution on the re-commencement of an interview where there has been a break (Code C para 10.8; Code H para 10.7; Code I para 10.6). Failure to do so may result in evidence obtained being

7 Although parts of PACE Code of Practice C apply specifically to people in custody in police stations, a suspect who is voluntarily interviewed, whether at a police station or elsewhere, should be treated with no less consideration (Code C note for guidance (NfG) 1A). For voluntary interviews, there is additional guidance issued by the National Police Chiefs' Council, *NPCC Voluntary Interview Guidance* (July 2024), available at: https://library.college.police.uk/docs/NPCC/Voluntary-interview-guidance-2024.pdf.

8 PACE 1984 s39(3B); and Code C paras 12.9A and 12.9B.

excluded at trial, although this is less likely if a lawyer is present.[9] The caution should be in the following terms (Code C para 10.5; Code H para 10.4; Code I para 10.3):

> You do not have to say anything. But it may harm your defence if you do not mention when questioned something which you later rely on in court. Anything you do say may be given in evidence.[10]

While minor deviations are permissible, the sense of the caution must be preserved (Code C para 10.7; Code H para 10.6; Code I para 10.5).[11] If the suspect does not understand the caution, the officer should explain it (Code C NfG 10D; Code H NfG 10C; Code I NfG 10C). The lawyer should already have explained the caution to their client, and if they are concerned that the client does not understand it, they should usually state this in the police interview. Any explanation given by the officer should be carefully noted, in particular because the officer may suggest that inferences will (as opposed to may) be drawn if the suspect refuses to answer questions. If the lawyer is still concerned that their client does not understand the caution, they should (if appropriate, after a further private consultation with the client) confirm in the interview that this is the case. The lawyer must be aware of the dangers of a suspect telling the police that they do understand the caution when they do not, or do not fully, understand it (see para 5.87 above). The lawyer should not normally indicate to the police that their client does understand the caution.

Reminder of the right to legal advice

7.7 The suspect must be reminded of their right to legal advice at the commencement or re-commencement of any interview at a police station or other authorised place of detention, and this reminder should be recorded in the interview record (Code C para 11.2; Code H para 11.3; Code I para 11.2).

Contemporaneous record

7.8 A contemporaneous record of a police interview must normally be made (Code C para 11.7).[12] While it is permissible for the record to be made at a

9 See *R v Armas-Rodriguez* [2005] EWCA Crim 1081; and see para 13.39 below.

10 Where, in exceptional circumstances, the police are permitted to interview a suspect who has asked to speak to a solicitor without them having received legal advice, or after charge, the caution is different. See Code C paras 10.6, 16.5 and Annex C; and para 5.69 above. Note that in *R v Pall* [1992] Crim LR 126, CA, it was held that while Code C does not require a caution if a statement is taken after charge, it should nevertheless be given.

11 *R v Saunders* [1988] Crim LR 521. Where an interpreter is used, precise interpretation is not necessary provided that the essential features of the caution are adequately conveyed to the suspect (*R v Koc* [2008] EWCA Crim 77).

12 Where a person is detained under TA 2000 s41, Code H para 11.8 provides that interviews conducted at a designated place of detention must be recorded in accordance with the code of practice issued under TA 2000 Sch 8 para 3. Where a person is detained under NSA 2023 s27, Code I para 11.7 provides that interview records should be made in accordance with the code of practice issued under NSA 2023 Sch 6 para 3. For voluntary interviews, further guidance can be found in chapter 7 of the *NPCC Voluntary Interview Guidance*, available at: https://library.college.police.uk/docs/NPCC/Voluntary-interview-guidance-2024.pdf.

later time in some circumstances, this is unlikely to apply to an interview conducted in a police station (Code C para 11.7(c)). If, for some reason, a contemporaneous record is not made, a record of the interview must be made as soon as practicable after completion of the interview (Code C para 11.8). If the interview is audio-recorded, the provisions of Code E apply (see para 7.10 below), and where it is visually recorded, the provisions of Code F apply (see para 7.11 below). If detention has been authorised under the TA 2000, the provisions of the Terrorism Act 2000 video recording code of practice apply (see para 7.10 below). If detention has been authorised under the NSA 2023, the provisions of the National Security Act 2023: video recording code apply (see para 7.10 below). Where, exceptionally, the record is made in writing, the suspect must be given the opportunity to read it (unless it is impracticable) and to sign it as correct or to indicate the respects in which the suspect considers it to be inaccurate (Code C para 11.11; see para 7.17 below). Failure by the police to comply with the recording and checking requirement may lead a court to refuse to admit evidence of what was said, although this is less likely if a lawyer was present.[13]

Significant statement or silence

7.9 At the beginning of an interview carried out at a police station, the interviewing officer must, after cautioning the suspect, put to them any significant statement or silence that occurred in the presence and hearing of a police officer or civilian interviewer before the start of the interview, and which has not been put to the suspect in the course of a previous interview that occurred before their arrival at the police station. The officer must ask the suspect whether they confirm or deny the earlier statement or silence and whether they wish to add anything (Codes C and H para 11.4; Code I para 11.3; and see para 5.116 above).

Audio and visual recording of police interviews

7.10 The audio-recording of police interviews is governed by Code C para 11.7 and Code E. There is a separate code for the audio-recording of interviews of persons examined under TA 2000 Sch 7 or arrested under section 41 and for persons examined under Counter-Terrorism and Border Security Act (C-TBSA) 2019 Sch 3 or arrested under NSA 2023 s27, and PACE Code E does not apply to such interviews. Interviews must be audio-recorded where one of the following conditions applies:

- interviews of a person cautioned under Code C section 10 in respect of any offence when an authorised recording device in working order and an interview room, or another room suitable for that device to be used, is available;[14]
- interviews that take place in respect of an indictable offence after charge or after the person has been told that they may be prosecuted;[15] or

13 *R v Dunn* (1990) 91 Cr App R 237, CA; and see para 13.23 below.

14 Code E para 2.1. For exceptions, see Code E para 2.3(a) and NfG 2E.

15 Which may only take place in limited circumstances. See Code C para 16.5; and para 10.31 below.

- where an interviewer wants to tell a person, after they have been charged or informed that they may be prosecuted for an indictable offence, about any written statement or interview with another person (Code E para 2.1).

Where audio-recording is mandatory, a 'relevant officer' (as defined in Code E para 2.4 and NfG 2E) may authorise a written interview where it is not reasonably practicable because of failure of or unavailability of recording equipment (or a suitable interviewing room), and the relevant officer considers on reasonable grounds that the interview should not be delayed (Code E para 2.3(c)).

7.11 Visual recording of interviews is not mandatory in any police force area, but where visual recording facilities are available and a police officer chooses to use them, the officer must comply with Code F.[16] Note that there is a separate code for visual recording of interviews of persons examined under TA 2000 Sch 7, or arrested under section 41 or persons examined under C-TBSA 2019 Sch 3 or arrested under NSA s27. There is also *NPCC Voluntary Interview Guidance,* which includes a section (7) on the interview recording system for voluntary interviews. These should be visually recorded or audio recorded (if video recording in not available).[17]

7.12 Occasionally, a client is reluctant or unwilling to be interviewed if it is to be audio or visually recorded, but is willing to be interviewed if the interview is recorded in writing. Code E para 3.9 and Code F para 2.10 effectively permit a suspect to object and provide that in these circumstances the interview must be recorded in writing. However, the police are permitted to proceed with audio or visual recording if the interviewing officer reasonably considers that they may proceed to put questions to the suspect with the recording equipment still operating. This would seem to be designed to allow the officer to test out how serious the suspect is about not wanting the interview to be recorded, so if a client does not want to be so recorded, they should be advised to remain silent until the officer has made clear that the recording equipment is not operating. A decision to continue to visually record an interview against the wishes of a suspect may be the subject of comment at court.[18]

7.13 The arrangements for ensuring that interviews are fully and accurately recorded, and that the recording is secure and made available to the suspect, differ depending upon whether the interview is recorded using a secure digital network or some other recording media.

7.14 The client should be advised of the possible consequences of an audio or visually recorded interview being heard or seen by a court. Everything said while the recording medium is switched on is recorded and, unless inaudible, may be transcribed. Therefore, the client should be advised not to treat the interview as if it were a private conversation, and should be made aware that the court may pick up cues from the way in which things are said. In the case of visually recorded interviews, there is the added dimension of non-verbal cues, such as facial expressions or physical

16 Code F para 2.2.

17 Available at: https://library.college.police.uk/docs/NPCC/Voluntary-interview-guidance-2024.pdf.

18 Code F NfG 2G.

gestures, which may have an effect on the way in which the court interprets what is said. In recent years, clips from police interviews have been made publicly available for the purpose of television shows or reporting.

7.15 A solicitor may use a digital device, including a laptop, mobile phone or Dictaphone, to create a recording of any police interview with their client.[19] This should be done overtly. If there are particular circumstances where the solicitor is unable to make an audio recording, they should attempt, as far as possible, to take a verbatim note of what is said by the interviewer and the client. This is often difficult, and may be impossible, because of the speed with which people usually speak, but the lawyer should try to record accurately the questions asked and what the client says. There are a number of reasons for this:

(1) It is a practical demonstration that the lawyer is taking an active part in the interview, which is important for both the client and the police to recognise. The questions asked in the interview may provide a significant indication of the evidence available to the police at that stage.
(2) If the lawyer confines the taking of notes to what they regard as the important parts of the interview, this may give valuable information to an observant police officer, who may recognise that certain lines of enquiry that they had not previously considered important may be worth pursuing.
(3) Particularly during a lengthy interview, or where there is more than one interview, the interviewing officer may refer back to an earlier part of the interview, or to an earlier interview, in order to try to show, for example, that the client is being inconsistent. The interviewing officer may not take adequate notes during the course of the interview, and referring back to the recording of an earlier part of the interview, or to an earlier interview, may not be feasible. The lawyer may, from their own record, be able to correct the officer. Similarly, what is said in interview may be relevant to other matters, such as an application to extend detention beyond 24 hours, or the point at which a decision whether to charge should be made.
(4) Although the suspect, or their lawyer, is normally entitled to be provided with access to, or a copy of, the recording after charge or after being informed that they will be prosecuted (Code E paras 4.12 and 4.16), it may not be provided immediately. A record of what was said may well be required before the recording is made available, for example, in relation to a bail application or in order to advise on plea.
(5) The summary of the record of the interview subsequently prepared by the officer may not accurately reflect the content of the interview.[20] The lawyer's notes of the interview will provide a quick reference to check

19 National Police Chiefs' Council and The Law Society, *Memorandum of Understanding Electronic Communication Devices being taken into Custody Suites by Solicitors* (July 2025) para 5.1(K), available at: www.npcc.police.uk/SysSiteAssets/media/downloads/publications/publications-log/criminal-justice/2025/mobile-telephones-and-laptops-being-taken-into-custody-suites-by-solicitors-and-their-usage.pdf.

20 See *Getting Cases Ready for Court: A joint review of the quality of prosecution case files by HMIC and HMICPS* (July 2013), available at: https://assets-hmicfrs.justiceinspectorates.gov.uk/uploads/getting-cases-ready-for-court.pdf, in which it was found that only 51 per cent of interview summaries were of 'adequate quality'.

the fairness of the summary, and will safeguard against difficulties caused by faulty or inaudible recordings.

(6) In deciding whether to draw a Criminal Justice and Public Order Act (CJPOA) 1994 s34 adverse inference and when assessing whether a suspect could reasonably have been expected to mention a fact, a jury is entitled to consider the length of questioning and to infer that if the interview lasted a considerable period of time, the questions are likely to have descended into a commensurate level of detail.[21]

Police interviews recorded in writing

7.16 If, exceptionally, an interview is not audio or visually recorded, it must normally be contemporaneously recorded in writing. This will frequently consist of one officer conducting the interview while another writes down what is said. Such interviews are usually slow and laborious, and often the result does not amount to a verbatim record of what has been said. They may be punctuated by statements like, 'Stop writing, and let's make this clear before we go on', which may come from the police, the suspect or the lawyer. Thus, a degree of negotiation occurs. While this does not necessarily work to the disadvantage of the suspect, the lawyer must take care to see that it does not. If the suspect, or the interviewer, is speaking too fast for what they say to be accurately recorded, the lawyer should ask them to slow down.

7.17 As with audio or visually recorded interviews, the lawyer should take their own note of what is said, and in this case it should, as far as possible, be a verbatim account. At the end of the interview the suspect must, unless it is impracticable, be given an opportunity to read through the interview record and to sign it as correct or to indicate the respects in which they consider it to be inaccurate (Code C para 11.11).[22] There is a temptation, particularly after a long interview or one conducted late at night, for the suspect to sign the record without reading it properly. This is potentially very damaging, since once it is signed the suspect will have little chance of persuading a court that it is inaccurate. The lawyer should also be aware that the client may not be able to read or the client's reading ability may be limited, a fact that the client may be reluctant to admit. For this reason, it may be appropriate for the lawyer to read the interview record out loud, although if the police are aware of a suspect's reading difficulty the senior interviewer present should do so (Code C para 11.11).

7.18 The client should be advised to sign the record of the interview only if they are absolutely satisfied that it is an accurate account of what was said. If they are not satisfied, the record should be endorsed accordingly. If the difference is minor, the interviewing officer may be willing to amend the written record. If, however, the disagreement is more significant and the police will not agree to change it even after reference to the lawyer's own notes, a full written record should be made of what the client disagrees with and what they believe the record should show. Furthermore, if the

21 *R v Harewood and Rehman* [2021] EWCA Crim 1936.

22 See, for example, *R v Parchment* [1991] Crim LR 626, CA; *R v Walsh* (1990) 91 Cr App R 161, CA; and *R v Waters* [1989] Crim LR 62, CA.

client wishes to add anything to the record (and this is something on which the lawyer may wish to give the client advice), this should be added. Only when these things have been done should the client sign the interview record. Code C para 11.12 provides that the lawyer must be given an opportunity to read and sign the record. While the lawyer should read it, they should not sign it unless absolutely satisfied that it is an accurate record of the interview.

Police objectives in interview

Introduction

7.19 The police interview of the suspect, as noted at para 7.1 above, is frequently the focus of a police investigation. The College of Policing states that professionally conducted interviews can 'direct an investigation and gather material, which in turn can lead to a prosecution or early release of an innocent person'.[23] While this suggests a neutral, objective 'truth-finding' process, interviewing officers often approach interviews of suspects in a more one-sided fashion. The principles of investigative interviewing, issued by the College of Policing, state the obvious when suggesting that investigators 'should recognise the positive impact of an early admission in the context of the criminal justice system'. All too often, the police interview is used as a mechanism for justifying the arrest and to confirm the police view that the suspect is guilty. Issues raised by the suspect that interfere with this belief may be regarded as 'irrelevant red herrings to be ignored or argued away', and inconsistencies in the account provided by the suspect may be exploited in order to demonstrate that they are lying.[24]

7.20 The College of Policing approach to investigative interviewing is based on the PEACE framework, which consists of five stages:[25]

- **Planning and preparation:** The interviewer should create and record an interview plan, taking into account the characteristics of the interviewee, whether and why an interview is necessary, the timing of the interview, and what the objectives are. This entails considering what is known by the police about the suspect, what evidence is available and what needs to be proved.
- **Engage and explain:** This is the first of the three stages of an interview, and involves establishing a relationship with the suspect and explaining the purpose of the interview, the suspect's rights, the ground rules and relevant procedures.
- **Account, clarification and challenge:** The second stage of an interview, which involves asking or persuading a suspect to provide an account in relation to the allegation(s), seeking clarification and challenging the

23 College of Policing, *Authorised Professional Practice: Investigation: Investigative interviewing* (October 2022), available at: www.college.police.uk/app/investigation/investigative-interviewing/investigative-interviewing.

24 See M McConville, A Sanders and R Leng, *The case for the prosecution* (Routledge, London, 1991) pp57, 61 and 76.

25 See note 23 above.

suspect in respect of any part of their account that conflicts with other evidence obtained.

- **Closure:** The third and final stage of a police interview requires the officer to consider whether the interview has covered all of the relevant issues, to summarise the interviewee's account and to explain what is going to happen next.
- **Evaluation:** After completion of the interview, the police interviewer(s) should consider what information has been obtained in the interview, compare it with other information received and what has to be proved, and consider what further action is to be taken.

7.21 An indication that the interviewing officer is using the PEACE interview strategy is the use of a written 'Interview Plan' containing prompts for 'Points to prove', 'Defences', 'Purpose [of the interview]' and 'Relevant issues'. However, while an interviewing officer may emphasise their desire to 'seek the truth', nothing can detract from the fact that the information they obtain from the suspect is available for the purposes of the prosecution.

Police tactics in interview

7.22 The police approach to interviewing differs in detail from case to case, and from officer to officer, but despite the fact that the PEACE interview strategy encourages officers to approach interviews with an open mind, experience suggests that they often do not do so, and may well use tactics based on an assumption of guilt. A number of specific police interview tactics are dealt with at para 7.49 below, but some more general issues are dealt with here:

- undermining the lawyer's advice;
- seating arrangements;
- 'phased' or 'managed' disclosure; and
- the 'no comment' interview.

Undermining the lawyer's advice

7.23 The interviewing officer may try to undermine the status of the lawyer or the lawyer's advice, or the relationship between the lawyer and their client, particularly if the officer believes that the lawyer has advised the client in a way that they regard as contrary to their interests. The officer may seek to achieve this by simple strategies such as introducing the lawyer to the client, or by ensuring that they select the seating position in the interview room so that there is no eye contact between the lawyer and their client. The lawyer should be aware of such strategies, and take appropriate action to avoid any adverse effects.

7.24 If the lawyer is an accredited or probationary representative, the police may try to undermine their status by referring to that fact in interview. Although accredited and probationary representatives are defined as solicitors for the purposes of the codes,[26] the significance of this may not be apparent either to the police officer or to the client. The lawyer should

26 Code C para 6.12; and see para 2.145 above.

explain their status in the initial consultation with the client, and this may help to minimise the impact of such a tactic (see para 5.10 above). If it is encountered, the lawyer (or the lawyer's firm) should consider taking the matter up with the police at senior level.

7.25 The interviewing officer may try to undermine the lawyer's advice by telling the suspect that they are not obliged to accept advice to remain silent. The lawyer should deal with this in the following way.

- Before the interview, warn the client that the interviewing officer may use this tactic, explaining the officer's aim – to make the client lose faith in the legal advice given – and what the lawyer will do if the officer attempts to do so.
- During the interview, if the officer attempts to use this tactic, intervene immediately to inform the officer that: (i) should the case go to trial, it will be for the court to decide on the merits of the legal advice given to the client and the client's decision; and (ii) the court will draw its own conclusions as to the appropriateness of the officer's conduct.

Seating arrangements

7.26 The way in which seating is arranged in the interview room may both undermine the status of the lawyer and effectively marginalise them, so that the suspect 'forgets' that the lawyer is there. Ideally, the lawyer should indicate where they and their client are going to sit. The best seating position for the lawyer is next to the client, but placed so that they can have eye contact with both the client and the interviewing officer. In this way the lawyer can establish their presence and be able to observe any non-verbal communication between the officer and the client.

7.27 If the police try to insist on the lawyer sitting in a place that marginalises them, they should consider advising the client not to answer questions until the matter is resolved. It may be advisable for the lawyer to see the client in private, if they have not already been warned of this possibility, so that the lawyer can explain what is going on, because it will not necessarily be obvious to the client. Another tactic the lawyer may consider is to sit where requested by the police until the recording device is switched on, and then move to where they wish to sit. It will then be more difficult for the interviewing officer to make an issue of it. There is no reference in Code F (visual recording of interviews) to seating position, but the fact that the interview is being visually recorded should not be used as a reason to prevent the lawyer sitting in an appropriate position.

'Phased' or 'managed' disclosure

7.28 The police strategy of phased or managed disclosure, and the suggested pre-interview response of the defence lawyer, is explained at para 4.30 above. In the interview, the lawyer should consider asking the interviewing officer:

- whether a phased disclosure strategy is being used or, where this is clear, asking them to confirm that the strategy is being used;
- to confirm what information has been disclosed to the suspect and/or the lawyer;

- to indicate whether they have information concerning the alleged offence that they have not disclosed and to remind the officer of the Code C para 11.1A, Code H para 11.1A and Code I para 11 right to information;
- to disclose the information that they have not yet disclosed; and
- to confirm whether they intend to introduce into the interview information or allegations that they have not disclosed.

This may persuade the interviewing officer to make further disclosure. Even if it does not, it helps to establish evidence of the level of police disclosure made and whether the police are deliberately withholding information, which may assist the accused in any subsequent argument as to inferences from 'silence'.

The 'no comment' interview

7.29 The lawyer should be prepared for particular challenges if the client is not going to answer police questions. Since the police interviewer may be seeking a confession, and a confession cannot be obtained if the client will not answer questions, the interviewer may try to step up the pressure on the client. Codes C and H para 12.5, and Code I para 11.19, specifically provide that the police do not require a suspect's consent or agreement to be interviewed even if they choose not to answer questions.[27] This is reflected in the College of Policing guidance, which states that even when a suspect exercises the right to silence, 'investigators have a responsibility to put questions to them'. The guidance goes on to state that the 'interviewer should try not to be swayed by the no comment response' and:

> should ask all the relevant questions as if the interviewee was responding. It is important that no gaps are left for the defence to fill at court. Failure to ask all the relevant questions in the first place may, but will not necessarily, preclude inferences being drawn in court.[28]

7.30 Thus, the police may still proceed with an interview of a suspect who does not intend to answer questions, whether or not a prepared statement has been submitted (see para 5.152 above). While it may be legitimate in such circumstances for the police to ask some questions, at some point such an interview may become oppressive if its purpose is to break the will of the suspect so that they speak despite their decision not to. Although it may be difficult to gauge the point at which an interview becomes oppressive, the lawyer should intervene if the interviewer goes beyond putting relevant questions, becomes repetitive, or if the client becomes distressed.

27 Although para 12.5 goes on to indicate that a suspect cannot be forced to go to an interview room.

28 See note 23 above. However, in *R v Green* [2019] EWCA Crim 411, an adverse inference was permitted when the police officer had provided an inaccurate account of the incident and asked the suspect whether he wanted to give an account before the CCTV footage was played, to which he responded 'no comment'. After the CCTV was played, he was asked if there was anything else he would like to say, to which he did not respond and no other questions were asked. The adverse inference was permissible as, 'if the circumstances are such that he is expressly or by necessary implication invited to give his account of the matter which has given rise to the interview. It is not necessary that specific questions are asked of him' (para 20).

7.31 One tactic designed to undermine the right to silence is for the police interviewer to try to get the suspect into the 'habit' of talking, for example, by starting the interview by asking about the suspect's family, or by completing the antecedent forms which are usually completed after an interview. The lawyer should try to persuade the officer not to do this by reference to Code C para 11.1A, which provides that an interview is the questioning of the suspect regarding an offence. Questions about antecedents do not relate to an offence. If the officer persists, the lawyer should consider advising their client not to answer the questions. There is, in any event, no obligation on the client to assist the police in completing the antecedent forms.

7.32 Another tactic is for the police interviewer to suggest to the suspect that a failure to reply to questions implies that they are guilty. The danger of such a suggestion is not the effect that it might have on magistrates or a jury. Rather, its danger lies in the fact that the suspect may feel forced to say something, or something other than 'no comment'. For this reason, the lawyer should intervene immediately, making it clear that that there are many reasons, consistent with innocence, why a person may remain silent in interview.

7.33 In a case where the police have seized property belonging to the suspect, they may imply that it cannot be returned until its true ownership has been established. This may be an astute tactic, particularly if they know that it is something valued by the suspect. The lawyer should intervene to reassure the client that the matter can be dealt with later, outside the context of the interview. Again, it is less likely to have an adverse impact if the client has received advice from the lawyer on this matter before the police interview begins.

The lawyer's objectives in the police interview

Introduction

7.34 As was suggested at para 1.3 above, defence lawyers need to be clear about their role. This is particularly true with regard to police interviews, not simply in view of their importance, but also because there are various factors that potentially inhibit the lawyer. Not only do interviews take place on police territory and according to a police agenda, but interviews are often highly emotionally charged, with police officers giving clear signals that they are in control and that lawyers are there on sufferance, for as long as they 'behave'. Given these circumstances, the lawyer should have in mind the definition of the lawyer's role set out in Code C NfG 6D (and Code H NfG 6C; Code I NfG 6D):

> The solicitor's only role in the police station is to protect and advance the legal rights of their client. On occasions this may require the solicitor to give advice which has the effect of the client avoiding giving evidence which strengthens a prosecution case. The solicitor may intervene in order to seek clarification, challenge an improper question to their client or the manner in which it is put, advise the client not to reply to particular questions, or if they wish to give their client further legal advice.

The lawyer should also consider the objectives set out below, which supplement the general requirement that lawyers must act in the best interests of their clients.

> **The defence lawyer's objectives**
>
> 1 To ensure that the police act fairly at all times and observe the requirements of PACE and the codes of practice.
> 2 To ensure that their client does their best in interview, whether or not they are answering questions.
> 3 To protect their client from unnecessary or inappropriate pressure and distress and, in particular, to protect vulnerable clients.
> 4 To ensure that an accurate account is kept of the interview, and that they keep their own record.

7.35 Underlying these objectives should be the clear understanding that the courts are likely to regard the involvement of the lawyer as a sufficient protection for the client, so that the lawyer's mere presence will, except perhaps in more extreme cases,[29] vitiate the effect of any unfairness or breach of PACE or the codes by the police. Therefore, lawyers must actively pursue these objectives – otherwise their presence will be of no positive effect and may even harm the interests of the client. In seeking to meet these objectives, the lawyer should have regard to a number of specific matters, dealt with below.

Ensuring that the police act fairly

7.36 In ensuring that the police act fairly and in accordance with PACE and the codes, the lawyer must be aware of the specific requirements of Code C, Code H and Code I relating to interviews, in particular the following.

(1) In any period of 24 hours, the suspect must be allowed a continuous period of eight hours' rest, free from interviewing or interruption, subject to limited exceptions. The rest period should usually be at night, but account should be taken of when the detainee last slept or rested (Codes C and H para 12.2; Code I para 11.16; and see para 5.27 above).

(2) The suspect must be fit to be interviewed, subject to exceptions in cases of urgency (Codes C and H para 12.3; Code I para 11.17).[30] The custody officer must consider the risks to the detainee's physical and mental state if an interview takes place, the risk that the interview may be considered unreliable by a court, and must also determine what safeguards are needed if an interview is to proceed (see para 5.22 above).

(3) The interview should, as far as practicable, take place in an interview room which must be adequately heated, lit and ventilated (Codes C and H

29 As, for example, in *R v Paris, Abdullahi and Miller (*1993) 97 Cr App R 99, CA; and see para 7.3 above.

30 See *R v Crampton* (1991) 92 Cr App R 369, CA (fitness to be interviewed of drug addict suffering from withdrawal symptoms).

para 12.4; Code I para 11.18), and the suspect must not be required to stand during the interview (Codes C and H para 12.6; Code I para 11.20).

(4) Subject to limited exceptions, there must be breaks in interviewing at recognised meal times (or at other times that take account of when the suspect last had a meal), and also short breaks for refreshment at intervals of approximately two hours (Codes C and H para 12.8; Code I para 11.22).[31]

(5) The right to information (Code C para 11.1A and NfG 11ZA; Code H para 11.1A and NfG 11ZA; Code I para 11 and NfG 11A) is written in subjective terms ('information sufficient for the person'). If a client is a child, neurodivergent or otherwise vulnerable, the sufficiency of information, in the context of that individual's needs, is a matter which requires particular attention.

The lawyer must also act promptly to deal with police tactics that are unfair (see para 7.49 below).

Ensuring that clients do their best in interview

7.37 Where the client does not intend to answer police questions, the lawyer should seek to ensure that this decision is respected. Tactics designed to undermine the decision should be firmly resisted (see para 7.29 above). If the client starts to answer questions, they should be reminded of their right to remain silent and, if necessary, the interview should be interrupted so that a private consultation can take place.

7.38 Where the client has decided to answer police questions, the lawyer should take any necessary action to see that the client's version is coming out, both clearly and in full. There are two aspects to this. First, the lawyer should listen carefully to what is being said so that if it is unclear or ambiguous, the lawyer can intervene to enable the client to clarify their position. It is not being suggested that the lawyer should try to take over the questioning, or that the lawyer should answer questions on behalf of the suspect. In fact, to do the latter could justify the lawyer's removal from the interview (see Code C NfG 6D; and para 7.50 below). However, it is legitimate for the lawyer to ask a question, or perhaps to summarise what they believe the client means to say and to ask the client if that is so. In many cases, such intervention may be accepted, or even welcomed, by the police officer. If the police do object, they should be reminded that Code C para 11.6, Code H para 11.7 and Code I para 11.6 require the officer to allow the suspect an opportunity to give an innocent explanation and that the lawyer is helping to achieve that requirement. The second aspect applies at the end of the interview. If it appears that the officer is preparing to wind up the process, and the lawyer knows that the interview has not covered all the matters that should have been dealt with, they should ask appropriate questions to elicit the necessary information. It may be that the interview has not adequately dealt with a defence, such as self-defence,

31 See *R v Trussler and Another* [1988] Crim LR 446 (failure to allow rest periods); *R v Gopee and Gopee* (1992) 89 LS Gaz 24 (three-hour interview without a break, where suspect had not eaten for four hours before commencement of interview).

which it is important to establish at this stage. If the client is admitting the offence, there may be important mitigating factors that the client has not been given the opportunity of fully explaining, or the client may wish to express regret. For guidance on strategy where a prepared statement has been, or is intended to be, submitted see para 5.152 above.

Protecting the client

7.39 Finally, the lawyer should take care to protect the client, especially if they are vulnerable. The various forms of vulnerability are dealt with in chapter 11 below. This section deals with the factors that may make a confession more likely.

Propensity to confess

7.40 Gudjonsson,[32] and Phillips and Brown,[33] have examined in detail the factors that are associated with confessions. While the factors are complex, and interrelated, some are worthy of particular note.

- Some studies suggest that younger suspects are more likely to confess than older suspects.
- Evidence suggests that suspects confess more readily to certain types of offences, such as property offences and, in particular, sexual offences.
- Suspects with no previous convictions are more likely to confess than those with previous convictions, although possibly those who have confessed before confess more easily.
- Women are significantly more likely to make admissions than men.
- Admission rates vary considerably between police stations.

False confessions

7.41 Four general categories of false confession have been identified:

- the 'voluntary false confession';
- the 'coerced-compliant confession';
- the 'coerced-internalised confession';[34] and
- the 'coerced-passive confession'.[35]

7.42 **Voluntary false confessions** occur without any externally imposed pressure or coercion, and may be associated with circumstances where a person attends voluntarily at a police station and tells the police that they have committed a particular crime. It is commonly believed that people do not voluntarily confess to crimes that they have not committed, but it is clear that this view is incorrect, although how often this occurs is unknown.

32 G Gudjonsson, *The psychology of interrogations and confession: a handbook* (Wiley, Chichester, 2003).

33 C Phillips and D Brown, *Entry into the criminal justice system: a survey of police arrests and their outcomes*, Home Office Research Study 185 (Home Office, London, 1998), especially p72.

34 Largely based on Gudjonsson's work.

35 Suggested by M McConville et al, *The case for the prosecution* (Routledge, London, 1991) p68.

Gudjonsson gives four reasons why a person might make a voluntary false confession:

(1) in order to draw attention to themself, driven by a 'morbid desire for notoriety';
(2) a need for punishment because of guilt in relation to a connected or unconnected matter, or because of generalised feelings of guilt;
(3) a belief in guilt because of a delusion, often (but not necessarily) associated with a serious psychiatric illness; or
(4) in order to protect the real culprit.

Shepherd adds a further reason:

(5) in order to deter the police from investigating some other, more serious, offence.[36]

7.43 **Coerced-compliant confessions** result from the nature of the interrogation. While a suspect knows that they are not guilty, they confess as a result of the coercive nature of the questioning coupled with a belief that they will achieve some advantage by confessing. If the suspect thinks of the long-term consequences at all, they may believe that the truth will come out later or that their lawyer will be able to sort it out. The advantages that a suspect may perceive include the following:

(1) **Being able to end the interview, or to leave custody, after confessing.** Code C para 11.5 provides that unless a suspect directly asks, a police officer must not try to obtain answers to questions by indicating what action the police will take if questions are answered.[37] However, the interviewing officer may suggest, directly or indirectly, that a confession may lead to certain consequences, or encourage the suspect to believe this.
(2) **Being able to cope with the pressures of the situation.** Such pressures may be many and varied, and may be internal as well as external. A confession is likely to please the interviewer, which in itself will relieve the pressure, but may also bring with it the prospect of more favourable treatment, such as refreshments, a visit or a telephone call. If a client is clearly distressed, the lawyer must consider intervening. This is not always easy, since the police are likely to believe that distress is a sign of guilt, and that it may be a prelude to a confession. However, distress may occur for a number of reasons unconnected with guilt.
(3) **Avoidance of being locked up in custody.** This may be of particular importance to suspects in certain situations. They may have a job to go to, an appointment to keep, a phobia about being confined in a locked cell, or they may have young children about whose care they are concerned (see para 5.27 above).

36 E Shepherd, *Police station skills for legal advisers: practical reference* (Law Society, London, 2004).

37 Although where failure by the suspect to co-operate may have an effect on their immediate treatment (for example, where refusal to provide a name and address when charged may lead to further detention), the officer may inform the person of any relevant consequences (Code C para 10.9; Code H para 10.9) (this is not replicated in Code I).

7.44 **Coerced-internalised confessions** occur where a suspect believes, or comes to believe, in their own guilt, even if only temporarily. Gudjonsson suggests that this is related to two distinct conditions:

(1) The first occurs where the suspect has no memory of the incident which, in particular, may result from amnesia or alcohol or drug-induced memory failure. Typically, the suspect may then think, 'If the police say I did it, I must have done it'.[38] Although, generally, suspects must not be interviewed if they are unfit through drink or drugs to the extent that they are unable to appreciate the significance of the questions put or their own answers (see para 5.22 above), this kind of internalised confession can occur when the suspect is not under such influence at the time of interview but was, or may have been, at the time of the incident.

(2) The second type of coerced-internalised confession occurs where a suspect, while having a clear recollection that they did not commit the offence, submits to a manipulative interviewing process which leads them to distrust their own recollection.

7.45 **Coerced-passive confessions** occur where the interrogation induces a suspect to 'adopt the *confession form* without necessarily adopting or even *understanding* the substance of what has been accepted or adopted'. An example would be where the interviewing officer persuades a suspect to accept a hypothetical possibility as a fact, for example, 'If you were attacked, you would have used the knife, wouldn't you?'.

The commencement of the interview

7.46 At the beginning of the interview, the interviewing officer must identify themself (Codes C and H para 12.7; Code I para 11.21[39]) and the suspect must be cautioned and reminded of their right to legal advice (Code C paras 10.1 and 11.2; Code H paras 10.1 and 11.3; Code I paras 10 and 11.2). If the lawyer believes that their client does not understand the caution, they should say so (see para 7.6 above). The officer must also put to the suspect any significant statement or silence which occurred before their arrival at the police station (Codes C and H para 11.4; Code I para 11.3; and see para 5.116 above).

7.47 The lawyer should make an opening statement, adapting the following suggested statement to the circumstances.

38 For an example, see *R v Brady* [2004] EWCA Crim 2230, where an innocent person whose memory was adversely affected by drug addiction admitted to a robbery of which she had no recollection because the police said that they had evidence that she had committed it.

39 In Codes H and I, an officer's identification may be by way of a warrant or other identification number and the name of their police station (Code H paras 2.8 and 12.7; Code I paras 2.8 and 11.21).

Defence lawyer's opening statement

1 My role is to protect and advance my client's legal rights. I will continue to advise my client throughout the interview where this is necessary.
2 I want you to address my client and me with appropriate formality throughout the interview.
3 [On my advice, my client is intending to answer questions.] or [I now advise my client not to answer questions in this interview.] Please do not try to undermine my client's decision in any way. If you do, I will intervene.
4 So that there is no room for doubt, I will [also] intervene if:
   - my client asks for legal advice;
   - you refer to evidence, or produce evidence, in respect of which you have not given me adequate information or access;
   - you try to put pressure on my client;
   - your questions are unfair or unclear;
   - a break in the interview is necessary.
5 Before the interview, you gave me the following information . . .
6 Please tell me:
   - what the purpose of this interview is;
   - whether you have evidence or information relating to the alleged offence that you have not told me about;
   - whether you consider that you have sufficient evidence to charge my client;
   - what you intend to do after the interview has finished.

7.48 An opening statement is a useful device for laying down ground rules for the interview and for establishing the fact that the presence of the lawyer is to be an active one. Intervening will be much easier if the interviewing officer has been warned to expect it. It is also useful, where the lawyer suspects that full disclosure has not been given, to ensure that the fact of lack of disclosure is recorded, especially where the police are using a strategy of phased disclosure (see para 7.28 above). In view of the dangers of waiver of privilege, reasons for advice to remain silent should not usually be given (see paras 5.99 and 5.164 above).

Intervening during interviews

Introduction

7.49 In this section guidance is given on the powers of the police to exclude lawyers from police interviews and on intervention in police interviews. It is essential that the lawyer takes a careful note of any intervention that they make and the reasons for it. If no intervention is made, the lawyer should make a note to this effect. Such a record may be important in the event of any complaint about the conduct of the lawyer or if the lawyer subsequently has to give evidence concerning the conduct of the interview.

Power to exclude the lawyer

7.50 Codes C, H and I make it clear that a lawyer can only be required to leave an interview if their conduct is such that the interviewing officer is unable properly to put questions to the suspect (Code C para 6.9; Code H para 6.10; Code I para 6.10). Code C NfG 6D, Code H NfG 6C and Code I NfG 6D indicate that, in carrying out their role, the lawyer may intervene in a police interview in order to seek clarification, or to challenge an improper question, or the manner in which it is put, or if the lawyer wishes to give the client further advice. It goes on to provide that the power to exclude the lawyer will only arise if the lawyer's approach or conduct prevents or unreasonably obstructs proper questions being put or the response from being recorded. The examples of misconduct warranting removal given in the NfG are answering questions on a suspect's behalf, or providing written replies for the suspect to quote.[40] Other examples might include conveying the answers to be given by gestures to the client; interrupting to such an extent that the interviewing officer is unable to put questions to the client; or using threatening or offensive words or behaviour. In any event, such behaviour is likely to be counterproductive, even if the police officer is also acting in such a manner. It will be better to 'let the interview record speak for itself' or, if the behaviour is non-verbal and the interview is being audio recorded or the non-verbal behaviour would not be captured by visual recording (where the interview is being visually recorded), for the lawyer to say something like, 'For the purposes of the interview record the officer is standing over my client in a threatening manner'. In most situations, the lawyer should ask the officer to stop the offending behaviour and, if necessary, should terminate the interview so that the issue can be dealt with outside the context of the interview and so that, if necessary, the custody officer can be involved.

7.51 It can be seen that the lawyer must go a long way in terms of intervening in an interview before it would be legitimate for the police to consider ejecting them, and in most circumstances if the lawyer is acting professionally, exclusion could not be appropriate.[41] Representatives face particular difficulty, since although once inside the police station there are no additional powers to eject them over and above those relating to solicitors (see para 4.4 above), they are particularly vulnerable to police threats to do so.

7.52 If the interviewing officer is acting in a grossly improper way, or the lawyer feels that they are in danger of losing their temper, the lawyer should suggest to the client that they wish to advise the client in private, which is always legitimate by virtue of PACE s58(1). In this way, the heat can be taken out of the situation and, if necessary, there will be time for the lawyer to regain composure.

40 This is not a reference to handing in a prepared statement, but drafting or suggesting answers for the client to quote in response to specific questions.

41 But note that PACE s58 grants the right to legal advice to the suspect, as opposed to giving a right to a particular lawyer to give advice (*Rixon and Others v Chief Constable of Kent* (2000) Times, April 11, CA).

Procedure for exclusion

7.53 The interviewing officer cannot take the decision to remove the lawyer themself. Code C para 6.10, Code H para 6.11 and Code I para 6.11 provide that before exclusion the officer must consult with a superintendent or above, or an inspector or above if a superintendent is not readily available. It is only that officer who can decide whether or not the interview can continue in the presence of the lawyer, and that officer can only take that decision after speaking to the lawyer. Furthermore, Code C NfG 6E, Code H NfG 6D and Code I NfG 6E provide that the officer must be in a position to satisfy a court that the decision was properly made, and in order to do this, may need personally to witness what is happening. Therefore, if the lawyer believes that their conduct has been entirely proper and that it is the interviewing officer who is acting improperly, they should consider asking the superintendent to sit in on the interview. However, before doing so, the lawyer should check with the client, since the client may object or may want time to calm down.

7.54 If the lawyer is ejected, the suspect must be given an opportunity to consult another lawyer and to have that lawyer present at the resumed interview (Code C para 6.10; Code H para 6.11; Code I para 6.10).

7.55 If such an incident does occur, whether or not the lawyer is ultimately asked to leave, the lawyer should take a careful note of what occurred as soon as possible, for this may be relevant at trial, or at any disciplinary proceedings taken against either the police officer or the lawyer. Code C para 6.11, Code H para 6.12 and Code I para 6.11 require the officer taking the decision to exclude the lawyer to consider reporting the matter to the Solicitors Regulation Authority (SRA) and, in the case of a duty solicitor, to the Legal Aid Agency (LAA). If this is likely, it may be better that the lawyer (or if a representative, the employing solicitor) takes the initiative and reports the matter to these bodies themself.

When should the lawyer intervene?

7.56 The opening statement set out at para 7.47 above indicates some of the circumstances in which the lawyer should intervene. Some of these, and some others, are now dealt with in more detail.

Breach of PACE or the codes of practice

7.57 If there is any apparent breach of PACE or the codes of practice, then unless the breach is very minor the lawyer should normally intervene. It has been suggested that it may be better to make no comment and to raise the breach at trial in order, for example, to seek the exclusion of damaging statements by the suspect. However, such a strategy is unlikely to be successful. If the suspect confesses or makes admissions as a result, they may feel under pressure to plead guilty. Furthermore, other than in extreme circumstances,[42] it is highly unlikely that a court would exclude evidence obtained in the presence of a lawyer as a result of a breach of

42 See, for example, *R v Paris, Abdullahi and Miller* (1993) 97 Cr App R 99, CA.

PACE or the codes and of which the lawyer was aware (see para 13.23 below).

7.58 If the interviewing officer gives an incorrect or misleading explanation of the caution, perhaps in response to the client or lawyer indicating that the client does not understand it, the lawyer should point out that it is incorrect or misleading (see para 7.6 above). However, the lawyer should not normally attempt to explain it to the client in the police interview. If the interviewing officer fails to administer the caution, this is unlikely to lead to exclusion of evidence of a police interview at which a lawyer was present.

7.59 As an exception to the general rule, if the interviewing officer fails to give the special warning under Code C para 10.11, Code H para 10.10 or Code I para 10.7 in circumstances where inferences may be drawn from failure to account under CJPOA 1994 s36 or 37, the lawyer should not intervene. Failure to give the suspect the information required by CJPOA 1994 s36(1)(c) or 37(1)(c) will mean that inferences could not be drawn under these sections (see para 5.90 above).

Introduction of evidence not previously disclosed

7.60 Prior to a police interview, the suspect and their lawyer must be given sufficient information to enable the suspect to understand the nature of the suspected offence and why they are suspected of committing it, in order to allow for the effective exercise of the rights of the defence. The information to be disclosed should normally include, as a minimum, a description of the facts relating to the suspected offence that are known to the officer, including the time and place in question (see para 4.27 above, which also deals with the modifications where a person is detained under TA 2000 s41 or NSA 2023 s27). In addition, the custody officer must make available to the suspect or their lawyer any documents and materials that are essential to challenging the lawfulness of the suspect's arrest or detention (see para 4.22 above). If evidence or documents that should have been disclosed under these provisions are introduced in the interview, or the client is asked to comment upon them, the lawyer should consider stopping the interview so that they can advise their client in private on the information or documents disclosed. The lawyer should also consider intervening even if the evidence or documents introduced were not covered by the disclosure requirements. Such an intervention will be made easier if the lawyer's opening statement included an indication that they would intervene in such circumstances (see para 7.47 above).

The client starts answering questions

7.61 The tactics employed by the police to try to persuade a suspect to answer questions are dealt with at para 7.29 above. The point to be made here is that if a client who has made a clear decision not to answer questions starts to do so in the police interview, the lawyer should intervene promptly. Even if the client has been carefully advised about the police interview, on commencing it or during the course of it they may find the pressure to answer too great. Of course, if a client changes their mind, the lawyer should not try to prevent them from doing so, but should ensure that this is a deliberate and informed decision. If the client appears to be about to answer a question, the lawyer should remind them of their decision not to do so. It may be that this will be sufficient, but if not, the lawyer should consider suggesting that the interview be interrupted for the purpose of giving legal advice. The interviewing officer may very well be annoyed by this, but a suspect in this situation is always entitled to receive legal advice (PACE s58(1)).

Unfair interrogation

7.62 PACE and the codes provide very little guidance on the question of what may amount to unfair interrogation. Codes C and H provide rules for the general well-being of the suspect while in the police station, and for the proper treatment of the suspect while in interview (see para 7.36 abovc), but say nothing of the nature of the interviewing other than to provide that 'oppression' must not be used (Code C para 11.5; Code H para 11.6; Code I para 11.5). PACE s76 provides that a confession is not admissible if (when raised by the defence) the prosecution cannot prove that it was not obtained by oppression or in circumstances likely to render the confession unreliable. PACE s78 gives a court a discretion to exclude evidence if to admit it would have an adverse effect on the fairness of the proceedings. However, apart from oppression, which is partially defined by PACE s76(8) ('"oppression" includes torture, inhuman or degrading treatment, and the use or threat of violence (whether or not amounting to torture)'), the sections do not offer any further guidance. Some indication of the courts' approach to unfair interrogation may be obtained from the many cases decided under these two sections (see para 13.19 below).

7.63 There is little agreement about what is and is not acceptable in a police interrogation, other than in respect of behaviour that is clearly oppressive. Fundamental questions remain unanswered – such as how long the police can continue questioning when the suspect is not answering; to what extent the police can continue asking the same or similar questions if they are not getting the answers that they want; to what extent the interviewing officer can raise their voice or use bad language; whether the police can legitimately seek to direct the suspect in terms of where the suspect sits, who the suspect looks at, etc; and to what extent the police can use tricks and subterfuge (see para 7.68 below). The lawyer must, therefore, intervene using as their guide the professional obligation to act in their client's best interests. The following account of unfair forms of interrogation is offered as guidance. A court would not necessarily exclude evidence obtained as a result of such forms of interrogation nor, indeed, conclude that they are unfair. In view of this, intervention by the lawyer is even more important.

7.64 Unfair interrogation may take a number of forms:

- a *specific question* may be unfair because, for example, it has been put in a confusing or an ambiguous way;
- the *form of a question* may be unfair because, for example, it is a leading question; or

- the *style of questioning* may be unfair because, for example, it is bombastic and bullying.

The lawyer must be prepared to deal with each kind of unfairness. Failure to do so may result in damaging admissions being made that are likely to be admitted at trial, however unfair the questioning was. If the lawyer does intervene, they must consider the possible impact of a refusal to answer the question in view of CJPOA 1994 ss34, 36 and 37 (see para 5.63 above), and must keep a careful note of the advice given and the reasons for that advice, since it may become relevant at trial.

Unfair questions

7.65 Specific questions may be unfair for a number of reasons.

(1) **Multiple questions:** These are questions that consist of a number of questions rolled into one. They are potentially misleading because an answer intended to be an answer to one part of the question may, at the time or subsequently, be taken to be an answer to another part of the question. For example, the answer 'yes' to the question 'You had the knife on you to use in case there was any trouble. You took the knife out with you when you left your house, didn't you?' may be intended by the suspect to relate to the second question but may be interpreted as an answer to the first.

(2) **Ambiguous questions:** These are questions that can have more than one meaning. The danger lies in the fact that an answer may be based on one meaning, but be taken by others to be based on another meaning. This may occur particularly where the police officer is using a word or phrase that is a legal term, but which is not necessarily understood as such by the suspect. The question 'Did you know it is wrong to steal?' may, in certain circumstances, be ambiguous because it confuses the distinction between taking something and stealing it, and because an affirmative answer may be taken to imply an acceptance by the suspect that it correctly describes their conduct.

(3) **Irrelevant questions:** An irrelevant question is one that has no logical connection with the offence for which the suspect has been arrested and detained. While an irrelevant question may not, in itself, be unfair or prejudicial, it may fit within a pattern of questioning that is. For example, questions about family or friends may be asked in order to try to get the suspect into the 'habit' of answering questions. They may be used to lull the unwary suspect into a false sense of security, and to break down adversarial barriers. While the lawyer may feel that a degree of latitude is acceptable, they should be wary of the purpose of such questions and intervene if necessary. If the officer objects to such intervention, it should be pointed out that Code C para 11.1A provides that an interview is the 'questioning of a person regarding their involvement or suspected involvement in a criminal offence or offences'. Irrelevant questions, it can be argued, do not relate to involvement in an offence. Questions about previous convictions or other misconduct may, depending on the circumstances – including the nature of the offence and the nature of the questions put – be regarded as irrelevant.

For guidance on questioning about bad character, see paras 4.64 and 5.173 above.

(4) **Questions concerning other offences:** One particular form of irrelevant question is that relating to offences other than that for which the suspect has been arrested and detained. It may be that the suspect wants to admit to other offences so that they can be taken into consideration when the matter comes to court. In this case, there will be no objection to such a question. However, questions about other offences may be introduced for the purpose of seeing whether the suspect will admit to them, even though the police have no evidence of involvement. They may also be asked in order to put pressure on the suspect. If the suspect believes that the police want to question them about offences that are more serious or more extensive than those for which they have been arrested, they may confess to the offence(s) for which they have been arrested in order to 'take the heat off' and to lead the police away from pursuing the other matters.

The codes of practice do not specifically prevent questions about offences for which the suspect is not under arrest. Intervention by the lawyer will often lead to the response, 'This is my interview, and I'll ask what questions I like'. However, PACE s31 provides that where a person has been arrested and detained, if it appears that the person would be liable to arrest for some other offence on release, the person must also be arrested for that offence. Therefore, if the officer begins to ask questions about an offence for which the suspect is not under arrest, the lawyer should ask whether the officer intends to arrest the suspect under PACE s31. If the answer is yes, then once that arrest has taken place, questioning about that offence will be legitimate.[43] However, if there is no intention to arrest, presumably this will be because the officer does not have reasonable grounds for suspecting commission of the offence by the suspect. This being the case, further questioning about such an offence should be resisted. If the officer persists, the suspect should be advised not to answer such questions.

(5) **Hypothetical questions:** A hypothetical question may be asked by the interviewing officer in order to try to establish a particular mental state, or to trap a suspect into accepting and responding to evidence that may not exist. With regard to the former, a suspect found with a knife in a public place might be asked, 'What would you have done if you were attacked?', in order to show that the suspect intended to use the knife to cause injury. In relation to the latter, a suspect arrested for burglary may be asked: 'What would you say if the fingerprints found at the scene of the burglary turned out to be yours?' In this situation, the lawyer should ask whether the police are in possession of such evidence before the client answers. It has been held that hypothetical questions, of the first type at least, are permissible.[44] Nevertheless, the dangers of a suspect answering a hypothetical question may be such that the suspect should be advised not to answer.

43 However, the lawyer will usually wish to terminate the interview in order to obtain more information from the officer about the alleged offence(s) and to advise the client before recommencing the interview.

44 *R v Stringer* [2008] EWCA Crim 1222.

(6) **Questions concerning co-suspects:** Questions concerning others arrested in connection with the same offence may be of two types: (i) the interviewing officer may ask about the involvement in the alleged offence of the other person(s) arrested; or (ii) the officer may ask the suspect to comment on what other co-suspects have said. In either case, it should be remembered that evidence implicating a co-defendant contained in a confession is normally not admissible at trial as evidence against the co-defendant (see paras 4.35 and 5.55 above).

With regard to questions concerning the involvement of a co-suspect, if the suspect is answering questions in interview, they will have to decide whether to answer such questions. In many cases, a suspect will not wish to implicate a co-suspect, either because of some perceived obligation towards that person or through fear. The suspect may require advice about the advantages of implicating a co-suspect, particularly if that person is more culpable. On the other hand, an over-readiness to blame another for the commission of an offence may also have disadvantages.

Care should be taken where the police ask the suspect to comment on a statement or record of interview of a co-suspect. While it is not prohibited by Code C, the lawyer should consider why it is being done. In a case where the suspect is denying the offence, or is not answering questions, the production of the record of an interview with a co-suspect may be designed to secure a confession, particularly if the co-suspect has clearly implicated the suspect. If the interview record shows that the co-suspect has implicated the suspect, while exonerating themself, it may be produced in the hope that the suspect will at least do the same. Such differences may then be exploited further so that either or both suspects may be led to confess, or at least to make damaging admissions.

While it would seem that the lawyer cannot object to the introduction into the interview of an interview record of another suspect, they should ask to see it and it may be advisable for the lawyer to advise the suspect in private on how to respond before the interview proceeds further.

(7) **Questions based on dubious or non-existent evidence:** Questions may be based, either expressly or impliedly, on evidence that does not in fact exist. This may involve deliberate misrepresentation by the police, or may be inadvertent, as where the officer themself has been misinformed about the existence of evidence. In *R v Mason*,[45] a confession obtained in the presence of a solicitor after the police falsely informed the suspect that his fingerprint was found on a piece of a bottle used to cause a fire, was subsequently ruled to be inadmissible.[46] This is

45 [1987] 3 All ER 481, CA.

46 However, the fact that the lawyer was also deceived is likely to have been an important factor. In *R v McLean and Kosten* [1993] Crim LR 687, it was noted by the Court of Appeal that not every trick will result in exclusion of evidence, although in *R v Imran and Hussain* [1997] Crim LR 754, the Court of Appeal held that there was a duty on the police not to actively mislead a suspect. See also *R v Christou and Wright* (1992) 95 Cr App R 264, CA; *R v Woodall* [1989] Crim LR 288, Crown Court; and *R v Beales* [1991] Crim LR 118.

probably one of the few situations where evidence obtained in breach of PACE or the codes, or as a result of other misconduct, is likely to be excluded despite the fact that it occurred in the presence of the lawyer. The fact that evidence does not exist is unlikely to be known to the lawyer at the time. A lawyer should certainly resist any attempt to solicit co-operation in a police deception of a suspect. If the lawyer does have any suspicion about the existence of evidence implied by a question, the lawyer should raise this with the officer before the suspect answers it and, if appropriate, ask to see the evidence. In due course, the lawyer should check whether evidence supposedly in existence at the time of the interview is subsequently forthcoming at trial.

Exaggeration of the strength of evidence is probably more likely than misrepresentation of its existence. The suspect may be told, for example, that there are several witnesses who have identified the suspect, when in fact what they have done is to give a description which may (or may not) fit the suspect. Any representation by the police about the existence of evidence should be treated with caution. If appropriate, the lawyer should question the officer about the precise nature of the evidence, and ask to see it, before the suspect answers the question in interview.

(8) **Questions that amount to an inducement to confess:** Interviewing officers should not ask questions that are designed, or are likely, to have the effect of inducing the suspect to confess by indicating what may or may not happen if the suspect answers a question or questions, or fails to do so. The police must not 'indicate, except to answer a direct question, what action will be taken by the police if the person being questioned answers questions, makes a statement or refuses to do either' (Code C para 11.5; Code H para 11.6; Code I para 11.5). A confession obtained by inducement should be excluded under PACE s76(2)(b), but exclusion is less likely if obtained in the presence of a lawyer (see para 13.23 below). One form of inducement that the courts may accept as legitimate, however, is an indication that an admission will result in a sentence discount. The client should be advised that there is no additional guilty plea discount for a confessional statement made in interview, but that a court may consider it as part of a defendant's mitigation (see para 5.143 above).

During the police interview, therefore, the lawyer should be aware of any improper inducement made and should intervene if necessary. References by the interviewing officer to bail, to the nature of charges that may be forthcoming, to the possibility of a caution[47] or to the fact that others may be arrested and interviewed, should all be watched out for.[48] As noted above, Codes C, H and I provide that if the suspect does

47 In *R (U) v Commissioner of Police of the Metropolis; R (R) v Durham Constabulary* [2002] EWHC 2486 (Admin)) it was held that the offer of a caution amounted to an unlawful inducement. This decision was overturned by the House of Lords ([2005] UKHL 21), but that part of the decision still stands. In *R v Commissioner of Police of the Metropolis ex p Thompson* [1997] 1 WLR 1519, QBD, it was held that a defendant should confess before the decision to give a caution is made and that a confession should not be sought as part of the cautioning process.

48 Even a reference to interviewing further witnesses has been held to be an improper inducement (*R v Howden-Simpson* [1991] Crim LR 49, CA).

ask the interviewing officer what action will be taken in the event of them answering questions, making a statement or refusing to do either, then the officer may inform the suspect what action the police propose to take, provided that such action is itself proper. If the suspect does ask a specific question, the lawyer should listen carefully to the answer given and, if necessary, should intervene to correct any false impression given. It may even be advisable to intervene before the officer answers and to tell the suspect that the lawyer will advise them about this when the interview has been completed.

An improper inducement does not necessarily involve the police in stating what action they intend to take. It may be more subtly, and perhaps unintentionally, offered by an expression of concern. In one instance, for example, a young single parent had been arrested and her baby left with a relative. During the course of the interview the woman became very distressed and the interviewing officer repeatedly asked her if she was worried about her baby and what she was going to do with her baby if she was kept in police custody for any length of time. In the circumstances, there was clearly a risk that such questions would induce the suspect to confess, and the solicitor rightly intervened. If the officer had really been concerned, it would have been appropriate to stop the interview or to release the suspect (with or without bail) so that she could make suitable arrangements for her child (see para 5.27 above).

It should be remembered that inducements may be made outside of the context of the interview and at a time when the lawyer is not present. The offer of bail, food and cigarettes, or social visits may all be made, directly or indirectly, conditional on 'co-operation', and the lawyer should be conscious of this when advising the client. It may even be that there has been no specific attempt by the police to offer such an inducement. It is commonly believed (and is often true) that co-operation with the police, particularly in the form of a confession, will ease the passage through the period of detention and will, in its turn, induce the police to look more favourably on the suspect when it comes to the issue of bail.

The form of questions

7.66 Quite apart from the unfairness of particular questions, the form or structure of a question or series of questions may make it more likely that the suspect answers them in the way the police want. While all the types of question specified below are permitted under PACE and the codes of practice, the lawyer should be aware of their potential for unfairness, and should be ready to intervene if necessary.

7.67 McConville et al identified four forms of question that 'overtly manipulate the suspect's decision-making':[49]

(1) **Leading questions:** These are questions that suggest the desired answer. An example would be: 'You did intend to steal the watch, didn't you?' While such questions are prohibited during evidence-in-chief in

49 M McConville et al, *The case for the prosecution* (Routledge, London, 1991) p69.

a trial, they are permissible during an interrogation. However, they may lead to unfairness precisely because they lead to the suspect giving a particular answer, while deterring other answers. Police training materials have, in the past, strongly suggested that interviewers should avoid using leading questions, except when summarising or confirming information that has already been given, because of the danger of misleading the suspect or planting a false memory.[50] They are particularly dangerous when questioning young children and those who are mentally vulnerable.[51]

(2) **Statement or 'tagged' questions:** These are statements put in the form of a question that the suspect is invited to adopt or defied to contradict. An example would be: 'What you did is, you went into town to meet your girlfriend, saw the car, noticed the expensive briefcase, and thought you'd have it out quick. The owner then came along, so you hit him and ran off. That's right, isn't it?' As with leading questions, it is quite clear what answer is wanted, and it discourages other answers or explanations. There has been sustained criticism of the use of 'tagged' questioning[52] of young suspects in criminal trials as the technique may produce unreliable answers.[53] There is no reason to believe that the reasoning does not apply equally to questioning under caution. If a client is either young or vulnerable, then a solicitor should be assiduous in ensuring that the questions asked are appropriate and easily understood.

(3) **Legal-closure questions:** These questions appear to invite the suspect to give information but, unknown to the suspect, have the effect of forcing that information into a legally significant category. This commonly occurs with an offence such as theft, where the suspect admits taking the item but without accepting that they were acting dishonestly or that they intended to deprive the owner permanently. The police response may well then be: 'So what you are saying is that you stole the item?' While appearing simply to confirm what the suspect has said, it introduces the legal concept of theft, which does not accord with a simple taking of goods. In this way, the suspect is led into accepting that they stole the item. The lawyer should be particularly alert when the interviewing officer appears to re-state what has been said, and should object if the re-statement does not accurately reflect what the suspect said.

(4) **Imperfect syllogistic questions:** Despite the name, the concept is relatively simple. This form of question seeks to persuade the suspect to

50 *A practical guide to investigative interviewing* (Central Police Training and Development Authority (Centrex), 2000) p32.

51 In *R (M) v (1) Leicester Constabulary (2) Crown Prosecution Service* [2009] EWHC 3640 (Admin), the court expressed concern about the use of leading questions during the interview of a child, making the point that questions put to children should be short and clear.

52 See, Lord Judge, *The Safest Shield Lectures, Speeches and Essays* (Hart, Oxford, 2015).

53 See, for example: *R v W and M* [2010] EWCA Crim 1926: 'It is generally recognised that particularly with child witnesses short and untagged questions are best at eliciting the evidence' (para 30); *R v Willis* [2011] EWCA Crim 1938; and the *Equal Treatment Bench Book* (May 2025 update), available at: www.sentencingcouncil.org.uk/wp-content/uploads/Equal-Treatment-Bench-Book.pdf.

accept a disputed fact (which is likely to be damaging to them) by persuading them that it logically follows from another fact or facts that have been accepted by the suspect. It may be illustrated by the following exchange.

Officer: You accept that you had been drinking, don't you?
Suspect: Yes.
Officer: And that you sat down next to the shop?
Suspect: Yes.
Officer: And you have said that you didn't see anyone else?
Suspect: Yes.
Officer: And that the shop window was broken when you woke up?
Suspect: Yes.
Officer: So it must have been you that smashed it, mustn't it?

Of course, it does not logically follow that the suspect smashed the window, but the suspect may be led in this way into accepting that they did. This form of questioning may be particularly effective from the police point of view where the suspect's recollection is unclear (perhaps through drink or drugs), or where for other reasons the suspect is susceptible to confession, albeit false. Again, the lawyer should be alert to the dangers of this form of question, and should intervene if necessary.

Style of questioning

7.68 The way in which questioning is conducted may have a significant impact on the outcome, and may have the effect of inducing an unwilling suspect to talk, or to make a false confession. Indeed, the style of questioning may specifically result from the officer's intention to produce such an effect. It must be remembered that the officer will frequently be working from an assumption that the suspect is guilty.

(1) **Domineering and bullying questioning:** There is plenty of evidence, both anecdotal and from research, that certain officers most of the time, and some officers some of the time, will resort to a style of questioning that is domineering, insulting, offensive, threatening or bullying.[54] This is contrary to the principles of investigative interviewing, published by the College of Policing,[55] which are set out opposite.

Two important questions for the defence lawyer are: (i) how far is an interviewing officer legally permitted to go? and (ii) when and how should the lawyer intervene? The provisions of PACE and the codes concerning oppressive or unfair questioning are set out in para 7.62 above. While the Court of Appeal has refrained from laying down rules, it is possible to derive some guidance on the interpretation of these provisions from decided cases. 'Oppression' was defined by the Court

54 See, for example, *R v Paris, Abdullahi and Miller* (1993) 97 Cr App R 99, CA.

55 College of Policing, *Authorised Professional Practice: Investigation: Investigative interviewing*, available at: www.app.college.police.uk/app-content/investigations/investigative-interviewing/#peace-framework.

of Appeal in *R v Fulling*[56] as 'the exercise of authority or power in a burdensome, harsh or wrongful manner; unjust or cruel treatment of subjects, inferiors, etc, the imposition of unreasonable or unjust burdens'. In a later case, evidence of a confession was rejected where it was obtained in an interview in which the suspect was 'hectored and bullied from first to last'.[57] However, in *R v Emmerson*,[58] the Court of Appeal held that questioning that was rude and discourteous, with a raised voice and some bad language, and that gave the impression of impatience and irritation, was not oppressive. An interviewing officer must never use abusive language and should never raise their voice or shout. While the officer may point out that the suspect is telling lies, it might be oppressive if this is repeated or shouted. Furthermore, if a suspect breaks down in the course of a police interview, they should be offered a break in the interview, although if 'the officer suspects that it is a mere sham he should put it specifically to the suspect to give him an opportunity to answer that'.

Investigative interviewing – Principles and ethics (College of Policing)

Principle 1

The aim of investigative interviewing is to obtain accurate and reliable accounts from victims, witnesses or suspects about matters under police investigation.

. . .

Principle 2

Investigators must act fairly when questioning victims, witnesses or suspects.

. . .

People with clear or perceived vulnerabilities should be treated with particular care, and extra safeguards should be put in place.

Principle 3

Investigative interviewing should be approached with an investigative mindset.

Accounts obtained from the person who is being interviewed should always be tested against what the interviewer already knows or what can reasonably be established.

. . .

Principle 4

Investigators are free to ask a wide range of questions in an interview in order to obtain material which may assist an investigation and provide sufficient evidence or information.

56 [1987] 2 All ER 65, CA.
57 *R v Beales* [1991] Crim LR 118.
58 (1991) 92 Cr App R 284, CA.

. . .

Principle 5

Investigators should recognise the positive impact of an early admission in the context of the criminal justice system.

. . .

Principle 6

Investigators are not bound to accept the first answer given. Questioning is not unfair merely because it is persistent.

. . .

Principle 7

Even when a suspect exercises the right to silence, investigators have a responsibility to put questions to them.

. . .

Bullying or offensive behaviour by the interviewing officer is less likely to be regarded as amounting to oppression, and is less likely to lead to exclusion of evidence, if it was conducted in the presence of a lawyer.[59] This does not mean, of course, that such behaviour will not have an adverse impact on the suspect simply because a lawyer is present. Indeed, its impact may be even greater if the lawyer is seen by their client to be intimidated, or is thought to be colluding with or indifferent towards such behaviour. The lawyer should normally intervene at an early stage, although the point of intervention requires careful judgment. Some suspects will not be unduly concerned about bad language or raised voices, whereas others will be intimidated by this. Generally, however, intervention should be sooner rather than later. Oppressive and similar forms of conduct can only be designed to obtain a confession. The officer should be reminded that Codes C, H and I, and the College of Policing's principles of investigative interviewing, require a police officer to act fairly, and that the stated purpose of an interview is to 'obtain accurate and reliable accounts' (Principle 1), not a confession. Furthermore, if the suspect is vulnerable for any reason, they must be treated with 'particular care' at all times (Principle 2). If the officer persists with such behaviour, the lawyer should consider interrupting the interview in order to advise their client in private and allow time for tempers to cool. If, however, the behaviour persists the lawyer should consider approaching the custody officer, or a more senior officer, with a view to another officer taking over the interview. The lawyer should also consider advising the client about lodging a formal complaint.

(2) **Failure to allow exculpatory statements:** A bullying or threatening style is not the only style of questioning that can lead to unfairness. The

59 See *R v Dunn* (1990) 91 Cr App R 237, CA (and see discussion at para 13.32 below); but contrast *R v Paris, Abdullahi and Miller* (1993) 97 Cr App R 99, CA.

officer may encourage statements by the suspect that are harmful to their interests, but move on quickly whenever the suspect tries to explain their behaviour in terms that may provide a defence or important mitigation. The College of Policing states that the interviewing officer should 'avoid interrupting the suspect while they are giving their account (interruptions may cause repercussions later and could result in miscarriage of justice, they may also inhibit the flow of information)'.[60] If the officer engages in such conduct, the lawyer should point out to the officer what they are doing, and ensure that the suspect has the opportunity to bring out the relevant information, either at the time or before the end of the interview.

(3) **Topic hopping:** This is a more generalised form of the kind of questioning described in (2) above. Changing topics before a suspect has had the chance to think about their response or to say all that they would wish to say is distracting and may cause confusion.

(4) **Maximising and minimising consequences:** This style of questioning is particularly likely where the suspect is not answering questions, but the officer believes that they may be persuaded to speak. It consists of maximising the advantages and minimising the disadvantages of a confession. The officer may seek to persuade the suspect that confessing could be in their interests, and/or that the consequences of confessing may not be as bad as the suspect believes. This tactic may contravene Code C para 11.5, Code H para 11.6 or Code I para 11.5, which provide that interviewing officers must not indicate what action the police will take if the person answers questions or gives a statement. Even if it does not, it may still amount to an improper inducement. The lawyer should intervene if this is the case, or if what is said by the officer in any way misrepresents the truth.

The end of the interview

7.69 Two separate, but interrelated, issues are involved here. First, at what stage should police interviewing cease? Second, what should the lawyer do at the conclusion of any police interview? A further question, of whether a suspect can be interviewed after charge, is dealt with at para 10.35 below.

At what stage should interviewing cease?

7.70 In the case of most suspects, there is only one police interview.[61] Code C para 11.6, Code H para 11.7 and Code I para 11.7 set out the circumstances

60 College of Policing, *Authorised Professional Practice: Investigation: Investigative interviewing: Structuring the suspect interview*, available at: www.app.college.police.uk/app-content/investigations/investigative-interviewing/#structuring-the-suspect-interview.

61 Research from the 1990s found that there was more than one interview in only one case in ten. See T Bucke and D Brown, *In police custody: police powers and suspects' rights under the revised PACE Codes of Practice*, Home Office Research Study 174 (Home Office, London, 1997) p31.

in which an interview, and interviewing, must stop, but the following provisions are of general relevance:

- In any period of 24 hours, a detained person must be allowed a continuous period of at least eight hours for rest, free from questioning, travel, etc. The rest period should usually be at night, but account must be taken of when the suspect last slept or rested (Codes C and H para 12.2; Code I para 11.16; and see para 7.36 above).
- There must be breaks in interviewing at recognised meal times, and also short breaks for refreshment at intervals of approximately two hours, subject to exceptions if the break would involve a risk of harm to others or damage to property, or would unnecessarily delay the suspect's release from custody, or would otherwise prejudice the outcome of the investigation (Codes C and H para 12.8; Code I para 11.22).
- Suspects must not be interviewed if the custody officer considers that an interview would cause significant harm to their physical or mental state (Codes C and H para 12.3; Code I para 11.17; and see para 5.22 above). Therefore, an interview should cease if the suspect becomes unfit during the course of an interview.

7.71 Code C, Code H and Code I give the police a significant degree of latitude in terms of determining when interviewing should cease. Code C para 11.6, Code H para 11.7 and Code I para 11.6 provide that interviewing must stop when:

(1) **The officer in charge of the investigation is satisfied that all the questions the officer considers relevant to obtaining accurate and reliable information about the offence have been put to the suspect.** The codes state that this includes allowing the suspect an opportunity to give an innocent explanation, and for the interviewer to test the accuracy and reliability of the explanation by asking further questions. Whether or not the suspect is answering questions, this provision is intended to enable the interviewer to continue asking questions until they have asked all questions that they believe to be relevant (although see para 7.72 below). If the suspect puts forward an explanation, it enables the officer to ask questions in order to test that explanation, for example, by reference to other evidence or by reference to what else the suspect has said. If the suspect is not answering questions, the provision is designed to enable the interviewer to ask all relevant questions, which is likely to assist in persuading a court in a subsequent trial that the accused did not act reasonably in failing to mention a fact relied upon in the accused's defence, an explanation for which should have been prompted by the questions asked (see para 5.87 above).

(2) **The officer in charge of the investigation has taken account of any other available evidence.** This appears to be designed to enable the police to have regard to other evidence that they have secured, or to seek other evidence (for example, in response to any explanation provided or assertion made by the suspect in interview), before concluding interviewing.

(3) **The officer in charge of the investigation, or in the case of a detained suspect, the custody officer, reasonably believes there is sufficient**

evidence to provide a realistic prospect of conviction for the offence in respect of which the suspect is being interviewed. A 'realistic prospect of conviction' reflects the evidential sufficiency test in the Code for Crown Prosecutors, which makes clear that the test involves consideration of what the defence case may be and how it is likely to affect the prosecution case. It further states that the test is an objective one: is a jury or court, properly directed in accordance with the law, more likely than not to convict the defendant of the alleged charge?

7.72 The structure of Code C para 11.6, Code H para 11.7 and Code I para 11.6 is such that interviewing does not have to cease until all three conditions are satisfied. Thus, even if the interviewing officer is satisfied that that there is a realistic prospect of conviction, it permits interviewing to continue if they are not satisfied that all relevant questions have been asked, or that not all available evidence has been taken into account. However, the effect of the code provisions is less straightforward than might appear for a number of reasons:

(1) If it can be established that the police intend to prosecute whatever further questions are put, or whatever the suspect might say in interview, it can be argued that a decision regarding prosecution should be made without further interviewing (see para 5.148 above).

(2) Code C para 16.1[62] provides that when the officer in charge of the investigation reasonably believes there is sufficient evidence to provide a realistic prospect of conviction, they must inform the custody officer without delay, who must then decide whether to charge the detainee. This suggests that the decisive factor in determining whether interviewing should cease is the sufficiency of the evidence, and that once the officer is satisfied that it provides a realistic prospect of conviction, interviewing must cease even if the officer is not satisfied that all relevant questions have been put to the suspect or that all available evidence has been taken into account.

(3) There is a contradiction between Code C paras 11.6 and 16.1 in that the latter states that it is the officer in charge of the investigation who must determine whether the evidence is such that there is a realistic prospect of conviction, whereas the former provides that in the case of a detained suspect this decision is for the custody officer. It is probable that the intention was to place initial responsibility on the officer in charge of the investigation to decide whether the realistic prospect of conviction test is satisfied, in which case the custody officer should be informed, who must then consider whether they are also so satisfied. However, the current version of Code C is unclear in this respect, but given the statutory responsibility placed on custody officers by PACE s37, a charge decision must be made if the custody officer is satisfied that there is a realistic prospect of conviction.

(4) There is arguably a conflict between Code C para 11.6 and PACE s37(7). The latter provides that if the custody officer determines that the officer has before them sufficient evidence to charge the person

62 Section 16 of PACE Code C applies to the charging process of persons detained under TA 2000 s41 (Code H para 14) and NSA 2023 s27 (Code I para 14).

arrested with the offence for which they were arrested, a decision about charge must be made. 'Sufficient evidence to charge' is not defined in PACE, but the Director of Public Prosecutions (DPP) guidance on charging[63] provides that the applicable standard is normally sufficient evidence to provide a 'realistic prospect of conviction' (sections 4 and 5) and Code C para 16.1A requires the custody officer to comply with that (PACE s37A) guidance in deciding how to act in dealing with a detainee. There is nothing in either PACE s37(7) or the Director's guidance on charging that permits the police to carry on questioning after the 'sufficient evidence to charge' threshold has been met (see para 10.9 below).

7.73 In practice, it is often difficult for the lawyer to judge whether the stage has been reached when interviewing should cease, since they will often not be fully aware of the evidence in the possession of the police. The lawyer may, in any event, be content for an interview to proceed in circumstances where it should stop if the client is answering questions in order to establish a defence or in order to lay the grounds for an effective mitigation. However, if the lawyer is of the view that continued interviewing is not in their client's best interests – for example, because the client is in danger of adversely affecting their position by what they say or because continued interviewing may make adverse inferences more likely – the lawyer should carefully consider whether the conditions for bringing interviewing to an end are satisfied and whether to make appropriate representations. If the lawyer believes that there is sufficient evidence to charge, they should consider interrupting the interview and making representations to the custody officer by reference to the factors set out in para 7.72 above.

7.74 Where a suspect has been arrested and detained for more than one offence, Code C para 16.1 provides that it is permissible for the interviewing officer to delay taking the suspect before the custody officer until the conditions have been met in respect of all of the offences. Michael Zander has argued that Code C para 16.1 cannot be reconciled with PACE s37(7) and that the provision may be ultra vires.[64] While a custody officer, and still less an interviewing officer, is unlikely to be impressed by argument about the ultra vires nature of Code C para 16.1, the lawyer could seek to bring interviewing to an end by persuading the custody officer that their duty to charge or otherwise under PACE s37(7) has arisen and cannot be delayed (see para 2.70 above). If interviewing does continue beyond the time when it should cease, it will be possible to argue that any resulting confession or other evidence adverse to the suspect should be excluded at trial under PACE s76 or 78 (see para 13.19 below). Furthermore, the police may be liable for false imprisonment if the detention goes beyond that permitted by PACE (see para 13.16 below).

63 Crown Prosecution Service, *Director's Guidance on Charging*, 6th edn (December 2020), incorporating the National File Standard, available at: www.cps.gov.uk/sites/default/files/documents/legal_guidance/Directors-Guidance-on-Charging-6th-Edition.pdf.

64 M Zander, *The Police and Criminal Evidence Act 1984* (Sweet & Maxwell, London, 5th edn, 2005) p150, although this does not appear in the current version of the book.

What should the lawyer do at the end of the interview?

7.75 At the end of a police interview the lawyer should:

(1) Ensure that the recording and checking requirements have been complied with (see paras 7.13 and 7.17 above).

(2) Take a note of:
- the time that the interview ended;
- the time that the various parties left the interview room; and
- the content of any conversation during this period.

This would help to prevent any allegation by the police that the suspect confessed after the recording medium was turned off from being accepted by a court.[65]

(3) Ask the officer how the investigation is to proceed after the interview. The information is necessary in order to enable the lawyer to advise their client on the future course of events, and it is normally helpful to obtain this information in the presence of the client.

(4) Consider whether to ask the police to pursue any particular lines of enquiry. If the client has put forward a defence in the police interview, or the lawyer is aware that the client has a defence that is capable of further investigation by the police, the lawyer should consider asking the officer in the case what action they intend to take to investigate these and, where appropriate, to press the officer to undertake such investigation. If the officer appears reluctant to do so, they should be reminded of the Criminal Procedure and Investigations Act 1996 Code of Practice para 3.4, which provides that in conducting an investigation the 'investigator should pursue all reasonable lines of enquiry, whether these point towards or away from the suspect'. The lawyer should keep a note of any such representations, and the response, since they may be relevant at trial. This is especially important if there is believed to be material (including communication material) held by a third party.[66]

(5) Consider whether pre-charge engagement[67] is an appropriate step (see para 10.14 below). Pre-charge engagement may be an appropriate route to explore potential lines of enquiry raised by the defence or the police. The (non-exhaustive) examples of pre-charge engagement include a suspect providing an encryption key (for example, the password for a mobile phone) or identifying potential witnesses. It is possible for pre-charge disclosure to take place to make sure that the process is fair and that the suspect is not misled as to the strength of the prosecution case.

(6) Arrange to speak to the client in private and:
- Evaluate the interview, in particular, whether the point has been reached when the police should make a decision about charge, and whether the client should request a further police interview. The latter may be necessary, for example, in order to deal with any matters missed in the interview or, where the client did not answer

65 Which occurred in *R v Dunn* (1990) 91 Cr App R 237, CA; and see para 13.23 below.

66 See *R v E* [2018] EWCA Crim 2426; and *Review of the efficiency and effectiveness of disclosure in the criminal justice system* (Attorney General's Office, November 2018).

67 *Attorney General's Guidelines on Disclosure* (2024) Annex B.

questions and the interview was used to obtain information about the police case, where it is now advisable to answer questions. Consideration should also be given to whether it is appropriate to submit a prepared statement, or a supplementary prepared statement (see para 5.152 above).

- Advise on the likely course of the investigation and detention. It is important that the client has as accurate an idea as possible about the likely course of the remaining period of detention in order to allay any unjustified fears and to minimise risks of the client becoming vulnerable to pressure. In particular, if the client has denied the offence in interview or made a 'no comment' interview, they should be warned that the police may visit them in the absence of the lawyer in order to persuade them to talk or confess. The importance of giving this warning is demonstrated by the case of *R v Williams*.[68] The defendant was arrested for burglary and was interviewed in the presence of his lawyer, making no admissions. After the lawyer left the police station, the interviewing officers paid an hour-long 'social visit' to the suspect in the cells. Subsequently, he agreed to be interviewed in the absence of his lawyer and confessed. The Court of Appeal upheld the conviction, finding that there had been no breach of PACE. In appropriate cases the client should also be warned of the possibility that they may be the subject of covert surveillance.
- Consider, in the context of CJPOA 1994 s34, what, if anything, should be said at the time of charge, or whether a prepared statement should be submitted at the time of charge (see paras 5.76 and 5.152 above).
- Take instructions on and give advice in respect of release without charge or following charge (see paras 10.113 and 10.136 below).
- Remind the client that they have a right under PACE s58 to legal advice at any time during the period of detention, and tell them how to exercise that right.

Port and border questioning

7.76 TA 2000 Sch 7 and C-TBSA 2019 Sch 3 allow an 'examining officer'[69] to stop, question, search and detain a person at a port,[70] or the border area in Northern Ireland, for the purpose of determining:

- under TA 2000 Sch 7, whether the person appears to be someone who is, or has been, involved in the commission, preparation or instigation of acts of terrorism;[71] and

68 (1992) Times, February 6, CA.

69 A constable, designated immigration officer or designated customs officer (TA 2000 Sch 7 para 1(1); C-TBSA 2019 Sch 3 para 64(3)).

70 Port includes an airport and a hoverport (TA 2000 Sch 7 para 1(2); C-TBSA 2019 Sch 3 para 64(4)).

71 TA 2000 Sch 7 para 2.

- under C-TBSA 2019 Sch 3, whether the person appears to be a person who is, or has been, engaged in hostile activity.[72]

The respective powers extend to the examination of goods for the same purpose. Each power has a detailed code of practice in force.

7.77 A person may be examined for a period of one hour without being detained under TA 2000 Sch 7 para 6 or C-TBSA 2019 Sch 3 para 4.[73] A person examined at a port, but not detained, is not entitled to consult a solicitor, but may do so at the examining officer's discretion and not at public expense. Where reasonably practicable, a private consultation with a solicitor should be allowed.[74] A person detained under TA 2000 Sch 7 or C-TBSA 2019 Sch 3 is entitled to consult with a solicitor.[75]

7.78 There is no right to silence in TA 2000 Sch 7 or C-TBSA 2019 Sch 3 interviews.[76] However, an answer or information given orally by a person in response to a question asked under TA 2000 Sch 7 para 2 or 3 or C-TBSA 2019 Sch 3 para 1 or 2 may not be used in evidence in criminal proceedings save for in the limited circumstances set out in TA 2000 Sch 7 para 5A(2) and C-TBSA 2019 Sch 3 para 6(2).[77]

72 C-TBSA 2019 Sch 3 para 1.

73 TA 2000 Sch 7 para 6A; C-TBSA 2019 Sch 3 para 5.

74 Home Office, *Examining officers and review officers under Schedule 7 to the Terrorism Act 2000* (July 2025) para 45, available at: www.gov.uk/government/publications/codes-of-practice-for-officers-using-examination-powers-at-ports/examining-officers-and-review-officers-under-schedule-7-to-the-terrorism-act-2000-accessible-version#examination-of-persons; Home Office, *Examining Officers and Review Officers under Schedule 3 to the Counter-Terrorism and Border Security Act 2019 Code of Practice* (July 2025) para 43, available at: www.gov.uk/government/publications/codes-of-practice-for-officers-using-examination-powers-at-ports/revised-schedule-3-code-of-practice-2023-accessible-version#examination-of-persons.

75 TA 2000 Sch 7 para 6; C-TBSA 2019 Sch 3 para 30.

76 See TA 2000 Sch 7 paras 2–3, 5 and 18; C-TBSA 2019 Sch 3 paras 1–3 and 23.

77 TA 2000 Sch 7 para 5A; C-TBSA 2019 Sch 3 para 6.

CHAPTER 8

Identification procedures

continued

Introduction

8.1 This chapter deals with visual identification and recognition procedures, and also with voice identification. Other methods of identification – such as fingerprints, footwear impressions, body samples, and examination to establish identity – are dealt with in chapter 6 above. The current version of Police and Criminal Evidence Act 1984 (PACE) Code of Practice D makes a fundamental distinction between the procedures to be followed in respect of visual identification by eye-witnesses (Part 3(A)) and those to be followed where the police are seeking to establish whether any person recognises a suspected offender (Parts 3(B) and 3(C)). This distinction is not entirely satisfactory, and may cause some confusion as to the circumstances in which they apply (see para 8.5 below). There is no separate code covering procedures to be followed in respect of voice identification, but Code D makes limited reference to voice identification.

8.2 It has long been recognised by the courts that visual identification evidence is problematic, and may be unreliable, even where a witness honestly believes that they have made a correct identification. As a result, not only must the correct identification procedure be observed in accordance with Code D, but in a trial on indictment the jury court must be warned of the dangers inherent in evidence of identification (known as a 'Turnbull warning').[1]

8.3 The complexities surrounding identification evidence mean that the lawyer must be diligent in ensuring that the appropriate method of identification is used, and that it is properly conducted. If the lawyer is unhappy about any aspect of the procedure, they should make appropriate representations at the time. The lawyer should also keep a note of such concerns, of representations made and of the police response, since these may be relevant both to the question of whether the identification evidence should be admitted at trial at all and, if it is admitted, to the direction to be given to a jury. As with intervention during the course of interviews, if the lawyer acquiesces in an identification procedure about which the they have reservations, the evidence of identification may be admitted on the basis that the presence (and implied consent) of the lawyer nullifies the effect of any breach of Code D.

8.4 The arrangements for, and the conduct of, identification procedures are the responsibility of an 'identification officer', who must be of the rank of inspector or above. However, generally the identification officer may delegate these functions to another police officer or to a civilian on condition that the officer provides effective supervision (Code D para 3.11). Code D does not apply to the powers under Terrorism Act (TA) 2000 Sch 8, National Security Act 2023 Sch 6 or the Counter-Terrorism and Border Security Act 2019 to take photographs, fingerprints, body samples and impressions, but it does apply to visual identification procedures conducted in respect of a person detained under that Act.

1 See *R v Turnbull* [1977] QB 224, CA.

Which type of procedure applies?

8.5 The three different forms of procedure specified in Code D are as follows:

(1) The procedures in Code D Part 3(A) 'Identification of a suspect by an eye-witness' apply when an eye-witness has seen a person committing a crime or in any other circumstances that tend to prove or disprove the involvement of the person they saw in the crime (Code D para 3.0). This part of the code sets out the procedures to be followed to test the ability of that eye-witness to identify a person suspected of involvement in the offence as the person they saw on the previous occasion.
(2) The procedures in Code D Part 3(B) 'Recognition by controlled showing of films, photographs and images' are for the purpose of testing whether a person recognises anyone in an image shown to them, but must not be used in respect of eye-witnesses (Code D para 3.34).
(3) The procedures in Code D Part 3(C) 'Recognition by uncontrolled viewing of films, photographs and images' are for the purpose of identifying and tracing suspects, and may involve both eye-witnesses and/or others who, by definition, are not known to the police.

Code D note for guidance (NfG) 3AA states that the eye-witness identification procedures in Part 3(A) should not be used to test whether a witness can recognise a person as someone they know but, rather confusingly, states that in such cases the procedures in Part 3(B) or (C) should be used. However, as noted above, the Part 3(B) procedure cannot be used in respect of eye-witnesses (although an eye-witness could be shown visual images by virtue of para 3.3 and Annex E). It is clear that Part 3(A) applies where an eye-witness known to the police may be able to identify the person they saw committing a crime, and that under Part 3(C) images may be seen by an eye-witness who recognises a person in the image, and who may then contact the police as a result. What is not so clear is which Part applies where an eye-witness known to the police may, or thinks that they may, recognise the person they saw committing the offence.

8.6 There is a number of reported cases on the question of whether an identification procedure should have been held in the case of recognition by an eye-witness, although most were decided in the context of previous versions of Code D.[2] It has been held that an identification procedure (of the sort governed by Code D Part 3(A)) is not required where a witness recognises a suspect in the sense that they know the suspect from previous contact with them.[3] However, it has also been held that if the recognition is less certain – and particularly if the suspect disputes the purported recognition – an identification procedure should have been conducted. Thus in *R v Fergus*,[4] it was held that an identification parade should have

2 For more recent cases concerning video recognition by police officers, see *R v Fitzsimmons, Duffy and McCrory* [2022] NICC 27; and *R v Bogie* [2023] EWCA Crim 1280.

3 *R (H) v DPP* [2003] EWHC 133 (Admin).

4 [1992] Crim LR 363, CA; and see *R v Byrne* [2004] EWCA Crim 979. Contrast *R v Clarke and Baker* [2003] EWCA Crim 718, where the evidence was treated as recognition rather than identification even though the witnesses knew the names of the suspects only because they had been told them by others; and see also *R v Folan* [2003] EWCA Crim 908.

been held where the witness had only seen the suspect once before and had been told his name by a third party. Similarly, in *R v Harris*,[5] although categorising the case as one of recognition rather than identification, the court held that an identification procedure should have been held where the suspect disputed the purported recognition, which was based on contact at school two years before the incident. Thus it would seem that in the case of tentative or uncertain recognition by an eye-witness, an identification procedure under Part 3(A) should be used and, depending on the circumstances, the lawyer may feel that this would be to the advantage of their client.

8.7 It has been held that the identification procedures in Code D (ie those in Part 3(A) of the current version (December 2023)) do not apply where the witness has merely given a description of the clothing worn by the suspect and has not described the suspect's features.[6] However, this case was decided in the context of a former version of Code D, and it may be that under the current version an identification procedure should be held in such circumstances if the identifying witness expresses an ability to identify the suspect or there is a reasonable chance of them being able to do so (Code D para 3.12).[7]

Eye-witness identification procedures under Code D Part 3(A)

Introduction

8.8 The procedures to be followed in respect of identification by eye-witnesses are set out in Code D Part 3(A) and Annexes A–E. The code distinguishes between:

(1) cases where the suspect's identity is not known; and
(2) those where it is known; and, in these cases, between:
 (a) cases where the suspect is known and available; and
 (b) cases where the suspect is known but is not available.

It is important to determine which of these applies, since this will determine which form of identification is applicable. A suspect is 'known' if there is sufficient information known to the police to establish that there are reasonable grounds to suspect a particular person of involvement in the offence (Code D para 3.1A(a)). This is the case whether or not the suspect has actually been arrested.[8] A suspect is 'available' where they are immediately available or will be within a reasonably short time, in order that they can be invited to take part in an eye-witness identification procedure and it is practicable to arrange an effective procedure (Code D para

5 [2003] EWCA Crim 174.

6 See *D v DPP* (1998) Times, August 7, DC; and *Parry v DPP* (1998) 12 October (unreported), CA.

7 Although see *R v Haynes* [2004] EWCA Crim 390.

8 See *R v Nunes* [2001] EWCA Crim 2283 (where the suspect had been arrested); and *R v Preddie* [2011] EWCA Crim 312 (where the suspect had been stopped by police with a view to arrest). For borderline cases, see *R v Haynes* [2004] EWCA Crim 390; and *B v DPP* [2006] EWHC 660 (Admin).

3.1A(b)). Note that the code uses the term 'suspect' to mean two separate things, and this may cause some confusion – while para 3.1A uses the term to mean a person who is suspected of committing the offence, para 3.12, for example, uses the term to mean the person whom an eye-witness saw committing the offence. The person whom the eye-witness saw committing the offence may not, of course, be the person who is known and available for an identification procedure. Indeed, the whole point of an identification procedure is to determine whether the eye-witness can identify the person arrested as the person they saw committing the offence.

8.9 The description of a suspect as first given by an eye-witness must normally be recorded before the witness takes part in an identification procedure (Code D para 3.1). A copy of the record must, where practicable, be shown to the suspect or their lawyer before a video identification, identification parade, group identification or confrontation is conducted. If it has not already been disclosed, the lawyer should request a copy of the description as soon as it becomes apparent that identification may be in issue. The lawyer should carefully examine the witness description, noting in particular the circumstances of the view and the nature and extent of the description given, and should ask the police whether it fully reflects the description given by the witness. In *R v Nolan*,[9] an identification was held to have been properly admitted even though the witness description provided to the defence lawyer omitted the fact that the witness had told the police that she had only seen the offender from the back.

Cases where the suspect's identity is not known

Street identification

8.10 Where the identity of the suspect is not known, a witness may be taken to a particular neighbourhood or place to see whether they can identify the person they saw in relation to the alleged crime. Code D para 3.2 provides that while the rules governing formal identification procedures do not directly apply to a street identification, the principles should be followed as far as practicable. It goes on to provide the following examples of the appropriate procedures to be followed:

(1) Where it is practicable to do so, a record should be made of the witness's description of the person they saw on the previous occasion before asking them to make an identification.
(2) Care must be taken not to direct the witness's attention to any individual unless, taking into account all the circumstances, this cannot be avoided.
(3) Where there is more than one eye-witness, every effort should be made to keep them separate and witnesses should be taken to see whether they can identify a person independently.
(4) Once there is sufficient information to establish that the suspect is 'known' – for example, after an eye-witness makes a positive identification – other witnesses should not be asked to make a street identification,

9 [2002] EWCA Crim 464.

and the case should be treated as one where the suspect is known and available.

(5) The officer or civilian support staff accompanying the eye-witness must record, in their pocket book, the action taken as soon as practicable, and in as much detail as possible.

Showing photographs or other visual images

8.11 If the identity of a suspect is known and they are available to take part in an identification procedure, an eye-witness must not be shown photographs or other visual images. If the other visual image is an 'e-fit' image (Code D para 3.3), then it is hearsay evidence and it is to be treated in the same way as a written record made by a police officer of a description provided by an eyewitness as to the appearance of someone the witness had seen.[10] However, if the suspect's identity is not known, an eye-witness may be shown such images to see whether they can identify a person whose image they are shown as the person they saw on the previous occasion, provided this is done in accordance with Code D Annex E (Code D para 3.3). In the case of a suspect who is known, but who is not available because, for example, they refuse to co-operate, the identification officer can make arrangements for a video or group identification (Code D para 3.21).

8.12 The showing of photographs or other visual images under Code D Annex E is quite separate from the procedure to be followed under Code D Part 3(B), which is not to be used in respect of eye-witnesses. Although Annex E is entitled 'Showing photographs to eye-witnesses', and largely refers to photographs, the procedures should also be followed where other visual images are shown to an eye-witness (which is clearly implied by Code D para 3.3). The showing of photographs and other visual images must be supervised and directed by an officer of the rank of sergeant or above, who must confirm that the first description given by the eye-witness has been recorded before they are shown the photographs. If this cannot be confirmed, the showing of photographs must be postponed, presumably in order for this to be done (Code D Annex E paras 1 and 2). Annex E provides, in particular, that:

(1) Only one eye-witness at a time may be shown photographs, and they must not be allowed to communicate with other witnesses in the case.
(2) The eye-witness must be shown at least 12 photographs at a time which should, as far as possible, all be of a similar type.
(3) The eye-witness must be told that a photograph of the person the witness saw may not be among them, and they must not be prompted or guided in any way.
(4) The witness must be told that they should not make a decision until they have viewed at least 12 photographs.
(5) If an eye-witness makes a positive identification from photographs, unless the person identified is otherwise eliminated from the enquiries or is not available, other witnesses must not be shown photographs. The identifying witness and any other witnesses must be asked to

10 *R v Thomasson* [2021] EWCA Crim 114.

attend a video identification, identification parade or group identification, unless there is no dispute about the identification of the suspect.

(6) Where the use of a computerised or artist's composite or similar likeness has led to there being a known suspect who can be asked to participate in a video identification, identification parade or group identification, that likeness must not be shown to other potential witnesses.

(7) The officer in charge of an investigation must inform the identification officer whether a witness to a video identification, identification parade or group identification has previously been shown photographs or computerised or artist's composite or similar likeness and, if this is the case, the suspect and their lawyer must be informed before the identification procedure takes place. There is no requirement for this to be done before a confrontation, but it is suggested that this requirement should also apply where practicable.

Implications for legal advice

8.13 A defence lawyer is unlikely to be involved at the stage of an investigation where the police carry out a street identification or show photographs or other visual images to a witness, although the lawyer may be in the latter case where the suspect has been arrested but refuses to co-operate with another form of identification procedure. When advising in respect of an identification procedure described in para 8.21 below, the lawyer should, where appropriate, ask whether there has been a street identification or whether any witness has been shown photographs or other visual images, and seek detailed information about the procedure used, whether there has been any social media identification (see para 8.88 below), and whether any identification was made. Note in particular that once a positive identification has been made by means of a street identification, or once a positive identification has been made from photographs, other witnesses should not normally take part in a street identification or be asked to view photographs (Code D para 3.2(d) and Annex E para 6). There is no prohibition on the identifying witness taking part in a further identification procedure, although the lawyer should consider whether it would serve a useful purpose (see para 8.20 below). Where a witness has previously been shown photographs or other visual images, the suspect and their lawyer must be told before the further identification procedure is carried out (Code D Annex E para 9). There is no similar provision in respect of a street identification, but the suspect will almost certainly be aware of it. If it appears that the provisions of Code D have not been observed, appropriate representations should be made, and a careful note taken of both the representations and any response. For the effect of any breach on admissibility of the identification evidence at trial, see para 13.41 below.

Cases where the suspect is known but not available

8.14 If a suspect is known but is not available (see para 8.8 above), or has ceased to be available (because, for example, they have withdrawn consent), the identification officer (Code D para 3.11) may make arrangements for a video identification (if necessary using still images rather than moving images); a group identification; or the showing of photographs or other visual images (Code D paras 3.3 and 3.21). As a last resort, the identification officer may consider a confrontation (Code D para 3.23). Any suitable moving or still image may be used for a video identification, and these may be obtained covertly if necessary (but see para 8.35 below). A video or group identification may also be used where, in the case of a child suspect, the consent of the child's parent or guardian to an identification procedure is either refused or reasonable efforts to obtain consent have failed.

8.15 Code D does not explicitly deal with the situation where a video or group identification has been conducted under Code D para 3.21 and the suspect subsequently becomes available. It would seem that an identification procedure should be held in respect of the witness who was asked to make an identification under para 3.21 if the conditions set out in Code D para 3.12 are satisfied (see para 8.18 below), but the key issue will be whether such a procedure would serve a useful purpose. In many circumstances, if the witness has picked out the suspect in a procedure conducted under Code D para 3.21, there would be no useful purpose in conducting another form of identification procedure. If there are other witnesses who have not taken part in an identification procedure under para 3.21, the usual rules under Code D para 3.12 will apply.

8.16 If a video or group identification has been conducted under Code D para 3.21, the lawyer should carefully consider whether the conditions for conducting a procedure under this provision were satisfied. Particular attention should be paid to the image of the suspect used, and whether there were any significant differences between this image and the images of the comparators used (for example, whether they were all still or moving images, the background of the images, etc).

Cases where the suspect is known and available

8.17 Where a suspect is known and available (see para 8.8 above), the police must decide whether to hold an identification procedure and select the form of procedure to be used.

When must an identification procedure be held?

8.18 The circumstances in which an identification procedure must be held are set out in Code D para 3.12, as follows. Where:

(1) an eye-witness has identified a suspect or purported to have identified them prior to the conduct of a video or group identification or identification parade;
(2) there is an eye-witness available who expresses an ability to identify the suspect; or
(3) there is a reasonable chance of an eye-witness being able to do so;

and:

(4) the eye-witness has not been given an opportunity to identify the suspect in a video or group identification or identification parade; and
(5) the suspect disputes being the person the witness claims to have seen;

an identification procedure must be held unless it is not practicable or it would serve no useful purpose in proving or disproving whether the suspect was involved in committing the offence.

8.19 If these conditions are not satisfied, an identification procedure may, nevertheless, be held if the officer in charge of the investigation, after consultation with the identification officer, considers that it would be useful (Code D para 3.13).

8.20 Thus, the conditions that make the holding of an identification procedure mandatory are as follows:

(1) **An eye-witness has identified a suspect.** Presumably, this means that an eye-witness has identified or purported to have identified a person as the person they saw committing a crime (or in any other circumstances that tend to prove or disprove the involvement of the person they saw in a crime) prior to a suspect becoming known, since if an eye-witness recognised the person they saw committing a crime, then an identification procedure will normally not be appropriate (see para 8.5 above).[11] Provided the other conditions are satisfied, an identification procedure must be held even though the witness has identified or purported to identify the suspect in a procedure conducted under Code D para 3.2 (suspect's identity is not known).[12] Code D para 3.2(d) states that once there is sufficient evidence to justify the arrest of a particular person, the provisions set out from para 3.4 onwards (ie the provisions that are applicable when a suspect is known and available) apply);

(2) **An eye-witness expresses an ability to identify the suspect.** An eye-witness says that they will, or are likely to, be able to identify a person as the person they saw committing the offence (or in any other circumstances, etc); or

(3) **There is a reasonable chance that an eye-witness will be able to identify the suspect.** Although an eye-witness does not express an ability to make a positive identification (as in (2) above), there is a reasonable chance of them being able to do so. In *R v Nolan*,[13] for example, the witness had told the police that she had only seen the gunman from the back. However, the police thought that she was frightened and that she had seen more than she had told the police. The case was decided on an earlier version of Code D, but it would seem that in similar circumstances under the current Code D, the holding of an identification procedure would, assuming that the other conditions were satisfied, be mandatory; and

11 If there is no identification but, for example, an accumulation of circumstantial evidence that points to the identity of the suspect, Code D does not apply (*Alabusheva v DPP* [2007] EWHC 264 (Admin)).

12 However, in *R v Crampton* [2020] EWCA Crim 1334, a social media (Facebook) identification was allowed in the absence of a Video Identification Parade Electronic Recording (VIPER) procedure, the court noting that the suspect would likely have been identified in the VIPER procedure and would likely have attempted to exclude the VIPER process on the basis that it corroborated the Facebook evidence and could lead the jury to form a false impression on the strength of the identification.

13 [2002] EWCA Crim 464.

(4) **The suspect disputes being the person.** This requires a factual basis upon which it can properly be said that the suspect disputes being the person the eye-witness claims to have seen.[14] It will clearly apply if the suspect denies having been present at the relevant time. It will also be relevant if the suspect accepts that they were present but denies participation.[15] It would not normally apply if the suspect merely disagrees with the eye-witness's account of their level of involvement in the alleged offence since the issue would be one of participation rather than identification. It may not apply if the suspect does not dispute identification during the investigation, for example, on arrest or in the interview.[16] If the suspect does dispute being the person the eye-witness claims to have seen, it is important that this is made known to the police before charge. If identification is disputed for the first time after charge, it may be that a court will permit some other, less satisfactory, form of identification such as a dock identification (but see para 8.80 below);[17] and

(5) **An identification is not impracticable.** The cases on practicability were decided before the development of video identification and were principally concerned with the practicability of holding an identification parade. Given the widespread availability of video identification, and the development of image libraries, it is now more difficult for the police to maintain that all forms of identification procedure would be impracticable. The police must make their decision regarding practicability on reasonable grounds, and must take all reasonably practicable steps to investigate the possibility of holding a video identification before moving to another form of identification.[18] However, a procedure may be impracticable if the suspect has distinctive features that cannot be effectively disguised.[19] Also:

(6) **Serving a useful purpose.** Even if all of the other conditions are satisfied, an identification procedure does not have to be held if it would serve no useful purpose in proving or disproving whether the suspect was involved in committing the alleged offence. This condition may cause difficulty for both the police and defence lawyers, and ultimately for the courts. In *R v Forbes*,[20] the House of Lords, in interpreting a former version of Code D, attempted to reduce the discretion of the police to decline to hold an identification parade on the ground that

14 *Grier v DPP* [2024] EWHC 1493 (Admin).

15 *R v Hope, Limburn and Bleasdale* [1994] Crim LR 118, CA; and *K v DPP* [2003] EWHC 351 (QB).

16 *Grier v DPP* [2024] EWHC 1493 (Admin). But see the critical commentary at [2024] Crim LR 864.

17 *Karia v DPP* [2002] EWHC 2175 (Admin).

18 *R v Britton and Richards* [1989] Crim LR 144, Crown Court (Leeds). The decision was made at a time when identification parades were the primary form of procedure, but the same principles should apply to video identification.

19 In *R v Marrin* [2002] EWCA Crim 251, it was held that the use of make-up, etc was not inherently unfair, but care was needed to ensure that its use could not be detected by the witness. The wearing of hats should be avoided if possible, but there may be circumstances where their use would enhance the fairness of the procedure.

20 [2001] 1 AC 473, HL.

they did not think it would serve a useful purpose. In their Lordships' view, the code was intended as 'an intensely practical document giving police officers clear instructions on the approach that they should follow in specified circumstances'. However, subsequent amendments to Code D explicitly re-introduced the 'no useful purpose' provision.

The police are most likely to decide that an identification procedure would serve no useful purpose where there has already been a street identification or other form of identification of the suspect (which was not a video identification, identification parade or group identification). However, as noted in (1) above, the wording of Code D para 3.12 suggests that a further identification procedure may be required in such circumstances, so the key question in such cases will be whether a further procedure will serve a useful purpose. This is principally a matter for the identification officer (Code D para 3.11), but if the defence lawyer believes that it would be in the interests of the client for an identification procedure to be held, they should seek to persuade the officer that a formal procedure would serve a useful purpose.

The decision on whether an identification procedure would serve a useful purpose is clearly fact-sensitive, but some useful guidance on interpretation of the provision may be gained from the case-law. It was held in *R v Callie*[21] that the 'no useful purpose' provision does not permit the police to carry out a proportionality exercise. The relevant question is whether an identification procedure might produce relevant evidence. The fact that one eye-witness has made a positive identification does not mean that inviting other eye-witnesses to view an identification procedure would not serve a useful purpose.[22] In *R v Harris*,[23] the Court of Appeal decided that a formal identification procedure would have served a useful purpose in circumstances where the accused disputed 'recognition' by the complainants, who had attended the same school as the suspect some years earlier. The court made the important point that in these circumstances there was a useful purpose from the defence point of view because there was a real possibility that one or both of the complainants would not have picked the defendant out at an identification parade.

Selecting the identification procedure

8.21 Where the conditions for conducting an identification procedure are satisfied, the suspect must initially be offered a video identification unless (Code D para 3.14):

(1) a video identification is not practicable;
(2) an identification parade is both practicable and more suitable than a video identification; or

21 [2009] EWCA Crim 283.
22 *R v Gojra* [2010] EWCA Crim 1939.
23 [2003] EWCA Crim 174. This was decided under the version of Code D that came into force in April 2002, which also provided that an identification procedure need not be held if it would serve no useful purpose.

(3) the officer in charge of the investigation considers that a group identification is more satisfactory than a video identification or an identification parade, and the identification officer considers it practicable to arrange.

In making the decision about which procedure to offer to the suspect, the identification officer and the officer in charge of the investigation should consult each other, but Code D para 3.14 makes it clear that video identification is the preferred option.

8.22 The suspect is entitled to legal advice as to whether to accept the procedure offered, and may also consult with the appropriate adult (if relevant, and if the adult is present). If the suspect refuses the procedure offered, they must be asked to state the reasons for refusal. The suspect and their lawyer may make representations as to why another procedure should be used, and the identification officer must then offer that procedure or, if the officer decides it is not suitable and practicable, must record the reasons for refusal to offer the procedure preferred by the suspect (Code D para 3.15).

8.23 It can be seen, therefore, that it is up to the police to decide which procedure is to be used, but they must listen to, and record, representations if the suspect wants a procedure other than that initially offered. It should be noted that only an identification parade requires active consent and co-operation of the suspect. A video identification can be arranged using images of the suspect that are not taken under identical conditions as the images of the comparators if the suspect fails or refuses to co-operate (Code D Annex A para 3). A group identification can take place without consent of the suspect, covertly if necessary (Code D Annex C para 2). The identification officer may arrange for a confrontation to take place, in accordance with Code D Annex D, if none of the other formal methods of identification are practicable (Code D para 3.23). There is no express provision for inferences to be drawn from failure or refusal to co-operate with a particular form of identification, but evidence of failure or refusal to co-operate could be given in evidence (Code D para 3.17(v)), and the court could draw its own conclusions from that failure or refusal.

Should the suspect ask for an identification procedure?

8.24 The conditions that make the holding of an identification procedure mandatory (see para 8.18 above) leave the police with considerable discretion, for example, as to whether it would serve a useful purpose. If the conditions are not satisfied, the police have the discretion to conduct an identification procedure if the identification officer considers that it would be useful (Code D para 3.13). Failure to hold a procedure where the conditions are satisfied may result in other evidence of identification being excluded at trial (see para 8.86 below). Therefore, advice on whether to request an identification procedure can have a significant impact on the subsequent course of the investigation and the eventual outcome.

8.25 The lawyer will need to take account of what is known about the facts of the case, and should ask for a copy of the original description given to the police by any potential identification witness. The lawyer is entitled to see this (see para 8.9 above), although while Code D para 3.1 states that it must be given to the suspect or their lawyer before an identification procedure is conducted, it does not specifically state that it must be given before a decision about whether to hold a procedure has been taken. The lawyer should also ask the police whether any identification witness has been shown photographs or video or other visual image (see para 8.12 above). If any material has been released to the media by the police for the purpose of recognising or tracing the suspect, the suspect or their lawyer must be allowed to view it before any identification procedure is carried out, provided that it is practicable and would not unreasonably delay the investigation (Code D para 3.39). The lawyer should also consider what, if any, other form of identification evidence will be available if a formal identification procedure is not held. If a successful prosecution is likely to be dependent upon adequate identification evidence, and none is likely to be available, it is unlikely to be in the suspect's interests to ask for an identification procedure to be held where it is not being proposed by the police. In considering whether other identification evidence is likely to be available, the lawyer should consider, in particular, the possible availability of CCTV footage.

8.26 If the suspect is reasonably confident that they will not be picked out, it is likely to be advisable to request an identification procedure. It is important, however, that the suspect is warned of the potential danger of being identified. A firm identification in a formal identification procedure by one or more witnesses is likely to weigh against the suspect very heavily at trial. If the police appear reluctant to hold an identification procedure, the lawyer should consider whether to advise the client to request one. It may be that the police are unsure of their identification witness(es) and are hoping for a confession, which would render it unnecessary. It may be that they do not want to go to the trouble of arranging an identification procedure and are hoping to get by without one. Alternatively, the police may not have adequate evidence to link the suspect with the crime, and the defence lawyer will not want to prompt an identification procedure that might give the police the very evidence that they need.

8.27 It follows that in advising their client about whether to request an identification procedure, the lawyer must take account of what information they have about the nature of the identification evidence and what method of identification the police are considering. The lawyer should seek details of how many potential identification witnesses there are, whether they say they have seen the suspect before, what description they gave to the police and the circumstances of the alleged identification. This information will enable the lawyer to make informed judgments concerning the factors referred to above.

Should the suspect co-operate with a police request for an identification procedure?

8.28 This section is concerned with whether the suspect should co-operate with a proposed identification procedure, and whether the lawyer should make representations about the form of identification procedure offered. With regard to the former, it was noted in para 8.23 above that only an identification parade requires the active co-operation of the suspect, and a failure to co-operate can be given in evidence. Other forms of identification can be carried out without the consent of the suspect. Therefore, it would normally be appropriate to advise a client to co-operate with an identification procedure proposed by the police, since if they do not, the police may be able to conduct an identification procedure in any event, and evidence of the refusal or failure to co-operate may disadvantage the client at trial.

8.29 However, before advising the client to consent to an identification procedure, the lawyer should consider what information is available, particularly as to the description given by the identifying witness(es). As noted at para 8.25 above, Code D para 3.1 does not specifically provide that the witness description must be supplied prior to a decision about an identification procedure (as opposed to the conduct of an identification procedure), and some police officers take the view that it does not have to be supplied until shortly before the procedure is conducted. If it has not been supplied, the lawyer should ask for the original description before giving advice to the client as to co-operation with an identification procedure. The lawyer should also ask whether any further relevant information has been obtained since the original description was given. If the police fail to disclose any, or adequate, information, the lawyer may decide that in view of the lack of information they are not in a position to advise their client about whether to co-operate with the identification procedure. If this is the case, bearing in mind the dangers to the client of failing to co-operate, the lawyer should make clear to the police that they cannot advise their client on whether to co-operate with an identification procedure because of the refusal of the police to provide any (or adequate) information. The lawye should try to ensure that this is accurately recorded on the custody recor

8.30 The police will normally offer a video identification in preference another form of identification procedure. Some lawyers believe that th are fewer witness identifications in video identifications than in ide ation parades, although there is no evidence for this. Given the ava of image databanks, it is certainly easier, in video identifications, that the comparators are sufficiently similar to the suspect reasons, it will normally be appropriate for the lawyer to adv to co-operate with a video identification rather than to seek of identification. If the choice is between an identificati group identification, most lawyers would probably ad with the former. A group identification may take a var less controllable than a video identification or Furthermore, while a group identification should from a police station (and for this reason some l tially fairer than a parade in a station), it may be on grounds of security, safety or practicality Although a group identification should, as f ciples and procedures governing parade group identification conducted in a polic down version of a parade with, perh potential for unfairness may, therefore, difficult successfully to discredit the identification at trial if the lawyer acquiesced in it. A group identification may be particularly problematic if the suspect is distinctive-looking for some reason, since the suspect is more likely to stand out in a crowd than in a video identification or identification parade composed of similar-looking people.

Video identification

Introduction

8.31 Video identification is governed by Code D paras 3.5 and 3.6 and Annex A, and is the responsibility of an identification officer (Code D para 3.11). Witnesses are shown images of the suspect together with those of at least eight other people who, as far as possible, resemble the suspect in age, general appearance and position in life (Code D Annex A para 2). The normal rule is that a moving image of the suspect, taken after they have been given the information and notice required by Code D paras 3.17 and 3.18, must be used (Code D para 3.5). However, this is subject to two exceptions.

(1) Where:
  (a) the identification officer, in consultation with the officer in charge of the investigation, is satisfied that because of ageing, or other physical changes or differences, the appearance of the suspect has significantly changed since the occasion when the eye-witness saw a person committing a crime;
  (b) an image (moving or still) which both officers reasonably believe shows the appearance of the suspect as it was on the previous occasion in question is available; and
  (c) having regard to the extent of the change and the purpose of eye-witness identification procedures, the identification officer believes that such an image should be shown to the eye-witness.

In such circumstances, that image may be used in addition, or as an alternative, to the image taken after the information and notice required by Code D paras 3.17 and 3.18 are given, although the suspect should be asked if they want to provide their own image (which may be used instead if the identification officer and officer in charge of the investigation believe it to be suitable) (Code D para 3.5(a)).

If, where the suspect has an unusual physical feature, the identification fficer does not consider that replication of that feature or concealment the location of the feature can be achieved using a moving image, a ll image may be used (Code D para 3.5(b)).

s possible, all persons on the set of images should be portrayed in e positions or carrying out the same sequence of movements, and entical conditions (Code D Annex A para 3).

police insist on a video identification?

can, in effect, insist on a video identification. It is for the officer, in consultation with the officer in charge of the investigation, to determine which form of identification procedure to offer to the suspect (Code D para 3.14). Although the suspect can make representations that another form of identification be used (Code D para 3.15), a video identification can still be held if the identification officer decides that an alternative procedure is not suitable and practicable. If the suspect then refuses to co-operate, the police can proceed with a video identification procedure, provided that they have or are able to obtain a suitable image (Code D para 3.21). The image of the suspect may be taken covertly if the police believe this to be necessary (see para 8.35 below).

Can the suspect demand a video identification?

8.33 The suspect cannot insist on a video identification, although this will normally be the method of identification offered by the police. Video identification procedures may have advantages for some suspects. A nervous suspect may find it easier to be filmed than to stand on a parade. Also, with the development of image databases, it is easier to arrange for the images of comparators to look similar to the suspect than it is to arrange for suitable members of the public to stand on an identification parade.

Conduct of a video identification

8.34 Before a video identification takes place, the identification officer must explain to the suspect a number of things about the conduct of the procedure, as set out in Code D para 3.17. The information to be given to the suspect must be recorded in a written notice, which must be handed to them and which they must be given the opportunity of reading. The suspect must then be asked to sign a copy of the notice to indicate their willingness to co-operate (Code D para 3.18). The lawyer should ensure that they are present while this is done, and that the client fully understands what is being agreed to. If necessary, the notice should be read over to the client.

8.35 The duties under Code D paras 3.17 and 3.18 may be performed in relation to a detained suspect by a custody officer (or another officer or police staff not involved in the investigation as directed by the custody officer) rather than an inspector if it is proposed to hold the identification procedure at a later date and an inspector is not available (Code D para 3.19). If the identification officer and the officer in charge of the investigation have reasonable grounds for suspecting that if the suspect is given the information and notice under these provisions they would take steps to avoid being seen by a witness in an identification procedure, the identification officer can arrange for a suitable image to be taken of the suspect for possible use in a video identification, and give the notice and information to the suspect after that has been done (Code D para 3.20). Note that, although not mentioned in Code D, covertly recording a suspect's image may amount to a breach of the suspect's right to private life under European Convention on Human Rights (ECHR) Article 8 unless properly authorised as 'directed surveillance' under Regulation of Investigatory Powers Act (RIPA) 2000 ss26 and 28.[24]

24 *Perry v UK* (App No 63737/00) (2004) 39 EHRR 3, ECtHR.

8.36 The suspect or their lawyer must, where practicable, be given a copy of the original description given by an identifying witness (see para 8.9 above). They must also be told whether a witness has been shown photographs or other visual images by the police before the identity of the suspect became known (see para 8.12 above). If any relevant material has been released to the media for the purposes of recognising or tracing the suspect, which has been broadcast or published, the suspect or their lawyer must be allowed to view it before a video identification is conducted (Code D para 3.39).

8.37 The suspect or their lawyer, friend or appropriate adult, must be given a reasonable opportunity to see the complete set of images to be used in the identification procedure before they are shown to any witness (Code D Annex A para 7).[25] While this provides for the suspect *or* the lawyer to view the images, the lawyer should, if possible, view the images together with their client. The set of images must show at least eight other people (or 12 if there are two suspects of roughly similar appearance to be shown on the same set of images) who as far as possible resemble the suspect in age, general appearance and position in life, although this does not require that the images be identical (Code D Annex A paras 2 and 7). If the suspect has an unusual physical feature (for example, a facial scar or tattoo) the police may take steps to replicate or conceal it, and if this is done, the reasons for so doing must be recorded (Code D Annex A paras 2A and 2B). The lawyer should satisfy themself that the images are sufficiently similar, and should ensure that there is nothing about the set of images, such as posture, lighting or background, that marks out the suspect's image as different from those of the comparators (see Code D Annex A para 3).[26] Particular attention should be paid to whether any attempt to mask or replicate an unusual physical feature is satisfactory.[27] If the suspect has objections to the set of images, such steps as are practicable must be taken to remove the grounds for objection (Code D Annex A para 7). If this is not practicable, the officer must explain why.[28] The lawyer should, therefore, make appropriate representations, bearing in mind that the officer may respond either by proceeding with the video identification or by abandoning it and proceeding with another form of identification if it becomes impracticable to hold it.

8.38 Provided it is practicable, the suspect's lawyer (but not the suspect) must be given reasonable notification of the time and place it is intended to conduct the video identification. The lawyer may attend only with the prior agreement of the identification officer, who is satisfied that the

25 For a video identification checklist and report form, see checklist 14 in appendix 2 below.

26 It was held in *R v Day* [2019] EWCA Crim 935 that it was not unfair to use an image of a suspect who habitually wore glasses without the glasses, where the victim had described her attacker as not wearing glasses and the other images were of men not wearing glasses.

27 See *R v Pecco* [2010] EWCA Crim 972, in which the suspect had a tattoo on her neck that was not concealed in the image used for the video identification, and where the comparators did not have such a tattoo.

28 In *R v Middleton* [2005] EWCA Crim 692, failure by the police to comply with Code D Annex A para 7 did not result in exclusion of the video identification evidence since, the court stated, the suspect and the lawyer do not have an unfettered right to object to the images to be used in the video identification.

lawyer's attendance will not deter or distract the eye-witness(es) from viewing the images. The suspect and/or their lawyer must, on request, be informed whether or not the eye-witness(es) identified the suspect. The viewing of the set of images by the witness(es) must be audio-visually recorded. For obvious reasons, the suspect cannot be present at the video identification (Code D Annex A para 9). Witnesses must not be able to communicate with each other before seeing the set of images, and must not be able to overhear a witness who has seen them (Code D Annex A para 10). The lawyer should satisfy themself that the arrangements are adequate to prevent this. No officer involved with the investigation may take part in the procedure and, in particular, officers must not view the set of images before they are shown to any witness (Code D para 3.11 and Annex A para 15). The identification officer must not discuss with a witness the composition of the set of images or indicate whether a previous witness has made an identification (Code D Annex A para 10). Further, the identification officer must avoid directing the witness's attention to any person on the film or give any other indication of the suspect's identity.[29] If the witness has previously made an identification from a photograph or similar, the witness must not be reminded of it, nor must the witness be reminded of any description of the suspect (Code D Annex A para 13).

8.39 Before viewing the set of images, the witness must be told that the person they saw on the previous occasion may or may not appear in the images shown, and that if they cannot make a positive identification they must say so. Furthermore, the witness must be informed that they can ask to see a particular part of the set of images again or to have a particular image frozen, and that there is no limit on the number of times they may ask to see the set of images or any part of them. However, the witness must be asked to refrain from making any positive identification or saying that they cannot make a positive identification until they have seen the entire set of images at least twice (Code D Annex A para 11). Where the images have been adapted to conceal or replicate an unusual physical feature (see para 8.37 above) and a witness asks to view an image without the feature being concealed or replicated, they may be allowed to do so (Code D Annex A para 2C). If this results in the comparators not being sufficiently similar, this may amount to a breach of Code D Annex A para 2.[30] Having seen the set of images at least twice, and having indicated that they do not wish to see it again, the witness must then be asked whether the person they saw on the previous occasion was shown on the set of images and, if so, to identify them by the number of the image (see para 8.55 below). If the answer is in the affirmative, the witness must be shown the image of the person identified and asked to confirm it (Code D Annex A para 12). Each witness must be asked whether they have seen any film, photograph or image relating to the offence, or description of the suspect that has been broadcast or published, and their reply recorded. If they

29 '[A] witness should not be told whether an identification is right or wrong until the witness has made any further statement that he may wish': *R v Willoughby* [1999] 2 Cr App R 82 at p83 per Lord Bingham CJ, CA.

30 *R v Marcus* [2004] EWCA Crim 3387.

have, they should be asked to give details of the circumstances and, subject to their recollection, a record must be made in accordance with Code D Annex A para 41 (Code D Annex A para 14).

8.40 There is no specific provision in Code D Annex A that, where there is more than one witness, the position of the suspect in the order of images can, or should, be altered after each witness has viewed the set of images. Compare this with identification parades (see para 8.50 below). However, it may be advisable for the lawyer to request such a change in the order of images, if this is possible. If after the viewing procedure has been completed a witness informs a police officer or police staff involved in the post-viewing arrangements that they have made a mistake in their identification, or did not make an identification when in fact they could have done so, an accurate record of the words used by the witness and of the circumstances immediately after the viewing ended must be made. If the witness has not had an opportunity to communicate with other eye-witnesses about the viewing, the identification officer has the discretion to allow the eye-witness a second opportunity to make an identification by repeating the viewing procedure (Code D Annex A para 13A). The code does not explicitly state that a second viewing procedure should consist of the same images as in the first, but clearly it should do so.

8.41 As with other identification procedures, if the lawyer is present at a viewing, they should take a note of the whole process, including the overall time spent, whether and for how long the witness lingered over any particular image, any request to see a particular image, any request to see an image without a feature being concealed or replicated, any other conversation during the course of the viewing, and the precise words used if the witness identifies any of the people in the set of images.[31] Although Code D Annex A makes no specific provision for representations to be made, the lawyer should make appropriate representations if the provisions have not been properly complied with or if, for any other reason, the process was potentially unfair to the client.

8.42 The police must make arrangements for all relevant material contained in the set of images to be kept securely, and their movements accounted for (Code D Annex A para 15). For the retention and destruction provisions regarding photographs taken or used in eye-witness identification procedures, see Code D paras 3.30–3.33.

Identification parades

Parade arrangements

8.43 Identification parades are governed by Code D paras 3.7 and 3.8 and Annex B, and since they are now relatively unusual it is a good idea for the lawyer to remind themself of the provisions before any parade takes place. The lawyer needs to pay particular attention to the physical arrangements for the parade and the information that is to be given by the police to the

31 A qualified identification, such as 'I think it's him' or 'I can't be quite certain' may have some probative value, although a person should not be convicted on qualified identification evidence alone (*R v George* [2002] EWCA Crim 1923).

suspect.[32] Parades can take place in a normal room or one equipped with one-way screens. In the latter case, the parade must be conducted in the presence of the suspect's lawyer, friend or appropriate adult (Code D Annex B para 2). In all cases, a video recording or colour photograph of the parade must normally be made or taken (Code D Annex B para 23). Use and retention of any images is governed by Code D paras 3.30–3.33. Care must be taken to ensure that the parade is not rendered unfair:

(1) by contact between the eye-witnesses;
(2) by contact between eye-witnesses and the suspect or others standing on the parade before it begins;
(3) by an eye-witness seeing, or being reminded of, any photograph or description of the suspect, or being given any other indication as to the suspect's identity; or
(4) as a result of intervention by the officers involved in the investigation (see Code D para 3.11 and Annex B para 14).

8.44 With regard to (1) and (2), the lawyer should satisfy themself, so far as is possible, that the arrangements by which the various parties are to arrive at, and remain at, the station are satisfactory. If the suspect has been released on police bail pending the parade, the lawyer should ensure that there is no risk of the suspect being seen by potential witnesses. Thus, their respective arrival times and, if possible, their point of entry to the station, should be quite separate. Furthermore, witnesses should not see any of the other members, or potential members, of the parade, and the lawyer should check that the witnesses are not within sight when the potential members of the parade arrive. The lawyer should normally ask to check the route to be taken by the witnesses from the room where they are kept waiting to the parade room, to ensure that they will not have the opportunity of seeing any member of the parade en route. Witnesses must not have contact with other witnesses who have already seen the parade, or have an opportunity to overhear them (Code D Annex B para 14), so the lawyer should check that once witnesses have seen the parade, they are kept well away from those witnesses still to view it.

8.45 The conduct of a parade is the responsibility of the identification officer, who may direct another officer or police staff to make arrangements for or conduct the parade, but no officer involved with the investigation may take part in the identification procedure (Code D para 3.11). Officers involved in the investigation must not take any witness to the parade,[33] including the victim,[34] although it appears that it is permissible for such an officer to take the suspect to the parade.[35] The lawyer may, therefore, consider asking where the investigating officers will be during the parade, and who will be escorting the witnesses to the parade.

8.46 If the lawyer is not happy with the arrangements for the parade, they should make appropriate representations and a note of the response. In many cases, any cause for objection can be removed so that the parade can

32 For an identification parade checklist and report form, see checklikst 13 in appendix 2.

33 *R v Gall* (1990) 90 Cr App R 64, CA.

34 *R v Ryan* [1992] Crim LR 187, CA.

35 *R v Jones* [1992] Crim LR 365, CA.

satisfactorily proceed. However, if this is not the case, the lawyer will have to consider whether to advise the suspect to withdraw consent to the parade, which can only proceed with their consent.[36] Such a decision will require careful consideration. If the lawyer acquiesces in a breach of the codes or in a procedure that is otherwise unfair, the trial court may decide to admit the evidence. On the other hand, a refusal of consent could lead to another, less fair, form of identification and could have adverse consequences for the suspect at trial (see para 8.23 above). If, despite any breach, the suspect decides to proceed with the parade, the lawyer should ensure that the identification officer has made a written note of the representations made.

Preparing the client for the parade

8.47 An identification parade that is conducted strictly in accordance with the provisions of Code D Annex B can still lead to an unreliable identification as a result of the actions of the client. The client must, therefore, be carefully advised on their conduct during the parade. Most clients will not have been on a parade before, and they should be told what is likely to happen, and how long it is likely to take. Parades, especially at the preparation stage, can be long winded and tedious, and clients should be prepared for this. They should also be prepared for the fact that they are likely to feel nervous during the parade. This in itself, if apparent to the witness(es), could result in them being identified, and the lawyer should be prepared to discuss appropriate strategies with them.

8.48 It is important that the client looks 'right' in the parade. If they have been in custody for some time, or if they were arrested in the early hours of the morning, they may look untidy and dishevelled. The objective is that they look as similar as possible to the other members of the parade. If, as is likely, the others do not look like this, the lawyer should ensure that their client is given the opportunity and the facilities to clean up and to make themself look reasonably tidy.

8.49 The client should be advised on how to conduct themself during the parade. Their stance should be as relaxed as possible, although they should be advised to take their cue from the other members of the parade. They should be told that the witness may well stand and stare at them for some time. Ideally, they should simply look straight in front of them, without following the witnesses as they move. They should not look at the lawyer. If the parade is to be conducted with one-way screens, the client should be advised about the effect of the screens, that they may be unaware of where the witness is and that they should not move until they are told that the witness has left the room.

8.50 The client should be told that they may choose where they stand in the line-up, and that if there is more than one witness, they may change position after each witness has left the room (Code D Annex B para 13). Furthermore, they should be prepared for the possibility that they are

36 An identification parade can only be conducted if the suspect is 'available', which means that the suspect is willing to take an effective part in the procedure (see para 8.8 above).

asked to speak, to move or to adopt a particular posture (see para 8.56 below). The client should be advised that if this does occur, they should comply with the request and leave any objection to the lawyer, since to object at the time (if only by facial expression) will make it more likely that they are identified. Finally, they should be advised that if they have any objection before the parade begins, or are unhappy about the way in which the parade was conducted, they should discuss this with the lawyer so that representations can be made to the police at the time.

Conduct of the parade

8.51 An identification parade must consist of at least eight people (in addition to the suspect) who so far as possible resemble the suspect in age, height, general appearance and position in life (Code D Annex B para 9). Only one suspect may stand on a parade, unless there are two suspects who look sufficiently similar, in which case they can both be part of the same parade provided that there are at least 12 other people on the parade. In no circumstances can more than two suspects stand on the same parade. Suspects may select their own positions in the line, and if there is more than one witness, they may change position after each witness has left the room (Code D Annex B para 13).

8.52 One of the most difficult tasks for the lawyer is to decide whether the other members of the parade do look sufficiently similar to the suspect. The lawyer should pay particular attention to features such as height, hair (colour, length and style), baldness, facial hair, eye colour, build, racial characteristics, jewellery and clothing (including footwear). If necessary, the members of the parade can be asked to alter their appearance. For example, they may all be asked to wear hats to hide their hair colour, or plasters to obscure tattoos or other marks (see Code D Annex B para 10; and para 8.56 below).[37] What is 'sufficiently similar' is frequently difficult to judge, but the views of the suspect are obviously important here. The lawyer should also take account of any information about the description originally given by witnesses to the police so that they can seek to ensure that any features noted by the witnesses are also to be found in the other members of the parade.

8.53 When the suspect is brought to the room where the parade is to take place, they must be asked whether they have any objections to the arrangements for the parade. If practicable, steps must be taken to remove any grounds for objection (Code D Annex B para 12). If the suspect or their lawyer believes that one or more of the members of the parade are not sufficiently similar, the lawyer should seek their replacement by others who are more similar. In doing so the lawyer must try to gauge how far the identification officer is prepared to go, and how long the officer is prepared to allow the process of forming the parade to continue. This may involve a careful process of negotiation, balancing the need to ensure that the parade

37 *R v Marrin* [2002] EWCA Crim 251 endorsed the use of make-up and props, but warned that care must be taken to ensure that they do not direct attention to the suspect. Hats might be used, but should be avoided if possible if they had not been worn during the offence. See also para 8.37 above regarding replicating or concealing unusual physical features in video identifications.

members are sufficiently similar against the fact that the identification officer will at some point decide that a parade is not practicable and move to an alternative form of identification. It may be in the client's interests for a parade to become impracticable if the alternative is likely to be a group identification in circumstances that are more favourable to them, but this requires careful judgment and full consultation with the client. Note that whereas it has been held that the lawyer is entitled to seek time to find appropriate people to stand on a parade,[38] they have no right to substitute someone of their choice for a person already obtained by the police.[39]

8.54 If the identification officer does decide that a parade has become impracticable because of the difficulty of finding suitable people to stand on it, the lawyer should take a note of the reasons given by the officer, the attempts made to find people and any suggestions for forming a suitable parade made by the lawyer. Once the line-up has been finalised, the lawyer should take a note of the appearance of the members of the parade, noting in particular any features that are significantly different to those of the suspect.

8.55 Witnesses must be brought to the parade one at a time. A note should be made of the number of the officer bringing the witness to the parade. Immediately before they inspect the parade, the identification officer must tell the witness that the person that they saw may or may not be on the parade and that if they cannot make a positive identification, they should say so. Witnesses must then be asked to look[40] at each member of the parade at least twice, taking as much care and time as they wish. The officer must ask each witness, having done so, whether the person they saw on the earlier relevant occasion is on the parade (Code D Annex B para 17). If a witness makes an identification, the identification officer may ask them what they had seen the person identified do on the relevant previous occasion. This is not provided for in Annex B, although it has been held that the answer given by the witness is admissible in evidence.[41] The lawyer should consider objecting to such a question on the ground that it is not mandated by Annex B. A note of precisely what is said to the witness by the identification officer should be taken. Any material departure from the requirements of para 17 should be noted and appropriate representations should be made at the end of the parade (see para 8.57 below). The exact words of the answer given by the witness must be noted, since they may well disclose any uncertainty: 'I think it is number 8' is obviously less strong an identification than 'It is number 8' (see para 8.41 above). The identification officer's record of what was said and done should be checked at the time. If possible, this should be agreed but, if this is not possible, the

38 *R v Britton and Richards* [1989] Crim LR 144, Crown Court (Leeds).

39 *R v Thorne* [1981] Crim LR 702, CA.

40 Under a previous version of Code D, the officer was required to tell witnesses to walk along the parade at least twice, and the current requirement must be regarded as a retrograde step. The current version of Code D therefore legitimates the kind of procedure that was held to be contrary to Code D in *R v Quinn* [1995] Crim LR 56, CA. The lawyer should carefully observe the witness to try to establish whether they have complied with the identification officer's request.

41 *R v Lynch* [2007] EWCA Crim 3035.

lawyer should make appropriate representations and ensure that they are noted by the officer.

8.56 If the witness wishes to hear any member of the parade speak, adopt a particular posture or see them move, the identification officer must ask the witness whether they can make an identification on the basis of appearance only, before complying with the request. If it is a request to hear a parade member speak, the officer must remind the witness that the parade members have been selected on the basis of physical appearance alone. Only then should members of the parade be asked to comply with the request (Code D Annex B para 18). The lawyer should normally object to such a request precisely because the parade was not arranged with this in mind (see para 8.82 below). If intervention is necessary, it must be done speedily and without identifying the suspect. If the identification officer proceeds with the request from the witness, the lawyer should ensure that all members of the parade do what has been requested, but any other representations may best be left until after the witness has left the room. Where props have been used to disguise a particular feature (see Code D Annex B para 10; and para 8.52 above), a witness may ask that a person on the parade remove it (Code D Annex B para 19). The lawyer can do little in such circumstances, since to object may direct attention to their client. All relevant conversation must be noted and, if appropriate, representations should be made to the identification officer after the witness has left the room. After the procedure, each witness must be asked whether they have seen any film, photograph or image relating to the offence, or any description of the suspect that has been broadcast or published, and any reply must be recorded (Code D para 3.40 and Annex B para 21)

8.57 Once the last witness has left the room, the suspect must be asked whether they wish to comment on the conduct of the parade (Code D Annex B para 22). If the lawyer has any reservations or objections to the way in which the parade was conducted, they should make these known to the identification officer and ensure that they are accurately recorded. Such representations might include anything in relation to the conduct of the parade itself, or other matters such as whether the suspect has seen a witness on a previous occasion. In *R v Ogundipe*,[42] for example, the Court of Appeal was critical of the conduct of a parade in which noise and laughter from waiting volunteers could be heard.

8.58 If a witness makes an identification after the parade has ended, the suspect and their lawyer must be told, and consideration must be given to allowing the witness a second opportunity to identify the suspect (Code D Annex B para 20). The code does not explicitly state that this should not be in a differently constituted parade, although this would not be appropriate since the identity of the suspect would become obvious. In any event, the lawyer should carefully examine the reasons given for such a request and, in particular, ask whether the witness spoke to any other witness, or any officer involved in the investigation, after viewing of the parade. If there is any risk that such contamination has taken place, the lawyer may advise the client not to agree to a further parade, and make the reasons clear to the identification officer.

42 [2001] EWCA Crim 2576.

Group identification

Introduction

8.59 Group identifications are governed by Code D paras 3.4 and 3.16 and Annex C. A group identification can take a variety of forms, ranging from a less formal kind of identification parade (perhaps containing fewer than eight members of the public) conducted in the police station, to a street scene which a witness is asked to observe. They must be conducted, as far as possible, in accordance with the principles and procedures for identification parades 'so that the conditions are fair to the suspect in the way they test the witness's ability to make an identification' (Code D Annex C para 1). This includes the requirement that no officer involved with the investigation may take part in the procedures (Code D para 3.11). Before conducting a group identification, a record of the first description given by eye-witnesses must, if practicable, be shown to the suspect or their lawyer (Code D para 3.1). A group identification may be video-recorded if this is practicable. If not, a video recording or colour photograph must be taken of the scene of the group identification immediately after it has been held or, if this is impracticable, at some later time (Code D Annex C paras 8 and 9). Use, retention and destruction of images of the suspect captured under these provisions are dealt with in Code D paras 3.30–3.33.

8.60 It is for the identification officer to decide where a group identification is to be held. In making the decision, the officer may take into account any representations made by the suspect, appropriate adult, lawyer or friend. A group identification should normally be held in a place where other people are either passing by or waiting around informally, in groups so that the suspect is able to join them and is capable of being seen by the eye-witness(es) at the same time as they can see other members of the group. The code gives examples such as people leaving an escalator, pedestrians walking through a shopping centre and passengers at railway and bus stations waiting in queues or groups (Code D Annex C para 4). A group identification should not normally be conducted in a police station (Code D Annex C paras 3 and 37). If a group identification is to be conducted covertly, the choice of location may be more limited, and Code D Annex C para 5 suggests that suitable locations might be along regular routes travelled by the suspect, including buses or trains or public places frequented by the suspect. In choosing a location, the officer must have regard to the general appearance and number of people likely to be present and must, in particular, reasonably expect that over the period the witness observes the group, they will be able to see from time to time a number of people whose appearance is broadly similar to that of the suspect (Code D Annex C para 6). Clearly, the lawyer should take these factors into account in making any representation to the identification officer and in considering whether the proposed location is satisfactory.

Can the police insist on a group identification?

8.61 The police can, in effect, insist on a group identification. It is for the identification officer, in consultation with the officer in charge of the investigation, to determine which form of identification procedure to offer to the suspect (Code D para 3.14). A group identification can be offered in preference to other forms of identification procedure if the officer in charge of the investigation considers it more satisfactory than a video identification or identification parade, and the identification officer considers it practicable to arrange (Code D para 3.16). Although the suspect can make representations that another form of identification be used (Code D para 3.15), the final choice rests with the police, and a group identification can be conducted covertly if the suspect is unwilling to co-operate (Code D para 3.21; and see paras 8.8 and 8.32 above). Force cannot be used to make a suspect participate in a group identification.[43]

8.62 The question of practicability in relation to identification procedures generally is dealt with at para 8.20 above. Having decided that a video identification or identification parade is not practicable, or that a group identification is more satisfactory, the police should consider whether a group identification is practicable (Code D para 3.16). Whether a group identification is practicable in a situation where the other two forms of identification procedure are not will depend, in part, on the form that the group identification is to take and the circumstances of the case. In *R v Ladlow, Moss, Green and Jackson*,[44] where there were 11 witnesses to a fight, following which 21 suspects had been arrested, the court held that the police should not have moved straight to a confrontation after deciding that a parade was impracticable (since it could have involved up to 231 parades on a bank holiday), without considering the practicability of a group identification. It is not clear, however, that a group identification in those circumstances would have been any more practicable than a parade. In some situations, the lawyer may prefer a group identification to a parade (see para 8.65 below) but, if not, the lawyer should carefully consider the police justifications for not proceeding with a video identification or a parade, and why a group identification is practicable whereas neither of those methods is.

8.63 If the police request a group identification, in considering whether the suspect should consent, the lawyer should have regard to the possible adverse consequences of failure to consent. The issues here are similar to those relating to identification generally (see para 8.28 above). However, since a group identification can take a variety of forms, the lawyer should consider the potential for unfairness of the form of group identification being suggested by the police. If this leads the lawyer to advise the suspect to refuse consent, they should make clear to the police the precise reasons for refusal. In appropriate circumstances, the lawyer may wish to propose an alternative form of group identification that would be fairer to the suspect.

43 See *R v Jones and Nelson* (1999) Times, April 21, CA, which concerned a confrontation, but the same principles apply.

44 [1989] Crim LR 219, although now such a case would almost certainly have been dealt with by way of a video identification.

Can a suspect demand a group identification?

8.64 A suspect cannot insist on a group identification. The police will normally offer a video identification, and although the suspect or their lawyer can make representations as to why another form of identification should be used (Code D para 3.15), in most circumstances it would be difficult to justify a group identification in preference to a video identification. If, however, the police have rejected a video identification and are proposing to hold an identification parade, it may be possible for the suspect to achieve a group identification since a parade can only be held if the suspect consents. For a discussion of the relative merits of parades and group identification, see para 8.30 above.

8.65 In considering advice on whether a client may refuse to co-operate in an identification parade in order to achieve a group identification, consideration must be given to whether a refusal to give consent to a parade can have adverse effects at trial. Evidence of failure or refusal to consent to or co-operate in a video identification or identification parade can be given in evidence (Code D para 3.17; and see para 8.23 above), although even if there is a danger of adverse comment at trial, the scope for such comment is limited if the client is willing to consent to a group identification. Nevertheless, the client should be advised of the potential dangers. If the client does not wish to give consent to a video identification or identification parade but does wish to consent to a group identification, this should be made absolutely clear to the identification officer to forestall the danger of the officer assuming consent is withheld to all. If the problem with other forms of identification procedure is practicability rather than consent, and the client wants a group identification in preference to a parade, the lawyer should be prepared to argue that a group identification is practicable. This will be particularly relevant where the police do not have suitable video images or are having difficulty in finding sufficiently similar-looking people to stand on the parade.

The conduct of a group identification

8.66 Code D Annex C provides detailed guidance on how a group identification should be conducted. The provisions are not set out here, but it should be noted that they deal separately with group identifications involving moving groups and stationary groups, those conducted with and without the suspect's consent, identifications involving prison inmates, and group identifications in police stations. With regard to the latter, a group identification should only be conducted in a police station for reasons of safety or security or because it is impracticable to hold it elsewhere (Code D Annex C para 37). After the procedure, wherever it is conducted, each witness must be asked whether they have seen any film, photograph or image relating to the offence, or any description of the suspect that has been broadcast or published, and any reply must be recorded (Code D para 3.40 and Annex C para 12).

8.67 Since group identifications must, as far as possible, be conducted according to the same principles and procedures as for identification parades, much of what is said about the conduct of parades is relevant here (see para 8.51 above). Group identifications are often less controllable than parades and, therefore, the lawyer should be particularly alert to anything that might make the identification unfair. The lawyer should note in particular:

- the relative position of the witness and suspect;
- how many other people were in the vicinity, and how many of those people were similar in looks to the suspect;
- the length of time the procedure took; and
- what was said by a witness if they made an identification.

After the procedure has been completed, the lawyer should, in consultation with the client, make appropriate representations to the identification officer, and ensure that they are recorded in writing.

Confrontation

Introduction

8.68 Confrontations are governed by Code D para 3.23 and Annex D. A 'confrontation' is defined as a procedure whereby the suspect is directly confronted by an eye-witness. Confrontations have significant potential to lead to an unsafe identification since the eye-witness will know that the person they are asked to look at is a suspect. A defence lawyer should, therefore, try to avoid a confrontation taking place. Although the courts have held that identification evidence based on a confrontation should be excluded where the confrontation should not have taken place,[45] such evidence may be admitted where the suspect demands a confrontation in the presence of their lawyer. Furthermore, it is likely that evidence of a confrontation conducted contrary to Code D would be admitted at trial if it was conducted with the knowledge and acquiescence of the lawyer.[46] Therefore, if the police are proposing to hold a confrontation in contravention of Code D, it is important that the lawyer explains to the identification officer why a confrontation should not be held, and ensures that these representations are noted in writing. As with other forms of identification, the suspect or their lawyer must, where practicable, be supplied with a copy of the first description given by any witness who is to attend before a confrontation takes place (Code D Annex D para 2; and see para 8.9 above).

Can the police insist on a confrontation?

8.69 A confrontation may only be held if none of the other formal methods of identification are practicable (Code D para 3.23), although this may be subject to any demand for a confrontation by the suspect.[47] If this condition is satisfied, the police may proceed with a confrontation, whether or

45 See, for example, *R v Britton and Richards* [1989] Crim LR 144, Crown Court (Leeds); and *R v Ladlow, Moss, Green and Jackson* [1989] Crim LR 219.

46 See *R v Dunn* (1990) 91 Cr App R 237, CA; and see para 13.23 below.

47 See *R v Miller* (1991) 23 March (unreported).

not the suspect consents, although the police are not permitted to use force to make the suspect take part, or to make their face visible.[48]

8.70 Evidence of a confrontation 'engineered' by the police may not be admitted at trial.[49] Furthermore, a confrontation should not be held in preference to another form of identification procedure simply because the witness concerned happens to be a police officer.[50]

Can a suspect demand a confrontation?

8.71 Strictly, a suspect cannot require the police to hold a confrontation. It may be possible to 'engineer' a confrontation by refusing consent to any other form of identification, but the police may be able to conduct a video identification or group identification in the absence of consent or co-operation (Code D para 3.21; and see para 8.14 above). Determined opposition to other forms of identification procedure, coupled with a demand by the suspect for a confrontation,[51] may achieve a confrontation, but it is unlikely to be in the interests of the suspect for a confrontation to be held in view of its inherent unfairness. Therefore, a lawyer would rarely, if ever, advise such a course of action.

Conduct of a confrontation

8.72 Where a confrontation is to be conducted, it must be arranged by an identification officer (Code D para 3.11). No officer involved in the investigation may take part (Code D paras 3.11 and 3.23). It has been held to be a significant breach of Code D for an officer involved in the investigation to accompany the witness to the confrontation.[52] However, the court decided that, as there was no evidence of unfairness to the defendant, the trial judge was entitled to admit evidence of the confrontation. The lawyer should, therefore, check the arrangements for the confrontation with the identification officer, including who is to take the witness(es) to it.[53]

8.73 Before the confrontation takes place, the identification officer must tell the witness that the person they saw may or may not be the person the witness is to confront, and that if the witness cannot make a positive identification they should say so (Code D Annex D para 1). The suspect must be confronted independently by each witness, who must be asked: 'Is this the person?' If the witness identifies the person but is unable to confirm the identification, the witness must be asked how sure they are that the person is the one the witness saw on the earlier occasion (Code D Annex D

48 *R v Jones and Nelson* (1999) Times, April 21, CA; and Code D Annex D para 3.

49 *R v Nagah* [1991] Crim LR 55, CA.

50 *R v Samms, Elliot and Bartley* [1991] Crim LR 197, Crown Court (Inner London); and see Code D NfG 3A.

51 See *R v Miller* (1991) 23 March (unreported).

52 *R v Ryan* [1992] Crim LR 187, CA.

53 One reason for the finding that there had been no unfairness in *Ryan* was the fact that the lawyer had asked the officer whether he had said anything about the appellant, and that he was also present at the confrontation so that he could have overheard anything said by the police officer to the witness. This reinforces the need to try to avoid such incidents by advance preparation.

para 5). The confrontation must take place in the presence of the suspect's lawyer, interpreter or friend, unless this would cause unreasonable delay (Code D Annex D para 4).[54] It must normally be conducted in a police station, either in a normal room or one equipped with a screen. In the latter case, it must be conducted with a solicitor, friend or appropriate adult present or be recorded on video (Code D Annex D para 6). It is clear, therefore, that a confrontation should not take place in a cell unless, perhaps, this is justified by the refusal of the suspect to leave the cell or by the suspect's violent behaviour.

8.74 The lawyer should take a careful note of precisely what is said by the participants in the confrontation, and take a particular note of what is said by the witness (see para 8.55 above). The lawyer should also note who is present, who conducted the witness to the confrontation and, particularly if there is more than one witness, check whether there was any opportunity for the witnesses to talk with each other before, during or after the confrontation.

8.75 After the procedure, each witness must be asked whether they have seen any film, photograph or image relating to the offence, or any description of the suspect that has been broadcast or published, and any reply must be recorded (Code D para 3.40 and Annex D para 7).

Controlled recognition procedures under Code D Part 3(B)

8.76 Code D Part 3(B) (ie paras 3.34–3.37) applies when, for the purposes of obtaining evidence of recognition, a person (including a police officer) who is not an eye-witness views a film, photograph or other visual medium and is asked whether they recognise anyone who is shown in the material as someone who is known to them (Code D para 3.34). The procedure is to be distinguished from the showing of photographs or other visual images to an eye-witness where a suspect is not known (see para 8.11 above). The procedures to be adopted under Code D Part 3(B), aimed at safeguarding against mistaken recognition and the possibility of collusion, are set out in Code D para 3.35. The recording requirements are set out in Code D paras 3.36 and 3.37.[55]

8.77 Procedures under Code D Part 3(B) will normally be carried out before a defence lawyer is involved or, at least, without consulting them. Since the procedure under this part of Code D is not to be used in respect of an eye-witness, there is no question of a person who takes part in the procedure subsequently being asked to take part in an identification procedure involving a person identified as a result. A police officer who does not

54 Although not noted in Code D para 4, this should also include the appropriate adult, where relevant.

55 The provisions in Code D para 3.36 largely deal with the concerns of the Court of Appeal expressed in *R v Smith* [2009] 1 Cr App R 521, which involved a police officer being asked to view CCTV footage to see whether they could recognise an offender. For other cases involving police officers who were asked whether they recognised an offender, see *R v McGrath* [2009] EWCA Crim 1758; and *R v Moss* [2011] EWCA Crim 252.

know a suspect can acquire 'special knowledge or skills' in relation to individuals appearing in a video recording (for example, CCTV) by the frequent playing and analysing of the footage resulting in evidence of identification from photographic materials being admissible.[56]

Uncontrolled recognition procedures under Code D Part 3(C)

8.78 Code D Part 3(C) (ie paras 3.38–3.41) applies when, for the purpose of identifying and tracing suspects, films, photographs of incidents or other images are shown to the public (which may include police officers and police staff) through national or local media, or social media, or are circulated through local or national communications systems, and the viewing is not formally controlled and supervised as set out in Part 3(B).[57] A copy of the visual media that are released must be kept (Code D para 3.39). The officer responsible for circulating or making available the visual media must make arrangements to ensure that where a person indicates in response to a viewing that they may have information relating to the identity and whereabouts of anyone they saw in the viewing, they are asked to give details of the circumstances, and that a record is made of the circumstances and the conditions under which the viewing took place, as soon as is practicable (Code D para 3.41).

8.79 A person who comes forward as a result of viewing the visual media released may be an eye-witness; that is, they saw a person committing a crime or in any other circumstances that tend to prove or disprove the involvement of that person in a crime (see Code D para 3.0). If, subsequently, an identification procedure is conducted in relation to a known suspect (see para 8.8 above), the suspect or their solicitor must be allowed to view the visual media released prior to the conduct of an identification procedure, provided this is practical and would not unreasonably delay the investigation (Code D para 3.39). Each eye-witness involved in such an identification procedure must be asked, after they have taken part, whether they have seen any film, photograph or image relating to the offence or any description of the suspect which has been broadcast or published, and their reply recorded. If they have, they must be asked to give details of the circumstances, and a record must be made (Code D para 3.41).

56 *R v Ulas* [2023] EWCA Crim 82. See also *R v Yaryare, Hassan and Osman* [2020] EWCA Crim 1314.

57 Part 3(C) was inserted into Code D as a result of the decision in *R v Lariba, Dos Santos and Hamilton* [2015] EWCA Crim 478, in which the Court of Appeal was critical of the arrangements whereby a number of police officers purported to recognise one of the appellants from images circulated by the police on public media. For other cases involving unregulated recognition procedures, see *R v JD* [2012] EWCA Crim 2637; *R v Selwyn* [2012] EWCA Crim 2968; and *R v Singh* [2013] EWCA Crim 669.

Identification procedures after charge

8.80 Whereas Code C prohibits (subject to exceptions) further questioning regarding an offence once a person has been charged with the offence (Code C para 16.5), Code D makes no reference to identification procedures after charge. It would seem that the power of the police to hold a procedure and the right of the suspect to request a procedure apply equally before and after charge.[58] The suspect may wish to consider requesting an identification procedure even after charge if, for some reason, a procedure was not held before charge or if an eye-witness has only come forward after charge.

8.81 If the police ask the suspect to co-operate with an identification procedure after they have been charged, it may be because they are genuinely unsure of the suspect's guilt or, perhaps more likely, they wish to strengthen the evidence that they have against the suspect. For this reason, such a request requires careful consideration, particularly given the possible adverse consequences of not co-operating. Since Code C para 16.1 requires the officer in charge of an investigation to be satisfied that there is sufficient evidence for a prosecution to succeed before bringing the suspect before the custody officer with a view to charging, it could be argued that the suspect should not be required to undergo further attempts to bolster the prosecution evidence. By analogy with interviews, there comes a point at which the investigative process should stop (at least insofar as it requires the co-operation of the suspect), and that point is at the stage of charging the suspect. If a procedure is held after charge, the police may be able to justify interviewing the suspect following the procedure under Code C para 16.5 on the basis that information has come to light since charge (that is, the fact that the suspect has been identified) which, in the interests of justice, should be put to the suspect. Note that inferences under Criminal Justice and Public Order Act (CJPOA) 1994 s34, 36 or 37 could not be drawn from silence in such an interview (see para 5.75 above).

Voice identification

8.82 Code D is primarily concerned with visual identification, and the rules governing the conduct of various methods of identification make it clear that the aim is to achieve fairness in respect of *visual* identification.[59] Code D makes no provision for cases in which an attempted identification is to be made on the basis of voice alone, but Code D Annex B para 18 does permit a witness at an identification parade to ask a member of the parade to speak, and lawyers should treat such requests with great caution (see para 8.56 above). The lack of regulation of voice identification is unfortunate since

58 This is implied in *R v Joseph* [1994] Crim LR 48, CA. See also *R v Collins* (1996) 23 July (unreported).

59 Although para 1.2 states that the Code does not preclude the use of aural identification procedures. It was confirmed in *R v Deenik* [1992] Crim LR 578, CA that identification of a suspect's voice was not directly covered by PACE or Code D.

there is clear evidence of the risks of mistaken identification.[60] If there is a voice identification then the risks may be considered to be appropriately met by way of a modified *Turnbull* warning.[61]

8.83 One approach is for the Code D provisions regarding visual identification to be adapted in order to hold a 'voice identification parade'. In *R v Hersey*,[62] the police held such a parade in which the suspect and 11 volunteers read out a piece of text. Evidence of the witness's identification of the suspect's voice was admitted at trial, a decision upheld by the Court of Appeal. In 2003, the Home Office issued Circular 57/2003, *Advice on the use of voice identification parades*, which stated that the Home Office was working on the development of reliable procedures for voice identification. However, no such guidance has been issued. The circular stated that the police should not attempt to conduct 'live' voice identification procedures. Instead, they should use a procedure involving recorded voices of both the suspect and comparators.[63]

8.84 If faced with a request by police for a 'live' voice identification procedure, whether or not within the terms of Code D Annex B para 18, the lawyer should carefully consider whether it is in their client's interests to consent to such a procedure. Refusal to co-operate with a voice identification procedure cannot lead to adverse inferences under the CJPOA 1994. Although evidence of refusal to co-operate in a 'live' procedure may be admissible, in view of the uncertainty about voice identification it is unlikely that this would have adverse consequences for the suspect. If the lawyer does advise the client to refuse to co-operate, the reasons for this advice should be recorded.

Intervention in the case of breach of Code D

8.85 Breach of Code D may occur where the police fail to hold an identification procedure in circumstances where they should do so or where, in conducting an identification procedure, they fail to observe the requirements of Code D. Breach does not automatically lead to exclusion of identification evidence, but it may be excluded under PACE s78 (see para 13.41 below).

8.86 The courts have not always been consistent in their approach to exclusion of identification evidence under PACE s78 where there has been a

60 See *R v Gummerson and Steadman* [1999] Crim LR 680, CA; *R v Roberts* [2000] Crim LR 183, CA; *R v O'Doherty* [2002] NI 263; *R v Chenia* [2002] EWCA Crim 2345; and *R v Flynn* [2008] EWCA Crim 970. For a discussion of the issues concerning voice identification see J Robson, 'A fair hearing? The use of voice identification parades in criminal investigations in England and Wales' [2017] Crim LR 36; and G Morrison, 'Admissibility of Forensic Voice Comparison Testimony in England and Wales' [2018] Crim LR 20.

61 *R v Crow* [2021] EWCA Crim 617.

62 [1998] Crim LR 281, CA. See also *R v Davies* [2004] EWCA Crim 2521.

63 In *R v Flynn* [2008] EWCA Crim 970 the Court of Appeal provided a critical assessment of the problems of voice identification, stating that it was more likely to be reliable when carried out by experts using acoustic and spectrographic techniques, and sophisticated auditory techniques, than by lay witnesses (including police officers).

breach of Code D. However, since the case of *R v Popat*,[64] the courts have generally adopted the approach that in considering whether to exclude identification evidence, the key consideration is not whether the police have complied with the detailed rules set out in Code D, but whether the overall purpose of the code – securing fair identification practices leading to reliable identification evidence – has been respected.[65] While the provisions of Code D are mandatory, breach of a particular provision of Code D may not frustrate the overall purpose of the code. Therefore, if a breach does not fundamentally undermine the overall purpose, it may be dealt with by appropriate directions to the jury rather than exclusion of evidence.[66] Such directions should make clear to the jury that the suspect has lost the benefit of the safeguards provided by the code, and that they should take that fact into account in their assessment of the whole case.[67] See further para 13.41 below.

8.87 Therefore, the defence lawyer cannot rely on a breach of Code D procedures leading to exclusion of evidence thereby obtained. Consequently, the lawyer should normally intervene if the police fail to comply with the provisions of Code D in a way that is, or is potentially, damaging to their client's interests. Equally, the lawyer should intervene if they are aware of police conduct that, while in conformity with Code D, is or may be unfair.

Identification through social media

8.88 Informal identification through social media is becoming an increasingly frequent aspect of the identification of suspects. It is not dealt with in Code D, although Code D Part 3(C) applies where visual images are circulated for the purpose of identifying and tracing witnesses (see para 8.78 above). In *R v Alexander and McGill*,[68] the Lord Chief Justice observed that it was 'incumbent upon the police and the prosecutor to take steps to obtain, in as much detail as possible, evidence in relation to the initial identification'. Following this judgment, the Association of Chief Police Officers (ACPO) (as the National Police Chiefs' Council (NPCC) then was) issued guidance

64 [1998] Crim LR 825, CA. *Popat* was disapproved of in *R v Forbes* [2001] 1 AC 473, HL, but in respect of other aspects of the decision.

65 For example, *R v Bogie* [2023] EWCA Crim 1280, where there were multiple and admitted breaches of Code D, but fairness did not require the exclusion of the officers' recognition evidence.

66 For example, in *R v Cole* [2013] EWCA Crim 1149, it was held that although the failure by the police to disclose the first description given by an eye-witness was a clear breach of Code D para 3.1, it did not render the conviction unsafe given the strength of circumstantial evidence supporting the identification. In *R v Yaryare* [2020] EWCA Crim 1314, the court held that the question of whether a failure to follow Code D will render a verdict unsafe will depend on the particular facts of the case, and the court will need to consider the extent and significance of any breaches of the code and any consequential unfairness that have been caused.

67 *R v Forbes* [2001] 1 AC 473, HL. See also *R v Charles* [2001] EWCA Crim 1698; *R v Williams* [2003] EWCA Crim 3200; *R v Donald* [2004] Crim LR 841; and *R v Hassan* [2004] EWCA Crim 1478.

68 [2012] EWCA Crim 2768.

on *Internet social media and identification procedures.*[69] The guidance provides that an identification through social media is covered by Code D para 3.12(i) (of the version of Code D then in force), which means that a formal identification procedure should normally be held unless it is not practicable or would serve no useful purpose. The guidance further provides that in order to minimise any subsequent difficulties, police officers 'must be alive' to:

- the duty to obtain as much detail about the informal identification as possible;
- the importance of keeping accurate records of what happened; and
- the need to ensure that any disclosure of unused material to the defence is carried out properly and promptly.

8.89 The guidance is essential reading for any case involving social media identification. Among other important considerations, it provides that:

- the failure to obtain social media identification evidence as a priority may undermine a related arrest, identification procedure or prosecution as the content can be changed;
- a copy of the image will not be sufficient and the provenance of that evidence will be required; and
- the evidence required from an identifying witness is twofold:
  - to capture as closely as possible exactly what the witness did; and
  - to capture why the witness did it.

The guidance sets out a list of evidential considerations ('Issues for the Investigating Officer' para 6), and recommends that all of the social media evidence is put to a suspect during an interview in order to obtain the suspect's view of the accuracy of any identification.

8.90 Identification by social media may be hearsay evidence, and the defence lawyer will need to understand how the witness came to recognise the suspect as the point at which hearsay evidence becomes recognition evidence is a matter of fact and degree.[70]

69 July 2014, available at: http://library.college.police.uk/docs/APPREF/NVVIS-Guidance-on-Internet-Social-Media-and-Identification-Procedures.pdf.

70 See *Bracher v Crown Prosecution Service* [2023] EWHC 3500 (Admin) at para 23:
An individual puts up a post on a social media platform that contains an assertion. When another person repeats that assertion in court he is giving hearsay evidence; it is the report of another person's words. If a person identifies a photograph on social media as the photograph of another person that identification is hearsay. It is often impossible on a social media platform to know who it is who is identifying the person in the photograph posted on the site, and so the basis for the purported identification may not be apparent.

CHAPTER 9

Warrant of further detention

Introduction

Detention under PACE

9.1 Detention without charge up to 36 hours from the relevant time is dealt with at paras 2.74–2.81 above. Detention without charge beyond 36 hours is only possible in respect of a person who was arrested for an indictable offence (see para 2.23 above) and on the authority of a warrant of further detention issued by a magistrates' court. Warrants of further detention are governed by Police and Criminal Evidence Act 1984 (PACE) ss43–45.

9.2 A suspect who is brought before a court on the hearing of an application for a warrant of further detention is entitled to be legally represented at the hearing. If they are not represented but wish to be, the hearing must be adjourned in order for this to be arranged (PACE s43(3)). A suspect who is the subject of an application for a warrant of further detention is entitled to advocacy assistance without application of the financial eligibility test, and the sufficient benefit test (see para 1.57 above) is deemed to be satisfied.[1] No application for legal aid is required, but a determination must be made by a qualified solicitor who is a designated fee-earner or a supervisor (other than a prison law supervisor).[2] Given the obligation under the contract to continue to act for a client until the end of the investigation,[3] the lawyer (or their firm) advising a client at the police station should provide advocacy assistance in respect of the application.[4] Remuneration covers any reasonable preparation and follow-up work.[5] The relevant duty solicitor scheme is the police station scheme rather than the court scheme. An accredited or probationary representative cannot represent the client at the hearing of a warrant application since they do not have a right of audience.

9.3 A person detained for an indictable offence may be denied access to a lawyer for up to 36 hours from the relevant time, provided that certain conditions are satisfied (see para 2.151 above). In theory, a suspect whose continued detention has been authorised by a court under PACE s43 may still be denied access to a lawyer for any period up to the expiry of 36 hours from the relevant time. However, if they were legally represented in respect of the application for a warrant, it would be virtually impossible for a superintendent to be satisfied that one or more of the grounds for delaying access to legal advice under PACE s58(8) is satisfied.

9.4 An application for a warrant of further detention provides the lawyer with an opportunity to obtain information from both the client and the police. If the lawyer has been advising the client at the police station in

1 Legal Aid, Sentencing and Punishment of Offenders Act 2012 (LASPO) s15(2)(b); and Standard Crime Contract (SCC) Specification 2022 paras 9.166–9.168 (draft SCC Specification 2025 paras 9.161–9.163). Note that remuneration is subject to an upper limit under the Criminal Legal Aid (Remuneration) Regulations 2013 SI No 435 (as amended).

2 SCC Specification 2022 para 9.169 (draft SCC Specification 2025 para 9.164); for the recording requirements, see para 9.171 (draft SCC Specification 2025 para 9.166).

3 SCC Specification 2022 para 9.51 (draft SCC Specification 2025 para 9.43).

4 Counsel or an in-house advocate may be instructed, but subject to the costs rules set out in SCC Specification 2022 para 9.186 (draft SCC Specification 2025 para 9.68).

5 SCC Specification 2022 para 9.172 (draft SCC Specification 2025 para 9.167).

respect of the matter that is the subject of an application, they will be in possession of much of the information needed to deal with the application. It may be, however, that the lawyer is only requested, or an earlier request for legal advice by the suspect only complied with, at this stage. If this is the case, the lawyer should seek the information from the client set out in chapter 5 above. In addition, the lawyer should seek information from them about what has occurred while they have been in police detention. In particular, the lawyer will want to know whether any admissions have been made, and will also want to assess whether the police have acted in breach of PACE or the PACE Codes of Practice. Particular attention should be paid to why a lawyer was not involved at an earlier stage.

9.5 Information that should be provided by the police, or which the lawyer should consider seeking from them, is governed by three separate provisions. First, Code C para 2.4A provides that where a suspect leaves police detention or is taken before a court, they or their lawyer are entitled to a copy of the custody record as soon as practicable after the request is made.[6] If the lawyer is not already familiar with the contents of the custody record, they should seek a copy of it. The custody record may, in particular, indicate whether PACE and the codes have been complied with and whether any aspect of the detention has been unlawful.

9.6 Second, PACE s43(2) provides that the suspect must be provided with a copy of the information supporting the police officer's sworn application for the warrant, and the information must state (PACE s43(14)):

- the nature of the offence for which the person has been arrested;
- the general nature of the evidence on which that person was arrested;
- what enquiries relating to the offence have been made and what further enquiries are proposed; and
- the reasons for believing that continued detention is necessary for the purpose of such further enquiries.

The lawyer should ensure that they see, and consider, the contents of the information and, if appropriate, seek further details from the police.

9.7 Third, Code C para 15.0 provides that documents and materials that are essential to challenging the lawfulness of the arrest or detention must be made available to the suspect or their lawyer. For an explanation of what documents and materials may be essential for this purpose, see paras 2.61 and 4.22 above. In some respects, this obligation goes further than that required by PACE s43(2) in that it concerns documents and materials, and not merely a police summary of relevant information. The officer making the application is responsible for determining what documents and materials should be disclosed (Code C para 15.0(b)), and sufficient time must be allowed to enable the documents and materials to be viewed and considered before the hearing (Code C note for guidance (NfG) 3ZA). The obligation to disclose documents and materials is not limited to those that, in the police view, do undermine the legality of the arrest or detention. Therefore, the lawyer should consider what documents and materials may be relevant, both to the legality of the arrest and detention before the warrant hearing and to continued detention under a

6 This is in addition to the right to see the custody record under Code C para 2.4.

warrant, and make appropriate enquiries of the officer making the warrant application.

Detention under the Terrorism Act 2000

9.8 A person detained under Terrorism Act (TA) 2000 s41 may be detained for up to 48 hours from the time of arrest (see para 2.83 above). The person can be detained beyond this period, for up to a total of 14 days[7] beginning with the time of arrest (or, if the person was detained for examination under TA 2000 Sch 7 when arrested, from the time that the examination began), only if a judicial authority grants a warrant of further detention.[8] Warrants of further detention under the TA 2000 are governed by TA 2000 Sch 8 paras 29–37 and Code H section 14. The rules and processes are similar to applications under PACE, including the provisions regarding legal aid and disclosure of documents and materials (Code H para 14.0), subject to the following modifications.

9.9 Application for a warrant of further detention is made to a judicial authority (a specially designated district judge) (TA 2000 Sch 8 para 29(4)(a)). The application must be made before the expiry of 48 hours from the time of arrest, or within six hours of the end of that period, but the judicial authority must dismiss an application under the latter provision if they consider that it would have been reasonably practicable to have made it within 48 hours (TA 2000 Sch 8 para 30). The detained person must be given a notice stating that an application is to be made, the times at which it is to be made and heard, and the grounds upon which further detention is sought (TA 2000 Sch 8 para 31).

9.10 The detained person must be given an opportunity to make oral or written representations to the judicial authority and is entitled to be legally represented (TA 2000 Sch 8 para 33(1)). However, the judicial authority may exclude from any part of the hearing the person to whom the application relates and anyone representing them (TA 2000 Sch 8 para 33(3)). TA 2000 Sch 8 does not set out any conditions or criteria for the exercise of this power, nor does it require that reasons be given. Furthermore, the officer making the application may apply to the judicial authority for an order that specified information upon which they intend to rely be withheld from the detained person and from their lawyer (TA 2000 Sch 8 para 34(1)). To make an order, the judicial authority must have reasonable grounds for believing that if the information was disclosed, one or more of the consequences set out in para 34(2) or (3) would occur (TA 2000 Sch 8 para 34(2)).

9.11 A judicial authority may only issue a warrant of further detention if satisfied that there are reasonable grounds for believing that further detention is necessary:

- to obtain relevant evidence (whether by questioning or otherwise);
- to preserve evidence; or

7 This can be further extended to 28-days by the enactment of the draft Detention of Terrorist Suspects (Temporary Extension) Bill or by the emergency provision set out TA 2000 Sch 8 para 38.

8 TA 2000 Sch 8 paras 29(3) and 36(3).

- pending the result of an examination or analysis of any relevant evidence, or of anything the examination or analysis of which is to be or is being carried out with a view to obtaining relevant evidence,

and that the investigation is being conducted diligently and expeditiously (TA 2000 Sch 8 para 32(1) and (1A)). 'Relevant evidence' means, in relation to the person to whom the application relates, evidence that relates to the commission of an offence under any of the provisions mentioned in TA 2000 s40(1)(a), or which indicates that they are a person falling within TA 2000 s40(1)(b) (ie is or has been concerned in the commission, preparation or instigation of acts of terrorism) (TA 2000 Sch 8 para 32(2)).

Detention under the National Security Act 2023

9.12 A person detained under National Security Act (NSA) 2023 s27 may be detained for up to 48 hours beginning with the time of arrest under section 27 or the time they were first detained under certain specified provisions (NSA 2023 s27(3) and see para 2.84 above). The person can be detained beyond this period, for up to a total of 14 days[9] beginning with the time of their arrest under NSA 2023 s27, if a judicial authority grants a warrant of further detention.[10] Warrants of further detention under the NSA 2023 are governed by NSA 2023 Sch 6 paras 37–45 and Code I section 13. The rules and processes are similar to applications under PACE, but subject to similar modifications as apply to persons detained under TA 2000 s41.

9.13 The remainder of the chapter deals with warrants of further detention under PACE, but the same principles apply to applications under the TA 2000 and the NSA 2023, subject to appropriate modifications.

Application process

Introduction

9.14 An application for a warrant of further detention must be made on oath by a constable and must be supported by an information (PACE s43(1)). The requirements regarding the content of the information are set out at para 9.6 above. A copy of the information must be supplied to the suspect (PACE s43(2)), who must be brought before the court for the hearing (PACE s43(2)) and who is entitled to legal representation (PACE s43(3)). The application is heard by a magistrates' court, which is defined as a court consisting of two or more justices of the peace sitting otherwise than in open court (PACE s45(1)).[11] The court has the power, subject to consent of the suspect, to direct that the hearing be conducted by way of live link (PACE s45ZB).

9 This can be further extended to 28-days either by way of emergency legislation or by the emergency provisions set out in NSA 2023 Sch 6 para 46.

10 NSA 2023 Sch 6 paras 37(3) and 44(4).

11 A district judge (magistrates' court) may exercise alone this power (Courts Act 2003 ss26 and 27).

Lawfulness of the detention

9.15 In order for a warrant to be issued, the detention itself must be lawful.[12] The detention, or continued detention, may be unlawful if:

(1) The original arrest was unlawful, for example, because it was made in the absence of reasonable grounds or was not necessary (see paras 2.15 and 2.18 above), or the arresting officer failed to give reasons (see para 2.44 above).
(2) There are no grounds for detention, or continued detention, without charge under PACE s37 or any other provision. In particular, if the custody officer is satisfied that there is sufficient evidence to charge, the suspect must be charged or released (see para 2.64 above).
(3) The decision to detain beyond 24 hours was made unlawfully. It has been held that a court had no jurisdiction to grant a warrant of further detention where the detention was unlawful because the decision to extend the period of detention beyond 24 hours by a superintendent had been made without giving an opportunity to the suspect or their lawyer to make representations, as is required by PACE s42(6).[13]
(4) The conditions for interviews to be ended and for a decision regarding charge are satisfied (see paras 7.70 above and 10.5 below).

Time limits

9.16 An application can be made at any time before the expiry of 36 hours from the relevant time (see para 2.76 above), and thus can be made before the expiry of the initial 24-hour detention time limit.[14] For the purpose of calculating the time limit, the time of the application is the time that the constable makes the application on oath and gives evidence.[15] The time limit may be extended for a further six hours (that is, up to the expiry of 42 hours from the relevant time) if it is not practicable for the court to sit before the expiry of 36 hours, but it will sit during the six hours following the expiry of 36 hours (PACE s43(5)(b)(ii)). However, the 36-hour time limit is a strict one, and the court must dismiss an application if it appears that it would have been reasonable for the police to have made the application before the expiry of 36 hours (PACE s43(7)). In *R v Slough Justices ex p Stirling*,[16] the application was lodged nine minutes before the expiry of 36 hours, but the application was not made until one-and-a-half hours later (when the magistrates returned from lunch). It was held that the court should have dismissed the application since the application could

12 See para 9.7 above regarding disclosure of documents or materials that are relevant to the lawfulness of the arrest or detention.

13 *Police v Mudd and McDonough* November 1987 *Legal Action* 19, also reported as *Re An Application for a Warrant of Further Detention* [1988] Crim LR 296. Note that it is a decision of a stipendiary magistrate and, although of persuasive authority, is not binding on other courts.

14 Note that time during which a person has been released on police bail does not count for the purpose of calculating the period from the relevant time (see para 2.76 above).

15 *R v Sedgefield Justices ex p Milne* (1987) 5 November (unreported), Lexis No CO/1318/87.

16 [1987] Crim LR 576, DC.

reasonably have been made before the 36-hour time limit expired. Code C NfG 15D provides that an application should usually be made between 10am and 9pm, and if possible during usual court hours. PACE s45(2) provides that any reference to a period of time is to be treated as approximate only, so that an application made within minutes of the expiry of the time limit will probably be accepted, but the cut-off point is uncertain.

Issue of a warrant

9.17 The court may issue a warrant of further detention if it is satisfied that there are reasonable grounds for believing that further detention is justified (PACE s43(1)).[17] The period of the warrant should be such period as the court thinks fit, having regard to the evidence before it, up to a maximum of 36 hours (PACE s43(11) and (12)). If the suspect is to be transferred to another police area, in fixing the period the court must have regard to the distance and the time the journey would take (PACE s43(13)).

9.18 A warrant can be extended for up to a further period of 36 hours if an application is made in the proper form (see para 9.14 above) and the court is satisfied that further detention is justified. However, this is subject to an overall maximum period of detention of 96 hours from the relevant time (PACE s44(3)). Successive applications for extension of the warrant can be made, subject to the overall maximum period of detention. Under no circumstances can a suspect be detained without charge for longer than 96 hours from the relevant time.

9.19 A suspect who is the subject of a warrant of further detention must still have their detention reviewed in the usual way (see para 2.86 above), and must be released before the expiry of the warrant if the grounds for detention cease to apply (PACE s34(2)). In any event, unless the warrant is extended, the suspect must be released or charged on or before expiry of the warrant (PACE s43(18)). Such release must be without bail unless the pre-conditions for bail (see para 10.116 below) are satisfied (PACE s43(18)).

Refusal of a warrant

9.20 If the court is not satisfied that further detention is justified, it must either refuse the application or adjourn the hearing of it until a time not later than 36 hours after the relevant time (PACE s43(8)). If the court adjourns, the suspect can be kept in police detention during the period of adjournment (PACE s43(9)). If the 36 hours has expired at the time of the application, and it appears to the court that it would have been reasonable for the application to have been made before the expiry of that period, the court must dismiss it (PACE s43(7)). If a warrant is refused, the police can continue to detain the suspect without charge up to 24 hours from the relevant time, or 36 hours from the relevant time if authorised by a superintendent under PACE s42, provided that grounds for detention without charge still exist under PACE s37 (PACE s43(16)). Furthermore, if a warrant is refused, no further application for a warrant of further detention can be

17 For the definition of 'justified' see para 9.25 below.

made unless supported by evidence that has come to light since the court's refusal (PACE s43(17)).

9.21 A question that arises is whether the police could, on the refusal of a warrant, extend the period of detention without charge by arresting the person for a further offence. Generally, this would not be possible, since PACE s31 provides that where a person has been arrested for an offence and it appears to a constable that, if released, the person would be liable to arrest for some other offence, the person must be arrested for that other offence as well. PACE s41(4) then provides that where a person has been arrested under PACE s31, the relevant time (see para 2.76 above) is the relevant time for the original offence. However, PACE s31 only applies where the person is at a police station in consequence of the arrest for the original offence.[18] It could be argued, therefore, that the police could prolong the period of detention if they were to re-arrest the person while they are still at court.[19] However, even if such an argument were upheld, any evidence obtained during the prolonged period of detention might be excluded under PACE s78 since the further detention would clearly be contrary to the spirit of PACE s41.

Hearing of the application

Introduction

9.22 Applications for a warrant of further detention are relatively unusual, and courts may be keen, particularly if the hearing is outside usual court hours, to deal with the matter as quickly as possible. This can result in pressure being placed on the lawyer to rush the preparation stage so that the hearing can commence. Such pressure should be resisted, and the magistrates may need to be reminded of the important issues at stake. Particular pressure may be applied if the time limit for making the application is about to expire since, as seen at para 9.16 above, the critical time is the time that the police officer makes the application and gives evidence on oath. Because the suspect is entitled to legal representation under PACE s43(3), the lawyer is in a relatively strong position to hold out for more time to prepare. If the time taken by the defence to prepare results in the application being made outside the 36-hour limit, the question will arise as to whether the court can still admit the application under PACE s43(5)(b)(ii) (see para 9.16 above). In making the decision about practicality, the court must have regard to PACE s43(7), which provides that the court must dismiss the application if it appears that it would have been reasonable for the police to make the application before the time expired. Since the police should have anticipated that the defence would need a reasonable period for preparation, it can be argued that the court cannot be so satisfied.

18 The suspect is still in police detention as defined by PACE s118(2), but section 31 only applies where the suspect is 'at a police station'.

19 A similar ploy used in relation to custody time limits has been accepted by the Divisional Court as starting time limits afresh, even though the new charge arose from the same facts as the original charge (*R v Waltham Forest Magistrates' Court ex p Lee and Lee* [1993] Crim LR 522, DC).

9.23 The issues of the legality of the detention, of whether the formal requirements have been satisfied (ie supplying a copy of the information to the suspect and their physical presence), and of time limits may be taken as preliminary points. If they are successful, the application cannot proceed further. If there are no such preliminary points, or the defence lawyer cannot persuade the court to uphold them, the court will proceed to hear the substantive application. In order for a warrant to be issued under PACE s43 (or to be extended under PACE s44), the conditions in PACE s43(4) must be satisfied (see para 9.25 below). The burden of establishing these conditions is clearly on the prosecution.

9.24 In considering an application for a warrant of further detention, a court cannot draw inferences from silence or failure to account under Criminal Justice and Public Order Act (CJPOA) 1994 ss34, 36 and 37, since an application for a warrant of further detention is not included in the list of stages of proceedings where the sections apply (CJPOA 1994 ss34(2), 36(2) and 37(2)). The power of a court to draw inferences from failure to give evidence or to answer any question under CJPOA 1994 s35 also does not apply.[20]

Is further detention justified?

9.25 The general requirement for a warrant to be issued or extended is that the court must be satisfied that there are reasonable grounds for believing that the further detention of the suspect is justified (PACE ss43(1) and 44(1)). The term 'justified' is defined so that the court must be satisfied in relation to all of the following three factors (PACE s43(4)):

(1) detention is necessary to secure, preserve or obtain evidence;
(2) the suspect is under arrest for an indictable offence; and
(3) the investigation is diligent and expeditious.

To secure, preserve or obtain evidence

9.26 The court must be satisfied that detention without charge 'is necessary to secure or preserve evidence relating to an offence for which he is under arrest or to obtain such evidence by questioning him' (PACE s43(4)(a)). This is the same test as applies at the time of initial detention and at the 24-hour stage (see para 2.56 above). At the hearing, the police officer(s) should be cross-examined, and appropriate representations made, in relation to the following questions.

(1) **Whether it is necessary for the suspect to be detained.** PACE s43(4)(a) requires that detention be necessary, not merely convenient. Why is it that the suspect cannot be released and questioned without being detained, or released while the police are gathering other evidence? Is there any evidence to suggest that the suspect will abscond or seek to interfere with witnesses or evidence, or otherwise interfere with the course of the investigation? Would a release on bail without charge (if necessary, subject to appropriate conditions) be sufficient?

20 See, in particular, CJPOA 1994 s35(3).

(2) **Whether the suspect has been charged.** It is clear from PACE s43(4) that if the suspect has been charged with an offence, an application for a warrant of further detention in respect of that offence cannot be entertained. If the suspect has been arrested and detained in respect of more than one offence, and has been charged in respect of one or more of the offences, it is doubtful whether the court can issue a warrant in respect of the offence(s) for which the suspect has not been charged. The reason is that once a suspect has been charged, PACE s38 provides that the custody officer must release the suspect unless the conditions for withholding bail are satisfied, and if this is so, PACE s46 provides that the suspect must be brought before a court as soon as practicable.[21] An application for a warrant would not count as a production before the court for these purposes. The proper course in these circumstances would be for the police to produce the suspect under PACE s46 in respect of the matter for which they have been charged, to oppose bail, and then to ask for a remand to a police station for up to three days under Magistrates' Courts Act (MCA) 1980 s128(7).[22]

(3) **Whether the suspect should have been charged already.** PACE s37(7) provides that a custody officer must make a decision about charge if they have before them sufficient evidence to charge the person. See the discussion of what amounts to 'sufficient evidence to charge' at para 10.9 below. If the evidence given at the hearing of the application discloses that there is sufficient evidence to charge, then in view of PACE s37(7) the court will have no power to issue the warrant. If the suspect has been arrested and detained in respect of more than one offence, Code C para 16.1 provides that it is permissible to delay bringing the suspect before the custody officer until there is sufficient evidence in respect of all the offences. Therefore, the police could apply for a warrant in respect of one offence even though there is sufficient evidence to charge in relation to another offence. Note, however, that this aspect of para 16.1 may be ultra vires (see para 7.74 above).

(4) **What evidence the police intend to secure or preserve during the period of the warrant.** While a court may be reluctant to require the police to divulge their plans in precise detail, the police should be prepared to indicate the nature of the evidence they hope to obtain, how they intend to obtain it and how long this is likely to take. Does this involve interviewing witnesses and, if so, are they likely to be available? Will it involve seeking information that may be held electronically and, if so, when will it be possible to obtain it? For example, if the application is being heard on a Friday night, it may be impossible to obtain information from banks and building societies until the following Monday morning – outside the 36-hour initial maximum period of the warrant.

21 Although if bail is not granted, it would seem that there is nothing to stop the police from interviewing a suspect about matters for which they have not been charged during the period before they are produced in court. The restriction on questioning after charge in Code C para 16.5 applies only to questioning in respect of the matter for which the person has been charged.

22 Or, in the case of certain drugs offences, remand for up to 192 hours under Criminal Justice Act 1988 s152.

It may be that the police wish to carry out tests on materials such as suspected drugs. If so, who will do this and when will it be done?

(5) **What evidence the police hope to obtain by questioning the suspect.** If the suspect has been answering questions in interview, the police should be asked what other matters they want to put to the suspect. This may, of course, depend on what other evidence they hope to obtain but, again, it may be appropriate for the lawyer to explore why the suspect needs to be in detention for this purpose. If the suspect has not been answering questions in interview, and has firmly indicated that they do not intend to answer them, it can be argued that this ground for issuing a warrant cannot be satisfied. Although the fact that a suspect does not intend to answer questions does not alter the police's entitlement to put questions to them, this cannot be authority for continuing detention which has as its sole or primary purpose the undermining of the suspect's right to silence.

Under arrest for an indictable offence

9.27 The suspect must be under arrest for an indictable offence (see para 2.23 above) (PACE s43(4)(b)). Whether an offence is indictable will usually be straightforward. However, the police may lawfully arrest a person without precisely specifying the offence for which the person is arrested (see para 2.15 above). In order to make an application for a warrant of further detention, the police must have specified the offence with sufficient precision to establish that it is an indictable offence.

Diligent and expeditious investigation

9.28 Further detention is only justified if 'the investigation is being conducted diligently and expeditiously' (PACE s43(4)(c)). A mere assertion by the police that this is so is not sufficient since, by PACE s43(1), the court must have reasonable grounds for believing that further detention is justified and, therefore, must have reasonable grounds for believing that the condition in section 43(4)(c) is satisfied. The expression 'diligently and expeditiously' involves the idea that the police are carrying out the investigation as quickly as possible and are approaching it in a careful and industrious manner. From the suspect's point of view, there are often periods when the police appear to be doing little or nothing to progress the investigation and, if relevant, this needs to be dealt with in cross-examination of the police. Furthermore, it may appear that the police are only dealing with one issue at a time, when they could be pursuing various lines of enquiry simultaneously. To some extent, this obviously depends on investigative resources, but again this may be an area worth pursuing in cross-examination. Although Code C sections 8, 9, 11 and 12 place limits on the times during which, and the periods for which, the suspect can be interviewed, they do not provide that the investigation should not proceed by other means during those fallow times. If, for example, the investigating officers went home at 6pm and did not return until 8am the next morning, during which time nothing was done to progress the investigation, it may be difficult for the police to satisfy the court as to diligence and expedition.

Such lack of progress should not be justified by the fact that the suspect 'was having their lie down'.

Period of the warrant

9.29 The foregoing paragraphs indicate the range of issues that may be included in a defence submission that a warrant of further detention should not be issued. The court may need to be reminded that it must be satisfied that there are reasonable grounds for believing that further detention is justified, and that for this to be the case, all three of the criteria in PACE s43(4) must be satisfied. If the court is so satisfied, the remaining issue is the period of the warrant. If possible, a defence submission as to the period of the warrant should only be made once the court has decided that a warrant is to be issued.

9.30 A warrant can be issued for such period as the court thinks fit, having regard to the evidence before it, subject to a maximum of 36 hours (PACE s43(11) and (12)). This clearly means that the period should not automatically be 36 hours, but should relate to what the police intend to do to progress the investigation. Inevitably, this will require the court to make an informed guess, but since the decision involves loss of liberty the court should be urged to issue the warrant for the minimum appropriate period. Since the police can, subject to the overall time limit, make an application to extend the warrant under PACE s44, the investigation would not be jeopardised by the issuing of a warrant for a shorter rather than a longer period.

CHAPTER 10

The decision to charge and afterwards

continued

Introduction

10.1 This chapter sets out the detailed provisions regarding the decision to charge; pre-charge engagement; the charging process; alternatives to charging (including out-of-court disposals); challenges to charge decisions; pre-charge bail, bail or detention after charge; and leaving the police station. To help make sense of these provisions, the chapter commences with a broad outline of the charge decision process.

The charge decision process

10.2 Responsibility for making the various decisions is divided between the custody officer and a Crown prosecutor, as follows:

- The decision about whether there is sufficient evidence to charge, and the initial action to be taken thereafter, must be taken by the custody officer.
- The decision as to *whether a person should be charged, and what they should be charged with*, may be made either by the custody officer or by a Crown prosecutor, depending on the nature of the charge and the likely plea.
- The decision regarding *alternatives to charging, such as simple and conditional cautions,*[1] may be made either by the custody officer or a Crown prosecutor, depending on the out-of-court disposal concerned.
- Where a person in police detention is charged, the decision regarding *whether they should be kept in custody or released on bail pending their first court appearance* rests with the custody officer, irrespective of who makes the charge decision.

In making decisions regarding charge, the custody officer must have regard to guidance issued by the Director of Public Prosecutions (DPP) under Police and Criminal Evidence Act 1984 (PACE) s37A(3). The guidance, *Director's guidance on charging,*[2] sets out the tests for determining whether there is sufficient evidence to charge, and also regulates whether the custody officer or a Crown prosecutor[3] respectively has responsibility for making the charge decision. In cases where a Crown prosecutor must make the charge decision, an officer involved in the investigation must supply relevant information to the prosecutor, and the prosecutor must decide whether there is sufficient evidence to charge and, if so, must decide whether the person should be charged and what they should be charged with or, alternatively, whether they should be cautioned (PACE s37B(1)–(3)). The prosecutor must then notify their decision to an officer involved in the investigation, and if the decision is that the person

1 Note that if and when Police, Crime, Sentencing and Courts Act (PCSCA) 2022 Part 6 is implemented, simple and conditional cautions for adults will be replaced by community and diversionary cautions. See further para 10.95 below.

2 Sixth edn (December 2020), available at: www.cps.gov.uk/legal-guidance/directors-guidance-charging-sixth-edition-december-2020-incorporating-national-file.

3 PACE s37B refers to decisions to be made by the DPP, but in practice they are normally taken by a Crown prosecutor.

should be charged or cautioned, they must be charged or cautioned accordingly (PACE s37B(4)–(7)). If the person is in police detention at the relevant time, they may be charged in the normal way, but if they are not in police detention (because, for example, they have been released without charge), they may be charged by means of the written charge and requisition procedure (PACE s37B(8)). If there is a judicial review of a charging decision (including a decision to offer an out-of-court disposal), the suspect is to be considered an interested party, including at the Pre-Action Protocol letter stage.[4]

10.3 The division of responsibility for charging between the custody officer and a Crown prosecutor has created a number of problems. Custody officers frequently make charge decisions in circumstances where the decision should have been referred to a Crown prosecutor, and often refer cases when they should have decided to take no further action on the grounds of insufficient evidence.[5] For defence lawyers, making representations regarding charge in cases referred to a Crown prosecutor has been made difficult because prosecutors are usually unwilling to speak to defence lawyers.[6] This is despite the fact that the Code for Crown Prosecutors (CCP) (October 2018) explicitly recognises that the defence may submit evidence or information for consideration to help inform the prosecutor's decision.[7] Nevertheless, the defence lawyer should, where possible, ask to speak to the Crown prosecutor making the charge decision and should ask for written representations to be given to them where they refuse to speak to the lawyer. Suspects and their lawyers often have to wait while the case is being considered by a prosecutor, and such delays can often be lengthy. The Standard Crime Contract (SCC) requires duty solicitors, in respect of cases they have accepted, to provide advice where a client is to be charged, and to consider attending at the time of charge, 'bearing in mind whether it is possible to give confidential telephone advice and the possible consequences of not making a statement when charged'.[8] Although not binding in own-solicitor cases, these obligations on duty solicitors should be regarded as establishing a minimum standard applicable in all cases.

4 See *R (Watson) v Chief Constable of Greater Manchester* [2025] EWHC 332 (Admin); and *R (YNG) v Chief Constable of Sussex* [2025] EWHC 1412 (Admin).

5 A joint inspection by His Majesty's Inspectorate of Constabulary (HMIC) and His Majesty's Crown Prosecution Service Inspectorate (HMCPSI) found that while over 90 per cent of charging decisions were in accordance with the Code for Crown Prosecutors (CCP), in over one-third of cases the charge decision was made by the custody officer when it should have been referred to the Crown Prosecution Service (CPS). It also found that many cases were referred to the CPS when the police should have decided to take no further action. See HMCPSI and HMIC, *Joint inspection of the provision of charging decisions* (May 2015), available at: https://assets-hmicfrs.justiceinspectorates.gov.uk/uploads/joint-inspection-of-the-provision-of-charging-decisions.pdf.

6 In 2005, the government said that it would pilot arrangements under which the Crown prosecutor would initiate discussions with the defence regarding charge, but this did not result in a national scheme (see *A fairer deal for legal aid*, Cm 6591 (July 2005) para 4.9).

7 CCP para 3.4, available at: www.cps.gov.uk/publication/code-crown-prosecutors.

8 SCC Specification 2022 para 9.42(b) (draft SCC Specification 2025 para 9.37(b)).

10.4 Unless, and until, a person is charged with a criminal offence, the police should not name them or identify them other than in exceptional circumstances where there is a legitimate policing purpose in doing so. A legitimate purpose may include avoiding or minimising a threat to life, the prevention or detection of crime, or where the police have issued a public warning about a wanted person.[9]

Decision regarding charge

When must a decision be made?

Introduction

10.5 The point at which a decision must be made regarding charge is governed by a number of provisions in PACE, the Terrorism Act (TA) 2000, the National Security Act (NSA) 2023 and PACE Code of Practice C.[10]

10.6 By PACE s37(7), if the custody officer determines that they have before them sufficient evidence to charge an arrested person with the offence for which the person was arrested, the person must be:

(1) released without charge and on bail, or kept in police detention, for the purpose of enabling the DPP (in practice a Crown prosecutor) to make a charge decision (PACE s37(7)(a)(i) and (ii));
(2) released without charge and, if the pre-conditions for bail are satisfied, on bail, but not for the purpose of enabling the DPP to make a charge decision (PACE s37(7)(b));[11]
(3) released without charge and, if the pre-conditions for bail are not satisfied, without bail, but not for the purpose of enabling the DPP to make a charge decision (PACE s37(7)(c)); or
(4) charged (PACE s37(7)(d)).

Section 37(7)(b) and (c) allows the custody officer to release a person who has not been charged (but in respect of whom there is sufficient evidence to charge) on bail, but only if the pre-conditions for bail are satisfied (see further para 10.117 below). If the conditions are not satisfied, the release must be without bail. However, a release under section 37(7)(a), to enable the CPS to make a charge decision, must be on bail.

10.7 PACE s37(7) is in mandatory terms, and contains no provision for delay in making a decision as to the appropriate course of action other than where the person is not in a fit state to be dealt with (PACE s37(9)). Where, under the *Director's guidance on charging*, the custody officer is required to refer the matter to a Crown prosecutor for a charge decision, the suspect is to be detained for no longer than is reasonably necessary (and subject to the applicable detention time limit) to decide on how they

9 College of Policing, *Authorised Professional Practice: Media Relations* (July 2022), available at: https://www.college.police.uk/app/engagement-and-communication/media-relations. See also *Bloomberg LP v ZXC* [2022] UKSC 5.

10 Note that Codes H and I do not contain separate provisions regarding charge, but confirm that charging is governed by PACE and Code C section 16 (Code H para 15.1 and Code I para 14).

11 For release without charge, see para 10.113 below.

are to be dealt with (Code C note for guidance (NfG) 16AB). Unreasonable delay is likely to render the detention unlawful even if it is within the maximum period of detention. If the suspect is unlikely, if charged, to be granted bail, the delay in making a charge decision may not prolong their detention. If, however, the suspect is likely to be granted bail, the defence lawyer may argue that prolonged, and possibly unlawful, delay can be avoided by releasing their client on bail under PACE s37(7)(a)(i).

10.8 Generally, where a person is released and the custody officer determines that either there is not sufficient evidence to charge or there is sufficient evidence to charge but the person should not be charged or given a caution for an offence, the custody officer must give them written notice that they are not to be prosecuted. Such a notice does not prevent prosecution of the person if new evidence comes to light after the notice was given. This applies where a person is released under PACE ss34(5), 37(2), 37(7)(b) or (c), 37CA(2), 41(7), 42(10), 43(15) or (18), and 44(7) (ss34(5B)–(5E), 37(6A)–(6C), 37(8ZA), 37CA(5)–(7), 41(10)–(12), 42(12)–(14), 43(20)–(22) and 44(9)–(11) respectively). Note that unlike the reference to 'new evidence' in relation to re-arrest (see para 2.52 above), the reference to 'new evidence' in these provisions does not explicitly extend to an examination or analysis of existing evidence that could not reasonably have been made before the person's release.

Sufficient evidence to charge

10.9 A key issue in determining when a charge decision under PACE s37(7) must be made is the meaning of 'sufficient evidence to charge'. When the custody officer determines that they have before them sufficient evidence to charge, they must deal with the suspect in accordance with PACE s37(7)(a)–(d). The phrase 'sufficient evidence to charge' is not defined in PACE itself, and is subject to different interpretations in Code C and in the *Director's guidance on charging*. Code C para 16.1 does not use the phrase 'sufficient evidence to charge', but states that when the officer in charge of an investigation reasonably believes there is 'sufficient evidence to provide a realistic prospect of conviction' they must inform the custody officer without delay. This implies that a decision under PACE s37(7) must be made *as soon as* the custody officer is in possession of information that leads the officer to conclude that there is sufficient evidence to charge, and that the relevant test is the 'realistic prospect of conviction' test.[12]

10.10 However, Code C para 16.1A states that the custody officer must comply with the *Director's guidance on charging* in deciding how to act in dealing with a detainee, and the guidance sets out two different tests for determining whether there is sufficient evidence to charge – the 'full code test' and the 'threshold test'.[13] The full code test is the normal test to be applied in determining whether there is sufficient evidence to charge (see further

12 For the point at which interviewing must cease, see para 7.70 above. For the contradictions between Code C para 11.6 and para 16.1, see para 7.71 above. For consideration of the meaning of 'sufficient evidence to charge' for the purpose of determining whether a person arrested and taken to a police station should be detained for investigation, see para 2.62 above.

13 *Director's guidance on charging* paras 5 and 6.

para 10.21 below). The threshold test may only be applied in exceptional circumstances (see further paras 10.20 and 10.24 below). In practice, the tests for determining whether there is sufficient evidence to charge give the custody officer a great deal of latitude in deciding whether there is sufficient evidence to charge for the purposes of triggering action under PACE s37(7).

Representations by the defence lawyer

10.11 If the lawyer concludes that it is in their client's interests for a decision about charge to be made, for example, because detention has been lengthy and/or there is evidence to justify charging and the lawyer wishes to avoid further interviews,[14] they should consider the following:

- If it is clear that the police have decided to charge the client in any event, the custody officer must proceed to make a charge decision under PACE s37(7), and further detention without charge is likely to be unlawful.[15]
- If it appears that the police have sufficient evidence to provide a realistic prospect of conviction but the interviewing officer cites Code C para 11.6 as authority for allowing further questioning of the client, the lawyer should cite Code C para 16.1 as authority for the requirement that the interviewing officer must take the suspect before the custody officer without delay (see para 7.71 above). If the interviewing officer refuses to do so, the lawyer should consider making appropriate representations to the custody officer and ask them to determine that there is sufficient evidence to charge.
- If it appears that there is sufficient evidence to charge (in accordance with whichever of the two tests is relevant), but the custody officer is reluctant to make a decision, the lawyer should make representations that under PACE s37(7) and the *Director's guidance on charging*, the officer must make a decision.

If it appears that there is insufficient evidence to charge, and there is unlikely to be sufficient evidence in the near future, the lawyer should consider making representations to the custody officer that charge be refused or that the client be released pending further enquiries (see para 10.113 below). All representations, and responses, should be recorded, and the lawyer should also ask that they be entered on the custody record.

Detention for more than one offence

10.12 PACE s37(7) does not deal with the situation where a suspect is detained in respect of more than one offence. Code C para 16.1 provides that where a person is detained in respect of more than one offence, it is permissible for the investigating officer to delay bringing them before the custody officer until the officer believes that there is sufficient evidence to provide

14 For limitations on questioning after charge, see para 10.35 below.

15 See *R v Elliott* [2002] EWCA Crim 931; and *R v Dervish* [2001] EWCA Crim 2789.

a realistic prospect of conviction in respect of all the offences.[16] There are two possible arguments here from the defence point of view. First, this provision may be ultra vires since PACE s37(7) is in clear mandatory terms (see para 7.74 above). Second, even if Code C para 16.1 is valid, while it may be used by the interviewing officer to justify a decision not to take the suspect before the custody officer until a later stage, if the custody officer becomes aware (for example, because the lawyer has informed them) that there is sufficient evidence to provide a realistic prospect of conviction, the custody officer is bound by the terms of PACE s37(7).

10.13 Arguably, if released, the suspect should not be at risk of arrest for the offence for which questioning was not completed, since PACE s31 provides that if a person is liable to arrest for an offence while at a police station having been arrested for another offence, they must be arrested. However, it should be noted that while there is a prohibition on re-arrest following release at the expiry of 24 hours (PACE s41(9)), 36 hours (PACE s42(11)), a warrant of further detention (PACE s43(19)), or having been released on police bail[17] (unless new evidence justifying a further arrest has come to light since the suspect's release), there is no similar provision preventing re-arrest where a person is released in the circumstances being considered here. It may be, therefore, that the argument is of more practical use in seeking to speed up the process rather than in trying to secure the immediate release of the suspect.

Pre-charge engagement

10.14 An important consideration for the defence lawyer in determining their approach to the point at which a charge decision should be made is whether pre-charge engagement (PCE) would be relevant and of potential benefit. PCE, as a formally recognised process, was introduced by amendments to the *Attorney General's Guidelines on Disclosure* in 2020, with the stated aim of assisting 'prosecutors, investigators, suspects and suspect's legal representatives who wish to enter into a discussion about an investigation at any time after the first PACE interview, up until the commencement of criminal proceedings'.[18] PCE is a voluntary process, which can be initiated by the police, prosecutor or the defence lawyer, and the guidelines state that the investigator should provide information on PCE to the suspect or their lawyer either before or following a PACE interview, although in practice this may not happen.[19] PCE may be conducted face to face or by way of correspondence, and whilst it will often take place following a suspect's release without charge (either on bail or without bail), it may be initiated 'immediately after interview, when the investigator and suspect's representative may agree on further lines of enquiry that have

16 Although the suspect must not be further questioned about any offence in respect of which the conditions in Code C para 11.6 are satisfied.

17 Subject to the power to arrest for failure to answer to police bail under PACE s46A.

18 *Attorney General's Guidelines on Disclosure 2024* Annex B para 1, available at: https://assets.publishing.service.gov.uk/media/65e1ab9d2f2b3b00117cd803/Attorney_General_s_Guidelines_on_Disclosure_-_2024.pdf.

19 *Attorney General's Guidelines on Disclosure* Annex B para 16.

arisen from interview'.[20] So it can be commenced whilst the defence lawyer is at the police station, or subsequently, provided a decision to charge has not been made. Non-means tested legal aid is available for work done on PCE, including preparatory work where the police or prosecution subsequently refuse to agree to it, subject to an extendable upper limit.[21]

10.15 The defence lawyer should consider, with their client, whether to make a request for PCE or, if the police or prosecution request it, whether to agree to it. PCE can only proceed if both parties agree to it, and a refusal by the suspect to engage should not have adverse consequences for them at a subsequent trial.[22] The fact that a suspect exercised their right to silence in interview does not preclude a subsequent request for PCE,[23] and since PCE does not involve an interview under caution, it is not possible for inferences to be drawn at trial under Criminal Justice and Public Order Act (CJPOA) 1994 s34 (see para 5.70 above) from failure to mention a relevant fact during the PCE process. Acknowledging this, the guidelines indicate that the police or prosecutor should not initiate or agree to PCE if they are likely to seek to rely on the suspect's answers as evidence at trial.[24] However, everything said and all information provided during PCE must be recorded,[25] and the defence lawyer should be aware, and advise their client accordingly, that anything said or done during PCE could, if relevant, be used at trial.

10.16 The guidelines set out examples of matters that may be covered by PCE at para 4:

a. Giving the suspect the opportunity to comment on any proposed further lines of inquiry.
b. Ascertaining whether the suspect can identify any other lines of inquiry.
c. Asking whether the suspect is aware of, or can provide access to, digital material that has a bearing on the allegation.
d. Discussing ways to overcome barriers to obtaining potential evidence, such as revealing encryption keys.
e. Agreeing any key word searches of digital material that the suspect would like carried out.
f. Obtaining a suspect's consent to access medical records.
g. The suspect identifying and providing contact details of any potential witnesses.
h. Clarifying whether any expert or forensic evidence is agreed and, if not, whether the suspect's representatives intend to instruct their own expert, including timescales for this.

This is not an exhaustive list, and it may be noted that the examples tend to refer to information or consent to be obtained from a suspect. However, importantly, it does give the suspect and their lawyer the opportunity to both comment on lines of enquiry and also to suggest lines of enquiry that the police should pursue. As the guidelines make clear, reflecting Criminal Procedure and Investigations Act (CPIA) 1996 Code of Practice para 3.5,

20 *Attorney General's Guidelines on Disclosure* Annex B para 20.

21 See SCC Specification 2022 paras 9.113–9.120 (draft SCC Specification 2025 paras 9.109–9.112).

22 *Attorney General's Guidelines on Disclosure* Annex B para 3.

23 *Attorney General's Guidelines on Disclosure* Annex B para 9.

24 *Attorney General's Guidelines on Disclosure* Annex B paras 7 and 8.

25 *Attorney General's Guidelines on Disclosure* Annex B paras 25–30.

'[i]nvestigators should ensure that all reasonable lines of inquiry are investigated, whether they point towards or away from the suspect'.[26] The defence solicitor may also use PCE to seek further disclosure from the police or prosecutor. Whilst the statutory disclosure rules are not engaged at this stage of the process, the guidelines state that the police or prosecutor should consider whether any further material should be provided, in particular having regard to any information disclosed during PCE.[27] This may include (insofar as it has not already been disclosed) information enabling the suspect to understand the nature of any offence of which they are suspected (Code C para 11.1A),[28] or documents and materials that are essential to challenging the lawfulness of the suspect's arrest or detention (Codes C and H para 3.4(b); Code I para 3.1(v)).[29]

Who makes the decision on charge?

10.17 As noted in para 10.6 above, it is the custody officer's responsibility under PACE s37(7) to decide whether there is sufficient evidence to charge, but the decision as to charge (or an alternative to charging) may be that of a custody officer or a Crown prosecutor under the terms of the *Director's guidance on charging.*[30]

10.18 A Crown prosecutor must make the charge decision in respect of all indictable-only offences, and any either-way offence in respect of which, under the *Director's guidance on charging*, a custody officer is not permitted to make a charge decision (see below). In cases where more than one charge may be appropriate, and at least one of them must be referred to a prosecutor for a charge decision, all matters must be referred to the prosecutor.[31]

10.19 A custody officer may make the charge decision in respect of:

- any summary-only offence (including criminal damage where the value of the loss or damage is less than £5,000) irrespective of likely plea;
- any offence of retail theft (shoplifting) or attempted retail theft irrespective of plea provided it is suitable for sentence in a magistrates' court; and
- any either-way offence where it is anticipated that the suspect will plead guilty and which is suitable for sentence in a magistrates' court, provided that it is not:
  - a case requiring the consent to prosecute of the DPP or a law officer;

26 *Attorney General's Guidelines on Disclosure* para 17; and see para 15 and Annex A paras 11–13.

27 *Attorney General's Guidelines on Disclosure* paras 22–24.

28 Or, as relevant, the nature of their suspected involvement in the commission, preparation or instigation of acts of terrorism (Code H para 11.1A), or the nature of their suspected involvement in foreign power threat activity (Code I para 11); and see para 4.27 above).

29 See para 4.22 above.

30 *Director's guidance on charging* section 4 and Annex 1.

31 A report by HMIC/HMCPSI in 2015 found that in over one-third of cases examined, custody officers took the charge decision in circumstances where the case should have been referred to a Crown prosecutor. See *Joint inspection of the provision of charging decisions* (May 2015).

- a case involving death;
- connected with terrorist activity or official secrets;
- classified as a hate crime or domestic abuse under CPS policies;
- a case of harassment or stalking;
- an offence of violent disorder or affray;
- an offence involving causing grievous bodily harm or wounding, or actual bodily harm;
- a Sexual Offences Act (SOA) 2003 offence committed by or upon a person under 18 years; or
- an offence under the Licensing Act 2003.

A guilty plea may be anticipated if:

- the suspect has been interviewed and made a clear and unambiguous admission to the offence and has offered no explanation that could be used as a defence; or has not made a clear and unambiguous admission but has offered no explanation that could be used as a defence, and either (i) the commission of the offence and the identity of the offender can be wholly established by police witnesses, or (ii) there is clear visually recorded evidence of the offence being committed and of the suspect being the offender; or
- the suspect has not been interviewed, but either the commission of the offence and the identity of the offender can be wholly established by police witnesses, or there is clear visually recorded evidence of the offence being committed and of the suspect being the offender.[32]

An either-way case may be considered suitable for sentencing in a magistrates' court unless the overall circumstances of the case make it likely that a court will decide that a sentence in excess of six months' imprisonment is appropriate.[33]

10.20 A custody officer may also, in limited circumstances, charge a person with an offence that under the *Director's guidance on charging* should normally be referred to a Crown prosecutor for a charge decision. The conditions for doing so are set out in the *Director's guidance on charging* para 4.35, which makes clear that this should only be done on rare occasions. Charging in these circumstances must be authorised by an inspector or above, where the continued detention of the suspect after charge is justified and it is not possible to obtain a prosecutor's authority for the charge before the expiry of any relevant detention time limit. The charging decision must immediately be referred to a Crown prosecutor for ratification. In making a charge decision under this provision, the custody officer may charge on the basis of the threshold test provided that the conditions for doing so are satisfied (see para 10.24 below). The threshold test cannot be used in respect of a summary-only, non-imprisonable offence, and if it is used in respect of a summary-only imprisonable offence, the police must record how each of the conditions is satisfied. A custody officer cannot charge a person with an either-way offence on the basis of the

32 *Director's Guidance on charging* Annex 1 para 4.

33 *Director's Guidance on charging* Annex 1 para 5. Sentencing Act 2020 s224(1A)(b) was amended as from 18 November 2024 so that the maximum sentence in a magistrates' court for an either-way offence is 12 months, but as at 30 June 2025 that had not been reflected in the *Director's guidance on charging*.

threshold test where a guilty plea is anticipated and it is suitable for sentence in a magistrates' court, even if a remand in custody is considered to be appropriate. There is special provision regarding the use of the threshold test where charges are being considered in respect of more than one suspect.[34]

The tests for deciding on charge

The full code test

10.21 The decision regarding charge, whether made by a custody officer or by a Crown prosecutor, must normally be made in accordance with the full code test set out in the CCP.[35] The full code test consists of two stages: the evidential stage and the public interest stage.

The evidential stage

10.22 The person making the charge decision must be satisfied that there is sufficient evidence to provide a realistic prospect of conviction. This means that an objective, impartial and reasonable jury, or bench of magistrates or judge hearing the case alone, properly directed and acting in accordance with the law, is more likely than not to convict the defendant of the charge alleged.[36] The decision must be based on an objective assessment of the evidence, including the impact of any defence and any other information that the suspect has put forward or on which they might rely. The person making the decision must consider:

- whether the evidence can be used in court – is it likely to be admissible, and how important is that evidence in the context of the evidence as a whole;
- whether the evidence is reliable – are there any reasons to question its reliability, including its accuracy and integrity;
- whether the evidence is credible – are there any reasons to doubt its credibility; and
- whether there is any other material which might affect the sufficiency of evidence.[37]

If the evidential stage is not satisfied, the case cannot proceed, irrespective of how serious or sensitive the suspected offence is. It has been held that in deciding whether there is a realistic prospect of conviction, rather than take a statistical approach the prosecutor (and the same would apply to a

34 *Director's guidance on charging* paras 6.12–6.15.

35 CCP paras 4.1–4.14; see also *Director's guidance on charging* section 5.

36 In *R (Smith) v DPP* [2024] EWHC 2032 (Admin), Fordham J explained the evidential test in the following terms: '. . . the Evidential Stage is satisfied where the prosecutor considers that there is a sufficiency of evidence as to guilt, applying the lower standard. That means asking a question about guilt on the balance of probabilities. It does not involve considering whether a jury could be sure, on the criminal standard . . . The predictive phrase "realistic prospect" of conviction (Code §4.6), when it is used in the particular context of the Code, means "more likely than not". Is it objectively assessed as more likely than not that a criminal court would convict? That is the use of the civil standard, which is different from the criminal standard, as the predictive threshold' (paras 19 and 22).

37 CCP paras 4.6–4.8.

custody officer) should imagine themself to be the fact-finder and ask whether, on balance, the evidence is sufficient to merit a conviction, taking into account what they know about the defence case.[38] Note that in cases where trafficking of human beings is an obvious possibility, the police should make appropriate enquiries which the prosecutor should take into account in deciding whether a person should be charged.[39]

The public interest stage

10.23 This stage is normally only relevant if a prosecutor or custody officer has determined that the evidential stage is satisfied. However, if a prosecutor is satisfied that the broad extent of the criminality has been determined and that they are able to make a fully informed assessment of the public interest and it is clear that the public interest does not require a prosecution, the case should go no further.[40] If the evidential stage is satisfied, a prosecution should usually proceed unless there are public interest factors that outweigh those in favour of prosecution, or the prosecutor or custody officer is satisfied that the public interest may be properly served by offering the offender the opportunity to have the matter dealt with by an out-of-court disposal.[41] In considering whether prosecution is in the public interest, the person making the charge decision should consider the following factors:

- The seriousness of the offence – the more serious the offence, the more likely it is that a prosecution is required.[42]
- The level of culpability of the suspect – the greater the level of culpability, the more likely it is that prosecution is required.[43]
- The circumstances of and the harm caused to the victim – the greater the vulnerability of the victim, the more likely it is that a prosecution is required. This includes where a position of trust or authority exists between the suspect and the victim. The need for prosecution is also more likely if the offence was motivated by any form of discrimination against the victim's ethnic or national origin; gender; disability; age; religion or belief; sexual orientation; or gender identity.[44]
- Whether the suspect was aged under 18 years at the time of the offence – the younger the suspect, the less likely it is that a prosecution is required. When applying this test, age should not be assessed in purely

38 *R (FB) v DPP* [2009] 1 Cr App R 580, DC.

39 See *R v GS* [2018] EWCA Crim 1824 at para 75 for a distillation of the relevant principles. See also *CPS policy for prosecuting cases of human trafficking* (May 2011), available at: www.cps.gov.uk/sites/default/files/documents/publications/policy_for_prosecuting_cases_of_human_trafficking.pdf; and the CPS legal guidance *Modern Slavery and human trafficking: offences and defences, including the section 45 defence* (July 2025), available at: www.cps.gov.uk/legal-guidance/modern-slavery-and-human-trafficking-offences-and-defences-including-section-45.

40 CCP paras 4.4–4.5.

41 CCP paras 4.9–4.10.

42 CCP para 4.14(a); although the public interest may not be served by prosecution even in the case of a serious allegation such as murder (*R (Joseph) v DPP* [2022] EWHC 131 (Admin)).

43 CCP para 4.14(b).

44 CCP para 4.14(c).

chronological terms, and maturity is a factor, even when the chronological age is 18 or over.[45]

- The impact on the community – the greater the impact on the community, the more likely it is that a prosecution is required.
- Whether prosecution is a proportionate response – taking into account the cost to the CPS and to the wider criminal justice system.[46]
- Whether sources of information require protecting.[47]

The threshold test

10.24 Exceptionally, a Crown prosecutor may charge on the basis of the threshold test. The prosecutor must initially determine that the following conditions are satisfied:

(1) there are reasonable grounds to suspect that the person to be charged has committed the offence;
(2) further evidence can be obtained to provide a realistic prospect of conviction;
(3) the seriousness or the circumstances of the case justifies making an immediate charging decision;
(4) there are continuing substantial grounds to object to bail in accordance with the Bail Act (BA) 1976 and in all the circumstances of the case it is proper to do so; and
(5) it is in the public interest to charge the suspect.[48]

For the circumstances in which a custody officer may charge on the basis of the threshold test, see para 10.20 above.

10.25 With regard to the *first condition*, the prosecutor must be satisfied that there is at least a reasonable suspicion that the person to be charged has committed the offence. In doing so, the prosecutor must consider the available evidence and, specifically, whether it is relevant, is capable of being put into a format that would be admissible in court, and whether it would be used in the case. The prosecutor must also consider the impact of any defence or information put forward by the suspect. If so satisfied, the prosecutor must proceed to the *second condition* of the threshold test. This requires that the prosecutor is satisfied that there are reasonable grounds for believing that the continuing investigation will provide further evidence, within a reasonable period of time, so that all the evidence taken together is capable of establishing a realistic prospect of conviction in accordance with the full code test. The further evidence must be identifiable and not merely speculative. In applying the second part of the test, the prosecutor must take into account a range of factors: the nature, extent and admissibility of any likely further evidence and the impact it will have on the case; the charges that all the evidence will support; the reasons why

45 CCP para 4.14(d); and see: *R v Clarke* [2018] EWCA Crim 185; *R v Hobbs* [2018] EWCA Crim 1003; and paras 1.2 and 1.4–1.7 of the Sentencing Council's *Sentencing children and young people: Definitive guideline* (March 2017) for a detailed consideration of the correct approach to maturity, available at: www.sentencingcouncil.org.uk/publications/item/sentencing-children-and-young-people-definitive-guideline.

46 CCP para 4.14(f).

47 CCP para 4.14(g).

48 CCP paras 5.1–5.10. See also *Director's guidance on charging* section 6.

the evidence is not already available; and the time required to obtain the further evidence and whether any consequential delay is reasonable in all the circumstances. The *third condition* requires the prosecutor to assess the seriousness and the circumstances of the case in relation to the alleged offending and the associated risk created by granting bail. The *fourth condition* must be based on a proper risk assessment and must consider whether bail would be suitable if substantial conditions were imposed. The *fifth and final condition* requires the prosecutor to apply the public interest stage of the full code test on the basis of the information available at that time.[49]

10.26 If the prosecutor decides that the threshold test is not satisfied, the suspect cannot be charged. If there is no prospect of the case ever meeting the criteria for the evidential stage, the case must be the subject of no further action. If there are further reasonable lines of enquiry, the police may, subject to the detention time limit, detain the suspect whilst further investigations are carried out, or release them on or without bail.[50] If the prosecutor decides that the threshold test is satisfied, the suspect may be charged, and the material or evidence identified as outstanding recorded in a shared action plan, including an agreed timetable.[51] The full code test must be applied as soon as the anticipated material or evidence is received, and in a Crown Court case, before formal service of the prosecution case.[52] For action to be taken where a suspect is charged by a custody officer on the basis of the threshold test, see para 10.20 above.

Charges that require consent

10.27 The institution of proceedings for certain offences, or for offences in certain circumstances, requires the consent of either the Attorney General or the DPP or, in some cases, some other person such as a relevant government minister. Consent of the Attorney General must be provided by that office-holder. In most cases, consent of the DPP is deemed to have been given if a Crown prosecutor has determined that there is sufficient evidence to charge, identified the relevant offence and notified the police of their decision; although in some cases, CPS policy requires consent to be given by a more senior prosecutor.[53] However, some cases require the personal consent of the DPP, although this may often be delegated to specified prosecutors. In any event, lack of consent does not prevent a person from being charged with such an offence, nor from being remanded in custody or on bail (Prosecution of Offences Act (POA) 1985 s25(2)). The CPS guidance *Consents to prosecute* contains useful information on the timing of consent, and Annexes 1 and 2 of the guidance contain a list of prosecutions requiring consent by the Attorney General or the DPP.[54]

49 CCP paras 5.3–5.10.
50 *Director's guidance on charging* para 6.11.
51 *Director's guidance on charging* para 6.15.
52 *Director's guidance on charging* para 6.15.
53 POA 1985 s1(7); and see *R v Walker* [2016] EWCA Crim 751.
54 Available at: www.cps.gov.uk/legal-guidance/consents-prosecute.

Charging the suspect

Negotiating the charge

10.28 The lawyer should consider whether, and if so how, to negotiate regarding possible charges. Custody officers and Crown prosecutors have broad discretionary powers as to the appropriate course of action, and there is no obligation on them to charge a suspect simply because the evidential stage criteria have been satisfied (CCP para 4.10). There are practical difficulties in negotiating with a Crown prosecutor since, as noted at para 10.3 above, they are usually unwilling to speak to the defence lawyer directly. Where a prosecutor is to make the charge decision, the lawyer should consider asking the relevant police officer to include any written representations in the pre-charge report that the officer must give to the prosecutor.

10.29 In addition to evidential and public interest considerations (see paras 10.22 and 10.23 above), the following provisions of the CCP may be relevant to the representations that may be made.

- Charges should be selected that:
  - reflect the seriousness and extent of the offending supported by the evidence;
  - give the court adequate powers to sentence and impose appropriate post-conviction orders;
  - allow a confiscation order to be made in appropriate cases, where a defendant has benefitted from criminal conduct; and
  - enable the case to be presented in a clear and simple way.[55]
- As the CCP states: 'This means that prosecutors may not always choose or continue with the most serious charge where there is a choice.'[56]
- A prosecutor (or custody officer) should not proceed with more charges than are necessary just to encourage an accused to plead guilty to a few, nor proceed with a more serious charge just to encourage an accused to plead guilty to a less serious one.[57]
- In making a charge decision, consideration should be given to alternatives to prosecution.[58]

However, care must be taken where the lawyer would wish to indicate that their client would admit a lesser offence than that likely to be charged, or would be willing to admit an offence on a certain factual basis, since any communication to this effect would not be privileged and could be adduced at any subsequent trial.[59]

10.30 Negotiation regarding the charging decision is important because the decision made may well affect the police attitude to bail which, in turn, will affect the court's attitude to bail. Furthermore, the emphasis on speed of processing cases once they reach court means that there may be limited scope for negotiation after the charge decision has been taken. In considering what representations to make, the lawyer should take account of:

55 CCP para 6.1.
56 CCP para 6.2.
57 CCP para 6.3.
58 CCP paras 7.1–7.2.
59 *R v Hayes* [2004] EWCA Crim 2844.

(1) **Whether the custody officer or Crown prosecutor may be persuaded to deal with the matter other than by charging the suspect.** Custody officers must take alternatives to prosecution into account in deciding whether to refer a case to a Crown prosecutor or in making a charge decision (Code C NfG 16A). A prosecutor should consider an out-of-court disposal if it is appropriate to the circumstances of the case.[60]

(2) **What charge(s) would be appropriate.** Custody officers and Crown prosecutors have a large degree of discretion in determining what charges are appropriate for any given set of facts, and there are CPS policies and charging guidance in respect of many offences.[61] Factors to consider include:
- the mode of trial implications of a particular charge;
- the possibility of an alleged offence(s) being treated as an offence to be taken into consideration (see para 5.145 above); and
- the fact that a conviction or caution for many (although not all) sexual offences will result in the offender being placed on the sex offender register (see para 10.72 below).

(3) **The sentence implications of particular charges.** The 'dangerous offenders' provisions in Sentencing Act (SA) 2020 Part 10 Chapters 3 and 4 mean that a person aged 18 years or over convicted of certain specified violent, sexual or terrorism offences, and who at the time the offence was committed had been convicted of certain specified offences, or in respect of whom (if sentenced to an extended term) the court would specify at least four years' imprisonment, may be made the subject of an extended sentence. The specified offences are set out in SA 2020 s306 and Sch 18. They are too extensive to set out here but, for example, assault occasioning actual bodily harm (Offences Against the Person Act 1861 s47) is specified, whereas common assault is not, unless it is racially or religiously aggravated. Putting a person in fear of violence under Protection from Harassment Act 1997 s4 is a specified offence, whereas putting a person in fear of violence under Public Order Act 1986 s4 is not. Separate provisions under SA 2020 Part 10 Chapter 7 provide for mandatory custodial sentences for certain offences involving firearms or threats with a weapon or bladed article; and mandatory minimum sentences in respect of specified offences involving a weapon, bladed article or corrosive substance; and certain drugs or domestic burglary offences, where the suspect has previous convictions for similar offences.

The process of charging

10.31 Responsibility for charging a person with a criminal offence rests with the custody officer. If a Crown prosecutor has made the charge decision, they must notify an officer involved in the investigation of the case (PACE s37B(4)). The person to be charged must, if still in police detention, be charged in accordance with the prosecutor's decision. If the person has been released, they must be charged when they return to the police station

60 *Director's guidance on charging* para 8.5; CCP para 7.1.

61 Available via: www.cps.gov.uk/prosecution-guidance.

to answer bail or by means of the written charge and requisition procedure (PACE s37B(6) and (8)).[62]

10.32 The process of charging is normally little more than a formality, although the lawyer should consider the potential for inferences to be drawn under CJPOA 1994 s34(1)(b) (see paras 5.71 and 5.76 above).[63] A person charged at a police station must be cautioned in the following terms (Code C para 16.2):[64]

> You do not have to say anything. But it may harm your defence if you do not mention now something which you later rely on in court. Anything you do say may be given in evidence.

The person must also be given a written notice showing particulars of the offence(s) with which they are charged, including the name of the officer in the case (or warrant number in cases where Code C para 2.6A, Code H para 2.8 or Code I para 2.7 apply), the police station and reference number for the case, and confirmation of the caution. As far as possible, the particulars of the charge must be stated in simple terms, but they must show the precise offence with which the person is charged (Code C para 16.3). If the custody officer has determined that the person requires an interpreter (see para 11.107 below), an interpreter must explain any offence with which the person is charged or for which they are informed they may be prosecuted, and any other information about the offence given to them by or on behalf of the custody officer (Code C para 13.10). In addition, the person must be supplied with a translation of the written notice as soon as is practicable, although the custody officer can authorise the information to be given by an interpreter orally (Code C Annex M paras 2 and 3).

10.33 Before the charging process commences, the lawyer should advise their client about whether they should say anything on being charged and whether to submit a prepared statement (see paras 5.76 and 5.171 above). If a prepared statement is to be submitted, it will normally not be appropriate to say anything further. If a prepared statement is not to be submitted, this will normally be in circumstances where the client has said all that they should say while being questioned, or where it has been decided that they should say nothing at all. In these circumstances, there would be little point in the client saying anything at charge unless there are specific reasons why they should say something orally rather than hand in a prepared statement. It may be appropriate, for example, for the client simply to deny the offence on being charged, although the evidential value of this is limited.

10.34 The lawyer should always discuss with their client whether the lawyer should be present at the time of charge, and if the lawyer is not to be present the client should be clearly advised on what they should do and say at charge. Duty solicitors are under an obligation, where a client is to be

62 Under Criminal Justice Act (CJA) 2003 2003 s29.

63 Note that where a person is charged under the written charge and requisition procedure, inferences may be drawn from 'silence' when they are officially told that they are being reported to the CPS with a view to a written charge (CJPOA 1994 s34(1)(b)).

64 Unless they have not been given the opportunity to consult a solicitor, in which case they must be cautioned in the terms set out in Code C Annex C para 2 (see para 5.69 above).

charged with an offence, to advise them on the implications of the caution at charge, and must consider whether to attend at the time of charge having regard to whether it is possible to give confidential advice by telephone and the possible consequences of not making a statement when being charged.[65] This should be standard practice in own-solicitor cases as well.

Questioning after charge

Questions about the offence charged

10.35 The police may, for a number of reasons, wish to question a person after they have been charged with an offence or informed that they may be prosecuted. If the person submitted a prepared statement, or made an oral statement, at the time of charge, the police may want to question them about it. Where a person has been charged on the basis of the threshold test (see paras 10.20 and 10.24 above), the police may want to interview them following the further investigations they carry out. However, the general rule is that the police are not permitted to interview a person about an offence with which they have been charged or informed that they may be prosecuted for it (Code C para 16.5).[66] This is the case whether the person was charged on the basis of the full code test or the threshold test. The prohibition would seem to extend to preventing an interview about an offence that is closely related to that with which the person has been charged or informed that they may be prosecuted for it.[67] There are three exceptions to the general prohibition on further interviewing, as follows.

10.36 First, if the police wish to bring to the suspect's notice a written statement or interview record of another person, they may do so, but must not invite comment other than to caution the suspect (Code C para 16.4). In most circumstances, the suspect should be advised not to comment unless the content of the statement or interview record changes the basis for the advice originally given to the suspect by their lawyer. In this case, the lawyer should speak to their client in private so that advice can be given on whether to respond.

10.37 Second, a person may be interviewed about an offence with which they have been charged or informed that they may be prosecuted for it if is necessary:

- to prevent or minimise harm or loss to some other person or to the public;

65 SCC Specification 2022 para 9.42(b) (draft SCC Specification 2025 para 9.37(b)).

66 Strictly, Code C para 16.5 prohibits the interview of a 'detainee' after they have been charged. It might be argued that the prohibition does not apply to a person who has been released on bail or produced in court following charge, since the person is no longer in police detention as defined by PACE s118(2). Even if this is correct, the person would not have to co-operate with such questioning, and inferences could not be drawn from 'silence' in response to such questioning.

67 It has been held to be a breach of Code C para 16.5 for a person to be interviewed about an offence of driving while under the influence of alcohol where they had already been informed that they would be charged with the offence of being in charge of a motor vehicle while under the influence of alcohol (*Charles v DPP* [2009] EWHC 3521 (Admin)).

- to clear up an ambiguity in a previous answer or statement; or
- in the interests of justice for the person to have put to them, and to have an opportunity to comment on, information concerning the offence that has come to light since they were charged or told that they may be prosecuted for it (Code C para 16.5).

10.38 Third, where a person has been charged or informed that they may be prosecuted for an offence set out in Counter-Terrorism Act (CTA) 2008 s27, or an offence that appears to the judge to have a terrorist connection, a Crown Court judge can authorise the questioning of the person about the offence (provided certain conditions are satisfied) (CTA 2008 s22; and Code H section 15). Such interviews must be video recorded with sound in accordance with the Code of Practice issued under the CTA 2008.[68]

10.39 Before showing the person charged a written statement or interview record under Code C para 16.4, or before interviewing under Code C para 16.5, they must be cautioned that they do not have to say anything but that anything they do say may be given in evidence. This caution differs from the caution that must normally be given before or at charge[69] because inferences under CJPOA 1994 s34, 36 or 37 cannot be drawn from failure to mention facts after charge. Failure to give the caution as required arguably amounts to a significant and substantial breach, which may result in exclusion under PACE s78 of evidence so obtained. The prohibition on inferences does not apply to post-charge questioning under the CTA 2008, so the normal caution must be given (unless the person has asked for legal advice but is interviewed before receiving it) (CTA 2008 s22(9) and (10); and Code H para 15.9).

10.40 There is no power to detain a person solely for the purpose of post-charge questioning under Code C para 16.4 or 16.5, or under the CTA 2008. Therefore, if the person has been granted bail following charge, the police will only be able to conduct such questioning if the person agrees to remain at, or return to, the police station for this purpose. If the person has not been granted bail, the police may interview under these provisions during the period between charge and production in court.

10.41 If the police indicate their desire to put further questions while the lawyer is present, the lawyer should establish why the police wish to do so, and the nature of the proposed questioning. The client should normally be advised in private before any further interview takes place. Whether the client should be advised to answer further questions will depend on the circumstances (for general principles, see para 5.105 above), although as noted above, inferences under the CJPOA 1994 cannot be drawn from failure to mention a fact, or failure or refusal to account, at this stage (except under the CTA 2008 provisions). If there is a genuine ambiguity in a previous answer or statement, it may well be in the client's interests for this to be clarified, although they should be warned that questioning may

68 See Counter-Terrorism Act 2008 (Code of Practice for the Video Recording with Sound of Post-Charge Questioning) Order 2012 SI No 1793. The code, which is the same as the code for video recording with sound of persons detained under TA 2000 s41, is available at: https://assets.publishing.service.gov.uk/media/5a78f5de40f0b6324769b82d/video-recording-code-of-practice.pdf.

69 See Code C Annex C.

go further than that required to resolve the ambiguity. If they do, the lawyer should intervene to ensure that the questions are kept to those permitted under the Code C provisions, or in CTA 2008 cases, the terms of the judge's authorisation. The lawyer should consider whether it would be more appropriate to submit a prepared statement rather than co-operate with further questioning. If the client has previously admitted the offence in interview, there may be mitigation advantages to providing information that will prevent further loss or that will lead to the recovery of goods. If the reason for the further questioning is the emergence of new information, the lawyer will want to know the nature of such information so that they may advise their client about whether to answer such questions.

10.42 If the police wish to put further questions after the lawyer has left the police station, the usual rules regarding the right to legal advice apply (see para 2.129 above). However, the police may assert that the suspect asked for a further interview following the departure of the lawyer. If true, it would be relatively easy for the police to justify further questions under Code C para 16.5. It has been held that in such circumstances it would have been preferable for the lawyer to have been present, although absence of the lawyer did not amount to a breach of PACE or the codes as they then stood.[70] Under the current Code C para 6.5, not only would the suspect have to be reminded of the right to legal advice, but would also have to be reminded that they can speak to the lawyer on the telephone, and asked why they do not wish to have legal advice if they refuse it (see also Code C paras 16.4(b) and 16.5(b)). In the case of a person detained under the terrorism provisions, there is no explicit requirement in Code H for them to be informed in advance of post-charge questioning of their right to consult a solicitor, although Code H para 15.8 does confirm that the person is entitled to consult a solicitor and that this may not be delayed. In any event, before leaving the police station the lawyer should routinely advise their client of the danger of such interviews, and may consider asking the custody officer to record in the custody record a request to be notified if any further interview is to take place.

Questions about other matters

10.43 The police may wish to interview a suspect about matters other than the offence(s) in respect of which they have been charged or informed that they may be prosecuted. The police may wish to interview about other offences allegedly committed by the suspect, or may be seeking specific or general intelligence. They may even wish to recruit the suspect as an informant.

10.44 The question arises as to whether the police have power to detain the suspect in order to interview for such purposes. A suspect who has been charged and granted bail can, of course, voluntarily agree to remain at the police station. Where the police wish to interview a suspect who does not agree to remain, they may be able to prolong detention by arresting the suspect on suspicion of another offence(s) by virtue of PACE s31 (see para 2.35 above). However, the position is unclear. PACE s31 provides that

70 *R v Williams* (1992) Times, February 6, CA.

the police must arrest a person who is 'at a police station in consequence of [the original] arrest' if the person would be liable to arrest on release. This suggests that they could be arrested after they have been charged in respect of the offence for which they were originally arrested. However, PACE s38 provides that following charge, the custody officer must order the release of the person unless one or more of the conditions for withholding bail applies. It could be argued that this implies that a person should not be arrested and detained in respect of another offence following charge in respect of the original offence. However, since a person granted bail after charge in respect of the original offence could be arrested when they leave the police station,[71] it may be preferable for them to be arrested while at the police station under the provisions of PACE s31 because the detention time limit will run from the relevant time relating to the original arrest (by virtue of PACE s41(4)). In principle, the same argument applies to a person who has been charged but refused bail, although the police may simply seek to interview them during the period between charge and production in court. There is nothing to prevent the police from doing this, although, as noted below, the lawyer may wish to ascertain whether the police are prepared to arrest in respect of the new allegation(s).

10.45 If, after charge, the police say that they wish to interview the suspect about an offence other than that for which they have been charged, the lawyer should consider asking the police whether they intend to arrest by virtue of PACE s31. If the police say that they do not intend to arrest, this is likely to mean that they have insufficient information to amount to reasonable grounds for suspicion. If, alternatively, the police respond by arresting the suspect, the lawyer and client will have a clearer idea of the basis on which the police wish to conduct the interview.

10.46 If the police wish to interview the suspect after charge for intelligence-gathering purposes or in order to determine whether they might act as an informant,[72] arrest under PACE s31 would not be possible. Therefore, the police could only conduct such an interview if the suspect agrees to remain at the police station for this purpose or if, having been charged, bail was denied. In the latter case, an interview could be conducted in the period between charge and production in court.

Questions concerning the proceeds of crime

10.47 Confiscation of the proceeds of crime, together with powers to enquire into and restrain a person's assets and income where it is suspected that they are the proceeds of crime, is governed by the Proceeds of Crime Act

71 Although arguably this would be unlawful if the conditions for arrest were satisfied while the person was in the police station, since the requirement to arrest under PACE s31 is in mandatory terms. However, 'liable to arrest' may not mean simply that there are sufficient grounds for arrest. A police officer may decline to arrest even if there are sufficient grounds, either at all or because the officer wishes to arrest at a later date in order, for example, to give an opportunity to gather further evidence.

72 Note that the recruitment of informants is governed by Regulation of Investigatory Powers Act 2000 Part II and the Covert Human Intelligence Sources Code of Practice 2022, available at: www.gov.uk/government/publications/covert-human-intelligence-sources-code-of-practice-2022.

(POCA) 2002.[73] The National Crime Agency (NCA) has responsibility for recovering unlawfully obtained assets, and the police, His Majesty's Revenue and Customs (HMRC) and the CPS have a statutory duty to co-operate with the agency. The NCA and other agencies have a wide range of powers to investigate, to search and seize, to apply for civil recovery orders, and to tax in relation to the proceeds of crime. Restraint orders, which prohibit a specified person from dealing with any realisable property held by them and enable such property to be seized, may be made by the Crown Court in a number of circumstances. These include where a criminal investigation has been commenced, or criminal proceedings have been started, and there is reasonable cause to believe that the alleged offender has benefited from their criminal conduct. Some powers apply irrespective of whether the person has been convicted of a criminal offence. The Crown Court may order confiscation of the assets of a person convicted of or sentenced for an offence, or committed to the Crown Court for consideration of such an order, where it is satisfied that the person has a 'criminal lifestyle' or in respect of the benefit obtained by the person's 'criminal conduct'. The POCA 2002 also creates a number of money laundering offences.[74]

10.48 The question that arises at the police station is whether the suspect should respond to questions purportedly put under the asset recovery provisions, and designed to obtain information about their financial resources. Code C para 11.6 provides that the conditions under that paragraph which determine when interviewing should cease (see para 7.70 above) do not prevent suspects being invited to complete a formal question-and-answer record under the proceeds of crime legislation after the interview concerning the alleged offence has concluded. Whether such questioning takes place before or after charge, a significant issue is whether information supplied by the suspect for confiscation purposes could be used as evidence in respect of the offence charged or to be charged. There is limited protection of information supplied by a person (preventing its use in criminal proceedings against them) under POCA 2002 s18 and Sch 6, but this is unlikely to apply to questioning at the police station stage. Therefore, it should be assumed that any information supplied by the suspect in respect of the proceeds of crime, whether or not it is supplied to officers unconnected with the investigation of the offence, may be used as evidence in respect of the offence itself. For this reason, it will normally not be in the suspect's interests to provide such information while at the police station. A refusal would not have adverse evidential consequences in respect of the criminal proceedings, and it is not an offence to fail to provide such information. It may be advisable, however,

73 It replaced the confiscation provisions of the CJA 1988 and Drug Trafficking Act 1994, although these Acts are still mentioned in Code C para 11.6. CPS guidance on proceeds of crime and asset recovery (January 2025) is available at: www.cps.gov.uk/legal-guidance/proceeds-crime.

74 Note that a number of these offences potentially affect defence lawyers, including failure to disclose information about money laundering activities of a client and tipping-off. See the Law Society, *Anti-money laundering guidance for the legal sector* (April 2025), available at: www.lawsociety.org.uk/topics/anti-money-laundering/anti-money-laundering-guidance.

for the suspect to indicate that they will consider the matter further once released from detention, when they have had the opportunity to take full legal advice on the matter.

Written charge and requisition

10.49 As an alternative to charging at the police station, the suspect may be released under PACE s37(7)(a)(i) (on bail) or s37(7)(b) (without bail) and informed that they may be prosecuted. If a decision is subsequently made to charge the suspect, this may be done by means of a written charge and requisition (CJA 2003 s29). The written charge and requisition procedure replaced the summons procedure in respect of criminal proceedings commenced by a 'relevant prosecutor', which includes the police and the CPS. A written charge is issued directly by the police or the CPS, and is accompanied by either a requisition or a single justice procedure notice. A requisition requires the accused to appear before a magistrates' court to answer the written charge. A single justice procedure notice, which may only be issued to an adult in respect of a summary-only offence that is not punishable with imprisonment, requires the accused to notify the relevant magistrates' court whether they wish to plead guilty or not guilty and, if the former, whether they wish to be dealt with under the single justice on the papers procedure (that is, under Magistrates' Courts Act (MCA) 1980 s16A). In relation to certain specified offences, a prosecutor may offer the automatic online conviction option (CJA 2003 s29(2C)). The written charge and requisition, or written charge and single justice procedure notice, must be served on the accused, and a copy must be served on the court named in the requisition or the designated officer specified in the notice (CJA 2003 s29(3) and (3A)).

10.50 If a client is released with a view to a written charge, they should be advised that if a written charge and requisition is subsequently served on them, they will be under a duty to attend court on the date specified in the requisition. If they are served with a written charge and single justice procedure notice, they will be under a duty to respond to it as required. Failure to do so would not amount to an offence, but could result in the court issuing a warrant for their arrest. The client should also be advised to contact the lawyer if and when a written charge is served on them so that initial instructions can be taken and, if appropriate, an application for legal aid made.

10.51 The general prohibition on further questioning after charge also applies where the suspect has been informed that they may be prosecuted for the offence (see para 10.35 above). The client should be advised that if, nevertheless, the police subsequently seek to question them further, they should ask to speak to the lawyer before answering any such questions.

Alternatives to charging

Introduction

10.52 The range of alternatives to charging a person, in circumstances where the relevant conditions for charge are satisfied (see para 10.21 above), has become more complex over recent years. There is a rough hierarchy of disposals which, in ascending order of seriousness, include:

- community resolution;
- simple cautions for adult offenders and youth cautions for youth offenders; and
- conditional cautions for adult and youth offenders.

Police, Crime, Sentencing and Courts Act (PCSCA) 2022 Part 6 contains provisions that are intended to replace adult simple and conditional cautions with diversionary and community cautions. This Part of the 2022 Act had not been implemented as at 30 June 2025, and it is not known whether or when it will be brought into force. However, adult simple cautions are not currently governed by statute, and it appears that some police forces have, in anticipation of implementation of the new provisions, already adopted the two-tier structure embodied in the Act.[75] Therefore, the sections on simple and conditional cautions under the existing regulatory regime are followed by a section on the provisions of the PCSCA 2022.

10.53 Other forms of disposal include deferred prosecution, protection notices, penalty notices for disorder. The police may also, of course, decide that there should be no further action (NFA).

10.54 Police forces often have their own policies on use of the various alternatives to prosecution, and police officers often do not fully understand the range of disposals, the relevant criteria or their force policies.[76] It is important, therefore, for the defence lawyer to know what alternatives are available in the circumstances of any particular case. This section will cover the following alternatives to charging:

- community resolution;
- 'simple' cautions for adults;[77]
- conditional cautions for adults;
- diversionary and community cautions (as provided for by PCSCA 2022 Part 6, but not (yet) in force);
- deferred prosecution;
- community protection notices;
- domestic violence and domestic abuse notices;
- penalty notices for disorder; and
- no further action.

The section concludes with release without charge. For the alternatives to charging available for children, see chapter 11 below.

75 See Ministry of Justice, *Police Use of Out of Court Disposals to support adults with health vulnerabilities* (2024), available at: www.gov.uk/government/publications/police-use-of-oocds-to-support-adults-with-health-vulnerabilities.

76 A joint report by HMIC and HMCPSI in 2011 found that one-third of out-of-court disposals examined did not comply with the relevant criteria. See *HMCPSI Inspection: Exercising discretion, the gateway to justice* (June 2011), available at: https://hmicfrs.justiceinspectorates.gov.uk/publications/exercising-discretion-the-gateway-to-justice.

77 Youth cautions and youth conditional cautions are dealt with in chapter 11 below.

Community resolution

10.55 Guidance on community resolution (CR Guidance) is published by the National Police Chiefs' Council (NPCC),[78] although each police force is able to develop its own policy. The CR Guidance states that community resolution, which may be used in relation to both adults and children, is intended for use in respect of 'low level crime' where:

- a case is capable of proof;
- an offender has been identified; and
- there is an acceptance of responsibility or admission of guilt (CR Guidance para 1.1).

Although the guidance uses the expression 'capable of proof', it seems clear that this means that the available evidence satisfies the evidential stage criteria of the full code test (CR Guidance para 2.1; and see para 10.22 above). However, the CR Guidance also states that 'acceptance of responsibility' does not mean that the suspect must have admitted the offence in a PACE interview, but there must be evidence (written or otherwise) 'that the suspect accepts the facts of the case and their responsibility for them or that they accept their actions contributed to the offence' (CR Guidance para 2.2). Care should be taken in advising on community resolution since the latter suggests a lower standard than the evidential stage of the full code test, and if the suspect does not agree to a community resolution, the police may not have sufficient evidence to charge. For example, if a suspect accepts that what they did contributed to an offence being committed, that does not necessarily mean that they had the necessary mens rea. Whilst their actions may have contributed to the offence, they may not have had the necessary intention or been reckless.

10.56 There is no definition of 'low level crime', but the CR Guidance states that account should be taken of the relevant gravity matrix, and that community resolution should not be used in respect of an indictable-only offence, intimate partner domestic abuse or other offences as defined by force policy. Community resolution should only be used in respect of hate crime or non-intimate domestic abuse in exceptional circumstances, and where approved by an inspector (CR Guidance para 2.3). Although community resolution is not prohibited where a suspect has previous convictions, offending within the previous 12 months may make community resolution inappropriate; and in the case of a child suspect, guidance should be sought from a sergeant and/or referral made to a youth justice service (CR Guidance para 2.1).

10.57 It is for the police to decide what intervention is required for a community resolution, although any identifiable victim should be consulted, and the suspect must consent (CR Guidance para 2.1). Intervention may be directed at rehabilitation or reparation, and may range from a written or personal apology to some form of restorative justice (CR Guidance para 2.4).

78 *Community Resolutions (CR) Guidance 2022*, available at: https://justiceinnovation.org/sites/default/files/media/document/2022/npcc_community_resolution_guidance_2022.pdf. See also College of Policing, *Authorised Professional Practice: Prosecution and case management: Possible justice outcomes following investigation*, available at: www.college.police.uk/app/prosecution-and-case-management/possible-justice-outcomes-following-investigation.

'Simple' cautions

Overview

10.58 Unless and until PCSCA 2022 Part 6 is brought into force (see para 10.95 below), there are two forms of caution for adults: 'simple' cautions (sometimes referred to as police cautions, dealt with here); and conditional cautions (see para 10.77 below). Simple cautions are only available in respect of persons aged at least 18 years. Suspects under the age of 18 may be dealt with by way of a youth caution (see para 11.44 below). Unlike conditional cautions, simple cautions are non-statutory and are currently governed by Ministry of Justice (MoJ) guidance, *Simple cautions for adult offenders*.[79] However, simple cautions are subject to statutory restrictions under Criminal Justice and Courts Act (CJCA) 2015 ss17 and 18. In addition, the police can give cannabis and khat warnings, which are not governed by the MoJ guidance or the statutory restrictions but by individual police force policy and guidance.[80] The various conditions and restrictions, and provisions on decision-making, in respect of simple cautions are set out below.

Decision-making and restrictions

10.59 Generally, the decision whether to offer a simple caution is for the police, and an officer who considers that a caution should be offered should refer the matter to an officer of at least the rank of sergeant who is not involved in the investigation for approval (MoJ guidance paras 18 and 61). However, the general approach is subject to a number of exceptions and variations.

- If a case is referred for a charge decision to a Crown prosecutor, whether or not this is required by the *Director's guidance on charging*, the prosecutor can direct the police to offer a caution. A prosecutor may also direct that a caution be offered when reviewing a case where a person has been charged by the police with a summary-only or either-way offence.[81]

79 The most recent version was issued in April 2015, available at: www.gov.uk/government/uploads/system/uploads/attachment_data/file/416068/cautions-guidance-2015.pdf. See also PACE s37B(6) and (7); CCP paras 7.1–7.2; the *Director's guidance on charging* section 8; and College of Policing, *Authorised Professional Practice: Prosecution and case management: Possible justice outcomes following investigation*, available at: www.app.college.police.uk/app-content/prosecution-and-case-management/justice-outcomes/#adult-caution-operational-considerations.

80 See College of Policing, *Authorised Professional Practice: Prosecution and case management: Possible justice outcomes following investigation* para 3.3 (Cannabis warning), available at: www.college.police.uk/app/prosecution-and-case-management/possible-justice-outcomes-following-investigation.

81 PACE s37B(6); MoJ Guidance paras 15 and 17. The *Director's guidance on charging* para 8.5 states that where a case is referred to a Crown prosecutor for a charging decision, they may decide that it is appropriate for an out-of-court disposal. However, the prosecutor has a statutory duty in such cases to consider whether a caution would be an appropriate disposal (PACE s37B(3)), and the effect of section 37B(6) is that the prosecutor can direct that a caution be offered to the suspect. For circumstances where a prosecutor directs that a caution be offered but the suspect refuses consent, see para 10.66 below.

- A caution cannot be offered in respect of an either-way offence that has been specified by the secretary of state unless an officer of at least the rank of inspector determines that there are exceptional circumstances relating to the offender or the offence (CJCA 2015 s17(3); MoJ guidance para 33).
- A caution cannot be offered in respect of an indictable-only offence unless a police officer of at least the rank of superintendent determines that there are exceptional circumstances relating to the offender or the offence, and a Crown prosecutor agrees that a caution should be given (CJCA 2015 s17(2); MoJ guidance para 32).
- A caution cannot be offered in respect of a summary-only offence or an either-way offence that has not been specified by the secretary of state if, in the two years before the offence was committed, the person has been convicted of, or cautioned for, a similar offence, unless a police officer of at least the rank of inspector determines that there are exceptional circumstances relating to the offender, the present offence or the previous offence (CJCA 2015 s17(4); MoJ guidance para 35). An offender is to be treated as having been cautioned for a previous offence if they were given a simple caution, a conditional caution, a youth caution or a youth conditional caution (MoJ guidance para 36). For repeat offending not covered by the statutory restrictions, see para 10.63 below.

10.60 The offences specified for the purposes of the CJCA 2015 are set out in Schedule 1 to the Criminal Justice and Courts Act 2015 (Simple Cautions) (Specification of Either-Way Offences) Order 2015[82] and include:[83]

- offensive weapon and bladed article offences;
- carrying a firearm in a public place;
- child cruelty;
- sexual offences against children (including those relating to child prostitution and pornography);
- sex trafficking offences;
- indecent and pornographic images of children; and
- importing, exporting, producing, supplying and possessing with intent to supply to another class A drugs (MoJ guidance para 34).

10.61 In determining whether there are 'exceptional circumstances' for the purposes of CJCA 2015 s17(2), (3) and (4), a decision-maker must be satisfied that, were the offender to be convicted of the offence, the court would be unlikely to impose a custodial sentence (whether immediate or suspended) or a high-level community order (CJCA 2015 s17(5) and (6); MoJ guidance para 37). The decision-maker must take into account the following non-exhaustive list of factors (MoJ guidance para 38):

- the level of culpability of the offender in committing the offence;
- any harm that the offence caused, was intended to cause or might foreseeably have caused;
- the offender's antecedents;
- any aggravating factors;

82 SI No 790.

83 The offences specified are also set out in MoJ Guidance Annex B.

- any mitigating factors;
- the overall justice of the case and whether the circumstances require it to be dealt with by way of prosecution (for example, for the protection of the public); and
- the range of sentences appropriate to the facts of the case.

10.62 In determining whether an offence is similar for the purposes of CJCA 2015 s17(4), the decision-maker must treat a previous offence as being similar to the present offence if it was of the same description or of a similar nature – for example, they were both of a sexual nature, they both involved violence against the person, they both involved dishonesty by the offender, etc. Two offences are of the same description as each other if the statement of the offence in a written charge or indictment would, in each case, be in the same terms (MoJ guidance para 39).

10.63 Subject to the restrictions on offering a caution to a repeat offender under CJCA 2015 s17(4), a caution may be appropriate where there has been a sufficient lapse of time (at least two years) following a previous conviction or out-of-court disposal for the same or a similar type of offence to demonstrate that it had a deterrent effect, and:

- the current offence is low level;
- the offender has previously complied with another form of out-of-court disposal; or
- giving a simple caution is likely to be the best outcome for the victim and the offender (MoJ guidance para 52).

Admission of guilt

10.64 A caution must not be offered to a person who has not made a clear and reliable admission (MoJ guidance paras 20–23).[84] The person making a decision about offering a caution must take particular care if there is any doubt about the mental state or capacity of the offender. An admission may be made verbally or in writing, and during or outside the context of a formal interview, but the method for obtaining and recording it must be compliant with the provisions of PACE and the Codes of Practice (see paras 5.115 and 7.8 above). A caution must not be offered in order to secure an admission, which means, in practice, that an admission must be made before an indication is given that a caution may be offered (but see para 10.66 below).[85]

Application of the full code test

10.65 There must be sufficient evidence to provide a realistic prospect of conviction in respect of the offence concerned, and it must be in the public interest to offer a caution, in accordance with the CCP full code test (MoJ guidance paras 24–26; and see paras 10.21–10.23 above). In considering aggravating and mitigating factors, police officers must use the National

84 There has been a number of cases, particularly involving sexual offences, where the courts have subsequently decided that an admission which resulted in a caution was not 'clear and reliable'. See para 10.64 below.

85 MoJ Guidance para 21; and see *R (R) v Durham Constabulary* [2002] EWHC 2486 (Admin).

Decision Model and the College of Policing Gravity Factors Matrix (MoJ guidance para 29).[86]

Consent of the suspect

10.66 A simple caution cannot be imposed on an adult who refuses to accept it. The person must not be induced to accept a caution in any way and must not be pressed to make an instant decision on whether to accept it (MoJ guidance para 77). If a Crown prosecutor directs the police to offer a caution and this proves not to be possible (for example, because the suspect refuses to accept it), the suspect must instead be charged with the offence (PACE s37B(6) and (7)). Despite the mandatory wording of PACE s37B(7), it has been held that there remains a discretion not to prosecute where a suspect refuses to accept a caution.[87]

Legal advice and disclosure

10.67 Before administering a caution, the police must ensure that the suspect has had the opportunity of receiving free and independent legal advice in relation to the offence (MOJ guidance para 78). The MoJ guidance goes on to state that the right to legal advice set out in PACE must be adhered to. Since PACE provides that the right to consult a solicitor applies from the outset of detention in police custody, this must mean that before administering a caution, the suspect must be reminded of their right to legal advice even if they have previously waived their right to consult a solicitor.

10.68 The MoJ guidance para 78 also states that the suspect must be informed of the evidence against them and the decision to offer a caution. In relation to the former, the MoJ guidance states that the suspect and their lawyer are entitled to seek and have disclosure of the evidence before the suspect agrees to accept a caution. Since a suspect, and their lawyer, are required to have been given sufficient information to enable the suspect to understand the nature of the suspected offence and why they are suspected of committing it before being interviewed (Code C para 11.1A; and see para 4.27 above), this suggests that the information about the evidence to be given before a suspect considers whether to accept a caution should be more extensive than that provided prior to the police interview. However, it has been held that the disclosure obligation does not extend to a requirement to disclose relevant documents that are in the possession of the police.[88]

Views of the victim

10.69 The police are required, where appropriate and possible, to establish and take into account the views of the victim about the offence and the proposed

86 See *Caetano v Commissioner of Police of the Metropolis* [2013] EWHC 375 (Admin), in which it was held that despite there being a clear and reliable admission, the police should have taken no further action rather than offer a caution.

87 *Caetano v Commissioner of Police of the Metropolis* [2013] EWHC 375 (Admin).

88 *R (Manser) v Commissioner of Police of the Metropolis* [2015] EWHC 3642 (Admin). For a critical comment on this decision, see E Cape, 'Police station: update' April 2016 *Legal Action* 16.

method of disposal, and the nature of any harm or loss caused by the offence and its significance to the victim (MoJ guidance para 54). However, while the views of the victim are important, they are not conclusive (MoJ guidance para 56), and the fact that a victim does not want any action taken against the offender does not mean that the police should automatically take no further action (MoJ guidance para 57).

Specific offence types

10.70 The MoJ guidance provides specific guidance on interpreting these provisions in respect of a number of offence types.

- **Domestic violence and abuse.** The guidance encourages the police to take a 'positive action' approach, which entails considering the incident in its entirety, and seeking evidence that does not rely entirely on the complainant's statement. If the evidence stage of the full code test is satisfied, a simple caution will rarely be appropriate. However, a caution may be appropriate if the victim does not support a prosecution and the available evidence would only support charging a very minor offence (paras 40–41).
- **Stalking and harassment (racial or otherwise).** In deciding whether to offer a simple caution, officers should take into account two additional factors. First, a caution may render all conduct on which the caution is based inadmissible as evidence of a course of conduct should this continue subsequently. Second, since a restraining order may only be issued by a court, the only way of protecting a victim against future conduct would be by seeking an anti-harassment injunction from a civil court. In cases of stalking or aggravated harassment, a prosecution should be pursued wherever possible. Therefore, the views of the victim should be fully considered, and a simple caution should only be offered where the police are confident that the stalking or harassment will not continue, and a harassment warning has not previously been issued (paras 42–43).
- **Multiple offences and mixed disposals.** The decision-maker should consider the totality of the offending in determining whether a caution is appropriate. It is possible to use different disposals where a person has committed multiple but unrelated offences as part of the same incident. For example, if a person arrested for being drunk and disorderly is found to be carrying a number of car keys and admits their intention to steal from cars, they may be given a simple caution for going equipped to steal and issued with a penalty notice for the drunk and disorderly offence (paras 44–46).
- **Group offences.** Where a number of people are involved in committing an offence, while consistency of treatment is an important consideration, the extent of involvement of each person and their individual circumstances may mean that one or more could be offered a police caution whereas others are not (para 47).
- **Offences committed by persons subject to bail and/or court orders.** It is generally not appropriate to offer a caution where the person was on police or court bail or subject to a court order at the time that the offence was committed (para 48).

- **Offences committed by serving prisoners and offenders on licence.** A caution will rarely be appropriate in relation to an offence committed by a serving prisoner or a person who is subject to prison recall (para 49).

Consequences of accepting a simple caution

10.71 A caution should be administered by a custody officer or other suitably trained person to whom authority to administer cautions has been delegated (MoJ guidance para 79). Before administering a caution, the officer must ensure that the offender understands that they do not have to make an immediate decision, that they have a right to legal advice, and the effect of the caution and the implications of accepting it (MoJ guidance para 80).[89] The person must be asked to sign the simple caution form, which sets out that they have made an admission of guilt in respect of the relevant offence(s), their consent to receiving the caution and the implications of accepting it. They should be given a copy of the form to take away with them (MoJ guidance para 82).

10.72 Although a caution is not a criminal conviction, it forms part of the person's criminal record, and if it is imposed for a recordable offence it will be entered on the Police National Computer (MoJ guidance paras 64–68). It may, therefore, be cited in any subsequent court proceedings, may be used as evidence of previous misconduct where this is permitted (see para 5.173 above),[90] and may also prevent a further caution being offered in the future (see para 10.59 above). Fingerprints and other identification data can be taken and retained if the caution is for a recordable offence (see paras 6.4 and 6.57 above). In the case of a sexual offence specified in SOA 2003 Sch 3, the offender is a 'relevant offender' for the purposes of the notification and registration requirements of the Act, and will be placed on the sex offenders register for two years (MoJ guidance para 72). A simple caution given in respect of certain offences may lead to the offender being included in lists maintained by the Disclosure and Barring Service relating to those barred from working with children and vulnerable groups (MoJ guidance para 69).[91] The fact that a caution has been administered does not prevent prosecution if new evidence comes to light suggesting that the offence(s) committed are more serious than was apparent at the time the decision to caution was made, and does not prevent a civil action or a private prosecution brought by the victim (although rare in practice) (MoJ guidance para 74; and see paras 10.133

89 In *R (Stratton) v Chief Constable of Thames Valley* [2013] EWHC 1561 (Admin), a caution was quashed where the person cautioned had not been fully informed of the consequences.

90 In *R v Cambridge* [2011] EWCA Crim 2009, it was held that evidence of a previous caution had rightly been admitted to rebut evidence of innocent association. A defendant may challenge evidence of previous misconduct based on a caution by adducing evidence to show that they were not guilty of an offence, but this is unlikely to be successful if the defendant was in receipt of legal advice when they accepted the caution (*R v Olu, Wilson and Brooks* [2010] EWCA Crim 2975).

91 Note that the scheme for disclosure of convictions and cautions has been held to be incompatible with European Convention on Human Rights (ECHR) Article 8 (*R (P) v Secretary of State for Justice* [2016] EWHC 89 (Admin); *R (G) v Chief Constable of Surrey* [2016] EWHC 295 (Admin)).

and 10.135 below).[92] Furthermore, a simple caution may have implications for obtaining an entry visa to certain countries (MoJ guidance para 76). Simple cautions are covered by the Rehabilitation of Offenders Act 1974, and are immediately spent when administered. However, while this means that the person will not normally have to disclose the caution if asked, it does not apply if they are seeking work in an occupation listed in the exceptions order to the 1974 Act (MoJ guidance para 70).

Advising on simple cautions

10.73 A number of issues arise for the lawyer in respect of simple cautions, many of which are also relevant to other out-of-court disposals. First, the possibility of a caution may affect the advice to be given about whether the client should answer questions in interview and, in particular, whether they should make admissions (see para 5.142 above). This needs to be approached with care. It was held in *R (R) v Durham Constabulary*[93] that the police must not induce an admission by offering a caution, and this reflected in the MoJ guidance (see para 10.64 above). The lawyer should avoid doing what the police are prohibited from doing. However, the lawyer is likely to know whether a caution is a potential disposal and may have already have canvassed the possibility with the officer in the case. Therefore, lawyers should take instructions from their client regarding the alleged offence, and consider whether the criteria for a caution are satisfied before discussing with them the possibility of a caution. Particular attention should be paid to whether the instructions from the client amount to a 'clear and reliable' admission of guilt, and to what other evidence of guilt the police have.[94] In addition, the client should be advised that if they admit the offence, the police may proceed to charge rather than caution and the admission may then be used as part of the prosecution case.

10.74 Second, in circumstances where the police have not suggested that they are considering a caution, the lawyer should consider whether to try to persuade them to caution rather than charge. This will only be appropriate where the client has admitted or is willing to admit the offence, and where the lawyer is satisfied that the other conditions for a caution are satisfied, and is satisfied that the client understands the consequences of a caution. Failure to persuade the police to caution is not necessarily the end of the matter since, if the case is referred to a Crown prosecutor to make a charge decision or when a case is reviewed following charge, the prosecutor has an independent duty to consider whether a caution should be offered (see para 10.59 above).

10.75 Third, in circumstances where the police are offering a caution, the client will need advice on whether to consent. Again, the lawyer should

92 See also, *R (Lowden) v Gateshead Magistrates' Court* [2016] EWHC 3536 (Admin).

93 [2005] UKHL 21.

94 There has been a number of appeals, particularly in respect of sexual offences, where a caution (or reprimand or warning) was accepted where there was no clear and reliable admission (see, for example, *R (Wyman) v Chief Constable of Hampshire* [2006] EWHC 1904 (Admin)), or where there was insufficient evidence to give a realistic prospect of conviction (see, for example, *R (Mohammed) v Chief Constable of the West Midlands* [2010] EWHC 1228 (Admin)).

take into account whether their client has admitted or is willing to admit the offence, whether the other conditions for a caution have been met and whether the client understands the consequences of a caution. The lawyer should also consider any danger that, having secured an admission, the police may change their mind and proceed to charge.[95] Most importantly, if the client has instructed the lawyer that they are not guilty, the lawyer should try to persuade them not to admit to the offence simply because a caution appears to be an easy way out. Note that where the police have interviewed the client in the absence of the lawyer, and the lawyer is asked to advise the client on whether they should accept a caution, the police should disclose the interview to the lawyer in order to enable the lawyer to give such advice.[96]

10.76 The decision regarding a caution is often not an easy one, either for the suspect or the lawyer, for although theoretically there may not be a realistic prospect of conviction, regard must be had to the possibility of a court convicting on less than convincing evidence. In any event, the lawyer should emphasise to the client the potential adverse consequences of accepting a caution (see para 10.71 above). Care is also needed because of the advantages to the police of securing a caution in circumstances where, in the absence of an admission, they do not have sufficient evidence to provide a realistic prospect of conviction. Offering a caution may mean that they get some kind of 'result', whereas if they cannot obtain an admission they may simply not have enough evidence to proceed at all. Moreover, if the officer in the case 'offers' a caution, that officer does not have the power to decide whether a caution or prosecution should follow (see para 10.59 above). The lawyer should, therefore, seek confirmation from the appropriate officer before giving advice to the client in these circumstances.[97]

Conditional cautions

Overview

10.77 Conditional cautions for those aged 18 years or over are governed by CJA 2003 Part 3 and the *Code of practice for adult conditional cautions* ('the Conditional Cautioning Code') issued under CJA 2003 s25.[98] In addition, the DPP has issued the *Director's guidance on adult conditional cautions*

95 Although the danger of this is ameliorated by the decision in the *Durham Constabulary* case, considered at para 10.64 above.

96 *DPP v Ara* [2001] EWHC Admin 493.

97 It was held in *Omar v Chief Constable of Bedfordshire* [2002] EWHC 3060 (Admin) that prosecution for an offence for which a person had been cautioned would not be an abuse of process provided that they had not been induced to make an admission and that they had not been expressly told that they would not be prosecuted. In *Jones v Whalley* [2005] EWHC 931 (Admin), a similar decision was made in respect of a private prosecution. See paras 10.133 and 10.135 below.

98 The current code was brought into force by the Criminal Justice Act 2003 (Conditional Cautions: Code of Practice) Order 2013 SI No 801. The code is available at: https://assets.publishing.service.gov.uk/media/5a7c73ae40f0b626628ac289/9780108512162.pdf.

under powers granted by PACE s37A.[99] As well as having a statutory basis, conditional cautions differ from simple cautions in that they may require the offender to engage in some kind of activity and/or pay a sum of money, and breach can result in the offender being prosecuted for the original offence. Where a person has been drug-tested under PACE s63B, information from the sample can be used for the purpose of informing a decision about the imposition of a conditional caution (see para 6.82 above).

Criteria for a conditional caution

10.78 A conditional caution may be imposed on a person aged 18 or over (see para 11.56 below for those under 18 years). In order for a conditional caution to be imposed, five requirements must be satisfied (CJA 2003 ss22(1) and 23):

(1) The *authorised person* has evidence that the offender has committed an offence.
(2) The *relevant prosecutor or authorised person* decides there is sufficient evidence to charge and that a conditional caution should be given. The prosecutor must apply the evidential and public interest stages of the full code test (see Conditional Cautioning Code paras 2.3–2.8; and para 10.21 above).
(3) The offender admits the offence to the *authorised person*. The Conditional Cautioning Code states that a decision-maker must not offer a conditional caution in order to secure an admission (para 2.4). Following the case-law on similar provisions relating to simple cautions, an admission must be clear and reliable, and must not be induced by an offer made by any police officer (see para 10.64 above).
(4) The *authorised person* explains the effects of the conditional caution to the offender and warns the offender that failure to comply with any of the conditions renders them liable to being prosecuted for the original offence.
(5) The offender signs a document that contains details of the offence; an admission that they committed it; their consent to the conditional caution; and the conditions that are attached to the caution.

An *authorised person* is a police officer, a designated civilian or a person authorised for this purpose by the relevant prosecutor (CJA 2003 s22(4)). A *relevant prosecutor* means the Attorney General, Director of the Serious Fraud Office, DPP, secretary of state or a person specified in an order made by the secretary of state (CJA 2003 s27). Where the police consider that a conditional caution is suitable in respect of an indictable-only offence, the case must be referred to a Crown prosecutor (*Director's guidance on adult conditional cautions* para 6). Where a person has been charged with an offence, a Crown prosecutor may direct the police to give a conditional caution instead where the prosecutor, on reviewing the case, decides

99 July 2025, available at: www.cps.gov.uk/legal-guidance/conditional-cautioning-adults-dpp-guidance. See also College of Policing, *Authorised Professional Practice: Prosecution and case management: Possible justice outcomes following investigation*, available at: www.college.police.uk/app/prosecution-and-case-management/possible-justice-outcomes-following-investigation.

that a conditional caution would be more appropriate.[100] The decision to offer a conditional caution for an indictable-only offence, an either-way offence routinely dealt with at the Crown Court, or an offence likely to attract a high level community order or sentence of imprisonment, may only be taken in exceptional circumstances where the decision-maker is able to conclude that the public interest does not require the immediate prosecution of the offender and that if it took place a court would not impose a period of imprisonment or high level community order (*Director's guidance on adult conditional cautions* para 14.1). In assessing whether exceptional circumstances exist, the decision-maker must have regard to the factors set out in the *Director's guidance on adult conditional cautions* para 14.3.

What conditions can be imposed?

10.79 Any condition can be imposed provided it has the purpose of (CJA 2003 s22(3)):

- facilitating the rehabilitation of the offender;
- ensuring that the offender makes reparation for the offence; and/or
- punishing the offender.

Conditions directed at rehabilitation may include a requirement to take part in a drug or alcohol misuse programme, or to take part in a scheme tackling other addictions or personal problems, such as gambling or debt management.[101] Reparative conditions could include those that require apologising, repairing or otherwise making good any damage caused, provided that this is acceptable to the victim; it could also require financial compensation to be paid (which is not limited to offences in respect of which a financial penalty can be imposed). Where the offending has resulted in damage to community property, reparation may take the form of unpaid work to repair that damage or of a payment to an appropriate local charitable or community fund.[102] The only punitive condition that can be imposed is a financial penalty, which may be imposed only where the conditional caution is imposed in respect of an offence specified in, and subject to a maximum set out in, an order of the secretary of state.[103] Conditions that impose restrictions on the offender – such as a prohibition on contacting individuals, visiting certain locations or participating in particular activities – can be used provided that they contribute towards rehabilitation, reparation or punishment, or the aims of a foreign offender condition.[104]

10.80 Conditions must be appropriate, proportionate and achievable.[105] Punitive conditions should only be used where there are no appropriate

100 Conditional Cautioning Code para 2.10.
101 Conditional Cautioning Code para 2.15.
102 Conditional Cautioning Code para 2.16.
103 See Criminal Justice Act 2003 (Conditional Cautions: Financial Penalties) Order 2013 SI No 615. In fact, all offences are specified for this purpose, and the maximum penalties are £50 (summary-only offences), £100 (either-way offences) and £150 (indictable-only offences).
104 Conditional Cautioning Code para 2.33.
105 Conditional Cautioning Code para 2.21.

reparative or rehabilitative conditions, or where such conditions would not provide a proportionate response to the offending behaviour.[106] Offenders must be able to complete the conditions satisfactorily within a reasonable time. In the case of cautions imposed for a summary-only offence, this should be within 16 weeks. This is also the normal period for completion in the case of either-way or indictable-only offences, although it may be extended to 20 weeks in exceptional cases.[107]

10.81 There are special rules, guidance or principles that apply to conditional cautions in relation to:

- foreign offenders;
- sobriety requirements; and
- domestic abuse.

10.82 Where a conditional caution is given to a relevant *foreign offender*, conditions can be attached that have the objective of bringing about the departure of the offender and/or ensuring that they do not return to the UK for a specified period of time (CJA 2003 s22(3D)–(3G)). A relevant foreign offender is an offender directions for whose removal have been, or may be, given under Immigration Act (IA) 1971 Sch 2 or Immigration and Asylum Act 1999 s10, or against whom a deportation order under IA 1971 s5 is in force. See further the Conditional Cautioning Code paras 2.18–2.20, 2.24, 2.32 and 2.51; and the *Director's guidance on adult conditional cautions* para 15.2. Note that a foreign offender condition cannot be used where there are reasonable grounds for believing that the offence is connected to human trafficking, whether the offender is either a victim or perpetrator, or where the offender has made an asylum or human rights claim to remain in the UK and that claim is outstanding (Conditional Cautioning Code para 2.20).

10.83 The Home Office has issued guidance regarding the use of conditional cautions with *sobriety requirements*.[108] A conditional caution with sobriety conditions can be offered where the following conditions are satisfied:

- the offence is one for which a conditional caution can be offered;
- the offender was under the influence of alcohol at the time the offence was committed;
- the offender has admitted the offence; and
- the offender agrees to accept a conditional caution with sobriety requirements.[109]

Where these conditions are satisfied, an offender should be offered the following conditions:

- to completely abstain from drinking alcohol for a specified period on the days when they are likely to offend as a result of drinking alcohol;
- to regularly attend a suitable venue for sobriety compliance testing; and
- not to reoffend.

106 Conditional Cautioning Code para 2.25.

107 Conditional Cautioning Code para 2.31.

108 *Using conditional cautions with sobriety requirements* (November 2013), available at: https://assets.publishing.service.gov.uk/media/5a7c3a98ed915d76e2ebbf39/Using_conditional_cautions_with_sobriety_requirements.pdf.

109 *Using conditional cautions with sobriety requirements* p3.

In addition, other conditions may be offered, such as attendance at an alcohol project or similar.[110]

10.84 Principles for domestic abuse conditional cautions have been agreed by the Ministry of Justice, the CPS and the NPCC.[111] Under these principles a conditional caution may be offered to a person where the following conditions are satisfied:

- the offender has made a full admission, has not raised the possibility of a defence and accepts full responsibility;
- the offender has no previous convictions or cautions for domestic abuse in the previous two years, is not under police investigation or on bail for another offence, and has no history of coercive or controlling behaviour in this or any other relationship (and there is no evidence of coercive or controlling behaviour, stalking or harassment on the part of the suspect in the current relationship);
- the offence under consideration for a conditional caution is not a serious offence (a conditional caution should not be offered if the likely penalty is an immediate custodial sentence or a high-level community order);
- the express wishes of the victim, who has been fully informed of the options and consequences would be met;
- a relevant risk assessment tool shows the risk to the safety of the victim and/or their family is no higher than the 'standard' classification; and
- the conditions that are under consideration are in line with those considered suitable and sanctioned by the National Police Lead on Domestic Abuse.

A risk assessment should be conducted by a trained officer, and the offer of a conditional caution must be approved by an officer of at least the rank of sergeant who has appropriate domestic abuse knowledge and experience.[112]

10.85 A range of conditions may be offered, depending in part on the nature of the abuse and the relationship between the offender and the victim:

- if the offence involves intimate partner abuse, the focus of the conditions must be on rehabilitation of the domestic abuse perpetrator and a specific domestic abuse intervention must be available (although this may not be appropriate if the offender is female);
- if the offence involves non-intimate partner abuse, whilst the focus may also be on rehabilitation, interventions may more general, such as those directed at anger management;
- whether the offence involves intimate or non-intimate partner abuse, the police should also consider onward referral and/or signposting to other services, such as drugs, alcohol or financial support; and
- restorative justice interventions should not be offered for intimate partner domestic abuse, but may otherwise be considered provided the

110 *Using conditional cautions with sobriety requirements* p3.

111 December 2024, available at: www.npcc.police.uk/SysSiteAssets/media/downloads/publications/publications-log/criminal-justice/2024/principles-for-domestic-abuse-conditional-cautions.pdf.

112 *Principles for domestic abuse conditional cautions* para 1.

offence does not involve violence, stalking, harassment or a sexual offence, it is extremely low level, and a risk assessment has been conducted by a specialist officer.[113]

Consent of the suspect

10.86 A conditional caution cannot be imposed without the informed, written consent of the suspect (see para 10.75 above).

Repeat cautions

10.87 Previous cautions, simple cautions or other out-of-court disposals in relation to earlier offences do not preclude a subsequent conditional caution. A conditional caution may be appropriate where:

- there has been a sufficient lapse of time following a previous caution or conviction for the same or similar type of offence to suggest that it had a sufficient deterrent effect;
- the current offence is low level;
- the current offence is not similar or the same as any previous offence;
- giving a conditional caution is likely to be the best outcome for the victim and the offender; or
- the offender has previously complied with another form of out-of-court disposal.[114]

However, a conditional caution is unlikely to be appropriate where the offence forms part of a pattern of offending.[115] A second conditional caution is not precluded, but should not generally be offered in the absence of exceptional circumstances indicating that it may be appropriate. A previous failure to comply with a conditional caution will normally mean that a further conditional caution should not be offered.[116]

Decision-making

10.88 The *Director's guidance on adult conditional cautions* states that an authorised person 'for the purpose of administering a Conditional Caution' is a police officer not below the rank of sergeant.[117] It is unclear whether this is intended to limit the decision whether to offer a conditional caution to a police sergeant or above, but since offering a simple caution is similarly limited, it seems likely that this is the intention. The decision regarding exceptional circumstances (see para 10.78 above) must be made by an officer of at least the rank of inspector.[118]

Views of the victim

10.89 The view of the victim should be obtained wherever possible, and should be taken into account in determining whether a conditional caution is

113 *Principles for domestic abuse conditional cautions* para 4.
114 Conditional Cautioning Code para 2.11.
115 Conditional Cautioning Code para 2.12.
116 Conditional Cautioning Code para 2.13.
117 *Director's guidance on adult conditional cautions* para 2.1.
118 *Director's guidance on adult conditional cautions* para 4.

appropriate, and the conditions to be imposed – but the victim's views are not conclusive. However, the Conditional Cautioning Code requires that the victim's consent must be obtained in any case where direct reparation or restorative justice processes are being considered or where the victim is directly involved in some way. If the victim does not consent to such conditions, the decision-maker may still consider giving a conditional caution with other conditions attached that do not directly involve the victim.[119]

Specific offence types

10.90 Generally, a conditional caution is not appropriate for hate crimes. However, exceptionally a conditional caution may be considered having regard to the nature of the crime or the circumstances of the offender. Any such case considered by the police as suitable for a conditional caution must be referred to a prosecutor.[120]

Consequences of accepting a conditional caution

10.91 A conditional caution may be administered in a police station, court building, the offices of any prosecutor or any other suitable location consistent with achieving the appropriate impact on the offender. Conditional cautions with a foreign offender condition may also be administered at a port or immigration removal centre or similar place.[121] Before administering a conditional caution, the authorised officer must inform the offender that they have a right to free legal advice, and inform them of the evidence against them and the consequences of accepting a conditional caution.[122] In addition, when administering the caution, the officer must ensure that the offender understands the information set out in the Conditional Cautioning Code para 3.7.

10.92 Although a conditional caution is not a criminal conviction, it forms part of the person's criminal record, and if it is imposed for a recordable offence it will be entered on the Police National Computer. It may, therefore, be cited in any subsequent court proceedings, may be used as evidence of previous misconduct where this is permitted (see para 5.173 above),[123] and may also prevent a further conditional caution being offered in the future (see para 10.87 above). Fingerprints and other identification data can be taken and retained if the conditional caution is for a recordable offence (see paras 6.4 and 6.57 above). In the case of a sexual offence specified in SOA 2003 Sch 3, the offender is a 'relevant offender' for the purposes of the notification and registration requirements of the Act, and

119 Conditional Cautioning Code paras 2.47–2.48.

120 *Director's Guidance on adult conditional cautions* para 3.1.

121 Conditional Cautioning Code para 3.1.

122 Conditional Cautioning Code paras 3.5–3.6.

123 In *R v Cambridge* [2011] EWCA Crim 2009, it was held that evidence of a previous caution had rightly been admitted to rebut evidence of innocent association. A defendant may challenge evidence of previous misconduct based on a caution by adducing evidence to show that they were not guilty of an offence, but this is unlikely to be successful if the defendant was in receipt of legal advice when they accepted the caution (*R v Olu, Wilson and Brooks* [2010] EWCA Crim 2975).

will be placed on the sex offender register.[124] Although the Conditional Cautioning Code is less explicit than the MoJ guidance on simple cautions (see para 10.72 above), a conditional caution given in respect of certain offences may lead to the offender being included in lists maintained by the Disclosure and Barring Service relating to those barred from working with children and vulnerable groups.[125] Conditional cautions are covered by the Rehabilitation of Offenders Act 1974, and are spent at the end of the 'relevant period for the caution', that is, usually three months after the date on which it was given. Normally, a person cannot be prosecuted for an offence in respect of which they have received a conditional caution. However, it has been held that where a conditional caution was given contrary to the *Director's guidance on adult conditional cautions*, it could be quashed, leaving open the possibility of prosecution for the original offence.[126]

10.93 Although failure to comply with the conditions is not an offence, it does render the offender liable to prosecution for the original offence (CJA 2003 s24(1)). If a constable has reasonable grounds for believing that the offender has failed, without reasonable cause, to comply with the conditions, the constable can arrest them without a warrant (CJA 2003 s24A(1)). Where a person is so arrested, various provisions of PACE apply, with modifications (CJA 2003 s24B). Following arrest, the offender must be charged with the original offence (assuming that it is within any relevant time limit), released without charge and on bail (if the pre-conditions for bail are satisfied – see para 10.118 below) to enable a charge decision to be made, or released without charge and without bail (with or without variation of the conditions attached to the caution) (CJA 2003 s24A(2)). On prosecution for the original offence, the document that the offender signed (see para 10.78 above) will be admissible in evidence (CJA 2003 s24(2)).

Advising on conditional cautions

10.94 Many of the considerations that apply when advising on simple cautions also apply to advice on conditional cautions (see paras 10.73–10.76 above). The client should be specifically advised of the consequences of non-compliance, and the other consequences set out in paras 10.91–10.93 above. The police have the power to offer a conditional caution other than in respect of an indictable-only offence (see para 10.78 above), so representations should be made to the custody officer, if relevant. If the officer does decide to charge the client, a prosecutor can, in effect, reverse that decision and direct that a conditional caution be offered (see para 10.78 above), so representations to the CPS should be made in an appropriate case.[127]

124 Conditional Cautioning Code para 3.6.

125 Conditional Cautioning Code para 3.6.

126 *R (Guest) v DPP* [2009] EWHC 594 (Admin).

127 Note that communications with the CPS are not privileged, so that an admission contained in any letter seeking to persuade the CPS to conditionally caution a client may be adduced in evidence if a prosecution proceeds. See *R v Hayes* [2004] EWCA Crim 2844.

Cautions under PCSCA 2022 Part 6

10.95 If and when PCSCA 2022 Part 6 is brought into force, adult simple and conditional cautions will be replaced by diversionary and community cautions (although the changes will not affect youth cautions and youth conditional cautions). Diversionary cautions will be the 'upper-tier' disposal, although they will not be available for indictable-only offences other than in exceptional circumstances and with the consent of the DPP. At least one condition must be attached, with a power of arrest for failure to comply, and the possibility of prosecution for the original offence. The 'lower tier' disposal of a community caution will be available for any offence other than those that are 'excluded' under regulations. Again, at least one condition must be attached. There is no power of arrest for failure to comply, but there is provision for a penalty for non-payment of a financial condition, and enforcement as a fine. A code of practice governing both forms of caution must be issued.

Deferred prosecution or caution

10.96 The term 'deferred prosecution' is used in two ways. First, deferred prosecution agreements (DPAs) were introduced by Crime and Courts Act 2013 Sch 17 in relation, broadly, to corporate crime. A DPA enables a prosecutor to make an agreement with an organisation that could be prosecuted allowing for prosecution to be suspended for a defined period, provided that the organisation meets certain specified conditions. DPAs are not dealt with further here.[128] Second, the terms deferred prosecution and deferred caution are used to signify a more informal approach adopted by some police forces aimed at diverting some people, both adults and children, suspected of relatively minor crime from more formal disposals. There is no formal code of practice or detailed national guidance on this form of disposal, but some limited guidance has been issued by the NPCC.[129] A decision to prosecute or to caution is 'put on hold' whilst the offender is given the opportunity to complete agreed diversionary activities. If the activities are completed as agreed, no further action is taken, and the offender will not receive a criminal record (although it will still be held on local police databases). If the activities are not satisfactorily completed, the offender may be prosecuted or cautioned depending on the nature of the arrangement.[130] The evidential stage of the full code test

128 A Deferred Prosecution Agreements Code of Practice, issued under Crime and Courts Act 2013 Sch 17 para 6, is available at: www.cps.gov.uk/sites/default/files/documents/publications/DPA-COP.pdf.

129 *Outcome 22 (O22) Guidance 2022* para 5, available at: www.npcc.police.uk/SysSiteAssets/media/downloads/publications/publications-log/criminal-justice/2023/npcc-outcome-22-guidance-2022.pdf. Freedom of information requests by the law firm Kingsley Napley in 2022 showed that the use of deferred prosecution and caution is something of a 'postcode lottery', and that the police forces that responded were using them almost exclusively in relation to children. See: www.kingsleynapley.co.uk/insights/blogs/criminal-law-blog/outcome-22-is-the-use-of-this-outcome-a-postcode-lottery-for-children-in-the-uk-criminal-justice-system.

130 See further Youth Justice Board, *How to use out-of-court disposals* (January 2024), available at: www.gov.uk/guidance/case-management-guidance/how-to-use-out-of-court-disposals.

(see para 10.22 above) must be satisfied in order for a prosecution or caution to be deferred, and victims should be consulted and their views taken into consideration.

Protection notices and orders

10.97 Three forms of protection notices and orders are dealt with here: domestic violence protection notices and orders; domestic abuse protection notices and orders; and stalking protection orders. Strictly, they are not alternatives to charging, since each case action taken under these provisions can be taken at the same time as criminal proceedings.

Domestic violence protection notices and orders

10.98 Domestic violence protection notices (DVPNs) and orders (DVPOs) are governed by Crime and Security Act (CSA) 2010 ss24–33. Where the conditions are satisfied, a superintendent or above can issue a DVPN to a person who is suspected of using or threatening violence to an 'associated person', requiring them not to molest the associated person and, where appropriate, requiring them not to approach or enter their premises and, if they are living in those premises, requiring them to leave. Once a DVPN has been served on the person, the police must make an application to a magistrates' court for a DVPO to be heard within 48 hours.[131]

10.99 In order to issue a DVPN, a superintendent or above must have reasonable grounds for believing that a person (P) aged 18 years or over has been violent towards, or threatened violence towards, an 'associated person' and that the issue of a DVPN is necessary to protect that person (V) from violence or the threat of violence by P (CSA 2010 s24(1) and (2)). An 'associated person' is defined by Family Law Act 1996 s62 (as applied by CSA 2010 s24(9)), and includes a person to whom P is or has been married, a civil partner with whom they are cohabiting or have cohabited, a person with whom P has or has had an intimate personal relationship that is or was of significant duration, or a child of whom P is a parent or has or has had parental responsibility. Before issuing a DVPN, the officer must consider a number of statutory factors, including any representations by P, the opinion of V (although a DVPN may be issued even if they do not consent), and the opinion of any other associated person living in the premises to which the DVPN would relate (CSA 2010 s24(3) and (5)). Breach of a DVPN is not an offence, but P may be arrested by a constable having reasonable grounds for believing that they have breached the DVPN. P must then be produced in custody before a magistrates' court within 24 hours, or earlier if the application for a DVPO is to be heard within that time (CSA 2010 ss25(1)(b) and 26).

131 For further information, see Home Office, *Domestic Violence Protection Notices (DVPNs) and Domestic Violence Protection Orders (DVPOs) guidance* (November 2022), available at: www.gov.uk/government/publications/domestic-violence-protection-orders/domestic-violence-protection-notices-dvpns-and-domestic-violence-protection-orders-dvpos-guidance-sections-24-33-crime-and-security-act-2010. See also College of Policing, *Authorised Professional Practice: Major investigation and public protection: Domestic abuse*, available at: www.college.police.uk/app/major-investigation-and-public-protection/domestic-abuse.

10.100 The DVPN, which must be served personally on P (CSA 2010 s25(2)), must contain a provision prohibiting P from molesting V (CSA 2010 s24(6) and (7)). In addition, if P lives in the premises also occupied by V, the DVPN may contain provisions preventing P from evicting or excluding V, prohibiting P from entering the premises, requiring P to leave the premises and/or prohibiting P from coming within a specified distance of the premises (CSA 2010 s24(8)). Having served the DVPN, the police must apply to a magistrates' court for a DVPO, the hearing of which must take place within 48 hours of service (CSA 2010 s27(3)). A DVPO must be for no less than 14 days and no more than 28 days from the date of the order.

Domestic abuse protection notices and orders

10.101 Domestic abuse protection notices (DAPNs) and orders (DAPOs) are governed by Domestic Abuse Act (DAA) 2021 Part 3. As at 30 June 2025, they were being piloted in three police force areas (Greater Manchester, the Metropolitan Police areas of Bromley, Croydon and Sutton, and the British Transport Police). If regarded as successful, they are likely to replace DVPNs and DVPOs. In many respects, the two forms of notice and order are similar, although in some respects the ambit of DAPNs and DAPOs is wider than that of DVPNs and DVPOs.[132]

10.102 In order to issue a DAPN an inspector or above must have reasonable grounds for believing that a person (P) who is aged 18 years or over has been 'abusive' to a person aged 16 years or over (V) to whom P is 'personally connected', and reasonable grounds for believing that it is necessary to give the notice to protect V from domestic abuse, or risk of domestic abuse, carried out by P. The abusive behaviour may have been carried out in the UK or elsewhere (DAA 2021 s22(1)–(6)). Behaviour is 'abusive' if it consists of physical or sexual abuse, violent or threatening behaviour, controlling or coercive behaviour, economic abuse, or psychological, emotional or other abuse. The behaviour may consist of a single incident or a course of conduct (DAA 2021 s1(3)). Behaviour may be regarded as behaviour 'towards' a person even if it is directed at another person, such as V's child (DAA 2021 s1(5)). 'Economic abuse' means any behaviour that has a substantial adverse effect on V's ability to acquire, use or maintain money or other property, or obtain goods or services (DAA 2021 s1(4)). 'Personally connected' has a similar meaning to 'associated person' (see para 10.99 above). Before issuing a DAPN, the officer must consider a number of statutory factors (DAA 2021 s24(1)), which are similar to those that must be considered for issue of a DVPN (see para 10.99 above). Breach of a DAPN is not an offence, but P may be arrested by a constable having reasonable grounds for believing that they have breached the DAPN. P must then be produced in custody before a magistrates' court

132 For further information, see Home Office, *Domestic Abuse Protection Notices (DAPNs) and Domestic Abuse Protection Orders (DAPOs) guidance* (March 2025), available at: www.gov.uk/guidance/domestic-abuse-protection-notices-dapns-and-domestic-abuse-protection-orders-dapos. See also College of Policing, *Authorised Professional Practice: Major investigation and public protection: Domestic abuse*, available at: www.college.police.uk/app/major-investigation-and-public-protection/domestic-abuse.

within 24 hours, or earlier if the application for a DAPO is to heard within that time (DAA 2021 s26).

10.103 A DAPN must be served on P personally (DAA 2021 s25(3)). Unlike a DVPN, a DAPN is not required to contain a non-molestation provision. A DAPN may contain provisions that P must not contact V and must not go within a specified distance of premises in which V lives. If P lives in the same premises as V, the DAPN may also contain provisions evicting or excluding them from those premises, prohibiting P from entering those premises and/or requiring P to leave those premises (DAA 2021 s23). Having served the DAPN, the police must apply to a magistrates' court for a DAPO, the hearing of which must take place within 48 hours of service (DAA 2021 s29). A DAPO has effect for a specified period, until a specified event or until further order (DAA 2021 s38).

Stalking protection order

10.104 Stalking protection orders (SPOs) are governed by the Stalking Protection Act (SPA) 2019, which is supplemented by statutory guidance.[133] Unlike the provisions relating to domestic violence and abuse, the police do not have the power to issue a notice, but they do have the power to make an application to a court for an SPO at any stage of an investigation, and whether or not a prosecution proceeds.

10.105 A chief constable (or other chief officer) can apply to a magistrates' court for an SPO if it appears to them that a person has carried out acts associated with stalking, or they pose a risk associated with stalking to another person, or there is reasonable cause to believe the proposed order is necessary to protect another person from the risk (whether or not that person was the victim of the acts associated with stalking (SPA 2019 s1(1)). A risk associated with stalking may be in respect of physical or psychological harm, or may arise from acts that the suspect knows or ought to know are unwelcome to the other person even if, in other circumstances, the acts would appear harmless in themselves (SPA 2019 s1(4)). It does not matter where or when the relevant acts were carried out (SPA 2019 s1(5)). The court may make an SPO, and may include any prohibition or requirement that it is satisfied is necessary to protect the other person from the risks associated with stalking (SPA 2019 s2). The order may be for a specified period (of at least two years) or until further order (SPA 2019 s3).

Penalty notices for disorder

10.106 Various offences are covered by fixed penalty schemes. Probably the most frequently used are fixed penalties for a range of road traffic offences under Road Traffic Act 1988 Part III.[134] This section focuses on penalty

133 Home Office, *Stalking Protection Orders: statutory guidance for the police* (May 2024), issued under SPA 2019 s12, available at: www.gov.uk/government/publications/stalking-protection-act-statutory-guidance-for-the-police/stalking-protection-orders-statutory-guidance-for-the-police-accessible-version.

134 A useful list of offences attracting fixed penalty notices is published by the Sentencing Council, available at: www.sentencingcouncil.org.uk/explanatory-material/magistrates-court/item/out-of-court-disposals/7-offences-for-which-penalty-notices-are-available/.

notices for disorder under Criminal Justice and Police Act (CJPA) 2001 Part 1, in respect of which the MoJ has issued guidance: *Penalty notices for disorder (PNDs)* ('MoJ PND Guidance').[135]

10.107 A penalty notice for disorder (PND) can be issued in respect of an offence specified in CJPA 2001 s1 (CJPA 2001 ss1 and 2). These include:

- being drunk on a highway, other public place or licensed premises (Licensing Act 1872 s12);
- disorderly behaviour while drunk in a public place (Criminal Justice Act 1967 s91);
- wasting police time or giving a false report (Criminal Law Act 1967 s5(2));
- theft, limited by guidance to retail theft up to £100 (Theft Act 1968 s1);
- destroying or damaging property, limited by guidance to damage not exceeding £300 (Criminal Damage Act 1971 s1(1));
- behaviour likely to cause harassment, alarm or distress (Public Order Act 1986 s5); and
- possession of cannabis or khat and related offences (Misuse of Drugs Act 1971 s5(2)).

10.108 The MoJ PND Guidance provides that a PND can only be given for a specified offence that is at the lower end of the spectrum in terms of seriousness, and which was not committed in association with another specified offence or does not overlap with another offence (see MoJ PND Guidance para 3.7 for an overview of relevant factors). Only one PND should be given to a person for shoplifting, and a PND should not be given to a shop worker who has stolen from their employer.[136] Similarly, only one PND should be given for cannabis or khat possession.[137] A PND is not appropriate for a known class A drug misuser.[138] The views of the victim should be sought, although their views are not conclusive, but the officer should be mindful of the fact that a PND removes the possibility of a court awarding compensation.[139]

10.109 Where a police officer has reason to believe that a person aged 18 years or over has committed a listed offence, they may give the person a penalty notice (CJPA 2001 s2(1)). Unless at a police station, the officer must be in uniform (CJPA 2001s2(2)). The notice must state the alleged offence, provide reasonable information about the circumstances of the alleged offence, specify the 'suspended enforcement period' and explain its effect, state the amount of the penalty and where it can be paid, and inform the recipient of their right to ask to be tried for the alleged offence and explain how that right may be exercised (CJPA 2001 s3). The amount of the penalty depends on whether the offence is listed in Part I or Part II of Schedule 1 to the Penalties for Disorderly Behaviour (Amount of Penalty)

135 June 2014, available at: https://assets.publishing.service.gov.uk/government/uploads/system/uploads/attachment_data/file/403812/penalty-notice-disorder-police-guidance.pdf.

136 MoJ PND Guidance paras 3.12 and 3.14.

137 MoJ PND Guidance para 3.38.

138 MoJ PND Guidance para 3.57.

139 MoJ PND Guidance paras 3.60–3.62.

Order 2002,[140] and is either £90 or £60 respectively. A PND may include an education option if it arises from an offence in relation to which there is an approved educational course (CJPA 2001 s2(1A); and see MoJ PND Guidance section 6). If the penalty is paid within the suspended enforcement period (ie 21 days beginning with the date on which the order was given), no proceedings may be brought for the offence (CJPA 2001 s5). The recipient of the notice can ask, during the suspended enforcement period, to be tried, and in this case proceedings may be commenced against them (CJPA 2001 s4). If the recipient of the notice does not ask to be tried and does not pay the penalty during the suspended enforcement period, a sum equal to one-and-a-half times the amount of the penalty may be registered against them as a fine (CJPA 2001 s8). These provisions are modified in the case of a PND with an education option (see CJPA 2001 ss4(6)–(10) and 5(2)).

10.110 A penalty notice is not a conviction, and does not amount to an admission of guilt nor to proof that a crime has been committed.[141] However, while a PND does not form part of a person's criminal record, if it is imposed in relation to a recordable offence, an entry may be made on the Police National Computer, which may be disclosed as part of an enhanced Disclosure and Barring Service check.[142] Where a PND has been imposed, prosecution for an offence arising from the same circumstances is permissible if evidence of a more serious offence than that for which the penalty was imposed comes to light.[143]

No further action

10.111 There is no legal rule that requires a prosecution or out-of-court disposal simply because there is sufficient evidence to charge, and in some cases formal action may not be appropriate. The CCP states that there has 'never been the rule that a prosecution will automatically take place once the evidential stage is met',[144] and one of the consequences of applying the public interest stage (see para 10.23 above) may be that formal action against the suspect is not required. As the *Director's guidance on charging* makes clear, such a decision could even be taken before evidence is reviewed if 'it is clear ... that the public interest does not require a prosecution'.[145]

10.112 A suspect should be notified in writing of a decision to take no further action (see para 10.8 above).[146] Where the police decide to take no further action, the lawyer should, if relevant, advise their client that the police may

140 SI No 1837, as amended, inter alia, by the Penalties for Disorderly Behaviour (Amount of Penalty) (Amendment) (No 2) Order 2013 SI No 1579.

141 *R v Hamer* [2010] EWCA Crim 2053.

142 MoJ PND Guidance para 1.9.

143 *R v Gore* [2009] EWCA Crim 1424.

144 CCP para 4.10.

145 *Director's guidance on charging* para 5.7.

146 College of Policing, *Authorised Professional Practice: Prosecution and case management: Possible justice outcomes following investigation*, available at: www.college.police.uk/app/prosecution-and-case-management/possible-justice-outcomes-following-investigation.

arrest them again in respect of the same matter if new evidence justifying a further arrest comes to light. Where appropriate, the client should be advised to retain any relevant documents or other evidence in case it is needed in the future.

Release without charge or other disposal

Overview

10.113 The police have a variety of powers and duties to release (with or without bail) suspects who have been arrested for an offence and detained at a police station under PACE, but who have not been charged. These were significantly modified by the amendments to PACE made by Policing and Crime Act (PCA) 2017 Part 4 Chapter 1,[147] and then modified again by further amendments to PACE by PCSCA 2022 s45 and Sch 4. Statutory guidance is issued by the College of Policing under PACE s50B.[148] A person exercising a function in relation to pre-charge bail[149] must have regard to the guidance, subject to an exception in the case of members of the Serious Fraud Office, staff of the Financial Conduct Authority, HMRC officers and officers of the National Crime Agency (PACE s50B(8)). The police do not have power to bail without charge a person arrested and detained under TA 2000 s41, nor a person arrested and detained under the NSA 2023.[150] For the power to grant bail to an arrested person without taking them to a police station, see para 2.48 above.

Powers and duties to release with or without bail

10.114 Bail from a police station without charge is sometimes referred to as 'section 47(3) bail', but in fact there is a number of different bail powers in PACE Part IV. PACE s34(2) provides that where a custody officer becomes aware, in relation to a person in police detention (see para 1.58 above), that grounds for detention have ceased to apply and the officer is not aware of any other grounds to justify detention, they must order the immediate release of the detained person from custody (unless it appears to the officer that the person was unlawfully at large when arrested: PACE s34(4)). Such release may be without bail, but must be on bail if it appears to the custody officer that there is a need for further investigation of any matter in connection with which the person was detained at any time during the period of detention or that in respect of any such matter proceedings may be taken against them (or, if a child, that they may be given a youth caution), and the pre-conditions for bail are satisfied (PACE s34(5) and (5A)).

147 Note that Code C does not contain provisions regarding release without charge, nor bail with or without charge, and has not been amended to reflect the provisions on bail in the PCSCA 2022.

148 *Pre-charge bail: Statutory guidance* (March 2023), available at: https://assets.publishing.service.gov.uk/government/uploads/system/uploads/attachment_data/file/1139539/Pre-charge-bail-statutory-guidance-web.pdf.

149 A release on bail without charge is normally referred to as pre-charge bail, although since many suspects released on such bail are never charged, it would be better described as bail without charge.

150 Code H para 1.6 and Code I para 1.5; and see *R (I) v Westminster Magistrates' Court* [2008] EWHC 2146 (Admin).

10.115 Where a person arrested either without warrant or under a warrant not endorsed for bail is taken before a custody officer under PACE s37(1), and the officer determines that they do not have before them sufficient evidence to charge, the person must be released, on bail if the pre-conditions for bail are satisfied or without bail if they are not satisfied, unless the officer has reasonable grounds for believing that detention is necessary for one or more of the specified grounds (PACE s37(2)–(3); and see para 2.56 above). If the officer determines that there is sufficient evidence to charge, the person must be dealt with in accordance with PACE s37(7) (see para 10.6 above).

10.116 If the officer conducting a review of detention under PACE s40 (see para 2.86 above) concludes that detention can no longer be justified by reference to the conditions in PACE s37, they must release the suspect on bail if the pre-conditions for bail are satisfied, or without bail if they are not satisfied (PACE s40(8) and (8A)). Where a detained person has not been charged at the expiry of 24 hours after the relevant time, they must be released on bail if the pre-conditions for bail are satisfied or without bail if they are not, unless further detention is authorised under PACE s42 or 43 (PACE s41(7)). A similar provision applies at the expiry of the 36-hour time limit (PACE s42(10)), or where an application for a warrant or extension of a warrant of further detention is refused, unless the 36 hours or the existing warrant has not expired (PACE ss43(15), (16) and 44(7), (8)), or where a warrant expires (PACE s43(18)). There is no similar provision where an extended warrant expires, although it is probable that the same principles must apply.[151]

10.117 Where a custody officer determines that there is sufficient evidence to charge a suspect, the officer may release the suspect on bail with a view to a charge decision being made by a Crown prosecutor (PACE s37(7)(a)(i); and see para 10.6 above). Alternatively, having determined that there is sufficient evidence to charge, the custody officer may release the suspect without charge, on bail if the pre-conditions for bail are satisfied or without bail if they are not (PACE s37(7)(b) and (c)). The purpose appears to be to permit the police to continue with their investigation of the offence for which the suspect was arrested and detained even though the custody officer has determined that there is sufficient evidence to charge (but see para 10.128 below).

10.118 The pre-conditions for bail in relation to the release of a person by a custody officer are:

(1) that the custody officer is satisfied that releasing the suspect on bail is necessary and proportionate in all the circumstances (having regard, in particular, to any conditions of bail which would be imposed); and
(2) that the custody officer has considered any representations by the suspect or their lawyer (PACE s50A(1)).

In determining whether bail is necessary and proportionate, the custody officer must have regard in particular to:

151 Note that if a detention time limit has expired, it is difficult to see why the police should then have the power to release the suspect on bail, as opposed to unconditionally, since they would not have the power to detain the suspect on their surrender to bail unless new evidence justified their further arrest.

- the need to secure that the suspect surrenders to custody;
- the need to prevent offending by the suspect;
- the need to safeguard victims of crime and witnesses, taking into account any vulnerabilities of the putative victim or witnesses;
- the need to safeguard the suspect taking into account any vulnerabilities identified by the custody officer; and
- the need to manage risks to the public (PACE s50A(2)).

For the maximum periods for which the police may grant bail, see paras 10.123–10.124 below.

Power to impose conditions

10.119 A release on bail under PACE Part IV (which includes all the powers to grant bail referred to in paras 10.114–10.117 above, but not bail granted without taking the suspect to a police station),[152] is deemed to be a release on bail in accordance with BA 1976 ss3, 3A, 5 and 5A, as those sections apply to bail granted by a constable. Conditions can be attached to bail granted under PACE Part IV, except s37CA(2)(b) or 37A(2)(b) (PACE s47(1A), as amended by PCA 2017 s62(3)). Such conditions can be imposed as appear necessary for the purpose of ensuring that the person surrenders to custody, does not commit an offence on bail, does not interfere with witnesses or otherwise obstruct the course of justice, and/or for their own protection (or where the person is aged under 18 years, for their own welfare or in their own interests) (PACE s47(1A); and BA 1976 ss3(6) and 3A(5)). Any condition may be imposed other than a condition that the person reside in a bail hostel, make themself available for the purposes of a court report or attend an interview with a lawyer (BA 1976 s3A(2)). It has been held in relation to a court's power to impose bail conditions that in considering whether and what conditions to impose, the court must perceive a real and not merely fanciful risk of the relevant outcome,[153] and it is suggested that the same principle must apply to a decision by a police officer. See further paras 10.144–10.146 below. An application to vary or remove conditions may be made to a custody officer or to a magistrates' court (see para 10.148 below).

10.120 If the custody officer is considering releasing the suspect on bail, the investigating officer must, if reasonably practicable, seek the views of the putative victim concerning whether relevant conditions should be imposed and, if so, what relevant conditions should be imposed. A 'relevant condition' is one that relates to the safeguarding of the putative victim. The investigating officer must then inform the custody officer of any views obtained. Note that the police are not required to consult the putative victim as to whether bail should be granted and, in any event, the police are not bound by their views as to relevant conditions. If bail is granted subject to relevant conditions, the investigating officer must, if reasonably practicable, inform the putative victim of those conditions (PACE s47ZZA(1)–(5)).

152 For the power to attach conditions to bail granted without taking the suspect to a police station, see para 2.48 above.

153 *R v Mansfield Justices ex p Sharkey* [1985] QB 613, QBD.

Consequences of bail without charge

10.121 Bail without charge is not subject to an overall time limit, but PACE ss47ZA–47ZM limit the periods for which bail may be granted and extended. The 'bail start date' is the day after the day on which the person was arrested, irrespective of the actual day on which the person is released on bail (PACE s47ZB(4)(a)). The maximum periods for which bail may be granted or extended differ depending upon a range of factors, including whether the 'relevant offence' is an 'FCA' case, an 'HMRC' case, an 'NCA' case, an 'SFO' case or none of these (hereafter, a 'standard' case):

- an 'FCA' case is a case in which the relevant offence in relation to the person is being investigated by the Financial Conduct Authority (FCA), and a member of staff designated for this purpose confirms that this is the case;
- an 'HMRC' case is a case in which the relevant offence in relation to the person is being investigated by an officer of HMRC, and an officer of HMRC confirms that this is the case;
- an 'NCA' case is a case in which the relevant offence in relation to the person is being investigated by the National Crime Agency (NCA), and an officer of the NCA confirms that this is the case;
- an 'SFO' case is a case in which the relevant offence in relation to the person is being investigated by the Director of the Serious Fraud Office (SFO), and a member of the SFO confirms that this is the case (PACE s47ZB(4)(b)–(c)).

For a chart showing time limits and levels of authorisation for pre-charge bail, see appendix 1.

10.122 The 'relevant offence' is the offence in respect of which the power to release the person on bail is exercised (PACE s47ZA(8)). The period of bail granted may be shorter than the relevant maximum period for which bail may be granted if the person is already on police bail and the custody officer believes that it is appropriate to align the return dates, or the custody officer believes that a decision as to charge would be made before the relevant maximum period expires (PACE s47ZA(3)–(5)).

10.123 The initial maximum period for which bail can be granted is three months, beginning with the person's bail start date in a standard case and six months in an SFO, NCA, HMRC or FCA case (PACE s47ZB(1)). Note that the bail period does not run, or is suspended, during the period when a person is released on bail under PACE s37(7)(a) or s37C(2)(b) in order for a Crown prosecutor to make a charging decision (unless the prosecutor requests further information from the police in order to make the decision, in which case the period is treated as running during the time that the police are gathering the further information) (PACE s47ZL).[154] If a person who has been bailed is in hospital as an in-patient at any time on the day on which the applicable bail period would end, the running of the bail period is treated as having been suspended for any day

154 If the prosecutor makes the request and the applicable bail period would end before the end of seven days beginning with the day on which the request is made, the applicable bail period ends at the end of the period of seven days beginning with the day on which the request is made (PACE s47ZL(7) and (8)).

on which the person is an in-patient (PACE s47ZM(4) and (5)). Where the person had previously been released under PACE s30A (street bail) in connection with the matter for which they are in police detention, the period spent on street bail counts towards the period of 28 days for the purposes of PACE s47ZB(1)(b) (PACE s47ZM(1)–(3)). Extension of the period of bail beyond the initial maximum periods depends upon whether some or all of the following conditions are satisfied:

- **Condition A:** The decision-maker has reasonable grounds for suspecting the person to be guilty of the relevant offence.
- **Condition B:** The decision-maker has reasonable grounds for believing:
  - in a case where the person is, or is to be, released on bail under PACE s37(7)(b) or 37CA(2)(b), that further time is needed for making a decision as to whether to charge them with the relevant offence;
  - or otherwise, that further investigation is needed of any matter in connection with the relevant offence.
- **Condition C:** The decision-maker has reasonable grounds for believing:
  - in a case where the person is, or is to be, released on bail under PACE s37(7)(b) or 37CA(2)(b), that the decision as to whether to charge the person with the relevant offence is being made diligently and expeditiously;
  - or otherwise, that the investigation is being conducted diligently and expeditiously.
- **Condition D:** That the decision-maker has reasonable grounds for believing that the release on bail of the person is necessary and proportionate in all the circumstances (having regard, in particular, to any conditions of bail which are, or are to be, imposed) (PACE s47ZC(2)–(5)).

10.124 In a standard case, an inspector or above may extend the period of bail to the end of the period of six months beginning with the person's bail start date, provided that they are satisfied that conditions A–D are met. Before making a decision, the officer must arrange for the person or their lawyer to be informed that a determination is to be made; consider any representations made; and subsequently inform them of the determination made (PACE s47ZD). Where an extension has been granted under section 47ZD, a superintendent or above may, before the expiry of that period, extend bail up to a total of nine months beginning with the person's bail start date, if they are satisfied as to conditions A–D (PACE s47ZDA). Further, where an extension has been granted under section 47ZDA, and the DPP has designated the case as being exceptionally complex, an officer of the rank of commander or assistant chief constable or above may authorise bail up to 12 months beginning with the person's bail start date if they are satisfied as to conditions A–D (PACE s47ZE). In an SFO, NCA, HMRC or SFO case, an appropriate decision-maker may extend the period of bail to the end of the period of 12 months beginning with the person's bail start date, provided that they are satisfied that conditions A–D are met. An 'appropriate decision-maker' is a designated member of staff of the FCA, an HMRC officer of a rank equivalent to a police superintendent or above, an NCA officer of a rank equivalent to a police superintendent or above, or a member of the SFO who is of the Senior Civil Service. Before making a decision, the appropriate decision-maker must arrange for the person or their lawyer to be informed that a determination is to be made (and if a qualifying police officer, consult a qualifying prosecutor), consider any representations made, and subsequently inform them of the determination (PACE s47ZDB).

10.125 Where an extension of bail has been granted under (i) PACE ss47ZDA, (ii) 47ZDB, or (iii) 47ZE (ie any of the extensions of bail noted in para 10.124 above except extension of bail in a standard case by an inspector under PACE s47ZD), an application may be made to a magistrates' court to extend the period of bail. In order to extend bail, the court must be satisfied that conditions B–D are met. If it is so satisfied, and it is likely that the decision or investigations referred to in condition B will be made or completed within12 months beginning with the person's bail date in the case of (i), or 18 months in the case of (ii) or (iii), the court may extend the period of bail for such a period (PACE s47ZF(4)). If, being satisfied that conditions B–D are met, but it is unlikely that the decision will be made or investigations completed if a longer period of bail is not granted, the court may extend bail to 18 months in the case of (i) or 24 months in the case of (ii) or (iii), beginning with the person's bail start date (PACE s47ZF). PACE s47ZG provides that a court can further extend the bail period if it is satisfied that conditions B–D are met. The period of extension is three months from the end of the current applicable bail period if it is likely that the decision or investigations referred to in condition B will be made or completed within that period, or six months if it is not likely that the decision or investigations will be made or completed with the three-month period. Provided the relevant conditions are satisfied, there is no limit on the number of extensions of bail that may be granted (PACE s47ZG(7)).

10.126 Applications to extend bail under PACE ss47ZF and 47ZG must be made before the applicable bail period expires,[155] and are normally to be determined by a single justice of the peace on written evidence (PACE s47ZI). However, an application is to be heard orally (but not in open court) if a single justice of the peace considers that the interests of justice require an oral hearing, and the effect of the application would be to extend the applicable bail period so that it ends at or before the end of the period of 24 months beginning with the person's start bail start date and either that person, or the suspect or the person making the application, requests an oral hearing (PACE s47ZI(2) and (3)). Where an oral hearing is held, the justices may direct that the person to whom the application relates and their lawyer be excluded from any part of the hearing (PACE s47ZI(5)). The applicant may apply to the court for it to authorise that specified information be withheld from the person to whom the application relates and their lawyer. The court can grant such an application if it

155 If an application is made before the end of the applicable bail period, but it is not practicable for the court to determine the application before the end of that period, it must determine the application as soon as is practicable. If it appears to the court that it would have been reasonable for the application to have been made in time for it to be determined before the end of the applicable bail period, it may refuse the application (PACE s47ZJ).

is satisfied that there are reasonable grounds for believing that the specified information is 'sensitive' information. Information is sensitive if its disclosure would have one or more of the following results:

- evidence connected with an indictable offence would be interfered with or harmed;
- a person would be interfered with or physically injured;
- a person suspected of having committed an indictable offence but not yet arrested for the offence would be alerted; and/or
- the recovery of property obtained as a result of an indictable offence would be hindered (PACE s47ZH).

An application under PACE s47ZH is to be determined by a single justice of the peace on written evidence unless the justice determines that the interests of justice require an oral hearing (PACE s47ZI(7)).

10.127 A person who has been released on bail under PACE s41(7), 42(10), 43(18) or 47(2) may be re-arrested if, since their release, new evidence has come to light or an examination or analysis of existing evidence has been made that could not reasonably have been made before their release (PACE ss41(9), 42(11), 43(19) and 47(2), respectively). With the exception of arrest under PACE s47(2), this applies irrespective of whether the release was on bail or without bail. It would seem that where a person has been released without bail, in the absence of new evidence, etc, they cannot be re-arrested for the offence in relation to which they were originally arrested since otherwise the provisions on re-arrest of a person released on bail would not be necessary. Where a person has been released on conditional bail, they may be arrested by a constable having reasonable grounds for suspecting that they have broken any of the conditions (PACE s46A(1A)). Further, a person granted bail to return to a police station (whether conditional or not) is under a duty to do so, and may be arrested if they fail to attend the police station at the appointed time (PACE s46A(1)). A person arrested under PACE s46A must be taken to the police station at which they were required to surrender as soon as is practicable (PACE s46A(2)), and is treated as having been arrested for an offence for the purposes of PACE ss30 (duty to take arrested person to a police station) and 31 (arrest for further offence) (PACE s46A(3)). If the person had been released under PACE s37(7)(a) and the Crown prosecutor has not made a charge decision under PACE s37B, the custody officer may either charge the person or release them on bail again (PACE s37C(2) and (3)). The duty to attend at the police station on the appointed date is subject to the power of a custody officer to give notice in writing to the person that their attendance is not required (PACE s47(4)). Unlike under BA 1976 s7(3), there is no power of arrest in respect of an anticipated breach of conditions or anticipated failure to surrender. Breach of conditions is not an offence (subject to the following exception), but failure without reasonable cause to surrender to custody is an offence (BA 1976 s6, as applied by PACE s47(1)). Where a person is released without charge and on bail under PACE 1984 Part IV, and the release is subject to a travel restriction condition, breach of the condition is an offence punishable with up to six months' imprisonment and/or a fine. A 'travel restriction condition' is defined in PCA 2017 s68(2).

10.128 Where a person returns to the police station in accordance with their bail (or fails to surrender and is arrested and taken to the police station), the custody officer may authorise their further detention only if the grounds in PACE s37 are satisfied (as a result of PACE s34(7)). This does not apply where the person was released on bail under PACE s37(7)(a), in which case they may be kept in police detention to enable a charge decision to be made in accordance with PACE s37B or 37C (PACE s37D(4)). Where the person was released on bail under PACE s37(7)(b) (see para 10.117 above), they may be kept in police detention to enable a charge decision to be made or for the purpose of determining a new date for surrender to bail (PACE s37D(4A)). However, it is difficult to see how the person could be lawfully detained for the purpose of further investigation or in order to interview them since a pre-condition for the person having been released on bail under PACE s37(7)(b) is that the custody officer had determined that there was sufficient evidence to charge them. That precludes detention for the purpose of investigation under PACE s37(2).

10.129 Where a person returns to the police station in accordance with the grant of bail, including live link bail under PACE s46ZA(4), or is arrested for failure to surrender to bail under PACE s46A(1) or 46ZA(5), time spent in police detention before the release on bail (but not any time whilst on bail) counts for the purpose of calculating the maximum period of detention without charge (PACE s47(6); and see para 2.76 above). However, this is not the case if they have been re-arrested on the grounds of new evidence, in which case the detention clock starts again.

Advising in respect of release without charge

10.130 The powers to release on bail without charge, taken together with the powers to impose conditions, give the police a great deal of flexibility in conducting investigations. Given the detention time limits, the defence lawyer may seek to use this to the advantage of their client in securing the client's release on bail, especially where the investigation cannot be proceeded with quickly. As noted at para 10.117 above, release on bail is possible even if the custody officer has determined that there is sufficient evidence to charge, and in appropriate cases a release on bail in these circumstances may give the lawyer the opportunity to secure evidence of assistance to the client or to seek to make representations to the prosecutor. On the other hand, as noted at para 10.125 above, there is no overall time limit on bail, or limit on the number of occasions on which bail can be renewed. Where a person is to be released without charge (other than under PACE s37(7)(a)), there is now no presumption that the release is to be without bail, although the release may only be on bail if the pre-conditions for bail are met. In considering whether to grant authorisation, the officer must consider any representations made by the lawyer. Therefore, the lawyer should consider making representations relevant to the question of whether bail is necessary and proportionate and, if a release on bail (as opposed to a release without bail) is likely, relevant to what conditions (if any) are appropriate.

10.131 Where the client is released on bail, they must be given a notice specifying the date and time on which they must surrender, and the police station at which they must attend (which may be different from that from which they were bailed). It is normally advisable for the lawyer to arrange to meet the client shortly before the time given for surrender, and to advise them to ensure that if they do not meet before surrendering that they make it clear to the police that they want legal advice. It is always worth checking with the police before the time for surrender to ensure that the client has not, in the meantime, been notified that they do not need to attend, and to check what action the police intend to take on the client's surrender. In view of the potential for inferences under CJPOA 1994 s34(1)(b), the lawyer should always consider whether to attend, even if it is understood that the client is simply to be charged without further interview (see para 10.34 above). On attending with the client, the lawyer should ensure that time already spent in police detention in connection with the matter is correctly taken into account (see para 10.129 above).

10.132 Where the client is released without bail but under investigation (RUI), there is no statutory obligation for the police to keep them, or their lawyer, informed of the progress of the investigation. However, the statutory guidance on pre-charge bail (see para 10.113 above) states that police forces should have a formal mechanism for notifying suspects that they have been RUI-d, and explaining what this means (para 13.5). It also states that that the suspect or their lawyer can expect to be regularly updated regarding progress of the investigation, and should be provided with 'an indication of the likely update intervals in writing or on the notice at the time of release' (para 13.5). The police should have a clear investigative plan, and the investigator's supervisor should endorse the investigation log with an initial expected finish date (paras 13.9 and 13.10). There is nothing to prevent the police from initially releasing a suspect on bail, and subsequently transferring them to RUI, and there is some evidence that this may be done to avoid scrutiny by superior officers or the courts.[156]

Challenges to charge decisions

Decisions to charge

10.133 Where a charge decision has been made by the police rather than a Crown prosecutor, the decision must be reviewed by a prosecutor prior to the first hearing. The case should be continued only if the relevant tests under the CCP are satisfied.[157] Even if the charge decision was made by a Crown prosecutor, the prosecutor has a duty to keep prosecution decisions under review, and to take into account any change of circumstances. In doing so, the prosecutor should take into account any information or evidence supplied on behalf of the accused.[158] A decision to prosecute is, in principle, susceptible to judicial review, but this remedy is in practice only rarely

156 A Hucklesby, *Pre-charge bail and Release Under Investigation: an examination of their use, effectiveness and impact on suspects' and victims' rights and confidence in the criminal justice system* (September 2024), available at: www.birmingham.ac.uk/Documents/college-artslaw/law/research/precharge-bail/pcb-rui-final-report.pdf.

157 *Director's guidance on charging* para 21.

158 CCP para 3.6.

available since a prosecution decision can normally be challenged within the trial process itself, notably by an application to stay proceedings on the grounds of abuse of process. Arguments relating to abuse of process may and should be raised in the course of the criminal trial itself save in wholly exceptional circumstances, such as where the decision was made in breach of an authority's clear and settled policy.[159] Another example is where the accused was prosecuted having admitted the offence following an indication by the investigating officer that a caution had been approved.[160] A decision to prosecute rather than to offer a conditional caution, on the grounds that the offence concerned was one of domestic violence and a conditional caution for such an offence was prohibited by the *Director's guidance on adult conditional cautions*, was quashed on the grounds that the guidance must be interpreted as permitting exceptions.[161]

10.134 A decision not to prosecute may be challenged by way of judicial review by the complainant, although the courts are generally reluctant to intervene.[162] Generally, the courts will only intervene if the decision not to prosecute was arrived at as a result of some unlawful policy, or from a failure to act in accordance with the DPP's settled policy, or because the decision was perverse.[163] Note that under the Victims' Right to Review Scheme, victims have a right to request a review of a CPS decision not to prosecute or to terminate criminal proceedings.[164] A decision by the police or a Crown prosecutor not to prosecute does not prevent a private prosecution (although rare in practice), and a private prosecutor is not bound by the CCP full code test.[165]

Decisions to caution

10.135 A decision to caution may be challenged by way of judicial review by the person cautioned if it is made in breach of settled policy, such as where no clear and reliable admission was made[166] or where a caution was not in the public interest.[167] Note that a decision to caution rather than to prosecute

159 *R (Pepushi) v Crown Prosecution Service* [2004] EWHC 798 (Admin); *R v Chief Constable of Kent and Crown Prosecution Service ex p GL* (1991) 93 Cr App R 416, DC; *R v Commissioner of Police of the Metropolis ex p Thompson* [1997] 1 WLR 1519, QBD; *R (Mondelly) v Commissioner of Police of the Metropolis* [2006] EWHC 2370 (Admin); *R v DPP ex p Kebilene* [2000] 2 AC 326, HL; and *DPP v Durham* [2024] UKPC 21, PC (Trinidad and Tobago).

160 *Mansfield v DPP* [2021] EWHC 2938 (Admin).

161 *R (Robson) v Crown Prosecution Service* [2016] EWHC 2191 (Admin).

162 See, for example, *R v DPP ex p Manning* [2001] QB 330, QBD; and more recently, *R (Monica) v DPP* [2018] EWHC 3508 (Admin) and *R (Monica) v DPP and Boyling (Interested Party)* [2018] EWHC 3469 (QB).

163 *R v DPP ex p C* [1995] 1 CR App R 136, QBD, followed in *R (O'Brien) v DPP* [2013] EWHC 3741 (Admin).

164 May 2021, available at: www.cps.gov.uk/legal-guidance/victims-right-review-scheme; and see *R (SY) v DPP* [2018] EWHC 795 (Admin).

165 *R (Charlson) v Guildford Magistrates' Court* [2006] EWHC 2318 (Admin).

166 *R (Wyman) v Chief Constable of Hampshire* [2006] EWHC 1904 (Admin). See also *R (Mohammed) v Chief Constable of the West Midlands* [2010] EWHC 1228 (Admin), where, on the facts, an unlawfully administered caution for a sexual offence was held to amount to a breach of the rights of the recipient under ECHR Article 8.

167 *Caetano v Commissioner of Police of the Metropolis* [2013] EWHC 375 (Admin).

may be challenged by the complainant by way of judicial review. If the complainant launches a private prosecution after the offender is cautioned it may be stayed for abuse of process, but a stay will not necessarily be ordered.[168]

Bail or detention after charge

Introduction

10.136 Where a person arrested for an offence otherwise than under a warrant endorsed for bail is charged with an offence, the custody officer must, subject to CJPOA 1994 s25 (see para 10.150 below), release the person from detention either on bail or without bail, unless one or more of the conditions in PACE s38 is satisfied (PACE s38(1)).[169] If released, the person will be given a date for the court appearance which, by PACE s47(3A), must normally be no later than the first sitting of the relevant magistrates' court after the person is charged.[170] Alternatively, the custody officer may bail the person to attend a police station pursuant to a live link direction under Crime and Disorder Act (CDA) 1998 s57C (PACE s47(3(b)(i)). If the person charged is not released, the first appearance in court is governed by PACE s46, which generally provides that the person must be brought before a magistrates' court as soon as practicable[171] and not later than the first sitting after charge.[172] This will normally mean that the suspect must be produced in court no later than the day following the date of charge, excluding Christmas day, Good Friday or a Sunday.[173] A decision to release a person under investigation (RUI) and deal with them by way of written charge and requisition does not in any way limit the power of a magistrates' court to remand them in custody at the first appearance.[174]

168 Compare *Jones v Whalley* [2006] UKHL 41, in which a private prosecution was stayed; and *Hayter v L* [1998] 1 WLR 854, QBD, in which it was not. For a successful challenge by a complainant of a decision to give a conditional caution, see *R (Guest) v DPP* [2009] EWHC 594 (Admin). See also, *R (Lowden) v Gateshead Magistrates' Court* [2016] EWHC 3536 (Admin).

169 If the person was arrested on a warrant endorsed for bail, release will be determined by the terms of the warrant. Where a person is charged under CJA 2003 s87(4) (charge under the re-trial for certain serious offence provisions of CJA 2003 Part 10), they cannot be released without bail, and if they are granted bail, must be bailed to the Crown Court and not a magistrates' court (CJA 2003 s88(1)).

170 Although by PACE s47(3A)(b) it can be later if the designated officer for the relevant local justice area has notified the police that the appearance cannot be accommodated until a later date.

171 For interpretation of 'as soon as practicable' see *Nikonovs v Governor of HM Prison Brixton and the Republic of Latvia (Interested Party)* [2005] EWHC 2405 (Admin).

172 Except where the person is charged under CJA 2003 s87(4) (charge under re-trial for certain serious offence provisions of CJA 2003 Part 10), in which case the person must be brought before a Crown Court as soon as practicable and no later than 24 hours after they are charged (CJA 2003 s88(2)).

173 On Saturdays, justices should be available to deal with cases arising after completing the list of cases before them (*R v Clerk to the Justices, Teesside Magistrates' Court ex p H* (2000) 19 October (unreported)).

174 *R (Iqbal) v Canterbury Crown Court* [2020] EWHC 452 (Admin).

Drug testing and bail

10.137 The drug testing powers, both before and following charge, are dealt with at paras 6.76–6.83 above. Information from a drug test can be used to inform the decision as to bail (PACE s63B(7)), which includes both the decision whether bail should be granted and, if it is, the decision about any conditions to be imposed. Where a sample could be taken under PACE s63B and the custody officer determines that the person should be released under PACE s37(2) or 37(7)(a) or (b) (PACE s37(7)(a) or (c)), the person can continue to be detained for up to 24 hours from the relevant time (see para 6.81 above) to enable a sample to be taken (PACE s37(8A) and (8B)). Furthermore, where such a sample could be taken, but the person is charged before a sample is taken and the custody officer would otherwise release them on bail under PACE s38, the officer can authorise their detention for up to six hours from the time of charge in order for a sample to be taken (PACE s38(1)(a)(iiia) and (2); and Code C para 17.10).

Making representations regarding the bail/detention decision

10.138 The decision whether to bail a person after they have been charged is a very important one, not least because for many suspects getting out of the police station may be more important at that stage than the eventual result of the proceedings. It is also important because the police decision regarding bail is likely to have an impact on whether the court will grant bail. If the police grant bail, the court will normally do so. If, on the other hand, the police withhold bail, the court is more likely to come to the same decision. It is also likely that, where bail is granted subject to conditions the court will be heavily influenced by the police decision on what conditions to impose. Note that the bail decision is that of the custody officer even in cases where the charge decision is made by a Crown prosecutor.

10.139 It is, therefore, vitally important for the lawyer to try, where appropriate, to persuade the custody officer to grant bail, with or without conditions. When making a bail decision, the custody officer must determine whether there are documents and materials that are essential to challenging the lawfulness of the arrest or detention, and make any such documents or materials available to the suspect and their lawyer (Code C para 16.7A; and see para 2.62 above). The lawyer should, therefore, ask the custody officer whether there are any such documents or materials and, if so, ask for a copy of them. Although there is no specific duty on the custody officer under PACE or Code C to receive representations, most of the criteria for denying bail under PACE s38 require the custody officer to have reasonable grounds for their belief. It may be argued that the custody officer cannot do so if they know that the lawyer has a relevant representation to make to which the officer is not prepared to listen. One problem, particularly in a busy custody office, is that it is easy for the custody officer to go through the motions of listening to the lawyer's representations without, in reality, considering the arguments put forward. Since the custody officer is, in effect, performing a quasi-judicial role, the investigating officer and the lawyer should make representations to the custody officer regarding bail in each other's presence.[175] The custody officer must give reasons for imposing conditions (although not for granting unconditional bail or for withholding bail), which must be noted in the custody record, and a copy of that note must be given to the defendant (BA 1976 s5A(2) and (3)).

10.140 The nature of the representations to be made will depend on the circumstances and documents or materials disclosed under Code C para 16.7A, and on the lawyer's judgment about the way in which the custody officer is likely to be thinking. If the primary issue is whether bail should be granted at all, the officer should be asked to consider PACE s38(1) (see para 10.150 below) and which of the criteria may be satisfied. This will enable the lawyer to concentrate on the issues of primary concern, and will also enable them to argue (as appropriate) that the concerns could be adequately dealt with by the imposition of appropriate conditions. If the issue is whether any conditions should be imposed, and if so what form they should take, clearly the lawyer should consider, and direct the custody officer's attention to, the criteria for the imposition of conditions (and for the taking of a security or surety) under BA 1976 s3A(5) (see paras 10.144–10.146 below). The lawyer should, where relevant, already have discussed possible conditions with the client. Conditions should be both realistic and proportionate to the risk and, as noted at para 10.145 below, the perceived risk must be a real one and not purely speculative. If the conditions imposed are onerous, it may be that the client will indicate that they do not intend to keep to them. It has been held, in relation to court bail, that in such circumstances the defendant should be given the opportunity to comply with the conditions, and it is suggested that the same principle applies to police bail.[176] However, it would normally be better for the client to agree with the conditions, and then seek review by another custody officer or a court (see para 10.148 below).

Bail after charge

Introduction

10.141 A release on bail under PACE s38(1)[177] is deemed to be a release on bail granted in accordance with BA 1976 ss3, 3A, 5 and 5A, as they apply to bail granted by a constable (PACE s47(1)), with the 'normal powers to impose conditions of bail' (as defined in BA 1976 s3(6)) applying (PACE s47(1A)). On granting bail, a custody officer can require a security or surety, or impose a condition or conditions, or a combination of these.

175 Note that it has been held to be an abuse of process for the investigating officer to oppose bail following charge where the officer had promised that, if the suspect voluntarily returned to the UK and surrendered to the police, bail would be granted (*R (Hauschildt) v Highbury Corner Magistrates' Court* [2007] EWHC 3494 (Admin)).

176 *R v Bournemouth Justices ex p Cross and Others* (1988) Times, October 24, DC.

177 This includes PACE 38(1), as applied by PACE s40(10) (ie where bail is considered in respect of a person whose detention is under review at some time following charge).

Securities

10.142 A security – that is, money or some other valuable item such as jewellery or a passport provided by the suspect or on the suspect's behalf before being released – may be required if it appears necessary for the purpose of preventing the person from absconding (BA 1976 ss3(5) and 3A(5)).[178]

Sureties

10.143 A surety is, in effect, a promise by a person (other than the suspect) to forfeit a sum of money if the suspect fails to surrender to custody at the appointed time. One or more sureties can be required if it appears necessary to ensure that the suspect surrenders to custody (BA 1976 ss3(4) and 3A(5)).[179] In the case of a suspect under 17 years of age,[180] if a parent or guardian consents to be a surety for the child, the surety may be required to ensure that the child complies with any condition imposed on them (see below). However, a parent or guardian cannot be so bound if the child will reach 17 years before the date on which they are due to surrender, nor be bound to any condition to which they do not consent. In any event, the person cannot be bound in a sum greater than £50 (BA 1976 s3(7)). In practice, sureties are rarely required by the police when granting bail.

Conditions

10.144 A custody officer cannot attach conditions to bail unless it appears to the officer necessary to do so:

(1) for the purpose of preventing the person from failing to surrender to custody;
(2) for the purpose of preventing the person from committing an offence while on bail;
(3) for the purpose of preventing the person from interfering with witnesses or otherwise obstructing the course of justice, whether in relation to themself or any other person; or
(4) for the person's own protection or, in the case of a child or young person, for their own welfare or in their own interests (BA 1976 s3A(5)).

If one or more of these requirements is satisfied, the custody officer may impose any relevant condition that a court could impose other than (BA 1976 s3A(2) and (5)):

- a condition that the person reside at a bail hostel;
- a condition designed to ensure that the person co-operates with the preparation of a court report;

178 Although BA 1976 s3A(5) states that a security can be required if it is necessary for any of the purposes mentioned in para 10.144 below, section 3(5) restricts their use to ensuring surrender to custody (confirmed in *R (Shea) v Winchester Crown Court* [2013] EWHC 1050 (Admin)).

179 Although BA 1976 s3A(5) states that a surety can be required if it is necessary for any of the purposes mentioned in para 10.119 below, section 3(4) restricts their use to ensuring surrender to custody.

180 The relevant age remains under 17, despite the relevant age being under 18 for most purposes under PACE. BA 1976 s2 defines 'young person' as a person under the age of 18 years, but BA 1976 s3(7) refers to a person under the age of 17 years rather than to a young person.

- a condition that the person attends an interview with the lawyer;
- electronic monitoring;
- medical examination in the case of a person charged with murder; or
- drugs assessment and follow-up.

10.145 The custody officer is not required to have substantial grounds for believing in the necessity of any conditions, only that such conditions 'appear' to be necessary for one of the specified purposes. The question arises as to what grounds the officer is required to have in order to decide to impose conditions. It has been held that a court, in considering conditions, must perceive a real and not merely a fanciful risk that the defendant will not surrender to custody,[181] and it is suggested that the same principle should apply to custody officers in respect of all of the relevant purposes of bail conditions. Therefore, the officer must be able to point to a concrete reason why a condition is necessary, and how it relates to one or more of the statutory purposes. The lawyer should consider how any proposed condition relates to the statutory purposes, whether it is realistic and whether it is proportionate to the perceived risk. It has been held that although a condition not to drive is lawful, the fact that it may have unjust results by, in effect, extending a subsequently imposed period of disqualification, should be considered.[182] In cases where there are simultaneous Family Court proceedings, the custody officer should take into account any order that the court has or may make.[183]

10.146 In view of the wide powers to impose conditions, it is not possible to provide an exhaustive list of possible conditions. Below is a list of commonly imposed conditions, by reference to the criteria for imposing conditions under BA 1976 s3A:

(1) Failing to surrender to custody:
- security;
- reporting to a police station;
- residence at a particular address;
- not to leave the UK (possibly combined with a condition of surrender of passport).

(2) Committing an offence while on bail:
- not to go to a particular place or area (for example, licensed premises, shopping centre, address of victim, etc);
- curfew;[184]
- not to drive;
- residence at a place some distance from scene of alleged crime.

(3) Interference with witnesses or obstruction of course of justice:
- not to contact, directly or through others, named witnesses;
- not to go within a specified distance of address of witness.

181 *R v Mansfield Justices ex p Sharkey* [1985] QB 613, QBD.

182 *R v Kwame* (1974) 60 Cr App R 65, CA.

183 In *Nottinghamshire CC v Mother and Others* [2024] EWHC 666 (Fam), it was held that in imposing a condition of no unsupervised contact with a child, the custody officer should have made it subject to any order to the contrary by the Family Court.

184 It was held in *R (Crown Prosecution Service) v Chorley Justices* [2002] EWHC 2162 (Admin), that where a curfew condition is imposed, a further condition requiring the person to present themself at the door of their home during the curfew to a police officer could be imposed.

(4) Own protection (or welfare):
- residence at a particular address;
- not to go to a particular place or area;
- curfew.

Enforcement of bail

10.147 Police bail granted under PACE s38 is enforceable in the same way as bail granted by a court. Failure to surrender to custody at the appointed time without reasonable cause is an offence under BA 1976 s6, and the suspect may be arrested if they fail to surrender or if a police officer has reasonable grounds for believing that the suspect is not likely to surrender to custody (BA 1976 s7). Breach of bail conditions is not an offence, but a person released on bail subject to conditions may be arrested if a constable has reasonable grounds for believing that they are likely to breach any of the conditions, or for suspecting that they have broken any of the conditions. Furthermore, if the person was released subject to a surety, they may be arrested if the surety notifies the police in writing that the person is unlikely to surrender to custody and that the surety wants to be relieved of the obligations as surety (BA 1976 s7(3)). The court at which the suspect is due to appear may extend bail by fixing a later time at which the suspect is to surrender, whether or not bail was granted subject to a surety (MCA 1980 s43(1)).

Review of bail decisions

10.148 If the custody officer grants bail subject to conditions, whether without charge or following charge, the suspect may make an application to the same or another custody officer serving at the same station for the conditions to be varied. That officer may vary or remove conditions, but may also impose new conditions, including more onerous conditions (BA 1976 s3A(4)). There is no prescribed procedure for making such an application. The suspect may, alternatively or in addition, make an application to a magistrates' court for variation of the conditions (MCA 1980 s43B(1)). As with application to a custody officer to review conditions, an application requires careful consideration since the court has the power to impose conditions that had not been imposed or impose more onerous conditions (PACE s47(1D) and (1E)). The procedure for reconsideration by a magistrates' court of a bail decision by a police officer, including a decision as to the imposition of conditions, is governed by Criminal Procedure Rules 2020[185] (CrimPR) r14.6. In considering variation or removal of conditions, a court can take into account a police officer's opinion that the suspect may not surrender to custody even though the source of the information giving rise to the officer's opinion has not been disclosed.[186] There is no appeal against the decision of a magistrates' court, but the decision is susceptible to judicial review.[187]

185 SI No 759.

186 *R (Ajaib) v Birmingham Magistrates' Court* [2009] EWHC 2127 (Admin).

187 *R (Carson) v Ealing Magistrates' Court* [2012] EWHC 1456 (Admin).

10.149 Note that where a custody officer has granted conditional or unconditional bail, a prosecutor may apply to the court for a condition to be imposed or varied, or for bail to be denied (BA 1976 s5B(1)). However, an application can only be made if it is based on information that was not available to the officer granting bail when the decision was first made (BA 1976 s5B(3)).

Detention in custody after charge

The 'right to bail'

10.150 Where a person is charged with an offence, they must be released pending their first court appearance unless one or more of the conditions in PACE s38(1) is satisfied.[188] The presumption of bail is subject to two significant restrictions. First, a custody officer cannot grant bail to a person charged with murder (PACE s38(1)(c)). Second, where the suspect is charged with any of the following offences, and the suspect already has a conviction[189] for any of those offences in any part of the UK (or a conviction for culpable homicide), bail may only be granted if the custody officer is satisfied that there are exceptional circumstances that justify the grant of bail (CJPOA 1994 s25).[190] The offences concerned are:

- murder;
- attempted murder;
- manslaughter;
- rape (under SOA 1956 s1 or SOA 2003 s1, or under the law of Scotland or Northern Ireland);
- assault by penetration (SOA 2003 s2);
- causing a person to engage in sexual activity without consent where the activity caused involved penetration within the SOA 2003 s4(4)(a)–(d) (SOA 2003 s4);
- rape of a child aged under 13 (SOA 2003 s5);
- assault of a child aged under 13 by penetration (SOA 2003 s6);
- causing or inciting a child aged under 13 to engage in sexual activity, where an activity involving penetration within SOA 2003 s8(2)(a)–(d) was caused (SOA 2003 s8);
- sexual activity with a person with a mental disorder impeding choice, where the touching involved penetration within SOA 2003 s30(3)(a)–(d) (SOA 2003 s30);

188 It was held in *Hutt v Commissioner of Police of the Metropolis* [2003] EWCA Civ 1911 that if the arrest leading to the detention was unlawful, bail could not be denied under PACE s38(1). This probably does not apply where the nature of the illegality was such that it could be, or has been, 'cured', for example, where failure to give the required information under PACE s28 is 'cured' by the arrested person subsequently being given this information.

189 Including a finding of not guilty by reason of insanity, a finding under Criminal Procedure (Insanity) Act 1964 s4A(3) (unfitness to plead) that a person did the act or made the omission charged against the person, or conviction for an offence for which the person was absolutely or conditionally discharged (CJPOA 1994 s25(5)).

190 It was held in *R (O) v Harrow Crown Court* [2003] EWHC 868 (Admin) that CJPOA 1994 s25 does not violate ECHR Article 5 (right to liberty and security), provided that it is not construed too narrowly.

- causing or inciting a person with a mental disorder impeding choice to engage in sexual activity, where an activity involving penetration within SOA 2003 s31(3)(a)–(d) was caused (SOA 2003 s31);[191] or
- an attempt to commit any of these offences (other the first three listed above) (CJPOA 1994 s25(2)).

10.151 Where the previous conviction was for any of the offences listed above or culpable homicide in any part of the UK, the restriction only applies if the person received a custodial sentence (CJPOA 1994 s25(3A)). No guidance is given in the CJPOA 1994 to the meaning of 'exceptional circumstances' or to the relationship between CJPOA 1994 s25 and PACE s38. It would seem that the custody officer would still have to be satisfied that one or more of PACE s38 conditions applies before withholding bail, but in practice it is highly unlikely that a custody officer would grant bail in the circumstances covered by CJPOA 1994 s25.

Grounds for withholding bail

10.152 In the case of an adult, PACE s38(1) criteria are as follows:

(1) The name or address of the person arrested cannot be ascertained, or the custody officer has reasonable grounds for doubting whether the name or address given by them is their real name or address (PACE s38(1)(a)(i)). The expression 'cannot be ascertained' imposes a strict test and more or less equates with a refusal by the person to give such details, and where there is no other information about their name or address. Doubt about the person's true name or address has to be reasonable, and the lawyer will want to know the grounds for such a belief. Mere suspicion is not enough. Doubt may occur where, for example, documents are found on the person containing a name different from that given. It may be that the person can offer an explanation, although they should be warned that any statement made at this stage could provide evidence to the police in respect of the offence for which they have been charged or any other offence. Sometimes the police may have visited the address given by the person and been told that they are not known and/or do not live there. Again, there may be a rational explanation for this that can be safely disclosed to the police.

(2) The custody officer has reasonable grounds for believing that the person arrested will fail to appear in court to answer bail (PACE s38(1)(a)(ii)). In considering this ground the custody officer must have regard to the following factors (PACE s38(2A)):
   - the nature and seriousness of the offence, and the probable penalty;
   - the character, antecedents, associations and community ties of the person;
   - the person's record in respect of previous grants of bail;
   - the strength of the evidence; and
   - any other relevant consideration.[192]

191 Plus a range of similar sexual offences under the Sexual Offences (Northern Ireland) Order 2008 SI No 1769 (NI 2).

192 Note that the custody officer is not required to consider whether there is a real prospect of a custodial sentence since PACE s38(2A) provides that BA 1976 Sch 1 Part 1 paras 1A and 2(2) are to be disregarded.

The officer must have reasonable grounds for their belief, and the lawyer should seek to ascertain what those grounds are. The grounds may derive from the nature and seriousness of the offence charged or from a record of previous failure to surrender to custody. The lawyer should consider whether those grounds are reasonable and, if they are, whether they may be suitably catered for by the imposition of conditions.

(3) Where the person was arrested for an imprisonable offence, the custody officer has reasonable grounds for believing that their detention is necessary to prevent them from committing an offence (PACE s38(1)(a)(iii)). There is room for confusion regarding this ground, since it is stated to apply to a person arrested for an imprisonable offence, rather than to a person charged with an imprisonable offence. It is suggested that the wording follows from the general structure of the section, and that it should only be applied where a person is charged with such an offence. This provision is similar to that relating to bail from a court under BA 1976 Sch 1 Part I para 1(2)(b).[193] In considering this ground, the custody officer must have regard to the same factors as under (2) above. Particular factors that will be relevant to whether a person may commit offences while on bail include a history of offending which is persistent and repetitive (where the current alleged offence is part of the same pattern), previous offending on bail, the fact that the current alleged offence was committed whilst on bail,[194] and factors regarding the current alleged offence (for example, a history of bad feeling between the person charged and the victim) that might suggest further offending. Since the officer must believe that detention is necessary to prevent the person from offending, it follows that the officer would have to be satisfied that the imposition of appropriate conditions would not be adequate to prevent offending.

(4) In a case where a sample may be taken under PACE s63B (see para 10.137 above), the custody officer has reasonable grounds for believing that the detention of the person is necessary to enable the sample to be taken (PACE s38(1)(a)(iiia)). In this case the suspect cannot be kept in police detention after the end of the period of six hours beginning when the person was charged with the offence (PACE s38(2)).

(5) Where the person was arrested for a non-imprisonable offence, the custody officer has reasonable grounds for believing that detention is necessary to prevent the person from causing physical injury to any other person or from causing loss of or damage to property (PACE s38(1)(a)(iv)). In considering this ground, the custody officer must have regard to the same factors as under (2) above, particularly in establishing 'reasonable grounds'. The comments regarding the requirement for a belief that detention is 'necessary' in (3) above also apply here. In

193 Although under the BA 1976 a court must have substantial grounds for believing that the defendant would commit an offence while on bail, whereas under PACE the custody officer must have reasonable grounds for believing that detention is necessary to prevent this.

194 Note that one ground on which a court may withhold bail where a person is charged with an imprisonable indictable offence is that it appears to have been committed while the person was on bail for another offence, but this is not the case under PACE s38(1).

some respects, fear of future injury, loss or damage is similar to fear of offences being committed. However, there may be a fear of offences in circumstances where it would not be possible for the custody officer to maintain that this amounted to a fear of injury, loss or damage. In any event, it should only be in rare circumstances that a person is denied bail when charged with a non-imprisonable offence.[195]

(6) The custody officer has reasonable grounds for believing that detention is necessary to prevent the person from interfering with the administration of justice, or with the investigation of offences or of a particular offence (PACE s38(1)(a)(v)). In considering this ground, the custody officer must have regard to the same factors as under (2) above. Note the comments on 'reasonable grounds' in (2) above, and on the requirement for a belief that detention is 'necessary' in (3) above.

(7) The custody officer has reasonable grounds for believing that detention is necessary for the person's own protection (PACE s38(1)(a)(vi)).[196] Once again, note the comments on 'reasonable grounds' in (2) above (although the officer does not have to have regard to the factors set out therein), and the comments regarding the requirement for a belief that detention is 'necessary' in (3) above. This ground may be relevant either because the person is at risk from others (perhaps because of the nature of the alleged offence), or because the person is vulnerable (perhaps through age or mental disorder), or because they have threatened to injure themself. In the former case, the lawyer should explore whether their client could move to another address, if only temporarily, away from the area of hostility. If appropriate, this could be made a condition of bail. In the case of vulnerability, if the problem is lack of any, or appropriate, accommodation, it may be possible to make arrangements for the client to be suitably housed.

Leaving the police station

10.153 The actions to be taken by the lawyer before leaving the police station will depend on the stage the investigation has reached and whether the client has been charged. If the client has not been charged, the lawyer should review the matters set out in para 7.75 above in order to check whether any further action should be taken at this stage. If the client has been charged, the lawyer should consider whether it is appropriate to ask the police to pursue any particular lines of enquiry, given their obligation to pursue all reasonable lines of enquiry including those that may point away from the suspect (under the CPIA 1996 Code of Practice para 3.5). Where relevant,

195 Note that PACE s38(1)(a)(iv) refers to a person having been arrested for (as opposed to charged with) an offence that is not imprisonable. See the comments regarding this distinction under (3) above.

196 Whether this ground is compatible with ECHR Art 5 is highly fact-specific: *Archer v Commissioner of Police of the Metropolis* [2020] EWHC 1567 (QB).

the lawyer should also consider the client's physical and mental well-being, and give appropriate advice and/or take appropriate action.[197]

10.154 If the suspect has been charged and bailed to court, the lawyer should ensure that their client is clear about any bail conditions, their obligation to surrender to custody and the consequences of not doing so, and the arrangements for representation in the court proceedings. If the client has been given a long bail date, it may be appropriate for an appointment to be made at the lawyer's office.

10.155 If the client has been charged and detained in custody, the lawyer should normally see them again before leaving the station. First, it will frequently be helpful for the lawyer to take initial instructions relevant to any bail application to be made at the first court appearance. The lawyer should, by this stage, know what the police objections to bail are, and although the prosecutor will not necessarily adopt the same approach, the police view is clearly important. If bail with conditions, or with a surety or security, is possible, instructions can be taken about what conditions would be acceptable to the client, what might be available as a security and/or who might be available as a surety. For a checklist of information to be obtained in respect of a bail application, see appendix 2 checklist 12.

10.156 A second reason for seeing the client at this stage is to ensure that they understand what is going on, and what is likely to happen, including the timescale. If the client is to be produced in court the following morning, or if they are to appear by way of live link, they need to know this. It should not be assumed that the police will tell the client, or that they will understand or believe what they are told by the police. The client may want to make arrangements for fresh clothes, food or reading material to be brought in. Usually there will be no objection from the police to such arrangements. Persons held in custody are normally entitled to speak on the telephone to a person nominated by them (Codes C and H para 5.6; Code I para 5.5), although visits are at the custody officer's discretion (Codes C and H para 5.4; Code I para 5.3).

10.157 The client should be told that they continue to be entitled to legal advice at any time. Furthermore, particularly if the client refused to answer police questions or if they have denied the allegation, they should be warned of the possibility that they will be visited by the officer in the case after the lawyer has left. Unfortunately, the courts do not always disapprove of such visits, even where the suspect subsequently agrees to be interviewed without the lawyer present, and then proceeds to make admissions. In *R v Williams*,[198] for example, the Court of Appeal held that a judge was entitled to accept that an hour-long 'social visit' by the investigating officers to the

197 Evidence shows that arrest and detention, particularly in respect of certain types of offences such as sexual offences, can be important factors in self-harm and suicide by suspects during or shortly after leaving police custody. The Independent Office for Police Conduct (IOPC) statistics on deaths during or following police custody are available via: www.policeconduct.gov.uk/our-work/research-and-statistics. See also J Phillips, L Gelsthorpe, N Padfield and S Buckingham, *Non-natural deaths following prison and police custody: Data and practice issues*, Research report 106 (Equality and Human Rights Commission, December 2016), available at: www.equalityhumanrights.com/sites/default/files/research-report-106-non-natural-deaths-following-prison-and-police-custody.pdf.

198 (1992) Times, February 6, CA.

suspect in his cell, followed by an interview in the absence of his lawyer during which the suspect made damaging admissions, was proper and not in breach of the codes of practice. The court did say, however, that such visits should usually be avoided.[199] Whether the police will take any notice of this view may be doubted, and the client should be strongly advised that in the event of such a visit, they should ask to see their lawyer. The client should also be warned in appropriate cases of the possibility that the police may conduct covert surveillance of their cell, a practice that has come to light in a number of cases, or that the police may recruit cell-mates or others in detention to act as informants.[200]

199 See also *R v Marshall* (1992) Times, December 28, CA, where it was held that evidence of a confession made in a subsequent interview with a 'borderline subnormal' suspect should have been excluded.

200 See *R v Ali* (1991) Times, February 19, CA; *R v Bailey* [1993] 3 All ER 513, CA; *R v Mason* [2002] EWCA Crim 385; *PG and JH v UK* (App Nos 44787/98 and 44787/98) [2002] Crim LR 308, ECtHR. In *R v Allan* [2004] EWCA Crim 2236, it was held that the use of a fellow prisoner as an informant to obtain admissions infringed the defendant's common law right to silence and the privilege against self-incrimination.

CHAPTER 11

Children and other vulnerable detainees

continued

Introduction

11.1 This chapter deals with issues that specifically relate to suspects who are vulnerable. This includes children; those with mental health difficulties; and those who experience physical or other learning disabilities, including neurodivergence. Finally, the chapter deals with language difficulties and suspects who are foreign nationals.

11.2 The UN Convention on the Rights of the Child defines a 'child' as a person below the age of 18 years. The Police and Criminal Evidence Act 1984 (PACE) and the PACE Codes of Practice use the terms 'juvenile' or 'child' and the Children and Young Persons Act (CYPA) 1933 uses the term 'young person' to describe a person under the age of 18. Notwithstanding the statutory meaning of those words, unless the statutory provision prevents it, the terms child or children are used throughout this chapter. The terms child, children and young persons are used in Ministry of Justice (MoJ) and other statutory guidance. Both PACE and the PACE Codes of Practice contain specific provisions regarding children. PACE makes no reference to mentally vulnerable suspects, and limited reference to mentally handicapped suspects,[1] but the codes do contain provisions relevant to mentally vulnerable suspects. The codes also contain specific provisions for suspects in the other special groups referred to above. Policing practice regarding suspects from vulnerable groups varies considerably. The report of a thematic review by His Majesty's Inspectorate of Constabulary (HMIC) in 2015 concluded that, while it found some good practices, too many children and vulnerable people were arrested and detained rather than being dealt with in a way that did not criminalise them; that police assessment of vulnerability was sometimes poorly conducted; and that the treatment of vulnerable people in custody sometimes fell below acceptable standards.[2] Subsequent force reports by His Majesty's Inspectorate of Constabulary and Fire & Rescue Services (HMICFRS) show improvement but stubborn problems persist, for example, children unnecessarily arrested and then detained rather than being moved to local authority accommodation.[3]

11.3 Lawyers will need to consider how they should adapt their practice to take into account the additional needs of clients from the groups considered in this chapter and, where appropriate, challenge police judgments as to vulnerability and the treatment of vulnerable suspects. The need for special consideration is recognised, to an extent, by the Legal Aid Agency's (LAA) Standard Crime Contract (SCC) 2022 (draft SCC 2025), which provides that payment for personal attendance at the police station may be

1 The only reference is in PACE s77, which provides for a warning to be given to a jury of the special need for caution where a case is substantially dependent on a confession by a mentally handicapped person made in the absence of an independent person.

2 *The welfare of vulnerable people in police custody* (March 2015), available at: https://assets-hmicfrs.justiceinspectorates.gov.uk/uploads/the-welfare-of-vulnerable-people-in-police-custody.pdf.

3 *North London – Joint inspection of police custody* (November 2017), available at: https://hmicfrs.justiceinspectorates.gov.uk/news/news-feed/police-custody-north-london-generally.

claimed where the client is eligible for assistance from an appropriate adult, or requires an interpreter, even in circumstances where a claim for personal attendance would not otherwise be met.[4]

Children

General considerations

11.4 The police – in common with other institutions such as local authorities, the NHS and organisations providing probation services – are under a duty in discharging their functions to safeguard and promote the welfare of children (Children Act (CA) 2004 s11). The National Police Chiefs' Council (NPCC) has adopted the Youth Justice Board 'Child First' policy[5] guided by child-centred policing. Under this regime, children ought to be considered as children first rather than mini-adults or offenders; encouraging collaboration with them and seeking to maximise opportunities to divert them away from the stigma of contact with the criminal justice system.[6] While this does not mean that the police cannot arrest and detain children, it does mean that in making decisions regarding arrest and detention, the police must actively consider their welfare.[7] In deciding whether to arrest a child, police officers must take into account their age in determining whether arrest is necessary (see para 2.18 above), and should seek to time any arrest in order to minimise the time that they spend in custody.[8] This should mean that the police do not conclude that arrest of a child is necessary for a minor offence or in circumstances where they may find arrest necessary in respect of an adult.[9] Arresting a child should be a last resort. Custody officers and reviewing inspectors should also 'anxiously scrutinise'[10] a child's age and welfare needs when considering whether it is necessary to detain them both pre and post charge (see

4 SCC Specification 2022 para 9.10 (draft SCC Specification 2025 para 9.4) (although this refers to suspects who are unable to communicate by telephone rather than those who need an interpreter); and see para 1.55 above.

5 *A guide to Child First*, available at: https://yjresourcehub.uk/wp-content/uploads/media/Child_First_Overview_and_Guide_April_2022_YJB.pdf.

6 *Children and Young Persons Policing Strategy 2024–2027* (October 2024).

7 The NPCC *Child centred policing Best practice framework* sets the strategic approach to be adopted by all police officers, available at: www.npcc.police.uk/search?q=child+centred+policing.

8 College of Policing, *Authorised Professional Practice: Detention and custody: Children and young persons* (March 2024) para 2, available at: www.app.college.police.uk/app-content/detention-and-custody-2/detainee-care/children-and-young-persons/#children-and-young-persons. See also See *ST v Chief Constable of Nottinghamshire* [2022] EWHC 1280 (QB).

9 In its report, *In harm's way: The role of the police in keeping children safe* (July 2015) (available at: https://assets-hmicfrs.justiceinspectorates.gov.uk/uploads/in-harms-way.pdf), the HMIC expressed 'surprise' at finding children having been arrested for offences involving 'pushing a sibling, criminal damage in their own (children's) home, or for wasting police time for running away from home' (at p11).

10 *ST v Chief Constable of Nottinghamshire* [2022] EWHC 1280 (QB).

para 2.70 above).[11] The College of Policing advises that in conducting a risk assessment in respect of a child (see para 4.24 above), custody staff should take into account specific risk factors that may affect individual suspects, such as physical and mental maturity and other vulnerability indicators, in addition to the general risk factors.[12,13]

Key aspects of the judgment in the case of *ST*[14]

In finding that the arrest of a 14-year-old at his home address before 6am, 12 days after an alleged offence of robbery and despite the child's father being willing to bring him to the police station, the court cited the following factors as critical:

1 The arresting officer had insufficient information independently to assess whether an arrest was necessary or whether, if he held such a belief, it was a reasonable belief (in line with PACE s24(5) and Code G para 2.8).
2 Neither the investigating officer nor the arresting officer considered whether the policing objective could be met or achieved by less intrusive means, taking into account:
   - the situation of the victim;
   - the nature of the offence;
   - the circumstances of the suspect; and
   - the needs of the investigative process.
3 Taken together, there should be a differentiation between children and adults when considering the necessity for arrest and detention – age being a material consideration in those decisions.
4 The police should not use an arrest as an alternative to a PACE s8 warrant. In a dynamic situation, a request for a voluntary search can be made as an alternative.
5 The decision to arrest is dynamic and ought to be reassessed in light of new information.
6 The timing of the arrest failed to ensure that the child was in detention for no longer that was necessary. The timing of the arrest can be a material consideration concerning necessity.
7 There is no distinction between 'older' and 'younger' children when considering necessity. Older children should not be treated as more 'robust' – everyone under the age of 18 is to be treated as a child.

11 See *ST v Chief Constable of Nottinghamshire* [2022] EWHC 1280 (QB), which provides very helpful support in representations concerning the necessity to arrest and representations to de-arrest or otherwise challenge detention. See also Dr V Kemp, N Carr, H Kent and S Farrall, 'Examining the impact of PACE on the detention and questioning of child suspects' (University of Nottingham, London, 2023), which indicated that custody sergeants failed to authorise detention in less than 1% of arrests, available at: https://nottingham-repository.worktribe.com/output/21148005 (see p36).

12 At para 3.

13 The Child First Custody Training and Research Pilot supported by the Mayor's Office for Policing and Crime (MOPAC) operated an 'opt out' rather than 'opt in' in respect of legal advice for detained children in London. The pilot is part of a wider Nuffield Foundation-funded research project piloting a 'Child first' approach led by Dr Vicky Kemp and Dr Miranda Bevan. Details are available at: www.nuffieldfoundation.org/project/child-first-children-in-police-custody.

14 *ST v Chief Constable of Nottinghamshire* [2022] EWHC 1280 (QB).

11.5 The obligation to safeguard and promote the welfare of children also means, where appropriate, that the police should consider whether a child ought to be treated as a victim rather than a suspect. This is particularly the case in relation to prostitution, sexual exploitation and human trafficking offences. Crown Prosecution Service (CPS) policy is that children who are involved in prostitution should be treated as victims of abuse,[15] and similar considerations apply where a child is the victim of human trafficking, exploitation[16] or modern slavery.[17]

11.6 Crime and Disorder Act (CDA) 1998 s37(1) provides that 'the principal aim of the youth justice system is [to] prevent offending by children and young persons'. Defence lawyers, in common with all others who carry out functions in relation to the youth justice system, have a statutory duty to have regard to that aim (CDA 1998 s37(2)). However, the lawyer's professional obligation to act in the client's best interests remains paramount.[18]

11.7 CDA 1998 s38 requires local authorities, in co-operation with the police, the providers of probation services and health authorities, to ensure that the following youth justice services are available in their area at the pre-court stage:

- appropriate adult services;
- the provision of assistance to persons determining whether youth cautions should be given;
- bail support; and
- placement of those remanded to local authority accommodation.[19]

11.8 In addition, local authorities must publish youth justice plans setting out how youth justice services are to be provided (CDA 1998 s40(1)), and must appoint one or more youth offending teams (YOTs) to co-ordinate and provide youth justice services (CDA 1998 s39). Defence lawyers should ensure that they are familiar with the services and schemes available in their area. Information is also available from the Youth Justice Board for England and Wales (YJB), which has published national standards requiring YOT managers to develop integrated remand management structures that include provision for appropriate adults, and for providing

15 CPS guidance, *Prostitution and Exploitation of Prostitution* (April 2024), available at: www.cps.gov.uk/legal-guidance/prostitution-and-exploitation-prostitution.

16 See the Youth Justice Legal Centre Toolkit, *Child Criminal Exploitation* for more information, available at: yjlc.uk/resources/legal-guides-and-toolkits/child-criminal-exploitation.

17 CPS guidance, *Modern Slavery and human trafficking: offences and defences, including the section 45 defence* (July 2025), available at: www.cps.gov.uk/legal-guidance/human-trafficking-smuggling-and-slavery.

18 See generally, K Aubrey-Johnson, S Lambe and J Twite, *Youth Justice Law and Practice* (Legal Action Group, 2019, new edition due out 2026).

19 The *Youth Remand Concordat* (February 2025) provides guidance for all partners involved in decisions regarding remand. Paragraph 6 sets out the process to be followed at the police station where a child is charged. Available at: www.gov.uk/government/publications/youth-remand-concordat.

accommodation where it is required under PACE s38(6) in respect of a child who had been denied bail following charge.[20]

Definition of 'child'

11.9 Anyone who appears to be under the age of 18 years must be treated as a child in the absence of clear evidence to the contrary for the purposes of PACE and the Codes of Practice (PACE s37(15); Code C para 1.5 and note for guidance (NfG) 1L; Code H para 1.11; Code D para 2.4; Code I para 1.10). The relevant age for the purposes of PACE ss30A (bail elsewhere than at a police station), 63B (testing for the presence of a class A drug) and 65 (supplementary provisions regarding the questioning and treatment of persons by the police), is also 18 years (as a result of amendments to these sections by Policing and Crime Act (PCA) 2017 s74). The actual age of the suspect is irrelevant, so that even if a suspect is 18 years old or older, but the available evidence points to them being younger, they must be treated as a child unless and until evidence to the contrary is available. If the lawyer is aware that their client is a child, the lawyer should normally advise them to disclose their true age. If, despite the lawyer's best efforts, the client is not willing to do so, the lawyer should consider whether it is necessary for them to withdraw for the same reasons as those which apply where a client gives a false name and/or address (see para 5.40 above).

Police powers

11.10 The minimum age of criminal responsibility in England and Wales is 10 years[21] and a child under that age should neither be arrested nor held in police detention. Generally, police powers in respect of persons between the ages of 10 and 17 years are the same as for adults. However, note the following powers in respect of children and young persons, some of which also apply to children under 10 years:

(1) A child under 18 years may be kept under police protection at a police station, as a place of safety, where a police officer has reasonable cause to believe that the child would be likely to suffer significant harm if not removed to suitable accommodation (CA 1989 s46(1)).[22] The child can be kept under police protection for up to 72 hours, although if they are taken to a police station they must be moved to local authority or other suitable accommodation as soon as reasonably practicable (CA 1989 s46(3)(f)).

20 YJB, *Standards for children in the youth justice system 2019*, available at: www.gov.uk/search/all?keywords=standards+for+children+in+the+youth+justice+system. See also the duties under CA 2004 s11, and for application to the police, *Castle v Commissioner of Police of the Metropolis* [2011] EWHC 2317 (Admin). Local authorities may enter into centralised arrangements with other local authorities to provide secure accommodation for children at risk of being detained in police custody (*R (AR (A Child)) v Waltham Forest LBC* [2020] EWHC 622 (Admin)).

21 CYPA 1933 s50.

22 See further concerning the balance between this provision and Article 5 of the European Convention on Human Rights in *Archer v Commissioner of Police of the Metropolis* [2021] EWCA Civ 1662.

(2) A court can make a child safety order in respect of a child under 10 years who has committed an act that, if they had been 10 years or over, would have constituted an offence (CDA 1998 s11). However, the police have no powers of arrest in relation to child safety orders.

(3) Where a local authority has designated premises, or a superintendent or above has authorised use of the power (CDA 1998 s16(1) and (2)), a police constable who has reasonable cause to believe that a child or young person found by the constable in a specified area during a specified period is of compulsory school age[23] and is absent from school without lawful authority, may remove the child or young person to the designated premises or to the school from which the child or young person is absent (CDA 1998 s16(3)).

Persons who must be informed

11.11 The police have a number of duties to inform people of the arrest and detention of a child, which is in addition to a child's right to have someone informed of their arrest under PACE s56 (see para 2.126 above):[24]

(1) Where a child or young person[25] is in police detention, the police must take such steps as are practicable to ascertain the identity of the person responsible for the child's or young person's welfare (CYPA 1933 s34(2)). If the child or young person is in the care of the local authority, it is the authority rather than the parent or guardian who should be informed (CYPA 1933 s34(8)). Unless it is impracticable, that person (or authority) must be informed that the child or young person has been arrested, why they have been detained and the place of detention. This must be done as soon as is practicable (CYPA 1933 s34(3) and (4); Code C para 3.13; Code H para 3.15; Code I para 3.18).

(2) If the child or young person is known to be subject to a supervision order as defined in CA 1989 Part IV, the responsible officer must be given the same information as in (1) above as soon as reasonably practicable (CYPA 1933 s34(7); Code C para 3.14; Code H para 3.16; Code I para 3.18(ii)). There is a similar requirement to inform the local authority where it is known that the child or young person is being provided with accommodation by or on behalf of a local authority under CA 1989 s20 (CYPA 1933 s34(7A)), or is subject to a youth rehabilitation order (CYPA 1933 s34(7B)).

(3) The appropriate adult, who may or may not be the parent or guardian, must be informed of the grounds for detention and the place of detention as soon as practicable, and must be asked to come to the police

23 A person ceases to be of compulsory school age at the end of the school year in which they attain the age of 16 years (Education Act 1996 s8).

24 CYPA 1933 s34(9) makes it clear that the right of intimation is separate from and in addition to the police duty to inform certain people of the child's arrest and detention.

25 A child means a person under the age of 14 years, and a young person means a person who has attained the age of 14 and is under the age of 18 years (CYPA 1933 s107(1)).

station (Code C para 3.15; Code H para 3.17; Code I para 3.20(d); and see para 11.17 below).[26]

(4) Where the police wish to interview a child who is subject to current family proceedings, leave of the Family Court is only required where such an interview may lead to the child disclosing information confidential to those proceedings and not otherwise available to the police. Where the child is a ward of court, leave of the court is not required. The following people must be informed directly, where applicable, the local authority and other carer (if any). The police together with the individuals above should ensure that any children's guardian (if appointed) is also informed.[27]

11.12 The lawyer should check with the custody officer to see who has been informed and, in particular, whether the appropriate adult is at the police station and, if not, what steps are being taken to secure the appropriate adult's presence. There is no provision for delay in informing the persons specified above even if the child is being held incommunicado under PACE s56 or legal advice is being delayed under PACE s58 (Codes C, H and I Annex B NfG B1).

Child's right to legal advice

11.13 The right to consult a solicitor under PACE s58, Terrorism Act (TA) 2000 Sch 8 para 7 and National Security Act (NSA) 2023 Sch 6 para 7 (see para 2.129 above) applies to children in the same way as it does to adults.[28] PACE s58(4), TA 2000 Sch 8 para 7 and NSA 2023 Sch 6 para 7 provide that where a person makes a request to consult a solicitor they must be permitted to do so as soon as practicable, and there is no provision for action on the request to be delayed until the request has been confirmed with the appropriate adult. Code C para 6.5A, Code H para 6.6 and Code I para 6.5 state that in the case of a child, an appropriate adult should consider whether legal advice from a solicitor is required – but go on to state that if the suspect wants legal advice, the police must take the appropriate action and not wait until the appropriate adult arrives.

11.14 Children have reported the isolation and fear that is amplified by having insufficient information and waiting for the solicitor and appropriate adult

26 It was held in *DPP v Evans* [2002] EWHC 2976 (Admin) that the police were not required to delay a breath test procedure to enable an appropriate adult to be present.

27 See Family Procedure Rules 2010 SI No 2955 Practice Direction 12D, *Inherent jurisdiction (including wardship) proceedings* para 5.1, available at: www.justice.gov.uk/courts/procedure-rules/family/practice_directions/pd_part_12d#:~:text=There%20is%20no%20requirement%20for,5.2. See *Re Ward of Court (Wardship: Interview)* [2017] EWHC 1022 (Fam).

28 Research by Dr V Kemp, N Carr and S Farrall, *Examining the impact of PACE on Detention and Questioning of Child Suspects* (University of Nottingham, May 2023) (available at: https://nottingham-repository.worktribe.com/output/21148005) found that just under 53,000 children were arrested in England and Wales in 2022 and that 80% of them requested legal advice compared with 61% for adults (p36). Black, brown and racialised children requested legal advice more often than other children and under 14-year-olds are the least likely to request legal advice (p37). Police stations in London are currently piloting an 'opt out' rather than 'opt in' scheme for children whereby detained children are presumed to require legal advice.

to arrive at the police station. Research by Dr Vicky Kemp[29] describes the trauma of being at the police station as analogous to a further adverse childhood experience. The child should have access to the appropriate adult and solicitor as soon as possible and throughout their time in custody. Steps taken to restrict this to the proximity of the interview should be resisted (see paras 3.55, 3.58 and 4.11 above)

11.15 Since there is no provision for the police to delay contacting an appropriate adult, once an appropriate adult has been contacted it would be difficult for the police to justify delaying access to a lawyer under PACE s58(8), TA 2000 Sch 8 para 8(1) or NSA 2023 s28 and Sch 6 or Code I para 6.6 (see paras 2.151 and 2.156 above). Unless the police have specific information that leads them to believe that the lawyer requested is dishonest,[30] once the appropriate adult has been contacted (or any other person who the police are required to inform), the fact of detention has been disclosed, and it will be difficult for a superintendent to maintain that contact with a lawyer will lead to one of the prohibited consequences. It has been held that it would be difficult for a superintendent to have a reasonable fear in respect of contact with a lawyer where the suspect had already spoken to his wife on the telephone, and a similar principle should apply to contact with an appropriate adult.[31]

The appropriate adult

Introduction

11.16 Where a child has been detained, the police must contact an appropriate adult as soon as is practicable and ask them to attend the police station (see para 11.11 above). Local authorities have a duty to secure the provision of sufficient appropriate adults for their area (CDA 1998 s38), and responsibility is also placed on YOT managers to ensure that appropriate adults are available (see para 11.7 above). PACE envisages that appropriate adults should play a key role during the detention of a child, although evidence suggests that they frequently do not understand their role, are often passive and may have an adverse impact on the interests of the person they are supposedly there to protect.[32] Increasing attention is being paid to better equipping appropriate adults to undertake this role effectively. A plethora of information, advice and support including an accessible video for appropriate adults can be found at: www.gov.uk/government/

29 See note 28 above.

30 See additionally Code I para 6.4, which permits the police to direct that a detainee cannot consult the solicitor of their choice if they have reasonable grounds to believe that to do so will result in any of the consequences set out in NSA 2023 Sch 6 para 8(4) or hinder the recovery of the benefit from their criminal conduct (see para 2.135 above).

31 *R v Davison* [1988] Crim LR 442.

32 A joint inspection report by HMIC and other inspectorates published in 2011 found that appropriate adults were frequently ill-prepared and passive (*Who's looking out for the children? The Home Office publishes a Guide for appropriate adults* (2011), available at: www.gov.uk/government/uploads/system/uploads/attachment_data/file/117682/appropriate-adults-guide.pdf), which encourages a more active role. The National Appropriate Adult Network is concerned to improve standards, and publishes national standards for appropriate adults (see: www.appropriateadult.org.uk).

publications/guidance-for-appropriate-adults/being-an-appropriate-adult.[33,34] Lawyers should be aware of the fact that appropriate adults normally do not owe a duty of confidentiality to the child, but the presence of an appropriate adult at a consultation between the lawyer and the child may not destroy legal professional privilege (see para 11.26 below).[35,36]

Appropriate people

11.17 The appropriate adult may be:

- the child's parent or guardian (or care authority if the child is 'in care');[37]
- a local authority social worker; or
- failing either of the above, another responsible adult aged 18 years or over who is not a police officer nor employed by, or under the direction or control of, the police (Code C para 1.7; Code H para 1.13; Code D para 2.6, Code I para 1.12).

In respect of the last, it was held in *R v Palmer*[38] that a 17-year-old attending on his 16-year-old brother could not be an appropriate adult because he was not 18 years or over and was too close in age. In *R v Morse and Others*,[39] it was indicated that the suspect's father, who had a low IQ, was virtually illiterate and who was probably incapable of appreciating the gravity of the situation, was not suitable.[40]

11.18 The definition of who may be an appropriate adult amounts to a hierarchy. The appropriate adult should, if possible, be a parent or guardian (or representative of the care authority); and only if they are unavailable or inappropriate should it be a social worker; finally moving to the third category if both the others are unavailable or inappropriate. In relation to availability, no guidance is given in the codes about what efforts should be made by the police and the extent of delay that should be countenanced. The custody officer will have to take into account the detention time limits and the general requirement that all persons in custody must be dealt with expeditiously. A balance is necessary between the need to protect the child

33 'Examining the impact of PACE on Detention and Questioning of Child Suspects', note 28 above, p95.

34 The video (*Being an appropriate adult*, available at: https://vimeo.com/672820069 developed by Miranda Bevan (Kings College London) and Chris Bath (National Appropriate Adult Network (NAAN)), provides an accessible explanation for parents and other appropriate adults.

35 *R v H* [2018] EWCA Crim 2868. See also N Dent and S O'Beirne, 'Inappropriate Adults? A review of the Current Use of Appropriate Adults in the Criminal Justice System' (2021) 85 *Journal of Criminal Law* 44.

36 See also V Cochrane and W Hayes, *Legal Professional Privilege in Criminal Investigations and Proceedings* (Oxford University Press, 2024) ch 6 generally re privilege in the police station; and paras 6.22–6.34 concerning appropriate adults and interpreters specifically.

37 The term 'in care' applies to all cases in which a child is 'looked after' by a local authority under the terms of the CA 1989 (Code C para 1.7(a)(i); Code H para 1.13(a)(i)). This includes those in respect of whom a care order has been made, and those who are 'accommodated' by a local authority.

38 September 1991 *Legal Action* 21.

39 [1991] Crim LR 195, Crown Court.

40 But see *R v W and Another* [1994] Crim LR 130, CA, where, on the particular facts of the case, a mother was held to be suitable despite being psychotic.

by ensuring the attendance of an appropriate adult and the disadvantages of prolonged detention in a police station.

Inappropriate people

11.19 Even if a potential appropriate adult is available, the adult may not be suitable. The following are either unsuitable to act as appropriate adults or are prohibited from doing so, discussed below:

- estranged parents;
- interested parties, such as persons suspected of involvement, social workers and custody visitors; and
- solicitors.

Estranged parents

11.20 A parent who is estranged from the child, and whose presence is expressly and specifically objected to by the child, should not act as the appropriate adult (Codes C and H NfG 1B; Code I NfG 1C). In *DPP v Blake*,[41] a confession was excluded where it had been obtained in the presence of the child's father, whom she had specifically rejected in favour of her social worker who was unavailable.

11.21 The question of estrangement is not necessarily an easy one, either for the custody officer or the lawyer. Parents are frequently annoyed or angry with their children at the police station, irrespective of whether the child is guilty of the offence for which they have been detained. The determining factor has to be the attitude of the child – does the child 'expressly and specifically' object to the parent's presence?

Interested parties

11.22 A potential appropriate adult may have an involvement with the case that renders them inappropriate or ineligible:

(1) Persons suspected of involvement. A person, including a parent or guardian, should not be the appropriate adult if they are suspected of involvement in the offence, are the victim, are a witness, are involved in the investigation or have received admissions before attending to act as the appropriate adult (Codes C and H NfG 1B; Code I NfG 1C). The meaning of 'involved in the investigation' is unclear, but could include a person who, while not a victim or witness, reported the offence or has knowledge of circumstances central to the case.[42] The exclusion of a person who has received admissions is also not without difficulty. The purpose of this provision (as with that relating to social workers – see below) must be to try to ensure that the adult advises the child fairly and does not simply pressurise them into confessing to the police. This could be important, for example, if a parent has unfairly pressurised the child into making admissions to them. It could have the effect of reinforcing an untrue confession. Alternatively, it may be that the

41 [1989] 1 WLR 432, DC.

42 This circumstance can easily arise. For instance, where parents, with the best intentions, question a child about the circumstances of the allegation and become privy to information relevant to the investigation or unbeknownst to them, a parent is in fact a witness to relevant events.

child quite truthfully admitted the offence to their parent, and that it is perfectly in order for the parent to accompany the child when they are interviewed by the police. Even then, however, the parent is likely to be unaware of the strength of the evidence in the hands of the police, and an uninvolved adult might advise the child quite differently. Note that the restriction only applies where the person received admissions before attending to act as appropriate adult.

(2) Social workers. If the child has admitted the offence to, or in the presence of, a social worker or member of a YOT other than while they are acting as the appropriate adult, another appropriate adult should be appointed 'in the interest of fairness' (Codes C and H NfG 1C; Code I NfG 1D). A social worker would also be inappropriate if involved in the same ways as applies to others (see (1) above). It has been held that a social worker who reported the offence to the police and who would be seen by the child as being 'on the side of the police' probably should not have acted as the appropriate adult.[43] However, in *R v Ward*,[44] while waiting for his solicitor to arrive, an adult suspect made confessional statements to his appropriate adult. Despite this, the appropriate adult continued to act throughout the consultation and interview – in which the suspect made no comment. At trial, an unsuccessful application was made to exclude the confession and this decision was upheld by the Court of Appeal.

(3) Custody visitors. An independent custody visitor who is present at the police station and acting in that capacity, cannot act as an appropriate adult (Codes C and H NfG 1F; Code I NfG 1G).

Solicitors

11.23 If it is proving difficult to secure the attendance of an appropriate adult, the police may ask the lawyer to act as the appropriate adult. Indeed, the child themself may be keen for the lawyer to do so because it raises the prospect of being released earlier than otherwise might be the case. However, there are difficulties, not only in terms of potential conflict of role, but also because it may not hasten the child's release unless the lawyer is willing to accept responsibility for the child after release, which is usually not advisable. In any event, Codes C, H and I specifically provide that a lawyer who is at the police station in a professional capacity cannot act as the appropriate adult (Codes C and H NfG 1F; Code I NfG 1G).

Role of the appropriate adult

11.24 The role of the appropriate adult is set out in Code C para 1.7A, Code H para 1.3A and Code I para 1.13 in the following terms:

> The role of the appropriate adult is to safeguard the rights, entitlements and welfare of juveniles and vulnerable persons . . . to whom the provisions of this and any other Code of Practice apply. For this reason, the appropriate adult is expected, amongst other things, to:

43 *DPP v Morris* (1990) 8 October (unreported).

44 [2018] EWCA Crim 1464.

- support, advise and assist them when, in accordance with this Code or any other Code of Practice, they are given or asked to provide information or participate in any procedure;
- observe whether the police are acting properly and fairly to respect their rights and entitlements, and inform an officer of the rank of inspector or above if they consider that they are not;
- assist the suspect to communicate with the police whilst respecting their right to say nothing unless they want to as set out in the terms of the caution;
- help the suspect to understand their rights and ensure that those rights are protected and respected.

The role is amplified in the Home Office guidance, *Being an appropriate adult*,[45] which states the following:

Amongst other things, the appropriate adult is expected to:

- support, advise and assist the person when they are given, or asked to provide, information or participate in any procedure
- help them to communicate, whilst respecting their right to say nothing unless they want to
- help them to understand their rights and make sure those rights are protected and respected
- observe whether the police are acting properly and fairly and tell a more senior police officer if they are not
- the Appropriate adult's role is not to provide the detainee with legal advice.[46] However, the appropriate adult can instruct a solicitor to provide advice to the detainee (see also para 11.25 below).[47]

The role of the appropriate adult during police interviews is set out in similar terms in Code C para 11.17, Code H para 11.10 and Code I para 1.12.[48] Generally, a child must not be interviewed by the police or asked to provide a written statement in the absence of the appropriate adult, unless to avoid an immediate risk of harm to persons or serious loss of or serious damage to property (Code C paras 11.1 and 11.15; Code H paras 11.2 and 11.9; Code I paras 11.1 and 11.12–11.14). The appropriate adult also has specific roles in relation to legal advice, searches and samples, and identification procedures (see paras 11.25, 11.69 and 11.70 below).

11.25 For the lawyer, the appropriate adult can be a useful ally, but the adult's presence may also cause difficulty for a number of reasons. It was noted above that a child suspect has a right to legal advice in the same way as an adult. The appropriate adult can make the request for legal advice on behalf of the child (Code C para 3.19; Code H para 3.20; Code I para 6.5), and this is so even if the child has declined legal advice (Code C para 6.5A;

45 December 2024, available at: www.gov.uk/government/publications/guidance-for-appropriate-adults.

46 See *Miller v DPP* [2018] EWHC 262 (Admin), in which the court appeared to elide the role of an appropriate adult with that of the solicitor; although it did decide that evidence obtained in the absence of an appropriate adult should have been excluded.

47 Even if the detainee does not avail themselves of the advice, once instructed, a claim can be made under SCC 2022 para 5.11 (draft SCC 2025 para 5.9) or the *Criminal Bills Assessment Manual* para 5.11.8. See also NAAN at: www.appropriateadult.org.uk/policy/legal-advice. It is essential that a clear note is made of the steps taken in good faith and that the note accompanies the claim.

48 The National Standards for appropriate adults are developed by the NAAN and approved by the YJB and Directors of adult social services, available at: www.appropriateadult.org.uk/national-standards.

Code H para 6.6; Code I para 6.5). This could cause a problem if the adult requests legal advice but the child does not wish to receive it, since the lawyer should not impose themself on an unwilling client. In such circumstances, the lawyer could treat the appropriate adult as the client.[49] A more common difficulty occurs where the adult is hostile to the lawyer requested by the child. The lawyer should remember that their client is the child and not the adult. This may mean, in an extreme case, that the lawyer should seek the exclusion of the adult.[50]

11.26 An important question is whether an appropriate adult can disclose, or can be required to disclose, what is said in their hearing during a consultation between the lawyer and their client. With regard to the latter, although the codes state that an appropriate adult is not subject to legal privilege (Codes C and H NfG 1E; Code I NfG 1F), it has been held that the presence of an appropriate adult does not necessarily destroy legal professional privilege (*A Local Authority v B*[51]). While *A Local Authority v B* arguably remains good law, the judgment should be treated with caution.[52] However, there is a separate question of whether the appropriate adult can voluntarily disclose what is said, and here the position is less certain.[53] Even if a social worker is bound by a duty of confidentiality, a parent is not, and in any event the law will provide scant protection if the appropriate adult proceeds to tell the police what they have heard.[54]

11.27 As a result, the lawyer should initially speak to their client in the absence of the appropriate adult in order to advise their client of the risk of disclosure, and to ask them whether they want the adult to be present during the consultation (see Codes C and H NfG 1E; Code I NfG 1E). If the client does wish the adult to be present, the lawyer should consider asking the adult to give an undertaking that they will not pass on to the police any information divulged during the consultation. Such an undertaking is unenforceable, but may serve to underline the importance of confidentiality to the appropriate adult.

49 Since the appropriate adult has attended voluntarily at the police station for the purpose of assisting with an investigation, they should qualify for advice under the police station advice and assistance scheme on the basis that they are a volunteer under PACE s29 (see para 2.164 above).

50 Note that the police may exclude an appropriate adult where their conduct is such as to prevent the interviewer from properly putting questions to the suspect or recording their answers (Code C para 11.17A; Code H para 11.10; Code I para para 11.11).

51 [2008] EWHC 1017 (Fam).

52 See *R v Ward* [2018] EWCA Crim 1464 at para 11.22 above. NAAN provides advice for appropriate adults regarding confidentiality on its website, at: www.appropriateadult.org.uk/policy/legal-advice.

53 In *A Local Authority v B* [2008] EWHC 1017 (Fam), the court held that the local authority which employed the social worker who acted as appropriate adult could not use the information so obtained in order to assess the needs of the family.

54 See also *Bozkurt v Thames Magistrates Court* [2001] EWHC Admin 400, where the court confirmed the duty of confidentiality as central to the perception of fairness, but drew a distinction between the confidentiality of what takes place in and outside of a client consultation.

Special considerations for the lawyer

Taking instructions from and advising children

11.28 A particular effort may be needed to establish a rapport with a child client since, for the child, the lawyer may be just another adult authority figure who is not to be trusted.[55] Although not necessarily the case, a child may be particularly nervous, scared and vulnerable, and in need of support and guidance. This may concern what is happening in the police station, but may equally concern matters outside and which might appear to them to be more pressing than their current circumstances. Equally, the child may fail to understand the seriousness of their predicament, or may believe that anything they say at the police station can be 'undone' later. In the consultation with a child the lawyer should:

- start by attempting to build a rapport and trust – listening carefully and being interested in the child's agenda;
- seek basic information about the client and their circumstances;
- be aware of indications of neurodiversity, additional learning needs or mental health difficulties by observing and asking questions where appropriate, for example, noticing signs of stress, fidgets or self-harm, or asking whether anyone helps them with their reading;[56]
- take time to prepare the client for the police interview, telling them how it will be conducted, how long it will last and who will be present;
- carefully explain the caution and its implications and, if necessary, ask the client to explain it back to the lawyer; and
- if advice to make no comment in the police interview is accepted, consider conducting a practice interview with the client.[57]

Capacity

11.29 A child under the age of 10 years is deemed unable to commit a crime (see para 11.10 above). At common law, a child between the ages of 10 and 14 was presumed not to be able to commit a crime (the presumption of doli incapax). This presumption could be rebutted by the prosecution by adducing evidence that the child knew that what they did was gravely or seriously wrong. The presumption of doli incapax was abolished by CDA

55 See Youth Justice Legal Centre and Institute for Crime and Justice Policy Research at Birkbeck University, *It's a lottery: Legal Representation of children in the criminal Justice System*, available at: https://yjlc.uk/resources/legal-updates/its-lottery-new-report-quality-legal-representation-youth-justice-system. The research found that representing children effectively is particularly time-consuming and requires special skill. Their report identified key attributes as specialist communication, information-gathering and empathy skills. Sir Christopher Bellamy's 2021 *Independent Review of Criminal Legal Aid* (available at: www.gov.uk/government/groups/independent-review-of-criminal-legal-aid) recommended additional training and a commensurate increase in fees payable under the SCC to reflect the complexity of dealing with young and vulnerable suspects (see para 8.30).

56 Important contextual information about the welfare needs of the child will also be available on the custody record. See para 4.20 and Checklist 6 above.

57 The Howard League has published a useful guide, *Representing looked-after children at the police station: a step-by-step guide for lawyers* (2019), available at: https://howardleague.org/wp-content/uploads/2019/09/Joint-guide-children-in-care-for-web.pdf.

1998 s34.[58] However, the age and maturity of a child suspect may still be relevant to issues such as intention, recklessness and dishonesty, and a child's age may be relevant to whether they are capable of committing certain offences (such as some sexual offences).

Changing age

11.30 The relevant age for the purpose of determining whether a suspect is to be treated as a child at the police station is dealt with at para 11.9 above. It is likely that it is the age of a suspect when they are arrested that determines whether they are to be treated as a child, so that they should be treated as a child if they are under 18 years on the date of arrest even though they become 18 during the period of detention. However, this does not appear to have been authoritatively determined.

11.31 If a person under the age of 18 years is charged, they must normally first appear in a youth court, unless they are jointly charged with an adult. However, if they have their 18th birthday before the date on which they are first due to appear in court, they should appear in the adult rather than the youth court. If a person under the age of 18 years is charged with an either-way offence and has their 18th birthday before plea is entered, they have the right to elect trial in the Crown Court even though they have appeared in the youth court.[59]

11.32 Given the significant differences in the disposals available for children (as opposed to adults) and the consequential impact on criminal records, a critical decision is whether or not to take steps designed to ensure that a disposal decision is made in advance of the child's 18th birthday (see paras 11.36–11.43 below re youth disposals).

11.33 With regard to sentencing powers that depend upon age, generally the relevant date is the date of conviction and not the date of the offence or first court appearance.[60] However, a defendant who was 17 years old at the date of commission of the offence and 18 years old at the date of conviction should receive a sentence commensurate to that which they were likely to have received if sentenced on the date of commission of the offence.[61]

Police interviews

11.34 Codes C and H NfG 11C, and Code I NfG 11D state the following.

> Although juveniles . . . are often capable of providing reliable evidence, they may, without knowing or wishing to do so, be particularly prone in certain circumstances to provide information that may be unreliable, misleading or self-incriminating. Special care should therefore always be exercised in questioning such a person, and the appropriate adult should be involved if

58 Confirmed in *R v JTB* [2009] UKHL 20.

59 Pursuant to CDA 1998 s47, the youth court may (at any time before the start of the trial) remit the defendant to an adult magistrates' court from which an election can be made.

60 That is, where the person is being sentenced for the offence for the first time. It may be different where the person is being re-sentenced following discharge, revocation or breach. For more detailed consideration of issues relating to age, see K Aubrey-Johnson, S Lambe and J Twite, *Youth Justice Law and Practice* (Legal Action Group, London, 2019, new edition due out 2026).

61 See *R v Ghafoor* [2002] EWCA Crim 1857; and *R v Allon* [2003] EWCA Crim 204.

there is any doubt about a person's age, mental state or capacity. Because of the risk of unreliable evidence it is also important to obtain corroboration of any facts admitted whenever possible.

This reflects research evidence which shows that children are particularly suggestible and that younger, more suggestible suspects are more likely falsely to take responsibility for offences that they did not commit.[62]

11.35 This underlines the importance of the lawyer being vigilant during the police interview in order to detect unfair, inappropriate or oppressive questioning, and the lawyer should intervene where necessary to protect their child client's interests. The courts have suggested that children should be interviewed using short, clear questions in order to avoid ambiguous statements or admissions.[63] Hypothetical questions are permissible, but in the case of child or vulnerable suspects such questions should be approached with care.[64] For intervention in interviews generally, see para 7.49 above.

Youth disposals

11.36 The combined policies of the CPS, the NPCC guidance and case-law coalesce around the evidence-based 'Child First' principles supporting diversion (see para 11.14 above). Wherever possible, an outcome that limits a child's interaction with the criminal justice system, provides opportunities for them to take responsibility for their actions and makes use of 'teachable moments' with a view to preventing further offending, is to be preferred and will be in line with the aims of the youth justice system. This can include taking no further action in matters that would otherwise be punished heavily, because the prosecution of a child should be the last resort.

11.37 Plainly a child whose instructions are not guilty should not be encouraged to accept an out-of-court disposal that requires culpability. Not all disposals require an admission of guilt as a condition of eligibility for the out-of-court disposal, for example, for a community resolution disposal, an acceptance of responsibility can be sufficient.

11.38 The out-of-court disposals do not constitute a hierarchy of escalating punishments and a decision to impose a similar outcome for a different offence, for example, a subsequent youth caution, is permissible. As indicated earlier, it is important for the lawyer be familiar with the diversionary options in their area.

11.39 A range of statutory and non-statutory out-of-court diversionary options are available (referred to collectively as out-of-court disposals, OOCDs).

11.40 Statutory outcomes (also known as out-of-court resolutions) include:

- youth cautions; and
- youth conditional cautions.

62 See, for example, G Gudjonsson et al, 'False confessions among 15 and 16 year olds in compulsory education and the relationship with adverse life events' (2009) 20(6) *Journal of Forensic Psychiatry and Psychology* 950.

63 *R (M) v (1) Leicestershire Constabulary (2) Crown Prosecution Service* [2009] EWHC 3640 (Admin).

64 *R v Stringer* [2008] EWCA Crim 1222.

The Centre for Justice Innovation has produced an accessible leaflet for children which explains the statutory outcomes.[65]

11.41 Non-statutory outcomes are commonly referred to as diversion and consist of a number of outcomes (based on the code entered in the Home Office reporting figures) which ultimately allow the police to record no further action as the case disposal.

11.42 The broad range of disposal options are set out in the Child Gravity Matrix (March 2025), available on the NPCC website.[66] The table on page 15 includes information about whether an acceptance of responsibility or admission of guilt is required, who the decision-maker is and the impact on the child's criminal record. Further detailed guidance is available on the gov.uk website.[67]

11.43 It is anticipated that a joint decision about disposal will be made by the police and the YOT, also referred to as Youth Justice Service or Youth Offending Service, particularly where the decision between whether or not to send the file to the CPS or to charge, is a fine one. However, the decision ultimately rests with the police.

Youth cautions

Introduction

11.44 Youth cautions, unlike adult simple cautions, are a statutory disposal governed by CDA 1998 ss66ZA and 66ZB. Guidance regarding the aims, approach and decision-making is directed at the police, CPS and Youth Justice Service.[68] Youth cautions are available in respect of children under the age of 18 years. The youth caution replaced the reprimand and final warning scheme,[69] but a reprimand or warning imposed before the provisions came into effect is to be treated as a youth caution (Legal Aid, Sentencing and Punishment of Offenders Act 2012 (LASPO) s135(5)).

Conditions for a youth caution

11.45 The statutory conditions for giving a child a youth caution are that (CDA 1998 s66ZA(1)):

- a constable decides that there is sufficient evidence to charge the child or young person;
- the child or young person admits to the constable that they committed the offence; and
- the constable does not consider that the child or young person should be prosecuted or given a youth conditional caution in respect of the offence.

65 The leaflet is available at: https://justiceinnovation.org/node/30096.

66 Available at: www.npcc.police.uk/SysSiteAssets/media/downloads/publications/publications-log/criminal-justice/2023/child-gravity-matrix-v2.2---september-2023.pdf.

67 Available at: www.gov.uk/guidance/case-management-guidance/how-to-use-out-of-court-disposals.

68 Available at: www.gov.uk/guidance/case-management-guidance/how-to-use-out-of-court-disposals.

69 As a result of LASPO s135.

In deciding whether there is sufficient evidence, the officer must be satisfied that there is sufficient evidence to provide a reasonable prospect of conviction. The child or young person must make a clear and reliable admission to all elements of the offence (the admission can be made in the interview, but can also be at some later stage; and see para 10.64 above).[70] In considering whether a youth caution is an appropriate disposal, the officer must take into account the seriousness of the offence (by reference to NPCC's Gravity Factors Matrix[71]), the suspect's offending history and relevant public interest factors. Best practice suggests the officer should consult with the YOT and anyone else who might hold information about the child and their circumstances which is relevant to the decision (see para 11.47 below re child information forms). A youth caution can be given in respect of more than one offence if, overall, a youth caution is an appropriate and proportionate response.

11.46 As with all OOCDs, the officer must follow the Child Gravity Matrix scoring tool (at p6) to take into account a number of factors specific to the offence or generally, both mitigating and aggravating (pp11 and 12), and also identify any aggravating or mitigating vulnerability factors, for example, care experienced children or previous OOCDs not completed, to determine a final gravity score. The final gravity score determines the range of OOCDs available when it is applied to the disposals table (p15).

11.47 If the file is to be sent to the CPS for a disposal decision, it must be accompanied by a child information form (p6). The form is designed to collate relevant background information about the child and their circumstances. The information can be provided by relevant agencies involved with the child, not just the police. The aim is to ensure that decisions about the child are not made in a vacuum and to identify other issues relevant to the offending behaviour and further opportunities for intervention. Completion of the form is mandatory. The lawyer should ensure, as far as possible, that all relevant information is fairly and accurately recorded. Consideration ought to be given to assisting the police either during the attendance or after, to ensure that the form is optimised; for instance, with the child's permission, by sharing contact details of a teacher, GP or youth worker.[72]

Consent

11.48 There is no requirement that the child or young person (or their parent or guardian) give their consent to a youth caution. It was held, in relation to the final warning scheme, that since a warning was not the determination

70 And see *R (M) v Leicestershire Constabulary* [2009] EWHC 3640 (Admin), a decision in respect of a final warning.

71 The matrix (v2.4, March 2025) is available at: www.npcc.police.uk/SysSiteAssets/media/downloads/publications/publications-log/criminal-justice/2023/child-gravity-matrix-v2.2---september-2023.pdf.

72 In principle, pre-charge engagement is an option to provide a structure and payment for this activity. See Attorney General's *Guidelines on Disclosure* Annex B regarding pre-charge engagement generally and in respect of payment, available at: www.gov.uk/government/news/legal-aid-payments-available-for-pre-charge-engagement. See also para 10.14 above for further information regarding pre-charge engagement.

of a criminal charge, the absence of a consent requirement did not breach fair trial rights under European Convention on Human Rights (ECHR) Article 6, and it is likely that this would also apply to the youth caution scheme.[73]

Previous cautions or convictions

11.49 There is no statutory prohibition on giving a youth caution to a child or young person who has previously been given a caution or youth conditional caution (or other OOCD), or who has a previous conviction. Factors that may be relevant, and which the lawyer may put to the police officer, include:

- a sufficient lapse of time to suggest that a previous caution or conviction has had a significant deterrent effect;
- the current offence being dissimilar or unrelated to any previous offence;
- the best outcome for the victim and offender dependent on the circumstances of the individual case; and
- current and previous willingness to comply with any possible interventions (for example, if they have complied with voluntary interventions as part of a previous youth caution).

Decision-making process

11.50 It is for the police, rather than a Crown prosecutor, to make a decision about whether to give a youth caution, although it is likely that, as with adult cautions, a prosecutor may advise on, or authorise, the giving of a youth caution. The restrictions on decision-making for adult cautions (see para 10.59 above) do not apply to youth cautions.

Administering a youth caution

11.51 A youth caution may be administered by any police officer, and this may be done at a police station, at YOT premises or on other premises (for example, at a school, youth club or the child's home). The officer administering the caution must specify the offence that led to it, the fact that a record of the caution will be kept by the police, the effects of the Rehabilitation of Offenders Act (ROA) 1974 on disclosure of the caution, the consequences if it is a relevant sexual offence, and the impact on the prospect of a subsequent youth caution and on the power of a court to give a conditional discharge in respect of a subsequent offence. If a youth caution is given in respect of a recordable offence, fingerprints and other identification data can be taken and retained (see paras 6.3 and 6.57 above).

The consequences of a youth caution

11.52 When a youth caution has been administered, the officer must refer the child or young person to a YOT as soon as practicable (CDA 1998

73 *R (R) v Durham Constabulary* [2005] UKHL 21, confirmed by the ECtHR in *R v UK* (App No 33506/05) (2007) 44 EHRR 228.

s66ZB(1)). If the child or young person has not previously been so referred and has not previously been given a youth conditional caution, the YOT may assess them and may arrange for them to participate in a rehabilitation programme (CDA 1998 s66ZB(3)). Otherwise, the YOT must assess the child or young person, and must arrange for them to participate in a rehabilitation programme unless it considers it inappropriate to do so (CDA 1998 s66ZB(2)).

11.53 A youth caution does not count as a conviction, but the caution and any report on failure to participate in a rehabilitation programme may be cited in criminal proceedings in the same circumstances as a conviction may be cited (CDA 1998 s66ZB(7)). Youth cautions are covered by the ROA 1974, and are immediately spent when administered. See further para 10.72 above regarding whether a youth caution may be used as evidence of previous misconduct, the implications where a youth caution is given for a relevant sexual offence, and the possibility of being included in lists kept by the Disclosure and Barring Service (DBS).

11.54 Where a child has:

- received two or more youth cautions and is convicted of an offence committed within two years beginning with the date of the last of those cautions; or
- received a youth conditional caution followed by a youth caution and is convicted of an offence committed within two years beginning with the date of the youth caution,

the court must not impose a conditional discharge unless it is of the opinion that there are exceptional circumstances relating to the offence or the offender that justify it doing so. If so justified, the fact that the court is of that opinion and the reasons for that opinion must be stated in open court (CDA 1998 s66ZB(5) and (6)).

Advising on youth cautions

11.55 Most of the considerations relevant to advice in respect of adult cautions are also relevant to advice regarding youth cautions (see para 10.73 above). However, since consent is not required, the scope for negotiation is less than for an adult in similar circumstances. It should be remembered that a youth caution may lead to the client being required to undergo a rehabilitation programme in circumstances where, if charged, the CPS may not have proceeded with the prosecution or where, if convicted, the penalty would not have been so onerous. Also, as noted earlier, a youth caution may have an adverse impact on the prospects of a future youth caution and may, if the conditions are satisfied, prevent a court from giving a conditional discharge for a future offence. Therefore, in circumstances where a youth caution is likely to be given if the offence is admitted, these additional considerations should be taken into account in formulating advice on whether to admit the offence. The lawyer should also consider whether the child welfare provisions referred to in paras 11.4 and 11.5 above provide a basis for arguing that no formal action should be taken or that an alternative OOCD would be more suitable, for example, because it would not criminalise the child or is more proportionate to the circumstances of the case.[74]

Youth conditional cautions

11.56 Youth conditional cautions, for offenders under the age of 18 years, are broadly the same as for adults (see para 10.77 above). However, they are governed by CDA 1998 ss66A–66H rather than by the Criminal Justice Act (CJA) 2003. There is also a separate code of practice issued under CDA 1998 s66G, the Code of Practice for youth conditional cautions,[75] and separate guidance issued by the Director of Public Prosecutions (DPP) under PACE s37A, the Director's guidance on youth conditional cautions.[76] The major differences from adult conditional cautions are:

- a youth conditional caution cannot be issued without the consent of the child;[77]
- where a youth conditional caution is given, the authorised person must refer the offender to the YOT as soon as practicable (CDA 1988 s66A(6A));
- where a financial condition is attached, the applicable amounts are lower than for adults and differ according to whether the offender is under 14 years, or over 14 years but under 18 years;[78] and
- a foreign offender condition (see para 10.82 above) cannot be attached.

Non-statutory outcomes, whatever their form, result in the crime report being returned as no further action: 'Sexting' and Outcome 21

11.57 The College of Policing has issued a briefing note on 'Police action in response to youth produced sexual imagery ('Sexting')'.[79] The note provides detail of 'Outcome 21', a resolution available in youth-produced sexual imagery cases where there was no abuse, exploitation, malice or inappropriate sharing. Outcome 21 allows the police to record a crime as being committed, but to take no further action. In some circumstances, Outcome 21

74 The Mayor's Office for Policing and Crime (MOPAC) has produced helpful guidance, *MOPAC Guidance on the use of Out of Court Resolutions for children in London* (March 2025), available at: https://yjlc.uk/resources/legal-updates/mopac-guidance-use-out-court-resolutions-children-london. Page 23 of the guidance includes practical considerations for solicitors.

75 MoJ (March 2013), brought into effect by the Crime and Disorder Act 1998 (Youth Conditional Cautions: Code of Practice) Order 2013 SI No 613. The code is available at: www.gov.uk/government/publications/code-of-practice-for-youth-conditional-cautions.

76 Available at: www.cps.gov.uk/legal-guidance/conditional-cautioning-youths-dpp-guidance.

77 CDA 1998 s66B(6)(c).

78 See Crime and Disorder Act 1998 (Youth Conditional Cautions: Financial Penalties) Order 2013 SI No 608.

79 November 2016, available at: https://library.college.police.uk/docs/college-of-policing/briefing-note-sexting-2016.pdf.

may be an appropriate route to resolution. However, careful consideration is still required as the disposal may appear on an enhanced DBS check. The briefing also identifies that in 'lower risk' cases (the examples given are where the sharing is believed to be consensual/age appropriate), the youth 'should not have their device seized as a matter of routine and other options may be available to preserve evidence which do not include seizure of a device' (para 15). In cases where a child has produced images of themself as a result of online bullying, Outcome 21 is not suitable and an alternative no further action code ought to be used.

Outcome 22

11.58 There are various forms Outcome 22 can take, but most common with children is the type referred to as a 'deferred prosecution'.[80] It is an informal resolution that avoids criminalising the child. The evidential threshold for charge must first be met. In reality, a wide range of activities can be undertaken that meet the aims of the outcome, that being some form of 'diversionary activity' relevant to the offending behaviour or its causes is undertaken to address the root causes of the offending. The police are entitled to check on compliance and, if there is sufficient evidence, enforce a formal disposal outcome. No admission of guilt or acceptance of responsibility is necessary for Outcome 22.[81] As such, if there is a failure to complete the diversionary activity, and there is sufficient evidence, the police can move to a charge. Successful completion of the activity allows the police to take no further action. It is possible that a disposal via Outcome 22 will be disclosed on an enhanced DBS check.

Other OOCDs

11.59 Other forms of out of court disposal[82] include:

- Community Resolution (Outcome 8) – is a non-statutory outcome. In order to be eligible, an acceptance of responsibility is required. Activity can range from a letter of apology or some form of reparation agreed with the police following consultation with the victim. Guidance on

80 NPCC, *Outcome 22 (O22) Guidance 2022*, available at: www.npcc.police.uk/SysSiteAssets/media/downloads/publications/publications-log/criminal-justice/2023/npcc-outcome-22-guidance-2022.pdf?_t_id=WpYxq0sS-dntqOCWMFgndA%3d%3d&_t_uuid=ocWJjFOQQbWCqntEybvNbg&_t_q=restorative+justice+guidance&_t_tags=siteid%3a3130f8ed-b1e8-4a26-ad29-148e2941a2bd%2clanguage%3aen%2candquerymatch&_t_hit.id=Cds_Soh_Web_Models_Media_GenericMedia/_e725bfac-cefc-4197-a1a5-aadb1c32407d_en-GB&_t_hit.pos=10. See para 10.96 above for further information about deferred prosecution.

81 This was in answer to the evidenced disproportionate numbers of ethnic minority adults and children who received formal OOCD when an informal resolution would have been sufficient or more productive. Those outcomes required an admission that they were unwilling to give during the investigation stage due to issues concerning trust. See *Lammy review: final report* (September 2017), available at: www.gov.uk/government/publications/lammy-review-final-report.

82 Further information about out of court disposals generally can be found in chapter 10 above.

Community Resolutions has been issued by the NPCC.[83] It is possible for a community resolution to be disclosed on an enhanced DBS check.

- Outcome 20 – is very similar to Outcome 22 in terms of its aims and criteria. The difference is that the activity is undertaken by another body or agency (as opposed to the police or YOT) and is therefore voluntary and unenforceable, though the failure to co-operate may be taken into account in future disposal decisions. A number of creative third sector organisations have developed innovative community-based schemes in this space. Lawyers should familiarise themselves with what is available in their area.[84]
- Restorative Justice – is a further no further action code. It is a victim-focused outcome that allows the victim an opportunity to share their experience with the person who caused the harm. Typically, a facilitated conference takes place with both parties in a controlled environment. It aims to allow the offender to take responsibility for their actions, improves outcomes for the victims of crime and diverts offenders away from the criminal justice system. No acceptance of responsibility or admission of guilt is required.[85]

Charging

11.60 Generally, subject to the provisions on youth cautions, the considerations and processes relating to decisions to charge are similar for children as they are for adults (see chapter 10 above). The *Director's guidance on charging* (see para 10.2 above) makes no special reference to charge decisions regarding children. However, the CPS legal guidance, *Children as suspects and defendants*, does set out principles guiding the decision whether to prosecute.[86] These include:

- the charging decision should be made by a youth justice specialist;
- that when making charging decisions, prosecutors will consider the key principles of the youth justice system and consider whether the case is suitable for diversion;
- that if the case is suitable to be diverted, it is always better for this to happen before the case enters the court system. Nevertheless, prosecutors 'will' identify and advise on cases that appear to have been

83 Specific NPCC guidance concerning community resolutions (*Community Resolutions (CR) Guidance 2022*) is available at: www.npcc.police.uk/SysSiteAssets/media/downloads/publications/publications-log/criminal-justice/2023/npcc-community-resolution-guidance-2022-v.1.1.pdf?_t_id=uEBmHikZgoLbSYh4nQQa9g%3d%3d&_t_uuid=2LlWj0dHSD27xyW-Ea9KbA&_t_q=community+resolutions&_t_tags=siteid%3a3130f8ed-b1e8-4a26-ad29-148e2941a2bd%2clanguage%3aen%2candquerymatch&_t_hit.id=Cds_Soh_Web_Models_Media_GenericMedia/_2c4d10fb-6327-47ba-b587-54df1ebcfadc_en-GB&_t_hit.pos=1. See para 10.55 above for further information.

84 Options include asking the local YOT (the gov.uk site hosts a contact list at: www.gov.uk/government/collections/youth-offending-team-contact-details) or search via the local authority website.

85 *Restorative Justice Guidance* (2011), available on the College of Policing website at: www.college.police.uk/app/prosecution-and-case-management/possible-justice-outcomes-following-investigation#restorative-justice.

86 August 2025, available at: www.cps.gov.uk/legal-guidance/children-suspects-and-defendants.

missed, sending them back for consideration where they are identified; and

- that a prosecution should only be brought in circumstances where it is a proper and proportionate response.

The Code for Crown Prosecutors[87] (CCP) requires prosecutors to take into account the best interests and welfare of a child or young person, including whether a prosecution is likely to have an adverse impact on their future prospects which is disproportionate to the seriousness of their offending. It also provides that prosecutors must have regard to the principal aim of the youth justice system, which is to prevent offending by children and young people (CCP para 4.14(d)). See also the factors set out in para 11.5 above. Custody officers should have regard to the same principles.

Choice between bail and custody

11.61 With one addition, if a child is charged with an offence, the decision whether to grant bail (conditional or unconditional) or to keep the child in police detention pending the first court appearance is subject to the same criteria as for adults (see para 10.136 above).[88] The additional criterion is that a child can be kept in detention if the custody officer has reasonable grounds for believing that the child ought to be detained in their own interests (PACE s38(1)(b)(ii)), although this should be a last resort.[89] The expression 'own interests' is not defined and is open to broad interpretation, so that the custody officer may argue that it includes situations where the child is homeless, or is from the Gypsy, Roma and Traveller community, or is living in conditions of which the custody officer does not approve and which the officer believes to be contrary to the child's interests.[90] The NPCC Child First policy clearly encourages the position that children are not kept in custody unless it is absolutely necessary, which would include post charge.

11.62 Where a child is kept in police detention after charge, they must be dealt with in accordance with PACE s38(6)–(7).[91] Section 38(6) provides

87 CPS (October 2018), available at: www.cps.gov.uk/publication/code-crown-prosecutors.

88 Except that detention for the purpose of administering a drug test under PACE s38(1)(a)(iiia) applies only if the child has attained the minimum age (PACE s38(1)(b)(i)). See para 6.79 above.

89 *Archer v Commissioner of Police of the Metropolis* [2020] EWHC 1567 (QB).

90 The release from custody (with particular attention to children and vulnerable adults) is a standing inspection area for HMICFRS following its 2015 thematic review, *The welfare of vulnerable people in police custody* (March 2015), available at: https://hmicfrs.justiceinspectorates.gov.uk/publications/the-welfare-of-vulnerable-people-in-police-custody/.

91 But not if detained under some other power, for example, a warrant not backed for bail, or following arrest for common law breach of the peace or for breach of bail conditions. It was held in *R (BG) v (1) Chief Constable of the West Midlands (2) Birmingham City Council* [2014] EWHC 4374 (Admin) that the requirement did not apply where a child had been arrested for breach of bail conditions under Bail Act 1976 s7.

that the custody officer must arrange for the child to be transferred to local authority accommodation unless they certify:

- that, by reason of such circumstances as are specified in the certificate, it is impracticable to do so;
- in the case of an arrested child who has attained the age of 12 years, that no secure accommodation is available and that keeping the child in other local authority accommodation would not be adequate to protect the public from serious harm from them.[92]

Despite the fact that PACE s38(6) means that transfer to local authority accommodation should be the norm, there is evidence of widespread non-compliance, so that children who have been charged are frequently wrongly detained at the police station pending their first court appearance.[93] In an attempt to reduce the number of children held in custody at a police station following charge, the Home Office, together with a number of relevant agencies, published a *Concordat on children in custody*,[94] which reinforces the point that children charged with an offence and denied bail must, wherever practicable, be transferred to local authority accommodation. The Concordat was updated in 2025 with more detail regarding the responsibilities of each agency.[95]

11.63 With regard to practicability, Code C NfG 16D provides that neither the child's behaviour nor the nature of the offence with which they are charged provides grounds for the custody officer to detain them in police detention rather than to arrange a transfer to local authority accommodation. A custody officer may argue that they are justified in deciding that transfer would not be practicable if they believe that the accommodation to be provided by the local authority would not be secure.[96] However, Code C NfG 16D makes it clear that lack of secure local authority accommodation does not make it impracticable for the custody officer to transfer the child, and notes that the availability of secure accommodation is only a factor in relation to a child aged 12 years or over where the local authority accommodation would not be adequate to protect the public from serious harm from the child. Furthermore, Code C NfG 16D provides that the obligation to transfer a child to local authority accommodation applies as much to a child charged during the daytime as to a child who is to be held overnight, subject to the requirement to bring a person charged and kept in police

92 The Home Office *Concordat on Children in Custody* (January 2020) includes an annex with handy flow charts that set out the process, available at: www.gov.uk/government/publications/concordat-on-children-in-custody.

93 An HMIC report in 2011 found that in two-thirds of cases examined the police did not seek local authority accommodation, even though in the majority of those cases it would have been appropriate for them to have done so (*Who's looking out for the children?* (December 2011)). Subsequent HMIC inspections have found that the problem persists.

94 January 2020, available at: www.gov.uk/government/publications/concordat-on-children-in-custody.

95 See note 19 above.

96 By reference to *R v Chief Constable of Cambridgeshire ex p Michel* [1991] 2 WLR 1226, QBD.

detention or detained in local authority accommodation under these provisions before a court as soon as is practicable (PACE s46(1) and (2)).[97]

11.64 In the case of children who have attained the age of 12 years, the custody officer can take into account the lack of secure accommodation where keeping them in other local authority accommodation would not be adequate to protect the public from the risk of serious harm from them (PACE s38(6)(b)). It is understood that this subsection was intended to apply only to children of that age who were charged with violent or sexual offences.[98] However, somewhat strangely, PACE s38(6A) provides that:

> . . . any reference, in relation to an arrested juvenile charged with a violent, sexual or terrorism offence, to protecting the public from serious harm from him shall be construed as a reference to protecting members of the public from death or serious personal injury, whether physical or psychological, occasioned by further such offences committed by him.

Therefore, the possibility of keeping a child in police custody after charge under PACE s38(6) is not confined to those charged with a violent, sexual or terrorism offence. Furthermore, the justification of 'protecting the public from serious harm' is defined only in respect of those charged with a violent, sexual or terrorism offence. It is suggested, however, that this definition gives an indication of the gravity of the threat of harm to the public that would be required in order to keep a child charged with any other offence in police detention.[99]

11.65 Note that although PACE s38(6)(b) refers to the non-availability of secure accommodation, the police cannot insist that the local authority place the child in secure accommodation even if it is available. 'Secure accommodation' has a technical meaning, and a local authority cannot restrict the liberty of a child in its care otherwise than in approved secure accommodation. However, a local authority may hold a child placed with it under PACE s38(6) in secure accommodation for up to 72 hours within any 28-day period. The authority may only do so if it appears that non-secure accommodation is inappropriate because the child:

- is likely to abscond from other accommodation; or
- is likely to injure themself or other people if kept in other accommodation.

A child aged 10 or 11 years who is detained under PACE s38(6) may not be placed in secure accommodation unless it appears that they have a history of absconding and are likely to abscond from any other description of accommodation; and are likely if they abscond to suffer significant

97 Unfortunately, the code requirements are somewhat undermined by some case-law. In *R (M) v Gateshead MBC* [2006] EWCA Civ 221, it was held that whilst local authorities should have a reasonable system in place to enable them to respond to requests under PACE s38(6), they were not under an absolute duty to provide secure accommodation. Where the request was made at 00:20am, with a view to the child being produced in court at 10am the same day, it was wholly impracticable for the local authority to provide accommodation. See also *R (AR (A Child)) v Waltham Forest LBC and Others* [2020] EWHC 622 (Admin).

98 A 'violent offence' means murder or an offence specified in CJA 2003 Sch 15 Part 1. A 'sexual offence' means an offence specified in CJA 2003 Sch 15 Part 2 (PACE s38(6A)).

99 A view supported by Home Office Circular 78/1992 at para 10.

harm; or it appears that if they are kept in any other description of accommodation they are likely to injure themself or other persons.[100]

11.66 Where the custody officer is considering keeping a child in police detention under PACE s38(6)(a), the lawyer should consider asking them what efforts they have made to place the child in local authority accommodation, and/or why it is not practicable to transfer the child to local authority accommodation, and to make representations as appropriate. The College of Policing *Authorised Professional Practice* requires the custody officer to contact a senior officer if the local authority is unable or unwilling to provide accommodation.[101] If the custody officer is considering detaining a child at the police station under PACE s38(6)(b), the lawyer will want to know what grounds there are for believing that the public would be at risk of serious harm if the child was placed in non-secure accommodation. This will involve consideration of the nature of the harm feared and what evidence there is that the child would inflict such harm. However, it is likely that the custody officer would be justified in keeping the child in detention if there are grounds for fearing serious harm to the public, even if the risk of such harm is small.[102] For example, the risk of a child accused of arson absconding and causing another fire may be small, but the danger to the public if they did so would be very serious.

11.67 If a child is kept in police detention under PACE s38(6)(a) or (b), the custody officer must certify the reasons, and this certificate must be produced to the court before which the child first appears (PACE s38(7)).

11.68 There is nothing to prevent the lawyer assisting in identifying alternative accommodation for the child, whether formally with social services or informally with the child's family or network, provided the lawyer has permission from the child and feels competent to do so. Where possible and appropriate, obtaining the assistance of the YOT or the liaison and diversion team as early as possible is advisable.

Miscellaneous issues

Interviews on school premises

11.69 Children should not be interviewed by the police on school premises other than in exceptional circumstances, and then only if the school principal or their nominee agrees. In these circumstances, every effort must be made to contact both the child's parents, or other person responsible for the child's welfare, and the appropriate adult (if different), and reasonable

100 For England, see CA1989 s25 and Children (Secure Accommodation) Regulations 1991 SI No 1505 reg 6, as amended by Children (Secure Accommodation) (Amendment) (England) Regulations 2015 SI No 1883 reg 2. For Wales, see Social Services and Well-being (Wales) Act 2014 s119 and Children (Secure Accommodation) (Wales) Regulations 2015 SI No 1988 (W 298) reg 15(1), as amended by Children (Secure Accommodation) (Wales) (Amendment) Regulations 2016 SI No 312 (W 102) reg 2(8).

101 College of Policing, *Authorised Professional Practice: Detention and custody: Children and young persons* para 10, available at: www.app.college.police.uk/app-content/detention-and-custody-2/detainee-care/children-and-young-persons/#pace-transfers.

102 See, for example, *R v Birch* (1989) 11 Cr App R (S) 202, CA, a case on an analogous point under Mental Health Act (MHA) 1983 ss37 and 41.

time must be allowed to enable the person who is to act as the appropriate adult to be present. However, if waiting would cause unreasonable delay, the principal or their nominee can act as the appropriate adult unless the child is suspected of an offence against the educational establishment (Code C para 11.16). The child is entitled to consult a solicitor since they are a volunteer as defined by PACE s29 (see para 2.130 above).

Searches

11.70 A search carried out at the time of initial detention, or during detention, under PACE s54 (see para 6.91 above) does not have to be carried out in the presence of the appropriate adult, unless it is a strip search. In this case, unless it is urgent, if the strip search involves exposure of intimate parts of the body, it must only take place in the presence of an appropriate adult unless the child requests, in the presence of the appropriate adult, that the search be conducted in their absence and the appropriate adult agrees. A record must be made of the child's decision, signed by the appropriate adult (Code C Annex A para 11(c); Codes H and I Annex A para 12(c)).

11.71 An intimate search under PACE s55 (see para 6.101 above) must generally only be conducted in the presence of the appropriate adult, who must be of the same sex, unless the child specifically requests a particular adult of the opposite sex who is readily available. However, an intimate search can be carried out in the absence of the appropriate adult if the child signifies in the presence of the appropriate adult that the child prefers it to be conducted in the adult's absence, and the adult agrees. A record must then be made of the decision and signed by the adult (Code C Annex A para 5; Codes H and I Annex A para 6).

Identification and other procedures

11.72 Where an identification or other evidential procedure requires appropriate consent, such consent must be obtained from both the child and their parent or guardian[103] (as opposed to the appropriate adult) unless the child is under 14 years, in which case consent of the parent or guardian is sufficient (PACE s65(1); Code D para 2.12; and see para 6.3 above). If the parent or guardian is not acting as the appropriate adult, they do not have to be present in order to give consent, but must be given an opportunity to speak to the child and the appropriate adult if they wish (Code D NfG 2A). If the only obstacle to conducting a video identification, identification parade or group identification is that a parent or guardian refuses consent or cannot be contacted after reasonable efforts to do have been made, the child may be treated as known but not available (see para 8.14 above). Identification procedures that require appropriate consent are:

- fingerprints, subject to exceptions (see para 6.3 above);
- photographs, subject to exceptions (see para 6.11 above);
- searches and examinations to ascertain identity, subject to exceptions (see para 6.19 above);

103 Or, if the child is in the care of a local authority or voluntary organisation, that authority or organisation (Code D NfG 2A).

- footwear impressions (see para 6.26 above);
- X-rays and ultrasound scans (see para 6.103 above);
- intimate samples under PACE s62 (see para 6.33 above);
- non-intimate samples under PACE s63, subject to exceptions (see para 6.57 above);
- video identifications, identification parades and group identifications, subject to exceptions (see chapter 8 above); and
- drug-testing procedures under PACE s63B (see para 6.76 above).

11.73 Samples of handwriting are not specifically covered by PACE or the codes of practice (see para 6.69 above). In practice, they cannot be obtained without the consent of the suspect, but it seems unlikely that consent of the parent or guardian is necessary.

Detention in a cell

11.74 A child must not be placed in a police cell unless no other secure accommodation is available and the custody officer considers that it is not practicable to supervise the child if they are not placed in a cell, or the custody officer considers that a cell provides more comfortable accommodation than other secure accommodation in the police station. Often, there is little to distinguish a cell from a child detention room. In any event, child suspects must be kept separate from adult suspects (CYPA 1933 s31; Code C para 8.8; Code H para 8.9; Code I para 8.8).

Autistic clients[104]

11.75 There are additional considerations when advising a neurodivergent, or suspected neurodivergent, client (see chapter 5 above), and the lawyer should consider whether there is any accessible information that may assist their understanding of their client's needs.[105] If a suspect has been diagnosed with autism then, when relevant, the lawyer will need to take particular care to identify behaviour that is, or may be, related to the individual's neurodiversity. The complex considerations are well illustrated by the Upper Tribunal, where it was observed that:

> . . . aggressive behaviour is not a choice for autistic children . . . an autism meltdown is not the same as a temper tantrum. It is not 'bad' or 'naughty' behaviour and should not be considered as such. Rather, such challenging behaviour is increasingly being described as 'distressed behaviour.' An autistic child who feels very anxious and stressed – for example, because they are experiencing sensory overload, or are overwhelmed by social demands and interactions – may behave in a way that cannot reasonably be described as a choice. They may not understand the effect of their

104 The advice in this section is applicable to adults and children, although the impact on children is amplified by their age and level of maturity.

105 For example, an 'autism card'. An autism card (or variations of an autism card) often includes information such as a list of things that make the individual anxious or stressed.

> behaviour and any prospect of punishment is unlikely to have any deterrent effect upon them . . .[106]

There is now a wealth of material designed to inform the police response and approach to autistic individuals including the National Autistic Society's guidance.[107]

11.76 The process of being arrested and/or taken to a police station may be overwhelming to an autistic person. Responses to over-stimulation can include stress, agitation, disruptive behaviour, difficulties in concentration, listening engagement, or a 'meltdown'.[108,109]

11.77 In general, the police and the lawyer should keep the situation calm and keep language clear, concise and simple. The lawyer should try to identify whether the suspect has any sensory sensitivities (for example, sounds, lighting, textures).[110] If an autistic child has been arrested, the lawyer should try to establish the reasons why an interview needs to take place at that moment (given the likely sensory overload for their client).[111] If an immediate interview is not necessary, it may be appropriate for there to be a release on bail so that the interview can take place in a more suitable location or when the suspect has had time to re-regulate.

11.78 When preparing for interview, the lawyer should take background information from the suspect so that appropriate modifications can be made to the interview process. These modifications may include ensuring that the interviewing officer has planned their questioning to take into account the suspect's particular needs, to secure an interview environment that takes into account the suspect's sensory needs, and that the interview has planned breaks.[112] The right to information (Codes C and H

106 *C v Governing Body of a School, Secretary of State for Education (First Interested Party) and National Autistic Society (Second Interested Part) (SEN)* [2018] UKUT 269 (ACC).

107 National Autistic Society, *Autism: a guide for police officers and staff* (revised 2020), available at: www.autism.org.uk/shop/products/books-and-resources/autism-a-guide-for-police-officers-and-staff.

108 See *Autism: a guide for police officers and staff* pp30 and 35.

109 *Autism: a guide for police officers and staff* p10:

A meltdown is 'an intense response to overwhelming situations'. It happens when someone becomes completely overwhelmed by their current situation and temporarily loses behavioural control. This loss of control can be expressed verbally (eg shouting, screaming, crying), or physically (eg kicking, lashing out, biting).

A meltdown is not the same as a temper tantrum. It is not 'bad' behaviour. When a person is completely overwhelmed, and their condition means it is difficult to express that in an appropriate way, it is understandable that the result is a meltdown.

110 *Autism: a guide for police officers and staff.*

111 HMICFRS inspections (see HMICFRS, *Metropolitan Police Service – Joint inspection of police custody* (January 2019) p49, available at: https://hmicfrs.justiceinspectorates.gov.uk/publications/metropolitan-joint-inspection-of-police-custody/; or HMICFRS, *South Yorkshire Police custody – a mix of positive findings and concerns for inspectors* (October 2019) p45, available at: https://hmicfrs.justiceinspectorates.gov.uk/news/news-feed/south-yorkshire-police-custody-a-mix-of-positive-findings-and-concerns-for-inspectors) and research by Vicky Kemp (see note 28 above), supported the idea that custody officers could exercise their discretion to allow family members to visit and remain with children in custody where to do so limited the overload or anxiety for particularly affected children.

112 *Autism: a guide for police officers and staff*, 'Dos and don'ts for before the interview' p33.

para 11.1A; Code I para 11) is written in subjective terms. Codes C and H para 11.1A and Code I para 11, state that the suspect and their solicitor 'must be given sufficient information to enable *them* to *understand* the nature of their suspected involvement in an offence' (emphasis added). The lawyer will also need to consider whether the pre-interview disclosure is sufficient in light of their client's needs.

11.79 During the interview, the lawyer will need to take particular care to identify whether their client is becoming stressed, overloaded or anxious, such as to require a break or additional modifications to the interview process (for example, a different location). The interview should be conducted in a calm, natural voice. Language should be clear and simple. The interviewer should avoid instruction questions (for example, 'I want you to tell me about . . .'), multi-part questions or tag questions. Suspects with autism may take time to process questions or they may repeat the question that was asked.[113] The lawyer will need to ensure that this is not misconstrued or misunderstood by the interviewing officer. If an autistic suspect has a sensitivity to sound, the lawyer may want to make their own electronic recording of the interview[114] or to have immediate access to the interview recording (to remove the need for typing during the interview).

Mentally vulnerable suspects

Introduction

11.80 Special provision is made in Codes C, D, H and I in respect of mentally disordered and vulnerable people and others whose understanding is limited by reason of additional needs or incapacity. A useful summary of the Codes C, H and I provisions may be found in Annex E of the respective codes. In addition, the Mental Health Act 1983: Code of Practice was issued by the Department of Health in 2015.[115] The code provides that when considering the use of police powers to detain people under the MHA 1983, less restrictive alternatives should be considered, including convening a mental health assessment without using powers under MHA 1983 s135 or 136 (para 16.22). The code also states that a police station should not be used as a place of safety other than in exceptional circumstances; for example, where it is necessary to do so because the person's behaviour would pose an unmanageably high risk to other patients, staff or other users if the person were to be detained in a healthcare setting (para 16.38). An official report published in 2013 found that in many police force areas, mentally disordered and mentally vulnerable people continued to be

113 *Autism: a guide for police officers and staff*, 'Dos and don'ts for before the interview' p33.

114 See National Police Chiefs' Council and The Law Society, *Memorandum of Understanding Electronic Communication Devices being taken into Custody Suites by Solicitors* (July 2025), available at: www.npcc.police.uk/SysSiteAssets/media/downloads/publications/publications-log/criminal-justice/2025/mobile-telephones-and-laptops-being-taken-into-custody-suites-by-solicitors-and-their-usage.pdf. See also at para 7.15(6).

115 Available at: www.gov.uk/government/uploads/system/uploads/attachment_data/file/435512/MHA_Code_of_Practice.PDF.

routinely detained in police stations, both as suspects and under the MHA 1983.[116] However, amendments introduced by the Policing and Crime Act 2017 were designed to reduce the use of police stations as a 'place of safety'. The *National Partnership Agreement: Right Care, Right Person (RCRP)* acts as a threshold to assist the police in making decisions about how to respond to incidents and is intended to reduce the number of people brought into custody when the predominant issue is their mental health.[117]

Determining whether a suspect is vulnerable

11.81 If a police officer has any reason to suspect that a person of any age may be vulnerable, in the absence of clear evidence to dispel that suspicion, the person must be treated as such for the purposes of Codes C, D and H (Code C para 1.4; Code D para 2.3; Code H para 1.10; Code I para 1.17(d)). Under the codes, the term 'vulnerable' applies to any person who, because of a mental health condition or mental disorder (Code C para 1.13(d); Code H para 1.17(d); Code I para 1.17(d)):

(1) may have difficulty understanding or communicating effectively about the full implications of any procedures and processes connected with:
   - their arrest and detention; or (as the case may be)
   - their voluntary attendance at a police station or their presence elsewhere for the purpose of a voluntary interview; and
   - the exercise of their rights and entitlements;

(2) does not appear to understand the significance of what they are told, of questions they are asked or of their replies; or

(3) appears to be particularly prone to:
   - becoming confused and unclear about their position;
   - providing unreliable, misleading or incriminating information without knowing or wishing to do so;
   - accepting or acting on suggestions from others without consciously knowing or wishing to do so; or
   - readily agreeing to suggestions or proposals without any protest or question.

'Mental disorder' is defined by MHA 1983 s1(2) as 'any disorder or disability of the mind'. The Mental Health Act 1983 Code of Practice describes the range of clinically recognised conditions that can fall within the meaning of mental health disorder for these purposes (Codes C and H NfG 1GB; Code I NfG 1H).[118] A person with a learning disability[119] is not considered as suffering from a mental disorder for certain purposes under

116 HMIC, HM Inspectorate of Prisons, Care Quality Commission and Healthcare Inspectorate of Wales joint report, *A criminal use of police cells? The use of police custody as a place of safety for people with mental health needs* (June 2013), available at: https://hmicfrs.justiceinspectorates.gov.uk/publications/a-criminal-use-of-police-cells.

117 Home Office and Department of Health and Social Care (April 2024), available at: www.gov.uk/government/publications/national-partnership-agreement-right-care-right-person/national-partnership-agreement-right-care-right-person-rcrp.

118 At p26.

119 Defined by MHA 1983 s1(4) as a state of arrested or incomplete development of the mind which includes significant impairment of intelligence and social functioning.

the MHA 1983 unless that disability is associated with abnormally aggressive or seriously irresponsible conduct (MHA 1983 s1(2A)). Such a person may, however, be vulnerable as a result of a mental health condition for the purposes of Codes C, D, H and I.[120] Dependence on alcohol or drugs is not considered to be a disorder for the purposes of determining whether a person is mentally disordered (MHA 1983 s1(3)). Nevertheless, a person who is so dependant may be vulnerable as a result of a mental health condition for the purpose of the codes, and they must be re-assessed after recovering from the effects of drink and/or drugs (Codes C and H NfG 1GC; Code I NfG 1K).

11.82 For the purpose of establishing whether a person suspected of an offence may be vulnerable, the custody officer (or the officer investigating an offence in respect of a person who has not been arrested or detained) must take, or cause to be taken, the following actions (Code C para 1.4; Code H para 1.10; Code I para 1.9):

(1) reasonable enquiries to ascertain what information is available that is relevant to any of the factors described in Code C para 1.13(d), Code H para 1.17(d) or Code I para 1.9(a) as indicating that the person may be vulnerable;
(2) a record describing whether any of those factors appear to apply and provide any reason to suspect that the person may, or may not, be vulnerable; and
(3) ensure that such a record is made available to be taken into account by police officers, police staff and any others who, in accordance with the codes, are required or entitled to communicate with the person in question.

The codes specifically include solicitors and appropriate adults as people to whom such a record must be made available. Codes C and H NfG 1GA and Code I NfG 1I set out examples of relevant information that may be available for the purposes of making an assessment of vulnerability, including information from professionals who have had previous contact with the person, such as their lawyer.

11.83 It is clear from the above that it does not have to be positively established that a suspect is vulnerable as a result of a mental health condition or mental disorder in order for them to have to be treated as such – a 'reason to suspect' is sufficient to trigger the obligation. At the time of authorising detention, the custody officer must determine whether the suspect is, or might be, in need of medical treatment or attention and whether, among other things, the suspect requires help to check documentation (Codes C and H para 3.5(c); Code I para 3.6(d)). The custody officer must also conduct a risk assessment (Codes C and H paras 3.6–

120 A joint inspection by HM Inspectorate of Probation, HMIC, HM Crown Prosecution Service Inspectorate and the Care Quality Commission, published in 2014, found that the police often did not assess suspects with learning disabilities adequately, and frequently did not call in an appropriate adult even if a learning disability had been identified. See *A joint inspection of the treatment of offenders with learning disabilities within the criminal justice system – phase 1 from arrest to sentence*, available at: https://hmicfrs.justiceinspectorates.gov.uk/publications/joint-inspection-of-the-treatment-of-offenders-with-learning-disabilities-within-the-criminal-justice-system.

3.10; Code I para 3.7; and see para 4.24 above). This involves assessing where the detainee is likely to present specific risks to custody staff or to themself. The College of Policing *Authorised Professional Practice* includes guidance on conducting risk assessments.[121] In addition, the custody officer (in respect of a detained suspect) or the investigating officer (in the case of a volunteer) must take the action set out in para 11.81 above if they have reason to suspect that the person may be vulnerable.

11.84 Having conducted the various assessments, the custody officer (or the investigating officer, as relevant) must determine the appropriate response and take the appropriate action. If the person appears to be suffering from a mental disorder or is otherwise in need of clinical attention, the custody officer must make sure that they receive appropriate clinical attention as soon as is reasonably practicable or, in urgent cases, immediately (Code C paras 9.5–9.5B; Code H paras 9.6–9.8; Code I paras 9.6–9.7).[122] The custody officer may fulfil this obligation by calling in an appropriate healthcare professional.[123] Where a healthcare professional is called in, the custody officer must ask them for their opinion about any risks or problems which the police need to take into account when making a decision about continued detention, when to carry out an interview and the need for appropriate safeguards (Code C para 9.13; Code H para 9.15; Code I para 16). For fitness for detention and fitness for interview, see para 5.22 above. If the detainee is vulnerable, the custody officer must call in an appropriate adult (see para 11.16 below).

The lawyer's assessment

11.85 It is important to remember that custody and other police officers are not medically trained and frequently do not make appropriate judgments concerning suspects' vulnerability.[124] Defence lawyers should always be aware of the possibility that a client may be vulnerable, and should look out for the following signs:

(1) apparent lack of comprehension;
(2) lack of coherence;
(3) unexpected levels of agitation, anger or other emotions;

121 College of Policing, *Authorised Professional Practice: Detention and custody: Risk assessment*, available at: www.app.college.police.uk/app-content/detention-and-custody-2/risk-assessment/#checklist-assessing-detainees-.

122 Liaison and diversion services are increasingly available in police stations, albeit their availability is subject to local priorities. They are designed to assist the police and courts in ensuring the right mental health outcomes are achieved as early as possible. See Home Office, *Liaison and diversion: Healthcare in police custody suites*, available at: https://assets.publishing.service.gov.uk/media/5a7acd48e5274a319e77ad26/dip-psl11-diversion.pdf. Where relevant, lawyers should check what is available at a given police station.

123 Defined as a clinically qualified person working within the scope of practice as determined by their relevant statutory regulatory body. Whether they are 'appropriate' depends on the circumstances of the duties they carry out at the time (Codes C and H NfG 9A; Code I Annex G).

124 See notes 118 and 119 above. Also, *Reports of HMICFRS police custody facilities – joint inspections* can be found at: https://hmicfrs.justiceinspectorates.gov.uk/our-work/article/criminal-justice-joint-inspection/joint-inspection-of-police-custody-facilities/#reports.

(4) physical signs such as lack of co-ordination, drowsiness or body movements;
(5) unexpected patterns of behaviour; and
(6) reference by the client to medication or hospitalisation.

11.86 If the lawyer is concerned that their client may be mentally vulnerable, they should usually pursue the matter with them by asking questions such as whether they:

(1) are, or have recently been, on medication and, if so, what for;
(2) have recently been in hospital and, if so, what for;
(3) are currently, or have recently been, a hospital or clinic outpatient;
(4) have ever been assessed as having additional learning needs or received special education;
(5) attend any kind of day centre; and
(6) have contact with a social worker or community psychiatric nurse.

11.87 If the lawyer concludes that their client may be mentally vulnerable but the police have not made such a determination, the question arises whether the lawyer should tell the police of their knowledge or suspicions. If the client consents, this will present no problem, but there may be difficulties if the client does not give consent. If the lawyer's knowledge or suspicion arises from previous professional contact with the client or from something the client said to them, the information should not be passed on to the police.[125] If, however, the knowledge or suspicion is based on the lawyer's observations, this is almost certainly not covered by the duty of confidentiality. In either case, the lawyer should normally discuss their suspicions with their client before deciding whether to say anything to the police, although there will be times when the lawyer will form the opinion that this would be unwise, for example, if they are concerned about their own safety. If the police are not notified, and they had no reason to believe that the suspect was mentally vulnerable, while arguably any confession obtained from a mentally vulnerable suspect may be unreliable for the purposes of PACE s76, an application at trial to exclude evidence of the confession made in the absence of an appropriate adult may not succeed.[126] If the lawyer does tell the police of their knowledge or suspicion, this should give the police the reason to suspect vulnerability and trigger the responses required by Codes C, H and I.[127]

11.88 A suspicion that a client is mentally vulnerable may only become apparent during the course of a police interview. In this case, the lawyer should normally stop the interview and speak to the client in private so that a decision can be made about whether to inform the police. Again, if

125 Because it is covered by the lawyer's duty of confidentiality. See para 1.16 above.

126 See, for example, *R v Campbell* [1995] 1 Cr App R 522, CA.

127 Note that in *R v Beattie* [2018] NICA 1, the court preferred the evidence of a forensic medical officer who had examined the defendant and determined that he was not mentally vulnerable, to that of a defence expert witness who had not examined the defendant at the time he was detained at the police station. For this reason, if a police forensic medical officer has made such a determination, with which the lawyer disagrees, the lawyer should consider instructing their own medical practitioner (see para 11.95 below).

the officer is given such information in good faith, they must act on the information given and treat the suspect as mentally vulnerable.

Right to legal advice

11.89 A suspect who is, or who is being treated as, mentally vulnerable has the same right to consult a solicitor as any other person who is in police custody (see para 2.129 above). The appropriate adult also has a right to seek legal advice on behalf of the suspect (Code C para 3.19; Code H para 3.20; Code I para 6.5), but if the suspect requests advice, the appropriate action must be taken straight away and must not be delayed until the appropriate adult arrives (Code C para 6.5A; Code H para 6.6; Code I para 6.3). For guidance on circumstances where the suspect and the appropriate adult take differing views about asking for legal advice, see para 11.25 above. Since there is no provision for the police to delay contacting an appropriate adult, once an appropriate adult has been contacted it would be difficult for the police to justify delaying access to a lawyer under PACE s58(8), TA 2000 Sch 8 para 8 or NSA 2023 s27 and Sch 6 (for the reasons given at para 11.15 above).

The appropriate adult

Informing the appropriate adult

11.90 If the police determine that a detained suspect is vulnerable, the custody officer must inform them that an appropriate adult is required, and identify and inform an appropriate adult and ask them to come to the police station (Code C para 3.15; Code H para 3.17; Code I para 3.20(d)). Similar action must be taken by a police interviewer in the case of a voluntary interview (Code C para 3.21B(d)). There is no provision for delaying informing the appropriate adult, even if the suspect is being held incommunicado under PACE s56 or TA 2000 Sch 8 para 8, or access to legal advice is delayed under PACE s58, TA 2000 Sch 8 para 8 or NSA 2023 s27 and Sch 6 (Codes C and H Annex B NfG B1; Code I Annex B). In practice, having concluded that a suspect may be mentally vulnerable, a custody officer may nevertheless decide not to call an appropriate adult on the ground that they believe that the suspect is capable of understanding questions. This is a misinterpretation of the relevant provisions, and is contrary to the code provisions.[128]

Appropriate people

11.91 The appropriate adult may be:

- a relative, guardian or other person responsible for the care or custody of the suspect;

128 See *R v Aspinall* [1999] Crim LR 741, CA. Also note the broader approach of the Court of Appeal in *R v Al-Jaryan* [2020] EWCA Crim 440, acknowledging that the custody officer was entitled to take into account additional information, including the presentation of the detainee, to form a view about whether the detainee was vulnerable within the meaning of PACE Code C para 1.4.

- someone who has experience of dealing with mentally disordered or mentally vulnerable people but who is not a police officer or employed by, or under the direction or control of, the police (for example, an approved social worker as defined by the MHA 1983 or a specialist social worker); or
- failing either of the above, some other responsible adult aged 18 years or over who is not a police officer or employed by the police (Code C para 1.7(b); Code D para 2.6; Code H para 1.13; Code I para 1.12).

11.92 As with appropriate adults for children, this list amounts to a hierarchy, although Codes C and H NfG 1D and Code I NfG 1E provide that in certain (unspecified) circumstances it may be more satisfactory if the appropriate adult is someone experienced or trained in the care of mentally disordered or vulnerable people rather that a person lacking such qualifications. However, the codes make it clear that the suspect's wishes should, if practicable, be respected.

Inappropriate people

11.93 The provisions governing those who should not act as appropriate adults are generally the same as for children (see para 11.19 above).

Role of the appropriate adult

11.94 The role of the appropriate adult, and the assistance the adult may give or the difficulties that the adult may present to the lawyer, are similar to those as for children (see para 11.16 above). If a confession made by a mentally handicapped person,[129] on which the case against them wholly or substantially rests, is made in the absence of an 'independent person', a jury must be warned of the dangers of convicting in reliance on it (PACE s77).[130] PACE s77 does not apply where the suspect is mentally vulnerable for other reasons, although a judge always has a discretion to give such a warning, and a confession may be excluded as oppressive, unreliable or unfair under PACE s76 or 78.

Special considerations for the lawyer

Interviews

11.95 The lawyer should act with special care when dealing with clients who are, or may be, mentally vulnerable. It is significant that in a number of well-known miscarriage of justice cases the defendant was described as being, or verging on being, mentally disordered or handicapped, although in none of these cases did this appear to have been identified at the time of the defendant's detention.[131] The relevance of Codes C and H NfG 11C and Code I NfG 11D – which warn that such people may be prone to giving information that is unreliable, misleading or self-incriminating and

129 'Mentally handicapped' is the term used in PACE.

130 PACE s77 refers to an independent person rather than an appropriate adult. See also *R v Lamont* [1989] Crim LR 813, CA; and *R v McKenzie (Practice Note)* [1993] 1 WLR 453, CA.

131 See, for example, *R v Paris, Abdullahi and Miller* (1993) 97 Cr App R 99, CA.

requires that special care be taken when questioning them – will not necessarily be appreciated or taken into account by the police.

11.96 In most cases where a client is suspected of being mentally vulnerable, a healthcare professional will have to be called in by the police (see para 11.84 above). The practitioner may be of some assistance to the lawyer, although not necessarily so. First, it must be remembered that the practitioner will not be bound by the same duty of confidentiality as the lawyer, and anything disclosed may not be covered by legal professional privilege.[132,133] Second, although the codes do not specifically say so, the practitioner's role is primarily to assess the suspect's medical condition on behalf of the police. Third, the practitioner called will be paid by the police, and may be directly employed by them, and experience suggests that practitioners do not always play a helpful role from the defence point of view. Healthcare practitioners called in to the police station do not always understand the meaning and significance of 'fitness to be detained', 'fitness to be interviewed', or the definition of mental disorder and vulnerability, although Codes C and H Annex G and Code I Annex E should assist in determining fitness to be interviewed. The suspect has a right to be examined by a medical practitioner of their choice, but at their own expense (Code C para 9.8; Code H para 9.10; Code I para 9.11). The cost, provided it is reasonable and was incurred in the best interests of the client, may be claimed under the SCC (draft SCC 2025).[134]

Mental Health Act 1983 s136

11.97 It is important to establish at an early stage whether a client has been arrested for an offence or detained under MHA 1983 s136. Section 136 gives a constable power to remove a person from a public place to a place of safety if they consider that the person is suffering from a mental disorder and is in immediate need of care and control. This power exists irrespective of whether the person is suspected of having committed an offence, and irrespective of their age. However, in order to exercise the power, the police officer must first obtain advice from a doctor, nurse or approved medical practitioner unless, in the officer's judgment, it would not be practicable to do so. The person may be detained for up to 24 hours for examination by a doctor and interview by an approved mental health practitioner in order that suitable arrangements can be made for their treatment or care; subject to an extension of up to 12 hours where authorised by the responsible medical practitioner (MHA 1983 ss136(2A) and 136B). A police station is included in the definition of a 'place of safety'. However, a child cannot be taken to a police station as a place of safety

132 See *R v McDonald* [1991] Crim LR 122, CA. See para 11.26 above in relation to appropriate adults for children. Arguably, if a healthcare practitioner is present during a lawyer/client consultation, this should not destroy privilege. However, anything disclosed to the healthcare professional by the suspect in the absence of the lawyer is unlikely to be covered by privilege.

133 See also V Cochrane and W Hayes, *Legal Professional Privilege in Criminal Investigations and Proceedings* (Oxford University Press, 2024) ch 6 generally regarding privilege in the police station, and paras 6.22–6.34 concerning appropriate adults and interpreters specifically.

134 SCC Specification 2022 para 5.38 (draft SCC Specification 2025 para 5.36).

(MHA 1983 s136A(1)), and a police station may only be used as a place of safety for an adult where:

(a) the decision-maker is satisfied that:
   (i) the behaviour of the person poses an imminent risk of serious injury or death to themself or to another;
   (ii) because of that risk, no place of safety other than a police station in the relevant police area can reasonably be expected to detain the person; and
   (iii) the requirement in reg 4(1)(b) (so far as is reasonably practicable, a healthcare professional is present and available to the detained person throughout the period that they are detained at the police station) will be met; and

(b) where the decision-maker is not an officer of the rank of inspector or above, an officer of that rank or above authorises the person to be removed to, kept at, or taken to a place of safety that is a police station.[135]

Before determining that the circumstances specified in reg 2(1)(a) exist, a decision-maker who is a constable must, if reasonably practicable, consult with a doctor, nurse or approved mental health professional (reg 2(2)). Regulations 4–7 make further provision concerning the welfare of the person while detained at a police station, and their removal to another place of safety.[136] A person who is initially taken to a police station as a place of safety can be taken to another, more suitable, place of safety during the 24-hour period, or any period of extension (MHA 1983 ss136(3)).

11.98 Code C applies to people detained at a police station under MHA 1983 s136, except for section 15 (concerning reviews and extension of detention) (Code C para 1.10). A person detained under section 136 is entitled to legal advice. If the assessment is to take place at the police station, an approved social worker and registered medical practitioner must be called to the station as soon as possible to carry it out. Once the person has been assessed and suitable arrangements made for their treatment or care, or if a registered medical practitioner determines that the person is not mentally disordered, they can no longer be detained under section 136 (Code C para 3.16).

11.99 It is possible for a person to be under arrest for an offence and detained under MHA 1983 s136 at the same time. If this is the case, the police or prosecutor may be persuaded not to initiate any criminal proceedings if suitable arrangements can be made either under the MHA 1983 or on a voluntary basis. The *Director's guidance on charging* sets out the public interest considerations relevant to culpability and includes 'mental or

135 Mental Health Act 1983 (Places of Safety) Regulations 2017 SI No 1036 reg 2(1).

136 Guidance on these provisions is set out in a document issued jointly by the Department of Health and Social Care and the Home Office, *Mental Health Act 1983: implementing changes to police powers* (March 2018), available at: www.gov.uk/government/publications/mental-health-act-1983-implementing-changes-to-police-powers.

physical ill health or disability' either at the time of the decision or at the time of the conduct.[137]

11.100 Further CPS legal guidance contained in *Mental Health: Suspects and Defendants* sets out the approach to be taken by prosecutors in deciding whether to prosecute, including considerations relevant to diversion.[138] However, prosecutors will also have to consider the seriousness of the suspected offence, whether it is likely to be repeated, and the need to safeguard the public or the persons caring for the suspect (see para 10.23 above).[139]

Cautions and other out-of-court disposals

11.101 There is no special provision for mentally vulnerable people in the legislation relating to conditional cautions, or youth cautions, or in the relevant guidance. However, as noted at para 11.100 above, the CPS legal guidance confirms that 'effective diversion should be as available to those with mental health conditions as with all other defendants'. As above, the public interest stage of the CCP involves consideration of the mental condition of the suspect.

11.102 Clearly, the additional possibility of a simple caution, youth caution or conditional caution, or of no formal action, should be taken into account when advising a client who is or may be mentally vulnerable whether to answer police questions. The lawyer may also refer to the public interest considerations when seeking to persuade the custody officer or prosecutor to take action other than charging the suspect. It may be appropriate to press for an assessment by the YOT or the liaison and diversion team[140] so that such issues can be adequately considered.

Bail or custody?

11.103 PACE s38 contains no specific reference to mentally vulnerable accused persons (see para 10.136 above). There may, however, be particular concerns arising from the person's mental state or from associated problems such as homelessness. This could potentially justify a decision not to grant bail for the accused's own protection, or in order to prevent injury or damage, or absconding. If the accused is kept in police detention, the lawyer should make appropriate preparations for any bail application to the court, bearing in mind the additional powers of the court in respect of people who are mentally disordered.

137 October 2018, available at: www.cps.gov.uk/publication/code-crown-prosecutors; see para 14.4(b).

138 October 2024, available at: www.cps.gov.uk/legal-guidance/mental-health-suspects-and-defendants.

139 CCP para 4.14(b).

140 Liaison and diversion services identify people who have mental health, learning disability, substance misuse or other vulnerabilities when they first come into contact with the criminal justice system as suspects, defendants or offenders. Further information on liaison and diversion is available at: www.england.nhs.uk/commissioning/health-just/liaison-and-diversion/about/#:~:text=Liaison%20and%20Diversion%20(L%26D)%20services,as%20suspects%2C%20defendants%20or%20offenders.

Miscellaneous issues

Searches

11.104 A search carried out at the time of initial detention, or during detention, under PACE s54 (see para 6.91 above) does not have to be carried out in the presence of an appropriate adult, unless it is a strip search. In this case, if the strip search involves exposure of intimate parts of the body it must, except in cases of urgency, be conducted in the presence of an appropriate adult of the same sex. It would appear that, unlike in the case for children (see para 11.70 above), there is no provision for a mentally vulnerable suspect to dispense with attendance of the appropriate adult (Code C Annex A para 11(c); Code H Annex A para 12(c); Code I Annex A para 6). An intimate search (see para 6.101 above) may take place only in the presence of an appropriate adult of the same sex unless the suspect specifically requests the presence of a particular adult of the opposite sex who is readily available (Code C Annex A para 5; Codes H and I Annex A para 6). There is no equivalent provision to that which enables a child to agree to the conduct of a search in the absence of an appropriate adult. Codes C, H and I make provision to dispense with the presence of an appropriate adult in cases of urgency where there is a risk of serious harm to the detainee or others.[141]

Identification and other procedures

11.105 Where an identification or other evidential procedure requires consent, consent is only valid if given in the presence of the appropriate adult (Code D para 2.12). There is no provision for consent to be given on behalf of the suspect by the appropriate adult. For procedures requiring consent, and for comment on handwriting samples, see paras 11.72 and 11.73 above.

People with communication difficulties

Introduction

11.106 The codes, especially Codes C, H and I, make extensive provision in respect of suspects who have visual or aural impairment, or who have communication difficulties for other reasons. If a person appears to be blind, seriously visually impaired, deaf, unable to read or speak, or has difficulty orally because of a speech impediment, they must be treated as such for the purposes of the code in the absence of clear evidence to the contrary (Code C para 1.6; Code H para 1.12; Code D para 2.5; Code I para 1.1). Inability to read or speak should be interpreted to include inability to read or speak English. The lawyer should be vigilant to ensure that appropriate action is taken. It has been held, for example, that where the police were not aware that the suspect was deaf, and had no doubts about their hearing ability, there was no breach of the code when the suspect was

141 PACE Code C Annex A para 11(c); Codes H and I Annex A paras 6 and 12(c).

treated as if they were not deaf.[142] If the lawyer is aware, or has doubts, about whether their client comes within one of these categories, they should initially attempt to speak to them in private to establish whether their belief or suspicion is correct. Since, to a large extent, the special provisions of the codes are protective, the client should normally be advised to make the problem known to the police. The major exception to this concerns clients who might have problems with their immigration status, or asylum-seekers who may not want their embassy or consulate informed (see Codes C, H and I para 7.4). See further chapter 12 below.

Inability to speak or understand English

Information about procedural rights

11.107 A person who is taken to a police station under arrest, or who is arrested at the police station having attended voluntarily, must be informed of their procedural rights, including the right to interpretation and translation. The information must be provided both orally and in writing (Codes C and H paras 3.1–3.3A; Code I para 12.2(b) and Annex J), and the written notice must be in a language that the suspect can understand (Code C para 3.12(c); Code H para 13.14(c); Code I para 3.16(b)).[143] All reasonable attempts should be made to make clear to the suspect that an interpreter will be supplied at public expense (Codes C and H para 13.1B; Code I para 12.3). The notice of entitlements required to be given to a suspect by Codes C and H para 3.2 and Code I para 3.1 should be made available in Welsh and the principal European and ethnic minority languages – these and an 'easy read' English version are available online.[144]

Determining the need for an interpreter

11.108 It is the responsibility of the custody officer to determine whether a suspect requires an interpreter, and to record their decision (Codes C and H para 3.5(c)(ii) and (d); Code I para 3.6(c)). In the case of a voluntary interview, responsibility rests with the interviewing officer (Code C para 3.21(b)). The codes do not prescribe a procedure for doing so, but provide that it is for chief officer to ensure that procedures are in place to ensure that suspects are able to understand their position and to communicate effectively with police officers, solicitors and appropriate adults (Codes C and H para 13.1A; Code I para 12.2(c)). Codes C and H NfG 13B states that such a procedure may involve using a telephone interpreter service, or the use of cue cards or similar visual aids. Codes H and I make provision for a wide array of interpreting services, including live link, at Annex L and Annex K respectively. Since the codes state that a suspect who appears to be unable to speak or understand English must be provided with an inter-

142 *R v Clarke* [1989] Crim LR 892, CA.

143 If a translation in the relevant language is not available, the information in the notice can be provided by an interpreter and a written translation provided without undue delay (Code C para 13.12(d); Code H para 13.14(d); Code I para 3.16(c)).

144 Available at: www.gov.uk/guidance/notice-of-rights-and-entitlements-a-persons-rights-in-police-detention.

preter (Code C para 13.12; Code H para 3.14; Code I para 3.16(a)), any significant doubt should be resolved in favour of calling in an interpreter.

11.109 If a suspect challenges the quality of interpretation provided, or of a translation provided, the custody officer or interviewer (as relevant) must decide whether to make arrangements for a different interpreter or for another translation (Codes C and H paras 13.10A and 13.10C; Code I para 12.12). If the suspect challenges a decision that they do not need an interpreter, or the decision made following a challenge to the quality of interpretation or translation, the issue must be referred to an inspector who is to deal with it as a complaint (Codes C and H para 13.10D; Code I para 12.15).

Assistance by an interpreter

11.110 If the custody officer determines that a suspect requires an interpreter, they must arrange for an interpreter without delay (Code C para 3.12(a); Code H para 3.14(a); Code I para 3.16). Normally, the arrangements should be such that the interpreter is physically present with the suspect (Codes C and H para 13.1ZA; Code I para 12.1). However, if the custody officer or interviewer (as relevant) is satisfied that live link interpretation would not adversely affect or otherwise undermine or limit the suspect's ability to communicate confidently and effectively for the purpose for which it is being used, interpretation may be provided remotely. If the suspect or their lawyer makes representation that live link should not be used, it can only proceed if authorised by an inspector or above (Code C para 13.1ZA and Annex N; Code H para 13.1ZA and Annex L; Code I Annex K para 5). If live link is used, the modifications to various procedures set out in Annex N and Annex L Part 2 apply. Code I para 6 and Annex K contains similar provisions. The provisions on live link interpretation mean, for example, that interpretation may be provided remotely for the booking-in procedure, but in person for an interview. The codes permit live link interpreting, but only where the fairness of the proceedings is not affected by the absence of the physical presence of the interpreter. The decision about whether or not live link is suitable will be fact-specific in each instance, considering the age, gender and vulnerability of the suspect, the nature and circumstances of the case, and the impact on the suspect according to the particular purpose(s) for which they require the assistance of an interpreter and the time(s) when that assistance is required. Whether or not the suspect requires the assistance of an appropriate adult will not be determinative, but rather an assessment ought to be made concerning the potential adverse effects or limitations the suspect may experience as a result. The meaning of 'live link interpretation' is set out in Codes C and H para 13.12, and Code I para 12.17. If live link interpretation is used for an interview, the recording of the interview must be audio and visual, allowing all participants to see and hear each other.[145] For all other purposes it may be audio only.[146] Where a custody officer determines that a suspect requires

145 Code C para 13.12(a), Code H para 13.12(a)(i) and Code I para 12.17(a)(i).

146 Save for interviews under NSA 2023 s27 and Sch 6, which must be video and audio recorded. Where live link is used in interview, the recording must include the additional modifications at Annex K para 9.

an interpreter, there is no provision for the suspect to waive the right to interpretation.

11.111 The codes provide that if a suspect cannot communicate with their lawyer because of language difficulties, arrangements must be made for an interpreter to enable communication (Codes C and H para 13.9; Code I para 12.2). The provisions described in para 11.110 above apply, so that while interpretation must normally be provided face to face, it may be provided by audio-only live link if the conditions are satisfied.

Translation

11.112 Translation of documents is governed by Code C para 13.10B and Annex M, Code H para 13.10B and Annex K and Code I para 12.2(c) and Annex J, which provide that 'essential' documents must be translated into a language that the suspect understands. See para 11.107 above regarding translation of the written notice of rights and entitlements. 'Essential' documents are records that are required to be made in accordance with the code (Code C Annex M para 1; Code H Annex K para 1; Code I Annex J para 1):

> . . . which are relevant to decisions to deprive a person of their liberty, to any charge and to any record considered necessary to enable a detainee to defend themselves in criminal proceedings and to safeguard the fairness of the proceedings.

The annexes contain a table showing the documents that are considered essential for these purposes, and the times when they must be created and provided. A translation of the grounds for detention, and the particulars of any offences charged, must be provided as soon as practicable, but the translation may be provided orally if authorised by the custody officer. Translation of written interview records and written statements made under caution should be created contemporaneously so that the suspect can read and verify them, although this is modified where an interview is interpreted by live link (see Code C Annex N Part 2; Code H Annex L Part 2; Code I Annex K). There is no provision in the codes for translation at the police station of electronically recorded interviews. The documents specified in the tables in Annex M, Annex K and Annex J should not be regarded as exhaustive since, in any particular case, there may be other 'essential' documents (see para 4.22 above). In particular, a document recording the grounds for arrest may be an 'essential' document.[147] The suspect or their lawyer may make representations that a particular document should be translated, and if the custody officer is any doubt they must seek advice from an inspector or above (Code C Annex M paras 8–9; Code H Annex K paras 8–9; Code I Annex J para 9).

11.113 A suspect may waive their right to translation of documents, but waiver must be voluntary and consent may only be given after they have received legal advice or they give unconditional and fully informed written consent

147 ECHR Article 5(2) provides that everyone arrested must be informed 'in a language which he understands' of the reasons for their arrest.

having full knowledge of the consequences (Code C Annex M paras 4–7; Code H Annex K paras 4–7; Code I Annex J paras 4–6).

Interpretation in interviews

11.114 A person in respect of whom it has been determined that an interpreter is required (see para 11.108 above) must not be interviewed in the absence of a person capable of interpreting, except where the urgent interview provisions of Code C paras 11.1 and 11.18(c), Code H para 11.2 or 11.11(c) or Code I para 11.1 or 11.12(c) apply (Codes C and H para 13.2; Code I para 12.5). If the suspect is a child or mentally disordered or vulnerable and the person acting as the appropriate adult does not appear to speak or understand English, arrangements must be made for an interpreter to assist communication between the suspect, the appropriate adult and the interviewer, unless the urgent interview provisions apply (Code C para 13.2A; Code H para 13.3; Code I para 12.6 or 11.1 or 11.12(c)). Where the interview is not audio or video recorded, the interviewing officer must ensure that the interpreter makes a note of the interview at the time, in the language of the suspect, and certifies its accuracy, and the suspect must be given the opportunity to read it and certify it as correct or indicate the respects in which they consider it to be inaccurate (Codes C and H para 13.3; Code E NfG 4C; Code I para 12.16 and Annex J). Where a statement is made in a language other than English, the statement must be taken down in the language in which it is made and the person making it must be asked to sign it. An English translation must be made in due course (Codes C and H para 13.4; Code I para 12.7). The arrangements to be adopted where interpretation is provided by live link are set out in Code C para 13.12(a) and Annex N, Code H para 13.12(a) and Annex L, and Code I Annex K.

Interpretation during identification procedures

11.115 Where an identification procedure is conducted in relation to a suspect in respect of whom there is doubt about their ability to understand English, the custody officer must make the necessary arrangements for an interpreter as required by Code C (Code D para 2.14). Where an identification parade is held, once it is formed, the whole parade must take place in the presence and hearing of an interpreter (Code D Annex B para 8). If a witness makes an identification after an identification parade has ended, the suspect, their lawyer and the interpreter, if present, must be informed (Code D Annex B para 20).

Hearing and speech difficulties

11.116 Many of the provisions relating to interpretation for a person who does not speak or understand English are also relevant where the suspect is deaf or has hearing or speech difficulties.

11.117 If a suspect appears to be deaf, they must be treated as such for the purposes of the codes in the absence of clear evidence to the contrary (Code C para 1.6; Code D para 2.5; Code H para 1.12; Code I para 1.11).

If a suspect appears to have a hearing or speech impediment, the custody officer must call an interpreter as soon as is practicable and ask the interpreter to give the suspect the information required in Codes C and H paras 3.1–3.5 and Code I paras 3 and 3.1 (Code C para 3.12; Code H para 3.14; Code I para 3.16). 'Interpreter' includes appropriate assistance to comply with those provisions. A suspect who requires an interpreter or other appropriate assistance for these reasons must not be interviewed in the absence of an interpreter unless the urgent interview provisions of Code C para 11.1 or paras 11.18–11.20, Code H para 11.11 or Code I para 11.1 or 11.12(c) apply (Code C para 13.5; Code H para 13.2; Code I para 12.5). Similarly, if the suspect is a child and the person who is present as an appropriate adult appears to have a hearing or speech impediment, the suspect must not be interviewed in the absence of a person capable of interpreting or providing other appropriate assistance, unless the urgent interview provisions apply (Codes C and H para 13.6; Code I para 11.1 or 11.12(c)).

11.118 If a suspect requests legal advice and cannot communicate with the lawyer because of hearing or speech difficulties, an interpreter, who must not be a police officer or a member of the civilian support staff, must be called to enable communication (Codes C and H para 13.9; Code I para 12). See further paras 11.107 to 11.110 above.[148]

11.119 Where a suspect appears to have a hearing impediment, and the interview is audio recorded, the interviewer must also take a contemporaneous note of the interview in accordance with the requirements of Code C (Code E para 4.7). Note that the Law Society has issued a practice note, *Use of interpreters in criminal cases*, which states that where a police interview involves a sign language interpreter, the lawyer should insist that it is video recorded, and in such a way that images of both the suspect and the interpreter are captured.[149]

11.120 If any identification procedure requires information to be given to or sought from a suspect who appears to be deaf or if there is doubt about their hearing or speaking ability, the custody officer or identification officer must make arrangements for an interpreter in accordance with the provisions of Code C (Code D para 2.14). Where an identification parade is held, once it has been formed everything must take place in the presence and hearing of the suspect and of any interpreter who is present (Code D Annex B para 8). If a witness makes an identification after the parade has ended, the suspect, and their lawyer and the interpreter if present, must be informed (Code D Annex B para 20).

Blindness, visual impairment and additional learning needs

11.121 If a suspect appears to be blind, visually impaired or unable to read, they must be treated as such for the purpose of the code in the absence of clear evidence to the contrary (Code C para 1.6; Code D para 2.5; Code H

148 For information about qualified sign language interpreters, see the Signature Directory, available at: www.signature.org.uk.

149 January 2023, available at: www.lawsociety.org.uk/topics/criminal-justice/use-of-interpreters-in-criminal-cases.

para 1.12; Code I para 1.11). In such cases the custody officer must ensure that the suspect's solicitor, relative, appropriate adult or some other person likely to take an interest in the suspect (and who is not involved in the investigation) is available to help in checking any documentation. Where Code C, H or I require written consent or a signature, the person who is assisting may be asked to sign instead of the suspect, if the suspect desires this (Code C para 3.20; Code D para 2.13; Code H para 3.21; Code I para 3.24).

11.122 If a police interview is recorded in writing,[150] the senior police officer present must read it over to the suspect and ask them whether they would like to sign the record as correct, or make their mark or to indicate the respects in which they consider it inaccurate. The officer must then indicate on the interview record what has occurred (Code C para 11.11). There is no special provision in Codes E and F in relation to the signing of the label of an audio or video recorded interview that is not digitally recorded, but it is suggested that a third party present in the interview should be asked to sign the label and that the interviewer should record what has occurred. Where the suspect makes a written statement in accordance with Code C, Code H Annex D or Code I Annex D and the suspect cannot read, the senior officer present must read it over to the suspect and ask them whether they would like to correct, alter or add anything and to sign or make their mark at the end. The officer must then certify what has occurred on the statement itself (Code C; Codes H and Annex D para 12).

11.123 If, after a suspect is charged, the officer wishes to bring to the suspect's notice a statement made by another person or the content of an interview with another person, if the suspect cannot read, the officer may read it to the suspect (Code C para 16.4A).

Practical considerations

11.124 Where an interpreter is required, there is no provision for delay in requesting one, or for conducting an interview in the absence of an interpreter other than in the case of an urgent interview (Code C para 11.18(c); Code H para 11.11(c); Code I para 11.1 or 11.12(c)). Where an interpreter does attend, it will be difficult for the police to justify holding the suspect incommunicado under PACE s56, TA 2000 Sch 8 para 8 or NSA 2023 Sch 6 para 9, or delaying access to legal advice under PACE s58, TA 2000 Sch 8 para 8 or NSA 2023 Sch 6 para 9.[151]

11.125 The Law Society has issued a practice note, *Use of interpreters in criminal cases*,[152] which provides that:

- the lawyer must ensure that the client's interpretation needs are met;
- the lawyer must decide whether the interpreter arranged by the police can also act as the interpreter for the lawyer/client consultation;

150 Note: Codes H and I para 11.8 require interviews to be audio and visually recorded. A written record should be made of any comments made by a suspect.

151 See, in relation to children, para 11.15 above.

152 January 2023, available at: www.lawsociety.org.uk/topics/criminal-justice/use-of-interpreters-in-criminal-cases. For information about qualified interpreters, see the National Register of Public Service Interpreters at: www.nrpsi.org.uk/.

- the lawyer should use a different interpreter if the interpreter arranged by the police cannot meet all of the client's needs, there are multiple suspects or the client knows the interpreter arranged by the police;
- other relevant factors for the lawyer to consider include whether the suspected offence is particularly sensitive and/or serious or there is a particular risk that the interpretation may be challenged, and whether community relations are such that the client has little confidence in the relationship between the interpreter and the police; and
- if the lawyer decides to use the interpreter arranged by the police, the lawyer should explain the position to the client, obtain the client's consent and confirm that the interpreter is bound by their code of conduct to maintain confidentiality.

The cost of a separate interpreter, provided it is reasonable and is incurred in the best interests of the client, may be claimed under the SCC 2022 (draft SCC 2025).[153] Note that the presence of an interpreter at a consultation between the lawyer and their client does not destroy legal professional privilege.[154,155]

11.126 Interpreters can be a source of difficulty for the lawyer, particularly where it is not feasible to use a second interpreter for the consultation. The onus is on the custody officer to obtain an interpreter (Code C para 3.12; Code H para 3.14; Code I para 3.16), and although Codes C and H para 13.1 and Code I para 12 require chief officers of police to ensure that there are appropriate arrangements in place for the provision of suitably qualified interpreters, they may not be available in any particular case. Since an interpreter obtained by the police will be paid by them, the problem of lack of independence from the police is obvious. This problem is not necessarily solved by using friends or relatives of suspects as interpreters, since their connection with the suspect may lead them to give a less than accurate account of what the suspect says. Similarly, if the interpreter comes from the same local community, the suspect may be reluctant to talk freely to that person.

11.127 Even if an interpreter is suitably independent, the lawyer should try to satisfy themself that the interpreter has a sufficient knowledge of, and competence in, both languages. The fact that the suspect and the interpreter may have a common national origin does not guarantee that they will speak the same language. Many countries have populations speaking diverse languages, and even if there is an 'official' language, only the formal form of the language may be known by some inhabitants, who may not fully understand the language when spoken colloquially.

153 SCC Specification 2022 para 5.38 (draft SCC Specification 2025 para 5.36).

154 *Bozkurt v Thames Magistrates' Court* [2001] EWHC Admin 400.

155 See also V Cochrane and W Hayes, *Legal Professional Privilege in Criminal Investigations and Proceedings* (Oxford University Press, 2024) ch 6 and paras 6.22–6.34 concerning appropriate adults and interpreters.

Foreign nationals

11.128 A citizen of an independent Commonwealth country or a national of a foreign country (including the Republic of Ireland) must be informed as soon as practicable of their right to communicate at any time with their High Commission, embassy or consulate, and of their right to have their High Commission, embassy or consulate informed of their whereabouts and the grounds for detention (Codes C and H para 7.1; Code I para 7). A request for consular access must be acted upon as soon as practicable (Codes C and H para 7.1; Code I para 7).

11.129 If a citizen of an independent Commonwealth country or a national of a foreign country with which a bilateral consular convention or agreement is in force[156] is detained, the appropriate High Commission, embassy or consulate must be informed as soon as is practicable (Codes C and H para 7.2; Code I para 7.1). However, if the suspect is a political refugee or seeking political asylum, this information should be given only at the express request of the suspect (Codes C, H and I para 7.4). Consular officials may visit suspects out of the hearing of police officers and may arrange legal advice (Codes C, H and I para 7.3).

11.130 The exercise of these rights may not be delayed or prevented, even where the suspect is being held incommunicado under PACE s56, TA 2000 Sch 8 para 8 or NSA 2023 s27 and Sch 6 para 9,[157] or where legal advice is delayed under PACE s58(8), TA 2000 Sch 8 para 8 or NSA 2023 Sch 6 para 9 (Codes C, H and I NfG 7A).

Human trafficking and modern slavery

11.131 The CPS has issued legal guidance[158] for cases involving human trafficking or modern slavery, which can also be a material consideration when dealing with 'county lines' drug cases.[159] Factors relevant to modern slavery should be explored as early as possible, including at the police station, as they can have a material impact on the eventual outcome.[160] The CPS guidance sets out a four-stage assessment for prosecution:

156 For information on such countries, see Codes C and H para 7.2 and Code I para 7.1.

157 As specifically set out in Codes C, H and I NfG 7A.

158 CPS legal guidance, *Modern Slavery and human trafficking: offences and defences, including the section 45 defence* (July 2025), available at: www.cps.gov.uk/legal-guidance/modern-slavery-and-human-trafficking-offences-and-defences-including-section-45.

159 'County lines' dealing has been described as: 'To avoid detection and promote the supply of drugs, drugs dealers run "county drug lines" using couriers, often teenagers, to take drugs from a large city to towns some distance away.' (*R v Karemera* [2018] EWCA Crim 1432) and 'the exploitation of vulnerable children and adults by violent gang members in order to move and sell crack and heroin across the country, often associated with city-based organised crime gangs.' (CPS legal guidance, *Modern Slavery and human trafficking: offences and defences, including the section 45 defence* (July 2025), available at: www.cps.gov.uk/legal-guidance/human-trafficking-smuggling-and-slavery).

160 *R v DS* [2020] EWCA Crim 285.

(1) Is there a reason to believe that the person is a victim of trafficking or slavery?
   - If yes, move to Question 2.
   - If not, you do not need to consider this assessment further.
(2) Is there clear evidence of a credible common law defence of duress?
   - If yes, then the case should not be charged or should be discontinued on evidential grounds.
   - If not, move to Question 3.
(3) Is there clear evidence of a statutory defence under Modern Slavery Act 2015 s45?
   - If yes, then the case should not be charged or should be discontinued on evidential grounds.
   - If not, move to Question 4.
(4) Is it in the public interest to prosecute? Even where there is no clear evidence of duress and no clear evidence of a section 45 defence or where section 45 does not apply (because the offence is excluded under Schedule 4) this must be considered. In considering the public interest, prosecutors should consider all the circumstances of the case, including the seriousness of the offence and any direct or indirect compulsion arising from their trafficking situation; see *R v LM and Others*.[161,162]

11.132 The police are obliged to notify the Home Office of any occasion where they encounter a potential victim of human trafficking.[163] Therefore, if the lawyer believes that their client is a victim of modern slavery, human trafficking or sexual exploitation then, with the client's authority, this should be brought to attention of either the investigating officer or the custody officer. This may be relevant whether or not the client is a foreign national. For instance, much of the recent case-law concerning modern slavery arises from facts concerning children and the possession or supply of drugs.[164] When advising clients who have been arrested in respect of immigration document offences, lawyers should be particularly aware of the potential defence under Immigration and Asylum Act 1999 s31. The courts have criticised lawyers in a number of cases for failing to advise clients about the availability of the defence.[165]

161 [2010] EWCA Crim 2327.

162 For further information concerning the impact on children, the Youth Justice Legal Centre legal guide, *Child Criminal Exploitation* (May 2023), provides further practical advice, available at: https://yjlc.uk/resources/legal-guides-and-toolkits/child-criminal-exploitation.

163 Modern Slavery Act 2015 s52; and see College of Policing, *Authorised Professional Practice: Modern slavery: First response and the national referral mechanism* (February 2022), available at: www.college.police.uk/app/major-investigation-and-public-protection/modern-slavery/first-response-and-national-referral-mechanism.

164 See notes 15 and 17 above.

165 See, for example, *R v N* [2019] EWCA Crim 984; *R v S* [2020] EWCA Crim 765; and *DPP v M* [2020] EWHC 3422 (Admin), in particular, where the defence was successfully advanced despite the differing accounts provided to the police.

CHAPTER 12

Immigration detainees

continued

Introduction

Overview

12.1 This chapter sets out to give criminal lawyers a basic understanding of how to assist people in detention with immigration-related problems when encountered in police stations, and also to try to identify issues that, for detainees, are likely to be most relevant both at the time of detention and immediately thereafter.

12.2 A comprehensive understanding of the immigration process is beyond the scope of this chapter, and the principal aim is to enable the lawyer to assist the detainee to identify the range of options that may be open to them, as well as potentially identifying the limitations on some of those options.

12.3 One practical problem for lawyers in the field of immigration, and consequently also for those practising in criminal work where there is an immigration component, is that the relevant provisions are not contained within one piece of legislation, but are governed by an ever-growing series of statutes, immigration rules, statutory instruments and other delegated legislation, defining the terms on which processes for appeals, administrative reviews and bail are to be governed. Furthermore, there is a number of Home Office policies giving guidance on how the provisions and the mechanisms (as interpreted by the Home Office) are to operate, but which unhelpfully are not all within one single document.[1]

12.4 The statutes empower the secretary of state, immigration officers (IOs) and entry clearance officers (ECOs – officials carrying out functions at embassies and consular offices abroad) to make decisions to grant or refuse applications. The Immigration Rules set out the criteria governing how those applications for entry clearance, for leave to enter or for permission to remain are to be determined. The most recent set of consolidated rules took effect from 1 October 1994 (Statement of Changes of Immigration Rules HC 395). These have been substantially amended very many times since that consolidation. The Home Office website maintains a current version of the Immigration Rules, which incorporates the amendments when they take effect.[2] Much concern has been expressed as to the complexity of the rules, given the way they are so regularly amended.[3] The Law Commission published a report in January 2020 making 41 recommendations aimed at increasing the transparency and consistency of the rules.[4]

12.5 The format of subsequent rules has in part followed some of the guidance with the introduction of new appendices containing complete

1 See, for example, *Deportation on conducive grounds Immigration Act 1971 and UK Borders Act 2007* (June 2025), available at: www.gov.uk/government/publications/deporting-non-eea-foreign-nationals/conducive-deportation-accessible.

2 Available at: www.gov.uk/guidance/immigration-rules, most recently updated as at time of writing on 18 August 2025.

3 Described unfavourably by Jackson LJ in *Pokhriyal v Secretary of State for the Home Department* [2013] EWCA Civ 1568 as follows: '[the] provisions have now achieved a degree of complexity which even the Byzantine emperors would have envied' and endorsed by the Supreme Court in *Mandalia v Secretary of State for the Home Department* [2015] UKSC 59.

4 *Simplification of the Immigration Rules Report HC 14*, available at: www.gov.uk/government/publications/simplification-of-the-immigration-rules-report.

provisions as to eligibility criteria, although even with the revised appendices there is still often the need to cross-refer to broader provisions, for example, Part 9: grounds of refusal.[5]

12.6 Despite the many legislative changes, there has been no consolidating statute, hence it remains necessary to examine legislation dating back to the Immigration Act (IA) 1971, which contains many of the provisions relating to the powers of detention and sets out the classes of persons who are likely to be afforded an entitlement to apply for immigration bail. (As at the date of writing the Border Security, Asylum and Immigration Bill[6] was being debated in Parliament and proposed changes to the powers of detention would include amendments to some of the statutory provisions within the IA 1971).

12.7 Detention at a police station under immigration legislation may have resulted from a raid carried out by IOs alone or in concert with the police. Alternatively, it may follow after a person has been arrested for a criminal matter when their immigration status was called into question. The police may have little subsequent interest in the matter (which may have followed a relatively minor offence), and the only obligation upon them would be to ensure that the detainee's treatment in detention is broadly consistent with the Police and Criminal Evidence Act 1984 (PACE) until such time as the detainee is released from custody or transferred into alternative immigration detention. Increasingly, detainees are being held specifically in relation to immigration offences relating to their mode of entry to the UK and lack of formal documentation (see para 12.36 below). There is a mechanism for police to contact the immigration service where they believe the individual may be an Immigration Act offender through the Command and Control Unit (CCU) based in Manchester.[7]

12.8 If the police do proceed to investigate an alleged offence, the provisions of PACE will apply as they would to other detainees. The immigration investigation may be deferred until after the criminal investigation has been concluded, although it is becoming increasingly common for detainees to be subject to parallel investigations. It should be noted that if the person is released without charge in relation to the criminal matter, that does not necessarily secure the person's release from custody, since the immigration service may, and often does, exercise powers to authorise continued detention. A further limited power of arrest enables a designated IO[8] to detain an individual at a port of entry for up to three hours where the officer believes that an individual has committed a criminal (non-immigration) offence or is subject to an arrest warrant.[9]

12.9 There has been some debate about whether PACE and the PACE Codes of Practice apply to immigration detainees in police stations. The

5 February 2016, available at: www.gov.uk/guidance/immigration-rules/immigration-rules-part-9-grounds-for-refusal.

6 See version as at date of writing: https://publications.parliament.uk/pa/bills/cbill/59-01/0205/240205.pdf.

7 See *Partnership Working* version 5.0 4 April 2025, available at: https://www.gov.uk/government/publications/powers-and-operational-procedure/partnership-working-accessible.

8 UK Borders Act (UKBA) 2007 s1(1).

9 UKBA 2007 s2(1).

general view is that while matters are being investigated and could constitute a criminal offence (including an immigration offence), PACE and the codes will apply. They may cease to apply from the time that it is clear that a person is being detained solely in respect of, and having been served with, a notice under the immigration legislation, or where the person has been arrested on the authority of an IO solely for the purposes of having their fingerprints taken (Code C para 1.12(ii)), or where the detention is authorised under IA 1971 Sch 2 or 3, or Nationality, Immigration and Asylum Act (NIAA) 2002 s62.[10]

12.10 Furthermore, under Immigration and Asylum Act (IAA) 1999 s145, when exercising the power to arrest, question, search the person, enter or search premises, or seize property found on a person, an IO must have regard to the relevant PACE code. A direction as to the applicability of PACE came into effect on 15 July 2013,[11] which clarifies instructions for Home Office staff undertaking enforcement action.

12.11 Within the context of immigration powers that are exercisable, different roles are played by those carrying out immigration functions under the overall responsibility of the secretary of state.

The role of entry clearance officers

12.12 Many people seeking entry to the UK require prior entry clearance in order to do so, commonly referred to as a visa. The ECO will consider an application made at a post abroad and, if satisfied, may grant the application, and if not, will refuse the application. This includes cases where the application may be referred to officials in the UK for consideration (as is the norm in a number of categories, including family members seeking entry to join partners or other family members in the UK). Persons entering the UK in the absence of an appropriate entry clearance (where required) are liable to be returned to the country from which they embarked and may be detained pending the determination of removal arrangements, but such detention would be authorised in the UK by an IO rather than by the police.[12]

12.13 The existence of carrier liability sanctions to penalise airlines, passenger ferries and travel operators,[13] together with the introduction of more points based system routes to the UK, has significantly reduced the number of such individuals gaining entry to the UK though legal routes.[14]

12.14 However the downside to the restrictions has led to a significant increase in the number of illegal arrivals, including dangerous crossings by boat.[15]

10 Code C para 1.12(iii).

11 Immigration (PACE Codes of Practice) Direction 2013 (July 2013), available at: www.gov.uk/government/publications/the-immigration-pace-codes-of-practice-direction-2013.

12 IA 1971 Sch 2 para 16(2).

13 IAA 1999 Part II.

14 Further extensive powers were introduced in respect of maritime enforcement under Immigration Act (IA) 2016 s75 and Sch 14.

15 The number of people arriving in Britain by small boats in 2024 was 36,816; see: www.bbc.co.uk/news/articles/c5y45dmg2pjo. In the 12 months ending June 2025, the number had risen to 43,309; see www.gov.uk/government/statistics/immigration-system-statistics-year-ending-june-2025/how-many-people-come-to-the-uk-irregularly? (para 2.1).

The role of immigration officers

12.15 In broad terms, IOs are responsible for dealing with and determining cases involving persons from abroad who arrive in the UK seeking lawful entry. The individual may have recently arrived at a port, or may have made an application at a port of entry and be awaiting consideration of the application, for example asylum, where the decision is unlikely to be made for several months. In the immigration context, the grant of leave to enter or leave to remain is key. The IO's powers extend not only to the grant or refusal of leave, but also to the power to authorise detention or immigration bail, and if the latter, to imposing conditions on that release.[16]

12.16 In addition to IOs working within the various ports of entry in the UK, there are also IOs operating within designated enforcement units, such as that at Croydon. Furthermore, under a policy directed at pushing border controls offshore, there are 'juxtaposed controls' operating outside the UK, enabling powers to be exercised by IOs, including power to take fingerprints in controlled zones within France.[17] Post Brexit, these juxtaposed controls continue to operate and there have been recent discussions to cement further the commitment to the continuation of these controls with a stated focus on disrupting smuggling gangs.[18] This resulted in a pilot project between the UK and France, introduced from August 2025, for a returns agreement for those making boat crossings and the so-called 'one in, one out' policy.[19]

The role of the secretary of state

12.17 In cases where an individual had previously been granted lawful leave to enter or remain in the UK, any 'after-entry' decisions in respect of that individual will be taken by the secretary of state through the Home Office. This may include the decision to grant or refuse an extension of time in the UK, or a decision to allow or refuse permission for the individual to switch to remain in a different capacity from that under which they initially obtained leave to enter (for example, a student switching to remain in the capacity of being a partner of a person settled in the UK).

12.18 The secretary of state has power to make a decision to deport where they deem it to be conducive to the public good.[20] The power to deport also extends to dependant family members, such as a partner or a minor child of the individual who faces deportation. In 'automatic' deportation cases, the secretary of state has not merely a power, but a duty, to make a deportation order (see para 12.27 below).[21] The secretary of state also has the

16 IA 2016 Sch 10 para 1(1).

17 Nationality, Immigration and Asylum Act 2002 (Juxtaposed Controls) Order 2003 SI No 2818, as amended by Nationality, Immigration and Asylum Act 2002 (Juxtaposed Controls) (Amendment) Order 2011 SI No 1786.

18 Statement of Home Office in response to small boat crossings (May 2025), available at: https://homeofficemedia.blog.gov.uk/2025/04/16/latest-statement-in-response-to-small-boat-crossings/#:~:text=%E2%80%9CWe%20all%20want%20to%20end,and%20bring%20them%20to%20justice.

19 CP 1337, https://assets.publishing.service.gov.uk/media/68909bb2486754ec288783c2/CS_France_2.2025_Dangerous_Journeys_Agreement.pdf.

20 IA 1971 s3(5).

21 UKBA 2007 s32(5).

power to sign a deportation order, or to revoke a deportation order that has been signed.[22] The deportation of foreign criminals (persons with sentences of 12 months or more, serious harm from offending or persistent offenders[23]) is said to be in the public interest.[24]

12.19 The secretary of state also has responsibility for determining applications for asylum under the UN Convention Relating to the Status of Refugees 1951 (the 'Refugee Convention'), or where it is alleged that removal would constitute a breach of an individual's human rights under the European Convention on Human Rights (ECHR). Further, the secretary of state has responsibility for considering applications made for citizenship.

12.20 The decisions of the Home Office are carried out at a variety of offices, the central unit being based at Croydon, with regional offices in Belfast, Birmingham, Glasgow, Leeds, Liverpool, Manchester and Sheffield.

Illegal entrants

12.21 An illegal entrant is a person who has entered or sought to enter the UK unlawfully, or who has gained or attempted to gain entry through their deception or through the deception of another party. A person who arrives on a false passport would be an obvious example of someone who is an illegal entrant, as would someone who seeks to arrive in a clandestine manner without going through immigration control at all. The Court of Appeal has gone so far as to state that if a person requiring leave to enter was not given that leave, they could be classified as an illegal entrant.[25] If it is clear that deception had been used in gaining the original leave to enter, any leave granted is treated as being void ab initio and consequently any subsequent permission to remain or decisions made thereafter (in ignorance of those facts) will not prevent the individual from later being treated as an illegal entrant.

Overstayers

12.22 An overstayer is a person who, having previously lawfully entered the UK, has remained beyond the time permitted either by an IO or, in the event of an extension, by the secretary of state. The initial entry for such an individual would have been lawful, and the fact that they overstayed does not mean that their presence in the UK throughout their residence is deemed to be unlawful, merely that period beyond the date of lawful leave (save where a valid in time extension was made before that date[26]).

Persons in breach of their conditions

12.23 This includes a person who has overstayed, since one of the conditions of leave will relate to the period of time granted, but it will also include those persons who breach some other condition. For example, the condition prohibiting them from taking up employment. Persons granted entry

22 HC 395 Part 13 section 4.

23 NIAA 2002 s117D(2)(c).

24 NIAA 2002 s117C(1).

25 *R v Secretary of State for the Home Department ex p Rehal* [1989] Imm AR 576, CA.

26 IA 1971 s3C; see para 12.43 below.

under Immigration Rules Appendix Student for full-time studies on a graduate course are normally permitted to take up employment during term time of up to 20 hours per week.[27] Any work in excess of the authorised period during term time would be a breach of the conditions of leave.

12.24 Whether an individual has been identified as an illegal entrant, an overstayer or in breach of their conditions of leave, they will be liable to administrative removal in accordance with IAA 1999 s10, and would not automatically benefit from an appeal right exercisable prior to removal. The entitlement to appeal before removal will only apply where the removal of such an individual would be a breach of the individual's rights under the Refugee Convention, obligations to grant them humanitarian protection or where the removal would otherwise breach Human Rights Act (HRA) 1998 s6.[28]

12.25 Since the introduction of IA 2016 s63,[29] the category of persons who would be guaranteed an entitlement to appeal from within the UK prior to removal has been reduced yet further (see para 12.48 below regarding certification).

Deportees

12.26 As observed at para 12.18 above, those who face deportation include those who have been recommended for deportation by a court, as well as those in respect of whom the secretary of state has made a decision that their removal is conducive to the public good. This can include persons who have been lawfully given settlement in the UK, as well as their family members. Persons who are subject to deportation action (as opposed to administrative removal under IAA 1999 s10 – see para 12.24 above) may be entitled to bring an appeal prior to removal, but only where the appeal is not certified (see para 12.48 below). Where a recommendation for deportation is made by a criminal court, the appeal right against that element of a sentence remains within the criminal courts' jurisdiction, but where the removal potentially engages either the ECHR or the Refugee Convention, the decision to remove will trigger an appeal to the immigration courts. Crucially, the existence of an appeal will not operate as an automatic bar on removal prior to the appeal in a significant number of cases, unless it can be shown that the removal prior to the appeal would give rise to a real risk of 'serious irreversible harm'.[30]

Automatic deportation

12.27 A person who is a foreign criminal and has been convicted in the UK and sentenced to a term of imprisonment of 12 months or more,[31] or who commits an offence that is specified by the secretary of state as being

27 HC 395 Appendix Student ST 26.1 for those studying full time; for those studying below graduate level a maximum of 10 hours per week; for those studying part time, no work is permitted.

28 NIAA 2002 s84(1).

29 Which came into effect on 1 December 2016.

30 NIAA 2002 s94B(3).

31 UKBA 2007 s32(2).

particularly serious,[32] is subject to automatic deportation, whereby the secretary of state must make a deportation order.[33]

12.28 There are limited exceptions where such an order does not need to be made, that apply:

- to persons who would be exempt due to meeting certain specific requirements (Commonwealth or Irish nationals resident in UK on 1 January 1973);[34]
- where removal would breach the Refugee Convention or the ECHR (subject to certification powers[35]);
- where the person is under the age of 18 on the date of conviction;[36]
- where there are extant extradition proceedings;[37]
- where the removal would contravene the Council of Europe Convention on Action against Trafficking in Human Beings 2005;[38]
- where the individual is subject to certain orders under the Mental Health Act 1983;[39] and
- EEA nationals, but only where convicted solely in respect of offences committed prior to 31 December 2020.[40]

12.29 In theory, where an order is signed, no appeal right is available. In practice, the appeal is against whether the exception on asylum or human rights grounds should apply.[41] However, whether an individual will be able to exercise that right of appeal prior to removal is becoming increasingly difficult, following the introduction of certification powers (see para 12.48 below).

Powers of arrest and detention for offences

Introduction

12.30 There are extensive powers of arrest given to police officers and IOs under the IA 1971 (as amended), where it is believed that an immigration offence has occurred, including the breach of any conditions of bail or facilitation of illegal entry.

12.31 IA 1971 s28A(1) empowers a police constable or an IO to arrest, without warrant, on reasonable grounds for suspicion any person who has committed or attempted to commit any of the following offences:

- knowingly entering the UK in breach of a deportation order[42] or without leave;[43]

32 UKBA 2007 s32(3).
33 UKBA 2007 s32(5).
34 UKBA 2007 s33(1)(b).
35 UKBA 2007 s33(2).
36 UKBA 2007 s33(3).
37 UKBA 2007 s33(5).
38 UKBA 2007 s33(6A).
39 UKBA 2007 s33(6).
40 UKBA 2007 s33(6B).
41 NIAA 2002 s82(1).
42 IA 1971 s24(A1).
43 IA 1971 s24(B1).

- knowingly overstaying[44] or breaching a condition of leave;[45]
- overstaying as a seaman or crew member;[46]
- failing to comply with a bail restriction (such as residence, reporting or taking up employment without reasonable excuse);[47] or
- obtaining or seeking leave to enter or remain, or avoiding, delaying or revoking enforcement action, by deception.[48]

12.32 In addition, IA 1971 s28A empowers an IO to arrest, having reasonable grounds to believe that an offence has been committed in respect of the following:

- knowingly and for gain facilitating the arrival or entry (or attempted arrival or entry) in the UK of a person who the individual knows or has reasonable cause to believe to be an asylum seeker;[49]
- obstructing an IO or other person in the execution of their duties under the Act where it is impractical to serve a summons because of a lack of certainty about an individual's address, or where arrest is otherwise necessary to prevent the individual causing or suffering physical injury or causing loss or damage to property;[50]
- making, altering, possessing without reasonable excuse, using or attempting to use with an intention to deceive, a false asylum application registration card (ARC)[51] issued to a person who has made a claim for asylum;[52] or
- possessing a genuine or replica immigration stamp[53] without reasonable excuse.[54]

12.33 IOs are empowered to enter premises in order to search for and arrest those suspected of having committed offences.[55] The power to search also applies to business premises,[56] with such power being exercisable upon the belief that the individual is on the premises, not because it is believed that the individual owns or has a financial interest in the premises. Powers are also given to an IO to search premises for documents relevant to persons liable to detention before a decision on whether to grant or refuse

44 IA 1971 s24(C1).
45 IA 1971 s24(1)(b).
46 IA 1971 s24(1)(c).
47 IA 1971 s24(1)(h).
48 IA 1971 s24A(1).
49 IA 1971 s25A(1).
50 IA 1971 s26(1)(g).
51 According to Home Office Guidance on Application registration card (updated March 2025): 'The ARC is a credit card-sized plastic card issued by the Home Office to individuals who claim asylum. It certifies that you are an asylum claimant and can remain in the UK while your claim is pending. The ARC contains information about your identity or claimed identity. It is not proof of identity.' See www.gov.uk/government/publications/application-registration-card-arc/application-registration-card-arc.
52 IA 1971 s26A(3).
53 This relates to the stamping device; see IA 1971 s26B(3).
54 IA 1971 s26B.
55 IA 1971 Sch 2 para 25A(2).
56 IA 1971 s28FA(2).

them entry to the UK, or to curtail (cut short) their leave,[57] including documents in electronic format.[58]

12.34 Search powers are also available for documents believed to be relevant in determining whether a premises is liable to a penalty arising from illegal employment, or leasing premises to persons who do not have a legal right of residence in the UK.[59] The Border Security, Asylum and Immigration Bill proposes extending powers to search for, seize and retain items that appear to relate to the commission of an immigration offence, including retention of any electronic data seized.

12.35 IOs also have arrest powers exercisable without a warrant where, in the exercise of their duties, they have a reasonable suspicion that a person has committed, or has attempted to commit, a variety of additional offences, including conspiracy to defraud, bigamy, perjury, theft, false accounting, handling stolen goods, certain fraud and forgery offences including under the Identity Documents Act 2010, modern slavery, and trafficking for sexual exploitation.[60]

12.36 In addition to the increase in powers given to IOs, more individuals are potentially subject to the criminal law in this area. Asylum and Immigration (Treatment of Claimants, etc) Act 2004 s2 makes it an offence to arrive in the UK without proper documentation, regardless of the purpose for which entry is being sought. Following the instructions of an agent to destroy the passport or using a false passport for any part of the journey will not necessarily constitute a defence.[61] However, if no passport was used for the totality of the journey, then a section 2 offence is not committed.[62] Those who are charged with the offence may need urgent immigration advice if they are also seeking asylum in the UK, since the consequences of failure to produce a passport, or destruction of a passport or ticket without reasonable explanation, may damage the individual's credibility in the context of the asylum claim.[63]

12.37 An IO or police constable also has power to arrest without warrant a person who has unreasonably refused to assist in their own departure from the UK, such as by refusing to attend an interview or complete an application form for a passport or a return travel document.[64]

Powers of administrative detention

12.38 As noted above, even if a potential criminal investigation (whether for an immigration offence or otherwise) has been concluded, the person will not necessarily be released, and their detention can be authorised by an IO (or the secretary of state in the case of deportees). Furthermore, the grant of bail by a magistrates' court in connection with any pending criminal

57 IA 1971 Sch 2 para 15A(2).
58 IA 1971 Sch 2 para 25A(7A).
59 IA 2016 s47(2).
60 Asylum and Immigration (Treatment of Claimants, etc) Act 2004 s14.
61 Asylum and Immigration (Treatment of Claimants, etc) Act 2004 s2(7)(b)(iii), though it might amount to a defence in some cases; see *R v Asmeron* [2013] EWCA Crim 435.
62 *Soe Thet v DPP* [2006] EWHC 2701 (Admin).
63 Asylum and Immigration (Treatment of Claimants, etc) Act 2004 s8(1).
64 Asylum and Immigration (Treatment of Claimants, etc) Act 2004 s35(5).

action will not result in the automatic release of the person, who may be required to apply to an immigration judge of the First-tier Tribunal (FTT) Immigration and Asylum Chamber (IAC) for bail. This is subject to a different process and determined by reference to different criteria than those applying in criminal proceedings (see para 12.106 below).

12.39 The power to detain administratively, whether before, during or after any criminal detention, applies to the following classes of person:

- persons arriving in the UK, pending a decision as to whether or not they should be given leave to enter, or where their leave has been suspended pending a decision as to whether the leave should be cancelled;[65] and
- persons refused leave to enter the UK (including those treated as illegal entrants), pending the setting of removal directions.[66]

These powers may be exercised by the secretary of state as well as by an IO.[67]

12.40 Further detention powers are exercisable only by the secretary of state in respect of the following:

- persons liable to deportation following a recommendation by a criminal court, even when granted bail by a criminal court pending appeal against conviction or against the recommendation;[68]
- persons served with the decision to deport, pending the making of the deportation order;[69]
- persons in respect of whom a deportation order has been signed, pending removal;[70] and
- persons in respect of whom consideration is being given as to whether or not the automatic deportation provisions apply to them following completion of a term of imprisonment,[71] or once an automatic deportation order has been made.[72]

(The Border Security, Asylum and Immigration Bill proposes to extend the detention power to any person in respect of whom the secretary of state is considering deportation on non-conducive grounds where they have not been recommended for deportation by a court.)

12.41 The power to detain consequently applies not only to those persons in respect of whom a decision has already been made, but also to those in respect of whom a decision has yet to be made. The lawyer needs to make clear to the client that detention does not necessarily mean that all is lost, and that there may be remedies to pursue regarding release, and regarding the circumstances more generally.

12.42 It is unlikely that the person will remain at the police station for a lengthy period. After five days, any further detention must be in either a prison, a removal centre or another designated place. In the case of those

65 IA 1971 Sch 2 para 16(1) and (1A).
66 IA 1971 Sch 2 para 16(2).
67 NIAA 2002 s62.
68 IA 1971 Sch 3 para 2(1) and (1A).
69 IA 1971 Sch 3 para 2(2).
70 IA 1971 Sch 3 para 3.
71 UKBA 2007 s36(1).
72 UKBA 2007 s36(2).

in respect of whom a removal direction has been issued, the maximum period is extended to seven days.[73] Guidance exists in relation to limiting the power of detention in respect of women who are pregnant (unless removal from the UK is imminent or there are exceptional circumstances),[74] as well as in respect of the detention of vulnerable adults.[75]

Awaiting a decision

12.43 In some cases, the person detained will already have made an application to the Home Office and be awaiting a decision. This may be someone who had leave and who has applied for an extension of stay. The fact that many weeks or even months have passed since the date on which the person made the application to the Home Office does not mean that they inadvertently become an overstayer if no decision has been made. IA 1971 s3C provides that a person who has made a valid application, either for an extension of their existing leave or for leave in a different capacity, has the original leave and conditions (apart from the one concerning time) extended by operation of law, until either the application is withdrawn or any appeal relating to it is disposed of (or where relevant an in-time administrative review (see para 12.66 below) could be sought or is pending), provided that during that time the individual does not leave the UK. As a consequence, individuals in this scenario ought not to be detained. However, there is power to cancel the statutorily extended leave under IA 1971 s3C if the individual has breached any conditions attached to that leave or if deception has been used in connection with an application seeking leave to remain.[76] Furthermore, if an application was made to the Home Office, but after their leave had expired, although the person may not necessarily be removed until after the application has been considered, they may be detained. They do not have the statutorily extended leave if either their application was submitted out of time or if that application was invalid.[77]

12.44 If an individual is initially detained in respect of a non-immigration related matter, that might trigger some action in respect of the pending application, although in such circumstances the outcome tends to be negative rather than positive. It will often be the making of the negative decision that triggers detention, since there is an increasing trend for the secretary of state to detain individuals for the purposes of serving refusal decisions. This is particularly so for those where the decisions would not be appealable from within the UK prior to removal.

73 Immigration (Places of Detention) Direction 2021, available at: www.gov.uk/government/publications/immigration-places-of-detention-direction-2021/the-immigration-places-of-detention-direction-2021-accessible-version.

74 IA 2016 s60(2); see Home Office, *Chapter 55a: Detention of pregnant women*, v1.0 (July 2016), available at: https://assets.publishing.service.gov.uk/media/5a82268f40f0b62305b92bfd/Chapter_55a_Detention_of_pregnant_women_v1.pdf.

75 See Home Office, *Immigration Act 2016: Guidance on adults at risk in immigration detention* (May 2024), available at: https://assets.publishing.service.gov.uk/media/664b753c993111924d9d3862/Guidance_on_Adults_at_Risk_in_Immigration_Detention.pdf.

76 IA 1971 s3C(3A).

77 *R (Mirza and Others) v Secretary of State for the Home Department* [2016] UKSC 63.

12.45 Until recently, the evidence to demonstrate the time period to which an individual had been granted leave to enter or remain would usually be by the individual producing a biometric residence permit (BRP). These were phased out as of 31 December 2024 in favour of an eVisa system enabling an individual to obtain digital evidence of the length of residence and any conditions applied.[78] This means that, increasingly, those encountered at police stations with immigration issues will no longer have a physical document to establish their residence, but theoretically an easier means of establishing that residence through the eVisa system.

Immigration decisions

Introduction

12.46 Most immigration decisions as to refusal of leave to enter or remain or removal no longer attract a right of appeal,[79] and in many cases where there is a right of appeal, it is not exercisable from within the UK before removal. Consequently, it will be important for the adviser to try to assist the detainee in determining whether there is an appealable decision exercisable prior to removal since this is likely to impact on, among other things, whether it is sensible to remain detained, particularly as in many cases the individual may be advised that they can be more swiftly removed if they agree to a voluntary departure.[80]

12.47 The only classes of cases that now attract a right of appeal at all are limited to:

- decisions refusing a protection claim (asylum);[81]
- decisions refusing a human rights claim;[82]
- decisions revoking protection status;[83] or
- decisions depriving an individual of citizenship,[84] and
- limited categories of appeal for EEA nationals.[85]

Certification

12.48 In respect of asylum claimants or those who argue that their removal would breach their human rights, refusal does not attract a right of appeal from within the UK if either the claim was certified by the secretary of state as being clearly unfounded on the grounds that it raises no legitimate Refugee Convention or human rights element;[86] or where the secretary of

78 See *eVisas: access and use your online immigration status*, available at: www.gov.uk/guidance/online-immigration-status-evisa.

79 Though there may be the right to seek an administrative review (see para 12.66 below).

80 UK Visas and Immigration (UKVI), *Voluntary and assisted departures*, v6.0 (March 2024), available at: www.gov.uk/government/publications/returns-preparation/voluntary-and-assisted-departures-accessible.

81 NIAA 2002 s82(1)(a).

82 NIAA 2002 s82(1)(b).

83 NIAA 2002 s82(1)(c).

84 British Nationality Act 1981 s40A.

85 See para 12.57 below.

86 NIAA 2002 s94(1).

state seeks to remove the person to a safe third country.[87] Since July 2014, the power available to the secretary of state to certify cases was significantly widened in the case of persons liable to deportation following criminal convictions pursuing human rights claims, and an appeal could be certified if the secretary of state was satisfied that an appellant (or prospective appellant) would not face a real risk of serious irreversible harm if removed before the appeals process was exhausted.[88] Efforts to remove persons to Rwanda, which were highly controversial (and believed to have cost more than £318 million[89]), were never implemented.[90]

12.49 The Supreme Court considered that the absence of effective mechanisms for the preparation and presentation of the appeal would render a certification unlawful.[91] The certification of human rights appeals was extended further from 1 December 2016 in respect of all appeals raising human rights issues, with the consequence that even fewer appeals will be capable of being pursued from within the UK prior to removal if based on human rights (as opposed to protection) grounds.[92] Certification is used increasingly in respect of asylum claims to prevent an appeal from being exercised prior to removal, and a delay in the making of the claim may make a significant difference to the outcome of any subsequent challenge.

12.50 In such cases, a challenge might be pursued by way of judicial review of the certification decision, or of the decision to remove to a safe third country. Although there have been no removals to Rwanda, the framework for removals to safe countries remains in place. Specialist advice would need to be sought swiftly in such a case, as merely expressing an intention to apply for judicial review will not normally operate to prevent or delay removal.[93]

12.51 In considering whether or not to make a deportation order of a foreign national criminal, the Immigration Rules require the secretary of state to start from the presumption that the public interest requires deportation.[94] The secretary of state will thereafter consider whether the relevant factors in a particular case outweigh this initial presumption, and it is clear that (in non-protection claims) where a person has received a custodial sentence of 12 months or more (or an offence causing serious harm or a 'persistent offender') it would only be in exceptional cases that such a presumption would be outweighed.[95]

87 Asylum and Immigration (Treatment of Claimants, etc) Act 2004 Sch 3.

88 NIAA 2002 s94B(3).

89 Migration Observatory, *Q&A: The UK's former policy to send asylum seekers to Rwanda* (University of Oxford, July 2024), available at: https://migrationobservatory.ox.ac.uk/resources/commentaries/qa-the-uks-policy-to-send-asylum-seekers-to-rwanda.

90 The Border Security, Asylum and Immigration Bill proposes repealing the legislative framework of the specific Rwanda plan.

91 *R (Kiarie and Byndloss) v Secretary of State for the Home Department* [2017] UKSC 42.

92 NIAA 2002 s94B, as amended by IA 2016 s63.

93 UKVI, *Judicial reviews, injunctions and applications to the European Court of Human Rights*, v3.0 (May 2024,) available at: www.gov.uk/government/publications/returns-preparation/judicial-reviews-injunctions-and-applications-to-the-european-court-of-human-rights-accessible-version.

94 HC 395 para 13.2.1.

95 Private life exception, family life exception or other very compelling circumstances: see HC 395 para 13.2.1(a) and (b).

12.52 Where automatic deportation applies, then subject to considering whether a relevant exception applies, no such balancing exercise is required, as the secretary of state must make such an order.[96]

12.53 In the context of deportation decisions which follow serious criminal offences committed in the UK, the Court of Appeal has accepted that the secretary of state has a wide margin of discretion in assessing what is in the public interest.[97]

12.54 The Immigration Rules make it clear that the starting point for considering deportation will be that the presumption is in favour of deportation as being conducive to the public good and in the public interest, where an individual has been sentenced to 12 months or more (or an offence causing serious harm or a persistent offender).[98] This will only be rebutted where the individual has been lawfully resident in the UK for most of their life, is socially and culturally integrated, and there would be significant obstacles to their integration to the proposed country of deportation[99] (private life exception), or there is a genuine subsisting parental relationship with a child who is British or who has lived in the UK for more than seven years,[100] or a genuine subsisting relationship with a partner formed at a time that the person's immigration status was not precarious[101] (family life exception). In either case it would need to be shown to be unduly harsh to require the individual or the connected family member to leave the UK. The statutory framework also differentiates between cases where the sentence of imprisonment is between one and four years and those where the sentence exceeds four years, with the prospects of being able to succeed on an appeal in the latter case being confined to circumstances where there are very compelling circumstances over and above the private life or family life exception.[102]

12.55 It will be critical for the lawyer to be able correctly to identify whether the detainee is likely to benefit from an appealable decision exercisable prior to removal (not all deportation decisions will give rise to an appealable decision prior to removal (see para 12.46 above)). If there is no entitlement to appeal prior to removal, the prospects for bail are reduced and the possibility of pursuing any other remedies, such as through representations (see para 12.94 below), will be severely limited.

Mandatory bans on return

12.56 One aspect that will need to be considered at a very early stage is whether the client has any intention to return to the UK in the future. If a person is an overstayer, illegal entrant, used deception or breached a condition attached to their leave, they face the prospect of a mandatory ban on returning to the UK for a specified period of time. The ban will not apply to those seeking to return where they have overstayed for not more than

96 UKBA 2007 s32(5).

97 *DW (Jamaica) v Secretary of State for the Home Department* [2018] EWCA Civ 797.

98 HC 395 para 13.2.1.

99 HC 395 para 13.2.3; and see NIAA 2002 s117C(4).

100 HC 395 para 13.2.5.

101 HC 395 para 13.2.6.

102 HC 395 para 13.2.2 and NIAA 2002.

30 days (if any time after 30 April 2017) and leave voluntarily at their own expense.[103] In other cases, the ban will be for a period between one and 10 years, depending on their level of co-operation and whether deception had been used in respect of any earlier application.[104]

Immigration appeals

Introduction

12.57 As observed above, the categories of decision giving rise to a right of appeal are limited to those involving protection issues, human rights, deprivation of citizenship (or limited EU rights in respect of applications made prior to 11pm on 31 December 2020 and the decision made after 5 May 2023[105]). Of these, appeals on human rights grounds will in a significant proportion of cases be likely to be certified, so as to prevent an appeal from being exercised prior to removal from the UK.[106] Those that do are subject to strict rules about time limits for bringing appeals and the grounds upon which it can be argued that a decision should be overturned.

12.58 The time limit for bringing an appeal is 14 days from the date the decision is served for persons in the UK[107] (although there is power to extend the time limit under para 20). The notice of appeal must be served on the FTT itself.[108]

12.59 Any appeal that is brought will be limited to grounds specified by statute.[109] NIAA 2002 s84 specifies that an appeal must be brought on one or more of the grounds listed:

- removal would breach the UK's obligations under the Refugee Convention;[110]
- removal would breach the UK's obligations in relation to persons eligible for a grant of humanitarian protection (essentially ECHR Article 2 or 3 cases);[111] or
- removal would be unlawful under HRA 1998 s6.[112]

12.60 Cases are heard by an immigration judge in the FTT (or occasionally a panel), and either party may request permission to appeal from the determination if it is believed that the FTT may have made an error of law.[113] Any

103 HC 395 para 9.8.5.

104 See table within HC 395 para 9.8.7.

105 Immigration (Citizens' Rights Appeals) (EU Exit) Regulations 2020 SI No 61, as amended by Immigration (Citizens' Rights Appeals) (EU Exit) (Amendment) Regulations 2023 SI No 441.

106 NIAA 2002 ss92, 94 and 94B.

107 Tribunal Procedure (First-tier Tribunal) (Immigration and Asylum Chamber) Rules (FTT Rules) 2014 SI No 2604 r19(2).

108 FTT Rules 2014 r19(1).

109 The appeal in cases including deprivation of citizenship or the limited class of available EU law rights are not restricted to those grounds set out within NIAA 2002 s84.

110 NIAA 2002 s84(1)(a) or 84(3)(a).

111 NIAA 2002 s84(1)(b) or 84(3)(b).

112 NIAA 2002 s84(1)(c) or 84(2).

113 FTT Rules 2014 r33(1).

such request must be made within 14 days of the receipt of the immigration judge's decision,[114] and a decision as to whether to grant permission to appeal is initially considered by the FTT.[115] If that application is refused, a dissatisfied party may renew an application for permission to appeal to the Upper Tribunal itself (including where permission was granted on limited grounds only).[116] In a statement to Parliament made on 1 September 2025, the then home secretary, Yvette Cooper MP, announced the intention of setting up an independent adjudicator system to aid the pressure on the appeals backlog, albeit the detail was not clearly set out.[117]

12.61 The FTT may, as an alternative to granting or refusing permission, order a review of the decision if it is satisfied that the original decision contained an error of law.[118]

12.62 Legal aid funding is only available on a retrospective costs basis for the making of an application for permission to appeal if granted by either the FTT or the Upper Tribunal.[119] This applies only where the request for permission to appeal is made by the individual and not where the Home Office seeks permission (and not in respect of cases under a specific detention advice contract).[120] In that event, the normal costs provisions under public funding apply (see para 12.116 below regarding funding).

12.63 Most clients are unlikely to be detained in a police station throughout the appeal process. However, it is possible that the lawyer will be contacted for advice by a person who has been detained following the rejection of their initial appeal and who may seek advice as to any onward appeal, for which the time limit is 14 days.[121]

12.64 Many criminal lawyers already have difficulty in being able to refer cases to immigration specialists. For detainees requiring legal aid the advent of retrospective costs orders makes this all the more difficult. Although cases involving (non-protection) human rights issues are theoretically able to attract exceptional case funding,[122] the withdrawal of most aspects of advice and immigration from the scope of legal aid funding will make the task even more onerous. However, advice on securing release, including applying for immigration bail, is still within the scope of funding,[123] even if the underlying decision prompting the detention is not.

12.65 Whilst most in-country appeals will be dealt with subject to the time limits and provisions above, cases that raise issues of national security or relations between the UK and other states are likely to be dealt with

114 FTT Rules 2014 r33(2).

115 *Joint Presidential GUIDANCE 2019 No 1: Permission to appeal to UTIAC*, issued by the IAC, indicates that the default position is that if in doubt, the FTT should refuse permission to appeal (available at: www.judiciary.uk/wp-content/uploads/2019/08/PTA-guidance-August-2019-1.pdf).

116 Tribunal Procedure (Upper Tribunal) Rules 2008 SI No 2698 r21(2).

117 HC Deb, 1 September 2025, vol 772, https://hansard.parliament.uk/commons/2025-09-01/debates/1CB78605-9A14-4CEE-B5CE-BA8836354FA7/BordersAndAsylum.

118 FTT Rules 2014 r34(1).

119 Standard Civil Contract 2024 Immigration Category Specification para 8.142.

120 Standard Civil Contract 2024 Immigration Category Specification 8.143.

121 FTT Rules 2014 r33(2).

122 Legal Aid, Sentencing and Punishment of Offenders Act 2012 (LASPO) s10(2).

123 LASPO Sch 1 paras 25 and 26.

through appeals to the Special Immigration Appeals Commission[124] (SIAC). The number of appeals proceeding under this mechanism is very small. If there is an issue of particular sensitivity, it is essential that the lawyer should seek to refer the case to a specialist practitioner without delay. The mechanism of the appeals process particular to that scheme is beyond the scope of this chapter.

Administrative review

12.66 With the removal of a right of appeal save in the very limited class of cases involving either human rights or protection issues (deprivation of citizenship and limited EU law matters), the framework in place enables an individual to pursue an administrative review to correct case working errors in respect of many of the other types of immigration outcome for which there is no longer a right of appeal, where such decisions are classed as eligible decisions.[125] There are strict rules about what amounts to a case working error,[126] and the time limit for pursuing the remedy is 14 calendar days,[127] but only seven calendar days where the person is detained under the Immigration Acts.[128] The 14-day period is extended to 28 days in the case of applications for administrative review involving applications under Immigration Rules Appendix EU[129] (though the timeframe remains seven days in respect of those in this category detained under the Immigration Acts[130]). The Home Office will not seek to remove a person who has a pending in time application for administrative review,[131] but that does not mean that they cannot continue to be detained pending the resolution of that review.

Asylum/human rights cases

12.67 With increasing numbers of criminal investigations regarding mode of entry and lack of documentation, a growing number of detainees are being processed through the criminal justice system without being afforded an opportunity to present their asylum claims at an early stage. It is understood that the Home Office has had concerns about spurious asylum claims being made at the last moment, largely to frustrate removal. It is crucial for the lawyer to be aware of the tensions that exist between bringing a claim that may lack merit and the danger in not pursuing a claim until it is too late. As immigration law and practice becomes increasingly complex, many lawyers at the police station may be faced with hard choices about how best to advise. If a client is clear that they do wish to present a

124 Established by virtue of the Special Immigration Appeals Commission Act 1997.
125 HC 395 Appendix AR para 3.2.
126 HC 395 Appendix AR para 3.1.
127 HC 395 Appendix AR para 2.6(c).
128 HC 395 Appendix AR para 2.6(a).
129 HC 395 Appendix AR (EU) para 1.8(a).
130 HC 395 Appendix AR (EU) para 1.8(b).
131 HC 395 Appendix AR para 2.8.

claim for asylum, the lawyer should, wherever possible, try to refer the case on to an immigration practitioner, as a delay in making a claim for asylum without good reason is a factor that is likely to damage the applicant's credibility.[132] Asylum claims made by persons who are nationals of an EEA member state will automatically have a claim for asylum declared inadmissible, unless able to show very exceptional circumstances.[133]

12.68 For those lawyers advising detainees in relation to documentation offences, the impact of a conviction on the client's credibility both in the assessment of their claim by the Home Office and/or at the FTT on appeal must be considered. Admission of the offence may be the best way of avoiding a lengthy sentence,[134] but there may well be serious consequences in relation to the protection or trafficking claim. Wherever possible, the lawyer advising at the police station should try to enlist the assistance of an immigration practitioner, whilst the criminal lawyer continues to represent the client in relation to the criminal charge.[135]

Access to detainees

12.69 Generally, there will be no difficulty in securing access to an immigration detainee at a police station, since the police will normally have no reason to object to legal advice being received, particularly if they believe that it will speed up the process of emptying the cell. Their function is restricted to acting as jailer for the immigration service once any immigration decision has been served. There are some restrictions on access to advice where offences are still being investigated, particularly if the matter that led to the detention is alleged to have a national security and/or terrorism element. The general policy of the Home Office is to allow persons being interviewed in connection with their status to have access to legal advice and to be entitled to a private consultation.[136]

12.70 Given that the client may not have English as a first language, the lawyer is frequently dependent on the police or the immigration service, and on

132 Asylum and Immigration (Treatment of Claimants, etc) Act 2004 s8(1); and HC 395 para 339L(iv).

133 NIAA 2002 s80A; and HC 395 paras 326E and 326F.

134 In *R v Lu Zhu Ai* [2005] EWCA Crim 936, the Court of Appeal indicated that a sentence of nine months would probably be excessive and subsisted that sentence for one of five months for a male adult aged 26. In *R v Wang* [2005] EWCA Crim 293, the Court of Appeal concluded that a sentence of two months would be appropriate for a person aged 18 who had an extant claim for asylum and had pleaded guilty at the first opportunity. In *R v Musse* [2024] EWCA Crim 1012, a 20-month sentence was reduced to 12 months for a person making a 'small boat' crossing despite serious previous convictions in Belgium, on the basis of the guilty plea.

135 Many criminal practitioners will be all too well aware of the criticism inherent in the judgement of Lord Justice Hughes in *R v LM and Others* [2010] EWCA Crim 2327 as to the lack of familiarity within the profession with the Council of Europe Convention on Action Against Trafficking in Human Beings 2005. If in doubt, it may be wise to seek specialist advice, as the range of potential defences to documentation offences was expanded, following the decision of the House of Lords in *R v Asfaw* [2008] UKHL 31.

136 Home Office, *Interviewing suspects: caseworker guidance*, v10.0 (October 2024) p31, available at: www.gov.uk/government/publications/interviewing-suspects.

friends or relatives of the detainee, for relevant information. In some cases, the lawyer at the police station may discover that the client already has an adviser assisting in connection with the immigration matter.

12.71 IAA 1999 s91 makes it a criminal offence for any person to provide immigration advice to another, unless the adviser (or their employer) is registered with the Immigration Advice Authority (previously known as the Office of the Immigration Services Commissioner (OISC)),[137] authorised by a designated professional body (such as the Law Society or the Bar Council)[138] or by a designated qualifying regulator.[139]

12.72 The range of organisations regulated by the Immigration Advice Authority (IAA) is broad and, as with most professionals, the quality of advice provided varies. There may be some cases in which an IAA registered adviser will indicate that they cannot assist further because of detention (advisers are regulated at differing levels and some may be prohibited from dealing with detention and bail issues). In other cases, the client might indicate a level of dissatisfaction with the original adviser (because of the detention). Despite the client's unhappiness, it may be detrimental to their interests for the police station lawyer to accept full responsibility for the case in place of a previous representative, particularly as the time limits are short.[140]

12.73 If access to a detainee is refused on the basis that the initial instructions came from a third party, the custody officer should be reminded of the provisions of PACE Code C Annex B para 4. Although in theory it would be open to a custody officer to take the view that Code C does not apply to an immigration detainee, other than provisions as to conditions of detention and medical treatment (Code C sections 8 and 9), in most cases access is not problematic. More importantly the Immigration (PACE Codes of Practice) Direction 2013[141] explicitly refers to the exercise of powers being in conformity with PACE.

12.74 The policy document in respect of criminal investigations certainly contemplates that PACE will apply where investigations are being undertaken by the Immigration Service.[142]

Advising the client before interview

12.75 Before advising the client the lawyer should, if possible, speak to the IO in order to establish what information is held about the client. At the very

137 IAA 1999 s84(2)(a).

138 IAA 1999 s84(2)(b).

139 IAA 1999 s84(2)(ba).

140 The pool of potential referrals was further reduced by the introduction of compulsory individual accreditation for those undertaking publicly funded asylum and immigration work, as well as removal from scope a significant area of non-protection-based immigration under LASPO.

141 Available at: www.gov.uk/government/publications/the-immigration-pace-codes-of-practice-direction-2013.

142 Home Office, *Interviewing Suspects*, v10.0 (October 2024) explicitly states that the guidance is based on PACE instructions for the conduct of interviews. See: https://assets.publishing.service.gov.uk/media/670cec1292bb81fcdbe7b76a/Interviewing+suspects.pdf.

least, the lawyer should try to ascertain this before the immigration interview takes place. The lawyer should also ask to see any documents that have been taken from the client, such as a passport, biometric residence permit (BRP)[143] or other identity document (such as an asylum application registration card (ARC)[144]), and any prior communication or application with the immigration authorities. This might include details of a previous immigration adviser who may not have been alerted to the fact of detention and who may be able to shed some light on the matter which would assist the lawyer at the police station, even if that adviser does not take over conduct at that stage.

12.76 Although the IO is not obliged to provide the lawyer with full details, a lack of co-operation would be a matter worth commenting on in an interview, particularly where it is clear there are no existing criminal proceedings. Where criminal proceedings are contemplated, the level of pre-interview disclosure would be more limited and will not include details of any previous convictions, intelligence reports, statements or other investigative material.[145]

12.77 At the initial interview with the client before an immigration interview is conducted, the lawyer should try to ascertain as much detail and information about the client as possible (see checklist 15 in para 12.123 below). This could assist in determining the likelihood of being able to pursue an appeal or administrative review in the event of a negative decision, prior to removal. The lawyer should also be aware that where an appeal (or where relevant an administrative review) is pursued unsuccessfully, this will not prevent the operation of a mandatory ban if the client is an overstayer. The question of whether an appeal can be brought and, if so, whether it can be brought in the UK, will also be relevant to the question of the chances of securing bail. Where information has already been gleaned from an IO prior to the meeting, the lawyer should still seek instructions from the client, since the information disclosed may not be accurate, and because the lawyer should formulate their advice on the basis of information and instructions from the client. It is possible that information obtained from the client will conflict, and reaching a conclusion about merits and whether a right of appeal exists may be premature until the conflict of information has been discussed with the client.

12.78 However, some clients believe that their best strategy is to provide a 'revised' version of their immigration history. This may not be because of any inherent desire to deceive or avoid responsibility, but may arise from advice proffered within their community, from a fear of being returned to another country, or from a desire to protect friends or family in the UK whose immigration status may also be precarious. In the event of receiving conflicting information, the lawyer should advise the client of the information held, so that the client is forewarned that if they choose to

143 These were phased out as at 31 December 2024, but are still being relied upon for the purposes of establishing identity since not everyone with residence in the UK has successfully created an eVisa, which was supposed to replace BRP. See: www.gov.uk/guidance/online-immigration-status-evisa.

144 See: www.gov.uk/government/publications/application-registration-card-arc/application-registration-card-arc (see also footnote 50 above).

145 *Interviewing suspects* v10.0 (see pp23–24).

present a revised version, they may be disbelieved. It would also be important to emphasise that the lack of availability of an appeal prior to removal may mean that there is no forum within which to debate whether the version relied on by the client is more reliable than that presented by the Home Office.

12.79 As with any detainee, gaining the trust and confidence of the client will be critical to being able to give proper informed advice and to enable the client to select realistic solutions as to how best to proceed. The lawyer should be aware that in some cases there will be little that can be achieved other than reducing the amount of time needlessly spent in detention when, in reality, there is no prospect of being able to avoid removal or enforcement of a deportation order, or where any appeal is unlikely to be available prior to removal, as is likely to be the case increasingly in non-protection human rights cases.[146]

12.80 It is for this reason that the lawyer should try to take as full an account as possible of all aspects of the client's circumstances. For example, it may be that while the client is an illegal entrant, having arrived some years earlier, they have subsequently formed a relationship with a person settled here and may have a child born in the UK.[147] Although liability to removal as an illegal entrant will not normally attract an appeal right,[148] it may be argued that removal in these circumstances would be a breach of the individual's human rights in that removal would interfere with the right to family life under ECHR Article 8. This may be information that will need to be advanced in support of a request to remain in the UK, so as to avoid any removal, and in assessing the question of proportionality of any family life issue, regard must be had to the impact on family members of any proposed deportation or removal.[149] The IO's file may not have details of the individual's family circumstances, and at the very least this information should be raised. These factors may not ultimately make a difference to the outcome of the IO's decision as to whether removal should proceed, but they might provide a basis upon which the individual may be able to assert an entitlement to bring an appeal against the decision prior to removal. However, the starting point in the consideration of any appeal considering the right to respect for family and/or private life under ECHR Article 8 is that little weight should be given to a relationship that commenced when the individual was unlawfully in the UK.[150] Critically, the courts have emphasised that in the context of claims by persons seeking to rely on a private life exception,[151] little weight should be given to private life established before an individual has acquired a right of indefinite leave to remain.[152] The absence of any information as to those

146 NIAA 2002 s94B.

147 In *ZH (Tanzania) v Secretary of State for the Home Department* [2011] UKSC 4, the Supreme Court accepted that where a child was British, the best interests of that child would be highly relevant in an assessment of proportionality when considering removal of a parent.

148 IAA 1999 s10.

149 *Beoku-Betts v Secretary of State for the Home Department* [2008] UKHL 39.

150 NIAA 2002 s117B.

151 HC 395 para 13.2.3 and see para 12.57 above.

152 *Rhuppiah v Secretary of State for the Home Department* [2018] UKSC 58.

circumstances will mean that there would be no chance of an appeal arising prior to removal; the existence of the certification powers means that even where such matters are raised, this will no longer guarantee that any appeal will take place within the UK before removal is enforced.[153] Nonetheless, these factors as to the existence of a family life and dependants may be relevant to whether the person would remain detained while pursuing a remedy. More frequently, however, once it is clear that the remedy is making some form of application or representation, they are likely to be moved to an immigration removal centre pending the resolution of any such consideration.

12.81 At the very least, these aspects should be explained as a means of establishing the relative merits of remaining in the UK to contest proceedings, albeit with the possibility of detention in the interim, or accepting that on the facts of the particular case an appeal would be unlikely to succeed, or unlikely to be available prior to removal. In such an event, the main issue may relate to seeking to minimise the impact of a mandatory ban on any prospective return to the UK in the future. Although the lawyer at the police station may not have sufficient knowledge as to whether a case is ultimately likely to succeed, the lawyer can at least advise the client of possible remedies to pursue. However, bare assertion that the removal will be a breach of the right to family life will rarely mean that an individual can pursue an appeal prior to removal, let alone that such an appeal before an immigration judge would succeed.[154] Similarly, the fact that the Home Office may not accept that removal would mean a breach does not mean that an immigration judge would be bound to reach the same conclusion, although the added emphasis afforded to the public interest in carrying out any such evaluation may mean that the number of cases able to succeed at an appeal at all (whether from within the UK or after removal) is likely to be relatively small and will have to involve exceptional characteristics.[155]

12.82 For this reason, as a rule of thumb, remaining silent during an immigration interview is unlikely to be advantageous, since if there is new information to present, the failure to present it at the earliest opportunity may mean that the chance of mounting a successful application or challenge to removal prior to any appeal is lost; and delay may lead to adverse inferences being drawn, given that the client would have had the opportunity of raising the matters with an IO before a decision was taken on whether to proceed with removal action.

12.83 In other cases, remaining silent would almost certainly be fatal to the prospects of success. For example, persons alleging that their removal would engage the Refugee Convention are already likely to be facing hurdles regarding credibility for not having made an application for

153 See NIAA 2002 s94B.

154 The statutory presumptions about the weight to be given and what is in the public interest under NIAA 2002 s117B are extended to include additional considerations for appeals involving deportation of foreign national criminals by virtue of NIAA 2002 s117C.

155 *HA (Iraq) v Secretary of State for the Home Department* [2016] UKSC 60: 'In general, only a claim which is very strong indeed – very compelling as it was put in *MF (Nigeria)* [*MF (Nigeria) v Secretary of State for the Home Department* [2013] EWCA Civ 1192] will succeed' (Lord Reed at para 50).

asylum at an earlier stage,[156] and waiting until after an interview to assert a fear of return would compound the problem even further.[157]

12.84 In contrast to criminal proceedings, as very few of those detained will have effective appeals against removal, prior to removal being enforced, failing to respond to questions put in an immigration interview is unlikely to be productive where it is clear that there is no likelihood of further criminal charges being brought. There will be no trial at which inferences from silence can be drawn. Failing to allege a breach of the individual's human rights where such breach would need to be shown at the higher end of the scale, given the weight attached to the public interest, will mean that increasingly removal will take place without a prior in country appeal. While there is no requirement to answer questions put by an IO regarding a person's immigration status, the issue for the lawyer to consider is what might be lost by failing to speak.

12.85 If the client has indicated that their primary reason for seeking to avoid removal is that they have a fear that, if returned to their home country they would face serious harm and they wish to make an asylum- or protection-based human rights claim, it would be sensible for the lawyer to indicate that to the IO, either in advance or at the commencement of the interview. It is not normally appropriate for a full asylum interview to be conducted at a police station, given the importance of the issues and the fact that the client may benefit from specialist advice. The IO may conduct a shortened interview to determine how best to proceed with the asylum claim (a screening interview), but invariably they would not normally seek to conduct a full asylum interview, instead referring the matter to the Home Office. In the unlikely event that an IO insists on proceeding with a substantive interview on the asylum claim, the lawyer should ask for the interview to be delayed and to be given an opportunity to speak to a senior IO, particularly as there is a specific policy document on the conduct of asylum interviews that emphasises the need to create 'an environment in which the claimant feels able to disclose relevant and potentially highly personal and sensitive information'.[158]

12.86 If the possibility of bringing criminal charges has not yet been ruled out and any interview is conducted under caution, the advice to the detainee would be no different from that given to any persons interviewed under caution, even if the interview is being conducted by an IO (see generally chapter 5 above). This will include documentation offences, even where the client has indicated a desire to claim asylum. While it may be sensible to make no comment so as to avoid the client implicating themself in terms of the commission of an offence (overstaying and illegal entry being offences), at the conclusion of the interview the client should provide details of their personal or other circumstances if it is sought to rely on information that would trigger an in-country appeal right (particularly in protection claims). Alternatively, if the interview is conducted under

156 Asylum and Immigration (Treatment of Claimants, etc) Act 2004 s8(6).

157 See also HC 395 para 339L(iv).

158 Home Office, *Asylum Interviews* v9.0 (June 2022), available at: https://assets.publishing.service.gov.uk/media/64d0ec63e5491a000d4b5933/Asylum_interview.pdf.

caution, it may be sensible to request that at its conclusion a further interview be conducted, not under caution, so as to enable the client to provide that information relevant to a potential 'family life' human rights claim.

12.87 As with any detainee, the presence of a lawyer ought to have a positive impact on the ability of the client to handle the interview, but this can only be achieved if a relationship of trust is built with the client in what will be strained circumstances. The lawyer should emphasise the confidentiality of the instructions and should seek to ensure that a client is not under the misconception that a willingness on their part to endure lengthy detention will mean that the Home Office will be more likely to accept that they are telling the truth. The lawyer should also point out that whereas in criminal proceedings the burden rests on the prosecution, in the immigration context the burden of establishing an entitlement to reside, that the client was granted lawful entry, that they have not overstayed, that they have family or significant private life connections that mean that there is an exception to removal, or that they are British,[159] all fall on the client. It is also important for the lawyer to explain their ethical duties, and were the client to make statements in interview which the lawyer knew to be false, the lawyer may have to withdraw from the interview.

12.88 If the client does not speak English, the lawyer should attempt to secure the attendance of an independent interpreter. Although an interpreter will be arranged by the police or immigration service, it would not be appropriate for the same interpreter to be used for the purposes of obtaining client instructions and advising in private. The Legal Aid Agency (LAA) recognises the need to maintain the impartiality of advice given and accepts that the costs of an interpreter can be met as a disbursement.[160]

12.89 It would be sensible to alert the IO, as well as the custody officer, where an independent interpreter is to be used during interview. Unless there are specific issues about the conduct of a particular interpreter in the past, or the fact that the interpreter is related to the detainee, there would normally be no difficulty.[161] If the IO or custody officer objects, the lawyer should ask for reason and record the response.

Attending the interview

12.90 Wherever possible, the lawyer should attend any interview conducted by an IO. This should help to ensure the client is more at ease and consequently feels better able to reveal any relevant information that may affect the outcome of any enforcement decision. As with any other police station interview, the lawyer's presence should ensure that the client does not feel

159 IA 1971 s3(8).

160 LAA, *Criminal bills assessment manual*, v21 (December 2024) para 7.8.4, available at: https://assets.publishing.service.gov.uk/media/682d8eae38753e5f0ce8ed5e/Criminal_Bills_Assessment_Manual.pdf.

161 UKVI, *Asylum interviews*, v9.0 (June 2022), available at: www.gov.uk/government/publications/conducting-the-asylum-interview-process/asylum-interviews-accessible#bookmark114; see also Home Office, *Enforcement interviews*, v2.0 (December 2020), available at: https://assets.publishing.service.gov.uk/media/5fe1fa84e90e07452ec36f16/enforcement-interviews-v2.0ext.pdf.

bullied or intimidated and is afforded the opportunity to respond to questions properly put. There is no statutory right to have a lawyer present where the interview relates solely to the issues of administrative removal. However, the Home Office's guidance *Interviewing suspects*[162] makes it plain that a person is permitted to seek legal advice,[163] and denial of legal advice for the purposes of such an interview or preventing a lawyer attending is a rare occurrence and can only be justified where the lawyer is acting in a manner that is unreasonable.[164] *Interviewing suspects*[165] makes explicit reference to the detainee's entitlement to take legal advice from a duty solicitor where the interview is for the purposes of examining potential offences. However, the absence of a lawyer will not invalidate any decision made on the basis of information obtained in such an interview.[166]

12.91 Enforcement interviews are normally electronically recorded using a secure digital network when conducted in a police station, provided such facilities exist and are working.[167] It is still advisable to take a record of the interview in case there is any dispute or difficulty securing a copy.

12.92 If the questions asked in the interview have not enabled the detainee to state everything that the lawyer believes to be relevant, the lawyer should ask the IO to permit the client to put forward any additional information. Where time allows, the lawyer might help the client with a pre-prepared statement, which they would normally be invited to read out (or to be read out by an interpreter) and have signed.[168] This is important given that the consequences of a decision that does not attract an appeal may result in swift removal from the UK without any prior judicial scrutiny of their circumstances.

Advising the client after the interview

12.93 In some cases, an immigration interview may already have been conducted by the time the lawyer is able to see the client. However, the lawyer may still have an important role to play, particularly in terms of assessing whether or not an appeal right, or right to pursue an administrative review, exists prior to removal and, if so, the (potentially) shortened time limits within which the right must be exercised. Any papers served on the client should be carefully examined since the decision as to how they are to be dealt with is likely to be made shortly after the interview. If the client was not forthcoming at the interview, either because they chose to remain silent or because they were not afforded an opportunity to put information about their family or other circumstances to the interviewing officer, it would be appropriate for written representations as to those circumstances to be sent urgently to the relevant immigration office, the details of which

162 Version 10 (October 2024), available at: https://assets.publishing.service.gov.uk/media/670cec1292bb81fcdbe7b76a/Interviewing+suspects.pdf.

163 See p42.

164 *Enforcement interviews*, v2.0 p24.

165 Version 10 (October 2024) available at: https://assets.publishing.service.gov.uk/media/670cec1292bb81fcdbe7b76a/Interviewing+suspects.pdf.

166 *R v Secretary of State for the Home Department ex p Lawson* [1994] Imm AR 58, QBD.

167 *Interviewing suspects*, v10.0 p17.

168 *Interviewing suspects*, v10.0 p 42.

should be apparent from any notices served on the detainee.[169] This might affect whether a client will have a right of appeal exercisable prior to removal, though as observed above, the powers to certify a case asserting human rights elements, whether arising from protection issues or family life, are extremely wide, and any delay in submitting the information after interview would compound the problems of any realistic challenge being pursued prior to removal. Where removal is to proceed without an in-country right of appeal (or administrative review), the only remedy would be judicial review, and as that is a discretionary remedy, the conduct of the applicant would be relevant to the chances of success.

12.94 If such issues are raised at interview or through representations, or if the client is to be removed, they are likely to be served with a 'one-stop' notice and required to set out in detail the basis of any claim to remain in the UK.[170] The onus remains on the individual to show that removal would be unlawful. There is a requirement that a person served should update the Home Office as their circumstances change, not just when initially served,[171] and the time limit for the return of the one-stop notice is 10 days. At an appeal, the issues that could have been, but were not, raised in response to a 'section 120 notice', cannot be considered by the tribunal without the consent of the secretary of state[172] or, where relevant, at an earlier appeal.[173] For the lawyer, it is imperative to impress upon the client the need to comply with any time limit as well as the onus being on the individual to set out any basis to remain in the UK as soon as reasonably practicable.

12.95 It may also be appropriate to contact the client's family members after the interview to keep them appraised of the situation. Close family members (partner, children in the same household, parent or other adult dependent relative) may also be at risk of enforcement action,[174] in which case they should be advised to seek advice, though they may have rights of residence in the UK independently. In any event, they are likely to want to be informed about whether anything can be done for the client. If the client raises new issues at interview relating to family members, it would be appropriate to ask for evidence of the relationship to be provided, such as a marriage or civil partnership certificate, evidence of cohabitation, or a child's birth certificate. Given the tight time limits for appeals (and the question of whether the appeal will only be exercisable after removal in certified cases), and section 120 one stop notices, it is important that the process of evidence gathering begins as soon as possible.

12.96 Many defence lawyers are understandably reluctant to engage too deeply with the client's immigration case once work at the police station has been

169 Contacting the Home Office by email for specific cases is far from straightforward and there is a general reluctance to provide direct email contact details, and in some cases in the experience of the author, even when provided with an email address it will not always work, or a document sent will not necessarily always be acted upon.

170 NIAA 2002 s120(2).

171 NIAA 2002 s120(5).

172 NIAA 2002 s85(5).

173 NIAA 2002 s96(1). This is another category of case subject to certification, but here the certification power exists in respect of material that has or could already have been considered.

174 See IAA 1999 s10(2).

concluded. This may not only be because of the potential complexity, but also as there is real doubt as to whether any work done beyond the police station will be remunerated under the legal aid scheme, bearing in mind the requirement to be accredited under the Law Society's Immigration and Asylum Accreditation Scheme (IAAS).[175] The LAA's draft Standard Crime Contract (SCC) 2025 makes clear that where there continues to be an investigation of a criminal offence (including an Immigration Act offence), the lawyer can continue to advise until it is clear that the investigation has been taken over by the immigration service,[176] and that the immigration-only elements must be referred either to an immigration firm or back to the defence solicitor call centre (DSCC),[177] unless the client already has another lawyer for these issues. If possible, the lawyer should try to refer the client on to an immigration specialist given that the time limits are tight and, if further action is required, the work is likely to be time-consuming. If the lawyer has advised the client that there may be an appealable decision, it would be unwise to offer a definitive view on the prospects of success, or even whether there is likely to be an entitlement to pursue that appeal in-country, bearing in mind that the client may unwittingly spend longer in detention pursuing (or attempting to pursue) an appeal where the prospects are poor, and may face a longer mandatory ban, or may be inadvertently persuaded to abandon an appeal or an entitlement to appeal prior to removal which might have succeeded.

12.97 If in real doubt, given the tight time limits, where there may be a right of appeal, it may be safer for it to be exercised by the client and for the client to be referred on to an immigration adviser so that, if relevant, the immigration adviser can assess at an early stage whether it is appropriate to pursue or abandon the appeal. This at least has the advantage of avoiding complications that may arise from an attempt to lodge an appeal out of time. Any such work would not be remunerated under a crime legal aid contract.[178] Many criminal practitioners are finding it increasingly difficult to secure a referral, particularly if the client is still at the police station, as the client could be relocated anywhere within the country while an appeal or other representations are being pursued.[179] For those transferred to removal centres, exclusive contracting arrangements narrow further the potential pool of practitioners restricted to those who have such a contract,[180] though that only applies in respect of those seeking legal aid services.

12.98 Whilst the adviser may wish to assist the detainee, the method of appeal has now largely been transferred to an online portal requiring the creation of an account with HM Courts & Tribunals Service (HMCTS)

175 Standard Civil Contract 2024 Immigration Specification (August 2024) para 8.16(a), available at: https://assets.publishing.service.gov.uk/media/66a9ff2d0808eaf43b50da63/4_8_2024_Immigration_and_Asylum_Category_Specific_Rules.pdf.

176 Draft SCC Specification 2025 para 9.58.

177 Draft SCC Specification 2025 para 9.60.

178 Draft SCC Specification 2025 paras 9.61 and 9.62; and *Criminal Bills assessment manual*, v21 (December 2024) (note 158 above) para 5.6.5.

179 Notwithstanding this, the draft SCC Specification 2025 para 9.63 requires firms to have a policy on referrals and an expectation of firms building up links with immigration providers.

180 Standard Civil Contract 2024 Immigration Specification para 8.6, although there are limited exceptions for some pre-existing clients, or close relatives of existing clients.

where the client has a representative.[181] Consequently, it may be wiser for the client to be invited to file an appeal either online or on paper[182] in order to avoid the police station adviser being 'locked in' to the procedure.

Immigration bail – from the Home Office

12.99 As observed at para 12.31 above, a power to detain exists in a number of circumstances, even where there is no question of pursuing a criminal investigation. With the power to detain, there is also a corresponding power to release. There is no obligation on an IO or the secretary of state to keep the person in detention in such cases. The term 'immigration bail' is used, whether bail is given to such person by the Home Office or by the tribunal. The fact that a person is released from the police station and given bail certainly does not mean that they are being given permission to remain in the UK, nor does it mean that they are any more likely to be given such permission in the future. A person without leave who makes an application to remain in the UK on any basis while on bail is not entitled to insist on the application being determined, and they would not always be able to assert that any refusal of an application would give rise to a right of appeal. The exception to this is if the application to remain arises from a decision refusing a protection claim, refusing a human rights claim or revoking protection status.[183]

12.100 At least one condition must be attached to the grant of bail, even where granted by the Home Office, such as a condition of residence, a condition requiring the person to report to an immigration reporting centre, or to the FTT (or such other person as may be specified), or a condition restricting the person from taking up employment, or study.[184] Unless impractical or contrary to the individual's ECHR rights, an electronic monitoring condition will be made in all cases involving persons liable to detention under IA 1971 Sch 3 (persons liable to detention pending deportation).[185]

12.101 The instructions given to immigration service staff suggest that detention should be used sparingly and for the shortest period necessary.[186] According to the current guidance, factors influencing a decision to detain include:[187]

- the likelihood of the person failing to comply with a condition;
- whether the person has been convicted of an offence (whether in the UK or not);

181 See HMCTS, *Make an immigration and asylum appeal using MyHMCTS* (October 2024), available at: https://www.gov.uk/government/publications/myhmcts-how-to-use-online-immigration-and-asylum-appeal-services/make-an-immigration-and-asylum-appeal-using-myhmcts.

182 See *Appeal against a visa or immigration decision*, available at: www.gov.uk/immigration-asylum-tribunal/appeal-from-within-the-uk.

183 NIAA 2002 s82(1), subject to any such claim being certified under section 94, 94B or 96.

184 IA 2016 Sch 10 para 2(1)(a)–(f).

185 IA 2016 Sch 10 para 2(3)(a).

186 UKVI and Immigration Enforcement, *Detention: general instructions*, v3.0 (April 2025), available at: www.gov.uk/government/publications/offender-management/detention-general-instructions-accessible.

187 *Immigration bail*, v21.0 (January 2025) p62, available at: https://assets.publishing.service.gov.uk/media/679a0ca085c5e43aa3d10dc6/Immigration+bail.pdf.

- the likelihood of the person committing an offence while on immigration bail;
- the likelihood of their presence in the UK causing a danger to public health or a threat to public order;
- whether the detention is necessary in that person's interests or for the protection of any other person;
- whether the person has failed without reasonable excuse to co-operate in the determination of their immigration status, conditions or prior removal; and
- such other matters as may be relevant to the decision-maker.

12.102 Whilst there are no specific timeframes within which detention would become unlawful, the powers given to maintain detention were broadened further by Illegal Migration Act 2023 s12.[188]

12.103 The power to detain remains subject to the limitation on the detention of pregnant women (only where removal is imminent or there are other exceptional circumstances),[189] as well as guidance issued by the secretary of state regarding the detention of vulnerable persons.[190]

12.104 The lawyer should consider making representations both orally and in writing to seek to secure the client's immediate release after the conclusion of the interview. Any decision on whether to keep the client in detention will normally be taken by a more senior officer than the one conducting the interview, usually a chief immigration officer (CIO) or higher executive officer (HEO) within the Home Office.[191] Detention must be reviewed regularly, and for those held at a police station in excess of two nights the guidance requires that such detention must be authorised by an IO of at least the rank of inspector (or a senior executive officer at the Home Office).[192] However, even if there were to be a breach of the procedure for review or authorisation, where detention would otherwise have been authorised, the failure to adhere to the correct policy and procedure would not necessarily result in release and is likely to be remedied by no more than nominal damages.[193]

12.105 It is also possible to make a formal request for bail from the secretary of state using form BAIL 401, which invites an applicant to provide details

188 At the time of writing, the Border Security, Asylum and Immigration Bill 2024 proposed the repeal of most provisions of the Illegal Migration Act 2023, but this provision is not amongst those proposed to be repealed.

189 IA 2016 s60(2).

190 IA 2016 s59, and see Home Office, *Adults at risk in immigration detention*, v10.0 (May 2024), available at: https://assets.publishing.service.gov.uk/media/664b61e0993111924d9d3844/Adults+at+risk+in+immigration+detention.pdf; and also UKVI and Immigration Enforcement, *Adults at risk: Detention of potential or confirmed victims of modern slavery*, v4.0 (May 2024), available at: www.gov.uk/government/publications/offender-management/adults-at-risk-detention-of-potential-or-confirmed-victims-of-modern-slavery-accessible-version#:~:text=Potential%20victims%20of%20modern%20slavery%20are%20considered%20adults%20at%20risk,this%20(see%20evidence%20levels).

191 UKVI and Immigration Enforcement, *Detention: general instructions*, v3.0 (April 2025), available at: www.gov.uk/government/publications/offender-management/detention-general-instructions-accessible.

192 *Detention: general instructions*, v3.0 (April 2025).

193 *R (Lumba) v Secretary of State for the Home Department* [2011] UKSC 12.

of persons who can act as financial conditions supporters (sureties).[194] For a client who has access to friends or family able to offer substantial sums (presently in the region of £2,000), such an approach may be a speedier alternative than waiting for a tribunal bail hearing to be fixed. If this is not possible or if, despite the availability of willing financial condition supporters, the Home Office is not persuaded to release the client, a bail application to the tribunal should be considered. It is not necessary to seek bail from the secretary of state as a prerequisite before applying to the tribunal.

Immigration bail – from the tribunal

12.106 The FTT (IAC) has jurisdiction to grant bail to most people detained under Immigration Act powers.[195] For persons newly arrived in the UK held pending a decision on whether or not they should be given leave to enter, the opportunity to apply for bail arises only after they have been in the UK for more than eight days.[196]

12.107 Unlike those appearing before criminal courts, there is no statutory presumption in favour of bail, and the Bail Act 1976 criteria do not apply. The relevant criteria in deciding whether to grant or refuse bail are the same as those applicable to a person granted bail by the secretary of state (see para 12.99 above).[197]

12.108 The obligation is on the individual, or their representative, to request a bail hearing. There is an obligation on the immigration service to ensure that regular reviews are carried out,[198] and to refer a detainee's case to the tribunal every four months (save for those held pending deportation),[199] but in theory there is no upper limit to the length of time for which an individual can be detained.[200]

12.109 In order to initiate an application for bail, it is necessary for the detainee or their representative to lodge with the FTT an application for bail setting out the specified information required,[201] using form B1.[202] The easiest way to do this is to complete the electronic form and send by email to the appropriate hearing centre. Often the only way of establishing the relevant centre is to contact the enquiry unit on 0300 123 1711, as the relevant centre will not always be the one closest to the place of detention. The FTT

194 See UKVI, *Application for Secretary of State immigration bail* (November 2020), available at: www.gov.uk/government/publications/application-for-secretary-of-state-immigration-bail.

195 IA 2016 Sch 10 para 1(3).

196 IA 2016 Sch 10 para 3(3).

197 IA 2016 Sch 10 para 3(2).

198 UKVI and Immigration Enforcement, *Detention and case progression review*, v2.0 (September 2023), available at: www.gov.uk/government/publications/offender-management/detention-and-case-progression-review-accessible.

199 IA 2016 Sch 10 para 11(1)(b).

200 Save for the limited possibility of applying for habeas corpus or judicial review if the detention can be said to be truly excessive, although this may now be limited to those pending deportation given the automatic referral of those held other than in deportation cases.

201 FTT Rules 2014 r38(3).

202 Available at: www.gov.uk/government/publications/apply-for-release-on-bail-from-immigration-detention-form-b1.

is then required to forward details of the application to the secretary of state[203] and to fix a bail hearing date.[204] In theory, a bail hearing will be fixed within three working days from the date on which the FTT receives the application form, although in practice this target date is not always met. The notice of hearing is generally sent from the tribunal by email. The secretary of state is required to set out any reasons for objecting to bail and serve the same on the detainee or their representative no later than 2pm on the working day prior to the hearing.[205]

12.110 Where bail is being applied for within 28 days of an earlier application that was rejected, the tribunal will dismiss the application unless there has been a material change of circumstances since the previous hearing.[206] Furthermore, where removal directions are enforced to take effect within a period of 21 days, the tribunal cannot grant bail without the consent of the secretary of state.[207]

12.111 If bail is granted, an immigration judge must impose at least one condition, such as a requirement of residence, electronic tagging, reporting or financial condition of support.[208] If bail is refused, there is nothing to prevent a further application being made (subject to the automatic rejection without a hearing absent a material change of circumstances if made within 28 days of a previous decision). Bail guidance for immigration judges is issued from time to time, most recently by the President of the FTT (IAC) on 31 January 2024.[209]

Further action

12.112 The lawyer who advised at the police station should try to refer the case to an immigration specialist adviser. Urgent steps to be taken may include contacting family members, making representations about issues not dealt with in interview or about factors that should lead to the client being served with a one-stop notice, or advising on the tight time limits and the opportunities for bail, including the limitations on the likelihood of securing release where removal directions to enforce a person's departure are in effect and removal is to take place within 21 days.[210] Where the case cannot be referred on, the lawyer may want to consider which, if any, of those steps can be undertaken by them, albeit not under the draft SCC 2025. As observed above, in practice there can be some difficulty in identifying firms that are willing to undertake such cases on a legal aid basis. In many cases, the lawyer at the police station may have little option other than to refer the case back to the DSCC, particularly as there is no requirement

203 FTT Rules 2014 r38(6).
204 FTT Rules 2014 r39(1).
205 FTT Rules 2014 r40(1)(a).
206 FTT Rules 2014 r39(3)(c).
207 IA 2016 Sch 10 para 3(4).
208 IA 2016 Sch 10 para 2(1).
209 Available at: www.judiciary.uk/wp-content/uploads/2024/03/Guidance-on-Immigration-Bail-for-Judges-of-the-First-tier-Tribunal-Immigration-and-Asylum-Chamber-Presidential.pdf.
210 IA 2016 Sch 10 para 3(4).

(and no opportunity to be paid under the legal aid scheme) to provide advice where there is no ongoing criminal investigation.[211]

12.113 It may also be important to try to track down the client's whereabouts if they are no longer at the police station. Custody officers may assume that if the detainee is transferred out of the police station by the immigration service, they have been removed from the UK. This may be incorrect given the limits on the length of time that persons can be detained at a police station and the requirements relating to the seniority of officers who can authorise continued detention.[212]

12.114 Any person aged 17 years or over who is not a British citizen may be recommended for deportation by a criminal court as part of the sentence imposed if the offence for which the person is convicted carries a term of imprisonment, regardless of whether a custodial sentence is imposed.[213] The power arises in relation to any offence and is not limited to cases with an immigration element. Notice of the possibility of such recommendation must be served at least seven days before the date on which the sentence is imposed (form IM3).[214] This is usually done at the police station. If the notice has not been served, then the court considering imposing a recommendation may adjourn the criminal proceedings for the appropriate notice to be served.[215]

12.115 Given that the automatic deportation provisions apply to persons aged 18 years or over as at the date of conviction, it is increasingly less relevant whether or not a recommendation is made in terms of whether removal will follow a conviction, where the sentence imposed is 12 months or more.[216] The emphasis increasingly is upon removal at the conclusion of the sentence, especially as the requirement imposed under the legislation is to require the secretary of state to make a deportation order in such cases unless the person falls within one of the exceptions,[217] coupled with wide powers of certification in human rights cases raising issues of family or private life.[218]

Legal aid

12.116 Where advice is being given to a person arrested in respect of an offence, whether an immigration offence or otherwise, the SCC 2022 will apply as

211 LAA, *Criminal bills assessment manual*, v21 (December 2024) para 5.6.5, available at: https://assets.publishing.service.gov.uk/media/682d8eae38753e5f0ce8ed5e/Criminal_Bills_Assessment_Manual.pdf.

212 UKVI and Immigration Enforcement, *Detention: general instructions*, v3.0 (April 2025), available at: www.gov.uk/government/publications/offender-management/detention-general-instructions-accessible.

213 IA 1971 s3(6).

214 Crown Prosecution Service, *Sentencing – Ancillary Orders* (August 2024) section on Deportation, available at: www.cps.gov.uk/legal-guidance/sentencing-ancillary-orders.

215 IA 1971 s6(2).

216 UKBA 2007 s32(5). See also the discussion as to appropriateness of making a recommendation in cases involving deportation in *R v Kluxen* [2010] EWCA Crim 1081.

217 UKBA 2007 s33.

218 NIAA 2002 s94B.

usual. Failure by a duty solicitor to accept such cases referred while on the rota could lead to suspension or removal from the scheme.[219]

12.117 Where the detainee is not subject to any ongoing investigation of a criminal charge, the position is that such work would not be recoverable under the criminal contract, given the requirement to be accredited under the Law Society's IAAS. Nonetheless there are matters for which advice would be required at the police station, if only to identify the range of options that may be open and the limitations of any potential remedies for a particular detainee.

12.118 Any significant work beyond the police station would certainly be out of scope of criminal legal aid (in the absence of a criminal charge), given the requirement of immigration accreditation.[220] Where it is not possible to refer a detainee on to an immigration adviser, it is difficult to see how the work done for the purposes of trying to secure an appeal or meeting an administrative review deadline, or securing a bail hearing, could be remunerated either under the criminal or civil legal aid contract unless the lawyer at the police station is also accredited under the IASS.

12.119 For lawyers working in firms that also hold an immigration contract, public funding would be available for the conduct of the initial appeal and any application for bail, subject to meeting the means and merits tests under controlled legal representation (CLR), provided that the work is being undertaken by an individual who is accredited[221] (and subject to the work being in scope post LASPO). If resisting an appeal brought by the secretary of state from a decision of the FTT, funding will continue to be available.[222] For cases in which a legally aided party is seeking permission to appeal from a decision of the FTT (other than in detained asylum casework (DAC) scheme cases[223]), funding is subject to a retrospective costs regime;[224] in either case this would be as licensed work, rather than CLR.

12.120 Funding for work done on progressing an immigration application that is within scope is available under Legal Help subject to means and merits, and in most cases this will be under a fixed fee scheme.[225] Where appropriate, firms with an immigration contract are also able to undertake applications for judicial review, onward appeals to the Upper Tribunal or applications for habeas corpus as licensed work that would be applied for using the Client and Cost Management System (CCMS).[226]

219 *Criminal bills assessment manual*, v21 (December 2024) para 5.6.2.

220 Standard Civil Contract 2024 Immigration Specification para 8.13.

221 As previously observed, the scheme requires individuals as opposed to entities to be accredited.

222 Standard Civil Contract 2024 Immigration Specification para 8.143(b).

223 Standard Civil Contract 2024 Immigration Specification para 8.143(a).

224 Standard Civil Contract 2024 Immigration Specification para 8.142.

225 Standard Civil Contract 2024 Immigration Specification para 8.73.

226 Retrospective funding will apply in judicial review cases, so that payment of costs or fees of counsel is restricted to cases that are at least partially successful where a decision is withdrawn, or where permission for judicial review was granted or a hearing directed by the court. See Civil Legal Aid (Remuneration) Regulations 2013 SI No 422 reg 5A. The retrospective scheme also applies to applications for permission to appeal to the Upper Tribunal (save for the exception under DAC).

The role of the embassy

12.121 Citizens of independent Commonwealth countries or nationals of any foreign country held in a police station have the right to contact their High Commission, embassy or consulate.[227] Many clients are unwilling to contact their own national authorities, fearing potential reprisals. There has also been a tendency on the part of some consular officials to advise their own nationals to leave the country without exercising any potential remedies that may be open to them. If contact with consular staff has been made, and advice given, the lawyer should check whether the advice was appropriate, having regard to the individual circumstances of the client. The lawyer can check with the custody officer as to whether any such contact has been made, since it should have been recorded.[228]

12.122 For nationals of certain countries, bilateral conventions or agreements exist, whereby notification of arrest and detention of a national will automatically be given to the relevant consular official,[229] except in cases where the individual has claimed to be a refugee or has or intends to apply for asylum, in which case contact should immediately be made with the Home Office.[230]

Summary

12.123 The issues discussed in this chapter can be summarised as followed.

- Wide powers of arrest and detention exist for both immigration and non-immigration offences.
- Detention at a police station where authorised by an IO will largely mirror PACE requirements.
- Interviews by IOs may be a mixture of those under caution and non-caution.
- Care will be needed to determine whether the client can or cannot pursue an appeal, and whether such an appeal is likely to be capable of being pursued from within the UK; or whether they are a person who would be permitted to pursue an administrative review.
- Advice will need to be given that whilst bail can be sought, it may not be granted (and cannot result in release without the consent of the Home Office if there are removal directions in force to take effect within 21 days at the date of the bail hearing) and there are limitations on what the police station adviser can do.
- Legal aid restrictions prevent payment for representation in respect of bail or at an appeal unless the police station adviser is personally accredited under the IAAS. The availability of public funding beyond

227 UKVI and Immigration Enforcement, *Detention: general instructions*, v3.0 (April 2025), available at: www.gov.uk/government/publications/offender-management/detention-general-instructions-accessible; and see also Code C paras 3.1(a)(iv), 3.12A and 7.1.

228 Code C para 7.4.

229 Code C para 7.2, and see *Detention: general instructions*, v3.0 (April 2025) pp60–61 for a list of countries with a bilateral consular convention.

230 Code C para 7.4.

detention is severely limited following the restrictions imposed by LASPO.

- Asylum- and protection-based human rights claims will, in general, enable an appeal to be brought (subject to certification). In most other cases raising no such issue, an appeal is less likely to be available, although there may be the possibility of an administrative review with a shorter seven-day deadline where the individual is detained under the Immigration Acts.
- Even where asylum or human rights claims are pursued, certification powers can prevent appeal rights from being pursued prior to removal.

Checklist 15: Questions to ask an immigration detainee

1 Full name, including any aliases previously used
2 Date of birth
3 Nationality(ies) and country of birth
4 Whether client requires an interpreter and if so language and dialect
5 Current address (other than detention), and any previous addresses covering at least the last six months
6 Contact details of any relative or friend
7 Date and place of most recent arrival in the UK
8 Whether travelling on own passport
9 Whether any questions asked at border by immigration and details
10 Whether any answers given on arrival were inaccurate and if so details of inaccuracies
11 If client had previously applied for entry clearance from overseas (visa), were any of the answers to questions raised inaccurate and if so details of inaccuracies
12 Whether client has previously instructed a lawyer or IAA (formerly OISC) adviser and if so contact details
13 Any reason not to continue with previous adviser for immigration elements arising from the detention
14 Whether client has been served with any papers
15 How has client supported themself to date
16 Is client likely to wish to return to the UK lawfully in the future
17 If client is forced to return, what does client think will happen to them

For clients with family or close ties in UK

18 What are client's present family circumstances
19 Where relevant, what is the immigration status of the family members
20 If any children born in the UK, what was the immigration status of the other parent at the time of birth and what is the regularity of contact with the child/children if not in the same household
21 Are the immigration authorities aware of family circumstances and if so when were they notified
22 What does client think will happen to family if client is forced to leave UK

For clients previously granted lawful entry

23 If client was given legal right to enter, when does it/did it expire
24 Does client have evidence in respect of pending application to the Home Office

25 Can client provide Home Office reference number[231] or access to an eVisa or an expired BRP
26 If not held by the immigration service, where is client's passport

For clients who have never previously been given lawful entry

27 Where and when did client enter UK and how (for example, lorry/false passport)
28 Has there been any previous application to remain and if so what was that, and is there proof of the pending application

For clients wishing to make an application/appeal prior to removal

29 If client expresses anxiety about threats to life or freedom on return, are there reasons why this has not previously been raised
30 If client now seeks to raise issues about family or private life, is there a reason for not having already made an application on these grounds
31 If client has overstayed for less than 28 days or is in breach of landing conditions, would they benefit from seeking to leave before operation of mandatory ban
32 Has client already lodged an appeal and if not could an appeal be pursued prior to removal
33 Does client have community ties other than as already identified
34 What if any evidence is available to show that there would be serious irreversible harm were an appeal not exercisable prior to removal

Where release from detention is being sought

35 Are there physical, other health issues, or other vulnerabilities that may be relevant to the question of detention (for example, pregnancy, age, specific vulnerabilities)
36 Does client have friends willing to act as financial condition supporters and if so what is their status
37 What if any address could client to be released to
38 Has client ever failed to attend any court or report to any authority such as police or immigration in the UK before
39 If there is an entitlement to appeal that has not yet been exercised, what is the time frame within which it can be exercised
40 Has client been made aware that bail would be automatically refused if there are current removal directions in effect within 21 days of any bail hearing date
41 Has client been advised that willingness to remain detained will not strengthen a claim to remain in the UK

Availability of representation by police station adviser or otherwise

42 Is the basis of any application (other than bail) likely to fall within the scope of the Civil Legal Aid Immigration Specification
43 Does client appear to be financially eligible bearing in mind the requirement to consider income of the household, not merely circumstances as at point of detention
44 If so, is the police station lawyer able to refer the matter on via contacts with other legal professionals with a legal aid immigration contract
45 If not, does client have means to instruct a lawyer privately if only to file an appeal or administrative review urgently

231 In the past, such reference numbers would be the first letter of the surname followed by six or seven digits, but more recently a new format of 16 digits.

CHAPTER 13

Complaints and enforcement

Introduction

13.1 One of the more difficult questions for the defence lawyer is how they should deal with police conduct that is illegal, unfair or improper. A client may feel aggrieved about the way they have been dealt with and may complain of incivility at one end of the scale, or serious assault or dishonesty at the other. The lawyer may witness police behaviour that is unacceptable, or may believe that the police are ignoring or misunderstanding legal or other provisions. One of the weaknesses of the Police and Criminal Evidence Act 1984 (PACE), the Terrorism Act (TA) 2000 and the National Security Act (NSA) 2023 is that they provide no mechanisms for enforcement that are effective at the time the problem is encountered. Those remedies that do exist – primarily formal complaint; civil action; abuse of process; and exclusion of evidence – come into effect only after the event, by which time the damage is likely to have been done. Judicial review of police and prosecution decisions may be available, but the Administrative Court is generally reluctant to intervene in respect of decisions made at the early stages of the criminal process.

13.2 For this reason, the lawyer will often have to rely on their skills of persuasion and negotiation. This is frequently not easy, since the lawyer is on police territory, with their permission, and in a situation where the police can ultimately use their proprietorial or law enforcement powers to remove a lawyer who is proving to be a nuisance. An argument with a police officer may quickly result in the lawyer being surrounded by other officers who, whatever their motives, may appear very intimidating. In this context, the lawyer must exploit what few aids to enforcement there are. In particular, it will often be appropriate to ask the custody officer to make a note in the custody record. This may at least show them that the lawyer is taking the matter seriously. There is, however, no right to insist on an entry being made. In the event of a refusal, the lawyer should make a note of the cause for complaint, and the fact of refusal to enter it on the custody record, and sign and date it. The lawyer should also consider asking the custody officer to place a copy with the custody record, although with computerised systems this may not be possible. If relevant, the lawyer should seek to ensure that any CCTV footage is preserved.

13.3 The other action the lawyer can take at the police station is to refer the matter to an officer of higher rank. Some provisions in the PACE Codes of Practice require the custody officer to refer a matter to a more senior officer, and others specifically require a more senior officer to deal with a matter referred to them by the suspect or their lawyer. In practice, an inspector is likely to be on duty, and there will always be an officer in charge of the station, usually at the level of superintendent. An officer of higher rank may be more amenable to arguments based on statutory provisions or the codes, or other legal authority, and the lawyer should, if possible, prepare such arguments carefully. Given the natural propensity for senior officers to support their staff, the lawyer should endeavour to prepare an argument so constructed that the senior officer would not, by agreeing with the lawyer, be seen to be critical of their junior officer.

13.4 However, it will often not be possible for matters of concern to the lawyer to be dealt with in this way. The matter may be one where there is a conflict over the facts, and in this situation a senior officer is highly unlikely to decide in favour of the suspect and their lawyer. It may be one that arose before the lawyer arrived at the police station, for example, a complaint by the suspect that they were assaulted at the time of arrest or on the way to the station. This chapter deals with the major enforcement mechanisms that take effect after the event:

- formal complaints against the police;
- criminal action against the police;
- civil action against the police; and
- abuse of process/exclusion of evidence.

The chapter finishes with a brief consideration of the Human Rights Act (HRA) 1998 as it relates to issues that may arise at the police station.

Complaints against the police

Statutory scheme

13.5 The scheme for dealing with complaints against the police is governed by Police Reform Act (PRA) 2002 Part 2 and Sch 3. Under the PRA 2002, a complaint is any expression of dissatisfaction with a police force or a person serving with the police that is expressed (whether in writing or otherwise) by or on behalf of a member of the public subjected to, who was adversely affected by or who witnessed the conduct that forms the basis of the complaint (PRA 2002 s12). Where the complaint relates to the conduct of a person serving with the police, this includes members of a police force, civilian employees of a police force, special constables, and community or policing support volunteers (PRA 2002 s12(7)).

13.6 The scheme covers complaints made by:

- members of the public who claim to be the person in relation to whom the conduct took place;
- members of the public who claim to have been adversely affected by the conduct; and
- members of the public who claim to have witnessed the conduct (PRA 2002 s12(1B)).

In most cases, the actions of individual officers in relation to a particular suspect will be susceptible to complaint. Indeed, complaint may be the only action available to a suspect where the behaviour complained of does not amount to a criminal or civil wrong, and the suspect is not prosecuted or is prosecuted and pleads guilty. Breach of PACE or the PACE Codes of Practice does not, in itself, render the officer concerned liable to criminal or civil action (PACE s67(10)), although such breaches are admissible in any such proceedings. Although disciplinary action may be taken against an officer for breach of PACE or the codes, neither a lawyer nor a member of the public can initiate such action.

Whose complaint is it?

13.7 If a complaint is to be considered, the initial decision to be made is whether the complaint should come from the lawyer or from the client. Generally, a complaint should be made on behalf of the client. A lawyer can make a complaint on behalf of their client, or make a complaint on their own account if the conduct complained of directly relates to the lawyer or if the lawyer witnessed the conduct or was adversely affected by it. If the lawyer makes a complaint on their own behalf, this may deflect unwelcome pressure from the client. However, it would normally be advisable for the lawyer to complain personally only where the behaviour directly concerns the lawyer, as where the officer conducting an interview improperly seeks to undermine the lawyer by questioning them about their qualifications; or where the lawyer wishes to complain against the wishes of their client. The lawyer would also need to consider whether a complaint, brought by them, could impact their ability to continue to act in the case.

How to complain

13.8 A complaint may be made orally or in writing, although it is always advisable for it to be made in writing or, if made orally, to be confirmed in writing. It may be made to the Independent Office for Police Conduct (IOPC), to the relevant police authority or to the chief officer of police (PRA 2002 Sch 3 para 2). A complaint does not have to be given to any particular officer, but if made at the police station it should normally be presented to the custody officer (unless the custody officer is the subject of the complaint, in which case it would be better to present it to a more senior officer). It should be addressed to the chief officer of police for the relevant police area.

13.9 Where a complaint is made by or on behalf of the client while they are still at the police station, the lawyer should, in particular, consider:

(1) Including a request that any interview of the client, whether while the client is detained or subsequently, should only take place after having given due notice to the lawyer, and in the lawyer's presence.
(2) Whether the client should decline to be interviewed about the complaint while still detained at the police station. The police sometimes imply that if a complaint is to be pursued, the complainant must be interviewed about it while still detained. This is not so. Codes C and I para 9.2 and Code H para 9.3 do provide that where a detained person makes a complaint, a report must be made to an inspector or above who is not connected with the investigation, but there is no requirement for immediate investigation either in PACE or in the codes. Normally, particularly if a civil action against the police might be considered (see para 13.15 below), the client should be advised to decline to be interviewed about the complaint at the police station. The major exception to this would be where a complaint has been made for tactical purposes, and there is good reason to believe that the matter might be resolved with the intervention of a senior officer.

(3) If the client complains of physical injury having been caused, whether a doctor should be called. Codes C and I para 9.2 and Code H para 9.3 provide that where a complaint concerns a possible assault or the possibility of the unnecessary or unreasonable use of force, an appropriate healthcare professional must be called as soon as practicable. However, if the police call in a healthcare professional, the client should be advised not to discuss the circumstances of the injury with them, and the lawyer or client should arrange for an examination by an independent doctor as soon as possible.[1] However, there is no provision in the Standard Crime Contract (SCC) for disbursements in respect of police station advice and assistance.

How a complaint should be dealt with by the police

13.10 As noted above, if a complaint about the police is made by or on behalf of a detained person about their treatment since arrest, a report must be made to an inspector or above as soon as practicable. It is suggested that this should also apply where the complaint is about treatment immediately before, or on, arrest. The police are under a duty to take any steps that appear desirable for the purpose of obtaining or preserving evidence relating to the conduct complained of (PRA 2002 Sch 3 para 1). On receiving the complaint, the police must determine whether they are the appropriate authority and, if not, must notify the complainant which is the appropriate authority (PRA 2002 Sch 3 para 2). If the complaint alleges conduct resulting in death or serious injury, or of a description specified in regulations, or the Director General of the IOPC notifies the appropriate authority that it must be referred to them, the complaint must be referred to the IOPC (PRA 2002 Sch 3 para 4). Otherwise, the appropriate authority must deal with the complaint in a reasonable and proportionate manner, which may be by investigating it or notifying the complainant that the authority will take no action. The complaint must be investigated if there is an indication that a person serving with the police has committed a criminal offence or behaved in a manner that would justify the bringing of disciplinary proceedings, or there may have been an infringement of a person's rights under European Convention on Human Rights (ECHR) Article 2 or 3 (PRA 2002 Sch 3 para 6). The appropriate authority may decide to deal with some complaints by local resolution, particularly if the behaviour complained of is not very serious. Clients should be warned that they may be approached by an officer following their release who may try to persuade them to deal with the complaint in this way. The lawyer should consider advising their client not to speak to the police about the complaint except in the lawyer's presence. At any such interview, the police station legal advice scheme will not apply, although the client may be eligible for assistance under free-standing advice and assistance if the client satisfies the financial eligibility criteria.

13.11 In complaints dealt with directly by the IOPC, the IOPC itself will determine the form that the investigation is to take (having regard to the

1 Code C para 9.8, Code H para 9.10 and Code I para 9.11 permit a detainee to be examined by a medical professional of their choice at their expense.

seriousness of the case and the public interest), which may be an investigation by the relevant police authority, an investigation by the police under the direction of the IOPC or an investigation conducted by the IOPC itself (PRA 2002 Sch 3 para 15). In other cases, the appropriate authority may generally appoint an officer from the relevant police force or a National Crime Agency officer to conduct an investigation (PRA 2002 Sch 3 para 16). The officer investigating the complaint will normally wish to interview the client, although this is unlikely to be until some time after they have been released from police custody. As indicated above, the client should agree to be interviewed by the officer only in the presence of the lawyer. The client should, in particular, be advised to be wary of any attempt to dissuade them from proceeding with the complaint.

Whether to make a complaint

13.12 The question remains whether the suspect should make a complaint against the police while they are still in police detention. This entails considering (i) whether a complaint is appropriate at all and (ii) if it is, whether it should be made before the client leaves custody or subsequently. In advising a client, the following factors may indicate that making a complaint would be appropriate:

(1) A complaint may be the only form of action open to the client if the police behaviour concerned is unlikely to give rise to criminal or civil liability, taking into account the problems of proving that the behaviour did occur. This may be particularly relevant if the complaint concerns lack of police disclosure (see paras 4.22 and 4.27 above) or relates to interpretation or translation (see para 11.107 above).
(2) Making a formal complaint may help the client feel better, and may help them feel that something is being done about the conduct that has caused the problem. Against this, however, must be set the possible adverse consequences (see para 13.13 below), and the fact that only a small percentage of complaints are upheld.
(3) Where the behaviour concerned may be relevant at trial, a failure to complain at the earliest opportunity may have an adverse impact. For example, if the client maintains at trial that the reason for confessing shortly after the arrest was because of an assault by the arresting officers, the prosecutor, on any application to have the confession excluded, is likely to suggest that a failure to complain at the time is evidence of fabrication.
(4) As noted earlier, where a complaint is received, steps must be taken to obtain or preserve evidence. This may be important where there is potential evidence that may disappear or deteriorate over time. For example, if the complainant alleges assault by an unidentified officer, identification procedures undertaken at an early stage may be important.

13.13 There are, however, a number of factors that may weigh against making a complaint while the suspect is in police custody:

(1) While in police custody, the client is particularly vulnerable. First, especially in the case of more serious complaints or where feelings are 'running high', the client is at risk of police pressure such as prolonging detention, delays in responding to calls from the cell, insults, threats or even assault. Second, in certain circumstances, it may make the likelihood of prosecution greater. For example, if the client complains of assault by the police at the time of arrest, the police may take pre-emptive action by bringing a charge of assault on police against them. In this way, any injuries to the client can be explained by the alleged need for restraint.

(2) If the conduct concerned may give rise to a civil action against the police – for example, in respect of an assault by the police – a complaint can have an adverse effect on the civil proceedings, although this danger is now limited. It was formerly the case that the police had access to statements and documents arising from the investigation of a complaint in preparing their defence to civil proceedings, but that access was denied to the plaintiff on the grounds that the documents were covered by public interest immunity. However, in *R v Chief Constable of the West Midlands ex p Wiley*,[2] it was held that public interest immunity does not apply to such documents as a class, although it might in particular circumstances. The result is that police officers can still have access to the documents in preparing their defence in civil proceedings, but that the claimant is also normally entitled to access to them. The complaints regime under the PRA 2002 imposes a number of disclosure requirements on both the IOPC and the police.

(3) A complaint may alert the police to the defence the client will use at the trial of the criminal case against them. In many cases, this will be obvious anyway, but the danger can be limited by giving only brief details of the behaviour complained of while at the police station.

(4) Even if a complaint is upheld, there is no provision for financial compensation to be paid to the complainant, although occasionally ex gratia payments are made.

Criminal prosecution of the police

13.14 Police officers are, in principle, subject to the criminal law in the same way as anyone else. However, in practice, a suspect would face considerable difficulty in trying to initiate criminal proceedings against a police officer, either themself or by reporting the matter to the police. In the case of a private prosecution, no legal aid is available to the complainant other than under free-standing legal advice and assistance. For these reasons, the prospect of a criminal prosecution of a police officer is of limited relevance to the lawyer advising at the police station. As noted above, breach of PACE or the codes of practice does not of itself give rise to criminal liability (PACE s67(10)).

2 [1994] 3 WLR 433, HL.

Civil actions against the police

13.15 Although breach of PACE or the codes does not, in itself, give rise to civil liability (PACE s67(10)), a breach may be relevant in determining whether the police are liable in civil proceedings. The codes are admissible in any civil proceedings and, if relevant, are to be taken into account by the court (PACE s67(11)).

13.16 Note, in particular, potential claims for the following:

(1) False imprisonment is a form of trespass to the person involving the complete deprivation of liberty without lawful excuse. False imprisonment could result, for example, from an unlawful arrest, unlawful stop and search or drug search, detention contrary to PACE s37, improper authorisation of continued detention at the 24-hour stage, or improper detention beyond a relevant time limit.[3]

(2) Trespass to the person consists of an assault or battery. It could result from an unlawful search or detention, or where unreasonable force is used.[4]

(3) Trespass to property is an unjustified direct physical intrusion onto property in possession of another. It could result from an unlawful search or entry on to property to effect an arrest, etc.

(4) Malicious prosecution requires proof that:
- there has been a prosecution that has caused them damage;
- the prosecution was instituted or continued by the police;
- the prosecution terminated in favour of the claimant;
- the prosecuting police officer acted without reasonable and probable cause; and
- the prosecuting police officer acted maliciously.[5]

(5) Negligence or breach of statutory duty. Negligence involves a breach of a duty of care owed to another and could result, for example, from a failure to take adequate care of a vulnerable suspect, or causing injury or damage in conducting a search of a person or property or in carrying out an arrest. Breach of statutory duty does not simply consist of breach of a statutory provision, but involves the idea that parliament intended a piece of legislation to confer a cause of action on members of a protected class.[6]

3 See, for example, *Roberts v Chief Constable of Cheshire* [1999] 2 All ER 326, CA, in which it was held that a suspect was unlawfully detained where a review was not conducted at the relevant time.

4 See, for example, *Chief Constable of Thames Valley v Hepburn* [2002] EWCA Civ 1841, where a person was unlawfully detained following the execution of a search warrant that did not include a power to search persons. Note that there are certain restrictions on claims for trespass to the person where the claimant was convicted of an imprisonable offence on the same occasion as that on which the act is alleged to have been done (Criminal Justice Act 2003 s329); and see *Adorian v Commissioner of Police of the Metropolis* [2010] EWHC 3861 (QB).

5 See, for example, *Rudall v Crown Prosecution Service* [2018] EWHC 3287 (QB).

6 It was held in *Cullen v Chief Constable of the Royal Ulster Constabulary* [2003] UKHL 39 that failure to inform a suspect why legal advice was being denied did not give rise to this form of tortious liability, although a minority of the judicial committee of the House of Lords were of the view that the statutory provision was of such importance that it should be actionable without proof of harm.

13.17 Civil action against the police has a number of advantages over making a complaint or criminal proceedings. Legal aid may be available, and a successful action may result in financial compensation, sometimes quite substantial, being paid to the applicant. Guidance on quantum was set out in *Thompson v Commissioner of Police of the Metropolis*.[7] The standard of proof is 'on a balance of probabilities', so that success is more likely than in criminal proceedings, which require the case to be proved beyond reasonable doubt.

13.18 As noted above, the lawyer should always consider the possibility of civil proceedings, including judicial review,[8] when advising a client whether to make a complaint against the police, although civil action is not covered by the Legal Aid Agency's (LAA) Standard Crime Contract (SCC). A stated intention to advise a client to initiate a civil action may, in appropriate cases, be helpful when negotiating with the police, particularly with more senior officers. The lawyer should be particularly careful to take full contemporaneous notes where civil action by the client is a possibility.

Exclusion of evidence

Overview

13.19 Probably the strongest means of enforcement in respect of police conduct is an application to stay proceedings as an abuse of process,[9] or to exclude improperly obtained evidence under PACE ss76 and 78. PACE s82(3) also preserves the common law discretion of a court to exclude evidence, but in practice PACE ss76 and 78 have rendered the common law powers almost redundant. There is also special provision regarding the evidential use of confessions obtained from a mentally handicapped person (PACE s77; and see para 11.1 above). Of course, exclusion of evidence does not directly affect police conduct, and it will only be of direct relevance if criminal proceedings are initiated against a suspect who then pleads not guilty. Nevertheless, the defence lawyer at the police station should be aware of the exclusionary provisions for a number of reasons, dealt with below. The intention here is not to provide a full explanation of the exclusionary provisions, but rather to indicate their utility from the point of view of the lawyer advising at the police station.[10]

13.20 If the lawyer is aware that evidence may potentially be excluded, they should take this into account when advising their client, and may use this

7 [1997] 2 All ER 762, CA.

8 If judicial review is a realistic prospect, it is important to be mindful of the strict time limits – the claim form must be filed promptly and in any event not later than three months after the grounds to make the claim first arose.

9 Abuse of process is not further considered here. See, for example, the most recent edition of D Ormerod and D Perry, *Blackstone's Criminal Practice* (Oxford University Press, Oxford, annual) Part D3.

10 For fuller consideration of PACE ss76 and 78 see, for example, M Zander, *Zander on PACE: The Police and Criminal Evidence Act 1984* (Sweet & Maxwell, London, 9th edn, 2023); or the most recent edition of D Ormerod and D Perry *Blackstone's Criminal Practice* (Oxford University Press, Oxford, annual) Part F.

possibility when negotiating with the police. For example, if an initial interview has been conducted in breach of PACE or the codes, the lawyer should consider not only whether evidence of the initial interview might be excluded, but also whether it might lead to evidence of a subsequent interview being excluded. In either case, this will be a relevant factor in considering whether to advise the client to answer questions in the interview at which the lawyer is present. If the oppression or other factor that caused the original confession is still operative at the time of the subsequent interview, the evidence of that interview will be inadmissible, or should be excluded, on the same grounds. If the factor is no longer directly operative in the subsequent interview, and the subsequent interview is properly conducted, evidence of that interview may still not be admitted if the first interview 'tainted' the second or subsequent interview. The fact that the suspect has received legal advice before the second interview will not necessarily remove the 'taint'. See further para 4.52 above.

13.21 The lawyer should be particularly vigilant if they are aware of breaches of PACE or the codes, and should ensure that they take a full, contemporaneous note of the conduct concerned. If the conduct subsequently provides grounds for an application to exclude evidence, the lawyer may have to give evidence, which will be more credible if a clear contemporaneous note has been taken.

13.22 Not every breach of PACE or the codes will result in the exclusion of evidence.[11] Conversely, evidence may be excluded even where there has been no breach. It was held in *R v Brine*,[12] that exclusion under PACE s78 (and the principle probably also applies to PACE s76(2)(b) but not to (a)) is not confined to circumstances involving improper conduct by the police. In that case, the court heard that the defendant was suffering from mild paranoid psychosis, the effect of which was that he was likely to tell lies – that is, falsely confess – under stress. The Court of Appeal held that evidence of his confession should have been excluded even though the police were unaware of his condition.[13]

13.23 If the lawyer is aware of a breach of PACE or the codes, or of other improper conduct, in their presence, they should normally intervene at the time.[14] If the lawyer fails to intervene at the time, evidence obtained as a result of even a clear and substantial breach may not be excluded at trial. In *R v Dunn*,[15] the prosecution alleged that the defendant, who had denied the offence in interview, admitted it in the presence of his lawyer during the signing of the interview notes. The alleged confession was not recorded contemporaneously and the defendant was not shown a note of it, which were clear breaches of Code C. At trial, the defendant denied that

11 See, for example, *Watson v DPP* [2003] EWHC 1466 (Admin).

12 [1992] Crim LR 122, CA.

13 However, contrast *R v Campbell* [1995] Crim LR 157, CA, where the confession of a mentally handicapped defendant obtained in the absence of an appropriate adult was admitted in circumstances where the police were unaware of the defendant's handicap at the time of interview.

14 As an exception to the normal rule, the lawyer should not intervene if an interviewing officer fails to give a special warning under Code C para 10.11, Code H para 10.10 or Code I para 10.7 (see para 7.59 above).

15 (1990) 91 Cr App R 237, CA.

the conversation had taken place, and this was supported by his lawyer, a solicitor's representative. The alleged confession was not excluded, and he was found guilty. The Court of Appeal held that the trial judge had rightly decided that the lawyer was present to protect the defendant's interests, that intervention by her would have been possible, and that her presence would have inhibited the police from fabricating the evidence. The trial judge said that he would have excluded the evidence had the lawyer not been present. The lawyer, of course, denied the conversation took place, but the court held that it was for the jury to decide whether it believed her, which it obviously did not. It follows from this decision that failure by the lawyer to intervene could jeopardise the chances of exclusion of improperly obtained evidence.

13.24 This will not always be so. In *R v Paris, Abdullahi and Miller*,[16] the Court of Appeal held that evidence of a confession made in interview should have been excluded even though a solicitor was present. However, this was an extreme case where Miller was described as being on the borderline of mental handicap and where the court said that it was hard to conceive of a more hostile and intimidating approach to a suspect by the police officers interviewing him. The court also castigated the solicitor, supporting the Law Society's advice that the lawyer should intervene if questioning is oppressive, threatening or insulting, and that the suspect should be advised to remain silent if improprieties remained uncorrected or continued. If the lawyer failed to do this, said the court, the lawyer's presence might actually render the suspect a disservice since the police may take the lack of intervention as an indication that their conduct was not improper.

PACE s76(2)

Introduction

13.25 PACE s76 is concerned only with confession evidence, which includes any statement wholly or partly adverse to the person who made it (PACE s82(1)).[17] The general rule is that evidence of a confession is admissible in any proceedings (PACE s76(1)). However, PACE s76(2) provides as follows:

> If, in any proceedings where the prosecution proposes to give in evidence a confession made by an accused person, it is represented to the court that the confession was or may have been obtained–
>
> (a) by oppression of the person who made it; or
>
> (b) in consequence of anything said or done which was likely, in the circumstances existing at the time, to render unreliable any confession which might be made by him in consequence thereof,

16 (1993) 97 Cr App R 99, CA. See also *R v Glaves* [1993] Crim LR 685, CA.

17 It was held in *R v Hasan* [2005] UKHL 22 that whether a statement is to be treated as a confession is to be decided in the light of the circumstances when the statement was made and not at the time that it falls to be considered. Thus, if the accused makes an apparently exculpatory or neutral statement in the police interview, a court will have no power to exclude it under PACE s76 (although it may do so under section 78) even though by the time of the trial it is adverse to the accused – because, for example, the prosecution can then prove that the statement was untrue.

the court shall not allow the confession to be given in evidence against him except in so far as the prosecution proves to the court beyond reasonable doubt that the confession (notwithstanding that it may be true) was not obtained as aforesaid.[18]

13.26 PACE s76(2) thus creates two grounds for the exclusion of confession evidence – oppression and unreliability – which are dealt with below, but a number of general points should first be made:

(1) Once a representation[19] has been made to the court that a confession was, or may have been, obtained in one of the prohibited ways, evidence of the confession cannot be adduced unless the prosecution establishes beyond reasonable doubt that it was not so obtained. See, for example, *R v Harvey*;[20] *R v Davison*;[21] and *R v Paris, Abdullahi and Miller*.[22]
(2) It is irrelevant for the purpose of deciding whether to exclude the confession that the confession is or might be true. Thus, in *R v Cox*,[23] the Court of Appeal held that evidence of a confession of a mentally handicapped defendant made in the absence of an appropriate adult should have been excluded even though the defendant admitted the offence to the trial court. The correct question to ask, said the Court of Appeal, was not whether the confession was likely to be true, but whether it was likely to be unreliable.
(3) Evidence obtained as a result of a confession that is excluded at trial may be admitted, although the prosecution is not allowed to adduce evidence that it was discovered as a result of the confession (PACE s76(4)–(6)). Thus, if a confession that is subsequently excluded enables the police to recover stolen property, evidence may be given at the trial of the finding of the property, but evidence may not be given that the police knew where to look because of the confession.

Oppression

13.27 'Oppression' is defined to include torture, inhuman or degrading treatment, and the use or threat of violence (whether or not amounting to torture) (PACE s76(8)). This definition is not exhaustive and other forms of behaviour may be treated as amounting to oppression. In *R v Fulling*,[24] the Court of Appeal held that the word 'oppression' should be given its ordinary dictionary meaning, namely the 'exercise of authority or power in a burdensome, harsh, or wrongful manner; unjust or cruel treatment of subjects, inferiors, etc; or the imposition of unreasonable or unjust

18 Note that PACE s76A enables a confession made by an accused to be admitted on behalf of another person charged in the same proceedings (because, for example, it strengthens the case of that person or undermines the case of the accused who made the confession), subject to similar provisions regarding oppression and unreliability.
19 A 'representation' does not have to be evidence adduced. Representations made to the court by defence counsel are sufficient (*R v Dhorajiwala* [2010] EWCA Crim 1237).
20 [1988] Crim LR 241, Central Criminal Court.
21 [1988] Crim LR 442.
22 (1993) 97 Cr App R 99, CA.
23 [1991] Crim LR 276, CA. See also *R v Kenny* [1994] Crim LR 284, CA; and *R v Mushtaq* [2005] UKHL 25.
24 [1987] 2 All ER 65, CA.

burdens'. It also held that the expression would almost certainly involve some impropriety on behalf of the interrogator. In *R v Paris, Abdullahi and Miller*,[25] the Court of Appeal accepted that a series of interviews totalling 13 hours over five days, where the defendant, although accompanied by his solicitor, was bullied and hectored, and where, short of physical violence, 'it was hard to conceive of a more hostile and intimidating approach', was oppressive. Similarly, in *R v Beales*,[26] an interview in which the defendant was 'hectored and bullied from first to last' was held to be oppressive. On the other hand, in *R v Emmerson*,[27] rude and discourteous behaviour on the part of the interrogator was held not to amount to oppression. In *R v Ridley*,[28] it was held that a three-hour interview of an accused who was described as naive, conducted in a manner that was tendentious, persistent, aggressive and prurient, should have been excluded on the grounds of oppression. For exclusion to follow, there must be a causal, or possible causal, link between the oppression and the confession.[29]

Unreliability

13.28 The unreliability provision in PACE s76(2)(b) does not require any impropriety on the part of the police.[30] There must, however, be a causal connection between what was 'said or done' and the confession, as where a suspect confesses as a result of an inducement.[31] What was 'said or done' refers to the police and not to what was said or done by the suspect,[32] so that, for example, the fact that the suspect was withdrawing from the effects of drugs would not in itself come within the subsection,[33] although the circumstances might render the result unfair for the purposes of PACE s78. It is likely that the expression includes things not said or done. The expression 'the circumstances existing at the time' includes the circumstances of the suspect, and applies whether or not the police were aware of them. For example, the fact that the suspect had a mental age of eight years could be relevant.[34] The following are examples of the kind of conduct that may, or may not, result in exclusion of a confession.

25 (1993) 97 Cr App R 99, CA.

26 [1991] Crim LR 118.

27 (1991) 92 Cr App R 284, CA. See also *R v L (Admissibility of Confession)* [1994] Crim LR 839, CA, in which evidence of aggressive questioning was not excluded.

28 (1999) 17 December (unreported), CA.

29 *R v Parker* [1995] Crim LR 233.

30 *R v Fulling* [1987] 2 All ER 65, CA. Note that section 76(2)(b) also applies to a confession made other than to a police officer (*R v Roberts* [2011] EWCA Crim 2974).

31 *R v Delaney* (1989) 88 Cr App R 338, CA. See also *R v Barry* (1992) 95 Cr App R 384, CA. It was held in *R v Samuel* [2005] EWCA Crim 704 that there is a distinction between making a confession 'in consequence' of something said or done (which did engage section 76(2)(b)) and making a confession 'in the light of' something said or done (which did not).

32 *R v Goldenberg* (1989) 88 Cr App R 285, CA.

33 *R v Crampton* (1991) 92 Cr App R 369, CA.

34 *R v Everett* [1988] Crim LR 826, CA.

Denying access to a lawyer

13.29 Wrongly denying access to lawyer has resulted in exclusion of a confession under PACE s76(2), although normally when associated with other improprieties. See, for example, *R v Davison*;[35] *R v McGovern*;[36] and *R v Moss*.[37] However, denial of access to a lawyer has more often been dealt with under PACE s78, and denial in itself will not result in exclusion. See, for example, *R v Oliphant*.[38]

Failure to secure attendance of appropriate adult

13.30 In circumstances where an appropriate adult should be called in (see paras 11.16 and 11.90 above), failure to do so, or calling in a person who is inappropriate, may result in exclusion of a confession. See, for example, *R v Dutton*;[39] *R v Cox*;[40] *R v W*;[41] and *R v Al-Jaryan*,[42] where no appropriate adult was called, and *DPP v Blake*;[43] *R v Morse*;[44] and *R v Palmer*,[45] where an inappropriate adult was in attendance.[46]

Misleading the suspect and inducement

13.31 Although often dealt with under PACE s78 (see para 13.33 below), a confession may be excluded under PACE s76(2)(b) where the suspect is misled by the police about the existence of evidence, for example, that the suspect has been identified where this is not so.[47] Similarly, a confession may be excluded where it has been obtained by inducement, as where an employee confessed after being told by their manager, who was investigating a theft from the company, that '[w]e can sort this out internally or get the police involved'.[48]

Conditions of detention and interview

13.32 A confession may be excluded where the provisions of Code C or H regarding the conditions of the suspect's detention or interview are contravened – for example, inadequate rest periods[49] or inadequate refreshment[50] – although there would normally have to be an accumulation of breaches to result in exclusion.

35 [1988] Crim LR 442.
36 (1991) 92 Cr App R 228, CA.
37 (1990) 91 Cr App R 371, CA.
38 [1992] Crim LR 40, CA.
39 (1988) Independent, December 5, CA.
40 [1991] Crim LR 276, CA.
41 [2010] EWCA Crim 2799.
42 [2020] EWCA Crim 440.
43 (1989) 89 Cr App R 179, DC.
44 [1991] Crim LR 195, Crown Court.
45 September 1991 *Legal Action* 21.
46 See also *Miller v DPP* [2018] EWHC 262 (Admin), in which it was held that failure to call in an appropriate adult had a clear adverse impact on the fairness of permitting evidence of the drug/drive procedure to be admitted.
47 *R v Blake* [1991] Crim LR 119.
48 *R v Roberts* [2011] EWCA Crim 2974.
49 *R v Trussler* [1988] Crim LR 446.
50 *R v Gopee and Gopee* (1992) 89 LS Gaz 24.

PACE s78

Introduction

13.33 PACE s78(1) provides for the exclusion of any form of prosecution evidence,[51] including confession evidence:

> In any proceedings, the court may refuse to allow evidence on which the prosecution proposes to rely to be given if it appears to the court that, having regard to all the circumstances, including the circumstances in which the evidence was obtained, the admission of the evidence would have such an adverse effect on the fairness of the proceedings that the court ought not to admit it.

13.34 PACE s78 provides a court with a sufficiently broad discretion to exclude evidence even though it was not obtained in breach of PACE or the codes.[52] If the challenged evidence has already been adduced, a challenge under PACE s82(3) will likely have regard to the wording of PACE s78 as a guide as to how such direction may properly be exercised.[53] Conversely, breach of PACE or the codes will not necessarily result in exclusion of the evidence thereby obtained. Although the Court of Appeal has been reluctant to lay down guidelines for the interpretation of PACE s78 generally, for a breach of PACE or the codes to result in exclusion of evidence, it must be a significant and substantial breach and must have such an adverse effect that justice demands its exclusion.[54] Where these conditions are satisfied, it is likely that the evidence will be excluded.[55] This may be illustrated by two cases involving confessions obtained following the wrongful denial of legal advice: *R v Samuel*;[56] and *R v Alladice*.[57] In *Samuel*, the solicitor gave evidence that he would probably have advised his client before the interview in which his client confessed (he had been interviewed a number of times previously) not to answer questions. The Court of Appeal decided that the confession evidence should not have been admitted. The court came to the opposite conclusion in *Alladice*, where the defendant gave evidence that although he wanted his solicitor present, he was well aware of his right to remain silent. Both cases involved a significant and substantial breach, but while in *Samuel* the court concluded that this breach adversely affected the accused, in *Alladice* it concluded that there was no adverse effect.

13.35 The significance of the breach does not, in itself, determine whether evidence will be excluded. Thus, evidence obtained in breach of a defendant's rights under the ECHR will not necessarily be excluded. In *R v Khan*,[58] the House of Lords held that in considering exclusion of evidence

51 Including evidence of a significant silence under Criminal Justice and Public Order Act (CJPOA) 1994 s34, 36 or 37, and evidence of lies told by the accused.

52 *R v Brine* [1992] Crim LR 122, CA.

53 See, the judgment of Mr Justice Turner in the Crown Court case of *R v AB and CD* [2025] EWCR 3.

54 See *R v Walsh* (1990) 91 Cr App R 161, CA; and *R v Keenan* [1989] 3 All ER 598, CA.

55 *R v Allen* [2001] EWCA Crim 1607.

56 [1988] 2 All ER 135, CA.

57 (1988) 87 Cr App R 380, CA.

58 [1996] 3 WLR 162, HL.

under PACE s78, breach of ECHR rights was of no greater significance than breach of domestic law. Since breach of domestic law does not necessarily lead to exclusion so obtained, breach of a Convention right should not do so either. This was effectively upheld by the European Court of Human Rights (ECtHR) in *Khan v UK*,[59] where the court held that although the evidence had been obtained in breach of the right to private life under ECHR Article 8, the right to fair trial under Article 6 did not necessarily require that the evidence so obtained be excluded. It could be argued that the ECHR, incorporating as it does rights that are fundamental, should weigh very heavily in a court's mind in considering exclusion under PACE s78. However, while a court may well take a breach of the ECHR into account, it will not necessarily result in the exclusion of evidence.[60]

13.36 What follows is intended to give some indication of the kinds of conduct and breaches that may, or may not, result in exclusion of evidence under PACE s78:

- withholding information on suspects' rights;
- wrongful denial of legal advice;
- failure to caution the suspect;
- conduct and recording of interviews;
- identification procedures;
- questioning amounting to an interview during a search of property;
- entrapment;
- deception; and
- inducements.

However, it must be remembered that the courts are not always consistent in terms of the underlying principles informing their decisions on exclusion of evidence under PACE s78; decisions are very fact-sensitive and the Court of Appeal is reluctant to interfere with the decisions of trial judges.[61]

Withholding information on suspects' rights

13.37 Evidence of an admission made in interview may be excluded if the defendant was misled about their rights, as in *R v Beycan*,[62] where the defendant was led to believe that interviews were usually conducted in the absence of a lawyer. A similar result may follow from a failure to inform a suspect of their right to consult a lawyer,[63] although not if they then 'genuinely' agree to speak to the police.[64]

59 App No 35394/97 (2001) 31 EHRR 45, ECtHR.

60 See the critical commentary on *Khan v UK* (App No 35394/97) (2001) 31 EHRR 45, ECtHR in the *Criminal Law Review* report ([2000] Crim LR 684); and D Ormerod, 'ECHR and the exclusion of evidence: trial remedies for Article 8 breaches' [2003] Crim LR 61.

61 *R v Jelen* (1990) 90 Cr App R 456, CA.

62 [1990] Crim LR 185, CA.

63 *R v Williams* [1989] Crim LR 66, Crown Court (Inner London).

64 *R v Hughes* [1988] Crim LR 519, CA.

Wrongful denial of legal advice

13.38 As noted at para 13.29 above, wrongful denial of access to a lawyer may result in exclusion of evidence under PACE s76(2)(b), but this is more likely under PACE s78.[65] Evidence is unlikely to be excluded if denial of advice is treated by the court as having no adverse effect on the fairness of the proceedings. See, for example, *R v Alladice*;[66] *R v Walsh*;[67] and *R v Dunford*.[68] These cases were all decided before the ECtHR decisions on the right to legal advice noted at para 13.55 below, but the key issue continues to be whether denial of access to legal advice had such an adverse effect on the fairness of the proceedings that the evidence so obtained should be excluded. Note that incompetent legal advice at the police station may result in exclusion under PACE s78, although there is in practice a heavy burden on the accused in demonstrating the adverse effects on fairness of such incompetence.[69]

Failure to caution the suspect

13.39 A person must be cautioned before any questions about an offence are put to them if there are grounds to suspect them of having committed the suspected offence, whether or not the questioning takes place at a police station[70] (see para 4.39 above). Generally, where the courts conclude that a caution ought to have been given, and was not, they are likely to decide that evidence of what was said should be excluded.[71] However, this is not always the case,[72] especially where the defendant could be expected to have been aware of their rights or if they were in receipt of legal advice.[73] The courts generally pay close attention to whether a caution was required. It was noted at para 4.39 above that the courts have limited the obligation to caution to circumstances where there are *reasonable* grounds for suspicion. It has also been decided that a caution is not necessary in advance of questioning about a particular offence if the suspect was cautioned about another matter shortly before, unless the suspect is further arrested.[74] Furthermore, it has been held that a caution was not necessary where a suspect, on being questioned by the police about a particular offence,

65 *R v Samuel* [1988] QB 615, CA.

66 (1988) 87 Cr App R 380, CA.

67 [1989] Crim LR 822, CA.

68 (1990) 91 Cr App R 150, CA. See also *R v Anderson* [1993] Crim LR 447, CA.

69 See E Cape, 'Incompetent police station advice and the exclusion of evidence' [2002] Crim LR 471; and *R v Wahab (Appeal against Conviction); R v Cromer* [2002] EWCA Crim 1570.

70 Codes C and H para 10.1.

71 *R v Hunt* [1992] Crim LR 582, CA. See also *R v Okafor* [1994] 3 All ER 741, CA; *R v Oransaye* [1993] Crim LR 772, CA; *R v Allen* [2001] EWCA Crim 1607; *R v Senior* [2004] EWCA Crim 454; and *R v Miller* [2007] EWCA Crim 1891.

72 *R v Abdurahman* [2019] EWCA Crim 2239.

73 *R v Hoyte* [1994] Crim LR 215; *R v Armas-Rodriguez* [2005] EWCA Crim 1081; and *R v Devani* [2007] EWCA Crim 1926.

74 *R v Oni* [1992] Crim LR 183, CA; and *R v Pall* [1992] Crim LR 126, CA. But contrast *R v Kirk* [1999] 4 All ER 698, CA, which held that where the police have arrested for one offence but question about another, more serious, offence they must, at least, ensure that the suspect is aware of the true nature of the investigation.

started to tell them about a completely different matter of which the police had no knowledge.[75] While Code C provides that minor deviations from the wording of the caution are permissible provided the sense of the caution is preserved (Code C para 10.7), it was held in *R v Ibrahim, Omar, Osman and Mohamed*[76] that administering the wrong caution would not necessarily lead to exclusion of evidence of the subsequent interview.

Conduct and recording of interviews

13.40 Evidence has been excluded where the recording requirements of Code C have not been complied with. The courts have recognised that the provisions in Code C dealing with the recording of interviews and other relevant conversations (see paras 4.50 and 7.8 above) were designed to prevent 'verballing' or suspicion of 'verballing'. Thus, in cases like *R v Canale;*[77] *R v Keenan;*[78] *R v Walsh;*[79] *R v Joseph;*[80] and *R v Rowe,*[81] the Court of Appeal held that evidence of interviews that were not contemporaneously recorded should not have been admitted in evidence. However, exclusion will not always follow where there has been such a breach, as was seen in *R v Dunn* (see para 13.23 above), and in the somewhat surprising decision in *R v White.*[82] Evidence of an interview conducted contrary to the provisions of Code C para 11.1 and Code H para 11.2 (that, following a decision to arrest, the interview must normally be conducted in a police station) will normally be excluded (see para 4.44 above). Similarly, an interview conducted in breach of PACE s37 or Code C para 11.4 or 16.1 may be excluded.[83]

Identification procedures

13.41 Failure to hold an identification procedure in breach of Code D has, in the past, frequently resulted in exclusion of other identification evidence obtained, particularly evidence from a confrontation.[84] However, this was not always the case, especially where the court was of the view that, in the circumstances, another form of identification had not worked to the disadvantage of the defendant.[85] In *R v Popat,*[86] the Court of Appeal held that decisions on exclusion should be based on whether, overall, the identification process was fair and reliable, rather than on whether the detailed rules of Code D had been complied with. This was overruled in relation to

75 *R v Purcell* [1992] Crim LR 806, CA.
76 [2008] EWCA Crim 880.
77 [1990] 2 All ER 187, CA.
78 [1989] 3 All ER 598, CA.
79 [1989] Crim LR 822, CA.
80 [1993] Crim LR 206, CA.
81 [1994] Crim LR 837, CA.
82 [1991] Crim LR 779, CA. See also *R v Courtney* [1995] Crim LR 63, CA; *R v Dures, Williams and Dures* [1997] Crim LR 673, CA; and *R v Heera* [2010] EWCA Crim 1779.
83 *R v Coleman, Knight and Hochenberg* (1996) 20 October (unreported), CA, briefly considered at (1998) NLJ, 3 July.
84 *R v Conway* (1990) 91 Cr App R 143, CA; and *R v Britton and Richards* [1989] Crim LR 144, Crown Court (Leeds).
85 *R v Penny* (1992) 94 Cr App R 345, CA.
86 [1998] Crim LR 825, CA.

other aspects of the decision by *R v Forbes*.[87] However, *Forbes* reinforced the point that courts should be concerned with whether the overall purpose of Code D had been respected. While the provisions of Code D are mandatory, a breach of a particular provision of the code may not frustrate the overall purpose.[88] In such circumstances a judge may admit the evidence of identification and direct the jury that there had been a breach, pointing out the consequences of that breach and that the accused had lost the possible benefit of the code provisions (see the cases referred to at para 8.86 above).

13.42 There is extensive case-law on evidence of visual identification, the distinction between recognition and identification, and the Code D identification procedures (see generally chapter 8 above). Examples of post-*Forbes* cases where it was held that identification evidence did not need to be excluded include *Marsh v DPP*[89] (breach of the obligation to take an original description from the witness); and *R v B*[90] (witness not told to view the array in a video identification at least twice). Cases where it was held that the trial judge should have excluded the identification evidence include *R v Pecco*[91] (distinguishing marks on the suspect not adequately disguised); and *R v Preddie*[92] (street identification of a known suspect). The courts are particularly likely to exclude identification evidence where they conclude that the police deliberately tried to circumvent the provisions of Code D.[93]

Questioning during a search of property

13.43 Where a search is carried out at which the suspect is present, questions should be confined to whether any article that is discovered that the police are entitled to seize and retain is property claimed by the suspect and, if it is, whether it is property that could amount to evidence of an offence (see para 6.130 above). If it goes further, it could be excluded.[94] If the right to delay taking the suspect to the police station while the search is being carried out (PACE s30(10)) is abused by the police or His Majesty's Revenue and Customs (HMRC) officers who use the opportunity to conduct an irregular interview, evidence of the interview should be excluded.[95]

Entrapment

13.44 Entrapment is not a defence but, depending on the facts, may lead to exclusion of evidence under PACE s78, although in some circumstances

87 [2001] 1 AC 473, HL.
88 See, for example, *R v Bogie* [2023] EWCA Crim 1280.
89 [2006] EWHC 1525 (Admin).
90 [2008] EWCA Crim 1524. See also *R v Selwyn* [2012] EWCA Crim 2968; *R v Cole* [2013] EWCA Crim 1149; *R v Lariba, Dos Santos and Hamilton* [2015] EWCA Crim 478; and *R v LT* [2019] EWCA Crim 58.
91 [2010] EWCA Crim 972.
92 [2011] EWCA Crim 312.
93 *R v Nagah* (1990) 92 Cr App R 344, CA.
94 *R v Langiert* [1991] Crim LR 777, CA. See also *R v Raphaie* [1996] Crim LR 812, CA.
95 *R v Khan* [1993] Crim LR 54, CA.

it is more appropriate for an application to be made to stay proceedings on the ground of abuse of process.[96] It is important to distinguish between cases where a person is effectively incited to commit an offence and those where the police use undercover strategies to secure evidence of a crime already committed. Only the former can properly be described as entrapment, although both the case-law and commentary are often confused by use of the term to describe both. In *R v Smurthwaite and Gill*,[97] the Court of Appeal identified five factors as being relevant to the question of whether such evidence should be excluded, although it did not specify how the factors were to be interpreted or what weight was to be placed on them:

- Was the officer acting as an agent provocateur in the sense that they were enticing the defendant to commit an offence which the defendant would not otherwise have committed?
- What was the nature of the entrapment?
- Is the evidence of admissions or of the offence itself?
- How active or passive was the officer?
- Is there an unassailable record of what occurred, or is it strongly corroborated?

Predisposition of the accused to commit a crime is not the deciding factor. A critical factor is whether the police did no more than present the accused with an unexceptional opportunity to commit a crime,[98] although the court will be concerned to examine whether the conduct of the police was so seriously improper as to bring the administration of justice into disrepute.

13.45 Two contrasting cases may help to illustrate the approach to entrapment. In *R v Christou and Wright*,[99] the police set up a bogus jeweller's shop in order to recover stolen property and to collect evidence against the thieves and handlers. Admissions obtained in the course of conversations with the suspects when they went to the shop to sell stolen property were held to have been properly admitted.[100] In *R v Bryce*,[101] an undercover police officer contacted the suspect to ask whether he could supply a stolen car, and it was held that admissions obtained during the course of this transaction should not have been admitted since it amounted to an inter-

96 See *R v Loosely (No 2)* [2001] UKHL 53 for guidance on which is appropriate. For the treatment of entrapment by non-state agencies, see *R v Shannon* [2000] Crim LR 1001, CA; and *R v Hardwicke* [2001] Crim LR 220, CA.

97 [1994] 1 All ER 898, CA.

98 *R v Loosely (No 2)* [2001] UKHL 53. See also *R v M* [2011] EWCA Crim 648.

99 [1992] 4 All ER 559, CA.

100 See also *Ealing LBC v Woolworth Plc* [1995] Crim LR 58, DC; *R v Morley* [1994] Crim LR 919, CA; *R v Pattemore* [1994] Crim LR 836, CA; *R v Edwards* [1997] Crim LR 348; and *R v Mann and Dixon* [1995] Crim LR 647, CA. See A Ashworth, 'Re-drawing the boundaries of entrapment' [2002] Crim LR 161; D Ormerod and A Roberts, 'The trouble with *Teixeira*: developing a principled approach to entrapment' (2000) 6 *International Journal of Evidence and Proof* 1 at p38; S Sharpe, 'Covert police operations and the discretionary exclusion of evidence' [1994] Crim LR 793; and G Robertson, 'Entrapment evidence: manna from heaven, or fruit of the poisoned tree?' [1994] Crim LR 805.

101 [1992] 4 All ER 567, CA. See also *R v Smith* [1995] Crim LR 659; and *R v Rajkuma* [2003] EWCA Crim 1955.

rogation with the effect, if not the design, of using an undercover pose to circumvent Code C.

13.46 The ECtHR has accepted that the use of undercover agents is legitimate, but has held that it should be subject to adequate safeguards and must not lead to the incitement of crime.[102] For a useful illustration of conduct that may or may not amount to incitement, see *R v Loosely (No 2)*.[103]

13.47 A distinction must be drawn between 'entrapment' by a law enforcement agency and 'entrapment' by a vigilante group (for example, paedophile hunters). In *R v TL*,[104] the court was clear in stating that:

> 31. . . . Involvement of agents of the state in unacceptable behaviour is at the heart of the reasoning [in *R v Loosely*]. It is the court's unwillingness to approbate seriously wrong conduct by the state . . . that is the foundation of this aspect of the abuse jurisdiction.

Deception

13.48 If a suspect is deceived by the police into believing in the existence of evidence that does not in fact exist, evidence of admissions made in consequence may not be admitted, especially if the suspect's lawyer is also deceived.[105] Exclusion may also follow where the suspect 'deceives' themself, as where the suspect misunderstands the nature of a police enquiry and believes that they are simply assisting with an investigation of the death of a friend as a witness and not a suspect.[106] However, a deception practised by the police in the form of 'bugging' a police interview room is unlikely to result in exclusion of evidence so obtained.[107] Indeed, the courts seem generally reluctant to exclude evidence obtained by trickery or deception. Thus, in *R v Maclean and Kosten*,[108] evidence obtained by pretending that a courier had been involved in a car accident was not excluded. Nor was evidence excluded in *Williams v DPP*,[109] where the police had left a van apparently unattended in the hope that someone might try to steal from it.

102 *Teixeira de Castro v Portugal* (App No 25829/94) [1998] Crim LR 751, ECtHR. This was distinguished in *Nottingham City Council v Amin* [2000] 1 WLR 1071, DC. See also *R v Syed* [2018] EWCA Crim 2809, in which it was held that there was no material difference between English law and the jurisprudence of the ECtHR such as to cast doubt on *Attorney General's Reference (No 3 of 2000)* [2001] UKHL 53 complying with ECHR Article 6.

103 [2001] UKHL 53. See also *R v Byrne* [2003] EWCA Crim 1073.

104 [2018] EWCA Crim 1821.

105 *R v Imran and Hussain* [1997] Crim LR 754, CA; and *R v Mason* [1987] 3 All ER 481, CA.

106 *R v Williams* [1991] Crim LR 708.

107 *R v Ali* (1991) Times, February 19, CA; *R v Bailey* [1993] 3 All ER 513, CA; *R v Roberts* [1997] Crim LR 222, CA; *R v Mason and Others* [2002] EWCA Crim 385; *R v Khan* [1997] AC 558, HL; and *R v Parker* [1995] Crim LR 233. However, these cases were all decided before the enactment of the Regulation of Investigatory Powers Act 2000 and an important issue now would be whether any covert surveillance was properly authorised (see para 2.148 above).

108 [1993] Crim LR 687, CA.

109 [1993] 3 All ER 365, DC. See also *R v Cadette* [1995] Crim LR 229; and *R v Chalkley and Jeffries* [1998] QB 848, CA.

Inducements

13.49 Code C para 11.5 provides that an officer conducting an interview must not 'indicate, except to answer a direct question, what action will be taken by the police if the person being questioned answers questions, makes a statement or refuses to do either'. To do so may amount to an inducement to confess, and any confession so obtained may be excluded. In *R v Howden-Simpson*,[110] a confession was excluded where a choirmaster accused of theft of money belonging to the choristers was told that if he admitted the offence the police would proceed on only two charges, but that if he did not do so, they would interview all the choristers and charge him separately in respect of each one. Indicating that a caution (or other out-of-court disposal) will be given if the suspect confesses may amount to an inducement.[111]

The Human Rights Act 1998

Introduction

13.50 It is unlawful for a public authority, including the police and Crown Prosecution Service, to act in a way that is incompatible with a right under the ECHR (HRA 1998 s6). Rights under the HRA 1998 are enforceable by taking proceedings in an appropriate court or by relying on the right in any legal proceedings, including criminal proceedings (HRA 1998 s7). An application may be made to the ECtHR only once all domestic remedies have been exhausted.[112]

13.51 The most significant ECHR rights applicable to suspects at the police station are:

- Article 3 (*prohibition of torture, degrading and inhuman treatment*);
- Article 5 (*right to liberty and security*);
- Article 6 (*right to a fair trial*);
- Article 8 (*right to respect for private and family life*); and
- Article 10 (*freedom of expression*).

The HRA 1998 may enable a number of aspects of arrest, detention and evidence-gathering to be challenged. In some cases, the effect of the HRA 1998 is to strengthen a claim for which there is an existing remedy; for example, a claim for wrongful arrest on the ground that the police officer did not have reasonable suspicion that an offence had been committed. In other cases, the effect will be to enable a challenge to be made to police conduct that is apparently lawful, for example, delaying access to a lawyer under PACE s58(8). The HRA 1998 may also be relevant to an application to stay proceedings for an abuse of process or to exclude evidence under PACE s76 or 78. Set out here is a brief survey of aspects of police investigation that may be susceptible to challenge under the HRA 1998:

110 [1991] Crim LR 49, CA.

111 See *R (R) v Durham Constabulary* [2005] UKHL 21; and para 10.55 above.

112 Note that the decision to leave the EU does not affect obligations under the ECHR or the HRA 1998.

- arrest;
- detention following arrest;
- access to a lawyer;
- the 'right to silence'; and
- ill-treatment in police custody.

Arrest

13.52 ECHR Article 5(1) prohibits deprivation of a person's liberty except, among other reasons, by means of a lawful arrest effected for the purpose of bringing the person before a competent legal authority on reasonable suspicion of having committed an offence, or when it is reasonably considered necessary to prevent the person from committing an offence.[113] Most powers of arrest under PACE and other legislation require the officer to have reasonable grounds for suspicion, and although the domestic courts have set a low standard for the level of suspicion required, this has been held to be sufficient by the ECtHR.[114] PACE s24(1)(a), (b) and (3)(a) do not require reasonable suspicion (see para 2.14 above). This may not satisfy the requirements of Article 5(1)(c), but the provisions do not appear to have been challenged by reference to the ECHR. The ECtHR has considered the power of arrest for breach of the peace, and held that the definition of breach of the peace is sufficiently certain to meet the requirements of Article 5, but that arrest for breach of the peace may contravene Article 5 if its effect is to deprive a person of their right to freedom of expression under Article 10 and is disproportionate to the perceived risk.[115] PACE Code G takes Article 5 into account by requiring that in exercising powers of arrest, officers must act in a proportionate manner, and should consider whether the 'necessary objectives can be met by other, less intrusive means' (Code G para 1.3).[116]

13.53 ECHR Article 5(2) provides that a person who is arrested must be 'informed promptly, in a language which he understands, of the reasons for his arrest and any charge against him'. This is broadly reflected by PACE s28(1) (see para 2.44 above), although section 28(1) requires the information to be given as soon as is practicable after the arrest, which, in a particular case, may not be the same as 'promptly'.[117] Article 5(2) requires the information to be given in a language the arrested person understands,

113 'Reasonable suspicion' means the existence of facts or information that would satisfy an objective observer that the person concerned may have committed the offence (*Fox, Campbell and Hartley v UK* (App No A/182) (1991) 13 EHRR 157, ECtHR).

114 *O'Hara v UK* (App No 37555/97) (2002) 34 EHRR 32, ECtHR.

115 *Steel v UK* (App No 24838/94) (1999) 28 EHRR 603, ECtHR. See also *McLeod v UK* (App No 24755/94) (1999) 27 EHRR 493, ECtHR, which considered breach of the peace in relation to ECHR Article 8. Note that the ECtHR takes its own, 'autonomous', view of what amounts to criminal proceedings, and proceedings for breach of the peace were deemed to be criminal even though they are not criminal proceedings under domestic law.

116 This provides important context for consideration of whether an arrest is necessary. See, for example, *R (TL) v Chief Constable of Surrey* [2017] EWHC 129 (Admin) at para 25.

117 Although in *Fox, Campbell and Hartley v UK* (App No A/182) (1991) 13 EHRR 157, the ECtHR held that in determining the content and promptness of the information conveyed regard must be had to the particular facts of the case.

whereas PACE s28(1) makes no reference to the language in which the information must be given. There is no explicit provision in Code C, G, H or I requiring interpretation of the reasons for arrest.[118] With regard to what information must be given, a mere reference to the statutory provision under which a person is arrested will generally not be sufficient.[119] Rather, the person must be informed of the facts that form the foundation of the decision to arrest.[120]

Detention following arrest

13.54 ECHR Article 5(3) provides that a person arrested or detained in criminal proceedings must be brought promptly before a judge or other judicial officer, and is entitled to trial within a reasonable time or release (which may be subject to conditions) pending trial. It was held in *Michalko v Slovakia*[121] that Article 5(3) is concerned with two separate stages – the early stage following arrest and the period pending eventual trial before a criminal court. In relation to the first, the presumption must be in favour of release, and when deciding whether a person should be released or detained the authorities are obliged to consider alternative measures of ensuring the defendant's appearance at court. Under PACE, a person who has been arrested but not charged must be brought before a court within 36 hours (see para 2.82 above). A person detained without charge under TA 2000 Sch 8 must be produced before a judicial authority within 48 hours, and a person detained under NSA 2023 s27 must normally be released within 48 hours (see paras 2.83 and 2.84 above). The ECtHR has not laid down a precise definition of 'promptly', but in *Brogan v UK*,[122] the court found that a delay of four days and six hours did not satisfy the requirement. Generally, the provisions under PACE, the TA 2000 and the NSA 2023 regarding the maximum period of detention without charge satisfy Article 5(3). However, this may not be the case where a person is released on bail without charge, where bail is subject to onerous conditions.[123] The restriction on the grant of bail after charge under CJPOA 1994 s25[124] is probably in compliance (see para 10.150 above). The inability of a custody officer to grant bail to a person charged with murder may

118 Although Codes C and H para 3.2 and Code I para 3.1 do require a detainee to be provided with a note containing key information, including a right to interpretation. The notice of rights and entitlements is, at the time of publication, available in 55 languages.

119 *Fox, Campbell and Hartley v UK* (App No A/182) (1991) 13 EHRR 157, ECtHR. For interpretation of the requirements of PACE s28(1), see para 2.44 above.

120 *X v Germany* (App No 7705/76) (1978) 16 DR 111, ECtHR.

121 App No 35377/05 [2010] ECHR 2078, ECtHR.

122 App No A/145-B (1989) 11 EHRR 117, ECtHR.

123 It was argued by E Cape and R Edwards, 'Police bail without charge: the human rights implications' (2010) 69(3) CLJ 423, that police bail without charge could amount to a breach of ECHR Article 5(3), but this was rejected in *Re HA's Application for Judicial Review* [2014] NIQB 115. However, it was accepted, but not ruled upon, that police bail with onerous conditions attached could amount to a breach of ECHR Article 8.

124 Which was amended following an adverse decision in *Caballero v United Kingdom* (App No 32819/96) [2000] Crim LR 587, ECtHR.

not be, although provided bail is considered by a court within a reasonable time following charge, this will probably be sufficient.[125]

Access to a lawyer

13.55 ECHR Article 6(3)(c) provides that everyone charged with a criminal offence has a right to legal assistance. In *Murray v UK*,[126] the ECtHR held that where the attitude of the accused during police questioning can have consequences at trial, Article 6 will usually require that the accused is allowed access to a lawyer at that stage. This resulted in the amendment of CJPOA 1994 ss34, 36 and 37 so that inferences from 'silence' cannot be drawn where a person in police detention asks for, but is not allowed to consult, a solicitor before being interviewed (see para 5.69 above). Since *Murray*, the right to legal assistance at the police station has been developed in a large number of ECtHR decisions following the decision in *Salduz v Turkey*.[127] Essentially, a suspect arrested and detained by the police has a right to legal assistance and, although this is not absolute, it can only be interfered with if it is demonstrated in the light of the particular circumstances of the case that there are compelling reasons to restrict access. Even if there are such reasons, the use of evidence obtained in circumstances where access to legal assistance has been denied may breach the right to fair trial under Article 6(1). Therefore, delaying access to a lawyer under PACE s58(8), TA 2000 Sch 8 or NSA 2023 Sch 6 (see paras 2.151, 2.156 and 2.158 above) may, depending on the circumstances, contravene Article 6 rights, as may the use of evidence obtained in an interview conducted in circumstances where access to a lawyer has not been permitted or where an interview is held in the absence of lawyer with a suspect who wants legal advice (see para 2.137 above).[128] However, it was held in *Ibrahim and Others v UK* that a 'safety interview' conducted in the absence of a lawyer, in circumstances where the 'compelling reasons' exception was satisfied, did not breach Article 6, and that in the circumstances admission in evidence of the record of the interview did not render the trial unfair.[129]

13.56 The ECtHR has held that while the right to legal assistance can be waived, any waiver must not only be voluntary, but 'must also constitute a knowing and intelligent relinquishment ... it must be shown that [the suspect] could reasonably have foreseen what the consequences of his conduct would be'.[130] Codes C, H and I require a custody officer to ask a suspect who declines legal advice why they have refused, but do not require

125 By Coroners and Justice Act 2009 s115, only a Crown Court judge can grant bail to a person charged with murder. There are provisions governing the maximum period within which the decision must be made (section 115(3)).

126 App No 18731/91 (1996) 22 EHRR 29, ECtHR. See also *Averill v UK* (App No 36408/97) (2001) 31 EHRR 36, ECtHR; and *Magee v UK* (App No 28135/95) (2001) 31 EHRR 35, ECtHR.

127 App No 36391/02 (2009) 49 EHRR 19, ECtHR.

128 *Sebalj v Croatia* (App No 4429/09) [2011] ECHR 1048, ECtHR.

129 App Nos 50541/08, 50571/08, 50573/08, 40351/09 [2017] Crim LR 877, ECtHR.

130 *Pishchalnikov v Russia* (App No 7025/04) [2009] ECHR 1357 at para 101, ECtHR. See also *Plonka v Poland* (App No 20310/02) [2009] ECHR 2277, ECtHR.

the officer to explain to the suspect the consequences of waiving their right (see para 2.133 above). Arguably, this does not go far enough to satisfy the 'knowing and intelligent relinquishment' requirement, although this will depend upon the particular circumstances.

13.57 In *S v Switzerland*,[131] the right to private consultation with a lawyer was described by the ECtHR as 'one of the basic requirements of a fair trial in a democratic society'. In *Brennan v UK*,[132] the ECtHR held that although the right to private consultation could be restricted for good cause, in the absence of good cause it would amount to breach of Article 6 without the need to demonstrate an actual adverse effect. Interference with the right to private consultation may also amount to a breach of the right to private life under Article 8.[133] Under PACE, the TA 2000 and the NSA 2023, a suspect has the right to consult a solicitor *in private*, but this is subject to certain legal limitations and, where legal advice is provided by telephone, certain practical limitations (see paras 2.146–2.149 above).

The 'right to silence'

13.58 See the references to ECtHR case-law in paras 5.63–5.69 above.

Ill-treatment in police custody

13.59 ECHR Article 3 provides that no one shall be subjected to torture or to inhuman or degrading treatment or punishment. Codes C and I para 11.5 and Code H para 11.6 provide that no interviewer may try to obtain answers or elicit a statement by the use of oppression, and Codes C, H and I section 8 set out the minimum requirements regarding the conditions of detention. Therefore, provided that the police comply with these provisions, there should be no question of breach of Article 3. The ECtHR has held that to admit evidence obtained in breach of Article 3 would amount to a breach of Article 6,[134] and this is reflected in PACE s76(2) (see para 13.25 above). It should be noted that it is well established by ECtHR jurisprudence that where a person is taken into police custody in good condition but is found to be injured on release, the onus is on the state to provide a plausible explanation as to how the injuries were caused.[135]

131 App No A/220 (1992) 14 EHRR 670, ECtHR, and see the critical commentary at [2002] Crim LR 215.

132 App No 39846/98 (2002) 34 EHRR 18, ECtHR.

133 *Heino v Finland* (App No 56720/09) [2011] ECHR 309, ECtHR.

134 *Austria v Italy* (App No 788/60) (1963) 6 YB 740, EComHR.

135 See, for example, *Aksoy v Turkey* (App No 21987/93) (1997) 23 EHRR 553, ECtHR; and *Selmouni v France* (App No 25803/94) (2000) 29 EHRR 403, ECtHR.

APPENDICES

APPENDIX 1

Pre-charge bail

	SFO, NCA, HMRC or FCA cases	Standard cases	Designated exceptionally complex
Initial period	6 months (custody officer)	3 months (custody officer)	Where a standard case has been designated exceptionally complex by the DPP, a further pre-court extension may be authorised
First extension	12 months (level of authorisation determined by investigating agency)	6 months (inspector)	
Second extension		9 months (superintendent)	
Designated exceptionally complex			12 months (commander or assistant chief constable in consultation with the DPP)
First magistrates' court extension	18 or 24 months (magistrates' court)	12 or 18 months (magistrates' court)	18 or 24 months (magistrates' court)
Subsequent magistrates' court extensions	An additional 3 or 6 months (magistrates' court)	An additional 3 or 6 months (magistrates' court)	An additional 3 or 6 months (magistrates' court)

DPP	Director of Public Prosecutions
FCA	Financial Conduct Authority
HMRC	His Majesty's Revenue and Customs
NCA	National Crime Agency
SFO	Serious Fraud Office

APPENDIX 2

Checklists

Checklist 1: Instructions from a third party

A full and accurate note must be taken of all information obtained and advice given, which should be timed and dated.

1 Date and time of call
2 Name of person taking the call

Details of the third party

3 Name
4 Address
5 Telephone number
6 Relationship to person arrested

Details of the arrested person

7 Name, age and date of birth
8 Address
9 Telephone number
10 Any aliases used
11 Any vulnerabilities, medication, etc
12 Whether the suspect requested legal advice

Details of the incident

13 Reason for the arrest
14 Time and place of arrest
15 Circumstances of the arrest
16 Involvement of the third party (if any)
17 Details of other persons arrested or suspected
18 Details of any other witnesses or relevant third parties
19 Is the third party aware of any search taking place

Details of the detention

20 Police station suspect taken to
21 Name(s) and/or contact details of officer(s) involved

Initial response/appraisal given and action taken

22 Information given to third party
23 Action taken in response to third party contact

Checklist 2: Finding the client

A full and accurate note should be kept of all information sought and obtained, including the date, time, and name and status of officers spoken to.

1 Contact the custody officer at the police station where it is believed that the suspect has been taken. Where an enquiry about the whereabouts of a suspect is made by a person with an interest in the suspect's welfare, that information must normally be given, provided the suspect agrees (Codes C and H para 5.5; Code I para 5.4).

2 If the custody officer is not willing to give the required information, it may be that a decision has been made to hold the suspect incommunicado under PACE s56, Terrorism Act (TA) 2000 Sch 8 para 8 or National Security Act (NSA) 2023 Sch 6 para 9 (see para 2.127 above). This presents a difficulty, since from the police point of view, disclosing to the lawyer that the person has been detained may defeat the purpose of the action they have taken. The lawyer may wish to give an undertaking not to disclose the whereabouts of the suspect to a third party. The lawyer should also ask whether a decision to delay access to legal advice under PACE s58, TA 2000 Sch 8 or NSA 2023 Sch 6 has been taken (see paras 2.151, 2.156 and 2.158 above), since if it has not, the police will be under a duty to inform the suspect of the lawyer's interest, although strictly only if the lawyer attends in person (see para 3.18 above). It is also possible that a custody officer may not be willing to give the required information to a specific solicitor in circumstances where a superintendent has given a direction under TA 2000 Sch 8 para 9 (Code H para 6.5) or NSA 2023 Sch 6 para 8 (Code I para 6.4).

3 If the custody officer says that the person is not detained at that police station, they should be asked whether the person has been at that station and, if so, where they have been taken. If this still draws a blank, the custody officer should be asked whether they are aware of an arrest having taken place recently, whether they are expecting a suspect to be brought into the police station in the near future and/or how many people are in the queue waiting to be booked in. It may assist if the names of any officers involved in the arrest are known.

4 If this still does not work, it is worth asking the custody officer to check the custody records, since although they should be aware of who is, or has been, in custody, there may have been a recent change of shift or there may be a temporary custody officer. If this still does not work, the custody officer should be asked to inform the lawyer if and when the person is brought in. If the suspect is not located but there is still reason to believe that they are in custody, checks should be made at regular intervals.

5 If all of the above fail, the lawyer should consider telephoning other stations and going through the same process. Depending on the circumstances, the lawyer may also consider contacting HMRC offices or other police forces such as the British Transport Police.

Checklist 3: Obtaining information from the custody officer on the telephone

A full and accurate note must be taken of all information requested and obtained, and the source of that information, which should be timed and dated.

Details of the suspect

1 Name
2 Address
3 Date of birth and age
4 Gender
5 Whether a risk assessment has been conducted, and its outcome
6 Whether child/vulnerable/other special needs (for example, interpreter)
7 Identity of appropriate adult and whether contacted (if relevant)
8 Education, employment and professional background

Police and investigation details

9 Name of custody officer
10 Station where held and custody record number
11 Name and contact details of officer in the case (request that the custody officer passes the lawyer's details to the officer in the case)
12 Whether client arrested or a volunteer
13 Time and place of arrest
14 Name or shoulder badge number of arresting officer(s)
15 Time of arrival at station
16 Time detention authorised
17 Reason for and circumstances of arrest, and why arrest necessary
18 Details of alleged offence(s)
19 Whether an indictable offence
20 Any exceptional police procedure (delay in advice/delay in informing relative or friend/intimate body search/drug test/identification procedure)
21 Reason for detention
22 Time solicitor requested
23 Reason for delay in contacting solicitor (if relevant)
24 Reason for proceeding without solicitor (if relevant)
25 Whether interviewed yet (if so, why)
26 Whether and when interview likely to take place
27 Whether search made/proposed and/or samples taken/proposed, and result
28 Any request for PIN or encryption codes made and/or information provided
29 Any significant statement or silence
30 Any other person(s) arrested/sought by police

Charge/release (if relevant)

31 If charged:
- time of charge
- nature of charge(s)
- bailed/detained in custody

32 If bailed following charge:
- date/time/place of court appearance
- any conditions attached to bail
- reason for bail being considered necessary and proportionate

33 If not bailed:
- reason for refusing bail
- date/time/place of court appearance
- police/ Crown Prosecution Service (CPS) attitude to bail from the court

34 If not charged:
- whether released unconditionally/reported for summons/bailed
- if reported for summons, what offence(s) anticipated

35 If released or bailed without charge:
- reason for police bail
- any conditions attached to bail
- date/time/place of surrender

Action

36 Arrange telephone access to client

37 Confirm with custody officer:
- expected time of arrival
- that the officer will contact the lawyer if plans change
- that the client will not be interviewed before the lawyer arrives
- that the above will be noted on the custody record
- whether the lawyer would like to be contacted on any review of detention

Checklist 4: Initial telephone conversation with client

A full and accurate note should be taken of all information obtained and advice given, which should be timed and dated.

1 Confirm that the suspect does want legal advice, and does want it from the lawyer concerned (or the lawyer's firm).

2 Inform the client of the lawyer's status, and confirm that legal advice is free (unless the client has chosen to instruct the lawyer privately, in which case they should, nevertheless, be advised that they may be eligible for advice and assistance under the legal aid scheme).

3 If appropriate, inform the client of the lawyer's role and, in particular, that the lawyer's role is to act in the client's best interests.

4 Obtain initial information from the client, the client's understanding of the reason for the arrest, and any particular concerns or complaints that the client may have. The lawyer may at this stage be asked to contact a third party to inform them of the suspect's arrest. In principle, there is no reason why this should not be done, but care must be taken to ensure that this message is not used to pass on information to a person evading arrest, or which might result in evidence or proceeds not being recovered, or which might otherwise lead to interference with the course of justice. If in any doubt, the lawyer should agree to contact the third party only on the understanding that the lawyer will first tell the custody officer what is intended.

5 Decide whether, and when, to attend in person (see para 3.55 above).

6 Give initial advice to the client, including advice about whether it would be advisable for the lawyer to attend in person. If the lawyer does intend to attend, or to arrange for attendance, in person, usually they should advise the client not to answer police questions, and not to sign any documents, until they have received advice in person. However, in drink/driving cases the client should not normally be advised to refuse to give a sample pending arrival of the lawyer (see para 2.142 above). If attendance is to be delayed, the client should be warned of possible attempts by the police to persuade them to proceed with an interview in the absence of the lawyer and reminded of their continuing right to advice should this or any other issue arise about which they are unsure.

Checklist 5: Deciding whether to attend the police station

Always consider whether attendance is mandatory and, if not, whether the sufficient benefit test is satisfied. Consider whether professional obligations to the client require attendance even though payment may not be made under the SCC.

A full and accurate note must be taken of all information obtained, advice given, reason for not attending (where attendance is mandatory) and reason for attending (where attendance is not mandatory).

1 The lawyer should normally attend if:
- the suspect has been arrested for an offence and is going to be interviewed;
- the police are intending to conduct an identification procedure;
- the client complains of serious maltreatment by the police;
- the client is a child or a person at risk.

2 If 1 above does not apply, the lawyer should still consider attending if:
- the client is apparently drunk, under the influence of drugs or complains of being seriously unwell (unless satisfied that the police have taken all appropriate action);
- the alleged offence (or circumstances, if the client has been arrested for other than an offence) is serious or may have serious consequences;
- there are important issues concerning searches of the person or property;
- there are important issues concerning the taking of samples;
- an interview has been conducted, but advice is necessary at the time of charge;*
- the circumstances of the client indicate that attendance is necessary – for example, the client is unfamiliar with police processes, or the client is particularly upset or nervous;
- detention is likely to be lengthy;
- the lawyer is not satisfied that advice by telephone can be given with sufficient confidentiality;
- the lawyer is not satisfied that they can adequately communicate with the client by telephone;
- representations need to be made to the police, and these cannot adequately be made by telephone or email.

3 Attendance may not be necessary or justified where the client:
- has been arrested for a road traffic offence (including excess alcohol);
- has been arrested on warrant and no further offence is suspected;
- has been arrested for breach of bail and no further offence is suspected;
- has been arrested under a civil order or warrant.

* Which may be claimed for under the SCC.

Checklist 6: Reading the custody record

A full and accurate note must be taken of all information obtained and further enquiries made, which should be timed and dated.

1 The custody record number
2 The name and address recorded for the suspect
3 The grounds and reasons for arrest
   - Is this the same as the information already given to the lawyer?
   - What is the statutory or common law authority for the arrest?
   - Why was arrest necessary?
   - Is the arrest lawful?
   - Is it an either-way offence?
   - Is it an indictable-only offence? This is relevant, in particular, to probationary representatives.
4 The age of the suspect
   - If the suspect is under 18 years, what action has been taken in respect of an appropriate adult?
   - Why was the arrest necessary (in light of the suspect's age)?
   - Why was the detention authorised (in light of the suspect's age)?
   - If there is a potential for remand, has the custody officer made enquiries as to local authority accommodation?
5 The time that a solicitor was requested
   - What time was this acted on by the police?
   - If there is a significant time lapse, why is this?
6 The time of arrest and the time of arrival at the police station
   - If there is a significant time difference, why is this?
7 The time detention was authorised and grounds for detention being authorised
   - Are the grounds for detention lawful?
   - Is there sufficient evidence to charge?
8 Whether documents or materials relevant to the lawfulness of the arrest or detention have been disclosed to the suspect, and the time of any such disclosure
9 The property found on the suspect, if recorded. This may give an important indication of evidence in relation to the offence for which the suspect has been arrested (for example, large sums of money, bunches of keys, self-sealing bags, etc), or of other offences about which the police may want to question the suspect
10 Any indication that the suspect is, or may be, neuro-divergent, has mental health difficulties or any other vulnerability, and the results of the risk assessment conducted by the custody officer
   - If so, what action has been taken in respect of an appropriate adult?
   - Has a healthcare professional been requested or called?
   - Are you satisfied that your client does not require further medical care?
11 Any indication that the suspect is, or may be, unwell or otherwise unfit through drink or drugs
   - If so, has a healthcare practitioner been requested or called?
   - If a healthcare practitioner has already examined the client, what was the purpose of the examination and what was the result?
   - Are you content that your client does not require further medical care?

12 Whether a property search has been authorised
  - If so, on what authority and for what purpose?
  - What, if anything, has been seized?

13 Whether the suspect has been asked to sign a police officer's notebook
  - If so, why was the suspect asked to do so before the lawyer's arrival?
  - What was in the officer's notebook?

14 Whether an interview has been conducted
  - If so, why was an interview conducted at that stage?
  - Was it conducted contrary to Code C para 6.6 or 11.1, Code H para 6.7 or 11.2, or Code I para 6.6 or para 11?
  - What was said in the interview?

15 Any authorities given or decisions taken in respect of the taking of samples, fingerprints, photographs or drugs-testing
  - Have these been conducted?
  - What was the result?
  - Why were they authorised/conducted before the arrival of the lawyer?

16 Have any requests been made of, or information provided by, the suspect (for example, for PIN numbers or encryption keys pursuant to the Regulation of Investigatory Powers Act 2000 or in respect of ID procedures)?
  - What was the result?
  - Why were they authorised/conducted before the arrival of the lawyer?

16 Actions taken in respect of the risk assessment required under Codes C and H para 3.6 and Code I para 3.7

17 Any unusual entries – for example, late entries, deleted entries

Checklist 7: Information from the officer in the case

A full and accurate note must be taken of all information sought and obtained, together with relevant times.

1 The reason for and circumstances of the arrest, and reason why arrest was necessary
2 Details of the suspected offence(s) for which the client was originally arrested
3 Details of any other suspected offence(s) and whether the client has been, or is to be, re-arrested under Police and Criminal Evidence Act 1984 s31 in respect of such offences
4 Whether any other person has been arrested in connection with the offence(s), and whether that other person implicated the client
5 Whether any other person is being sought in connection with the offence(s)
6 Whether the client has been interviewed and, if so, why and what was said
7 Whether the client has made any admissions, or any significant statement or silence, outside the context of an interview
8 Whether any question has been put to the client under Criminal Justice and Public Order Act 1994 s36 or 37 and any reply made
9 Details of the evidence the police have that allegedly implicates the client
10 Whether the investigating officer has brought to the custody officer's attention any Code C para 3.4(b), note for guidance (NfG) 3ZA documents or material which appear to undermine the need to keep the suspect in custody.*
11 Whether a search of property has been conducted
- If so, whether anything of evidential significance has been found
- If not, whether and when it is proposed to carry out a search

In both cases, the legal authority for the search should be ascertained and checked against the offence for which the client has been arrested
12 Whether it is intended to carry out any other procedure such as:
- removal of clothing
- an intimate or non-intimate search
- taking an intimate or non-intimate sample
- taking a handwriting sample
- conducting an identification procedure

and the reasons for and legal authority for such procedures
13 What other investigations are being conducted or are intended
14 Whether the client has any previous convictions or other forms of previous misconduct
15 The purpose of any forthcoming interview
16 Whether the officer has any other relevant information that has not been disclosed to the lawyer and, if relevant, whether a strategy of phased disclosure is being used
17 Is there additional evidence that will be put to the client in the interview, for example, documents/CCTV (implications for children and vulnerable clients)
18 Is the interview being audio and visually recorded
- If visually recorded, why?
- Will anyone be watching a live stream of the interview?

19 The officer's view of the client's fitness for interview and whether the client may come within the categories requiring an appropriate adult

20 Whether the officer has sufficient evidence to charge (if relevant), and what is likely to happen after the interview
21 (Where appropriate) the attitude of the officer to diversion from prosecution
22 Whether the officer is aware of any indications that the client may present a risk to the safety of the lawyer
23 Whether the officer has turned their mind to the question of bail and/or any concerns relating to bail or proposed bail conditions

* While Codes H and I have an equivalent to Code C para 3.4(b) (Code H para 3.4(b); Code I para 3.5), they do not have a direct equivalent to Code C NfG 3ZA. Instead, Code H (NfG 3G) and Code I (NfG 3F) recognise that there may be circumstances where the arrest has been based on sensitive information which cannot be disclosed.

Checklist 8: Summary of police evidence to be requested

A full and accurate note must be taken of all information sought and obtained, together with relevant times.

1 A history of the case, or 'case narrative', including whether and how the case was reported to the police or whether and why the police initiated the investigation, how the client came to be arrested and what happened on arrest, and what has happened in the case so far from the officer's point of view.
2 What investigations have been made at the crime scene (if relevant), including who has attended (arresting and other officers, scene of crime officers, forensic specialists, etc).
3 What relevant communications have taken place (for example, between members of the public and the police, and between police officers), what was said, and how this has been recorded. Where appropriate, the lawyer should ask to see or hear records made.
4 Who has been interviewed in relation to the case, and who has made a statement. The lawyer should ask to see relevant statements, including those of any identifying witness. Where appropriate, a detailed note should be taken of descriptions given of relevant events and relevant people, especially possible suspects.
5 What searches have been conducted, samples taken, photographs or other recordings made. The lawyer should ask to see the product of such activities.
6 What relevant real evidence or objects the police have in their possession (for example, weapons, documents, clothing, CCTV recordings, etc). Again, where appropriate, the lawyer should ask to see such items.
7 What forensic examinations or tests have been conducted, and the results of such examinations or tests.
8 What other investigations, forensic tests, etc, are planned.
9 What information the officer has concerning the client's circumstances, including any previous convictions or other forms of previous misconduct.

Checklist 9: Structure of initial consultation

1 Explain who you are, your status, the fact that legal advice and assistance is free (or, if acting on a privately funded basis, set out your fees and also explain that free advice is available via the duty solicitor scheme), and how the consultation will be conducted.
2 Seek out any immediate preoccupations or specific needs – for example, medication, food – and take appropriate action.
3 Take client's background details. This may help the client to settle down and develop confidence in you, and enables you to assess the client. However, it may be more appropriate to do this later in the consultation, particularly if the client is known to you.
4 Tell the client what information you have obtained from the police, give an outline of what the prosecution would have to prove (if appropriate) and (where appropriate) an initial indication of the apparent strength of the police case.
5 Take the client's account of the relevant facts, including the circumstances of the arrest, the suspected offence(s) and whether the client has already said anything relevant to the police.
6 Give advice on the client's legal position.
7 Give advice on whether the client should answer questions in the police interview.
8 Give advice (as appropriate) on search, samples, identification procedures, etc.
9 Brief the client on the conduct of the police interview and your role during the interview.
10 Prepare the client for the police interview.

Checklist 10: Initial consultation with client

Confirm the following information

1 Full name (including any aliases)
2 Address
3 Date of birth or age
4 Telephone number (mobile and landline)
5 Email address

Inform the client

6 Name and status of the lawyer
7 The fact that legal advice is free (if relevant) or an estimate of their likely costs
8 That the conversation is confidential and covered by legal professional privilege (LPP should also be explained to the client)
9 The role of the lawyer
10 What the lawyer has been told about the suspect and/or the alleged offence(s)
11 The power of the police to detain the client
12 What is likely to happen during police detention
13 The meaning of the police caution and adverse inferences

Give the client

14 The 'client care' letter
15 A business card

Ask the client

16 What they know about the matter for which they have been arrested (including involvement of any co-accused)
17 Whether they have said anything relevant to the police and/or whether they have refused to answer any questions put to them by the police
18 Whether the police have found or removed any item:
- on arrest
- on detention
- during any search of the person or property
- from any other person

19 Whether the police have told them about evidence in their possession
20 What happened at the time of arrest
21 Whether they have received any injuries
22 Whether they are currently under the influence of drink/drugs
23 Whether they suffer from any other relevant disability or neurodiversity (including name and address of doctor where relevant)
24 Whether there are previous convictions
25 Whether currently on police or court bail
26 Whether currently on licence or subject to return to prison
27 Information about personal circumstances:
- marital/cohabitee status and whether any children or dependants
- employment status
- whether currently taking medication
- any relevant medical condition
- details of accommodation, including occupation status and length of residence
- details of any probation officer or social worker involved

28 Whether they wish a friend or relative to be contacted

Advise the client

29 What the police have to prove
30 The client's legal position
31 Whether to answer questions in the police interview
32 How to handle the police interview
33 What is likely to happen after the police interview, including the possibility of police approaches in the absence of the lawyer

Checklist 11: Dealing with more than one client in respect of the same or a related offence

Keep a full and accurate note of what is said to the clients, and their responses, and consider asking the clients to endorse the notes.

1 Ask the investigating officer and/or custody officer to provide the name of other individuals under arrest.
2 Take instructions from Client 1 and tell them the names given to you by the investigating officer and/or custody officer. Tell them that you have also been asked to act for one of the other individuals under arrest and ask whether Client 1 is aware of any conflict or potential conflict of interests. If Client 1 says that there is, you cannot act for Client 2, although you should take action to ensure that Client 2 is able to secure access to legal advice.
3 If Client 1 says that they are aware of no conflict or potential conflict, consider for yourself whether the instructions given by Client 1 disclose a conflict or potential conflict, and if you conclude that they do, you cannot act for Client 2.
4 If you are satisfied that there is no conflict or potential conflict, advise Client 1 that if you receive information that is confidential to Client 1 but which is relevant to Client 2, you will have to disclose that information to Client 2, and will seek permission from Client 1 to disclose that information if the situation arises. If Client 1 does not agree to this, you cannot act for Client 2.
5 If Client 1 is content with this approach, see Client 2 and advise them that you are acting for Client 1, and that if there is a conflict or potential conflict of interests, you cannot act for Client 2. Ask Client 2 if they are aware of a conflict or a potential conflict with Client 1. If Client 2 says that there is, tell Client 2 that you cannot act for them, although you can take action to secure legal advice for them.
6 If Client 2 says that they are not aware of a conflict, or potential conflict, inform Client 2 that if they give you any information, or you subsequently receive information, that is relevant to Client 1 you will have to disclose it to Client 1. If Client 2 does not agree to this, you cannot act for Client 2.
7 If Client 2 is content with this, take instructions from Client 2. In view of the danger of concoction, do not give any information to Client 2 that you have obtained from Client 1 before you have taken instructions from them.
8 Consider whether the instructions obtained from Client 2 disclose a conflict or potential conflict of interests. If they do, you cannot continue to act for Client 2, and must also consider whether you can continue to act for Client 1 having regard to the principles set out in paras 5.42 and 5.43 above.
9 Continue to keep the issue of conflict of interests under review, and if a conflict of interests becomes apparent, consider whether you should cease to act for either or both clients.

Checklist 12: Information for a bail application to custody officer or court

1 Full name
2 Address
3 Date of birth or age

Failure to surrender to custody

4 Does the client have previous conviction(s) for Bail Act 1976 offences?
If yes:
- when?
- penalty imposed?
- what were the circumstances?
- have they been granted bail since the last Bail Act 1976 offence?

5 Has the client previously surrendered to custody satisfactorily?
If yes:
- when?
- in what circumstances?
- what offence was under investigation?
- penalty imposed for relevant offence(s)?

6 If the client is married/cohabiting:
- how long have they been living together?
- how stable is the relationship?

7 If the client has children or other dependants:
- where do they live?
- how often does the client see them?
- in what way does he/she support them?

8 In respect of the client's accommodation:
- how long have they lived there?
- does s/he own/rent/squat in it?
- who pays the rent/mortgage?
- if they cannot return there, do they have other available accommodation?

9 How long has the client lived in the area?
10 Where were they brought up?
11 If there are parents and/or siblings, where do they live and what contact do they have with them?
12 If the client is in employment:
- where do they work?
- what job do they do?
- how long have they had the job?
- is it a permanent job?
- what is the employer's reaction likely to be to the arrest and charge?

13 Possible sureties, securities and conditions:
where appropriate, the following information in respect of possible sureties:
- name
- address
- telephone number
- occupation
- length of time known to the client
- relationship to client
- any previous convictions

- likely financial circumstances
- appropriate police station if reporting condition imposed
- any problems with a condition of residence
- if client has no, or unsuitable, accommodation, would they agree to stay in a bail hostel?
- does client have a passport?

If yes:
- would they agree to surrender it to the court?
- do they have any plans to travel abroad?
- would they be willing to deposit a security of money or valuables?

Fear of further offences

14 Is client currently on bail?
If yes:
- date(s) imposed
- whether police or court bail
- alleged offence(s)
- how long on bail

if court bail, whether conditional:
If yes:
- conditions already imposed
- whether conditions have changed since bail originally granted

15 Does client have previous convictions?
If yes:
- when, where, sentence(s) imposed
- were any of them committed whilst on bail?
- were any of them for similar offences to offence(s) now charged?
- have client's circumstances changed?

16 Have client's circumstances materially changed since current alleged offence(s)?

17 Possible conditions:
- if a curfew is appropriate, would client agree to it?
- if a condition is made not to go to scene of alleged crime, would client agree to it?
- are there other conditions that may be appropriate?

Interference with witnesses

18 Does client have previous convictions for serious assault/perverting the course of justice?

19 Has the client made any threats against the witness(es) in the current case?

20 Possible conditions:
- if a condition was made not to contact the witness(es), would the client agree to it?

Own protection

21 Does the client have access to accommodation away from the relevant area?

Checklist 13: Identification parade checklist and report form

1 Is identification in dispute?

2 Is an identification parade practicable, and would it serve a useful purpose, having regard to:
- whether it could be held at a later time/date
- whether the police have made sufficient effort
- whether the lawyer should offer to help find persons to stand on the parade – any purported identification already made?

3 Should the suspect ask for/agree to a parade, having regard to:
- what is known about the initial view by the witness
- what is known about other, non-identification evidence
- what alternative method of identification is likely?

4 Original description of identifying witness(es) provided?

5 Has there been any informal identification (for example, social media identification)?

6 Any material released to the media and, if so, copies provided?

7 Arrangements for taking photograph or video of parade checked?

8 Arrangements for witnesses to attend the police station checked?

9 Arrangements for other members of the parade to attend the police station checked?

10 Route taken by witnesses from waiting room to parade room checked?

11 Arrangements to keep witnesses who have viewed parade separate from other witnesses checked?

12 Location of officers in the case checked?

13 Suspect informed by the identification officer:
- purpose of the parade?
- right to free legal advice?
- right to have lawyer present?
- whether any witnesses have been shown photographs, photofits, identikits or similar?
- fact that suspect does not have to agree to parade?
- fact that if suspect refuses parade, refusal may be given in evidence and police may proceed covertly to test whether witness makes an identification?
- fact that if they significantly alter appearance between taking of photograph and ID parade, this may be given in evidence?
- fact that a video/photograph may be taken of them?
- fact that if suspect changes their appearance other ID arrangements may be made?
- fact that suspect or their lawyer will be provided with original description given by identifying witness(es)?

14 Suspect given notice setting out the above, and asked to sign copy?

15 Suspect given advice by lawyer regarding parade, including:
- how it will be conducted
- stance
- where to look
- right to decide on where to stand
- not to speak while witness is in the room

- effect of one-way screens
- to tell lawyer if dissatisfied with conduct of parade?

16 Whether other persons on the parade are satisfactory, including:
- number
- age
- height
- race
- position in life
- hair
- facial hair
- eyes
- build
- clothing
- distinguishing marks (for example, visible tattoos)
- any feature given in original description by witness(es)?

17 Suspect informed by identification officer:
- of conduct of the parade?
- about caution?
- to indicate whether they object to any of the arrangements for the parade?

(If yes, note what is said and any action taken to deal with the objection(s))

18 Suspect asked at end of parade whether they have any comments on the conduct of the parade?
(If yes, note precisely what is said)

19 Any representations made by the lawyer?
(If yes, note precisely what is said)

20 Time parade started and finished

21 Any other relevant comments

22 The conduct of the parade (complete one copy of this questionnaire for each witness)

1		2	3	4	5	6	7	8	9	10	11	12	13	14	15	16

(Note position of suspect with an X and give brief description of other persons on the parade)

Other persons present in the parade room

Name of witness

Suspect told they can choose where to stand?

Time witness brought into parade room

Number of officer bringing witness in

Witness told:
- to look at each person on parade at least twice?
- to take their time?

- that parade contains the suspect(s) and others who cannot have been involved?
- that they will be asked if the person that they saw is on the parade and, if so, their number?
- that the person they saw may not be on the parade, and that if they cannot make a positive identification they should say so?

Note what the witness does and says (use diagram if helpful)

Any identification made by the witness?
(If yes, note precisely what is said)

Any comment by the suspect while the witness is in the room or after they leave?
(If yes, note precisely what is said)

Time witness left the parade room

Any representations made by the lawyer?
(If yes, note precisely what is said)

Was a photograph/video taken of the parade?

Checklist 14: Video identification checklist and report form

1 Is identification in dispute?
2 Is an identification parade or group identification more suitable?
3 Does the suspect consent to a video identification?
4 Arrangements for witnesses to attend the police station checked?
5 Arrangements for selection of video ID images checked?
6 Route taken by witnesses from waiting room to viewing room checked?
7 Arrangements to keep witnesses who have viewed film separate from other witnesses checked?
8 Location of officers in the case checked?
9 Suspect informed by the identification officer:
- purpose of the video procedure
- right to free legal advice
- right to have lawyer present
- whether any witnesses have been shown photographs, photofits, identikits or similar (including any informal viewings using social media)
- fact that suspect does not have to co-operate with the video identification
- fact that if suspect refuses to co-operate, refusal may be given in evidence and police may proceed covertly to test whether witness makes an identification
- fact that if suspect significantly alters appearance this may be given in evidence
- fact that a video/photograph may be taken of them
- fact that if suspect changes their appearance, other ID arrangements may be made
- fact that suspect or their lawyer will be provided with original description given by identifying witness(es)

10 Suspect given notice setting out the above, and asked to sign copy?
11 Suspect given advice by lawyer regarding video identification procedure including:
- how it will be conducted
- to tell lawyer if dissatisfied with the arrangements

12 Whether images for the video ID are satisfactory, including:
- number
- age
- height
- race
- position in life
- hair
- facial hair
- eyes
- build
- clothing
- distinguishing marks (for example, visible tattoos)
- any feature given in original description by witness(es)
- background
- lighting

13 Any objections made to the set of images before it is shown to the witness(es)?
(If yes, note what is said and action taken to deal with objection)

14 The conduct of the video identification procedure (complete one copy of this questionnaire for each witness)

Other persons present in the viewing room

Name of witness
Time witness brought in to viewing room
Number of officer bringing witness in

Witness told:

- that the person they saw may or may not be on the video?
- to refrain from making an identification or saying that they cannot make an identification until they have seen the entire film at least twice?
- that at any point they may ask to see a particular part of the film again, or to have a particular frame frozen for them to study?
- that there is no limit to the number of times they may view the whole film or any part of it?

Note what the witness does and says

Any identification made by the witness?
If yes, was the film of the person identified shown to the witness again?
(Note precisely what is said)

Time witness left the viewing room

Any representations made by the lawyer?
(If yes, note precisely what is said)

---

15 Any representations made by the lawyer when all witnesses have viewed the video?

(If yes, note precisely what is said)

---

16 Time viewing completed

---

17 Any other relevant comments

Checklist 15: Questions to ask an immigration detainee

1 Full name, including any aliases previously used
2 Date of birth
3 Nationality(ies) and country of birth
4 Whether client requires an interpreter and if so language and dialect
5 Current address (other than detention), and any previous addresses covering at least the last six months
6 Contact details of any relative or friend
7 Date and place of most recent arrival in the UK
8 Whether travelling on own passport
9 Whether any questions asked at border by immigration and details
10 Whether any answers given on arrival were inaccurate and if so details of inaccuracies
11 If client had previously applied for entry clearance from overseas (visa), were any of the answers to questions raised inaccurate and if so details of inaccuracies
12 Whether client has previously instructed a lawyer or Immigration Advice Authority (formerly Office of the Immigration Services Commissioner) adviser and if so contact details
13 Any reason not to continue with previous adviser for immigration elements arising from the detention
14 Whether client has been served with any papers
15 How has client supported themself to date
16 Is client likely to wish to return to the UK lawfully in the future
17 If client is forced to return, what does client think will happen to them

For clients with family or close ties in UK

18 What are client's present family circumstances
19 Where relevant, what is the immigration status of the family members
20 If any children born in the UK, what was the immigration status of the other parent at the time of birth and what is the regularity of contact with the child/children if not in the same household
21 Are the immigration authorities aware of family circumstances and if so when were they notified
22 What does client think will happen to family if client is forced to leave UK

For clients previously granted lawful entry

23 If client was given legal right to enter, when does it/did it expire
24 Does client have evidence in respect of pending application to the Home Office
25 Can client provide Home Office reference number* or access to an eVisa or an expired biometric residence permit
26 If not held by the immigration service, where is client's passport

For clients who have never previously been given lawful entry

27 Where and when did client enter UK and how (for example, lorry/false passport)
28 Has there been any previous application to remain and if so what was that, and is there proof of the pending application

* In the past, such reference numbers would be the first letter of the surname followed by six or seven digits, but more recently a new format of 16 digits.

For clients wishing to make an application/appeal prior to removal

29 If client expresses anxiety about threats to life or freedom on return, are there reasons why this has not previously been raised

30 If client now seeks to raise issues about family or private life, is there a reason for not having already made an application on these grounds

31 If client has overstayed for less than 28 days or is in breach of landing conditions, would they benefit from seeking to leave before operation of mandatory ban

32 Has client already lodged an appeal and if not could an appeal be pursued prior to removal

33 Does client have community ties other than as already identified

34 What if any evidence is available to show that there would be serious irreversible harm were an appeal not exercisable prior to removal

Where release from detention is being sought

35 Are there physical, other health issues, or other vulnerabilities that may be relevant to the question of detention (for example, pregnancy, age, specific vulnerabilities)

36 Does client have friends willing to act as financial condition supporters and if so what is their status

37 What if any address could client to be released to

38 Has client ever failed to attend any court or report to any authority such as police or immigration in the UK before

39 If there is an entitlement to appeal that has not yet been exercised, what is the time frame within which it can be exercised

40 Has client been made aware that bail would be automatically refused if there are current removal directions in effect within 21 days of any bail hearing date

41 Has client been advised that willingness to remain detained will not strengthen a claim to remain in the UK

Availability of representation by police station adviser or otherwise

42 Is the basis of any application (other than bail) likely to fall within the scope of the Civil Legal Aid Immigration specification

43 Does client appear to be financially eligible bearing in mind the requirement to consider income of the household, not merely circumstances as at point of detention

44 If so, is the police station lawyer able to refer the matter on via contacts with other legal professionals with a legal aid immigration contract

45 If not, does client have means to instruct a lawyer privately if only to file an appeal or administrative review urgently

Index